LEVEL THREE LEADERSHIP

Fifth Edition

LEVEL THREE LEADERSHIP

GETTING BELOW THE SURFACE

James G. Clawson

The Darden Graduate School of Business Administration
University of Virginia

Prentice Hall

Boston   Columbus   Indianapolis   New York   San Francisco   Upper Saddle River
Amsterdam   Cape Town   Dubai   London   Madrid   Milan Munich   Paris   Montreal Toronto
Delhi   Mexico City   Sao Paulo   Sydney   Hong Kong   Seoul   Singapore   Taipei   Tokyo

Editorial Director: Sally Yagan
Editor in Chief: Eric Svendsen
Director of Editorial Services: Ashley Santora
Editorial Project Manager: Meg O'Rourke
Editorial Assistant: Carter Anderson
Director of Marketing: Patrice Lumumba Jones
Marketing Manager: Nikki Ayana Jones
Marketing Assistant: Ian Gold
Production Manager: Fran Russello
Art Director: Jayne Conte
Cover Designer: Suzanne Duda
Cover Art: Fotolia: Fire over the mountain © Ronnie Howard
Media Editor: Denise Vaughn
Media Project Manager: Lisa Rinaldi
Full-Service Project Management: Hema Latha / Integra Software
  Services, Ltd.
Printer/Binder: RR Donnelley
Text Font: 10/12 Times

Credits and acknowledgments borrowed from other sources and reproduced, with permission, in this textbook appear on appropriate page within text.

Library of Congress Cataloging-in-Publication Data
Clawson, James G.
  Level three leadership: getting below the surface / James G. Clawson.—5th ed.
    p. cm.
  Includes bibliographical references and index.
  ISBN-13: 978-0-13-255641-5
  ISBN-10: 0-13-255641-3
  1. Leadership.   I. Title.
  HD57.7.C545 2012
  658.4'092—dc22

                                              2010037198

17   16

Prentice Hall
is an imprint of

www.pearsonhighered.com

ISBN 10:   0-13-255641-3
ISBN 13: 978-0-13-255641-5

This edition is dedicated to Bob Johnson, former CEO of Honeywell Aerospace and Dubai Aerospace Enterprises and former president of the Aerospace Industry Association. Bob has an effervescent zest for life and seemingly unbounded energy—an example of how leadership is about managing energy, first in yourself, and then in those around you.

BRIEF CONTENTS

CONTENTS

PREFACE

Level Three Leadership (L3L) prepares students and practicing managers to understand and apply principles of leadership. This is not a book that surveys the various leadership theories out there for the sake of intellectual knowledge and repetition on an exam (although the Appendix does that), rather L3L is about providing guidance to students of leadership in creating their own, practically applicable, model of influencing others. In that regard, this book presents a flexible leadership model and related concepts that work in a variety of settings, much like a four-wheel-drive vehicle can navigate multiple types of terrain. In addition to its use in undergraduate and MBA programs, the book has been used to work with practicing managers in executive education programs in the United States, Brazil, Canada, Costa Rico, Thailand, Japan, Germany, Greece, Netherlands, the United Kingdom, Turkey, Egypt, and South Africa. It also forms the basis for an executive education program, *Power and Leadership*, which has been running continuously at the Darden Graduate School of Business at the University of Virginia for more than 15 years. The contents are field tested as well as classroom tested.

In general, the book introduces the following key concepts:

1. A Leadership Point of View (LPV). (a) Do you *see* what needs to be done? (b) Do you *understand* all the forces at play? (c) Do you have the *courage to act* to make things better?
2. A Diamond Model of leadership that includes the self, strategic tasks, influencing others, designing functional organizations, and managing change. The model posits that leadership is a function of *all* of these elements taken together and that *together* they produce results that include, in a balanced scorecard perspective, customer satisfaction, internal efficiency, learning, and financial return.
3. Self-leadership is the foundation of leading others; if you can't lead yourself, how can you lead others?
4. People behave at three levels: visible behavior, conscious thought, and semiconscious values, assumptions, beliefs, and expectations (VABEs) about the way the world is or should be. People who try to influence others work naturally at all three levels, but in differing proportions. Your leadership level profile will influence your ability to lead others.
5. Strategic thinking, ethical behavior, managing globally, and managing change are critical aspects of leading so there are significant chapters on these topics.
6. There are two main reasons for a lack of leadership: lack of strategic story to tell and the fear of rejection. The book guides students to think about how much they have become habitually afraid of the judgments of others.
7. Leadership is about managing energy, first in yourself and then in those around you. Self-leadership begins with learning how to manage your energy to higher levels. Resonance and flow are key elements here. Energy is perhaps another more direct way to think about motivation.
8. There are different techniques and approaches used to manage/lead at Levels One, Two, and Three. There are chapters on each of these to help students sort out their personal profile.
9. The book also includes chapters on the Language of Leadership and how to lead through speech more effectively and on managing teams.

10. Self-awareness is a key element of effective leadership, so there is an extensive workbook with a number of self-assessment instruments and exercises.
11. Every chapter ends with a summary of the key concepts introduced in the chapter, questions to guide further reflection on those concepts, a short caselet designed to help students apply the concepts (in case you'd rather not use more lengthy cases from Darden, Harvard, NACRA, ICCH, and/or Ivey), guidance for workbook related activities, and an invitation to submit more caselets online.

NEW TO THE FIFTH EDITION

The fifth edition is significantly enhanced with additions based on recommendations from reviewers and users. There are no new chapters, but every chapter has been enhanced in minor or major ways. New research, new books, and new authors have been added and referenced. The workbook has been reduced somewhat and simplified for reasons of space and usage.

Changes in this edition include the following:

1. First chapter is shortened for easier reading.
2. A new six-point decision model has been included in the chapter on leadership and ethics.
3. Kaplan and Norton's concepts on strategy mapping have been added to the chapter on strategy frames.
4. References to new insights on neuro-plasticity have been added to the chapters on why people behave the way they do.
5. Introductions to DeBono's six thinking hats and Buzan's mindmapping have been added to the chapter on leadership and innovation.
6. The section on listening has been buttressed in the chapter on the language of leadership.
7. A discussion of stress management has been added.
8. The role of goal setting is more explicit and clear.
9. Additional references have been added to the Appendix on theories of leadership.
10. The workbook has been shortened to make it more manageable.

ACKNOWLEDGMENTS

Publishing a book is an enormous undertaking that involves teams of people in many different constituencies. I'm grateful to my colleagues at the Darden School and at other schools, and in particular in the Organizational Behavior Teaching Society. Numerous students, associates, and readers have contributed thoughts and ideas to various parts of the book. A special thanks to Tony Mento. The support and encouragement at Prentice Hall has been wonderful, especially of Jennifer Collins and Ashley Santora.

LEVEL THREE LEADERSHIP

SECTION

1

INTRODUCTION

1 THE LEADERSHIP POINT OF VIEW

The task of a great leader is to get his people from where they are to where they have not been . . . Leaders must invoke an alchemy of great vision. Those leaders who do not are ultimately judged failures, even though they may be popular at the moment.

—HENRY KISSINGER

Leadership is about managing *energy,* first in yourself and then in those around you. This is not the usual academic definition. When you walk into an organization, you can tell quickly what the energy level is—and therefore the quality of the leadership in the place. If the energy level is low, the leadership is likely to be weak. If the energy level is high, there is likely good leadership in place. This book is about how to manage human energy, first in yourself and then in those around you. Most leadership discussions assume that the goal is to motivate others; here, we'll begin with self-leadership and then move to motivating (or energizing) others. Although we will explore and dissect multiple perspectives on leadership, in the end this book is an invitation to think at three levels about developing your personal leadership style. And in that context, I invite you to remember and think about this unusual definition of our topic: *Leadership is about managing* energy, *first in yourself and then in those around you.*

Let's begin with the fairly simple observation that being a leader depends on one's point of view, not on title or status. People who inhabit positions of power may or may not be leaders. Society tends to think that people who occupy leadership positions are leaders. If we meet a "president" of an organization, we are encouraged to think of that person as the leader of the organization, which may, in fact, not be true. We've all met many people with leadership titles who were not strategic thinkers, who had little influence, and who weren't sure where they were going—or how to get there! Some of the most powerful leaders in history—for example Mother Theresa, Jesus, and Gandhi—never held titular offices, yet they led millions of people. At the same time, some of the incumbents of the most powerful leadership positions were—and are—viewed as weak or ineffectual leaders with little influence. We can refer to people who occupy positions of authority as "authoritors." Whether they are leaders or not depends on their point of view.

Point of view, in large part, determines a person's attitude about everything they see including leadership. In essence, a point of view is a habitual way of seeing the world around us. Each individual develops over time a habitual point of view. This view may be a follower's point of view, an administrator's point of view, a bureaucrat's point of view, or even a contrarian's or devil's-advocate point of view. As we watch and listen to people, it often becomes apparent which point of view they are employing, whether consciously or not; they make it apparent in their speech. People who take the follower's point of view, for example, tend to ask questions like "What do you want me to do?" "How will you measure me?" "What resources do I have to do the job?" "Can you give me more authority to match my responsibility?" "Can you remove the obstacles I face?" People with a bureaucratic point of view tend to say things like "That's not my job" or "Our procedures require you to fill out this form." Table 1-1 provides some common language associated with these various points of view. The language for each is consistent with and reflects the underlying mental framework and perspective (point of view) that the person takes toward the surrounding world. Perhaps your experience has already familiarized you with these language clues.

TABLE 1-1	Language Cues of Various Points of View
Point of View (POV)	**Language Cues**
Follower's POV	What do you want me to do?
	Will you give me more authority?
	I need you to clear the obstacles for me.
Bureaucrat's POV	That's not my job.
	I'll pass that on to so-and-so.
	Our procedures don't allow that.
	We've never done it that way.
	This hasn't been approved.
	I can't do that without my supervisor's permission.
	Have you filled out the form yet?
Administrator's POV	What did they do last time?
	We've never done it that way.
	Let's see, what was the rule on that?
	How can we maintain our present position?
	This is too different from what we've done before.
Contrarian's POV	That'll never work!
	We tried that before.
	That's a terrible idea.
	You won't be able to fund it.
	You'll never be able to do it in time.
	Well, to play the Devil's Advocate . . .
	Yeah, but . . .

ELEMENTS OF THE LEADERSHIP POINT OF VIEW

The Leadership Point of View (LPV) is something different from the points of view and cues listed in Table 1-1. The LPV consists of three elements:

1. *Seeing* what needs to be done
2. *Understanding* ALL the underlying forces at play in a situation
3. Having the *courage to initiate action* to make things better

Does this perspective make sense to you? Think about it for a minute. What do leaders do? They enter or engage a situation, "somehow" see what needs to be done, ensure that they understand the situation well—not just their "favorite" perspective—and then exercise courage to initiate action to make things better. This process may seem simple. Adopting and employing an LPV is not necessarily easy; it is demanding, yet powerful. It demands broad, strategic thinking, careful analysis and insight, and careful planning mixed with lots of courage. Taking an LPV requires a willingness to focus your attention, your efforts, and your time and energy (Table 1-2).

Seeing What Needs to be Done

Most people rely on someone else to tell them what needs to be done. The problem with this approach is that eventually *someone* must make that decision. Someone asks someone else, explicitly or implicitly, "What should we do?" And then that person asks the next person, who asks the next person, and eventually, the person who decides what to do next, for better or worse, is the "leader."

How does one decide what to do next? What should the priorities be? These questions have no easy answers, yet the truth is that sometime, somewhere, someone has to say, "Well, let's go left instead of right." It may be that the higher level people in some organizations have better information, better experience, and better judgment and that they are better prepared to make those decisions. Or you may say, "They developed their leadership capacity after they got the leadership job/title." It's true that people often grow into their jobs, but sometimes they don't. This reality is the genesis of the widely mentioned Peter Principle—that a person will be promoted to the level of his or her incompetence. In other words, people are promoted for doing well, and when they don't do well, they stop getting promoted, so organizations tend to fill up with people who are incompetent at their jobs.[1] When a senior position in an organization opens up, who will be chosen to fill it? Usually, the person *perceived* to have performed the best at the next level down is the one promoted.

TABLE 1-2 The Leadership Point of View

1. Do you *see* what needs to be done?
2. Do you *understand* the underlying forces at play?
3. Do you *have the courage to initiate action* to make things better?

---

[1] Laurence J. Peter and Raymond Hull, *The Peter Principle: Why Things Always Go Wrong* (New York: Bantam, 1970).

So we might ask, When does one begin to take the LPV, that is, to begin looking around and deciding what needs to be done and then exercising the courage to get it done? If you wait until you have been promoted to a "leadership position" to begin thinking about developing your LPV, the odds are it's too late. You've spent too many years waiting for others to tell you what needs to be done to make a sudden professional and psychological jump to figuring that out for yourself—and others. For many, the habits of following are so ingrained that they may never become comfortable or good leaders.

Some people who have a Follower's Point of View or a Bureaucratic Point of View take exception to this thought. They defend themselves by attributing leadership characteristics to a title or position rather than to themselves. They argue, for example, "Well, my boss has more data than I do, so it's not possible for me to have a view of what needs to be done." This statement may be true, but in today's world, it is increasingly less likely. Today, with the Internet, intranets, and other forms of mass media, we have access to oceans of information. The challenge amid all of these data is to develop the vision, perception, wisdom, and judgment to sift the information for what is relevant to you and your organization—the information that contains implications for your future—and then to clarify and expose those implications for those around you.

Your boss carries no magic wand. Bosses are faced, like you, with scanning the environment, sifting through these oceans of information, and making choices about what's important and what's not. If you think you'd like more responsibility but you don't enjoy or aren't motivated to do this kind of mental homework, I invite you to rethink your ambitions. Leaders by their nature—and, I say, by definition—are charged with seeing what others commonly do not. This vision does not come overnight. It's the result of lots of reading, lots of scanning, lots of conversations, and lots of thinking. If you look around your work and cannot see what needs to be done to make the place a beehive of productivity and value creation, look again. And again. And again.

Another aspect to recognizing what needs to be done comes from seeing what needs to be done *in yourself.* Most would-be leaders look out there for ways to change the world. Few are wise enough to realize that unless they change the way they deal with the world, nothing much is likely to change. At a minimum, it means changing the way you interact with the outside world. At a more profound level, it may mean changing some of your core assumptions about who you are and how the world works. In fact, we could argue, and we will later, that if you want to change something around you, you must first begin with yourself. Being able to see what needs to change in yourself is the key to becoming an effective leader.

Understanding All the Underlying Forces at Play

One of the reasons the suggestions of junior- or middle-level people are dismissed is that their proposals are made from a limited perspective that fails to take into account the broader issues that the more-senior people see. This limited perspective is particularly apparent when middle-level employees are called on to identify problems and offer solutions. In my experience, the proposals that are ultimately accepted show a more in-depth analysis of current conditions and situations and what aspects of the organization might be affected if these were changed. The proposals that are ultimately rejected tend to be narrowly focused and ignorant of related issues and forces affecting the situation. You cannot responsibly propose a new plant without considering the costs. You cannot realistically propose expanding a facility without understanding local zoning regulations and the size of the local labor pool. Sometimes what seems obvious and important to one employee is sheer folly to another who sees the big picture.

Leaders must continually work to broaden their vision and deepen their insight into the global, societal, market, competitive, consumer, and related issues that surround any organization. If they miss these or any underlying forces, their choices about what to focus on and what to do will be met with surprises, unanticipated obstacles, and perhaps failure. The same result is true for senior people who hold strong opinions not based on analysis. Sometimes subordinates must obey senior leaders while remaining convinced that their leaders don't see the whole picture; the malaise of seeing less clearly or comprehensively is not limited to lower levels of an organization. Again, your title does not guarantee your leadership capability.

Can you ever understand all that is required to make informed leadership choices? Probably not. You can stack the odds, though, by doing your homework, soliciting other viewpoints, and developing your judgment as to what works and what doesn't. Leaders must operate in conditions of uncertainty, and that reality implies the need for even more careful analysis and ultimately for some faith and courage. The fields of risk analysis and quantitative analysis in business schools help leaders-to-be to assess uncertain conditions and think about alternatives and potential outcomes. And although "paralysis by analysis" is not a good thing, many would-be leaders merely shoot from the hip and hope for the best.

If you take a real LPV, you'll do what you can to ensure you understand what's going on in a situation before you jump in. Some Americans believe that the worst thing is to do nothing, but sometimes, if you understood what was going on, you would realize it was the best thing. Although inaction is often deadly, so, too, can be the stereotypical North American approach, "Fire, Fire, Fire, Aim!"

Having the Courage to Initiate Action to Make Things Better

The final aspect of the LPV is having the courage to initiate action to improve the situation. Again, most people are unwilling to develop the requisite courage. Perhaps it's because they are comfortable in their current lifestyles and don't want the hassle that leadership brings. The "hassle factor" is one reason leaders make more money: they do things that others cannot or will not do (for whatever reason).

Many people don't want to be leaders. I see two main reasons for this lack of leadership initiative. The first is lack of strategic insight (the person has nothing to say about what we should do) and the second is fear of rejection (generally abbreviated FoR). Let's be blunt: Leadership requires courage. People in leadership roles are in crucibles of public scrutiny. Those who are comfortable with the current way of doing things will not like you suggesting changes, particularly if you're not seen as a leader. "Who are you to say?" they may comment. "What gives you the right?" If you've done your homework, at least you won't have to rely on that tired, old saw, "Because I said so, and I'm the boss." Instead, you can lay out your vision of why your strategic approach is important (what you see), explain why your solution addresses all the forces at play (political, economic, environmental, consumer, employee, etc.), and in the process, begin to persuade people to accept your way of thinking.

Presenting your case takes courage. Plain guts. What if you're wrong? You may be. What if they don't agree with you? I'm sure at least one contrarian won't! At that point, the weight of real responsibility will settle on your shoulders, and you'll know what it means to be a true leader, not just one in title alone.

A large proportion of society, the large majority of people, lives life in fear of rejection. Most people react negatively to this statement. Let's explore this reaction for a moment. Julian Rotter developed a concept he called the *Locus of Control*. Locus of Control is a rough measure of how much

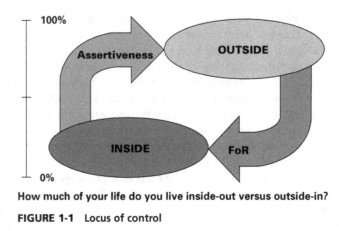

How much of your life do you live inside-out versus outside-in?

FIGURE 1-1   Locus of control

a person lives his or her life "inside-out" versus "outside-in." People who live their lives outside-in tend to think more about the opinions of others than about their own opinions of themselves. People who live more inside-out tend to think more of their own opinions than those of others (Figure 1-1).

Living "outside-in" means that a person thinks about what others will think or say in response to their own behavior. If you dress to please others, if you conform your desires to fit what others expect or demand, you're living, to that extent, outside-in. On the other hand, if you tend to assert your beliefs without worrying about what others will say, you'd be living more inside-out. Consider the extremes of the scale on the left side of the figure. Those who live their lives completely outside-in or are at the bottom of the inside-out scale, we could call "spineless, wishy-washy, opinionless." James Joyce wrote an interesting short story about a young woman in Dublin entitled "Clay." His thesis was that this person was so malleable that whatever group she was with, she molded herself to fit them . . . instead of the other way around.

At the top of the scale, people who live completely inside-out, we'd have narcissistic, ego-centric, self-centered, obnoxious boors. These are people who have no concern whatever for the thoughts and concerns of others. Where would you place your own behavior on this scale? How much do you worry about what other people say? Does that focus change what you say or do? On balance, are you more concerned about what others think of you? Or are you more likely to do what you want and let the chips fall where they may? For example, do you ever (how often?) change what you're thinking before you speak in order to be more socially "acceptable"? Do you ever (how often?) not do things you really want to do because of what others might think? If this behavior is not fear of rejection, what is it?

The fear of rejection is a powerful thing. As social beings, we humans contain within us a pow-erful, probably genetic, force that makes us want to belong to, to be a part of, a group of some kind. In prehistoric times, this predisposition probably kept us alive. Over the course of history, it became the basis for the fundamental sanction that humans in power imposed on those who were, in their view, misbehaving: removal or rejection from society. The only question was, for how long? Five minutes in a parental "time-out." Thirty years in prison for rape or armed robbery. Indefinitely in the case of life imprisonment or capital punishment. In the religious world, excommunication was, and is, the ultimate sanction. So, if you were so inclined, don't dismiss the importance of the concept of the fear of rejection out of hand—we all want to be accepted by somebody. The questions are, by whom and how many and how often? You may ask yourself if your fear of rejection keeps you from behav-ing more like a leader, and whether you'd like to work on that aspect of your dealings with others.

Conclusions

This opening chapter introduced a number of important concepts beginning with "Leadership is about managing energy, first in yourself and then in those around you." One implication of this assertion is that before you start thinking about influencing others, you might want to think about reflection and introspection. Reflection has become an important part of the current research on leadership. Throughout this book, I will invite you to reflect, to self-assess, on a number of aspects and dimensions of leadership. The workbook at the end of the book will help you in these self-assessments. The premise is that the person who knows him- or herself well is better equipped not only to lead, but to lead well. Executive coaching is big business; more and more executives realize that the issues we've begun to develop in this chapter are not just rudimentary, low-level, introductory concepts, but rather leadership-related concepts that extend to leaders in their mid-fifties and older and even those who serve on the executive committees.

I've also said that people develop a point of view during their lives and that those who have an LPV, regardless of their title, are more likely to succeed in leadership positions. If you can size up a situation quickly, have the ability to understand all the forces at play, and have the internal courage to initiate action, you can develop your leadership capacity. This perspective includes being aware of how you need to change if you want to become an effective leader.

We also argued in this chapter that people shrink from leadership roles for two main reasons: not having a strategic story to tell and the fear of rejection. The first can be remedied with study, practice, and active learning, but the latter is a deeper issue. Learning to trust your conclusions when others disagree is a fact of life for people in leadership roles. Finding the balance between being open to the opinions of others and being confident of your views is a central leadership challenge.

If you want to develop your LPV, you can begin by developing your own strategic thinking capacity. Rather than waiting for someone else to tell you what needs to be done, do your own mental homework. Where do you think the organization to which you belong should be going? Why? What data do you have? What's your rationale? You don't need to wait until you are assigned to the leadership role to begin thinking about these things. In fact, if you do, the odds are you'll never make it there. Don't wait for someone else to tell you what the strategic future of your department or division will be. By then, it may be too late—as they announce the closing of your division, the sale of your section, or the outsourcing of your department's services to a subcontractor. Look around. Look beyond your present circle of responsibilities. Devote time weekly to thinking about where your organization should be going. At a minimum, you'll be a much better conversationalist at receptions and in the hallway. More likely, you will come to be viewed as a person who goes beyond the current job, beyond the bureaucratic mind-set, to a proactive view of the business as a whole—the stuff of which leaders are made.

The times, as Bob Dylan wrote, are "a-changin'." In some ways things are different, and in some ways they are the same. The next chapter will explore the challenges of these changes for leaders and would-be leaders.

Concepts Introduced in This Chapter

1. Leadership is about managing energy, first in yourself and then in those around you.
2. People take habitual points of view, some as leaders, some as followers, some as bureaucrats.
3. The Leadership Point of View (LPV) consists of *seeing* what needs to be done, *understanding* all forces at play, and having the *courage* to initiate action to make things better.

4. People lack in leadership for two main reasons: a lack of strategic thinking (no story to tell) and a fear of rejection (the desire to be accepted by others).
5. People live their lives balanced in some way between inside-out and outside-in. Leaders live more inside-out than outside-in.
6. Self-leadership involves the realization that to change the world around us, we must be willing to change things in ourselves—in the way we think, the way we communicate, the way we believe the world is or should be.

Questions for Personal Reflection

1. What is your average daily energy level? How does your energy level affect those around you?
2. Can you manage or change your energy level? Or do surrounding circumstances tend to determine how you feel?
3. What things will you have to change in yourself in order to become an effective leader?
4. In most situations, are you able to see what needs to be done? Or do you find yourself waiting to be guided or nudged one way or another?
5. Do you enjoy learning about a broad range of issues and forces in society? Or would you rather focus on your favorite subject?
6. How much of your life do you live inside-out versus outside-in? Why? Where did this style come from? What, if any, change would you like to make in this balance?
7. Suppose you were just asked to be the president of your current organization (university or company or other organization). What would your strategy be for the organization?
8. How much do you worry about or consider what other people think when you speak or act? Why? How much does the fear of rejection shape your behavior?

CASELET FOR DISCUSSION

George Hendrickson had just been asked to be the new CEO of the Rocky Mountain Box Company. He was the first person who was not a member of the founding family to be in charge of the company. Competition was fierce in the industry and margins were small, often just pennies a box. George and his colleagues, former peers and now employees, knew the cardboard box business inside and out. Yet many competitors were developing all kinds of new container options, including plastics, plastic coatings, linings, enclosures, odd shapes and sizes, and so on. George had a strong loyalty to his company and its employees, and he wanted to ensure their future.

Research the paperboard container business on the Internet and then be prepared to offer advice to George.

WORKBOOK

Note on page 343 of the workbook the ways that you've used the fear of rejection in the past week and what the impact of that tendency is on your ability to lead.

CONTRIBUTING YOUR OWN CASELETS

Have you seen or experienced a situation involving the concepts introduced in this chapter? If so, and if you'd like to contribute your experience/situation to our case data bank, please visit http://faculty.darden.virginia.edu/clawsonj/ and click on the "Contribute new caselets" button.

2 | THE DIAMOND MODEL OF LEADERSHIP IN ORGANIZATIONS

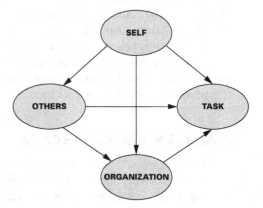

(Before you read this chapter, I encourage you to complete the exercise, Survey of Managerial Style, on page 352.)

In a learning organization, leaders are designers, stewards, and teachers. They are responsible for building organizations where people continually expand their capabilities to understand complexity, clarify vision, and improve shared mental models—that is, they are responsible for learning.

—PETER SENGE,
Fifth Discipline, 340

We live in a rapidly changing world that needs leaders at every level of society. We need leaders at the international, national, local, neighborhood, and family levels. We need leaders in businesses at all levels regardless of the overall size of these businesses. We need these leaders because until we all become perfectly and uniformly able to perceive the meaning of present and future events clearly and to act on them effectively, leaders help us see things differently, help us to organize our efforts, and help us to accomplish things that we might not be able to accomplish otherwise. Unless one has a model of leadership—that is, a mental map of what leadership is and how one employs it—one's attempts to influence others will be ad hoc, inconsistent, and wandering. Note that everyone has *some kind of model* about leadership in their minds. I invite you here to begin making your model of leadership more explicit.

Do you want to *be* a leader in society or just *know about* leadership in society? Some people say they are uncomfortable trying to influence others, or they are too shy, or they are more interested in doing their work than in getting involved in "office politics." An alternative way to think about this question is to ask whether you'd like to have more positive influence on those around you. You could consider thousands of employees, a few team members, colleagues in a professional firm, other citizens on a local committee, or members of your family. If the answer to that question is yes, then think about strengthening your small "l" leadership skills. You can learn something here that will help you develop that positive influence among your peer group. Having a flexible but powerful way of thinking about developing that influence will guide your efforts, and that's our goal in this chapter.

LEADING STRATEGIC CHANGE

Our model begins with a key concept that leadership only has meaning if it has a direction and a means of achieving that direction. Leaders take initiative; they are proactive. In other words, leadership without a strategy is aimless, and leadership without the ability to manage change is powerless. Thus, while we speak separately of leadership, strategy, and managing change, we could—and should—also speak of *leading strategic change* as a more comprehensive concept. We really cannot talk about leadership without talking about strategy and managing change. The overlap of these domains is shown in Figure 2-1.

First we must ask, leadership for what? This is the strategic question. Once a person has developed the answer to this question, the next question is, how can we get there? This question usually involves three other domains: the environment, others (the potential followers), and the organization (the setting in which the leader and the followers work). Finally, one must look at the issue of managing change, another important leadership initiative. In fact, one could argue

FIGURE 2-1 Leading strategic change

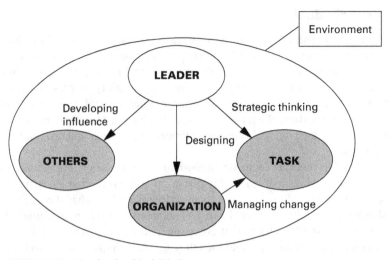

FIGURE 2-2   Key leadership initiatives

that no change means no leadership. Leadership is not about protecting the past, but rather about building the future.

One way to diagram the view of leadership outlined just now is shown in Figure 2-2. The potential leader must address all three directions, or vectors, to solve his or her fundamental problems of "What?" and "How?" These three initiatives provide the basis for a comprehensive, four-wheel-drive utility model of leadership.

KEY ELEMENTS OF LEADERSHIP

Each of the four basic elements introduced in Figure 2-2—the individual leader, the task facing the organization, others working in the organization, and the organization itself—clearly creates an impact on the outcomes of a leadership situation. The characteristics of the leader, the individual, will make a difference. The nature of the tasks or challenges facing the organization will have an impact, so will the nature of the people in the organization. The impact caused by the organization's design is often overlooked; however, structure, systems, and culture play a huge role in the outcomes of a leadership situation. Further, if we examine the relationship between these four basic elements, we can say that leadership is not just a result of any one of them *but of how all the elements work together.* In other words, leadership is only in part about the qualities of the leader: one must consider the strategy envisioned, the relationships with the followers, the organizational context in which the leader will attempt to influence those followers, and the environmental context in which the efforts to lead take place.

In this view, leadership is the result of a confluence of the characteristics of these four main domains and of the relationships between and among them, a total of at least 11 essential factors. Each of these factors as much as the traits of any potential leader will influence the outcomes of a situation and help determine whether those outcomes are positive. Let's examine each of the elements.

Leader: The Individual

Clearly, the individual leader in a leadership situation possesses characteristics that will influence the outcomes. Who you are and how you present yourself, your voice, your language, your demeanor, your energy level—all of these things and more will have an impact on the outcomes. Each individual leader brings to a situation a variety of personal characteristics, including preferences, skills, values, goals, education, interpersonal style, and a psychological makeup. These attributes shape the leader's abilities to observe, to make sense of and deal with the environment, to understand and relate to followers, to manage change, and to define and work toward a goal.

Many leadership theories focus on individual characteristics, but research shows that the so-called great-man theory of leadership doesn't work; which characteristics are effective depends on the situation. Many modern corporations develop what they call competency models, a shorter list usually of about 10 to 20 characteristics that management believes are essential to be a successful leader in that company. Although a great deal of overlap occurs among these competency models, sometimes they are too complex to use well or too simple to be comprehensive.

Either way, *who you are makes a difference.* Although who you are makes a difference on leadership outcomes, your personality is not *all* that is necessary for effective leadership. Strategic thinking, influencing others, designing organizations, managing change, and building commitment between employees and the organization are also key elements in leadership outcomes.

Task: What Should We Do?

As we described in Chapter 1, people who take the Leadership Point of View (LPV) can size up a situation and see what needs to be done. This assessment is not always easy. Chief executives responsible for large corporations must size up an enormous array of alternatives and select the ones they believe to be most important. This process includes competitive issues, financial options, operating alternatives, hiring practices, and a host of other possible "tasks" to consider. From that bewildering array, *someone* must choose what's most important and what we are going to focus on. In this first step in the LPV, the individual leader's view of those tasks—of what the organization should be working on—sets the agenda for an organization and is critical to the leadership outcomes in that situation.

Clearly, one person's view of those tasks can vary from another's. Outside observers may see another set of tasks or challenges that the organization "ought" to be addressing. An individual's ability to read and assess what is taking place around them guides their conclusions about what is important and what the organization could do—and should do. This view, or vision, of what *needs* to be done, what *can* be done, or what *should* be done will shape virtually all of the leader's behavior as well as the agenda for the rest of the organization. The way a person assesses the challenges facing an organization is clearly a function of that person's vision and of the "realities"—or issues that come into focus when the leader recognizes them and places priority on them—facing the organization.

Depending on what the leader(ship) sees, what the leader believes he or she can do, and how the leader behaves, the situation might be transformed from a no-change situation into one in which dramatic and positive things begin to happen. Leadership involves sensing, seeing, and *appreciating* what is taking place around us. The capacity to appreciate what's happening around you is not an innate gift, but rather a skill that you can develop and strengthen. Like strategic thinking in general, environmental appreciation is part science and part art.

Others: Working Together with Followers

Leadership doesn't happen without followers, so any map or model of leadership must include the "others" or followers. The employees of an organization also bring to the situation a set of characteristics, including values, preferences, experience, skills, goals, educational background, and concerns. Environmental pressures affect them as well as the leader, but perhaps in different ways. Their personal and collective characteristics help determine whether the leader will be able to develop an influential relationship with them. The quality of the leader–follower relationship (the north–west axis in Figure 2-3) will determine in large part whether the followers will develop a view of the tasks facing the organization similar to the view held by the leader (the east–west axis in Figure 2-3). If the others don't trust or respect the leader, it will be difficult for them to develop commitment for and energy to work on the leader's view of what can be or should be done.

Organization: Designing the Right Context

As the leader and employees develop convergent views of what the firm should be doing, the structure of the organization and the systems that hold it together become increasingly important. At a minimum, organizations consist of a predictable set of features: a structure, a series of human resource management and other kinds of subsystems (introduced later), and a culture. Organizational culture is the result of the collision between the design decisions managers make and the people they hire into the organization. The leadership of an organization decides what they want the structure and systems of a business to be. The people who populate that design determine consciously what the culture of the organization will be.

This organizational design subcontext can either enable the leader and the employees to move ahead toward their objectives or constrain them from realizing their vision. If the organization's structure and systems do not fit the demands of the task as defined, the organization and its leadership will be at a severe disadvantage. Effective leaders are constantly working with questions of whether the organizational context is favorable to the task or mission they defined. Stan Davis, in

FIGURE 2-3   Elements in leadership

his book *Future Perfect,*[1] asserts that *all* organizations are obsolete by definition because of the time lag between the development of a strategic vision and the implementation of an organization to work toward it. By the time the organization is in place, he says, especially in a turbulent environment, the changes in the strategic picture require that the organization change again to try to keep up. Peter Senge reinforces this message with his concept of the learning organization in *The Fifth Discipline.*[2] Unless an organization is a learning organization, he notes, it will be unable to keep up with the rapidly changing world as we now know it. Similarly, if the attitudes and abilities of the employees are not matched to or aligned with the systems and structure of the organization, their efforts to achieve the goals of the firm will be diluted and diffused.

A DIAMOND IN THE ROUGH

These four elements—the leader, the task, the followers, and the organization—can be arrayed in the shape of a diamond as shown in Figure 2-3. Each of the four elements and their characteristics are important to understand if one wants to be an effective leader. This basic four-point mental model or map of leadership provides the basis for a flexible framework that can be applied to a variety of settings and used to understand a multitude of situations. It's a "diamond in the rough" because one does not need to specify exactly which characteristics need to be addressed in each element: the model is flexible. As times change, as knowledge increases, our understanding of the importance of different dimensions in each element might evolve. Plus, the context in which these elements combine may change. That said, I assert that every leadership situation has these basic elements in it. If one ignores or discounts any of these elements, one is likely to fail as a leader.

Environment: The Context

All leadership situations occur within an environmental context that includes, among other things, political forces, legal forces, labor market realities, financial vicissitudes, increasingly diverse demographics, advancing technology, investor inquiries, an international arena, and competitive pressures. Although these forces are often overlooked or only given cursory attention, they affect all other elements of a leadership situation, individually and in concert. Effective leaders are adept at scanning and interpreting these external forces and their impact. Chapter 1 described how important these environmental changes are in setting a context for one's attempts to lead or influence others. Environmental factors affect *all* of the elements of the model. They certainly affect the possible tasks that a leader must consider and hence his or her strategic thinking. They affect the "others" in the organization—the employees and members whom one is trying to lead. They affect the nature of the organization, including its shape and culture. And they certainly affect one's ability to manage change. So we illustrate this pervasive influence by showing the leadership situation being embedded in the circle of surrounding environmental factors.

Results: Outcomes of Leadership

In the end, leadership is about results, about outcomes. The choices leaders make about *what outcomes* to focus on reflect their values and assumptions. These outcomes include profitability, customer satisfaction, operational effectiveness and efficiency, and employee growth, learning,

---

[1] Stanley M. Davis, *Future Perfect* (Reading, MA: Addison-Wesley, 1987).
[2] Peter Senge, *The Fifth Discipline: The Art and Practice of the Learning Organization* (New York: Doubleday, 1990).

and morale. Most leaders in private-sector businesses include profitability high on their list. Profitability, however, is a function of a series of important steps: satisfying customers who purchase, developing the organizational capabilities to service those customers, and building an organization that is sustainable. When these three other elements are aligned, profits emerge.

The balanced scorecard model developed at the Harvard Business School by Robert Kaplan and David Norton presents this "balanced" way of thinking about outcome measures.[3] If customers are not satisfied or delighted, one is not likely to make money in the long run. If your internal processes are not efficient, you are not likely to make money in the long run. And if your organization is not learning, you are not likely to continue making money in the long run. If you're familiar with American baseball and the baseball diamond consisting of first base, second base, third base, and home plate, you can make these elements analogous to the bases. Customer satisfaction is the first base; if you don't have happy customers, you might as well stop right there. If you have happy customers, then we can ask, are you making them happy efficiently? If so, you'll get to second base and in "scoring position" by improving your efficiencies. Third base is the capacity to learn regardless of how the environment changes. And if you do all these things, you're likely to make it home, to score, and that's the financial payoff. So, selecting the "right" measures of leadership situation outcomes becomes an important leadership issue in and of itself. We address this topic in greater depth later.

INTERELEMENT RELATIONSHIPS ARE IMPORTANT

The four basic elements—the leader, a set of strategic challenges or tasks, the followers, and the organization—set in an environmental context, form the key building blocks of leadership outcomes. The characteristics of these elements provide the basic raw materials of a leadership situation, but it is the *relationships* among them that determine how it will all turn out. Consider again the diamond-shaped model shown in Figure 2-3.

On the northeast corner, the line between Leader and Task represents the relationship between the leader and the challenges facing the organization. This relationship is the substance of what the leader pays attention to and *sees* as critical as well as forming the crux of the leader's vision of what the organization should be doing. If this axis is broken (i.e., if the leader has not developed a vision of what needs to be done and set priorities for self and organization, that is, if the leader has no strategic story to tell), the leader has no purpose, no direction, and no outlet for attempts to lead or influence. In short, a leader cannot get somewhere if he or she doesn't know where he or she wants to go. From an array of tasks, what the leader chooses to focus on and work on defines the leadership agenda.

On the northwest corner, the line between Leader and Others represents the relationship between the leader and the followers. We can analyze and examine the quality of those relationships and determine whether they are healthy or "broken." If they are broken—that is, if the leader doesn't have influence with the followers—not much will happen in the way of leadership, no matter how clear the vision (north–east axis) is.

The north–south axis, the line between Leader and Organization, represents the leader's design decisions about how the organization should be structured and operate. If a leader has a good strategic story to tell and a strong relationship with the followers but makes bad organizational design decisions, the energy of the organization can be drained away amazingly fast. Further, when

[3] See, for example, Robert S. Kaplan and David P. Norton, "The Balanced Scorecard: Measures That Drive Performance," *Harvard Business Review,* July 1, 2005, R0507Q.

boards of directors hire new leaders, if the new leader's style and skills don't match the organiza-tion's culture, one or the other will have to change. If the leader is a good organizational designer and a master of managing change, this north–south link will be strong. If the leader comes from the outside and has a style that is at great variance with the characteristics of the organization, it will be difficult to create a positive leadership outcome. Numerous situations reported in the press describe an outside leader who came in and was clearly at odds with the culture, structure, costing systems, and other features of the organization and who, even though he or she was hired to make changes, was eventually rejected by the organization as a human body might reject a poorly conducted transplant.

On the southwest corner, the line between Others and Organization represents the quality of the connection between the followers and the organization. Here we can assess the strength of the bonds between the organization and its members. If this relationship is basically a mercenary one in which people trade time and talent for money, it will be more difficult to lead toward world-class performance, for instance, than if that relationship were a committed one in which the systems and processes of the organization encourage a deeper attachment to the organization.

On the southeast corner, the line between Organization and Task represents the match between the various aspects of the organization (structure, systems, processes, culture, etc.) and the strategic challenges facing the organization. If the organization is ill-structured to meet those challenges, it will be difficult to create a positive leadership outcome. As already noted, this axis is constantly changing as the environment changes, and the leadership tries to reorganize the business to keep up. Employees who resist these changes probably don't have a clear view of the strategy of the organization (east–west axis) and, therefore, are less committed to doing what the organization wants and needs.

On the east–west axis, the line between Others and Task represents the followers' take on what they are trying to do. A gap between what the leader sees (the northeast corner) and what the followers see (the east–west link) decreases the likelihood of a positive leadership outcome. If the leader's view of the task (northeast corner) is strong and the leader's relationships with the followers (north–west axis) are strong, but the east–west link is broken, management will have to constantly supervise what the employees are doing. If the east–west axis is strong, though, (i.e., the employees have a clear picture of the strategy and are committed to it) the need for management to supervise begins to melt away. Many not-for-profit organizations benefit from this congruence between employees' values and visions and those of the organization—and the leaders just have to keep out of the way.

Each of the circle elements portrayed in Figure 2-4, including the environment that surrounds them all, contributes a variety of features or characteristics that affect the outcome of the leadership opportunity. Leaders who ignore any of them may not get the desired results. Further, understanding the relationships between and among those elements is essential to under-standing leadership. So, leadership is more than just personal character traits and habits. It involves a leader's ability to think strategically, to bond with followers, and to design an organi-zation that people believe in and, ultimately, the capacity to manage change.

How the Diamond Model Relates to Other Models of Leadership

The diamond framework presented here is flexible enough to incorporate many of the features of the main leadership models present today, but in a way that is simple and useful for the practic-ing manager. The Diamond Model allows a focus on the individual characteristics of the leader

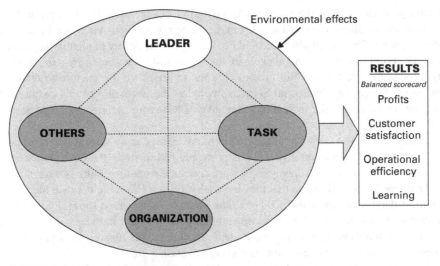

FIGURE 2-4   Diamond Model of leadership

and leaves room to include the useful elements of the great-leader theories. It focuses on leader–follower relationships (northwest corner). It also contains a strong contingency flavor and asserts that the fit between the leader and the situation is a critical part of a positive leadership outcome. The model includes the importance of leaders as designers in shaping their organizations. Although the model doesn't give all the details related to each element or of the relationships that connect them, it does point out the key areas of attention that leaders need to be aware of and understand.

Basic Definitions

Before we continue, we need to establish some working definitions that will clarify what we mean by leadership in talking with others about what it is and isn't. We asserted in Chapter 1 that "leadership is about managing energy, first in yourself and then in those around you." We expand that definition by considering the relationship between power and leadership. First, simply put, *power* is the ability to make something happen. Power in organizations is the ability to get others to do what you want them to do. This definition simply states that when you make a change in something, you are exerting power in that thing. If you exert power, you get something done, you move a person, an organization, a project from here to there.

First, the ability to influence others can be taught. In fact, in *The West Point Way of Leadership,* Col. Larry Donnithorne notes that one West Point commandant once said that he could make a leader out of anyone who was not a schizophrenic.[4] To the extent that leadership includes the ability to think strategically, to communicate effectively with others, to design supportive organizations, and to lead change, leadership can be taught.

We can think of leadership skills as clustering around three areas: strategic thinking or visioning, garnering the commitment of others to that vision or strategy, and monitoring and

---

[4] Larry Donnithorne, *The West Point Way of Leadership* (New York: Currency Doubleday, 1993).

measuring progress toward the vision. The visioning cluster includes gaining an historical perspective, identifying trends in the present, and perceiving their outcomes in the future. It includes a concern for what might and could be. It includes the ability to identify signposts along the way that point one way or another. It includes the ability in some sense to dream, to see clearly a picture of the future you'd like to see, and to articulate that picture to others. If you completed the Survey of Managerial Style as invited at the beginning of this chapter, you can review your own data and the indications they give of how your preferences range across these three dimensions.

The first big reason why we cannot find as many leaders as we want is that most people do not do their strategic homework. That is, most people fail to study the environment carefully enough and, in the midst of that analysis, simply conclude what they think is what the business should be doing. Many will argue that they have a low vision (V) score because their jobs don't demand it. A database of more than 700 practicing managers, however, showed no clear correlation between the size of a person's V score and that person's level in the organization. In other words, you can and should develop your strategic-thinking skills regardless of your level in the organization. Others—your competitors in the organization—are.

The skills that cluster around "garnering the commitment of others" (the north–west axis) include communication style, patterns, and abilities. This skill cluster includes the level of trustworthiness a person has and the quality of the relationships an individual develops with others. It includes the ability to listen, to understand and respect the goals and dreams of others, and to find ways to match those goals with your own. All of these things can be taught.

The monitoring and measuring skills cluster includes the ability to design and follow significant measures of what you're trying to accomplish so you can attend as the organization begins to drift from your vision and to praise and celebrate those who contribute toward the goal.[5] This tripartite view of leadership skill development, what we could call the VCM perspective (for visioning, commitment gathering, and monitoring and measuring), is shown in Figure 2-5.

Not everyone will have the same proportion of these three skill clusters. Some people might have more visioning skills and fewer managing skills. Others might be excellent and inspiring communicators but not so good at coming up with the vision in the first place. Each of these skill clusters, however, includes specific skills that you can learn. By studying these skills and practicing them, you can increase your ability as a leader. Progress in this area also depends on some other factors that we'll discuss later.

The second element of our leadership definition is *willingness*. Some individuals with the ability to be leaders choose not to exert influence for a variety of reasons. Perhaps they are uncomfortable being center stage, laying out their thoughts and beliefs for others to see and accept or reject. Another reason for the lack of leaders is the *fear of rejection*. The issue here is that many people are so concerned about what others think of them, even if they have done their strategic homework, that they are afraid to speak honestly. Why? Fear of rejection. Sometimes, their reluctance is based on an ethical conclusion that believes in self-determination above all else. Regardless of the reason, each of us must decide whether we will accept or seek leadership responsibilities—and many are not willing to do so.

In some respects, leadership is like a crucible that either refines or incinerates a person's soul and being. At times, it feels like being the figurehead on the prow of a clipper ship, arms

---

[5] See James Kouzes and Barry Posner, *The Leadership Challenge* (San Francisco, CA: Jossey-Bass, 1987).

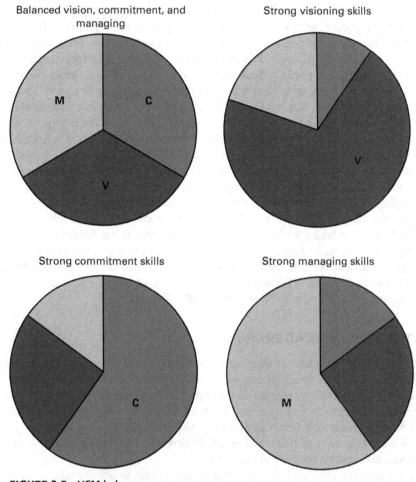

Balanced vision, commitment, and managing

Strong visioning skills

Strong commitment skills

Strong managing skills

FIGURE 2-5   VCM balance

and legs pinned back against the hull, face and chest exposed to the elements of the sea. The only buffer or protection is simple determination to persist and reach the goal. This aspect of leadership, the loneliness and vulnerability to attack and criticism, justified or not, often causes otherwise capable people to shrink. Even in smaller group settings, the process of exposing one's thoughts, feelings, beliefs, and analyses to others can be daunting. Clearly, in order to be a leader, one must develop some mental toughness and ability to endure criticism. Ultimately, to be a leader, one must be willing to overcome the fear of rejection and attempt to influence others.

The third key element of this definition lies in the choice of the followers to follow. When the agency of the followers is compromised or removed—when followers are forced or coerced into doing something—leadership ceases to exist and something else takes its place. If you threaten people with their jobs and thereby force them to do what you want, you may indeed be exerting power, but by this definition, you're not leading. If you get people to do what you want them to do but they don't know about it, you've moved into the realm of manipulation, which also is *not* leadership. If people feel that they *have* to do what you want them to do for fear of their jobs or their well-being, you've moved out of leadership into coercion. True leadership is more than about winning the behavior of people; it is about winning their minds and their hearts.

People in positions of potential leadership, such as CEOs, vice presidents, or supervisors, sometimes borrow authority from their titles and order people to do things on threat of their livelihoods. Many years ago, Stephen Covey likened it to using a crutch to walk: unable to influence on one's own merits, the person who borrows power from his or her title to force people to do things is using a leadership crutch. Although the short-term job may get done, it is not leadership. It is intimidation and coercion, and in the end, it undermines one's ability to lead others.

Manipulation and leadership are distinctly different. Manipulation is when you get someone to do something without them knowing it. You use this method because deep down you believe that they won't do it if they knew what you were doing. The deceit involved in manipulation removes the element of voluntary followership. If people don't know what you're getting them to do, how can it be leadership? The question becomes, If the followers knew what you were doing, how you were doing it, and what your motives were, would they still follow you willingly? If the answer is yes, then you don't need to use the manipulative techniques and you can claim to be a leader. If the answer is no, you're not leading, you're manipulating, and when the "followers" find out, your "leadership" will collapse.

TARGET LEVELS OF LEADERSHIP

When people talk about leadership, they most often think of the organizational or institutional level and refer to the titular heads of companies or foundations or institutions as their leaders. True organizational leaders have a broad impact; their decisions can affect thousands of lives. Yet much research and experience suggest that we need leaders at many levels in organizations.[6] Surely, each work group within an organization needs leadership to guide and manage its daily activities. We can also think of individual or self-leadership.[7] If we are unable in some sense to lead ourselves, how can we presume to lead others?

The general model in Figure 2-4 applies to organizations, to work groups, and to individuals as well as society writ large. These four levels of attention are important to remember throughout the discussion in the remainder of the book. The concepts later introduced about the ethics of leadership, the need for strategic thinking, and the ability to influence others and to redesign structures to unleash potential all relate to each of these levels—society, the organization, the work group, and you, the individual.

Leadership occurs at four levels:
* 1. Societal*
* 2. Organizational*
* 3. Work Group*
* 4. Individual*

---

[6] See John Kotter, *The Leadership Factor* (New York: The Free Press, 1988), for a discussion "little l leadership" needed everywhere in organizations.
[7] See Charles Manz, "Self-Leadership," *Academy of Management Review* 11, no. 3 (July 1986): 585.

Conclusions

As you reflect on the model in Figure 2-4 and contemplate your own goals and aspirations of leadership, note that leadership is the *result* of a situation in which people have worked together voluntarily with energy to accomplish some purpose. In this view of leadership, leaders respect the dignity of their followers and recognize the importance and power of self-determination. They work openly rather than covertly to convince, persuade, and guide others to a view of what needs to be done and, in so doing, build commitment to that view. This approach depends on a strong ethical foundation. Further, leaders' attempts to influence occur in environmental, national, and organizational contexts that can shape or severely handicap their efforts.

The view of leadership presented here incorporates a broad view of leadership potential situations in which various forces are at play. These forces include the characteristics of the leader, those of the followers, the organization, and the environment (and its bewildering array of strategic possibil-

ities). This view is optimistic about the internal capacities of the followers and the leaders' confidence in and acceptance of their own role in guiding those capacities. This view asserts that leadership begins when a person recognizes all of the elements of the situation and is willing to work to unlock the potential in each of those elements to make something happen. This view contends that leadership requires significant, assertive personal attributes, intense effort, and a deep sense of respect for the environment and people. It requires an ability to see and formulate strategy, an ethical foundation on which to build relationships, and a clear sense of appropriate measures and the ability to manage change.

All these features take place at three levels: that of the individual, the work group, and the organization. Effective leaders are aware of and active at all three levels; they are not only willing to influence organizations and work groups around them, to lead strategic change, but also willing to initiate equally disruptive change in themselves.

Concepts Introduced in This Chapter

1. Leadership is the result of much more than personal characteristics of the potential leader. Leadership includes defining a task (setting a strategy), the quality of relationships with followers, designing organizations, and managing change within the organization and in relationships with followers in order to achieve the desired outcomes of the task/strategy.
2. Leadership is different from exercising power. Power gets others to do what you want them to do; leadership involves ability (skill in influence), willingness to be in the leadership role, and influence that creates voluntary response. Many people who

have the skills to lead choose not to because they don't want to be in the leadership role with all of its pressures and difficulties.
3. One cannot talk about leadership without talking about strategic thinking, managing change, and ethics. Effective leaders are strategic thinkers, masters of the change process, and ethically grounded.
4. Leadership involves a cluster of skills around creating a vision, a second cluster of skills around garnering commitment, and a third cluster of skills around managing progress toward the vision.
5. Leadership occurs at four levels: externally, in the organization, in the work group, and in one's self.

Questions for Personal Reflection

1. To what extent do your efforts to influence others rely on your position or title (exercising power)? If your title or position were taken away, would others listen to you? Why or why not?
2. How much time do you spend in strategic thought, creating a vision for yourself, your workgroup, or your organization? What would you need to do to increase this time?

3. How comfortable are you with the change process? Do you understand it? Do you feel like you are a master at managing it?
4. Why is it important for a potential leader to have a clear vision or dream in order to become an effective leader?
5. Recall a person with authority over you who used power rather than leadership as defined here to influence you. How did you respond to that person? What were your thoughts about that experience? What did you learn from that experience?

CASELET FOR DISCUSSION

Consider the profiles presented in Figure 2-5. Can you identify individuals that fit each profile? Who are they and how does their behavior reflect the profiles laid out in the figure?

WORKBOOK

Complete the Survey of Managerial Style on page 352. As requested at the end of the exercise, consider how you'd like to develop your leadership skill set while you're working through the book and the program or course associated with it. Please contribute your data to our growing database at http://faculty.darden.virginia. edu/clawsonj/index.htm.

CONTRIBUTING YOUR OWN CASELETS

Have you seen or experienced a situation involving the concepts introduced in this chapter? If so and if you'd like to contribute your experience/situation to our case data bank, please visit http://faculty.darden. virginia.edu/clawsonj/ and click on the "Contribute new caselets" button.

3 | LEVELS OF LEADERSHIP

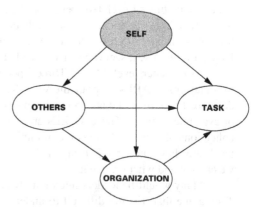

For every thousand hacking away at the leaves of evil, there is one striking at the root.

—Henry David Thoreau[1]

Before we address the details of the various aspects of the general Diamond Model in detail, an important set of ideas needs consideration. These ideas concern the difference between focusing on the superficial and focusing on the deeper, more powerful aspects of leadership. Leadership is about affecting human behavior, which can be thought of as occurring at three levels: visible behavior, conscious thought, and semiconscious or preconscious basic values and assumptions. Visible behavior, what I will call "Level One," is simply what others say and do, the things that you can capture on a video camera. People speak and act. They make gestures and movements that we can see and hear. This visible behavior is Level One behavior.

---

[1] Quoted in Stephen Covey, *Spiritual Roots of Human Relations* (Salt Lake City, UT: Desert Book Co., 1971).

TABLE 3-1 Levels of Human Behavior
1. <u>Visible behavior</u>
2. Conscious thought
3. Values, assumptions, beliefs, and expectations (VABEs)

At "Level Two," people have conscious thoughts, which they may or may not reveal at Level One. Although we may not be aware of these thoughts, the person very much is. They decide what to show to us and what to keep to themselves. They *think*, and they are aware. Of course, sometimes Level Two behavior "leaks" to Level One in tiny ways—a sigh, a grimace, a grin, a twitch. In our attempts to lead others, we may or may not pay attention to what others are thinking—in fact, often we do not. Many authoritors only pay attention to what others do, in large part, because it seems consistent with a "results-oriented" perspective.

At a deeper level, "Level Three," people hold a set of values, assumptions, beliefs, and expectations (VABEs[2]) about the way the world is or should be. These values and beliefs developed over time and are so much a part of the person that they may be only partially visible or available to them. These VABEs are, therefore, often semiconscious or partially conscious collections of what we have come to think of as the way the world is or should be. These three levels are shown in Table 3-1, in which the double underline denotes a separation between what we can see and what we cannot.

Many would-be leaders intentionally choose to try to influence people at Level One only. They argue that it is too difficult to understand Levels Two and Three, and, in fact, they don't really care what's happening at Levels Two and Three, so they focus on Level One. Dealing with people only at the level of their visible behavior is, they argue, simpler and seemingly more accurate. In fact, many theorists and observers argue strongly that leaders can *only* deal with Level One and that attempts to influence Levels Two and Three are unethical and an invasion of privacy. This is the essence of the Skinnerian view. B. F. Skinner, the famous psychologist, conducted research and wrote extensively arguing that we could condition animals and people to behave in certain ways by managing the mechanisms by which they were rewarded.[3] You may remember, he put (among other things and in his work's simplest form) a chicken in a box with a button; when the chicken pecked on the button, it was rewarded with a kernel of corn. By reinforcing the pecking behavior with the corn, Skinner was able to teach the chicken to peck in a certain way. Skinnerians, then, tend to argue that leadership should focus on behavior and not think about or worry about what goes on *inside* a person. There are several issues with this approach, not the least of which is that this model relies on the assumption of the consistency of the chicken's underlying value on a kernel of corn. Satiated chickens likely have little interest in the marginal piece of corn.

Visible behavior is clearly the most readily available. Levels Two and Three, on the other hand, are available to us only through two means: (1) when the other person decides to reveal him-or herself to us, and (2) through our observations of their behavior, which enable us to *infer* what the underlying VABEs might be. Both of these methods are imprecise. We cannot always be sure that what someone says is an accurate reflection of what they are thinking or experiencing.

---

[2] Some scholars may find this terminology weak, yet over a dozen years, it has proven effective in executive education settings as a means for consolidating several ideas and making them memorable.

[3] See B. F. Skinner, *Beyond Freedom and Dignity* (New York: Bantam, 1971).

Of course, others may or may not be *able* to tell us their thoughts and feelings as well. They may be hesitant to tell us the truth or they may not be very clear in their own minds about their thinking. When we observe people, if we are careful, we may get some vital clues about why people behave the way they do. In fact, sometimes our observations may give us a clearer picture than if we just listened to what they said. People don't always behave at Level One consistently with what they say they believe.

The model presented in this book is decidedly not Skinnerian. Rather, it recognizes the levels of conscious thought and of somewhat vague but strongly held values, assumptions, beliefs, and expectations and argues that effective leadership must take into account Levels Two and Three. Unless one does, one has little hope of understanding why people behave the way they do and therefore, of influencing them in profound ways, ways that move beyond monitoring and constraining superficial behavior.

BODY, HEAD, AND HEART

Because visible behavior is decidedly physical and observable, we can liken Level One to the body. Some companies and managers explicitly state their wish that employees would check their thoughts and emotions at the door, and just do their jobs. In essence, this philosophy is focused on Level One and attempts to manage visible behavior in isolation from what people think (head) and believe (heart). Many managers express frustration because they try to hire "workers" and "people" keep coming to work; that is, because of what they think and believe, they often do things that managers don't want them to. Most managerial systems since the beginning of the Industrial Revolution (around 1800) focused on Level One, on visible behavior, with much less attention on Levels Two and Three. Frederick Taylor's work on time–motion studies around the turn of the twentieth century, for instance, focused largely on managing the behavior of employees with little attention given to their inner thinking and feeling.[4] The underlying assumption of those who seek to influence only visible behavior is that people are like machines in that they can be programmed to behave consistently. The goal of Level One managerial systems is to minimize variance from work objectives by managing people to behave in the most efficient manner and in concert with the "corporation's values."

Increasingly, in a changing world with enormous volumes of information available to employees at every rank, the centralized, Level One control mentality is outdated and unworkable. People keep bringing their heads and their hearts to work, which influences their behavior constantly. Further, as competition increases, corporations are concerned about building high-performance workplaces where employees at all levels are committed to and engaged in serving customers, where their heads and hearts as well as their bodies are focused on high-quality work. Unless management can tap into the human potential at Levels Two and Three, it will be unable for the corporations to compete with the best of its competitors. Leading at Level One is a formula for mediocrity—not for world-class performance. It's a simple concept: unless the whole employee is engaged in the work, the work won't be as high quality as it otherwise would be. Focusing on Level One is insufficient for getting this kind of commitment and engagement and for competing against those who have learned how to get more out of their employees.

---

[4] See Frederick W. Taylor, *The Principles of Scientific Management* (New York: Harper & Brothers, 1911).

Effective leadership also needs to influence Level Two. Level Two, or conscious thought, is thought we are immediately aware of in ourselves. We think thoughts and choose whether to communicate them and if we do, whether to communicate them accurately. We are aware of Level Two activity within ourselves almost constantly, and we presume it in others. We can liken Level Two to the mind because that's where it occurs. Would-be leaders who ignore what people think are undermining their own capacity for influence.

Level Three refers to the deep-seated beliefs that we hold about what is true in life and that we generally take for granted and no longer need to think about or reflect upon. Level Three includes our hierarchy of priorities, our list of what we value more than other things. It includes our summary of the "shoulds" and "oughts" in the world, the way the world and the people in it should behave. Level Three probably also includes the influence of the enteric "brain." Emerging research is learning more and more about this ancillary nervous system that resides literally in our alimentary canal. It seems to be an evolutionary residual of the central nervous system of our distant invertebrate ancestors. The enteric "brain" includes something like 100 million neurons, many more than in your spinal column, and is capable of producing more serotonin than the brain that sits atop your spinal column. We are learning more about the reality of "gut feel." Taken together, the beliefs we hold in our primary brain and the influence of our secondary brain form the domain of Level Three.

Our Level Three VABEs are, by nature, highly cultural and family specific. The circumstances of where we were born and grew up, the quality of our relationships with our parents, and what they taught us—in fact, all of our life's experiences—contributed to the set of VABEs we hold as adults. I'll explain more about this process later.

In a sense, our VABEs are like limestone caverns (Figure 3-1). The interior of these limestone caverns is dark and wet. Over time, tiny drops of limestone-laden water drip from the ceilings and land on the floors. As they do, evaporating partially each time, they leave a small deposit. After millions of repetitions, these deposits form into stalactites and stalagmites. Some of these structures are thin and easily broken. Others are thick and may even have formed into solid columns extending from ceiling to floor. Our VABEs are like these limestone structures. Some are pretty weak; others are pillars central to our personality and views of the world. Further, some are so familiar to us that we no longer notice them. These stalactites and stalagmites and pillars form the structures of our personality—yet we may not see them clearly because they are so much who we are.

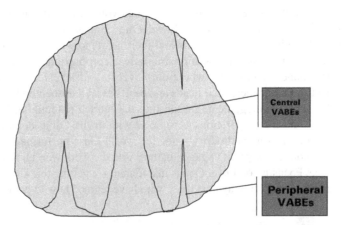

FIGURE 3-1   Our Level Three VABEs form much like limestone caverns . . . a drop of experience at a time.

To see our own Level Three VABEs, we often need assistance. Like fish swimming in water or birds flying in air, we have come to take for granted our more fundamental VABEs and assume them to be "true." Honest conversations with others, particularly people who are skilled in recognizing VABEs when they see them, can be helpful in clarifying what a person's—or an organization's—VABEs are. This does not mean that you have to be a psychologist to be a Level Three Leader—that is, one skilled at influencing at Level Three. Psychology is the study of where a person's VABEs come from. Management and leadership have to do with *recognizing* the most influential VABEs and then working with a person or organization to accomplish some goals with those VABEs. Note that VABEs are not just an individual phenomenon; they also have a major influence in the collective organizational level. "Cultures" at the organizational, national, or regional level are collections of shared VABEs.

Types of VABEs

VABEs come in a variety of forms. We can think of VABEs of distinction, VABEs of association, and VABEs of strategy.[5] Distinction VABEs help us to distinguish between one concept and another. We accept, for example, that one country's boundaries begin here or end there. Yet the ground shows no lines, just continuous dirt. That country, France perhaps, is an assumption of distinction. Association VABEs reflect our priorities and values. "France is good," we may think, or "France is bad." Finally, strategy or what we might call "conditional" VABEs involve action. "If I turn left, we can get there faster," we may believe, or "If I lie, no one will find out." Strategy VABEs usually have the basic "if-then" structure.

VABEs are usually clearest and most available for examination when they are stated as declarative normative sentences, such as "People should tell the truth," "The early bird gets the worm," "Be respectful to your elders," or "Don't spit in public." The basic structures of distinction, association, and strategy VABEs are shown in Table 3-2.

We carry thousands of VABEs around with us. Some we inherited from others (see Chapter 10 for a discussion of how VABEs or "memes" are transmitted), whereas some of them we developed uniquely from our experience. Some of them are relatively weak, and others quite strong and central to our way of living. The collective structure of our VABEs forms the nature of our personalities in a powerful way. Even so, it may not be so easy to recognize another person's VABEs.

VABEs are often manifest at Level One when people act or speak. Whenever you hear a person say "should" or "really oughta wanna" or "Good Xs do it this way," a blip should appear on your personal VABE radar because that person just revealed to you a portion of his or her list of VABEs. If you watch and listen carefully and with intent, you can pick up a lot about a person's VABEs.

Peoples VABEs are not necessarily consistent; they may espouse one VABE and live another. This gap between *espoused* theories or VABEs (what a person says) and *actual* behavior (what a person does) has been the subject of much research and practical speculation.[6] Books have been written too about the difference between "knowing and doing," the gaps between Level Two and Level One—which suggest some conflicts at Level Three. Bob Quinn's work at Michigan on the Competing Values Framework recognizes this reality.[7] Quinn observes that we have many competing values within us and that two of the

---

[5] See Richard Brodie, *Virus of the Mind* (Seattle, WA: Integral Press, 1996). Brodie, building on the work of Richard Dawkins, refers to these "mental viruses" as "memes" instead of VABEs.

[6] See, for example, Chris Argyris, *Reasoning, Learning, and Action* (San Francisco, CA: Jossey-Bass, 1982).

[7] See, for example, Robert E. Quinn, *Beyond Rational Management* (San Francisco, CA: Jossey-Bass, 1991).

TABLE 3-2 Basic Structure of VABEs		
Distinction VABEs	→	"This is X."
Association VABEs	→	"X is (good, bad)."
Strategy VABEs	→	"If A, then likely B."

biggest ones are the tensions between inside and outside and between control and autonomy. Some of these competing values are predictable and universal; some are unique to regional cultures, to families, and to individuals.

Level Three, then, is a gray area between conscious thought and the subconscious; it is an area that *may* be available to us, but about which we seldom think and into which we seldom delve in detail. Yet, it controls our lives, our thinking, and clearly our judgments about what we view to be right or wrong. We can liken Level Three to the heart, although no physiological evidence other than the enteric nervous system indicates that our VABEs in any way reside there or near there.

Please note that these three levels of human activity are closely intertwined. Clearly our VABEs affect our thinking, and clearly our thinking affects our behavior. Others argue that our behavior affects our thinking and feeling—the view taken by Skinnerians. The effective Level Three Leader will be aware of these recursive influences and strive to influence all three levels, not just one. It requires a willingness to think about all three levels and to consider how one might begin to influence them in others. A singular focus on behavior ignores two-thirds of what makes individuals do what they do. See Figure 3-2 for a visual diagram of the relationship between behavior, thoughts, and VABEs.

CONNECTING THE THREE LEVELS TO SCHOLARLY VIEWS

This three-level view of human behavior is relatively straightforward and well understood by scholars and many practicing leaders. In discussing the development of leadership in ethnic and organizational cultures, for instance, Ed Schein, one of the world's leading authorities on the subject, introduces what he calls three levels of cultural manifestation: (1) artifacts, the visible structures and processes of a culture; (2) espoused values, the justifications for behavior; and (3) basic underlying assumptions, the "unconscious taken-for-granted beliefs, perceptions,

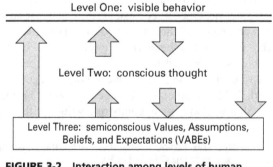

FIGURE 3-2   Interaction among levels of human behavior

thoughts, and feelings" that drive culture.[8] If you're interested in exploring this concept further, Schein's book contains an excellent description of how these underlying basic assumptions are formed and shape individual and organizational behavior. Our three-level leadership model parallels Schein's cultural model in many ways.

Learning Level Three Leadership

If you accept the assertion that human behavior occurs at these three levels and that leaders should pay attention to all three, the question emerges, how do I learn to attend to all three? The first step is in recognizing your own VABEs and then those of others. This is consistent with our opening assertion that strong leadership begins with self-leadership. Developing skill at observing and inferring is critical to "seeing" VABEs.[9] If we recollect that the issue of "What do you see?" is the first step in developing a Leadership Point of View, then we can see the importance of developing better VABE vision. If we can "see" what others overlook, we have a head start on developing influence. Second, we may need to unlearn some of the VABEs we already developed thus far in life. This learning and unlearning is particularly important in an era of paradigm shift from a bureaucratic to an infocratic society. This process is difficult for many people. By definition, people are comfortable with their VABEs; in fact, a person's VABEs tend to define who that person is. To a large degree, our present VABEs are what they are because they have "worked" for us so far in life and got us to where we are. The rest of the book will invite you to be thinking about these three levels of human behavior as you work through the sections on strategic thinking, self-leadership, influencing others, organizational design, and managing change.

Techniques for All Three Levels

Attempts to lead or influence at each of these three levels imply the use of different techniques. Although some techniques may have affect on more than one level, many leadership approaches or recipes clearly target one level more than another. Table 3-3 shows some common techniques employed at each level. You may be able to add more techniques to this basic list. We all use all of these techniques in one proportion or another. The point is not that we should use only the techniques at Level Three or Level One, rather that if we know what our habitual tendencies are, we can develop our leadership style more appropriately for the careers we choose. We'll explore these concepts further in subsequent chapters.

ORGANIZATIONAL IMPLICATIONS

So far, we have looked at Level Three Leadership primarily from individual and interpersonal perspectives. We can also speak of three levels of activity in a broader, organizational sense. A Level One, visible behavioral focus in organizational leadership is reflected in the

---

[8] Edgar H. Schein, *Organization Culture and Leadership* (San Francisco, CA: Jossey Bass, 1985).
[9] This approach encourages the development of inductive logic skills—seeing patterns in raw data. Much of our educational system is focused on deductive logic—giving patterns and practicing applications. "Pattern recognition" is a critical managerial skill set because managers often operate in rapidly changing environments in which there are no proven recipes for behavior.

TABLE 3-3	Some Common Techniques Employed at Levels One, Two, and Three	
Level of Intended Influence	**Influence Technique**	**Usual Impact**
Level One: Visible behavior	Orders, commands, threats, intimidation, incentives, bonuses	L1: Short-term compliance, possible sabotage, passive aggression L2: Obligatory agreement L3: Anger, resentment
Level Two: Conscious thought	Arguments, rationale, data, citations, references, evidence, manipulation	L1: Short-term compliance L2: Begrudged agreement L3: Anger, resentment, resistance
Level Three: VABEs	Visioning, purpose definition, honesty, openness, emotional story telling, anecdotes, tender emotions	L1: Commitment

application of the latest fads or techniques. Level One Leaders read about the latest technique in the literature and try to apply these techniques over the top of their existing organizations without considering of how these new techniques affect other interrelated systems and the structures and cultures of the organization. Sometimes it manifests itself when executives commission expensive educational programs but then never attend personally.

Level Two at the organization includes the organizational design of its structure, its key systems, and the formal design of the firm. These historically designed aspects of the organization are the result of conscious thought; hence, we can align them with Level Two.

The way in which an organization's design factors combine with the people who work in it, including the managerial or leadership style of the people in charge, to create a set of values, assumptions, beliefs, and expectations about how people in the organization should behave, results in the organizational culture (and subcultures). Level Three in the organization is the organizational culture, the set of commonly held values and operating principles that people take for granted as the "way we do things around here." These cultural realities may or may not line up with the formal organization and its subordinate designs. When they don't, "unintended consequences" are the result.

Level Three in the organization, as in the individual, is semiconscious. Some employees may be able to talk about aspects of the extant culture, while others may not be clear enough about it to articulate it—although they behave it. Using Chris Argyris's terms, Level Two is the "espoused theory" of the organization, while Level Three is the theory in action. These elements are shown in Table 3-4. They differ somewhat from Ed Schein's characterization, yet they illustrate the point that what managers do (trying to apply the latest fad in the literature), how they think about the organization (its structure and processes), and what they believe deeply about how to manage and organize are all potentially quite different things.

Level	Personal	Organizational
One	<u>Visible behavior</u>	Artifacts, buildings, physical things, and the "walk" and the "talk"
Two	Conscious thoughts	Espoused theories, the thoughts that support the "talk," rituals, ceremonies, fads, systems, routines, processes
Three	Values, assumptions, beliefs, and expectations	Theories in action, the underlying assumptions that generates "walk"

TABLE 3-4 Levels in Personal and Organizational Analysis

Conclusions

To speak of human behavior is confusing because we don't know whether we're referring to visible behavior, cognitive behavior, or subconscious values related behavior. It's helpful therefore to think of human behavior as occurring at three levels. Each of them has their strengths and weaknesses which we'll explore in great detail later in the section Leading Others. As you continue your reading and thinking, please keep these three levels in mind.

Concepts Introduced in This Chapter

1. Level One Leadership that focuses only on behavior ignores two major sources of motivation for most people: what they think and what they believe and feel.
2. Level One is visible behavior, Level Two is conscious thought, and Level Three contains the preconscious, semiconscious, or subconscious values, assumptions, beliefs, and expectations about the way the world is or should be.
3. Level Three Leadership, which is aware of and influences people's values and basic assumptions, has the potential to be far more powerful than Level One Leadership.
4. Even though Level Three Leadership does not imply that one must be a psychologist (who studies where values and assumptions come from), it does imply that effective leaders will be skilled in recognizing and clarifying VABEs in those with whom they work.
5. VABEs affect thoughts, and thoughts affect behavior; probably the reverse is also true. Consequently, effective leaders will pay attention to all three levels.
6. Levels One, Two, and Three apply to organizations as well as to individuals. Most organizational leaders focus on Level One and ignore the realities of Levels Two and Three.

Questions for Personal Reflection

1. How do people leak their Level Two conscious thought at Level One visible behavior?
2. What are your five most important VABEs?
3. What are your boss's VABEs? Your coworkers'? Can you write them down? If you listened more carefully, could you figure them out?
4. What are the main physical artifacts of your organization? What are the main processes that govern behavior in your organization? What are the VABEs that underlie those processes and artifacts?

5. Identify the ways that you behaved as a Level One Leader during the past week. At home? At work? In your avocation? What was the impact of these behaviors?
6. How could you have behaved as a Level Three Leader during the episodes you identified in question 3?

CASELET FOR DISCUSSION

Al was walking down the hall in the office. As he turned a corner, he saw John, his subordinate, come out of Al's boss' office, stop, look both ways, and then stride the opposite direction down the corridor. As John turned to walk away, Al noticed that he was carrying a thick file with the name of John's biggest client on the label.

WORKBOOK

Complete the Leadership Levels Assessment on page 344 of the workbook. Try to answer as honestly as you can about how you influence others.

CONTRIBUTING YOUR OWN CASELETS

Have you seen or experienced a situation involving the concepts introduced in this chapter? If so and if you'd like to contribute your experience/situation to our case data bank, please visit http://faculty.darden.virginia. edu/clawsonj/ and click on the "Contribute new caselets" button.

SECTION II

STRATEGIC THINKING

4 THE CHANGING CONTEXT OF LEADERSHIP

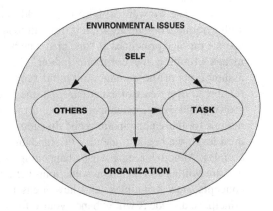

Those who do not remember history are condemned to repeat it.

—GEORGE SANTAYANA

Things aren't what they used to be, especially when it comes to understanding what it means to be an effective leader. Most observers agree that the industrialized world is in the midst of a major managerial paradigm shift that is changing the way we think about business, the way we organize to do business, and the problems and dilemmas that business presents.[1] These changes are as significant as those experienced during the last major paradigm shift—the Industrial Revolution—when the western world moved from agrarian-based to manufacturing-based economies. Now, 200 years later, we are in the midst of another similarly significant and fundamental transition: moving from the Industrial Age to the Information Age in an increasingly integrated global economy.

---

[1] Although one can find support for this premise in many places, one good support is Edwin C. Nevis, Joan Lancourt, and Helen G. Vassallo, *Intentional Revolutions* (San Francisco, CA: Jossey-Bass, 1996).

Understanding and becoming effective in this third and emerging new context requires a fundamental shift in management thinking and modes of leadership. Principles of organization and leadership that worked well for the past 100 years are being replaced with new principles based on new assumptions about people, economies, and how to organize. Understanding this new paradigm is essential to becoming a leader in the world of today leading to tomorrow. Many of the existing basic assumptions about leadership and management may be ill-suited for the emerging Information Age business world. Your perspective on the world around you and the way in which you plan and execute your business in that world will surely determine your success. Not understanding the new emerging realities will put you at a disadvantage compared with your peers and competitors.

Because we were all born in a world dominated by the bureaucratic mentality and filled with pyramidal organizations, it is difficult to appreciate the changes taking place. Bureaucracies operate on such principles as "one man, one boss," "follow the chain of command," and "success means climbing the corporate ladder." Many of us learned these and other underlying assumptions of the bureaucratic mind-set/point of view at an early age, and they were then reinforced over years of experience. At one level, we see corporations combining and dividing, growing and dying, much as they have for a long time. At a second level, we observe that the reasons for those combinations and divisions, for the growth and decline, are changing. And at a third level, we begin to identify the fundamental differences in the belief systems causing the changes. Although seeing what's happening in the larger picture of today's world is difficult, if you are willing to reexamine some long-held beliefs and to extend yourself, you can add new concepts, new principles, and new ideas to your present skill sets. These new concepts, principles, and ideas will enhance your efforts to lead. If you take that opportunity, you'll be a more effective leader.

GLOBAL BUSINESS ISSUES

As you think about your society and the world in which you live and work, you may see a series of trends that will affect your environment and your ability to lead in it. In fact, I invite you to take a moment and jot down the trends you see that are affecting your world today. Building on our concept of the Leadership Point of View introduced in the first chapter, what do you *see* with regard to the following?

What are the major trends affecting my career today?	
What are the issues that my generation will have to deal with?	
What are my biggest concerns for the future?	
What will I have to be careful of as my career unfolds?	

When we ask these questions of clients and MBA students, we find that one of the most evident trends is the shift from a bureaucratic, manufacturing-based economy to a high-tech, information-based economy. A second major trend is the globalization of the world's economies. We are rapidly becoming a global economy in which events in one part of the world dramatically affect the rest of the world and in which businesses cannot afford to think of themselves as "domestic" businesses. Third, the profitable margins in the world seem to be shifting from services to the next kind of economy, what Pine and Gilmore call an "experience economy."[2] Fourth, the twenty-first century is already being called "the China Century." The growing economies of China and India will have a huge impact on the business context over the next 100 years. Fifth, the population of the world continues to grow, despite the observation that in industrialized countries, birthrates drop. The growing global population puts pressure on society's infrastructure. Sixth, one of the major pressures is the use of energy. When petroleum runs out, what will be the impact on businesses and on society? Some say that we have already passed "peak production," meaning that we now use more petroleum than we are finding and the supply is beginning to dwindle. Seventh, what about the tensions between the haves and the have-nots? Will the tensions between the poor and the wealthy continue to escalate and produce a future laden with terrorism and violence? Eighth, what about the health of the earth? What impact will global warming have on your generation?

A recent MBA class discussion developed 27 trends that the students felt their generation—the current new generation of leaders—would have to deal with during their lifetimes. For example, the Baby Boomer generation dealt with reconstruction after World War II and the development of the automobile industry and the computer industry. What major challenges do you see on the horizon facing your generation? In order to strengthen your perspective on the sweep of events shaping the world you live in, let's review some basics of the development of human business activity.

THE BEGINNING OF HUMAN ECONOMIC ACTIVITY

The prehistoric shift from hunter/gatherer society to farming, the Industrial Revolution, and the Information Revolution were behind the three major worldwide paradigm shifts in management. We are living in the midst of this third shift, a transition period between the Industrial Age and the developing Information Age. If you understand the dynamics and implications of this turbulent period and can put your personal efforts at leadership in that context, you'll be better prepared for making the transition, understanding the seeming chaos about you, influencing those around you, and helping, not hindering, your organization's efforts to make the transition as well. This book, then, is about enhancing your ability to influence others amid changing times.

Hunter/Gatherer

The hunter/gatherer era in our prerecorded history was dominated by our race's focus on food for survival. Tribes were relatively small and widely separated to allow sufficient territory for hunting and gathering. Because this era was prerecorded history, we do not have detailed accounts of life and leadership among hunter/gatherer groups. We learned a lot from archeological studies, though, and are able to infer some things about society among these small tribes. What is clear is that about 13,000 years ago, a blossoming of human creativity, innovation, and population growth occurred. Best-selling author Jared Diamond calls this transition the

---

[2] Joe Pine and James Gilmore, *The Experience Economy* (Boston, MA: Harvard Business School Press, 1999).

beginning of "farmer power."[3] When humans learned to farm, they no longer had to roam the countryside looking for food. They could, by cooperating and concentrating their efforts, generate enough food to last them through the winter and with some to spare so that they could turn their attention to other pursuits like music, art, religion, writing, toolmaking, and so on. Only a few moments' reflection is needed to imagine how the nature of leadership, the skills that would be respected, and the organization of the human groups would change dramatically. Tribes could grow in size and complexity. "Spare" time would increase. Leaders would be those with a seasonal perspective, with an understanding of horticulture instead of hunting, and society would be increasingly organized around stability and responsibility, rather than bravado and daring. Well-known organizational theorists Paul Lawrence, Nigel Nicholson, and Rod White wrote about these prehistoric roots to modern management thought.[4] One of the features of the new agrarian society was the importance of land ownership that gave rise to the elements of aristocracy, the dominant management model as written history emerged in the world.

Aristocratic Society

From the cultural bloom at 11,000 B.C.E. until the nineteenth century, much of the society around the world was stratified according to the aristocratic agricultural model.[5] The word *aristocracy* comes from Greek and means "rule by the best," which meant those born to noble families who owned productive land. In Japan, for example, wealth was determined by the number of bags of rice (*koku*) one's land would produce. With few exceptions, societies around the world before 1800 assumed that royal birth meant royal abilities and royal rights to power and authority. One's birth determined one's likely standing in society, one's wealth, one's educational opportunities, and one's ability to influence events. Societal and organizational power and authority were largely distributed according to family lineage as they related to land holdings. The random process of birth selected the next generation's kings and queens and emperors and empresses. In the effort to consolidate power and authority, great houses in Europe and Asia sought alliances through political means, military means, and arranged marriages, hoping to bind their fortunes and build greater stability in society. Structurally, the aristocratic model meant that certain families tended to rule and dominate the social and political landscape. At a second, mental level, it meant that people thought that this system was normal and that the noble families were the rightful rulers. At a third level, the tacit, central assumption in the aristocratic paradigm was, practically speaking, "father knows best." Royal fathers were the center of political and economic activity in most of the world. Fathers who were also titular heads of states, nations, and great estates made the decisions and the laws, arbitrated disputes, and administered justice and punishment. Fathers dreamed of conquest, alliance, or economic expansion and then established the funds for and recruited others to fulfill those dreams. The sons, the princes, held hopes of ascending to the father's throne by royal right, a right for the most part recognized by the people.

---

[3] Jared Diamond, *Guns, Germs and Steel* (New York: Norton, 1999).

[4] All three authors presented papers at the Academy of Management 2000 meetings in Toronto. Subsequently, Nicholson published *Executive Instinct* (New York: Crown Business Publishers, 2000), an exploration of our genetic tendencies in leadership. To explain their thinking, White coauthored a paper with Barbara Decker Pierce entitled "The Evolution of Social Structure: Why Biology Matters," *Academy of Management Review* 24, no. 4 (1999), 843–853. Lawrence and Nitin Nohria, in *Driven* (San Francisco, CA: Jossey-Bass, 2001), describe their interpretation of what happened during this flourishing of human behavior.

[5] Human groups, like chickens with their pecking order and many other groups in the animal kingdom, always stratify themselves. We have yet to find a human group that is not stratified. The only question seems to be, along what criteria?

TABLE 4-1	Characteristics of Aristocratic Society

- Orderly society
- Limited information
- Limited transportation
- Homogeneous followers
- Limited opportunities
- Limited education
- Limited technological advances
- Male domination
- Limited resources

Among its many positive aspects, the aristocratic model gave stability to society because people knew their place in the world virtually from birth and were molded and educated to accept and grow in that place (see Table 4-1). With enormous wealth and lots of leisure time, monarchs and royal families searched for interesting employment and entertainment. Artists, musicians, sculptors, and writers all benefited from this search and thus were able to add to the world's treasures. The aristocracies supported the development of some of the world's greatest literature, philosophy, art, and music.

Despite these advantages, the aristocratic model had many disadvantages. It left millions of people feeling disenfranchised. Even though many accepted their "natural" positions as servants or subjects, others longed for a more fluid, free society. The revolutions for freedom and independence in the eighteenth century were manifestations of humankind's dissatisfaction with a society that felt increasingly confining, unfair, and anachronistic. The aristocratic system tended not to recognize individual talents if the person possessing these talents was not in the proper class. It limited education to a few, inhibited the movement of talent into key positions in a multitude of organizations, inhibited the distribution of wealth in a fair and equitable way, and, importantly, was not flexible enough to meet changing times. These factors contributed to the burgeoning dissatisfaction among the underprivileged classes.

The Industrial Revolution and Bureaucratic Society

These dissatisfactions led to the political upheavals of the late eighteenth century, including revolutions in the Americas and France. Powerful as the political changes were, an equally profound but quieter change was gathering momentum. In the second half of the eighteenth century and the first half of the nineteenth century, the invention of the steam engine, the discovery of petroleum, and the development of mass manufacturing techniques for clothing, guns, shoes, utensils, and tools revolutionized the economic world. This transformation made a host of durable goods available to an ever-wider subset of the population and created a new, more powerful merchant class. The Industrial Revolution also caused a major shift in the nature of leadership in organizations as it became clear that the aristocrats could no longer keep up with the changes that were occurring nor could they be counted on to provide the best leaders for the new organizational forms that were taking shape. These realities, along with the increasing economic and political gaps between the noble class and the working classes, created a tension between the old system and the emerging new reality. Wars of independence in the United States, France, and Russia were the social earthquakes that occurred along the fault line of this tension between the old and new ways of thinking and were symptomatic of an aristocratic paradigm giving way to a new worldview.

Another significant precursor to the bureaucracies that we know today was Frederick the Great, who needed to find quick and efficient ways of molding uneducated poor people into effective fighting units. His efforts to assign specific jobs to members of teams, to develop uniforms and systems of rank, and to centralize decision making, all provided strong models for future organization designers.

The Industrial Revolution forced a paradigm shift to a new model of management for society in which "common" people were given authority and power by virtue of their abilities and skills. The people who were more familiar with the techniques of manufacture and wealth creation than the political and societal niceties of the elite held more and more of the powerful positions in these new companies. Power was distributed according to the office one held, not one's birthright. The French word *bureau*—meaning "office"—was joined with *-cracy* to convey the novel idea (at the time) that power was fixed to the office one held and not one's last name. This term signaled a key difference between the old and new paradigms: power accrued to the office, not to the individual. Today, vestiges of the aristocratic model remain, although in both England and Japan, as well as elsewhere, these vestiges are under increasing scrutiny and are mostly considered outdated and expensive residues of a previous world order.

This transition from the Aristocratic Age to the Industrial Age was a major paradigm shift. Although we speak of a paradigm "shift," the process seems painstakingly slow when viewed from the vantage point of the span of a single lifetime: most people are born, live, and die in one dominant model. When we look at the structure of society over several generations, however, paradigm shifts represent dramatic disruptions in the stability of society and dramatic changes in its thinking and organizational forms.

Ironically, one of the best summaries of the new bureaucratic system was written by a man born in 1864 into the highly cultured upper middle class in Europe—the German sociologist Max Weber. By that time, the Industrial Revolution had been gaining momentum for almost a hundred years, so the world into which Weber was born was already largely "industrialized." Weber summarized the key assumptions that represented a break with the aristocratic system and clarified the way that the bureaucratic system was already taking hold. In *The Theory of Social and Economic Organization,* Weber took great pains to describe his view of the new *legitimate* authority as opposed to aristocratic authority. His writing, considered a milestone in describing the shift from aristocratic thinking to bureaucratic thinking, clarified the view of what largely had already happened.

In describing the new bureaucratic system, Weber concluded that a new order of society was growing out of a widely accepted set of laws that "are formally correct and have been imposed by accepted procedure"[6] and were distinct from the aristocratic view. These "laws" were not necessarily documented but became the new underlying assumptions upon which the new economy was built. The key components of this new idea of legitimate authority included mutually agreed upon rules, equal application, and authority existing in an "office" and not in the incumbent.

The institutionalization of the bureaucratic model produced enormous momentum and commitment throughout societies worldwide. Aristocracies depended on the good health and skills of the heirs, whereas bureaucracy allowed organizations to continue even without a particularly key family member or individual. Bureaucracy changed the aristocratic handing down of power by allowing nonfamily members to fill the offices of power subject to the rules of the organization. Hence, institutions could be created and continued to exist even though their individual members and surnames changed with time.

---

[6] Max Weber, *The Theory of Social and Economic Organization* (New York: Free Press, 1947), 131.

In bureaucracies, power and authority were distributed according to the office or the structural relationships of the offices in an organization. When promoted, one received additional power, authority, and usually wealth. Decision making was often consolidated at the top of these organizations, and implementation of those decisions was assigned to the middle and bottom. Organizations continued to come and go as they did in the aristocracies, and people continued to think of the established organizations as the "right" ones. The basic assumption of the aristocratic model was, "father knows best." The basic assumption of the bureaucratic model became, "the boss knows best."

Although similar to the aristocratic model in some respects, the bureaucratic model expanded the range of individuals who could fill the power roles. As in the aristocracies, new bosses were primarily men, but now not necessarily the sons of previous bosses. The new leaders were better educated than others and often more experienced, thus lending a general credence to the underlying assumption that "the boss knows best." Employees and middle managers in most bureaucracies looked to the executive ranks for vision, guidance, control, encouragement, rewards, and information about the nature and status of the organization. Raw data flowed up, analysis and decision making took place at the top, and instructions and orders flowed down.

This common pattern spawned a range of bureaucratic phrases like "We don't pay you to think; just do it" and "That's on a need-to-know basis only," which are now common, everyday expressions. As these expressions became a part of our everyday language, we took them for granted as the way things were. This taking for granted, in fact, reflects the reality that the new paradigm was set and was no longer considered a change.

Bureaucracies, which worked well for over two centuries, were a powerful influence and produced many positive changes. Talented people had greater freedom of upward socioeconomic movement than in the aristocratic model. Bureaucracies provided a structure for mobilizing large labor pools. The development of new industries was no longer dependent on the whims of aristocratic individuals. Bureaucratic society as a whole was more flexible to meet the challenges of changing times. Bureaucracies dampened the effects of ignorance improperly promoted and, importantly, reduced the dissatisfaction associated with the aristocratic model (although bureaucracy supplanted aristocracy in many ways with a new resentment for those with "new" money).

Bureaucracies also generated a stream of organizational research and theory building, much of it based on a desire to reduce the variance between job description and human performance. Much of Frederick Taylor's work on scientific management, along with the dominant leadership models of the bureaucratic era, revolved around finding ways to fragment, prescribe, and control human behavior.[7] The goals of management during these times included standardizing human behavior and minimizing variance in human work. It was, in Gareth Morgan's term, the "machine company."[8]

With bureaucracies, as with many systems, sources of historical success became the seeds of future decay. The system of assumptions and principles that formed bureaucracies generated some unfortunate outcomes. The ability to continue business without a particular individual and eventually to create institutions as more or less fixed parts of society led some organizations to focus more on survival as an objective of their existence—diverting their efforts from customer service goals. The fitting of people into predefined job descriptions tended to alienate them from their work, to encourage a one-way, top-down communication pattern, and to discourage learning activities. In their worst form, bureaucracies came to serve few, if any, beyond their employees.

---

[7] Frederick Taylor, *Principles of Scientific Management* (New York: Harper, 1911).

[8] Gareth Morgan, *Images of Organization* (Newbury Park, CA: Sage, 1986).

Bureaucracies also, as they grew, allowed moderate or lesser talents to remain and hide within the labyrinthine structures. Sometimes, the new, prescribed legal order of things codified by Weber blurred the vision of good people who were properly promoted, so that they couldn't *see,* much less attend to, the customer needs. Bureaucracies also tended to discourage creativity and entrepreneurial behavior in favor of low-risk, previously conceived, and planned behavior. These problems of bureaucracies now loom large for North American and European firms as they wrestle with the underlying principles, technological breakthroughs, and ferocious competition in a new, emerging paradigm.

THE PRESENT PARADIGM SHIFT

Today, rapid change is the order of things. In many respects, this speed of change not only is a function of the turbulence as we move from the Industrial Age into the Information Age, but also represents the nature of a society connected by instant information and ready means of travel. During the twentieth century, we experienced the development of electricity, petroleum products and fuels, nuclear energy augmented by wind and sun, and unanticipated volumes of technological breakthroughs in chemistry, physics, machinery, biogenetics, biochemistry, miniaturization, nutrition, energy use, data transfer, computers, and hundreds of other fields. The pace of change represented by these breakthroughs and innovations continued to accelerate in the last 50 years. Most managers agree that the relationship between time and change in our society is exponential (Figure 4-1), that things are changing at an ever-increasing rate. Of course, no system can maintain an exponential rate of change, because eventually the change approaches a vertical line; however, during the transition period between the Industrial and Information Ages, the rate of change has been enormous.

The task of keeping current in any field has become overwhelming. We are bombarded with more books to read, theories to comprehend, sensors creating more data, observers drawing more conclusions, television channels, and political, scientific, and socioeconomic situations and commentary. Citizens of many countries can watch at their leisure the inner workings of foreign governments around the world as they happen. Our ability to integrate the disparate tidal waves of information and new knowledge is overtaxed.

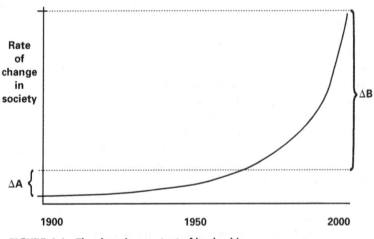

FIGURE 4-1   The changing context of leadership

The implications of this information and change explosion for our generation and succeeding ones are many and enormous. Perhaps first on the list is the realization that although our parents may have had the luxury of continuing their careers in the same fields over the course of a typical 40-year career, our generation does not have that luxury. We cannot expect to finish our careers doing the same things we started out doing. In almost every field, new materials, tools, theories, techniques, substitutes, and ways of organizing are needed, meaning that *we must all be constant learners* or we'll soon be obsolete and out of work.

Now, more than ever before, lifelong learning is critical to survival. Expect that whatever you learn now will soon be displaced and replaced and that you must be engaged in learning—not passively, but actively—seeking to gain an advantage by learning faster than others. Reading, thinking, ingesting, digesting, pondering, struggling, skimming, researching, and investigating, all with a sense of urgency, represent the new *normal* way of life, the necessary means of keeping up. This learning orientation is especially important in leadership, in developing the ways you think about and manage your influence on others.

A new framework for organizations that differs significantly from bureaucracies is emerging in response to these dramatic changes. Organizations are re-forming around information systems and communication systems that support them. Power is now emanating from people who know how to access and digest volumes of information. As with the previous paradigm shift, this shift is not instantaneous, although it is happening much faster than the previous shift from the Aristocratic Age to the Industrial Age. The causes for this new shift, like the last one, are rooted in technological change.

Many aspects of the new Information Age shape our thinking about organizations and leadership. In this new age, power revolves around the people who coordinate resources to meet customer needs. Information becomes the key competitive and managerial advantage, as markets and customer demands change much more rapidly than before. Companies such as Wal-Mart, Capital One, and BancOne used information systems as powerful strategic weapons in building competitive positions that are difficult for others to assail. With increasing size and shrinking intervals between customer orders and expected fulfillment, internal product development and delivery cycle times are much shorter than before. These phenomena, in turn, mean that management can no longer know and understand what needs to be done at each interface between the organization and its environment.

Managers increasingly rely on employees to get relevant data and to make decisions in order to respond to demands and challenges more quickly than bureaucratic structures would allow. This trend introduced the popular term of the late 1980s and early 1990s: *empowerment*. Organizations unable to wield bureaucratic structures to compete effectively are turning to their employees and trying to "empower" them to make decisions, to take responsibility for corporate results, and to show initiative in recognizing and solving the problems confronting their firms. This flattening of organizations is a natural outcome of the Information Revolution, but many managers still see it as an isolated fad that they can choose to ignore or treat superficially; they fail to understand the larger context in which these changes are occurring.

As information networks proliferate, the boundaries of any organization begin to blur. Writers recently described this emergence of "boundaryless" or virtual organizations that exist primarily in concept but whose boundaries or edges are hard to find. Large numbers of part-time employees, commingled computer systems that automatically place orders to stock shelves, and alliances between competitors and vendors of all kinds are examples of this emerging boundaryless phenomenon in corporations.

One concern in these new, emerging organizational forms is the danger that employees will lose a sense of being, a sense of participation, and a sense of being part of a large organization.

If people don't see who they work for and don't understand the larger picture of how their work fits into an ethereal, virtual organization, they may not be able to commit enough energy to contribute world-class work. Effective leaders in these new organizations will be able to find ways to hold the people in these organizations together. Traditional kinds of organizational "glue" are becoming less adhesive. In this respect, many private-sector companies are learning from nonprofit organizations, which historically pioneered structures that deal with fluid employee roles and fuzzy boundaries.

Another symptom of this paradigm shift is the wave of "delayering" or "flattening" of organizations that occurred in the 1980s and 1990s as the ranks of middle managers were eliminated. Nineteenth-century railroad companies greatly influenced the growth of middle management and the rise of bureaucracy. They built multiple layers of management primarily to process information coming in from a geographically diverse organization, move it up through the organization, process it, refine it, summarize it, and pass it on to the top. A decision was made, which then traveled back down through these organizational layers, and was disseminated to the ranks.

Modern information systems are rapidly replacing these vertical organizational forms. Customers' use of similar systems in dealing with competitors also means that an organization doesn't have the time to follow that involved of a chain; instead, many organizations are learning to become instantaneously responsive. As a result, the need for a vertical hierarchy of decision makers is disappearing.

These pressures are turning more and more companies to experiment with and deploy empowered, team-oriented structures. As the middle levels are cut out, people at lower ranks of the organization gain authority to commit the resources of the firm to meet customer needs. Not coincidentally, this trend parallels a similar one in the political realm, as so many countries recently exerted their independence from former protectors and dictatorships. Centralized systems are breaking down all over the world as people at all levels are confronted with frenetic technological change, instant information, and the need to act.

As we can see in the transition from the Aristocratic Age to the Industrial Age, organizations continue to come and go and re-form. Most people are beginning to mentally accept the emerging reality that change is a fact of life and that the new, flatter organizations are the "right" ones (although many still resist this recognition). At this third level, however, the newly emerging assumptions about management are not that "father knows best" or "management knows best," but that "people close to the work know best." These "key process contributors" are the people closest to the customer and who know the key customer-serving processes best and know what needs to be done to manage those processes to the best effect. Although some executives and managers continue to resist any shift from the bureaucratic mind-set, the de facto reality is that the power to make effective decisions is migrating to these key process contributors.

Organization designers are struggling to find structures that recognize and accept this new reality. Business executives in the nation's largest corporations are now talking about speed, boundaryless organizations, project teams, concurrent engineering, and the importance of listening rather than telling. In the late 1980s for instance, Jack Welch, CEO at General Electric Company, initiated an enormous corporate change called "WorkOut," which was intended to help the business leaders of his divisions get in touch with the ideas and perspectives of people at various levels. Through initiatives such as WorkOut, Welch was working to transform his company from an Industrial Age bureaucracy into an Information Age organization. Welch is not alone in this effort, as more and more of his peers in industry after industry seek to do the same.

Everywhere, new interest is emerging in the key information-based processes that produce goods and services and in the organizational structures that support them. Enlightened corporate executives are examining how these processes work and are looking for ways to speed up the production and creative processes with higher quality and increased levels of customization to meet customer needs. Those who were raised in bureaucracies and are uncomfortable with the new context tend to be reluctant and resistant to understand what they need to learn to be effective in the new surroundings.

Observers call this new context the Information Age or the Post-Industrial Era. One wonders what the emerging organizational forms for distributing power will be called, because they will not be pure bureaucracies. Although these emerging organizational forms will have some lingering bureaucratic characteristics, they will look more like neural networks. Whether they are called team forms, empowered organizations, circles of influence, virtual organizations, infocracies, custocracies, boundaryless organizations, or fluid collections of processes, they will be the face, the image, of the new paradigm. It may be that we will settle on Peter Senge's simple but powerful term, *the learning organization*.[9] Another term, *infocracy*, captures much of the reality that information provides the basis of power in these new forms.[10] No longer does the family or the office hold the source of the power that determines organization. The information explosion redistributes the power in these new organizations. Whatever the new approach is called, it will be characterized by widely distributed power and structures that better recognize the value of all organization members receiving, processing, and making decisions from new and exploding oceans of information.

In these new structures, leadership power will migrate in seemingly chaotic fashion to the people who are close to the key challenges of each organization and who have the talent and abilities to resolve them. Employees in surviving companies will ignore and avoid the historical, formalized ways of functioning; titles will become less meaningful, whereas relationships between people assigned to different areas or functions will become more so. Management will support rather than direct teams, and the artifacts of steeply stratified bureaucracies (e.g., executive parking places, dining rooms, washrooms, suits and ties, isolated offices, one-way performance evaluation, and disparities between employee and executive compensation) will continue to shrivel and disappear. Organizational boundaries will continue to blur as vendors and customers alike demand and tolerate organizational representation, data, mainframe access, team membership, and influence on what used to be internal decisions. Alliances made possible by vastly superior communications will continue to grow in number around the world. The distinction between what is internal and what is external to an organization will continue to fade.

The paradigm shift from bureaucracy to infocracy has been described and predicted by many others, one of the first being Warren Bennis, who, in a 1966 article in *Think* magazine, wrote about "The Coming Death of Bureaucracy."[11] He characterized bureaucracies as having well-defined chains of command, standardized operating procedures for dealing with virtually every contingency, divisions of labor based on specialization, selection and promotion systems based on technical competence, and high levels of impersonality when dealing with employees.

Bennis identified four threats that spelled the demise of bureaucracies: rapid and unexpected changes, growth to the point that historical procedures would no longer work, increased complexity in modern technology, and growing discontent with the impersonality of management–employee relationships.

---

[9] Peter Senge, *The Fifth Discipline* (New York: Doubleday Currency, 1990).
[10] James G. Clawson, "The New Infocracies: Implications for Leadership," *Ivey Business Journal*, May–June (2000): http://www.iveybusinessjournal.com/view_article.asp?intArticle_ID=219.
[11] Warren Bennis, "The Coming Death of Bureaucracy," *Think*, November–December, 1966, 30–35.

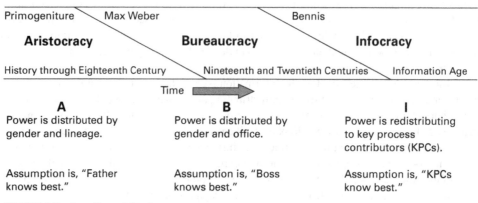

FIGURE 4-2 Paradigm shifts in management

The new organizations replacing bureaucracies, Bennis said, would be temporary in nature and would shift rapidly to meet changing demands. He called them "organic-adaptive" structures. In them, employees would be highly motivated but experience less commitment to a particular work group because these connections would rapidly change. Organizational designs would evolve to the point that rather than repressing ideas and creativity, they would encourage play and creative thinking as organizations struggled to keep pace with environmental changes. Today, as we watch the changes taking place in organizations around us, we cannot help but be impressed with Bennis' 30-year prescience. Others as well described this transition.[12] There is a debate, however. Hal Leavitt at Stanford argues that bureaucracies are here to stay.[13]

A visual representation of this paradigm shift is shown in Figure 4-2. The diagonal lines separating the three major paradigms described here show the gradual nature of the shifts; however, the shift from bureaucracy to infocracy will surely happen much more quickly than the shift from aristocracy to bureaucracy. The impact of new fuels and new sources of information will be key stimulants to the shift. The models used to distribute power in organizations appear at the bottom of the figure with the key assumptions about who knows what to do.

The new information-based paradigm requires new thinking, values, systems, and skills, as well as new kinds of leadership. Members in the new organizations will also need to develop broader ways of thinking about their work. No longer will they be able to say, "That's not my job" and expect to have either a job or a company that will survive. They will have to find ways of sending information from the bottom up as well as enhance sending it from the top down. Managers and employees alike will need to recognize every employee's potential for contributions that may go beyond the formal job description. Less and less will leadership be an exercise in conveying the message, "Listen up folks, here's how we're going to do this!" It will require thinking in terms of inclusive answers instead of exclusive ones. We will learn in organizational terms and in leadership terms, "fuzzy logic" and "and/also" answers instead of "clear logic" and "either/or" answers. Employees and leaders who will thrive in these new organizations will be comfortable with these less certain kinds of influence.

---

[12] For example, see Gifford and Elizabeth Pinchot, *The End of Bureaucracy and the Rise of the Intelligent Organization* (San Francisco, CA: Berret Kohler, 1994).

[13] Harold J. Leavitt, *Top Down: Why Hierarchies Are Here to Stay and How to Manage Them More Effectively* (Boston, MA: Harvard Business School Press, 2005).

The new paradigm also demands of its leaders that they develop some new core values and skills. The new leaders will focus more on listening compared with talking than they did in the past. In consulting settings with a wide variety of clients, almost always, participants declare that one of the implications of the challenges is that their leadership needs to listen better. This capacity is becoming more and more important in the new paradigm. Leaders will learn to value cooperation more than competition, talent more than title, and teamwork more than individual effort and glory. To value service to customers more than (but not at the exclusion of) profits, they must accept, deep down, the fact that customers come *before* profits, that profits come *after* customers, and that without customers they are without revenues or profits. Collins and Porras, in their classic book *Built to Last,* call this orientation "purpose beyond profit."[14] Many of us, striving for positions of leadership, will have to, as Davidow and Malone put it, "reverse our thinking." Rather than trying to create customers for our present products, we must value and understand customer needs and then reorganize our firms to meet those needs faster and with higher quality than others.

The leaders in this new context will have to learn to value fixing things that apparently aren't yet broken. Hal Leavitt introduced this notion by explaining that new leaders will be problem creators as much as they are problem finders or problem solvers.[15] The new leaders will value anticipation, risk-taking, and new ideas. They will *develop a value for change,* a deep-seated belief and trust in the change process, and an enthusiasm for embracing it. Hugh McColl, CEO at Bank of America (then NationsBank), taught the motto "We will savagely embrace change."[16] Effective leaders in the new paradigm will understand and live this new philosophy as they relinquish their values for stability and control and the present distrust for surprises. They will learn to love learning, change, diversity, and the challenges of being alert and ever-present in order to see and respond to surrounding changes.

The new paradigm will also require the designing and implementation of new organizational systems. The new leaders will implement and experience new organizational forms, like the spaghetti organization in Denmark reported by Tom Peters.[17] They will implement "spherical" performance evaluations (that go beyond the groundbreaking 360-degree evaluations done in some companies now) done by team members, subordinates *and* customers, and suppliers and community citizens, rather than single superior officers. These spherical evaluations will include relevant data from all who have a stake in a person's or a team's contributions to the organization. We will see working hours shift to meet the needs of customers and team members, not predictable working hours in our time zone as standardized by bureaucracies. We will see computer data links worldwide at all levels of organizations, not just at the pinnacles.

The new paradigm is dependent in many ways on speed of travel and speed of information transfer. Without these elements, the knowledge necessary to build loyal and trustworthy alliances and partnerships would break down. We will see increasingly sophisticated cost-accounting and tracking systems that match cost causes with total costs rather than spreading costs across departments. We will see promotion systems that allow for changes in the strategic and competitive tactical demands facing firms. We will see recruiting systems that increasingly focus on social skills as much as or more than technical skills (that can be taught and developed more easily).

---

[14] James C. Collins and Jerry I. Porras, *Built to Last* (New York: HarperBusiness, 1994).

[15] Harold Leavitt, *Corporate Pathfinders* (Homewood, IL: Dow-Jones Irwin, 1986).

[16] From a private conversation with a NationsBank executive.

[17] Tom Peters, *The Tom Peters Seminar* (New York: Vintage, 1994), 29.

Infocracies will require new internal organizational skills. Employees and managers alike must be better at listening, eliciting, discussing, encouraging, recognizing feelings, informal influence, persuasion rather than commanding, foreign languages, using computers, focusing on customer-oriented priorities, and searching out causes. Paradoxically, they will be better at attending to more by attending to less—that is, by *focusing* in a way that one can see *more* of what is happening. The new paradigm will require employees and managers who are more facile at intercultural understanding and communication, and better at seeing what people have to offer rather than what they look like. They will become better at sharing, at taking personal risks in order to model, at praising rather than criticizing, at helping rather than telling, and at process observation and intervention. We must learn how to be patient up front in order to be more effective later on. More empathy (i.e., ability to see the world the way others see it) and less sympathy (i.e., trying to solve others' problems with our own core of beliefs and values) are required.

The new leaders will be learners who are open to new ideas and who value change. The new leaders will be trustworthy, respectworthy, and changeworthy. They will value what others can do, and they will know how to highlight and build on those capabilities. In the face of the changes ahead, they will be clear on who they are and what they stand for. Unlike aristocratic and many bureaucratic leaders, they will be deeply respectful of the value and dignity of individuals in and near their organizations.

The new leaders of tomorrow will be systems thinkers, able and eager to see ever larger pictures of systems within systems. They will respect the individual regardless of race, gender, or religion, for what the individual can do and how he or she does it. They will be designers and initiators, always looking for a better way, always willing to fix things that aren't yet broken, but with a specific purpose in mind. The new leaders will be and/also thinkers instead of either/or thinkers.[18] The new leaders will be coaches and caretakers, teachers and students, workers as well as managers, and role models as well as instructors.

Timing is important in this shift. Trying to move too soon is as deadly as moving too late. The Nash Metropolitan was a compact car designed for urban traffic and ease of parking, with lots of storage space, high gas economy, and sturdy construction. Unfortunately, it was introduced in the early 1950s rather than 1973, when the oil shock taught people worldwide the value of such cars. The picture telephone was introduced about the same time, but is only now coming into its own as a desired technology. Companies that succeed in the new paradigm will demonstrate a good sense of timing as well as take into account the parameters in their industries that either facilitate or inhibit the introduction of the new paradigm. Unfortunately, too often the usual error will be in changing too late, and the usual inhibiting factor will be senior- or middle-level management.

THE CONTEXT OF MODERN INFOCRACIES

Infocracies create a series of implications for the kind of leadership necessary for today's world. The trends listed earlier will surely affect you and your ability to lead in these new organizations. Let's review quickly the key trends that are likely to affect you.

Virtually, every business today has some kind of international connection. This connection may be suppliers, manufacturers, call centers (now often done in India or Pakistan), customers, or accounting and payroll. The immediate implication is that you will need to know how to handle yourself in

---

[18] See, for example, Charles Handy, *The Age of Paradox* (Boston, MA: Harvard Business School Press, 1995).

other cultures. If you've had experience overseas, you will be one step ahead. If you can speak more than one language and are comfortable with the business protocols, the food, the relationship to time and space, and the social niceties unique to each culture, you'll have a big advantage. If you're hosted in Indonesia, for example, as an important visitor, are you prepared to eat raw, fresh, and steaming monkey brain? Are you aware of when to take your shoes off in Japan or how to exchange business cards? Do you know not to show the bottom of your shoes to your opposites in Saudi Arabia? Learning how to deal in different cultures is a necessity of doing business in the new infocratic era.[19]

Next, as you look for profit margins in the world, the theories of Joe Pine and Jim Gilmore mentioned earlier may be helpful to you. They note that during the agricultural era, humans exchanged things they took from the soil. As these farmed goods became common, their profit margins fell; today we call them "commodities." In the Industrial Era, we made things from the stuff we took from the earth. When people bought durable goods, they had something they could hold on to. Then the margins on goods began to erode as well. With the advent of the Information Age in the 1950s, companies found higher margins in the services sector. In the service economy, customer paid for things you did for them. However, stiff competition continues to erode those margins. Today, the main place we find high margins are in the "experience" sector, where people will pay for something that is gone as soon as it's over: Super Bowl tickets, soccer games, music concerts, and entertainment. This notion of paying for experience extends dramatically to the business world. If another company can offer your goods and services (meaning your industry has become "commoditized"), why would a customer choose to do business with you? Primarily, it is because of a superior experience dealing with you. Companies may think they are selling goods and services, but in a global economy with stiff commoditizing competition, what they are really selling is the experience of dealing with that company.

China is expected to dominate the twenty-first century. With the world's largest population, a strong entrepreneurial spirit, and an increasingly encouraging regulatory environment, China will influence virtually every economy in the world. If the Chinese make favorable trade agreements with other Asian countries and Latin American countries, the United States could find itself increasingly hemmed in by Chinese business success.

World population continues to grow. Even as birthrates in industrialized countries taper off, the overall population of the world continues to climb. What is the sustainable capacity of the earth? We are at about 6.5 billion now. Can we support 13 billion? 33 billion? How many people will be alive during your children's life span? What effects will the growing population density have on your business and on your family's lifestyle? World population figures show that the population of the earth grew at a stable rate (minus the Black Plague era) until about 1800, when the slope of the growth curve shifted upward dramatically. The Industrial Revolution triggered a worldwide uptick in population. Another major inflection point occurred at the Information Revolution about 1950 with the advent of better medical research and data processing. Although economists show that birthrates in the industrialized nations tend to drop, the total population of the world continues to climb exponentially.

Concurrently, the world continues to consume petroleum at a huge rate. Optimists declare that when the time comes, we'll find alternative sources of energy. Pessimists conclude that we're already on the downhill slide toward an economy without oil. What will happen to your business if fuel costs continue to rise? What if oil hits $100 per barrel again?

---

[19] See, for example, Terri Morrison, Wayne A. Conaway and George A. Borden, *Kiss, Bow, or Shake Hands: How to Do Business in Sixty Countries* (Avon, MA: Adams Media Corp., 1995).

The gaps between the haves and the have-nots continue to persist. The enormous loss of human potential and recurring conflicts between the rich and poor continue to drag on our economic and social growth. Do you see these trends continuing? Will terrorism be a more common and "acceptable" part of your future lifestyle? How would this reality affect your ability to lead and what it would require to lead successfully?

Conclusions

The world continues to change rapidly around us at a rate that is not likely to slow down in the near future. Organizations are scrambling to invent new structures and systems to respond and are discovering that the changes are so profound that they require new thinking, values, skills, designs, and leadership. This book is about what that leadership might look like and the organizations that those leaders will design and implement. Our goal is to help you begin to prepare in earnest for the changes that you will encounter during your career and lifetime. The next chapter introduces a simple conceptual framework of leadership that will provide a structure for the book and invites you to visualize it and use it to guide your efforts to develop new skills of leadership.

Concepts Introduced in This Chapter

1. As the millennium turned, we were and are in the midst of a major paradigm shift in the way business is done, the way organizations are structured, and the way leadership works.
2. The Information Revolution is creating new organizational forms—*infocracies*—that are flatter, are more dependent on fast and accurate information, demand more participation from all members, and must respond more quickly than ever before.
3. The Information Age demands new kinds of leadership that are substantially different from the leadership of the bureaucratic Industrial Age.
4. Many leaders trained and experienced in the Industrial Age will find it difficult to let go of old leadership habits and to learn new ones.
5. Effective leaders in the new Information Age will understand and be masters of the change process.
6. Effective leaders in the new Information Age will be able to coordinate diverse subunits of ethereal, boundaryless organizations that often defy description.
7. Leadership today occurs in a context of sweeping changes and trends that include shifts in global information sharing, population growth, the rise of China, the decline of oil, persistent differences between the rich and poor, and an emergent "experience" economy.
8. To be an effective leader in the new Information Age, one must learn new skills and develop new perspectives.

Questions for Personal Reflection

1. What kinds of changes have you noticed in your work and organization over the last several years? What trends and issues will face your generation of leaders?
2. What role does accurate, current information play in your ability to do your job, to become a more effective leader, and to shape your organization in the future? How well are you able to collect, understand, and utilize that information?
3. Which people in your organization seem to be working on an old, bureaucratic paradigm, and which seem to be moving ahead with fresh thinking?
4. Where does your organization rank with the competitors in your industry in terms of moving into the Information Age? Are you ahead? Middle of the pack? Behind?

5. What is your emotional reaction to the changes you see taking place around you? Do you feel threatened or invigorated? Why?
6. What would it take to get your organization moving decisively into the Information Age?
7. What would it take to get you prepared to lead in a global, populous, high-tech, rapidly changing world?

CASELET FOR DISCUSSION

The CEO of Triple Four Corporation (TFC), a global conglomerate, was new in her post and was thinking about what mark her administration would leave on the company. She wanted to develop and enhance the strategy for her company, a mixture of defense and high tech, but wanted to ensure that she'd be making the right decisions. She asked her executive team to come up with a list of the trends they saw that they thought would have significant influence on TFC over the next 20 years. If you were a member of that executive team, what trends would you identify for her and your collective consideration?

WORKBOOK

Use the Strategic Challenges section of the workbook on page 346 to clarify the challenges you see facing your organization. You may wish to interview a few respected colleagues to see what they think and then meld your views with theirs to get a balanced view.

CONTRIBUTING YOUR OWN CASELETS

Have you seen or experienced a situation involving the concepts introduced in this chapter? If so and if you'd like to contribute your experience/situation to our case data bank, please visit http://faculty.darden.virginia.edu/clawsonj/ and click on the "Contribute new caselets" button.

5 | STRATEGIC FRAMES

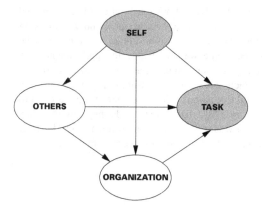

There are two parties, the establishment and the movement.

—RALPH WALDO EMERSON

We begin our tour of the Diamond Model with the north–east axis—strategic thinking—because leadership without strategy is nothing. Without strategic thinking, leaders have nowhere to go, nowhere to point, no story to tell. Effective leaders, by definition, have a strategic view and direction. To become an effective leader, one needs to become a strategic thinker.

Great leaders have great strategic dreams, visions of what could be and what they think should be. Robert Greenleaf, in *Servant Leadership,* noted, "Not much happens without a dream. And for something great to happen, there must be a great dream. Behind every great achievement is a dreamer of great dreams. Much more than a dreamer is required to bring it to reality; but the dream must be there first."[1] Although you may not have thought of yourself as a strategic dreamer, unless you are able to develop powerful strategic dreams, your abilities as a leader will be greatly undermined. To be a powerful leader, you must first have a dream,

---

[1] Robert Greenleaf, *Servant Leadership* (Mahwah, NJ: The Paulist Press, 1977), 16.

a strategic dream that defines and describes what could be—or rather what you believe should be. This chapter will explore frameworks for strategic thinking as a way of organizing your thinking, and the roles of innovation and ethics in strategic thinking. First, though, we need to establish some common language.

DEFINITIONS

When people begin thinking and talking about strategy and strategic thinking, they often get confused by the terminology. Some simple definitions and concepts can help us be clear in our conversations. First, the term *strategy* often conjures up thoughts of "long-term," "broad scope," and "high level." Yet these descriptions miss an important point. A **strategic issue** is *any* issue that affects one's ability to develop and maintain a competitive advantage. If one has no competitive advantage, one does not have much of a strategic future. Eventually, the organizations with a competitive advantage will exercise that advantage and put those who are at a disadvantage out of business. Strategic thinking is about conceiving ways to build and sustain competitive advantages.

A strategic issue is any issue that affects one's ability to develop and maintain a competitive advantage.

A **competitive advantage** in turn has three components.[2] First, it is the ability to offer superior value to customers. Inability to offer superior value to those who use an organization's goods and services means no advantage over others who would fill those customers' needs—and eventually they will do so. Superior value may be defined by the customer in terms of quality of the product or service, convenience of access to it, cost, unique features, or many other ways. Unless a firm knows what its customers value, it will have difficulty identifying what provides superior value in its offerings to customers and how.

A competitive advantage is a function of three elements:

(1) Superior value added
(2) Difficulty in imitation
(3) Enhanced flexibility

Second, competitive advantage means offering superior goods and services that are hard to imitate. If this ability is not hard to imitate, others will quickly copy what the firm does and its advantage will disappear. Difficulty in imitation can come from several sources. Patent protection is a common source, although it expires after a set period. Financial resources can be another. Large installed product base can be another. Quality of service based on careful employee hiring practices, intensive and consistent training, and advanced human resource management policies can also be a source of competitive advantage that can take years or

---

[2] George S. Day, "The Capabilities of Market-Driven Organizations," *Journal of Marketing*, 58 (October 1994): 37–52.

decades to imitate. Brand recognition and reputation, geographic dominance, and government subsidy and support are also examples of sources of difficulty in imitation.

Third, the ability to offer superior goods and services must be, paradoxically, hard to imitate and yet enhance a firm's flexibility. If a firm learns to do things in a superior but fixed way and the market environment changes quickly so that the firm is unable to respond or adapt, the advantage vanishes. The very systems that make a firm's offerings hard to imitate can also make it inflexible in its ability to adapt. The paradox and management challenge here is the desire to establish delivery capabilities that are hard to imitate yet not hard to modify or adapt. Unless a firm's management style and organizational realities include the capacity to learn and grow rapidly, that firm will, in a rapidly changing world, quickly become obsolete.

The definition of strategy is based on *"one's* competitive advantage." Then, who is that "one"? Strategic issues and thinking do not just apply to large organizations. Every organism faces strategic challenges, and if an organism is not able to meet and overcome those challenges, it will lose its competitive advantage and begin to die out. In the biological world, if rabbits are unable to figure out how to live in the presence of wolves, they begin to die out. If the wolves are unable to learn how to hunt better than cougars or to live among humans, they begin to die out. In the business world, units that cannot meet their competitive challenges begin to disappear.

FRAMES FOR STRATEGIC THINKING

Bruce Henderson, founder of one of the world's great consulting firms, the Boston Consulting Group, summarized strategy succinctly this way: "Strategy is the management of natural competition."[3] He then pointed out five basic elements of strategic competition:

1. The ability to understand the interaction dynamics of competitors in an arena
2. The ability to predict how action will affect those dynamics
3. The ability to commit resources to future outcomes
4. The ability to predict risk and return on those commitments
5. The courage to act

These principles relate directly to your skills and abilities at strategic thinking. As it turns out, several different and related approaches taken in the last 50 years build on this foundation and seek to strengthen our understanding of strategic competition. Each of these approaches can add to your ability to think strategically. The challenge is not to memorize and regurgitate them all, but to understand the basic perspectives of each and incorporate them into your strategic Level Three thinking and view of the world. Then you can use your integrated set of strategic values, assumptions, beliefs, and expectations (VABEs) to formulate a strategy for your organization, your work group, and yourself.

FIT MODELS

Ken Andrews was one of the earliest modern strategy observers and commentators.[4] Andrews popularized the separation of strategy formulation and implementation in which he argued that corporate leaders must first create strategy and then lead and manage so as to implement it. He proposed nine criteria for evaluating the strength of corporate strategies:

---

[3] Bruce Henderson, "The Origin of Strategy," *Harvard Business Review*, November 1, 1989, 89605.
[4] Kenneth Andrews, *The Concept of Corporate Strategy* (Homewood, IL: Irwin, 1971, 1980).

1. Has the strategy been made clear and identifiable?
2. Does the strategy fully exploit domestic and international opportunities?
3. Is the strategy consistent with current and future corporate capabilities?
4. Is the strategy internally consistent?
5. Does the strategy present a manageable risk level?
6. Does the strategy match the personal values and goals of senior management?
7. Does the strategy match the company's societal contribution goals?
8. Does the strategy stimulate to action?
9. Does the marketplace seem to be responding to the strategy?

Even though they tend to be yes/no rather than descriptive questions, considering them carefully can help one assess the clarity and appropriateness of one's own strategic thinking. You could use this list as a template for assessing the strength of your strategic communication.

Andrews's approach was essentially a fit model in that it encouraged management to find appropriate niches in the world of opportunities and to use their strengths to exploit those opportunities. Andrews's views led to a widely used model of strategic analysis commonly referred to as the SWOT (strengths, weaknesses, opportunities, and threats) model. The idea was that managers should examine all the four carefully and find areas in which their particular strengths and weaknesses could be brought to bear most effectively. Figure 5-1 shows a diagram of how the SWOT model was often presented and conceived. The SWOT model often provided the basis for discussion of four additional, related, action-oriented questions that corresponded to the SWOT analysis:

1. What *new* capabilities do we want to develop?
2. How do we create *new* possibilities?
3. What do we need to learn in order to develop *new* capabilities?
4. How do we partner to build shared expectancies?

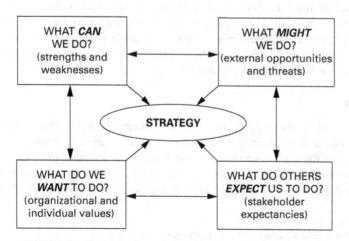

FIGURE 5-1   Four questions that guide strategic choices

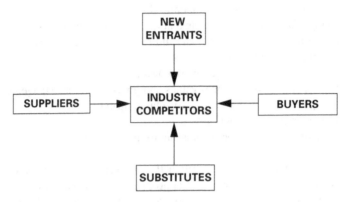

FIGURE 5-2 Porter's Five Forces Model

Porter's Five Forces

During the 1980s, Michael Porter, at the Harvard Business School, introduced what he called a Five Forces Model (shown in Figure 5-2). Porter's economics background led him to focus more on industries than Andrews's corporate perspective did. Porter's model assessed a firm's advantages compared with other firms in an industry.[5] The five forces that shaped an industry, he said, were new entrants (held at bay by barriers to entry), the power of suppliers, the power of customers, the threat of substitution, and a company's core capabilities to compete amid the other companies in an industry and the other four forces. Porter also extended the concept of strategic competitive advantage to another layer (above individual, work group, and company) to consider countries.[6]

Barriers to entry make it difficult for new entrants to compete in an industry. Barriers to entry may include patent protection, geographic proximity, established share of market, and huge but necessary initial investment costs in plant and equipment. Customers have power (as a "force") over a company to the extent that they want additional products or services that a given company may not offer. Suppliers can influence a firm's ability to compete to the extent that the firm is dependent on them for their outputs in order to meet customers' demands. Industry innovations that leapfrog a firm's products and services and provide substitutions for them can be a major threat to a firm's survival. Finally, if a firm's internal skills and abilities don't compare favorably with those of competitors in an industry, that firm's position in that industry will erode. Porter's work seemed to build well on Andrews's model, and managers accepted the Five Forces Model as a natural extension of SWOT analysis.

Value Chain

Porter also clarified another important strategic concept, the value chain. In Porter's model, each company had a value chain that enabled it to compete against others. A *value chain* is a stream of activities that add value to inputs and make them desirable to others. One can examine the strength of one's ability to compete by understanding the economics of each link in the value chain. In Porter's view, one could identify a generic value chain consisting of nine basic

---

[5] Michael Porter, *Competitive Advantage* (New York: The Free Press, 1985).
[6] Ibid., *The Competitive Advantage of Nations* (New York: The Free Press, 1990).

elements. These elements include five primary links and four supporting structures. The five primary links are inbound logistics, operations, outbound logistics, marketing and sales, and service. Basically, Porter asserted, every organization followed this pattern, taking something in, manipulating it, and then delivering it to others through marketing and sales groups and finally servicing it if necessary. The quality of the value added at each of these steps collectively defines the company's strategic competitive advantage. If value is lacking at each step or is easy to imitate, the organization realizes little competitive advantage.

The four secondary support structures are organizational infrastructure, human resource management practices, technology employed and its development, and procurement methods. These basic supporting structures make it possible for an organization to add value at each of the five links in the value chain. If any of the four supporting structures is weak or unable to contribute to the five links, then an organization's strategic competitiveness is reduced.

Revisions of the value chain concept recently applied the concept to a larger, industry-based view. In this view, one traces the major value-adding activities of a class of products or services and tries to analyze where the economic opportunities are and how one's own capabilities and strengths apply to those segments of the chain. In the automobile industry, for instance, a simple value chain could include mining, shipping, steel production, shipping, component fabrication, subassembly, shipping, assembly, storing, shipping, marketing, sales, financing, and service. Henry Ford decided in the 1920s to integrate his firm to each and every step in this chain, but over the years he discovered that it was not a profitable venture. The skills, competencies, and capabilities demanded in each step of the value chain were different, and Ford Motor Company eventually narrowed its automobile business to focus on fabrication, subassembly (although much is subcontracted), assembly, and financing.

This broader view of an industry's or a class of products' value chain helps a management team decide where their organization's particular skills and abilities might best add value and hence better serve customers. If one analyzes the economics of each of the steps in an industry value chain, one may find opportunities or, alternatively, segments of the business where competition doesn't make much sense (e.g., because margins are low, barriers to entry are high, and competition is stiff).

Deciding what the discrete links in a value chain should be is not an exact science. One tries to identify all of the separate activities that add value in the series of processes from raw material to consumption and then analyze the economics of each one. If an activity has trivial impact on the overall value added throughout the chain, it might be grouped with another activity until the grouping becomes a significant link in the value chain that delivers value to customers. The goal is to create a sequential list of value-adding activity clusters, each of which having a significant impact on the value of the final product or service.

With such a list in place, one can then begin to analyze each link in the chain to see where the economic opportunities are. In this analysis, one looks at special skills or technology demanded by the activity, what the cost structures in that activity are, and what the related margins might be and then compares these with the organization's capabilities. If the skills and experience demanded by a link, for example mining in the preceding Ford example, are inconsistent with the organization's core capabilities and hence ability to add significant value, then the firm should choose, strategically, to compete elsewhere. If the margins in that link (mining) are narrow and shrinking because competition is high, barriers to entry are relatively high (cost of new equipment and remote location costs), and power of customers is high, as it might be in mining, then the firm should choose to compete at a different point in the value chain. James Moore, principal at GEO Consulting, for example, developed an analytic procedure that helps organizations clarify whether they have what it takes to succeed in business at any point in a product's value chain.

Core Capabilities

A key concept in the evolving fit strategy models was that of core capabilities. First popularized by C. K. Prahalad and Gary Hamel,[7] core capabilities referred to the collection of organizational skills a firm developed over time that enabled it to compete and made it difficult for others to imitate its success. Core capabilities, or clusters of skills, are often intangible competencies, related to technology and its development and to internal organizational processes around innovation, production and financial management efficiencies, and marketing. An example of successful core capabilities identification and application would be Canon's expertise in optoelectronics, a term used to signify the ability to marry optical skills with electronic skills effectively to create new products through efficient internal organizational processes. The recognition of this core capability took Canon from being a "camera company" to being the leading firm in the birth of the laser-jet printer industry. Recognition of core capabilities can transform the way a company views itself. Caterpillar's extraordinary capability to manage the production, financing, and distribution of first-rate construction equipment worldwide is an example of a cluster of organizational skills in design, manufacturing, global relationships, financing innovation, and dealer relations that complement each other intricately to sustain the world's most successful construction equipment company. Wal-Mart's ability to manage inventories across a vast retail distribution system is another example of organizational core competitive capability.[8] Honda's expertise and innovation in designing and applying high-power, high-efficiency, small engines led to competitive advantages in several industries, including motorcycles, lawn-care products, and automobiles. Disney's ability to imagine and create animated stories that appealed to children and adults alike was the central factor in the creation of an empire of entertainment, which now includes amusement parks, broadcasting companies, toys, hotels, golf courses, and various related pieces.

The central question posed to a firm's management by this kind of strategic thinking is, what are your unique core capabilities? If a firm can identify something that it does better than anyone else and is able to focus on that capability in responsive markets, the firm will realize a competitive advantage—for the moment. By definition, core capabilities take time to develop and are so complex, weaving together competencies from various divisions of an organization that they tend to be difficult to imitate, especially in the short run. This key finding was described in *Built to Last*.[9] As firms tried to find places where their particular core capabilities might compete successfully, they found themselves fighting for increasingly narrow niches. This strategic-fit thinking was ultimately limited, which caused some firms to think about ways of changing the relative mix of competitive advantages in industry according to their desires.

Growth

Most strategists are convinced that businesses must grow. Population specialists, environmentalists, and conservationists continue to argue about whether growth is unlimited or sustainable, but most business leaders actively seek to grow. The motivation for growth may be in part a natural human desire to extend one's experience and boundaries.[10] Ram Charan and Noel Tichy summarized Igor

---

[7] C. K. Prahalad and Gary Hamel, "The Core Competence of the Corporation," *Harvard Business Review*, May 01, 1990, 90311.
[8] See George Stalk Jr., Philip Evans, and Lawrence E. Shulman, "Competing on Capabilities: The New Rules of Corporate Strategy," *Harvard Business Review*, March 01, 1992, 92209.
[9] James C. Collins and Jerry I. Porras, *Built to Last* (New York: HarperBusiness, 1994).
[10] See, for example, Mihalyi Csikszentmihalyi, *The Evolving Self* (New York: HarperCollins, 1993). See also Paul Lawrence and Nitin Norhria, *Driven* (San Francisco, CA: Jossey-Bass, 2001), in which they argue that the first fundamental human desire or drive is to acquire.

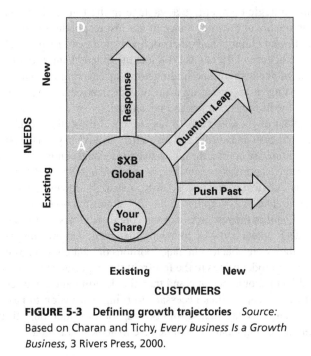

FIGURE 5-3 **Defining growth trajectories** *Source: Based on Charan and Tichy, Every Business Is a Growth Business, 3 Rivers Press, 2000.*

Ansoff's diversification matrix and argued that every business can be a growth business, even in what seems to be a saturated market.[11] They build their argument on a 2 × 2 grid showing old and new customers and old and new products as depicted in Figure 5-3. They point out that no matter how "mature" your current market with current customers and current products is, you can find ways to identify broader potential opportunity. One way is to realize how much, in total, your customers are spending on products like your own and view that as your target "share of wallet"—that is, the total amount of spending of your customers. In addition to seeking to gain a larger share of wallet, one can think about new customers for existing products and services. Most sales forces take this route, trying to find ways of pushing out what we already know, do, and make. The third route, offering new products and services to existing customers, demands a willingness to look at customers' total wallet of all spending, not just on products and services like your own, and your willingness to develop capabilities to capture more of that spending. This approach requires research and development, close customer ties, and a strategic innovation mind-set. The fourth avenue for broadening potential is moving into the new customers–new products cell, where both elements are new. This high-risk strategy implies a greater leap from your current platforms of competency and customer base—and the risk of falling down in the process.

INTENT MODELS

Even though Andrews, Porter, and others emphasized finding the right time and place to compete, Hamel and Prahalad[12] began to wonder about how to develop core capabilities as a

---

[11] Ram Charan and Noel M. Tichy, *Every Business Is a Growth Business* (New York: Times Business/Random House, 1998). Ansoff's matrix was first published in "Strategies for Diversification," *Harvard Business Review*, 1957.
[12] Gary Hamel and C. K. Prahalad, *Competing for the Future* (Boston, MA: Harvard Business School Press, 1994).

means of developing strategic competitive advantage in the future. They built on the ideas of Karl Weick,[13] who wrote about the importance of not just responding to one's environment, but of enacting it. James Bryant Quinn[14] and others defined strategy retrospectively as the path made apparent by a series of historical decisions ("logical incrementalism"), but Prahalad and Hamel asserted that strategic thinkers should be finding ways of enacting or shaping their competitive environments by investing in and creating a set of organizational capabilities that would give them, at some time in the future, a competitive advantage.

This strategic intent might take years to realize, but if carefully conceived and managed, it could reshape the economics of an industry and give a firm an advantage that would take others years to duplicate. In the meantime, of course, the innovative firm would continue to develop its core capabilities. This more proactive approach was called *the strategic intent model.* One shining example of this way of thinking is manifest in the history of Komatsu, the Japanese construction equipment maker, which decided to take on Caterpillar in the global construction market. At the time of this decision, Komatsu had neither the resources nor the core capabilities to do so effectively. Yet they formed a serious, strategic intent and—by following that intent and investing year by year in their targeted capabilities—they were able to win major portions of their chosen business.[15]

The strategic intent model brings to the forefront the importance of having a vision of what the organization could and should become and then the determination and resources to invest in developing the competitive capabilities necessary to bring that vision to pass. If it takes years, even decades, to build an advantageous set of core capabilities, then only firms with the vision and resources to continue doing business will be able to achieve that goal.

The BCG Model

In the 1970s the Boston Consulting Group developed a strategic planning matrix for categorizing business units. The group argued that if you compared a market segment's growth with the share of the market that a company had, you could identify desirable and undesirable positions (Figure 5-4). Business units that were operating with high market share in high-growth segments were "stars." Those operating with high market share in low-growth industries were "cash cows," because it would be difficult for competitors to take away established share. Business units operating with low market share in low-growth industries were "dogs" to be sold, and units with low shares in high-growth segments were "problem children" that either needed to do something fast or die. The reasoning behind BCG's matrix is similar to Jack Welch's famous late-twentieth-century dictum to operating executives, "If you're not Number One or Number Two in your industry, you'll be sold."

Although some problems exist with the assumptions underlying the BCG matrix, it has many strong features. First, it helps managers think about whether a particular business unit has a bright future and how it might strive to capture that future. Second, it suggests a normal development among business units from "problem child" to "star" or to "cash cow" or to "dog," a concept that also encourages long-term thinking. BCG analysts argued for positioning of business units and then management decisions that would develop each toward the more advantageous category. Executives leading "problem children" had to figure out how to capture share in growing segments, or they die. Those leading "stars" were encouraged to think about their position and the growth of their segment to ensure that they would settle into "cash cows" and not into the "dogs." Leaders of "cash cows" were forced to think about how to maintain their dominant position and

---

[13] Karl Weick, *The Social Psychology of Organizing* (Reading, MA: Addison-Wesley, 1979).

[14] James B. Quinn, "Strategic Change: Logical Incrementalism," *Sloan Management Review* (Summer 1989): 45.

[15] See "Komatsu Limited," Harvard Case Services 9-385-277, for further details.

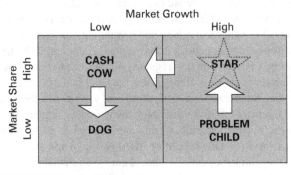

FIGURE 5-4 The BCG matrix

avoid becoming low-share, low-growth "dogs." Related thinking appears in Christensen's Innovator's Dilemma introduced later.

The Ecological Model

A fourth approach emerged in the work of James Moore at GEO Consulting. Moore postulated that the concept of business industries was dying and that a more descriptive metaphor of what was happening in the business world at the turn of the millennium was the concept of business ecosystems.[16] Moore argues that, in reality, Company A may be competing with Company B in one region of the world, selling to Company B in another region, and in a joint venture alliance with Company B in another region. Each company, in this ecological view, was living and thriving in a complex relationship with the other, and the destruction of either might lead to disastrous results for the one that remained. In biological terms, they were in a symbiotic relationship—if either one died, so did the other.

This view is decidedly different from the common "business is war" mentality that most managers have about their strategic planning and that usually involves finding ways to minimize or destroy competitors' positions. In the ecological view of business, putting other companies out of business may be the worst thing for a company, which has multiple relationships around the world, to do. The more long-lasting approach would be to view their businesses as ecosystems with ill-defined boundaries between industries or companies and to approach their competitors as necessary parts of the business ecosystem, rather than as enemies to be exterminated. Companies that can compete on one hand and ally on the other are developing core capabilities that allow them to deal with ambiguity, contradiction, and competing internal pressures in ways that give them an advantage that are hard to imitate and that build their flexibility for the future. Those that persist in fighting their competitors may, in fact, be sowing the seeds of their own destruction—naturally or through antitrust regulation as in the case of the former AT&T before the 1984 court ruling.

STRATEGY AS REVOLUTION

Gary Hamel offered a more radical view of strategic thinking in his book *Leading the Revolution*.[17] Hamel argued that most established businesses are at risk from revolutionaries. Eventually, he said, revolutionary companies would steal customers and markets, then employees, and finally assets.

---

[16] See James F. Moore, "Predators and Prey: A New Ecology of Competition," *Harvard Business Review*, May 1, 1993, 93309.

[17] Gary Hamel, *Leading the Revolution* (Boston, MA: Harvard Business School Press, 2000).

Ralph Waldo Emerson once noted, "There are two parties, the establishment and the movement." In that spirit, Hamel posited two kinds of leaders: value squeezers who tried to milk additional profits out of an "old" business model or value proposition and revolutionaries who created new value propositions and businesses. Eschewing continuous improvement, Hamel argued, strategic leaders should search for revolutionary new business models regularly—always searching for ways to challenge and destroy their old mental business models. If they don't, they will find their profits asymptotically eaten away until they finally die, as other revolutionaries find new ways to service their customers.

Hamel proposed a series of rules for designing revolutionary organizations that might be constantly reinventing themselves. First, he said, set unreasonable expectations. This notion is consistent with Collins and Porras's *Built to Last* insight of BHAGs (big, hairy, audacious goals) that stretch people to do more than they think they can. Second, Hamel recommended using elastic business definitions. Don't get locked into one view of what kind of company you are. If Canon had always thought of itself as a "camera company," it likely would never have invented the laser-jet printer. Third, create energy by defining your activity as a cause, not a business. People would rather work for something important and powerful than to make others wealthy. Again, this idea is consistent with Collins and Porras's concept of "purpose beyond profits." Fourth, listen to revolutionary voices. Most companies are led by people who want more of the same and are not sensitive to or sympathetic with discordant voices. Yet those voices (e.g., that of Steven Jobs and Steven Wozniak at Apple, trying to build their "personal computer") may well be the voices of the next generation.

Fifth, create an open market for new ideas. If the organization does not systematically and openly find and reward new ideas, it will die. Sixth, create an open market for capital to fund those new ideas. Let managers invest freely in the ideas they believe will serve their customers. Seventh, create an open market for talent. Attracting and retaining talent is one of the key strategic challenges in the twenty-first century. Organizations that encourage mobility and allow highly talented people to work on projects they are moved by are much more likely to attract and keep the highly talented. Eighth, encourage low-risk experimentation. If you have free markets for ideas, funding, and talent, then the next step is to encourage rather than punish people for trying small experiments in growing revolutionary ideas.

Ninth, grow by cellular division. When a little experiment succeeds, don't stifle it and bureaucratize it, let it grow naturally and independently. The Johnson & Johnson (J&J) family of businesses is a good example of this. J&J is a collection of more than 200 businesses, each formed from a new idea brought forward internally, then grown and spun off into a separate business, still a part of the J&J family. Tenth, let the revolutionaries participate in the wealth creation. Hamel wrote, "You can't reward entrepreneurs like you reward stewards." If a revolutionary comes up with a great idea, he or she naturally wants to enjoy the benefits of that idea.

Hamel's ideas about strategy invite all leaders to rethink their commitments to innovation and self-reinvention. Profit-squeezing leaders, trying to get one last drop out of a system, a process, or a business model, may be ignoring larger strategic dangers. They would do better to find and listen to the revolutionaries who exist on the periphery of their organizations and who may have a vision of the next new, radical model of creating superior value.

THE EXPERIENCE ECONOMY

Pine and Gilmore offer a broad, sweeping way of thinking about economic development and related strategic thinking.[18] They argue that if we look at the whole of human economic activity

---

[18] Joe Pine and James Gilmore, *The Experience Economy* (Boston, MA: Harvard University Press, 1999).

historically, we can observe at first that humans made profits from things they took out of the earth. Eventually these things became so common in the agricultural society that they became easy to get (commodities)—and profit margins on them declined. In about 1800, with the advent of the Industrial Revolution, people began to make things out of the material they took out of the earth, in part because they got higher margins from adding value to iron ore by making it into goods. The advent of the Information Revolution (about 1950) produced another shift in economic focus, when people realized that margins on goods were shrinking as they became commodities, so they shifted to services. Now, they argue, as margins on services shrink (as the services are outsourced overseas), we enter a new experience economy where the higher margins are not for raw materials, goods, or services, but for ethereal experiences that evaporate when they are over. Note how much people are willing to pay for tickets to a rock concert, to a World Cup Soccer game, to the Super Bowl, and related events. Pine and Gilmore assert that the next major economic phase will be a transformational one in which the high margins will be available to those who can promise to transform us while we are with them, not just give us commodities, goods, services, or experiences. We can see this trend emerging today in the margins commanded by consultants, universities, and mergers and acquisitions.

THE INNOVATOR'S DILEMMA

Clayton Christensen at the Harvard Business School discovered a strategic pattern with which most companies wrestle. He calls it the Innovator's Dilemma because although this strategic pattern is a natural rational process, it produces a real conundrum for strategists. In Figure 5-5, we show the basic elements of the Innovator's Dilemma. Notice that the vertical axis is an unusual measure, the proportion of a product's features that customers can use. Over time, companies hope that customers will be able to use more and more of their products' features, as represented by the rising dark line. At the same time, at any given time, companies have a range of customers, those who can use many of a product's features and those who can use few, represented by the bell-shaped curve to the right. As a company begins selling its products and services, it rationally wants to add features and services because that's what customers want and it can realize higher margins. The problem is that over 10, 20, or 30 years, a company naturally and rationally learns a "high-margin culture," a way of doing business that seeks higher and higher margins. This pattern leads to two dangers.

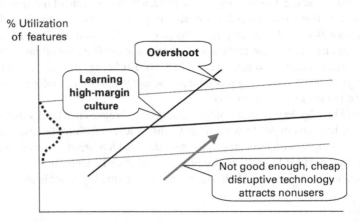

FIGURE 5-5 The innovator's dilemma

The first danger is "overshoot"—when a company offers products that customers don't want and cannot afford. For example, one company, with a distinctly inside-out engineering culture, built two very expensive, top-of-the-line telecommunications satellites. The problem was that their customers didn't need or want, nor could they afford those satellites. Consequently, they sat unused in a warehouse and the huge, multimillion-dollar investment went unutilized.

The second danger is that when an unsophisticated, lower-technology-based company offers a competing product at the lower end of the feature spectrum (as represented by the upward sloping line on the right), the first company isn't interested in competing for low-margin, low-end business. Such a goal is just not rational. So the second company gets a toehold, and then the rational thing to do is to add features so they can command higher margins. Mercedes and Cadillac, for instance, were not so interested when Kia or Hyundai entered the U.S. automobile market. As time went by, however, we saw Mercedes, Volvo, and Cadillac begin offering smaller and smaller and cheaper and cheaper models to compete with the companies slowly eating away at their market shares from the bottom up.

The Innovator's Dilemma is that when an established company is faced with cheap, low-tech, unsophisticated competitors, the company often doesn't want to compete with them because they attack in low-margin segments. The danger, though, is that down the road, their margins are eaten up from the ground.

GOOD TO GREAT MODEL

Jim Collins asserted that six basic elements are necessary to take a company from a consistently mediocre position in an industry to a consistently superior position.[19] In the 1,100 companies included in his study, the six elements form a solid basis for thinking about a strategy for moving from mediocrity to industry leadership. The six elements are as follows:

1. Level Five leaders
2. First who, then what
3. Confront the brutal facts
4. Hedgehog concept
5. Culture of discipline
6. Technology accelerators

If a company could get these things, he argued, a virtuous cycle of momentum would build a "flywheel effect" that would propel a company to greatness. We can think of this move from good to great as a Boeing 747 getting ready to take off. First, you need a good pilot, then you need a good crew. Before rotation and takeoff, you need to confront the brutal facts like airspeed, weight, flaps indicators, and so many others. Then, once airborne, you have to focus on what you do well (flying), obey all safe-flying procedures, and use the latest technology (flight control and navigation, etc.) to get to your destination.

The Level Five leadership that Collins recommended relates to a totally different scale than the Level Three Leadership put forward here. Collins's levels are simply levels of management from employee to supervisor, to manager, to organizational leader, to a special kind of organizational leader characterized by will and humility. Level Five Leaders, in Collins's view, have a deep determination to accomplish their vision and are remarkably humble about their progress,

---

[19] Jim Collins, *Good to Great* (New York: HarperCollins, 2001).

eschewing personal celebrity in favor of a strong team. Clearly, one could argue that will and humility are VABEs (Level Three concepts) that drive their behavior.

The "first who, then what" element refers to the importance of finding the best "athletes" you can and then letting them define their own work. This finding flies in the face of organizations that try to define job descriptions or key competencies at higher levels and then force fit the next generation of leaders into it.

"Confront the brutal facts" is akin to Jack Welch's dictum, "Face reality as it is, not as it was, or as you wish it were."[20] This problem of vision, of "seeing what needs to be done," was outlined in our earlier definition of the Leadership Point of View. Too many people at all levels try to discount, distort, or ignore the brutal facts. It's not a healthy way to think about strategy.

Collins uses a hedgehog concept to prescribe finding something that you're good at and sticking to it. He says the hedgehog concept consists of the intersection of three things: something you love to do, something you're good at, and something that people will pay you to do. It's an excellent piece of advice for the individual as well as the work group or corporation.

The culture of discipline element is the care that managers throughout the organization take to sticking to their core hedgehog concept, and not trying to do other things. Criticisms of Peters and Waterman's classic *In Search of Excellence* often pointed out how the companies touted there later tried to do other things and fell off their pedestals. Discipline in decision making, again, is a challenge at all three strategic levels. How many individuals struggle with discipline in their personal lives, discipline around eating, drinking, smoking, exercise, reading, and managing expenses? The same is true of work groups and organizations.

The technology accelerators in Collins's summary are particular technological solutions to specific problems. Too often, companies get enamored of the latest Information Age systems when what they really need is a simpler, perhaps in-house-developed system to do a particular thing—at a much lower cost.

Collins argued that the 11 companies that made the jump from good to great all demonstrated the six factors, which together produced a flywheel effect of positive momentum. Minimizing or hindering any of these six factors puts a drag on the flywheel and slows down performance. Ensuring that all six are in place and in shape is likely to produce the opposite effect, touching a turning hoop so that it revolves or turns over faster and faster. All of these concepts are summarized in Figure 5-6.

STRATEGY MAPS

One more strategic perspective, that of Robert Kaplan and David Norton, deserves our attention.[21] This perspective is built on the balanced scorecard framework but with a set of causal linkages. The reasoning is relatively simple and powerful: money comes from customers, customers are made happy by the abilities of companies to please them, and the abilities of companies to do things are based on their people and processes. The balanced scorecard was first introduced by Kaplan and Norton to encourage corporate management teams to focus on more than just the bottom line. When driving a car, for example, you must pay attention to many things, not just your speed. In fact, if you pay proper attention to those other things, the other dials on your dashboard, you can actually increase your speed. Conversely, if you focus just on your speed, you can damage your car and destroy your ability to go fast.

---

[20] Noel Tichy and Stratford Sherman, *Control Your Destiny or Someone Else Will* (New York: HarperBusiness, 2001).
[21] Robert S. Kaplan and David N. Norton, *"Strategy Maps: Converting Intangible Assets into Tangible Outcomes,"* (Boston, MA: Harvard Business Press, 2004).

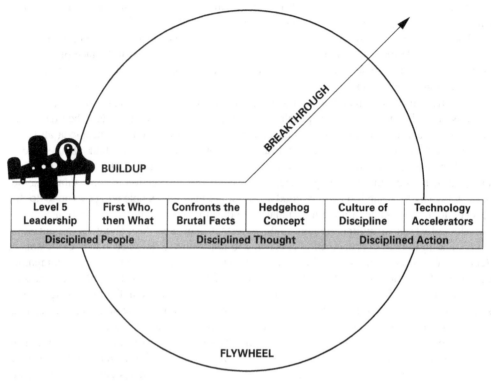

FIGURE 5-6   Good to Great Model

The original balanced scorecard consisted of a focus on four elements: customers, internal operations, and the learning and development of an organization's people as well as the finances. With their strategy mapping concept, Kaplan and Norton enrich the original balanced scorecard framework by showing how investments in the other three elements, in a causal map, enhance profitability.

Profits (**P**) are what's left when you subtract expenses (**E**) from revenues (**R**). Revenues come because customers like what you do. So one major way to enhance profits is to please customers. It seems simple, yet many management teams lose sight of that linkage. (The other way to enhance profits, of course, is by managing costs.) This is the "financial perspective."

The customer perspective is to identify what it is that your customers (segmented, of course) want. Is it quality? Low cost? Dependability? Reliability? Brand image? Convenience? Or some mixture of these elements (and more)? When a company goes to market, the strategy map perspective will ask, "What's your customer value proposition (CVP)?" That is, on what basis do you plan to please and delight your customers so that they want more of what you have? The CVP for Starbucks originally, for example, was a "third place," a place between work and home where, coming and/or going, you could stop, get a warm drink to your exact liking, read the paper, check your e-mail, and compress or decompress—make the transition. This CVP proved very profitable for Starbucks as they grew rapidly into a global brand.

The internal operations perspective then asks, "What internal capabilities do you have to have in order to please your customers with your CVP?" In essence, each organization in the strategy map view would need to identify the key elements in its internal value chain that in turn produced customer satisfaction. With Starbucks, this began with high-quality raw materials (coffee beans), high-quality roasting processes, and high-quality employees. So, purchasing, roasting, and serving became centrally important links in the Starbucks effort to build internal capabilities. Each of these required large investments—relationships and ultimately education for the best coffee growers in the world, proprietary roasting facilities kept under secret wraps (like the Coca Cola formula), and human resource policies that attracted the cream of the temporary labor pool (who wants to be a barista for life?). These significant, multimillion-dollar investments (e.g., $10,000,000 in a coffee growing education center in Latin America) would only be worth it if they made happy customers who in turn would buy more at Starbucks.

Finally, the "intangible assets" (not on the balance sheet) who made the organizational capabilities actually function were the people, what many call today "human capital (**HC**)." Think of the original conception of the modern corporation—it had capital (money), labor (people), and plant and equipment. Today, we speak of "human capital" (the sum of all of the talents, skills, and abilities of organization members), "social capital (**SC**)" (the sum of the value of the *relationships* among all those people), and "organizational capital (**OC**)" (the value added by the way an organization manages information, activity, and decision making). The strategy map perspective suggests that one should only invest in these three elements IF those investments will produce stronger, deeper organizational capabilities that directly and in turn satisfy customers who in turn buy more.

In this way, intangible assets like people, their skills, the way they work together, the information infrastructure, and a host of related elements can be directed at improving profits, several links down the strategy map chain. Investments in training programs, education, computer systems, reorganizations, and even acquisitions could now be evaluated in terms of how well each element was contributing to the strategy map causal chain. Now, managers could ask questions like, "How will this training program cost contribute to our bottom line?" Figure 5-7 depicts the key questions at each level in the strategy map perspective and the very high level (non-detailed) vertical linkage among them.

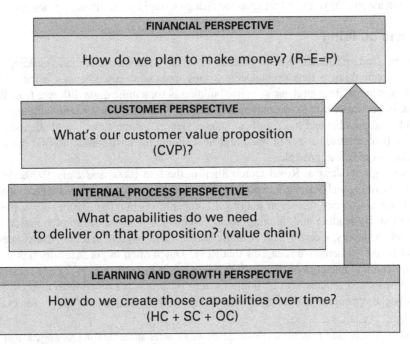

FINANCIAL PERSPECTIVE

How do we plan to make money? (R–E=P)

CUSTOMER PERSPECTIVE

What's our customer value proposition (CVP)?

INTERNAL PROCESS PERSPECTIVE

What capabilities do we need to deliver on that proposition? (value chain)

LEARNING AND GROWTH PERSPECTIVE

How do we create those capabilities over time? (HC + SC + OC)

FIGURE 5-7   The strategy map key questions

DEVELOPING YOUR STRATEGIC THINKING

As you can see from this discussion, the main elements of the fit, growth, intent, ecological, revolutionary, experience, innovator's dilemma, good to great, and strategy map models of strategic thinking build on and are related to each other. Modern strategic thinkers work hard to understand the influential forces in the world around them, to assess and develop their relative competitive strengths vis-à-vis their competitors, to develop clear visions of where they want to go, and to maintain the flexibility and even contradictory nature of countervailing relationships in order to develop a sustainable strategic competitive advantage.

Strategic thinking is hard work. It requires reading about and following trends in the general and trade presses to keep current on forces that influence the present and future. It demands a keen awareness of the basis upon which one unit competes with others. A strategic thinker must be open to learning and developing new ways of competing. Strategic thinking depends not only on the vision, but on the courage to choose a path and then the fortitude to stick to it over years of effort, perhaps with modest results at first.

Two modern strategists, Jeanne Liedtka and John Rosenblum, call strategic conversations the building blocks of strategy.[22] Business leaders get together and talk. In the course of those conversations, they try to clarify their view of what the organization can and should become and how that might happen. Sometimes these conversations are fuzzy, sometimes quite sharp.

Strategy building is difficult in rapidly changing environments. When the context is chaotic, strategic thinkers need to develop alternative, flexible courses of action. This approach will be effective only if those courses of action are built on a strong value base and are consistent with what Collins and Porras called the firm's "purpose beyond profits." The recurring turbulence in the economic world has led to a rapid erosion of trust in strategic planning departments. Many companies that developed strategic plans, had strategic intent, and bet large resources on those plans discovered in the past 20 years that things often change so rapidly that strategic plans cannot be trusted.

Scenario Building

A proven, effective alternative to the practice of strategic planning is scenario building, a process in which strategic thinkers develop plausible stories about what could happen in the changing environmental context. True strategic scenario building is something quite different from the common practice of best-case, worst-case, and most-likely-case scenarios. In scenario building, each story is plausible and possible and has significant consequences for the firm. The challenge is to identify these likely alternatives and then find ways of scanning the environment to find out which one is occurring as quickly as possible.

Strategic thinkers at Royal Dutch Shell in the late 1960s and early 1970s developed the scenario planning technique to the point where they were able to prepare their company to move from being last among the seven major oil companies to number one or two at the end of the millennium. By reading and thinking about economics, politics, geography, nationalism, and a host of other factors, Pierre Wack, Peter Schwartz, Les Grayson, and their colleagues were able to identify likely alternative scenarios that Royal Dutch Shell might face and then to specify the kinds of leading indicators or signals they might see in the newspapers for each scenario.

When small articles about Middle Eastern oil producers meeting to discuss international affairs began appearing in the international papers, they scanned regularly: for example, they

---

[22] Jeanne M. Liedtka and John W. Rosenblum, "Shaping Conversations: Making Strategy, Managing Change," *California Management Review* 39, no. 1 (Fall 1996): 4.

recognized a leading indicator of one of their scenarios, which included the formation of an oil cartel. What was to others a trivial news item in the middle of the paper was to the scanners at Royal Dutch Shell a clear predictor of their "cartel" scenario and its enormous implications for getting stable supplies of crude. Seeing these articles and having already worked through what might happen if such a cartel were formed, Royal Dutch Shell was able to change its strategic course to one of gaining direct access to oil supplies before the oil shock of 1973 hit and, in so doing, laid the foundation for the company's dramatic rise among its competitors.[23] Scenario planning, therefore, demonstrates the capacity for helping strategic thinkers approach the process of strategy building with a disciplined and grounded foresight that includes flexibility.

Broad Reading

From the preceding examples, it is clear that a key activity in the development of good strategic thinking is wide-ranging reading and thinking. Sometimes impending opportunity or disaster can best be seen from a different and distant vantage point. Strategic thinkers are skilled at viewing situations from multiple points of view and at collecting data on and perspectives of those different points of view. One way, for instance, that MBA students can develop this "ability to see the alternative" is by learning to play the Chinese/Japanese game of Go.

Go is played on a board with 19 lines each across and down, creating 361 squares. Unlike chess in which players have many different kinds of pieces to move, Go players have only stones, black and white, which they may place as they wish on the intersections of the lines. The objective in chess is to capture or kill the opposing king, but in Go the objective is to control more territory than an opponent, but not to annihilate him or her (consistent with the ecological view of strategy). Because it includes so many more squares (chess has only 64) and the object of the game is different, Go turns out to be much more complex than chess. Linear thinking that anticipates several moves down the line becomes a liability. Rather, the ability to see the development of strong and weak shapes of stones as they evolve on the board becomes more important. Western students report that learning to play Go caused them to realize that the majority of the world's population, those living in Asia, might think about things in ways fundamentally different from Westerners and that the depth of those differences is significant.

ESSENTIAL ELEMENTS OF STRATEGIC THINKING

Jeanne Liedtka helps summarize this discussion with her perspective on strategic thinking, which includes five key elements: a systems perspective, intelligent opportunism, intent focus, driven by hypothesis, and thinking in time.[24]

Systems thinking begins with a systems perspective, an ability to see how the various forces and components of an industry fit together. Systems perspective helps individuals rise above satisfying their own departmental goals to see how all parts of an organization or industry fit together and how changes in one affect others. An understanding of these various components—the parts of the value chain in an industry, for instance—allows an intelligent opportunism to help find the

---

[23] For more information on scenario planning, see Les Grayson and James Clawson, "Scenario Building" (UVA-G-260); Paul Shoemaker, "Scenario Planning: A Tool for Strategic Thinking," *Sloan Management Review*, Winter (1995): 25; Pierre Wack, "Scenarios: Uncharted Waters Ahead," *Harvard Business Review*, September 01, 1985, 85516; and Peter Schwartz, *The Art of the Long View* (New York: Doubleday Currency, 1991).
[24] Jeanne Liedtka, "Strategic Thinking: Elements, Outcomes, and Implications for Planning," working paper, Darden Graduate School of Business Administration, Charlottesville, VA.

profitable places to do business. Intelligent refers to the ability to analyze and interpret the various parts and pieces of an industry or business segment. Here is where the analytic techniques we described earlier in the chapter come in. These tools provide a way to develop an intelligent view of where the opportunities might lie. This analysis presents an opportunity for strategic thinkers/leaders to make a decision about what they want to do. This choice forms the core of their intent. Unless this intent is clear, the strategy will vacillate and wander.

The implementation of an intent is based on some hypothesis about cause-and-effect relationships in the industry or business. Recognition of the hypothetical nature of this element is the difference between stubbornness and persistence. As individuals implement their intent, if things don't work out, those with a hypothesis-driven perspective will be willing to try something else. Sometimes it means a change in method, other times a change in intent.

Strategic thinkers understand the importance of timing. They understand that the right product or strategy at the wrong time will fail, as will being too soon or too late, or rushing or delaying unduly. Good strategic thinkers develop a sense of when to act and when to wait.

Finally, strategic thinkers need to make some serious choices about innovation and ethics. With regard to innovation, Gary Hamel above noted that there are two main kinds of strategists, "juice squeezers" and "innovators." Juice squeezers and innovators think differently about how to manage a business. It's interesting to observe that in the history of General Electric, Jack Welch's administration seemed to focus primarily on driving up efficiencies (juice squeezing) whereas his successor, Jeff Immelt, seems to focus more on innovation. Can the two strategies be melded? Perhaps, but they have inherently competing values: drives to be more efficient leads one to avoid "unnecessary" cost and waste, whereas innovation is an inherently inefficient and unpredictable process that often leads to costly experimentation.

At the same time, leaders make de-facto or explicitly strategic choices about their ethics. Will they be "compliant" with the letter of the law but always looking for ways to circumvent it? Will they follow the popular sports dictum, "If you're not cheating, you're not trying"? Will they strive to stay well within the law or even to lead law making in a way that serves multiple stakeholders? Or will they do everything they can to make as much money as they can regardless of the impact on others? These major questions are the subjects of subsequent chapters.

Conclusions

Effective leaders are strategic thinkers; they recognize a deep value in thinking ahead. They develop the skills of clarifying their purpose, of having a vision of what they could become if that purpose were realized, and of exploring ways and means of reaching that vision. They understand the importance of investing in and developing the core capabilities necessary to execute and implement their strategic intent. Increasingly, they understand the importance of managing their strategic intentions with enough flexibility that allows them not only to coexist with competitors in a global market, but to thrive in a symbiotic way with them.

Strategic thinking is part art and part discipline. You can develop your strategic thinking skills. This development, however, will require effort, study, hard thinking, many conversations, and a wide range of reading and reflection. It will require practice in articulating what may be only fuzzy thoughts occasionally illuminated by brief flashes of insight. It will require learning to capture those thoughts and flashes in your conscious verbal mind and on paper. It will require revolutionary reflection and energy, and if you are to implement and realize your strategic dreams, it will require you to develop consummate skills in leadership and managing change.

Principles Introduced in This Chapter

1. A strategic issue is any issue that affects the ability to develop and maintain a competitive advantage.
2. A competitive advantage has three parts: superior value added, difficulty in imitation, and enhanced flexibility.
3. Strategic thinking applies to at least three levels: organizational, work group, and individual.
4. Strategically, individuals can think of their fit in the environment (fit model) or of creating an environment in which they can fit (strategic intent).
5. Each link in the value chain for a product or service has its own strategic value or lack of it.
6. Competitive advantage is built upon core capabilities that take time to develop.
7. Most businesses have lots of room for growth.
8. Effective strategic thinking is usually revolutionary.
9. In the successive waves of economic development in human history, the margins always shrink. This propensity has been true through the Agricultural Age and the Industrial Age and is recurring again in the Information Age. Today, large margins are available in experiences. Tomorrow, they may be in transformations.
10. Strategists often fall prey to the logical traps of the Innovator's Dilemma. It's a huge challenge to strive to gain larger margins through upgrading your products and services and at the same time remain nimble enough to compete at the bottom of the customer spectrum.
11. To move from average to exceptional, strategists should consider Collins's six elements: Level Five leadership; first who, then what; confronting the brutal facts; establishing a hedgehog concept; being disciplined about decision making; and using appropriate technology accelerators.
12. Strategic scenario building can help position an individual or an organization effectively for the future.
13. Effective leaders are good strategic thinkers.
14. Strategic thinking involves an ability to analyze competitive advantages and to devise means of developing and maintaining them.
15. Strategic thinkers are familiar with several perspectives including SWOT analysis, five forces analysis, building strategic intent based on core capabilities, long-term scenario building, businesses as ecosystems, and strategy as revolution.
16. Strategic thinkers make, intentionally or not, decisions about how much to innovate vs. drive up efficiencies and how much to stretch the legal and ethical boundaries of sustainable business.

Questions for Personal Reflection

1. How much time do you spend thinking strategically about your own position, your work group's position, and your company's position?
2. If you avoid strategic thinking because (a) your job doesn't demand it or (b) you don't have time for it, what impact will this avoidance have on your career over the next 10 to 20 years?
3. How does your organization treat its revolutionaries?
4. How, if at all, revolutionary are you in your thinking?
5. What kind of experience do you give your customers? Is that experience a commodity or something unique and competitively advantageous?
6. Could you compete at the bottom of your customer range today if you had to, or have your cost VABEs become too expensive?
7. What's your hedgehog concept?
8. How much does fame factor into your desire to lead?
9. How disciplined are you in your decision-making processes?
10. What could you do to develop your strategic thinking skills?
11. How can you allocate regular time to strategic thinking?
12. What do you need to read in order to develop a different perspective on your industry, company, and work group?
13. What are the key competitive forces at play in your industry? Where are they headed?
14. What scenarios can you imagine that are plausible and yet potentially disrupting to your firm or work group? How could you prepare for those alternatives?

CASELET FOR DISCUSSION

Assume you own a small (US$15,000,000) manufacturing company that makes equipment for the automobile industry. At present, your company only makes metal components. What are the strategic challenges you face? What decisions will you have to make? Where will your profits come from? How will you ensure that stream of profits?

CONTRIBUTING YOUR OWN CASELETS

Have you seen or experienced a situation involving the concepts introduced in this chapter? If so and if you'd like to contribute your experience/situation to our case data bank, please visit http://faculty.darden.virginia.edu/clawsonj/ and click on the "Contribute new caselets" button.

6 ETHICAL DIMENSIONS OF LEADERSHIP

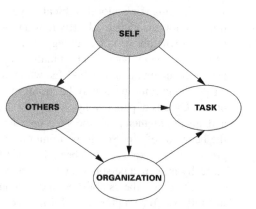

What you do thunders so loudly in my ears,
I cannot hear what you say.

—RALPH WALDO EMERSON

All leadership involves a moral dimension in why and how people exert influence over others—and the stance that one takes in this regard is a strategic choice. The moral issue is also a Level Three consideration: that is, how one influences others depends on the values, assumptions, beliefs, and expectations (VABEs) of the people involved. Because leadership is about influencing others, to study leadership is to beg the moral and strategic questions of whether it is right to influence others and what means one should employ. Some people strongly feel that they have no right or desire to influence others and prefer that others be left alone to determine the path of their lives without external pressures. Others strongly feel that they have not only the right but the God-given responsibility to change the way others think and believe. In an increasingly electronically, economically, and environmentally connected, crowded, and potentially hostile world, the freedom to determine one's own life path is becoming increasingly difficult. Decisions made by strangers minutes, miles, or continents away affect our daily lives in many ways. Yet, within our sphere of contacts and acquaintances, this dilemma of whether we will choose to influence others to change the way they behave, think, and believe remains.

SIX DIMENSIONS OF LEADERSHIP MORALITY

In my discussions with upper-level executives in countries all over the world, it is clear that global managers see at least six issues related to leadership, decision making, and morality: strategic, financial, moral, ethical, legal, and cultural. *Strategic* refers to the efforts of an organization's leaders to identify how and where they want to function or do business. *Financial* refers to whether or not a strategy, a tactic, a behavior, or a choice is likely to be profitable. *Morality* is the individual determination of what's right and wrong. An act may be immoral to a person based on his or her VABEs, while not viewed as unethical or illegal by other authorities. At the same time, what may be moral to one person may be immoral, unethical, or illegal to others. Groups of people may or may not share views of what's moral, or what's right and wrong, and attach judgments of others to those determinations. Typically, if members of a group judge the behavior of a person to be immoral or wrong, they will ostracize that individual from the group. In fact, exclusion has been the main means of punishment in human history. Exclusion is basically moving a person away from the center of the society or group.

Ethics are the established and accepted guidelines of behavior for established groups or institutions. To be a physician, for instance, you must accept the code of ethics set down by the licensing board of the medical profession. If you violate that code, you may lose your membership in that professional group. Ethical behavior varies from professional group to professional group. Ethical considerations have to do with right and wrong, as does morality, but in the context of a professional group's explicit and written standards. Where the criteria for membership in a particular professional group are fuzzy (as in business management, which is not under a comprehensive governing body as is medicine or law), the definition of ethical behavior becomes more problematic. Nevertheless, as with morality, violation of the ethics established by a group usually results in expulsion from that group. A violation of the bar association's ethical standards, for example, can result in a person being disbarred.

Legality obviously concerns obeying the established laws of a society. Technically speaking, violations of the laws are illegal, but they may or may not be viewed by members of that society as immoral or unethical. For instance, many people violate the posted speed limits on major highways almost with impunity, obviously not believing that doing so is wrong, immoral, or professionally unethical.

Finally, every leadership action takes place in a *cultural context*. Leadership tactics and approaches taken in one culture may be prohibited or offensive in another. What seems unethical and/or illegal in one culture may be generally acceptable in another. Effective leaders will be sensitive to these nuances and realize how their style may or may not work well as they move from culture to culture. Cultures are communities of shared VABEs, so, again, it's hard to imagine a situation in which Level Three considerations do not come into account. Further, each of these four dimensions interacts with each other: the legal boundaries do not necessarily match the moral boundaries or the ethical boundaries—and they certainly migrate from culture to culture. Effective global leaders will understand how these elements interact and affect their ability to lead (Figure 6-1).

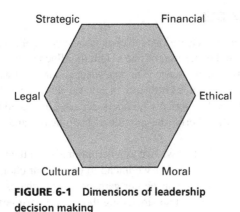

FIGURE 6-1   **Dimensions of leadership decision making**

Given these definitions, we can explore the overlaps and the differences between the dimensions. We can go further, however, and use a stakeholder perspective[1] to analyze the "ethical" nature of any situation, including those involving leadership. In the stakeholder perspective, we speak of the harms and benefits to others as we strive to clarify the moral dimension of a leadership situation. Ed Freeman identified the key stakeholders in an ethical perspective on the corporation as management, employees, customers, owners, suppliers, and the surrounding community. If we can first identify all who would be influenced by an act—the stakeholders—we could then begin to assess the consequences in terms of whether the act is harming or benefiting them. Does the act attempt to influence another harm or benefit? If the act harms another, we have a case that the act may be unethical in a broader moral sense (not the narrower professional group sense). Table 6-1 shows a rudimentary way to set up this kind of analysis with regard to any individual leadership action under consideration (layoffs, mergers, changes in reward system, etc.). No final list defines all the relevant stakeholders; they will vary from situation to situation.

TABLE 6-1   Basic Stakeholder Analysis

For any given or proposed strategy or policy . . .

Stakeholder	Benefits	Harms
Management		
Employees		
Shareholders		
Customers		
Community		
Environment		
Unions		
Others		

---

[1] See Ed Freeman, *Strategic Management: A Stakeholder Approach* (Marshfield, MA: Pitman, 1984).

MORALITY AND LEADERSHIP

Given that every leadership act affects various stakeholders, every act of leadership raises many moral questions. We can begin with the question of one's right to influence another. Is there such a right? Clearly, parents presume a right to influence their dependent children. At what point does this "right" begin to dissipate?[2] When does another's influence in any way abridge what Thomas Jefferson called "unalienable rights" that he and America's founders declared allocated to all humankind? Does everyone have a right to "life, liberty, the pursuit of happiness," and freedom from unwanted influence?

We live in a social world. Unless we live as a hermit (and even then), we are unable to escape the influence of others' decisions. Whether we intend to or not, our choices influence others. The routes we take in traffic, the way we manage our garbage, the purchases we make, at one level or another, all have influence. Some, perhaps including those who have been abused in one way or another, resent the notion of leadership, of one person intending to influence and guide another's behavior. Nevertheless, anyone who chooses to lead is choosing to influence others and should be aware of the moral responsibilities of that role. If the impact of a leader is negative, the leader must bear at least part of the responsibility for the outcomes. This explains why, as argued earlier, some people who have the talent may shrink from leadership situations.

Embedded in our earlier three-part definition of leadership are several moral issues. First, individuals *choose* whether they wish to influence others. Many are not willing to do so and yet are thrust into positions of leadership. These people often wrestle with the emotional and moral burden of their roles, yet because of the desire to be "successful," they may continue in the position. Others choose to be in leadership positions but are seemingly unaware and uncaring about the *consequences* of their leadership decisions. Leaders need to be aware of the impact of their leadership and work at assessing whether it is a "harm" or a "benefit" and to whom.

Second, not all individuals have the same *ability* to influence, should they choose to try. Leadership ability varies, and one may or may not choose to develop that ability. This type of development usually includes finding a vision, a goal toward which the community should, in the eyes of the leader, work. The leader exercises his or her skills to the end of that goal and engages the efforts of others in this cause. Some with strong leadership abilities, like Hitler and Stalin, may choose goals that we would say are immoral or wrong. Others, like Gandhi or King, may choose more worthy goals. The use of an individual's skills as a leader invites them to consider the value of their objectives.

Third, leadership involves, I say, *choice*, not coercion, so that followers follow *willingly*. Leaders have, on various levels, a moral obligation to use influence, not force. Further, when people use force, they are no longer practicing leadership. They may be using power, but they are not leading. Some viewpoints clearly disagree with this perspective.[3]

However you approach it, leadership involves a very strong moral dimension with many moral questions embedded in it. Level Three Leadership purports to influence not only what people do and think, but also what they believe and feel. In some sense, this intention is an invasion of privacy, an exploration into the basic assumptions and values of another. Whether we do it and how we go about it are also moral issues. This recognition requires a few additional definitions.

---

[2] See William Glasser, *Choice Theory* (New York: Harper Perennial, 1999), for a discussion of how parents naturally begin their children's lives under the influence of control theory.

[3] For example, Edwin C. Nevis, Joan Lancourt, and Helen G. Vassallo, *Intentional Revolutions* (San Francisco, CA: Jossey-Bass, 1996).

Some view values-based leadership as a kind of manipulation. **Manipulation** comes in two forms: deceptive manipulation and coercive manipulation. *Deceptive manipulation* is maneuvering events in ways that get people to do certain things when they are not *aware* of the forces influencing them. *Coercive manipulation* is maneuvering events so that people are forced to choose what we want them to do when they would have chosen freely otherwise. The film *Sophie's Choice* (in which a woman is forced by her Nazi tormentor to choose one of her two children to live or else they both die) illustrates this latter kind of manipulation.

> Manipulation is getting people do what you want them to do without them agreeing to or knowing what you're doing.

Both kinds of manipulation are immoral or wrong in the sense that they violate our definition of leadership, in which the followers respond voluntarily. Only when people have full information and freedom to choose can they be enabled or labeled as followers. Further, manipulations involve violations of several moral principles and undermine our ability to lead. When people discover at some point, as they always do, that they have been manipulated, "had," or treated unfairly, their motivation and interest in following the so-called leader drops precipitously. Manipulation is not leadership. Manipulation is counterfeit leadership that some people use believing that they are getting what they want out of a situation by leading, but the net result is distrust, lack of respect, and weak relationships that will not produce quality over the long run. Manipulation is a short-term fix, used by people who don't have the ability to lead to cover up their own inadequacies.

THE MORAL FOUNDATION OF LEVEL THREE LEADERSHIP

If Level Three Leadership involves moral issues, we need to find a moral foundation for exercising this kind of leadership. Rich Teerlink, former CEO of Harley–Davidson, asserted four cornerstones to what we can call the moral foundation of leadership. Without these four cornerstones in place, leadership is not likely to be effective or long lasting. The foundation of leadership includes truth-telling, promise-keeping, fairness, and respect for the individual[4] (Figure 6-2). We could actually distill these four ideas down to the last principle, respect for the individual, because if one had respect for another individual, one would not lie, break promises to them, or treat them unfairly. In a sense, then, these four principles are different windows onto the same core moral concept of "integrity in relationships." It is useful, however, to look at respect for the individual in greater detail by breaking out the other three dimensions. In the end, though, one's answer to the question, are you showing respect for the individual? is a good indicator of the other three.

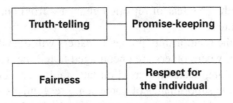

FIGURE 6-2 The four cornerstones of the foundation of ethical leadership

---

[4] This concept was first introduced to me by my colleague Alex Horniman, who developed it while as head of the Olsson Center for Business Ethics at the Darden School. The ideas are also apparently used by Rich Teerlink, CEO of Harley–Davidson, as noted in Tom Peters, *The Tom Peters Seminar* (New York: Vintage Books, 1994), 81.

The truth, as you see it
and communicate it to
others, is a great crucible
that burns out would-be
leaders and hardens
effective and true leaders.

Truth-telling in leadership means telling the other the truth as you see it when the truth you see will have an impact on the other. Although it may seem trite to say that truth-telling is a moral foundation for effective leadership, not all managers or would-be leaders believe it. In one seminar when senior managers of a major firm were gathered together to discuss leadership and influence, they were considering the question, should one tell the truth in business? As the discussion progressed, the group became violently divided on this question—so much so that at one point individuals were literally standing on chairs and pounding the table and pointing and shouting at their "colleagues" across the room. Those who argued in favor of truth-telling, whether it be to employees, customers, suppliers, the press, the parent company, or whatever stakeholder, said that business is based on trust and that if the ability to trust another (either to behave consistently or to behave with our best interests at heart) erodes, the ability to do business disappears. People may do one deal, but they won't do two. Those who argued against truth-telling said that if you told people the truth (how much you're making on a deal, the quality of the product, etc.), you wouldn't be able to do any business, in part because deals are based on margins: margins are a product of people's perceptions ("value-based pricing"), and truth-telling destroys perceptions.

Truth-telling is essential to effective leadership. If you are unwilling to tell people the truth, you will not be able to lead them, if for no other reason than they will be unable to respond to your ultimate goals willingly. The truth, as you see it and communicate it to others, is a great crucible. It refines relationships by cleaning out hidden goals, ulterior motives, suppressed resentments, manufactured conclusions, and uncertainties about the values of the other. Telling the truth as you see it is an essential part of the mutual, fair exchange that must occur for business to function and for leadership to emerge.

People feel that they need to withhold the truth for a variety of reasons. Sometimes people feel pressured to withhold or distort the truth of bad news—bad news from an objective viewpoint, from a personal viewpoint, or from an imagined viewpoint of the other—in part, because we sometimes give data more evaluative power than exists inherently in them. In another view, though, data are simply data. Some data may be disconfirming to our present style of behavior; some may be confirming, but in the end, whether we accept or reject the data is entirely up to us.[5] People are constantly accepting, rejecting, discounting, distorting, or ignoring the information that they receive based on their core VABEs.

When we expect that others will attribute to our data a negative, evaluative overtone, or when we fear that the receiver will punish us for telling the truth as we see it, we are under influence to not tell the truth. This fear of rejection emanates from our core VABEs developed over the course of our lifetimes.

On the other side of the relationship, potential leaders will note that if they cannot create an atmosphere around them where others are encouraged to tell the truth and find it safe to do so, the business will be making decisions based on late, faulty, or incomplete information far too often. Interviews with the subordinates of some senior executives indicated that they were fearful of raising new ideas and bringing forward new suggestions because of the typically negative and aggressive responses they receive. The senior executives, on the other hand, argued that their subordinates needed to be more "tough and thick skinned" and aggressive in bringing

---

[5] Daniel Goleman explores this leadership talent in *Emotional Intelligence* (New York: Bantam, 1995). Albert Ellis and Robert Harper also describe it in *A Guide to Rational Living* (North Hollywood, CA: Wilshire Book Company, 1975).

their ideas forward. They could not see that their brusque, aggressive style was stifling new ideas and the generation of new leadership. Their underlying VABEs explicitly stated were that "strong leaders with strong ideas will fight back and make them happen regardless of push back." Effective, moral leaders will realize that their own demeanor clearly affects the organization's response—even to ideas and proposals that they say they want but signal in other ways that they don't want.

In a nonevaluative view, feedback from others is simply information, neither moral nor immoral, neither right nor wrong, until we respond to it, accepting it or rejecting it or beginning to do something about it. People tell a joke about three baseball umpires having a drink together. One says, referring to their job of calling "strikes" and "balls" in a ball game, "I call them as I see them." The second umpire argued, "No, I call them as they *are!*" The third umpire wisely said, "They aren't anything until I call them!" Our responses to others are the same. What other people do is neither good nor bad until, using our core VABEs, we judge them to be so.

The challenge for the person listening to another person's truth-telling is to remain both nonjudgmental and nondefensive, with ears and hearts open, listening carefully to what is being communicated. Too often people in leadership positions begin to get defensive immediately and miss the main message or its meaning. The underlying VABE, stated or not, is "it's your job to listen to me, not mine to listen to you." If you can also view the information you give to others in this light, you can learn to tell your truth more effectively.

Promise-keeping is another cornerstone of effective moral leadership. Promises today often seem made to be broken. Management leaks information from confidential meetings to the press, executives in offices of public trust are indicted for insider trading and other forms of fraud, and commitments to employees are routinely changed or broken outright. Worse, executives seem willing to make whatever promises are necessary to "keep the lid on" a management situation and all too ready to abandon those promises a few short months later. Broken promises are destructive to trust, respect, and ultimately to leadership. They are also characteristic of addictive behavior in which people promise without intention of following through in order to get what they want in the short run.

To the extent that willing followership is a function of trust, the promise-keeping that encourages trust is an essential skill and a part of the moral foundation of effective leadership. People who make promises or commitments and then break them are like the boy who cried "wolf" too many times; before long the community won't believe them anymore. Potential leaders need to be careful of making commitments—and then careful of keeping the ones they make. Broken promises undermine potential leader–follower relationships quickly.

Fairness is also a part of the moral foundation of effective leadership. Fairness ensures that followers will get their share of the rewards of the enterprise. When employees begin to perceive that they are not being treated fairly, their motivation to follow declines drastically. Much has been made recently about the gaps between first-line employees' and CEOs' salaries in manufacturing firms. Various estimates have shown that the multiples in the United States far exceed by a factor of 2 those in the rest of the industrialized world. For example, in Japan, CEO salaries average about 9 to 10 times that of production employees. In Europe, the figure ranges from 10 to 20 times, whereas in the United States, the figure is closer to 45 times.[6]

---

[6] Towers Perrin, Worldwide Total Remuneration Study, 2003–2004.

You may think that this differential is "fair" in that the senior managers are more experienced, are better trained, add more value to the firm, are brighter, and are for numerous other reasons. Whether these characteristics are true, though, if the workers perceive an imbalance between their compensation and that of their managers up the organization, distrust will set in and productivity and performance will suffer. Why should a person follow another whom the person believes is not only likely but proven to withhold fair compensation for value added and who is likely, therefore, to be exploiting the organization and its members for personal gain?

Fairness was less of an issue in traditional organizations than it will be in the new organizations because information about the health of the firm will be much more broadly distributed. If the employees don't know the financial picture of the firm, they might be "managed" or "manipulated" to accept lower wages and still work hard. In the new organizations, though, with large and readily available information networks, employees will have better information about the health of the firm and its industry, so it will be increasingly difficult to manipulate what stakeholders know about a firm and its distribution of resources.

Respect for the Individual

The first three moral cornerstones of effective leadership can be distilled into the last, *respect* for the individual. One who respects another will tell that person the truth. One who respects another will keep promises made to that person. One who respects another will treat that person fairly. Respect for the individual means viewing and treating others as human beings with dignity, who have added and are adding value to the mission of the enterprise. Respect for the individual means believing that all individuals have some intrinsic worth and should be treated accordingly with courtesy and kindness. In a common Buddhist greeting in Southeastern Asia, the greeter brings palms together in front, slightly bows, and says, *"Namaste,"* which means "I respect the part of god that is within you." Every person has something divine within; Level Three Leadership invites a recognition of that assertion.

The preceding argument does not mean that all individuals should have equal influence on self or others, only that all should be treated with a basic human courtesy. The assumption is that because they live, they deserve to be treated with dignity. Paradoxically, treating people with respect accrues respect to the leader and enhances the leader's circle of influence, because all who observe this quality in the leader will respect the leader more. Yet many "leaders," people in positions of influence, begin to lose sight of and respect for people in the lower ranks of the organization. They begin to judge the relative contributions of employees to the firm's outcomes according to their rank and to treat people based on that judgment. Those they judge to be in the lower end of the distribution of contributors they treat with some disdain and perhaps even outright disrespect. This ethical choice can have disastrous results.

THE NORMAL DISTRIBUTION OF EMPLOYEES' VALUE ADDED

It is clear that any given group of people will be distributed from high performers to moderate performers to weaker performers compared with the other members of that group. This comparative distribution is true of any organization. Regardless of the organization, members will vary in their contributions to the organization's mission. This distribution of performance will likely approximate a normal distribution, as shown in Figure 6-3, with a small group of extraordinary

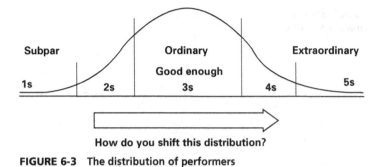

How do you shift this distribution?

FIGURE 6-3   The distribution of performers

performers (5s), a large group of good-enough performers (4s, 3s, and 2s), and a small group of subpar performers (1s). One of the challenges for the effective leader is to shift the distribution to the right—to move the good-enough group toward the extraordinary tail. How can one encourage good-enough workers to work extraordinarily? In other words, how can one shift the performance distribution to the right? Recognizing and using the moral foundation of leadership are essential to this movement. Unless you are able to engage good-enough people and get them to perform as 4s and 5s, your organization will continue to perform at the good-enough, but not great, level. Without a moral foundation in your leadership attempts, you will not be able to get more people to perform at the 4s and 5s levels.

Let's test that assertion. Ask yourself: If I tell my people or if we tell each other the truth half of the time, can we become an extraordinary team? If we keep our promises to each other half of the time, can we become world-class performers? If we treat each other fairly half of the time, can we become the competitor to beat in our business? If we show respect for each other half of the time, can we be world-class leaders? My guess is that you answered "no" to each of these questions. In that case, you agree that the moral rock or foundation is essential to effective leadership. Then the question is, What kind of scores on these dimensions would you have to get to establish a moral foundation for leadership? If you polled your colleagues, what would the average score be? (A short one-page survey on these questions is included in Workbook on page 395 to be used with your team if you wish.) You would need Olympic gold-medal numbers (9.9, 9.8, 9.9, 9.7, etc.) to have a foundation for seeking higher levels of engagement and performance.

If you establish a moral foundation, it does not guarantee that you will be able to shift the performance curve to the right; doing so only enables that shift. We can think of leadership as having two main foci: first, the moral foundation. If the four cornerstones are not in place, one will not have the basis for a shift to the right. Without that foundation, you can practice traditional leadership skills (i.e., strategic thinking, effective speaking, and good organizational design work) until you're blue in the face and still have no chance of moving the group's performance to the right. On the other hand, if you establish the moral foundation and then exercise the traditional leadership skills, you have a good chance of getting performance to improve. In this view, the moral foundation is a necessary precondition for an improvement in performance, and traditional leadership skills are the superstructure that can encourage better performance; the more leadership skills you pile on top of the moral foundation, the more efficiently you can get the performance distribution to shift.

Over time, the rational approach for any management team would be to strive to get more energy, and hence performance, out of its employees (Figure 6-4). The challenge—referred to as

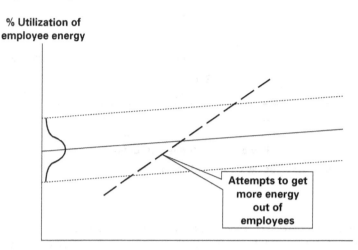

**% Utilization of
employee energy**

**Attempts to get
more energy
out of
employees**

FIGURE 6-4 The motivator's dilemma

"the Motivator's Dilemma"—is to find and use that energy.[7] As we described earlier, some use cheerleading approaches; others rely on goal setting. Some focus more on recruiting and selection, believing that high performance is either innate or not.

Some think that the 2s and 3s in an organization are not motivated, that they lack in ambition and energy. As soon as you begin believing and operating on this principle, you begin to lose respect for the individual and your communications and actions will belie your beliefs. It may be that these people simply are not motivated by what's happening at work or the way in which that work is presented and organized. What if you were to follow these people home? You might find that many of them perform in nonwork activities with extraordinary quality, performing well in activities that engage them deeply. It may be as a rescue-squad volunteer, softball player, bowler, church administrator, or Little League coach. The challenge to the effective leader is to find ways to engage the extraordinary capabilities of the employees and channel that energy in part toward the goals of the enterprise.

One of the most direct ways of motivating and directing employees, and therefore to develop Level Three Leadership skills, is to build one's leadership attempts on the moral rock described earlier, consistently telling the truth, keeping promises, and treating people fairly and with respect. Figure 6-5 illustrates this relationship, with the four dimensions of the moral rock displayed below the normal curve of performance. The more leaders believe and behave the moral rock dimensions, the more powerful their relationships with their employees and the more extraordinary the performance of those employees will be. You can see in Figure 6-5 that each of the four cornerstones has been put on a 10-point scale. You might do a little self-assessment of

---

[7] Clayton Christensen and Michael Raynor, *The Innovator's Solution* (Boston, MA: Harvard Business School Press, 2003), provided the inspiration for this thought and how the application of the basic principle of Christensen's "innovator's dilemma" might apply to the motivation of employees in a business. One of Christensen's insights was the value of assessing the percentage of utilization of features by customers that is adapted here to focus on the percentage of energy of employees engaged by management. More thoughts on this topic later and also in James Clawson, "The Motivator's Dilemma," in *The Future of HR: 50 Thought Leaders Call for Change*. Edited by Michael Losey, Sue Meisinger, and David Ulrich (New York: Wiley, 2005).

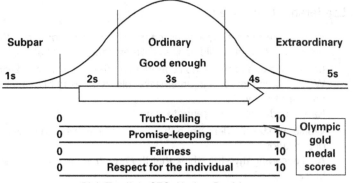

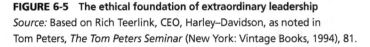

Rich Teerlink, CEO, Harley–Davidson

FIGURE 6-5   The ethical foundation of extraordinary leadership
Source: Based on Rich Teerlink, CEO, Harley–Davidson, as noted in
Tom Peters, *The Tom Peters Seminar* (New York: Vintage Books, 1994), 81.

your work group and rate your team on each of these four dimensions. A score of 10 means that you practice that dimension 100 percent of the time; a score of 5 would mean that you practice that dimension 50 percent of the time; and so on. (See the Assessing the Moral Foundation of Your Leadership exercise on page 395 in Workbook.)

UNIVERSALITY OF THE MORAL FOUNDATION OF LEVEL THREE LEADERSHIP

Is the moral foundation described here possible for all? Does respect for the individual mean that we must like all of our employees or strive to have them all like us? Is this general approach a reasonable one? Does it apply to other cultures and nationalities? What do you think?

The direct answer is "Yes." Moral leadership is possible for all, and it does not require that you like each individual on your team. It does require that you recognize the potential of every individual and find it a worthy challenge to bring that potential to the fore. Sterling Livingston's classic article "Pygmalion in Management" cites the My Fair Lady story as a powerful example.[8] Professor Higgins was able to bring out of Eliza something others could not see and did not work to bring forth. The challenge of effective leadership is to bring out the best in others.

Public society at the beginning of the twenty-first century is clamoring for moral, legal, and ethical leadership. Scandals in numerous large corporations affected employees and customers worldwide and undermined the public trust, again, in corporate leadership. Effective leaders, especially in these turbulent times, will recognize that in the end, the truth always comes out and that no long-term benefit accrues to any of the key stakeholders of the corporation, including themselves, in violating the principles of the four cornerstones of ethical leadership. Table 6-2 suggests some simple litmus tests that would-be leaders could consider as they reflect on what to do and what to say.

---

[8] Sterling Livingston, "Pygmalion in Management," *Harvard Business Review*, September 1, 2002, 1768.

TABLE 6-2 Ethical Leadership Litmus Test	
Truth-telling	Would I like to have my actions reported tomorrow morning in the national newspaper? What would happen if others found out what the truth is?
Promise-keeping	Before I make a promise, do I consider whether I can, in fact, keep it? Would my employees and other stakeholders argue publicly that I kept my promises to them? Have I made promises I cannot keep?
Fairness	Would my stakeholders argue that they are being treated fairly in this organization? Am I deceiving myself to think that those who argue otherwise are just unreasonable?
Respect for the individual	Do I know the names of the people I meet daily? Do I look the people I meet daily in the eye and am I "with" them for that brief moment? Do I listen to what others say, or do I interrupt and interject my own thoughts? Am I convinced my VABEs are more important than others'?

Let's acknowledge that many choose not to treat others with respect. Numerous individuals in the business world do not show respect for others and at the same time claim to be leaders of "integrity." Level Three Leadership is leadership that recognizes and deals with people's core VABEs. If a would-be leader's VABEs do not include the principles of the moral foundation, the odds are that he or she will have to resort to manipulation, deceit, and coercion to get things done, which moves us out of the realm of ethical influence. Adherence to the principles of the moral foundation is a good definition of integrity. People often claim integrity and vigorously defend their own possession of it, yet never stop to examine what it is and how it plays out in dealings with suppliers, employees, and customers. Integrity means to be whole, to be unified. How can one not tell the truth and have integrity? How can one not tell the truth and have employees respond willingly to their attempts to influence? How can one break promises and claim integrity? How can one treat people unfairly and say that they are leading with integrity?

This line of reasoning doesn't necessarily mean that all will like the leader or that the leader will like all the employees. This framework provides plenty of room for disagreements and, at the same time, for mutual respect for each other and the basic beliefs upon which their relationship is built. Even though disagreements occur, with the moral foundation in place, those disagreements are clear, on the table, and well understood. Out of respect, people spend time striving to understand all of the aspects of the disagreements among all stakeholders so that the issues are clear to all. Obviously, if the topic of disagreement is major, it may lead to a parting of ways, but the parting will be based on mutual understanding rather than manipulation, deceit, jealousies, or contempt.

Commitment to the principles of a moral foundation is evident in an effective leader's behavior. This commitment emanates from a person's center so that in speeches, conversations, meetings, plans, and programs the four principles are evident. It is rather easy, if you can get their attention, to have senior groups pause and assess themselves on these four dimensions. When they do, the insight of the group jumps another level. In one senior management meeting, it was evident that the people in the room were not using the moral principles and that their company was suffering from ordinary performance. At a first meeting with the group, a consultant interrupted and introduced the moral dimensions and then asked the group to rate privately its past and present behavior on each of the four dimensions on a scale of 1 to 10 as described earlier. A few minutes later, the reported average score of the senior executives in the room was between 3 and 5 for each of the four dimensions. A lively discussion then ensued as to whether the group would be able to manage itself, much less the company, unless dramatic changes were made in the ways that they dealt with each other. This senior group began working immediately on improving their abilities to use the moral foundation dimensions. They discovered that making that kind of Level Three change was not easy, yet each agreed that it was necessary if they hoped to move the company from ordinary to extraordinary performance.

This point is portrayed powerfully by survey results reported in *Industry Week* magazine. Two independent national polling firms conducted two independent surveys of American middle managers over a 10-year span, 1973 to 1983. In these controlled samples of middle managers from many industries across America, two basic questions were asked: Do you trust senior management? Do you respect senior management? In the 1973 results, the yes answers averaged about two-thirds. By 1983, the yes answers had fallen to about one-third. One wonders how one can manage, much less lead, a business if two-thirds of middle managers don't trust or respect senior management.[9] A 2004 survey in the United Kingdom reported that nearly 80 percent of employees of U.K. firms don't trust their senior management.[10] After all these years, the fundamental issue remains: At what level of trust and respect can a leadership team expect to get world-class performance from their employees?

Another indicator of the universal applicability and impact of morally founded leadership comes from my own research, in which we surveyed and interviewed more than 100 matched pairs of superiors and subordinates in a large insurance company. Both individuals in the relationships rated how much the subordinate learned in the relationship, a measure of the superior's influence on the subordinate at Levels Two and Three. In addition, measures of more than 50 characteristics of the individuals and their relationship were included in the survey. The results indicated that the combined levels of trust and respect accounted for about 75 percent of the variance in the amount of learning in the relationship.[11] Both of these studies suggest that trust and respect are key factors in successful management and leadership relationships.

The inherent ethical nature of leadership raises questions about how leadership develops and appears in different national cultures. Do leaders in the various regions of the world have similar values and ethics in their leadership choices? Do truth-telling, promise-keeping, fairness, and respect for the individual "count" in Japan, Australia, India, China, Africa, Europe, and Latin America? At the surface, leadership behavior seems to vary widely in these regions. Americans are viewed as being too aggressive or too personal too quickly, whereas to Americans, Japanese leaders seem inscrutable and too slow to decision. To what degree are principles of leadership universal? Certain things are universally human and some are unique to certain groups. Consider Table 6-3, which contains a list of levels ranging from the universal to the unique.

---

[9] Bruce Jacobs and William Miller, "The Verdict on Corporate Management," *Industry Week*, July 25, 1983, 58.

[10] Reported by *HR & Management Research* at www.managementissues.com/display_page.asp?section=research&id=1154 (accessed February 4, 2005).

[11] James G. Clawson, "The Role of Interpersonal Respect and Trust in Developmental Relationships," *International Journal of Mentoring*, Spring 1990.

TABLE 6-3 Examples of Cultural Commonalities

Levels of Universality	Examples
Human (universal)	Laughter, humor, love, fear, desire to improve one's situation
Global Region (Asia, Africa, Latin America)	Weddings, language, religions
Nation (China, Venezuela, etc.)	Laws, regulations, social customs
National Region (Southern United States)	Dialects, social customs, use of time and space
Organizations and neighborhoods (South Boston, West Bank, IBM, British Aerospace)	Recreation, biases, work habits, focus of attention, use of time and space
Family	Values, work, manners, etc.
Individual	VABEs related to all of these examples

In any leader's background, all of these levels of influence will have a shaping effect. How much of this ethical foundation is in the "universally human" layer as opposed to the national or neighborhood level? Do Chinese care about truth-telling in distinctively Chinese ways? Do Ugandans care about promise-keeping in uniquely Ugandan ways? Do Argentineans believe in fairness in Argentinean ways? Do Germans have respect for the individual in uniquely German ways? Surely the global regional influences, the national influences, and the subnational influences shape people's VABEs. In the end, though, if a leader lies to Russian employees, will they tolerate this behavior? If a Brazilian leader breaks promises to employees, will their levels of trust go up or down? If an Indian manager takes more than a fair share of the rewards, will the employees' energy go up or down? Despite the assertion that the four principles of moral leadership are universal and that violating them will erode the strength of a leader's influence, it's best that you explore these questions for yourself. Japanese leaders may tend to be more "quiet" early in discussions in order to learn the general opinion of the group; but make no mistake, Japanese leaders can be top-down, hierarchically oriented, just like North American leaders. A lack of transparency worldwide also seems to lead to lower levels of trust and respect.

Legal Constraints

Because not all authoritors behave ethically or morally and because of the rash of such unethical behavior in the early part of the twenty-first century, the U.S. Congress has passed some laws designed to "legislate the ethics" of business leaders. One of the most important of these was the Sarbanes–Oxley Act of 2002, commonly referred to as SOX or Sarbox. This act established a new agency, the Public Company Accounting Oversight Board (PCAOB), which must oversee the actions of executives of publicly held firms on behalf of the government and the shareholders. One of the major effects of this act was to make chief executives of publicly held firms legally and criminally accountable for overseeing and reporting on the quality of their internal accounting and reporting procedures. That CEOs and CFOs now had to "certify" the verity of their public reports, over and above what their accounting firms declared, made the top jobs much more risky and open to prosecution. Companies were also required to have fully independent audit committees on their boards of directors. Companies were not allowed to make loans to their executives. The act also provided protection for insiders who blew the whistle on infractions.

The Foreign Corrupt Practices Act of 1977 and its revision in 1998 (The International Anti-Bribery Act of 1998) made it illegal for American companies or companies doing business in the

United States to engage in bribes or payments to officials for the sake of getting preferential treatment or business. This act also has no amount specified so that even small bribes can be construed as attempts to gain unfair advantage: the intent of the payment is the primary issue in this law. The law does, however, allow "facilitating payments" or "grease payments" to officials in countries where this is not against the law and only to expedite duties already assigned to that official.

The United Nations Declaration of Human Rights also comes into play when one considers doing business in the global arena. This declaration, drafted by John Peters Humphrey and Eleanor Roosevelt in 1948, includes 30 articles delineating what "we" today consider to be the basic rights of all human beings. Clearly, today, there are still many parts of the world where these rights, political, physical, and economic, are being debated, denied, and abridged. The global business leader (see Chapter 7) makes strategic choices about how to conform to, or comply with, these laws and rights.

Compliance is a challenging term. One can comply with the letter of a law while morally and ethically disagreeing with it and continuing to try to find ways around the law. Many companies today find that compliance with the law is not enough to win them respect in the eyes of the public. Consequently, the degree of compliance or leadership in the related realm of ethics, morality, legality, and culture is a strategic decision forced upon all those who choose to do business in the global marketplace.

Conclusions

Effective leadership, worldwide, is built on a foundation of moral and ethical principles—and moral and ethical principles are a Level Three phenomenon. One cannot manage effectively without learning to deal with the VABE-based foundation of business ethics, morals, laws, and their cultural surroundings. If you try to ignore these principles, your attempts to lead will be relatively weak. On the other hand, if you can establish trust and respect among your colleagues by practicing the four cornerstones of moral leadership—truth-telling, promise-keeping, fairness, and respect for the individual—then you will have a solid foundation from which your leadership attempts can spring. Leading morally won't ensure dramatic results, but it will enable your other leadership skills to have influence.

Concepts Introduced in This Chapter

1. All leadership includes strategic, financial, moral, ethical, legal, and cultural issues.
2. A modern view of the corporation takes a stakeholders' approach to analyze the harms and benefits of various constituencies and how they are affected by the corporation's actions.
3. One can analyze the ethical nature of a situation by assessing various stakeholders' harms and benefits.
4. Effective leaders tell the truth.
5. Effective leaders keep their promises.
6. Effective leaders treat people fairly.
7. Effective leaders have and show respect for the individual.
8. People worldwide have strong views on ethical issues. We can analyze those differences by looking for the similarities and differences at several levels.
9. Various legislative bodies around the world continue to make laws to constrain the unethical and immoral behavior of some business authoritors.
10. Compliance with legal constraints is not the end of the discussion about the relationship between profitable, sustainable, ethical, moral, legal, and culturally sensitive business. One should also consider the long-term impact of their behavior.

Questions for Personal Reflection

1. Describe to a friend an incident in your experience where authoritors (people in positions of authority) behaved unethically.
2. Could you be an effective leader if you told your people the truth half of the time? If you kept your promises to them half of the time? Why or why not?
3. Rate your current work group on the four cornerstones of the moral foundation on scales from 0 to 10. (See the exercise in Workbook.)
4. What could you do to strengthen the moral foundation of your leadership base and of the leadership base of your organization?
5. What is the relationship between the moral foundation principles and the concept of Level Three Leadership?

WORKBOOK

You can use the simple form "Assessing the Moral Foundation of Your Leadership" on page 395 in Workbook to get a sense of the moral/ethical foundation you have in your team. You can make copies and distribute one to each of your team members and ask them to rate the qualities of your team. Then, have a third party collect and summarize the data anonymously. Then you can meet to discuss the results.

CASELET FOR DISCUSSION

As an MBA intern working for an international company during your summer break, you travel to a foreign country. While there, your boss asks you to do two projects, one involving interviewing corporate counterparts in other companies. He asks, however, that you not reveal that you're working for your company, only that you're a graduate student doing research. When you ask why, he says because if they know you're working for our company, they won't give you any data. You say you're concerned about this deceit. He says, "Well then, pay your own way home"—which you cannot do and still go to school.

CONTRIBUTING YOUR OWN CASELETS

Have you seen or experienced a situation involving the concepts introduced in this chapter? If so and if you'd like to contribute your experience/situation to our case data bank, please visit http://faculty.darden.virginia.edu/clawsonj/ and click on the "Contribute new caselets" button.

INNOVATION AND LEVEL THREE LEADERSHIP

Creativity is your best path to creating value.

—JEFF deGRAFF AND KATHERINE LAWRENCE[1]

Strategists must decide the degree to which they will emphasize innovation. Strategist Gary Hamel argues that there are two kinds of strategists: squeezers and innovators. The squeezers are looking for ways to get rid of wasted energy, inefficiency, and redundancy. Innovators are looking for ways to create new products, new technologies, and new market segments. Squeezers want to have the lowest cost base and tend to do better in stable industries. Innovators are willing to invest in finding the next new thing and tend to do better in changing industries. The two are not necessarily mutually exclusive; however, there are some natural inhibitions to doing both. Innovation is inherently inefficient and costly and hence puts pressure on the desire to manage costs downward. In rapidly changing industries, innovation is essential to maintaining a competitive advantage. If one overemphasizes efficiency at the expense of innovation, sooner or later, the competition

---

[1] Jeff deGraff and Katherine A. Lawrence, *Creativity at Work: Developing the Right Practices to Make Innovation Happen* (San Francisco, CA: Jossey-Bass, 2002).

or Clayton Christensen's cheap, unsophisticated, low-technology substitutes will attack.[2] An overemphasis on efficiency and productivity measures will eventually squeeze out creativity and innovation, and when that happens, one loses the "enhanced flexibility" that we noted earlier as a fundamental element of competitive advantage.

One can think about innovation *in* squeezing—that is, about how to innovate processes that will lower costs and improve productivity (essentially the measure of inputs over outputs). Squeezing innovations tend to be in the arena of process improvements, total quality management, just-in-time inventory controls, and Six Sigma manufacturing, which is common in today's environment. Although these efforts are indeed "innovations," they are not what Hamel was referring to in setting up the dichotomy. Innovation in strategy—finding new market segments, leapfrogging technology, and substituting products—requires investment in research and development, market knowledge, basic research, and ventures with unknown outcomes. These ventures are more costly than finding better ways to do what you already know how to do.

We can think about innovation or its cousin, creativity, at the same levels we introduced in our discussion of strategic challenges: societal, organizational, work group, and individual. In other words, are organizations innovative? Is our work group innovative? Am I, as an individual, innovative? To begin, let's note that it's difficult to institutionalize innovation at the organizational level because to do so, one must create routines (organizational habits) that produce routine disruptions; this is an oxymoron. Many companies have tried to do this, some with more success than others. But even at the much vaunted 3M Company, attempts to produce consistent and predictable creative innovation have slowed in recent years. 3M Company's experience with a former GE executive as CEO and an emphasis on increasing efficiencies created a slowdown of innovative output.[3]

Given the complexities of managing efficiency and innovation at the organizational and work-group levels, we'll focus here, for the moment, on enhancing your individual creativity— your ability to think innovatively. If you can develop stronger personal skills of innovation, you'll likely be able to find ways to implement your ideas in your work-group and organizational contexts.

Creative thinking involves the need to attend to different ways of thinking and different foci of thought. Edward DeBono popularized the notion of "six thinking hats," that is, characteristic ways in which people think (Level Two).[4] He "colored" these hats as follows: white hat = facts and figures, red hat = emotions and feelings, black hat = cautious and careful, yellow hat = speculative positive, green hat = creative thinking, and blue hat = control of thinking. A social scientist would recognize that these "hats" are not really different kinds of thinking, rather a memorable way to note different modes people might be in or emphasize from time to time. Someone with their "yellow hat on" might be overly optimistic about the prognosis of a pending acquisition while another "black hatted person" might be "always" putting on the brakes. In some ways, these hats might be temperaments. As such they are habitual ways of behaving. DeBono's insight was to help people think about how their central repeating patterns might either be helpful or hurtful to their purposes and therefore invite them to think about ways to "rebalance" their thinking.

---

[2] See the discussion of the Innovator's Dilemma in the chapter on strategic frames.
[3] Brian Hindo, "3M's Innovation Crisis: How Six Sigma Almost Smothered Its Idea Culture," *Business Week*, June 11, 2007, cover article.
[4] Edward DeBono, *Six Thinking Hats,* New York: Little, Brown and Company, 1985, 1999.

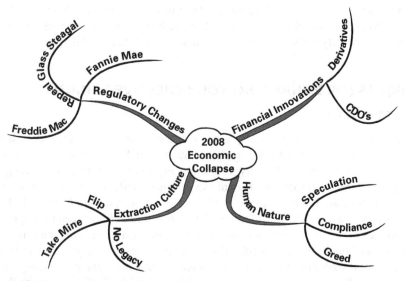

FIGURE 7-1   Sample mind map

Tony Buzan has stimulated people to rethink the way they think and their education with the concept of "mind mapping." In a mind map, one draws visual connections to concepts rather than listing them formally in a linear outline. Buzan's argument is that a mind map is a more accurate representation of the way information is stored in the brain than the bullet list or outline that most of us were taught in school. A mind map allows a more flexible free flowing way of capturing ideas.[5] A sample mind map appears in Figure 7-1.

Innovation at its core is about challenging underlying habits often based on one's values, assumptions, beliefs, and expectations (VABEs) and is therefore an inherently Level Three process. By this we mean that, as we discuss shortly, humans tend to be creatures of habit and many, if not most, of those habits are rooted in our Level Three VABEs. Gary Hamel confirms this view in his book *The Future of Management*, in which he claims that the innovative leader's primary "pickax" is questioning underlying beliefs.[6]

1. Is this a belief worth challenging? Is it debilitating? Does it get in the way of an important organizational attribute (like strategic adaptability) that we'd like to strengthen?
2. Is this belief universally valid? Are there counterexamples? If there are counterexamples, what do we learn from those cases?
3. How does this belief serve the interests of its adherents? Are there people who draw reassurance or comfort from this belief?
4. Have our choices and assumptions conspired to make this belief self-fulfilling? Is this belief true simply because we have made it true—and, if so, can we imagine alternatives?

To innovate, then, is to challenge our VABEs in ways that allow us to see things differently and from different perspectives. The rest of this chapter will offer suggestions for how you might

---

[5] Tony Buzan, *The Mind Map Book: How to Use Radiant Thinking to Use Your Brain's Untapped Potential* (New York: Plume, 1996).
[6] Gary Hamel, *The Future of Management* (Boston, MA: Harvard Business School Press, 2007), as reported in *Fortune*, October 1, 2007, 122.

enhance your ability to do this. There are multiple techniques for developing one's ability to think innovatively or creatively. Whether they become habitual or not depends on you. Here are some of the more widely recognized techniques that you may find useful.

TECHNIQUES FOR ENHANCING YOUR CREATIVE THINKING

Observe Mindfully

One of the common habits that people lapse into is that of going through their day without really observing or thinking about what's taking place around them. Saul Alinsky once noted that most people go through life without really collecting experiences, rather just having a set of happenings, and those happenings become experiences only when one digests them and incorporates their meaning into one's point of view as we described in Chapter 1. The skill of doing this is what many call "critical thinking." By *critical thinking* I mean the degree to which an individual can listen to or read a thought, a concept, or a perspective and then assess its "truthfulness" or "functionality" in life. There are many spurious arguments in life, and the innovative business leader must develop skills at recognizing them and challenging them. James Kouzes and Barry Posner in their seminal work *The Leadership Challenge* declare that the first of five key leadership skills is "challenging the status quo."[7]

When you hear a news report, read an article, or are engaged in a conversation, are you constantly looking for the quality of logic and data? Are you able to describe the issues from both sides of the fence? Do you find yourself constantly thinking about how a product or service could be improved? This is not so much a "devil's advocate" point of view as it is constantly looking for better ways to do things.

Consider the Opposite

Chic Thompson—in his book *What a Great Idea!*—offers one way to do this.[8] At one point in his career, Thompson was employed by the founder of Gore-Tex®, who expected him to come up with a new use for the technological innovation once a day for a year—and he did it. One of the techniques he used was to consider the opposite. If you get stuck when you're thinking about an issue or a topic, try asking yourself, what's the opposite? This approach can be very useful in any number of settings. For example, if you're arguing or fighting with someone about who's right or how to win, think about the opposite: Could you let them be right or could you both win or could you give them what they want and still "win"?

Avoid Deadline Stress

Deadlines can kill creativity. Many believe the opposite—that a deadline or an arbitrary parameter can stimulate new ways of thinking about things—and there's some truth to that. Repeated stress of meeting deadlines and end-of-quarter reporting periods can, however, cause the body's natural fight-or-flight chemical reactions to kick in and cause innovation shutdown. Thompson notes that most creative ideas tend to come in those times and places when one is not focusing intensely on the problem. This is a well-known phenomenon that leads to the dictum

---

[7] James M. Kouses and Barry Z. Posner, *The Leadership Challenge*, 4th ed. (San Francisco, CA: Jossey-Bass, 2007).
[8] Charles "Chic" Thompson, *What a Great Idea!* (New York: HarperCollins, 1992).

"let's sleep on it." Thompson claims that the majority of new ideas come in the shower, while driving, or while working on something else.

At the same time, it's hard to avoid deadline stress in today's business world. One way to move in that direction is to avoid procrastination. Keep a notebook and when you get a new assignment, capture your thoughts immediately on what or how you might fulfill it. Let those thoughts ruminate in your mind as you attend to your other routine items and while the deadline approaches, continue to add notes to your notebook. I often find that the spontaneous outline that I made during a phone conversation or during a meeting with a new challenge sets the stage for the final project. The initial stimulation and your mind's immediate creative responses should not be overlooked. The central point is that to encourage innovation, it helps to calm your mind.

Calm Your Mind

It's not that easy for most people to calm their minds and allow the full faculties of the amazing human brain to come into play. The Eastern tradition of meditation and the Western tradition of prayer are common ways that many use to calm their minds and allow new ideas to bubble to the surface. Martial artists also use quiet or dynamic meditation to allow them to be able to apprehend the whole and to respond to multiple attacks or situations without focusing too much on one at the expense of another. Outside-in stress tends to reduce creativity. Learning to manage your thought processes so that you can utilize all your faculties can help you enhance your creativity.

Always Search for a Better Way

At one time, it was generally thought that business managers tried to maximize. Formulae and decision-making frameworks were designed to get the best out of every situation. Herb Simon, however, won a Nobel Prize for identifying the reality that most managers did not maximize, rather they satisficed—they found the first acceptable option and went with it.[9] This tendency, to find an acceptable solution and then move on, has strengths and weaknesses associated with it. On the one hand, it makes for faster decisions, and on the other hand, it leads to average or mediocre solutions. One way to avoid this tendency is to pay attention to the customer's experience.

Consider the Customer's Experience

Much has been written about delighting the customer, exceeding their expectations, and leaving them with a world-class experience. In the chapter on strategic frames, we introduced Pine and Gilmore's notion of an experience economy. Although these ideas seem compelling, my guess is that your experience in the world is that there remain enormous opportunities for improving customer experience.

Consider, for example, what happens when a woman discovers a lump in her breast and begins to worry about breast cancer. In most health management organizations, it takes about two weeks from the time the patient presents herself to the point when she receives a definitive diagnosis and can gain some relief from her uncertainty. One organization, Park Nicollet in Minneapolis–St. Paul, however, decided that having patients worry about the uncertainty with the sleepless nights and anxiety was unacceptable. They put together a cross-functional, interdisciplinary team to tackle the problem and design a new system. The process they came up with reduced the uncertainty from two

---

[9] Herbert Simon, *Administrative Behavior*, 4th ed. (New York: Free Press, 1997).

weeks to four hours. If a woman presents with symptoms of breast cancer at 8:00 A.M., she knows by the time she leaves the clinic at noon whether or not she has breast cancer and what her options might be. That's innovation. And what's amazing is that Park Nicollet did this in 1992, and by 2010, most health-care organizations had not yet mimicked the approach. Utilizing the customer perspective is one way to augment your thinking. There are other ways to stimulate your curiosity.

Stimulate Your Curiosity

One way to stimulate your curiosity is to constantly ask yourself how things work. This concept is akin to the earlier notions of observing mindfully and seeking better ways. Many people have limited curiosity and do little to stimulate its growth. If you have studied history or, as in my case, languages earlier in life, do you have an interest in biology, manufacturing, chemistry, and other topics that influence our lives daily? My MBA program was an eye-opening experience, learning how the business world "works." Do you ever ask yourself, how do they do that? If not, I encourage you to do so daily. How do they make things? Where do products come from? How do they manage that process? How would I organize it if were me? If I were "Congress," what laws would I make and why? What consequences would they have? Why do people behave the way they do? Practicing to ask these questions daily over and over again will tend to stimulate the development of your curiosity. And one way to heighten your curiosity is to heighten your sensual awareness.

Use Mind Mapping

Try using mind mapping instead of bullets and outlines for your note taking and idea brainstorming. You can practice anytime anywhere. As you listen to a speaker, take your notes in mind map form and observe how this changes the way you think and/or recall the information. Preparing to give a speech, use mind mapping to generate your ideas and notes. Observe how this changes your thinking and ability to generate new thoughts and quickly plan out a talk. Try the Buzan computer-based mind-mapping program and see how it changes the way you generate ideas and writing plans.

Heighten Your Senses

Michael Gelb, consultant and author, has written a very interesting stream of books on poise (the Alexander Technique) and creative genius. In describing the multiple talents of Leonardo da Vinci, one of the brightest intellects in human history, he notes da Vinci's attention to his sensory experience.[10] By paying attention to the tastes as you eat, by noting more mindfully the colors surrounding you, by allowing pleasant sounds to engulf you, by practicing your sensitivity to the surfaces you touch, you develop your neural nets and bring what otherwise might have been semi- or subconscious to the fore. This heightened sensitivity can enhance your ability to hear what people are really saying or presenting, to see what's happening, and to experience events more completely.

Fight Killer Phrases

Thompson also argues that creativity is often dampened unnecessarily by what he calls "killer phrases," words that squash fledgling ideas and insights. Perhaps you've heard some of these:

---

[10] Michael Gelb, *How to Think Like Leonardo da Vinci: Seven Steps to Genius Every Day* (New York: Dell, 2000).

We've never done it that way. That'll never work. That's a stupid idea. Get out of the Pleistocene era! What a dumb idea. We could never afford that. It may be easy for you to recognize these phrases as uttered by others. Are you aware, however, of how often you say them to others? Do you dampen the creative ideas of others by virtue of your creativity-killing comments? Sometimes, being less judgmental and more open to undeveloped ideas can encourage creativity—in yourself and others.

Allow Fuzziness

Another of da Vinci's characteristics is what Gelb called "Sfumato," an Italian word for smoky or fuzzy or indistinct. Premature pushing to clarity can limit creativity. Letting the fuzziness linger for a while can encourage less stressed or less deadline oriented minds to come up with new thinking.

You'll note that there are some paradoxes in the list we're developing here: the tension between deadlines and calm minds, the tradeoffs between satisficing and looking for a better way, and the balance between immediate stimulation and tolerating uncertainty for a while. There are no known formulae for describing exactly how much of these contradictory tensions one should cultivate. Recognizing them, though, may help you think about whether or not you're leaning too far in one direction or the other and need to do something to tip the scales in the other direction.

Look for Unexpected Connections

We'll note here one more of Gelb's insights into da Vinci's life and work looking for unexpected connections. Are there concepts or principles that work in one field that might apply or clarify processes in another? This is the principle underlying analogies. Can you find analogies that at once clarify, stimulate, and satisfy? Roger von Oech touted this principle in his book *A Whack on the Side of the Head.*[11] One of the exercises he had readers do was to develop an analogy for life: for example, "life is like a maze in which you try to avoid the exit" or "Life is like a bagel. It's delicious when it's fresh and warm, but often it's just hard. The hole in the middle is its great mystery, and yet it wouldn't be a bagel without it."

Finding connections between math and art, marketing and manufacturing, biology and business, or drama and leadership can be very stimulating exercises. I have one colleague, Ed Freeman, who teaches leadership through the process of selecting and presenting plays. Students must decide what play to produce, then divvy up the roles that they share from scene to scene, manage the rehearsals, team work, logistics, marketing, and production, and learn on-stage presence. Twenty years ago, most managers would not have imagined the connections between theater and leadership. What's more, his class is very popular because students thoroughly enjoy what they're doing.

Look for What's Fun

Innovating is exhilarating. Here's another bipolar tension in life: routine and variety. On the one hand, we tend to be creatures of habit; on the other hand, we tend to enjoy variety as the spice of life. Business managers in general tend to be serious and focused on hard work to get results. Although this focus can be productive, it can also squelch innovation

---

[11] Roger vonOech, *A Whack on the Side of the Head* (Menlo Park, CA: Creative Think, 1983).

and creativity. In the chapter on resonance, we discuss the relationship between feel and performance. If you can find ways to make work more fun, the odds are you'll be more creative and innovative as well. Fun is not necessarily unproductive. Robots may be productive, but they lack creativity.

The Four I's

Jeff deGraff and Katherine Lawrence identify four principles that they've used successfully in their work at the University of Michigan and in their consulting. These four "I's" are imagination, investment, improve the current, and incubate. We've touched on these at various times earlier in this chapter. Most of our suggestions have been about how to increase your imagination. We've noted that investment in creativity pushes against the desire to enhance productivity among squeezers. Looking for a better way opens the whole literature surrounding process improvements and incremental *kaizen* advancements. And finally, organizing projects and ideas so that they can incubate and gestate is important. We've taken a more individual approach here. DeGraff and Lawrence offer processes that one can use in organizations to broaden innovative activity.

INNOVATE LIKE EDISON

Gelb and Caldicott's latest book, *Innovate like Edison*,[12] also explores the processes by which creative thinking becomes business innovation. In exploring Caldicott's great-grand uncle's life and activity as America's greatest inventor and innovator, the authors identify five bundles of competencies that Edison's life exemplified: solution-centered mind-set, kaleidoscopic thinking, full-spectrum engagement, mastermind collaboration, and super-value creation. Edison himself commented on the important difference between creative thinking and business innovation. He'd invented a system for immediately capturing and recording votes in large groups like legislatures. His system was functional and easy to produce but rejected by the political leaders of the time because they wanted the time the old process took between vote and counting to lobby and affect the outcome. Edison declared, then, that he'd never again waste his time on innovations that no one wanted. Most successful business innovations are combinations of creative thinking, multiple inventions, process innovation, intense collaboration across traditional boundaries, mobilization of unusual resources, and a tight connection with the market place. Gelb and Caldicott identify five underlying skills that relate to each of the five Edisonian competencies.

Gelb and Caldicott summarize the challenge facing modern organizations and business school curricula in their quote from Professor Vijay Govindarajan from the Tuck School of Business at Dartmouth:

> We've got to get every member of the organization, from top to bottom, literate in innovation just like we make them literate in finance, or literate in marketing, or literate in any other management discipline. Innovation is not only about ideas and creativity; it's a whole discipline about how you turn an idea into reality.[13]

---

[12] Michael J. Gelb and Sarah Miller Caldicott, *Innovate Like Edison: The Success System of America's Greatest Inventor* (New York: Dutton, 2007).
[13] Ibid., 10.

Conclusions

Are there any new ideas? Many business observers comment about how the latest "fad du jour" often seems like repackaged ideas from 20, 30, or 50 years ago. Part of the challenge is that each new generation has to find ways to learn what has been discovered in history. That learning can contribute to idea ossification. Does one learn along the way to challenge the status quo? Does one develop habits of reading widely and looking for interdisciplinary connections? Does one learn to manage one's own mind to be constantly looking for better ways of doing things? Or does one learn to fit into the way we've always done it? Innovation begins with the individual, you. If you have the skills and habits related to innovating, you can bring those to your work group and to your organization. The odds are you won't be encouraged to do this. You'll find innumerable killer phrases along the way. Whether you succumb to those will depend on whether you're living too much outside-in.

Concepts Introduced in This Chapter

1. Strategist must decide the degree to which they will emphasize innovation. In rapidly changing industries, innovation is essential to maintaining a competitive advantage.
2. Innovation at its core is about challenging underlying VABEs and is an inherently Level Three process.
3. It is difficult to institutionalize innovation. To do so, one must create routines that produce routine disruptions.
4. Effective leaders will be innovative thinkers.
5. There are multiple techniques for developing one's ability to think innovatively or creatively. Whether they become habitual or not depends on the individual.
6. Managers, employees, teachers, and students must learn the disciplines of innovation in order to survive in today's business world.

Questions for Personal Reflection

1. How many processes can you find in your organization in one day that could be improved? How would you improve them?
2. If you were the president of your organization, what three things would you want to change and why? How would you go about changing them?
3. Write down three main concepts from your college major and think about how they might apply to leading a business. If you majored in management, think about how they might apply to your national government.
4. Think about your weekly routine. When do your best ideas tend to bubble up? How could you protect and cultivate your creative-thinking processes?
5. How could you develop a personal model of innovation whether it at the individual, work-group, or organizational level? Where could you read and learn to develop such a model?
6. What kinds of books would you normally not want to read? What might you learn if you read one or two?
7. Write down a one-page description of your daily commute. How many details can you remember about the route and surroundings?
8. What are your favorite foods? Why? What are your favorite colors? Why? Can you describe three different surfaces, and how they feel to your touch?
9. How would you revise the health-care system in your country? What changes would you make, and how would you organize and pay for your design?

CASELET FOR DISCUSSION

Sara was a chemical engineer. Her manager asked her to devise a new compound that would have great market potential. He asked her to describe the target characteristics of her compound, and how it might be used before he would be willing to consider investing in the research to find and develop the compound. If you were in Sara's position, what kind of a compound would you want to develop, and how might it be used?

CONTRIBUTING YOUR OWN CASELETS

Have you seen or experienced a situation involving the concepts introduced in this chapter? If so, and if you'd like to contribute your experience/situation to our case data bank, please visit http://faculty.darden.virginia.edu/clawsonj/ and click on the "Contribute new caselets" button.

8 | PERSONAL, WORKGROUP, AND ORGANIZATIONAL CHARTERS

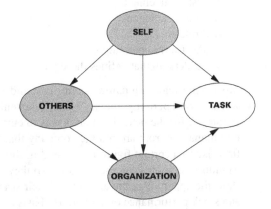

*Mission statement work is the single most important work
because the decisions made there affect all other decisions.*

—STEPHEN COVEY

Leaders involved in strategic discussions often get confused by
the strategic language. They begin to use *strategy*, *vision*, *mission*,
business, *values*, and other related terms loosely or interchangeably,
which can lead to miscommunication and misdirection. The range of
strategic frameworks as introduced in Chapter 7 surely contributes to
this confusion. One way you can begin to distill your personal
summary of these frameworks and then develop your strategic thinking
skills is to work through personal, workgroup, and organizational
charters.

CHARTERS

Charters in the colonial era were documents that outlined the purpose, scope, and range of authority for a particular expedition. These details included geographic definitions, goals, expected outcomes, and certain powers delegated for implementation. Similarly, we can consider an organizational charter as a set of documents that outlines the present and future intentions of the organizational expedition. Organizational charters, as shown in Figure 8-1, include six distinct and sequential parts:

1. Mission statement
2. Vision statement
3. Values statement
4. Strategy
5. Short-term operating goals
6. Leadership that defines these parts

Most American companies seem to spend most of their time and energy attending to and working on operating goals. In fact, one senior executive told employees that the company's "strategy" for the next six months was to curtail sales costs. Another executive of a major firm told managers from around the company that their business was to make the stock price of the firm rise to a certain figure by the end of the year and that if they didn't, the senior executives wouldn't get their year-end bonuses, so they needed to get their rears in gear. These examples show the apparent nature and sum of their strategic thinking. Although concern for profitability and stock performance on a quarterly basis are important, Collins and Porras[1] and others assert that focusing on these measures to the exclusion of customer service and value delivered undermines the long-term viability of a firm and can actually harm the company by encouraging people to make decisions and take actions that hurt customer relationships and eventually profitability.[2] Other more strategically oriented CEOs will note that giving in slavishly to the

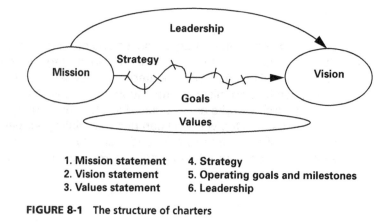

1. Mission statement   4. Strategy
2. Vision statement   5. Operating goals and milestones
3. Values statement   6. Leadership

FIGURE 8-1   The structure of charters

[1] James C. Collins and Jerry I. Porras, *Built to Last* (New York: HarperBusiness, 1994).
[2] Robert S. Kaplan and David P. Norton, "The Balanced Scorecard—Measures That Drive Performance," *Harvard Business Review*, February 1, 2000, 92105.

analysts' pressure is tantamount to yielding management to them. The challenge for effective leadership is to clarify the organization's purpose and vision and to do so in a compelling, even inspiring way.

This focus is a relatively new phenomenon. Most of management research and effort during the nineteenth and twentieth centuries was directed at Level One, visible behavior. Job descriptions and other features of the bureaucratic management paradigm were directed at controlling the behavior of employees regardless of their thoughts and feelings. Henry Ford, for example, once declared in exasperation, "I keep trying to hire a pair of hands and they keep coming with heads and bodies attached!" The new, emerging organizational forms, however, which seek to create high-performing workplaces, are increasingly and appropriately targeted at Levels Two and Three. Today's managers realize that they need to get employees' minds and hearts, as well as their bodies, engaged in their work if the organization is going to compete successfully.

Level Three Leadership begins with what we may call an organizational charter. As presented here, organizational charters are composed of a mission statement, a vision statement, a values statement (all of which are Level Three statements), a strategy, and short-term operating goals. Each of these elements is unique and serves a different purpose. Many organizations either confuse these terms or don't use these statements as the powerful leadership tools they can be. Furthermore, many organizations focus almost exclusively on the short-term goals. When they do, Level Three opportunities to inspire employees are lost, and the leadership retreats to a Level One influence structure.

One may also consider personal charters and work-group charters. In other words, if you cannot write down your personal charter, how can you expect to do so for your work group or your organization? In fact, based on the example of the Matsushita Leadership Institute described earlier, unless you can put your personal charter on paper, succinctly and powerfully, you're not really prepared for leading others. To begin this process, complete the exercise and worksheet in Workbook on page 351 in Chapter 26 to help you.

MISSION

The mission statement comes first because it defines what the organization will and will not do: the organization's reason for existence. Organizations, work groups, or people don't require a mission statement to exist. Some even argue that mission statements can get in the way of doing business.[3] Many executives were, at one time, pushed through a mission statement process that left them skeptical and vehemently opposed to this approach. These people generally have a difficult time answering the question as to why their people go to work. Further, they leave large amounts of untapped energy latent in their organizations. Perhaps their conclusion stems from an expensive organizational process in which a committee with subcommittees grinds for months and comes up with the following statement: our mission is to deliver world-class goods and services which delight our customers beyond their expectations while giving our investors an above-industry-average return on their investments. Statements like these may be true at some high level, but are vanilla, nondistinctive, and unmotivating.

---

[3] Barbara Bartkus, Myron Glassman, and R. Bruce McAfee, "Mission Statements: Are They Smoke and Mirrors?" *Business Horizons*, November–December (2000): 23.

A *mission statement* is a concise declaration of the reason for the organization's existence and of the kind of activity the organization will pursue. This statement helps to concentrate the efforts of organizational members and helps preclude attention from other activities and enterprises. Effective mission statements are action oriented and revolve around a core that offers something to customers rather than something that primarily benefits the organization.

"To Make Money," You Idiot: Causal Mapping

When asked about the mission of their company, many managers today reply, "To make money!" and then look at you as if it's a dumb question. The problem with this kind of thinking is that it encourages Level One behavior that undermines itself. Here's how. Consider a simple causal map like the one shown in Figure 8-2. You can see that many things on the map contribute to profitability, but the two immediate contributors are revenues and costs. Each of the nodes no doubt involves other inputs and outputs. The simple ones, the + and − signs on each relationship, show whether the previous causal node adds to or detracts from the next node. An increase in price, for example, likely has a negative effect on customer satisfaction (although among certain upper-end segments, the opposite is true).

Each of us carries implicit causal maps that explain our view of how the world operates. We may or may not be able to articulate them or write them down. Sometimes, we use these semiconscious or preconscious mental causal maps (that reside at Level Three) without questioning their validity or impact. The first step in using them effectively, and perhaps in modifying them, is to make them explicit so we can examine them at Level Two. This step amounts to bringing Level Three VABEs (values, assumptions, beliefs, and expectations) up to Level Two conscious awareness. Once individuals know clearly what they believe about what will affect profitability (or anything else), they can begin to plan interventions at various places on the map that could have strategic impact.

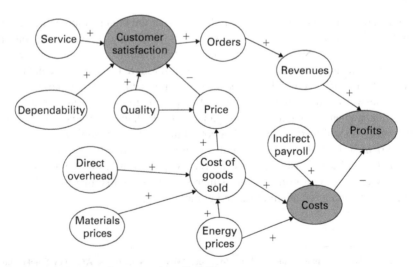

FIGURE 8-2   Causal maps and profitability

A critical issue is where individuals choose to focus their attention on their causal map. *Focus* here is like putting a spotlight on different relationships on the map, thus highlighting one area while leaving the other areas on the map in the shadow. We do this same type of focusing naturally all the time with our implicit causal maps of how the world, our relationships, or our businesses operate. Again, this prioritization is a Level Three phenomenon, a manifestation of our values. Our decisions about where to focus our attention are critical to our ability to find and solve problems and to make strategic interventions. When we shine our mental spotlight on a part of our causal map, we begin "attending" to certain parts or processes of the organization rather than to others. This attention shapes what "we see that needs to be done," the first step in the Leadership Point of View (LPV). This focusing of attention is a key leadership activity—and, in fact, central to purpose clarification.

When the *primary* and relatively *exclusive* focus or spotlight is on profits, employees are encouraged to do things that may not be good, paradoxically, for profitability. For instance, in one $600-million firm, employees were so focused on profits and meeting their targets, period by period, that they began to ship next month's orders to customers in order to include them in the current month's accounting figures. They began to postpone training and maintenance activities and to eliminate time spent dealing with customer complaints and inquiries in order to focus more time on the efficiency of their design and production processes. One month, after several years of this behavior, their orders suddenly dropped by almost 50 percent. Panicking, they called their major customer, a distribution firm, and learned after several conversations that they had shipped so much finished product to the distributor's warehouses under their old operating guidelines that the distributor simply couldn't carry any more of "your finished goods inventory" and couldn't sell any more. Oblivious to what was happening among end users and insensitive to the realities faced by its distributors, this producer had focused its attention on its sales at the next link in the value chain to the exclusion of subsequent links. The firm faced the cataclysmic realization that focusing on short-term profits severely eroded the firm's ability to stay in business. This classic example shows a de facto mission statement that revolved around making money and hitting the "numbers" rather than serving customers.

A more productive approach is to look back in the causal chain map to the Customer Satisfaction node. You can see in Figure 8-2 that this node is somewhat removed from the Profits node, and yet its impact on Profits has a direct line. Turning our spotlight here does not ignore the importance of profitability, but it does put it in a larger context and in a different light. If we attend more to the Customer Satisfaction node, we can begin to think energetically about "which customers?" and "what do they want?" Although profit is, in this light, no longer the *central* reason for existence (mission) of the organization, profitability becomes a predictable and stable by-product of the attention given to customer satisfaction.

Of course, one doesn't ignore cost structures, either. The point is that *where you focus in your implicit mental causal map makes a huge difference.* If you focus on Profits exclusively, you are likely overlooking large amounts of energy in your organization that could otherwise be directed, ironically, at making profits. The Level Three message to employees when management says, "The purpose of the business is to make money," is "Your work here is to make other people wealthy." It is not a motivating value. On the other hand, with a mission statement presented in terms of how the organization will serve customers, leaders and employees can begin to join in a common purpose of sorting out how to fulfill the mission, and organizing to accomplish it.

We call this kind of mission statement a *service-oriented mission statement.* This way of thinking about and presenting the organization's mission is intrinsically uplifting and energizing. Most people feel larger when they are part of a morally powerful and serving purpose. "Service to customers" takes an outward focus that speaks to an employee's sense of contribution and draws on his or her sense of connection to society. "Making money" as a core mission creates an inward focus and attends to what the organization can take from society and will in the long run be a less powerful motivator.

When the mission of an organization is morally focused and clearly understood and people are committed to it, they may make decisions that seem, in the short run, to erode profits. Compared with our earlier example, this different focal point in the business's causal map may lead to postponing shipments rather than accelerating them in order to meet customer needs or to acceleration of training and maintenance activities so that customer needs can be met more quickly and with higher quality in the future. This approach may also lead to a greater propensity to listen to people who are in active conversation with the customer, people who may not have organizational status or power, but who in reality possess the information the organization needs to meet customer needs. This trend is observable in many high-performing service organizations throughout the world today.

This approach suggests that a mission statement should identify a customer group, which is different from focusing on a product area. If, for instance, at the beginning of the twentieth century, you had focused on a product grouping, say, "carriage accelerators" as your (overly narrow) definition of your industry, you might have continued to see your mission as building buggy whips, but have missed the market's encouragement to do research and development on new types of transportation, like automobiles. If you had focused on serving people who wanted to travel independently, automobile research would have easily fit into your mission and your thinking. The mind-sets that would-be leaders bring to their efforts to establish mission statements either allow them to respond to changes around them or inhibit their ability to see what they need to attend to. Going back to the LPV, your statement of mission for yourself, your work group, or your organization will be a powerful indicator of what you "see."

A good mission statement declares what your organization intends to do, and for whom. The actual organization will vary from person to person. For conglomerates, each division needs a mission statement that defines these foci. Likewise, each department can articulate a mission statement that helps employees understand *why* they come to work each day.

Conceiving a good mission statement is not an easy thing. Perhaps you have seen corporate mission statements laminated in plastic and distributed to all employees. It's a sure sign of the lack of power of the statement if you ask employees, what's the mission of your company? and they have to fish in their wallets for the card. Good mission statements are powerful, crisp, memorable, and easy to connect with. Writing them is more than stringing together trite clichés like "world-class," "provider," "customer-oriented," and "balanced returns to all our constituencies." If you'd like to see a whole volume of mission statements to compare and get some examples, read *The Mission Statement Book* by Jeffrey Abrahams.[4] Note, however, that the challenge of effective leadership is to *define* these things. Who will clarify the purpose or the center of the organization if not the leader?

What is your mission or purpose in life?

Consider the following examples. The mission of the Commonwealth of Virginia Department of Transportation (VDOT) was to get thousands of people spread all over the state in a variety of roles, including administration, painting stripes, laying asphalt, putting up traffic signals and signs, and doing research on roadways, to have a common purpose when they go

---

[4] Jeffrey Abrahams, *The Mission Statement Book* (Berkeley, CA: Ten Speed Press, 1995).

to work. After a year and a half of careful reflection, VDOT came up with its mission: "Keep Virginia moving." This clear, simple, pointed statement allows everyone in the system to see how their work might connect to this purpose. Another firm states its mission as "We protect those who protect us." For this defense company engaged in making radar-jamming equipment, the central purpose is direct, simple, powerful, and broad enough to relate to virtually every employee.

The Darden Graduate School of Business Administration has a powerful mission, one that enables all those involved to connect with daily. What do you suppose the mission of a large well-known business school might be? The clichéd formula for mission statements might suggest something like "To be a world-class provider of leading-edge research to academicians, managers, students in a customer-oriented, Six Sigma way." Blah, blah, blah. Rather, it chose the following: "The mission of the Darden School is to better society by preparing principled leaders in the world of practical affairs." The school may on occasion fall short of that lofty mission, but it is clear, crisp, and morally sound. Your organization *deserves* a similarly short, concise, memorable, broadly applicable, inspiring mission. One of the key roles of leadership is to set and clarify that mission or purpose.

Gary Hamel, as noted in the previous chapter, asserted that mission statements should be flexible. His concern, a good one, was that narrow mission statements created mental barriers to innovation, flexibility, and seizing opportunities. The examples given here are broad enough that they allow for multiple visions, multiple strategies, and lots of creativity, but they are focused enough to define a purpose, a cause, and a raison d'etre that any member or employee can identify with and choose to engage in.

It's one thing to write the mission statement for a company. It's quite another to write your own personal life's mission statement. Before we end this section, consider drafting your personal mission in life. What is your purpose on the earth? Some believe this question is silly, that it has no answer. Others believe that God gives one a mission in life and the goal is to figure that out. Others believe that you can live with or without a purpose. I believe that having one lends clarity and energy to your daily activities. Lily Tomlin, the great American comedienne, once said, "I always wanted to be somebody. I guess I should have been more specific!" This statement is one that far too many humans find themselves thinking at mid- and late-career stages.

Do you have a personal mission statement? If not, can you craft one that captures what you're trying to do with your life? Again, the worksheet on page 351 in the Workbook in Chapter 26 can help you begin this process. Perhaps a couple of examples will help get you thinking. Two university professors articulated their mission statements: "to make people think" and "to help people create powerful futures." Both of these seem like very appropriate mission statements for university professors.

If you find "What is your purpose or mission in life?" a compelling question, ask a number of people you respect what their life's mission is. Some may not be able to state one. Some will have clear ones. Either way, you will learn from the conversation.

One last point here. One danger is that when people try to draft a personal mission statement, they will ignore the thing they have spent 30 years of their life doing. If you are involved in manufacturing airplanes and draft something like "to serve others" or "have a happy family," it sounds very lofty but really doesn't distinguish you from a doctor or a McDonald's franchise owner. I encourage you to find a way to incorporate your life's chosen profession into your mission statement, so your statement says something not only about what you hope at Level Three but also about what you *do* at Level One. In this case, an alternative might be, "to help people by building better airplanes" or more simply, "to build better airplanes." For a pilot, it might be, "to fly." For a surfer, it might be, "to experience the biggest and best waves."[5] For an insurance executive, it might be, "to give people peace of mind." For a spirits manufacturer, it might be, "to help people party."

You'll spend one-third or more of your waking life at work. If your mission statement ignores that fact, you're fooling yourself and taking something less than your full purpose to work. When you write a mission statement that distills how you spend your time and energy, you may, seeing that, decide either to reinforce or to change it.

VISION

Given a mission or purpose, most people need a view of where they're going. If a mission is about what we do or why we exist today where we are, a *vision* is the view that we take of what the organization can and should become if it followed and succeeded in that mission. A visionary leader looks ahead and "sees" what the organization should become and uses that dream or panoramic view to guide communications with others in the organization—a key element in leadership.

Would-be leaders who cannot envision the future and what their organization can do in it have a difficult time talking and behaving in ways that inspire and motivate others at Level Three. In the same way that short-term financial goals make weak mission statements, short-term financial visions of the future make weak visions. Stan Davis, in *Future Perfect*, explores this concept well.[6] Davis describes how effective leaders cast their minds into the future and then look back on the present state of the organization. The gap in between is the progress that the organization must make in order to achieve the vision. Leaders who think in this way, Davis notes, tend to talk in the *future perfect* tense; that is, they will use phrases such as "When we achieve our vision, we *will have done x, y*, and *z*." The *x, y*, and *z*, of course, are the things that the leader recognizes need to be done in order to move toward the vision. They become the shorter-term goals and objectives for the organization that are described later.

The more descriptive, detailed, and passionately held the visions are, the more power they hold. If leaders talk just about becoming a "world-class" organization (which has become a trite and almost meaningless phrase), they overlook the myriad details required to describe to others what "world-class" in their business looks like. Effective leaders will imagine, see, and then describe in minute detail the view they have of what is possible—and not just once, but hundreds of times in hundreds of settings.

Where do you believe you or your organization ought to be in 10 (or 30) years?

Often, midlevel managers and employees claim that their lack of vision is a function of the work they do and that if they had the CEO's job, they too would be able to see things in broader, visionary terms. The data developed from the *Survey of Managerial Behavior* (included in the Workbook on page 352), a self-assessment instrument that measures in part an individual's interest in visioning, however, suggest little correlation between a person's level in an organization and the time and energy the person spends on creating a powerful vision. In this database, many senior managers spent little time thinking about the future, and many lower-level employees worked to

---

[5] *Riding Giants* (Columbia TriStar Home Entertainment, 2005).
[6] Stanley M. Davis, *Future Perfect* (Reading, MA: Addison-Wesley, 1987).

develop a clear view of what they were doing. The clear conclusion is that the mental effort to define a vision is person specific, not job specific. Those who are appropriately promoted to strategic positions have already developed personal beginnings of a corporate vision and will get the strategic jobs *because of* their demonstrated visionary capacity rather than their potential to develop it. Although we don't say it's too late to develop a vision when you get a "visionary job," you'll be better off in the promotion pool and more effective as a leader wherever you are promoted if you've developed a personal vision of what your department and your organization can and, in your mind, should become. This process develops in you the mental capacity for strategic, visionary thinking.

A second excuse that people offer for not being more visionary is that the world is changing so fast no one can see where it's going. This excuse is a cop-out. Visioning doesn't necessarily mean being able to predict the future, rather it means envisioning what you think the future could, and should, be. Without this kind of vision, it is virtually impossible to develop the strategic intent described in Chapter 7. Do you know and are you able to describe what you believe your company should be in 10 years' time? In 20 years? How about yourself? Remember Lily Tomlin's line: "Maybe it's time to be more specific."

Visioning is a learned behavior that can be developed, but it doesn't come easily. Visions grow out of study, reading, comparing, traveling, seeing, imagining, seeking, analyzing, and a host of other activities that give the individual a base from which to create and receive new views of what is possible. If you want to become an effective leader, you should be practicing visioning *now*. You can do this by thinking regularly about where you or your organization is going, what you or it will look like, or should look like, in 4, 10, 20, 30, or 100 years; by reading broadly; or by formulating your own broad answers to the pressing problems of the day—personally, nationally, or organizationally.

A complete vision statement would include visions for the various aspects of the charter you're working on. For a society, it might include visions for defense, health care, the economy, and culture. For an organization, it might include visions for financial condition, customers, public reputation, internal processes, employees, indeed, all of the major disciplines found in modern businesses. For a team, it might include vision of culture, membership, productivity, activities, etc. For a person, it might (should) include visions of the physical, intellectual, social, professional, financial, marital, parental—all of the –AL aspects of life.

You might begin your efforts to develop your visioning skill by regularly asking yourself difficult questions such as "How would I respond to the economic situation today if I were the nation's chief executive? How would I see my company operating in the next century? What would its reputation be? What do I plan to be doing when I am 45? 55? 65?" Shower time, commuting time, end-of-day reflection time are all good times to pause and think about what you would do if you were in the chief strategic job in your country, region, organization, or department—or in your life.

If you really get serious about this exploration, you may begin scheduling time to read and think about these issues and begin developing on paper your view of what's possible. Of course, your first drafts may not be your last; the point is to get started and to develop your capacities by practice and revision. A stellar example in this regard is Konosuke Matsushita, founder of Matsushita Electric (Panasonic in the United States), the global Japanese electronics firm. His vision extended 250 years into the future and was divided into ten 25-year pieces, each with its specific goals and strategic targets.

Visioning is more than daydreaming; it is demanding, mental *exercise*. Like physical exercise, it is hard work. In this effort, you must stretch your thinking, your view, and your basic assumptions about what could be. You must also be realistic and take into account all of the factual data available to you. If you daydream or practice visioning by assuming away thorny realities, you aren't helping your skills to develop at all.

Visions are like targets: they give organizational members something to shoot at. If the mission statement defines what we do, the vision statement puts an element of striving into it by giving people something to reach for. We present these two steps—defining a mission and creating a vision—as steps 1 and 2 of building an organizational charter. They become the bookends of the strategic manuscript of the organization; they frame what comes between. They rest, however, on the foundation of a set of values.

Values

A values statement addresses the question, "What principles will guide us as we strive to accomplish our mission and realize our vision?" *Values statements* are the declaration of the principles by which an organization will work on fulfilling its mission and realizing its vision. Values are arbitrary in that they may not be based purely on effectiveness; the ways to go about creating a future are unlimited.

What do you and your company stand for in terms of how you conduct your business?

A values statement outlines which ways or principles we will choose and which ways we will not. For example, one major company recently declared, along with many others, that Southeast Asia was going to be an area of emphasis over the next several decades. The company also declared that despite the widely held rule of thumb that political payoffs and kickbacks were common practice in many of these areas, they would walk away from business that required *that* kind of "unethical" behavior. This values statement is one that will surely impact profitability in a variety of ways.

In another example, the heads of the subsidiaries of a global communications firm that had grown by acquisition met to discuss strategy. As they talked about their futures, they began to discuss a small part of one business leader's activities that involved producing and broadcasting satellite programming. They discovered in the meeting that one of the acquired firms produced, among other things, adult films. The discussion recognized that this segment was growing and highly profitable. They talked about whether the firm wanted to be in this part of their industry's business. It was not purely a matter of "making money" because this subsidiary was highly profitable. It is another example of a values discussion that sets a tone for the rest of the organization as it implements its mission and strives toward its vision.

Walking the Values Talk

Many companies explicitly write down their values in published values statements; these statements are intended to help members and outsiders alike understand what the leadership stands for and how members of the organization should act. If these statements match the behavior of the managerial and leadership ranks of the organization, then the values are likely to become more and more instilled in the thinking and behavior of the rest of the organization. If actual leadership behavior contradicts stated values, employees and outsiders alike will begin to see the hypocrisy and attempt either to find other companies to do business with or to ignore the public statements and try to discern the underlying "true" values that guide the leaders' behaviors. For this reason, we cannot talk about leadership without talking about values and ethics—as discussed earlier.

A major challenge for leadership is to act in accordance with stated values. Few things are more demoralizing to a workforce than to see a gap between a leader's walk and his or her talk. When you reflect on, identify, and declare your values or your company's values, you need to be sure you are a good role model of them. If you are not, it would be better not to declare them.

Perhaps you have seen values statements before. One company printed a core values pamphlet that declared integrity, communication, accountability, respect, and excellence with helpful statements under each about how an individual might behave those values (e.g., "I act with integrity when I stand up for what I believe is right"). Another company prints unique cards that say, "Create a safe involved workplace; Passion for growing with our partners; Recognize and reward strong performance; Measurement defines progress; Speed a hallmark; Motivated, productive, and diversified workforce is our goal; and Honesty and integrity" as its guiding principles. Kwon Jae-Hwa's federation of 80 or so Tae Kwon Do schools offers five core values—Courtesy, Integrity, Perseverance, Self-Control, and Indomitable Will—hung for all to see on large signs in their practice areas.

When thought through carefully and modeled consistently, values statements can be especially useful. They can guide recruiting and promotion activities, daily decision making, product development, production activity, customer relationships, organization design efforts, daily work habits, government relations, advertising, and almost every feature of an organization's activities. They tell us how we might make decisions, but they don't tell us what to do. We still have to figure out how to get from mission to vision.

Strategy

A strategy statement is different from a mission statement, a vision statement, and a values statement. A strategy is a choice about the broad approach an organization is going to take toward executing its mission statement and, in so doing, develop a competitive advantage. In that sense, it is a "how" answer to the mission statement's "why" and the vision statement's "what." Rather than focusing on principles of activity as the values statement does, the strategy states explicit broad decisions about targets of business activity. In that sense, a strategy is more specific than a values statement, but less specific than a goals statement. A strategy distinguishes between the routes we take as we move toward a vision, yet allows the values we espouse to continue to govern our activities as we move along that route.

Strategy: What path will you take toward implementing your vision?

Strategies may relate to the various functions of the firm or to its overall direction. Strategy questions in finance, operations, marketing, and human resources need to be answered: "What is our financial strategy? What is our customer strategy? What is our related operational strategy? What is our employee relations strategy? Will we take the high-equity or the high-debt road? Will we go public? Will we take the *make* or *buy* road? Will we take the head-on or the niche competition road? Will we attack the high-margin or the low-margin segments? Will we source here or there? How will we attract and retain talent?" And so on. Strategies, by definition, are far-reaching in their implications and cannot be changed easily. Because most organizations formulate functional as well as corporate strategies to govern their financing, production operations, marketing, and organizational areas, effective organizations also create ways of tying these strategies together so that all are working in concert to support the overall strategy of the firm. The purpose of a strategy is to create a high-value-added, difficult-to-imitate, and relatively unique set of organizational capabilities.

So, in the end, this collection of strategies should target the development of relatively unique capabilities within the firm that focus on a set of customers. Note that capabilities are not competencies. We may think of *competencies* as relatively discrete and individual skills existing in various parts of the organization. They may have to do with technical aspects, customer relationships, process management, computer management, data collection, or other narrow areas. To become true competitive capabilities, though, competencies must be bound together and integrated in ways that augment each other in a powerful synergy. For example, a company may collect lots of data on customers; however, only when account managers are selected and trained to utilize those data in a timely fashion is the potential power of the organization unleashed (see, e.g., the story of Capital One[7]). These larger capabilities (in the Capital One case, the capability was segmenting and serving the financial credit market almost customer by customer) grow out of the individual specialized competencies, the encompassing organizational structures, the processes that bind them, and the leadership behaviors that grow them. Developed over time, these capabilities become hard to imitate and give the firm a distinction and a foundation for competing in the marketplace. Clearly, effective leadership has to do with working directly in the process that defines this strategic focus and in overseeing the way in which an organization develops its competitively advantageous capabilities.

The effective leader, then, is a leader of strategic change, who understands the mission, who sees and communicates relentlessly a clear vision, who stands on a solid values foundation, and who knows how to initiate and effect changes that will have a long-lasting and productive impact on the organization. This perspective begins to define the most common target areas for leading strategic change efforts: interventions in mission, vision, technology, organizational design, and acquiring, developing, and deploying human resources.

Operating Goals

Goals, of course, come in both short-term and long-term forms. Long-term goals begin to approach what constitutes a vision statement, whereas short-term goals provide milestones for the organization as they move toward the vision. Short-term goals help people decide what to do today and tomorrow and help them link mission and vision statements with their own work.

What indicators will you use to signal progress along the path toward your vision?

---

[7] Capital One Financial Corporation, Harvard Business School Case 700124.

For that reason, goals can be dangerous. If organizational members don't see, understand, and connect the mission, vision, values, and strategic statements, explicit or implicit, of the firm, they can easily lock onto short-term goals and begin to focus their activities on achieving those goals. As long as the short-term goals in place are carefully aligned with the other statements, this focus is fine. In a world that is changing at an increasingly frenetic pace, however, it is more and more difficult to select specific goals that are always aligned with meeting customer satisfaction. Political, economic, and social events now change so quickly that many firms find it harder and harder to establish realistic annual goals, much less two- or three-year plans.

Nevertheless, short-term (monthly, quarterly, or annual) goals *based on the right measures* can enormously help guide day-to-day efforts. Books have been written about how to select goals, how to write them, and how to work on them. The distillation of many of these books is that effective goals (personal or organizational) are tied directly to the mission and vision; they are specific, are clear, have deadlines, and are attainable. As noted in Chapter 7, though, seeking continuous improvement through the attainment of short-term goals may actually be the path to a lingering strategic death. Quarterly goals do not represent strategic vision. Indeed, quarterly results need attention; however, they are not the end, not the purpose of the organization. Executives who mistake quarterly goals for strategic vision lack the latter.

Conclusions

Leaders who confuse the concepts, content, and wording of missions, visions, values, strategies, and goals present an unnecessarily confusing picture to their organizational members. If you understand the differences between each of these elements of a comprehensive organizational charter, you will be better prepared to create content for each, to communicate the purpose of each, and to use them in organizing and energizing your organization's members. The process is diagrammed in Figure 8-3. If a would-be leader does not have a clear vision of what he or she thinks the organization should become, the north–east axis in our basic model is broken. Without this clarity, the leader's communications to the employees along the north–west axis will also be broken. This disruption results in employees who are unable to form their own view of what we're working on here—the east–west axis fails to form and the leader is relegated to constant supervision in guiding the employees toward short-term goals.

On the other hand, if leaders have a clear mission and vision in mind for the organization, they are much better prepared to talk with employees (and other constituents) at that level.

Then they can talk about why they're in business, what they're trying to create, and which customers they're trying to serve. This clarity helps employees to "see" the purpose of their work—a purpose that extends beyond the creation of wealth for other people. This vision begins to create the east–west axis and reduces the need for constant supervision. If the organizational design, including the selection, work design, appraisal, reward, and learning systems, of the organization supports the vision, the east–west axis will be strengthened, and further, the ties between employees and the organization, the south–west axis, will be strengthened.

The sixth and final element in an organizational charter, therefore, is the leader who defines the other elements. If the first five elements are fuzzy, uninspiring, or misaligned, we can only look to the leadership and ask, "Why don't you work on clarifying these elements?" This direct question can be threatening. Sometimes people will answer, "Because the questions are irrelevant to running the business." Usually, the executive does the "mission work" or "visioning" as a program that someone convinced him or her to do—rather than as something he or she believed in.

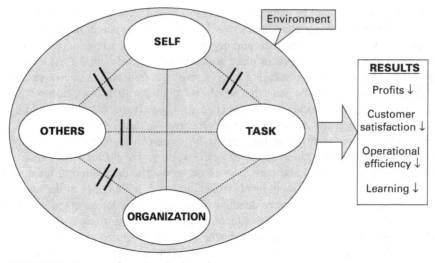

FIGURE 8-3   Impact of weak or broken charters

At the same time, interviews with employees often reveal that they are confused about where they are going and what they should be doing besides putting in time and collecting a paycheck. It is the widely known and well-used formula for mediocrity.

Sometimes executives will admit, "I don't know how," in which case, there's hope. The leader may be willing to learn and to invite colleagues to learn as well. As they work on developing their joint views on mission, vision, values, strategy, and goals, they build stronger teamwork and, more importantly, shared understanding of what the organization is all about. After working through

their charters, many individuals feel a renewed sense of purpose and energy for their work. Developing an organizational charter provides a powerful step toward learning and implementing Level Three Leadership.

An exercise with some work space in Workbook will allow you to work on your personal, work-group, and organizational charters. If you continue to refine your charters, revisiting them regularly and polishing and updating the language, your clarity of strategic thinking and intent will improve and your ability to communicate with your employees at Level Three will also expand.

Concepts Introduced in This Chapter

1. Many leaders confuse between the terminologies of strategy, often mistaking short-term operating goals for mission, strategy, or even vision.

2. The concept of a *charter* is a good way of clarifying this confusion. Charters consist of a mission statement, a vision statement, a values statement, a strategy, operating goals, and the leadership that defines them.

3. A mission statement defines the reason for the existence of the organization and, in a memorable, artful way, states its purpose.

4. A vision statement is a mental and verbal picture of what the leadership believes the organization could and should become. Vision does not result from the "right answer"—it is a question of desire, faith, and values.

5. A values statement makes explicit the principles upon which the company will do business. Values statements can be dangerous if leadership does not behave in accordance with the espoused or stated values.
6. A strategy is a broad set of decisions, functional and organizational, that define how the company is going to go about working toward its vision. Strategies may change from decade to decade in established firms, but yearly or quarterly changes are hardly strategic because of the time and effort it takes to mobilize resources to develop corporate capabilities to support the strategy.

7. Operating goals are often mistaken for strategic intent. They consist of short-term, quarterly targets on key indicators of progress along the strategic pathway. Poor choice of measures can sidetrack a strong strategy by sending mixed signals to the employees and encouraging behavior that may actually be self-defeating.
8. The charter concept can be applied to an organization, to the various divisions and work groups within it, and even to individuals. A strong personal charter will help a would-be leader select career opportunities, communicate effectively with others, and build a stronger plan for the organization.

Questions for Personal Reflection

1. What is the purpose of your life?
2. What is your vision for your future?
3. What values do you stand for—in your behavior as well as your speech?
4. What strategy are you pursuing in order to reach your vision?
5. What are your short-term annual goals that will indicate your progress along this strategic pathway?
6. What is the purpose of your work group? Can you articulate this purpose in a powerful, memorable way?
7. What is your vision for your work group or your organization? What do you think it should look like in 5 or 10 years?
8. What values are you modeling in your work group? What would your associates say if they were interviewed independently?
9. What is your strategy for moving toward the vision you see for your work group or your organization?
10. Why are you waiting and letting other people set the mission, vision, and strategy statements for your work group and/or organization?
11. What will you have to do differently to create clearer mission, vision, values, and strategy statements for your work group or organization?

CASELET FOR DISCUSSION

Andy was just assigned to lead the product development group at his company. He'd managed other departments before but always felt uncomfortable as to how to guide his people most effectively. The company produced a wide array of products for consumption worldwide. Andy had employees under his direct supervision at corporate headquarters and employees with matrixed responsibility in some 20 other facilities around the world. As he contemplated his new responsibilities, he wondered how best to organize his thoughts and how to begin his administration.

WORKBOOK

There are three forms in Workbook on pages 349–351 designed to help you think through your charters at the organizational, workgroup, and personal levels. The forms are too small to contain complete charters, but they may help you get started with notes as you sort through your strategic thoughts with regard to all three levels. You can construct them from simple two-column tables in any word processor.

CONTRIBUTING YOUR OWN CASELETS

Have you seen or experienced a situation involving the concepts introduced in this chapter? If so, and if you'd like to contribute your experience/situation to our case data bank, please visit http://faculty.darden.virginia.edu/clawsonj/ and click on the "Contribute new caselets" button.

SECTION III

SELF

9 SELF-LEADERSHIP

*The first step to wisdom is to realize that we cannot trust
implicitly our sense and our beliefs, yet to still be eager to
understand the reality that lies behind our partial
perceptions of it.*

—Mihalyi Csikszentmihalyi,
The Evolving Self, 242

This section explores the northern ball in our diamond ball of leadership,
the nature of human behavior. Humans tend to be creatures of habit. By
"habitual," I mean unthinkingly repetitive. We develop routines that tend
to dominate our lives. If you doubt this, ask yourself if you've ever been
on your way to the movies and found yourself half way to work instead.
The daily pattern of commuting creates in us a routine pattern that we
tend to re-create without thinking once we begin the pattern—by driving
out of the driveway. Or ask yourself if you've ever been sitting in class or
a meeting and seen someone about to speak and think to yourself, "I
know exactly what's coming—it's predictable."

Consider this question: Given all the people you've met thus far in life, what proportion of their visible (Level One) behavior would you guesstimate to be habitual? What do you think? Go ahead . . . write your guess here: _____ percent

Now that you've thought about Level One visible behavior, let me ask you about all these people you've met so far again: Given all the people you've met thus far in life, what proportion of *the way they think* would you guesstimate to be habitual? Again, write your estimate here: _____ percent

Finally, let's move to the shadowy world of semiconscious, preconscious, or subconscious values, assumptions, beliefs, and expectations (VABEs) about the way the world is or should be: Given all the people you've met thus far in life, what proportion of their underlying VABEs would you guesstimate to be habitual? Answer: _____ percent

You might imagine these would be difficult questions to answer in research. I have not yet found a definitive study that clarifies these questions. But I can tell you what nearly 2,000 upper-level managers and leaders worldwide would say. That is, if you ask these questions of practicing managers (country managers, functional managers, brand managers, etc.) in executive education settings, here's what they say:

These are high numbers. They suggest that the perception of managers all over the world is that most of the people they've met are creatures of habit. That is, we, you, tend to do things over and over again without thinking.

Level of Behavior	Global Average of Upper-Level Executives
Visible behavior	75%
Conscious thought	85%
VABEs about the way the world is or should be	95+%

There is a robust and fascinating literature on the topic of attention and mindfulness. One of the best summaries comes from Harvard professor Ellen Langer in her book *Mindfulness*. She notes, as have many others, that so many people go through life without really attending to what's taking place around them. And she gives guidance on how one might begin to develop a life that is more *mindful* of what's happening in one's environment.[1] Saul Alinsky, as reported by the noted organizational behavior scholar Henry Mintzberg, once noted, "Most people do not accumulate a body of experience. Most people go through life undergoing a series of happenings which pass through their systems undigested. Happenings become experiences when they are digested, when they are reflected on, related to general patterns, and synthesized."[2]

---

[1] Ellen Langer, *Mindfulness* (Reading, MA: Addison-Wesley, 1990).
[2] Saul Alinsky, *Rules for Radicals*, quoted by Jonathan Gosling and Henry Mintzberg in "The Five Minds of a Manager," *Harvard Business Review*, November 1, 2003, R0311C.

Many have attempted to help us humans become more mindful. These include not only university professors like Langer, but also martial artists who teach the value of "soft eyes" in order to attend to the *whole* simultaneously, futurists, who invite us to see broad trends before their impact burrows down into our individual lives so that we may prepare for them, and journalists, who always look for a story that reflects social and other patterns that emerge in society. Despite all of these efforts, we tend to learn habits early in life and then to perpetuate them throughout our adult and senior years.

Most of these patterns are rooted in repetition. It's oft said that repetition is the key to learning, and in a physiological sense this is true. At birth, a human child is utterly dependent on those around it for safety, care, and growth. As the child begins to become aware of its surroundings and of "objects" (like parents) in its surroundings, connections between some neurons are used and stimulated and others are not. Over the course of the first six years or so of life, the neural–neural and neural–muscular connections that are used repeatedly grow stronger and more active, whereas those that are not used tend to wither, atrophy, and eventually become resorbed into the body. Researchers measure the length of human activity cycles as an indicator of learning. Declining cycle times (the time it takes to perform a task) imply a "learning curve." The more one practices, the better one gets—the data suggest.

So, by "habitual" we mean "unthinkingly repetitive." And the relationship of this concept to leadership is this: If you or anyone cannot manage his or her own habits, much less the habits of others, how in any world could we be considered "leaders"?

THE NUMBER ONE QUESTION IN LIFE

This brings us to what I will assert is the most important question in life. I realize that's a bold statement. I discovered this question in what I consider to be one of the best books I've ever read, *The Evolving Self*, by the former chair of the Department of Psychology at the University of Chicago, Mihalyi Csikszentmihalyi.[3] Csikszentmihalyi's (pronounced chick-sent-mee-high-ee) basic reasoning is this: Given the level of habituality that we humans exhibit and given that much of these habits come from two main influences or "legacies" that we inherit—our genes and our VABEs (or as Richard Dawkins calls them "memes")—will you or any other individual ever be anything more than a vessel transmitting the genes and memes of previous generations on to the next?

The most important question in life: Will you ever be anything more than a vessel transmitting the genes and VABEs (memes) of previous generations on to the next?

Sadly, for most people, he argues, the answer is no, and the reason is that most of us are unwilling or unable to reexamine the VABEs we were taught as little children. Csikszentmihalyi notes that becoming a truly free adult means "transcending" some of the VABEs we, in our limited experience, accept as true.[4] As long as we are unwilling or unable to reexamine our core VABEs, we are unlikely to change our view of the world and the way we behave in it. Reflection to identify our core VABEs so that we can examine them as adults and not defenseless children is

---

[3] Mihalyi Csikszentmihalyi, *The Evolving Self* (New York: Harper Perennial, 1993).
[4] See Ibid.

critical to self-awareness and to effective self-leadership.[5] Next, we need to develop skills of influence based on our new insights about why people behave the way they do. The way we speak, our habits of communication, our habits of thinking, our measures for right and wrong, based on our historic VABEs, may no longer in a changing world be functional. Finally, we need to reexamine our roles and strategies in designing and leading change in organizations because organizations tend to reflect the VABEs of their leaders. People who are unwilling or unable to change or even think about changing will de facto repeat their past behavior in the future. And their lives will unfold as repetitions of previous habits developed early in life.

The definition of insanity is expecting different results while you continue doing the same thing.

EVERY ORGANIZATION IS PERFECTLY DESIGNED TO PRODUCE THE RESULTS IT'S PRODUCING

The same principle is true of organizations. Edward Deming, a process improvement consultant who worked first for the U.S. military following World War II and then for Japanese industry, is attributed with this statement: every organization is perfectly designed to produce the results it's producing. The logic is obvious: you get the results you're getting because of the way you behave in the world. If you want different results, you have to behave differently. Alcoholic Anonymous makes a similar statement when they say (probably quoting Albert Einstein), "The definition of insanity is expecting different results while you continue doing the same thing."

We can apply this principle to our own behavior as well: Every person is behaving in a way in the world to get the results they are getting. If we want different results, we need to do something differently. The implication of this is that all change begins with the individual (Figure 9-1). And this implies that "self-leadership" is the beginning of effective leadership in teams, organizations, and society.

The willingness and the capacity to reexamine habits are a sign or symptom of maturity. In other words, as small children, most of our VABEs and our habits are repetitively drilled into us. At

FIGURE 9-1 Can you change anything in the world "out there" without changing yourself first?

---

[5] Henry Mintzberg, *Managers Not MBAs: A Hard Look at the Soft Practice of Managing and Management Development* (New York: Berrett-Kohler, 2004).

some point, we make some kinds of transitions (not all the same) from defenseless children to adolescents to young adults to adults to seniors. If, along the way, we don't learn how to examine our habits and our VABEs, can we ever said to be "thinking for ourselves"? Clearly, if you and I had been born and raised in Central Africa, Scandinavia, Australia, Pakistan, China, or any of a hundred other regions in the world, we would likely, as adults, have a different worldview. Yet, as adults, most of us cling to those early habitual ways of thinking and believing we gained in *our* region with vigor. The willingness to examine our routines at all three levels is a sign that one is beginning to become an independent thinker. All thought and belief up to that point takes place within the confines of the outside-in–imposed thought structure of the surrounding culture and family. So, in that sense, the ability to, in Csikszentmihalyi's terms, "transcend" our genetic and memetic inheritances is a sign of maturity or adulthood or wisdom—and the beginnings of self-leadership.

Others besides Csikszentmihalyi have noted the importance of learning to lead oneself first. Charles Manz was one of the first to make this concept book title.[6] He's expanded that insight with Chris Neck more recently.[7] Ken Blanchard has linked this to his interest in the "one-minute manager."[8] In the end, one may ask, Okay, how do I begin to think about enhancing my self-leadership?

WHAT TO DO?

Csikszentmihalyi's term "transcend" does not mean throw out all of your childhood legacies. We can use the popular convention of "Keep, Lose, Add" here to say that when one examines (or reexamines) one's habits, there are some that are functional in today's global economy (and should be retained), perhaps some that are dysfunctional (and should be lost), and some that we don't have that we might acquire. There is a simple template in Workbook on page 362 that will help begin to make notes on these differences. You can begin to make entries there of the behaviors (at all three levels) that you want to "Keep, Lose, Add" as you work through the book, your course, or your career.

Keeping a journal of your thoughts and feelings is another excellent technique for gaining insight into your own thinking and believing. It's easier to "see" yourself when you're reading something you've written down previously. The ability to see oneself, to examine oneself with new, more adult and informed eyes, and to decide, intentionally, how to grow is a sign of maturity, wisdom, and a strong foundation for beginning to think about leading others.

One thing you might record in your journal would be your efforts to manage your Level One habits. That is, how well are you able to manage your routines about sleeping, drinking, eating, exercising, socializing, studying, and so forth? Many of these, including eating, smoking, drinking, exercising, and socializing, affect your health in significant ways. Despite that, many have not been able to change their habits to their own benefit. And this can lead to reduced energy in life and at work. The "Managing Your Energy" exercise on page 364 in the Workbook will also help you begin to think about which of your habits add to your energy level and which detract from your energy level. If, indeed, leadership is about managing energy, first in yourself and *then* in those around you, this is a great place to start.

---

[6] Charles Manz, *The Art of Self-Leadership: Strategies for Personal Effectiveness in Your Life and Work* (Englewood Cliffs, NJ: Prentice Hall, 1983).
[7] Chris Neck and Charles Manz, *Mastering Self-Leadership: Empowering Yourself for Personal Excellence* (Upper Saddle River, NJ: Prentice Hall, 2007).
[8] Ken Blanchard, *Self-Leadership and the One-Minute Manager* (New York: HarperCollins, 2006).

Stress

One of the key elements of self-leadership is the ability to manage one's own stress. Leadership roles are very demanding; the larger they are, the more demanding they become. Notice how the hair of the political leaders of major countries tends to gray quickly while in office. Stress has been shown to have significant impact on weight, cardio-vascular disease, various addictions like smoking, and performance. Effective leaders have learned how to manage their own stress so that they can continue to do their jobs well. They know that a little stress (eustress) is good, but that too much can be a killer.

I'm sure you've heard many of the common suggestions for managing stress; perhaps you've tried some or many of them. The fundamentals include proper sleep, proper diet, reduction of stimulants (like caffeine), frequent and regular exercise, meditation, healthy intimate relationships with significant others, hobbies, and regular breaks including vacations. While the research is pretty clear on how to manage stress, many manager/leaders do not implement these fundamentals in their lives. They get busy, they travel, the phone rings, the text messages flock in, problems arise, and the fundamentals get pushed aside. One former CEO of Honeywell Aerospace noted that he got so interested in his job that he often skipped lunch and dinner and worked well into the night. Then his travel schedule was very full which meant less sleep, rich dinners, entertainment engagements, and little to no exercise. When his cardiologist called into one of his meetings and said you need to get here now, he was forced to realize that while he may not have been cognizant (at Level Two) of his stress level, his body was. The cortisol was pumping, his waist was expanding, and his arteries were slowly clogging. Fortunately in his case, the doctors transplanted three arteries from his arm to his heart and prevented a major life threatening heart attack. He might have asked himself at one point, "Are my daily habits helping me to do more or are they shortening my career and my life?" We all could benefit from that "self-discussion" frequently. It is a question of self-leadership.

Conclusions

We humans tend to be creatures of habit and unless we confront that issue and learn to manage more intentionally our own behavior, our attempts to lead others may be seen as hypocritical and dictatorial. It takes an adult with a strong self-concept, an ability to live more inside-out than outside-in, and a determination to grow intentionally instead of reactively to excel in self-leadership.

Self-leadership implies the need for every individual to confront the question of whether they are acting in a truly adult and independent way or whether they are mere passengers riding on the tips of spears thrown by previous generations. Rising to this occasion creates a foundational platform for later inviting others to change—that is, for leading them.

Principles Introduced in This Chapter

1. Humans tend to be creatures of habit.
2. "Habitual" means unthinkingly repetitive.
3. Every organization is perfectly designed to produce the results it is producing. This may also be said of humans.
4. A central question is whether a person or an organization will ever have the capacity and the interest in reassessing its habits and restructuring them. Most people and most organizations tend not to.
5. Unless people, or organizations, can see, examine, and evaluate their underlying habits, they are likely to spend the rest of their lives repeating their history.
6. The willingness and the capacity to reexamine habits can be said to be a sign or symptom of maturity.

7. Bad habits can exacerbate the problems associated with stress. Effective leaders learn to manage their stress effectively through sleep, exercise, diet, relationships, and meditation.

8. Self-leadership seems like a contradictory term; however, the ability to lead or influence one's own behavior at every level is a precursor to becoming an effective leader among others.

9. Although we cannot always influence the world around us in the way we wish, we can always learn to lead ourselves to deal with the world around us in more productive ways. Unless we do so, we will live our lives as mere passengers on the tips of spears thrown by previous generations.

Questions for Personal Reflection

1. List the 10 most important values that guide your life. Where did you learn them? Who taught them to you?

2. See if you can identify five habits (at any level) in your daily routine. What are the repeating, mindless patterns do you follow from day to day? Assess each of these patterns on their contribution to your maturity and well being. Do they help or hinder and how?

3. Complete the "Keep, Lose Add" and "Managing Your Energy" exercises in Workbook at the end of the book.

CASELET FOR DISCUSSION

Every morning, Pat got up, made a cup of coffee, read the paper over a leisurely cigarette. After showering and dressing, he went out the door, turned to the right, got on the subway, and rode the 40 minutes to the station near work. On the train, Pat read from his latest novel. At the base of Pat's building, he bought a croissant and another cup of coffee and rode up the elevator. At his desk, he went through the mail in the inbox and spent an hour responding to overnight e-mails. Then he began to dive into the stack of paper associated with his latest project. Mid morning, Pat looked up. The clock said 10:23. Thirty feet away, a senior executive 30 years his senior was doing what Pat was doing only with larger numbers and behind a glass wall. Pat twitched his toes to get some blood back in them and went back to work. When Pat got home that night, he was exhausted. He prepared a short meal, heavy on carbohydrates, watched television for an hour and went to bed.

WORKBOOK

Complete the "Managing Your Energy" exercise on page 364 and the "Balancing Your Life" exercise on page 371 of Workbook. Consider how well you manage yourself on various dimensions of life. Are you "leading yourself" so that you'll be prepared to do the things in life that you want to? What would you like to do better to become better prepared?

Online versions of the "Managing Your Energy" and "Balancing Your Life" exercises are available at www.CareerNextStep.com. A simple version of the "Balancing Your Life" exercise in spreadsheet form is available online at http://faculty.darden. virginia.edu/clawsonj.

CONTRIBUTING YOUR OWN CASELETS

Have you seen or experienced a situation involving the concepts introduced in this chapter? If so, and if you'd like to contribute your experience/situation to our case data bank, please visit http://faculty.darden.virginia.edu/clawsonj/ and click on the "Contribute new caselets" button.

10 A LEADER'S GUIDE TO WHY PEOPLE BEHAVE THE WAY THEY DO

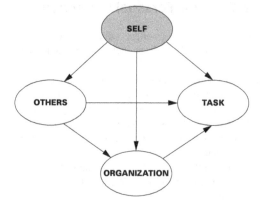

*To be autonomous means to act in accord with one's self—
it means feeling free and volitional in one's actions. When
autonomous, people are fully willing to do what they are
doing, and they embrace the activity with a sense of
interest and commitment. Their actions emanate from their
true sense of self, so they are being authentic. In contrast,
to be controlled means to act because one is being
pressured. When controlled, people act without a sense of
personal endorsement. Their behavior is not an expression
of the self, for the self has been subjugated to the controls.
In this condition, people can reasonably be described as
alienated.*

—EDWARD DECI,
Why We Do What We Do[1]

---

[1] Edward L. Deci and Richard Flaste, *Why We Do What We Do* (New York: Penguin Books, 1996), 2.

Leaders want to influence people, so unless they understand why people behave the way they do, their efforts may have random, perhaps unpredictable, even alienating effects. Despite the fact that leaders want to get more energy out of people, they may, in fact, do just the opposite. For instance, perhaps you have been trying to get subordinates to do something at work, and no matter what you do, they just won't respond. On the other hand, maybe your boss has been asking you to do something, and you resist. When people don't do what we want, we are often perplexed by their visible behavior. If you've ever asked yourself, Now, why did he do that? you've wrestled with this problem. At home, at work, or at play, you have no doubt observed people doing things that were, to you, unexpected, unusual, or totally illogical. And you have probably seen two people in similar situations respond in different ways.

All of these incidents raise the question for would-be leaders of why people behave the way they do. Volumes have been and continue to be written about this complex subject, but leaders must have—in fact, we could say *do* have—some kind of mental map of human behavior. Even if it's not conscious (at Level Two), everyone carries a mental model or map of human behavior. The question is whether your conscious (Level Two) and not-so-conscious (Level Three) understanding of human behavior is accurate and therefore functional.

This chapter will build on the concept of habituality introduced in Chapter 9, by introducing some fundamental principles about human behavior that should help you understand people no matter where you encounter them. In Chapter 11, then, we offer a summary framework that has proved pragmatic and powerful for leaders in a variety of situations.

TWO LEGACIES

We are all born with two powerful legacies. The first is our genetic inheritance. We live in an era in which the human genome—30,000 genes strong—was mapped for the first time. We have a map of these blueprints of life, but we are still learning what they do. And that understanding is changing rapidly. What *do* our genes determine?

Any parent will tell you that children, even those raised in the same environment, have innate and unique tendencies. Clearly we inherit a variety of characteristics from our parents. They include not only physical characteristics like eye and hair color, metabolism, and body shape, but also behavioral templates or tendencies. Our genes, it appears, may affect much more than our stature, hair color, and the more fundamental species-specific instincts or drives such as breathing, eating and drinking, reproducing, and socializing.

Nigel Nicholson at the London Business School, for example, makes a case that many aspects of our human behavior, including the seemingly universal tendency to create hierarchies, is an inherited trait that is "hardwired" into our DNA strands.[2] Is there a leadership gene? Are people who "rise to the top" driven by their makeup to do so? What if people do not have the leadership gene? Can they, too, learn to lead more effectively?

Sorting out the balance between nature and nurture is a difficult and interesting question.[3] It may be, for example, that we can no more "teach" a hard-nosed, autocratic leader to be kind and

---

[2] Nigel Nicholson, "How Hardwired Is Human Behavior?" *Harvard Business Review,* July–August (1998): 135, 98406. See also Ibid., *Executive Instinct* (New York: Crown Business, 2000).
[3] See, for example, Matt Ridley, *Nature via Nurture: Genes, Experience, and What Makes Us Human* (New York: HarperCollins, 2003).

gentle than we can "teach" a person not to be allergic. It may be that we can no more teach a quiet, shy, unassuming person to be a firebrand of inspiration than we could teach a person to grow a tail. Humans remain, however, one of the most adaptable species on earth. Ridley points out that in some remarkable ways, our "nature" is actually shaped by the way we are "nurtured" or raised and taught.

THE BRAIN

At the same time, our genes determine, among other things, the modus operandi of that most amazing of human organs, the brain. At birth, human brain cells are proliferating at the rate of 250,000 cells per minute. Each of these cells or neurons has the capacity to connect with 10,000 other neurons. The number of possible connections is staggering. Consider also that the brain is awash in some 300 hormones. The function of these hormones and how they relate to each other is an ongoing focus of intense research and study. And it appears that the imbalance of some of these hormones can have significant effects on human behavior.

John Ratey describes what he calls "shadow syndromes," the mild forms of major mental disorders that many of us carry around with us.[4] These shadow syndromes include depression, hypomania, rage disorder, attention deficit disorder (ADD), obsessive compulsive disorder (OCD), bipolar disorder (BPD), social anxiety disorder (SAD), and other similar conditions. One either has these conditions or does not. Rather they exist on continua, so that a person may have mild, moderate, or severe symptoms of these various conditions. Ratey and Johnson assert that these symptoms are largely, interestingly, milder forms of autism. Autism is, oversimplifying, getting stuck on one aspect of emotional existence that affects an individual's ability to relate to others and to the world.

Although all these various kinds of shadow syndromes are observable around us almost daily, one of the most common is ADD. ADD is a set of symptoms that includes difficulty focusing on one thing at a time. One way to think of it is that people with ADD don't have a "buffer" between them and the outside world like other people do. Most people, for example, can go to the grocery store or the video store and browse peacefully among the multitude of options. People with ADD, however, often find those kinds of environments overstimulating and overwhelming. Their minds cannot filter out all the options, so they experience them all at once, and it's mentally exhausting. The buffer that most of us have allows us to screen out the irrelevant stimuli surrounding us and helps us focus on one thing. This capability is a big help in relationships, because most of us can overlook or screen out the little interpersonal mistakes that people often make. People with ADD tend to get overly angry at little things and often conclude that others are conspiring against them or being rude or cruel when they are not.

Further, this buffer also allows us to censor our thoughts—it provides a screen between our Level Two thoughts and our Level One behavior. People with ADD experience difficulty with this task, so they tend to blurt out whatever they are thinking or feeling—and in ways that others often find confusing and disconnected. People with ADD may struggle to find the right words or link multiple arguments in a single sentence—or sentence fragment.

Children with ADD can be exasperating to parents and teachers; employees with ADD can be equally exasperating to employers and would-be leaders. Approaches that work for people with milder forms of the shadow syndromes may not work for those with moderate forms, which raises the issue of medication. It's a controversial issue; many feel that society overprescribes

---

[4] John J. Ratey and Catherine Johnson, *Shadow Syndromes: The Mild Forms of Major Mental Disorders That Sabotage Us* (New York: Bantam, 1998).

pills for children and adults as "the answer for everything." Those who have not lived or worked with people with ADD, SAD, or OCD may not understand how challenging these disorders, even in their milder forms, can be.

To the extent that these syndromes are genetically derived—that is, a manifestation of biochemical imbalances in the brain—all the psychological counseling and coping mechanism training in the world won't help. If your pancreas doesn't produce enough insulin, you cannot will your pancreas to do so; it requires medication. Likewise, if your brain's chemicals are a bit out of balance, straining to cope with life won't make it easier. Because the brain contains so many chemicals and our knowledge of their function and interplay is limited, those who seek medication to help often find that it's usually a process of trial and error to find the right medication for their particular imbalance. People who have mild forms of these syndromes may benefit from reading Ratey and Johnson's book. They should also not feel any stigma attached to trying to find the right medication blend that will help them deal with the vicissitudes of life with poise.

Whatever your genetic legacy is at birth, you also get a second inheritance—the "gift" of your parents' and your surroundings' memes.

YOUR MEMETIC LEGACY

Memes are the ideas and beliefs, the values, assumptions, beliefs, and expectations (VABEs), that people develop and pass on to others over time.[5] Memes are what Richard Brodie called "viruses of the mind."[6] Memes, like genes, are packets of information passed on from generation to generation.

Memes also behave in many ways like genes. Memes reproduce, like viruses, until their environment is no longer hospitable and they die.[7] Sometimes they seem to have a life of their own and spread wildly; other times they fade away. "Waste not, want not" is a meme that developed during economically difficult times. "Never touch a person with your left hand" is a meme that spawned in nomadic nations without modern hygiene facilities. The "stirrup" is a meme (mental concept) that was born in medieval times, spread, and ultimately changed the whole face of the global political and military power structure.[8]

We can think of memes as the mental building blocks (complementing the genetic physical building blocks) upon which we erect our behavior. We are quite aware at Level Two of some of our memes. Other memes are so common and essential to us that they are invisible to us, like water to swimming fish. Ideas that we take for granted, electricity for one, were unknown for much of human history. Our current set of memes, wherever we were born, were propagated, refined, and passed on from previous generations.

REFLECTION

One of the fundamental challenges in life, and especially in leadership, is to become more aware of our personal memes and to decide, as adults, which we will perpetuate and which we will work to eradicate, in ourselves, our progeny, our associates, and our subordinates. If we do not undertake this reflective reexamination, we live our lives as little more than riders on the tips of spear thrown by previous generations, perpetuating their thoughts, beliefs, and assumptions about the way the world

---

[5] Richard Dawkins, *The Selfish Gene* (Oxford: Oxford University Press, 1976).
[6] Richard Brodie, *Viruses of the Mind* (Seattle, WA: Integral Press, 1996).
[7] Susan Blackmore, "The Power of Memes," *Scientific American*, 283, no. 4 (October 2000): 52–61.
[8] Jared Diamond, *Guns, Germs, and Steel* (New York: Norton, 1999).

is and ought to be. To consciously transcend our memetic endowment, in ways that we cannot do with our genetic endowment, is the mark of a truly mature adult and of a visionary leader.[9] Because memes, whether conscious, subconscious, or preconscious, guide our behavior and shape our motivations, unless we see and examine them, we are not truly architects of our own lives, much less the lives of others. Instead, we are mere executors of the blueprints of previous generations.

Most leaders, however, take a decidedly simpler view of human motivation. They simply focus on what they can see and not what might cause it. This willingness to ignore cause and effect in leaders' thinking can lead to disastrous results. Most leaders in history, particularly business leaders, I assert, have been Level One Leaders who targeted only Level One, visible human behavior. They tended to ignore both the genetic and the memetic endowments that people have. Was it Einstein who said, "For every complex problem there's a simple answer that's both elegant and wrong"? Level One Leadership is the simple approach that gets one to "good enough"—and it's a formula for mediocrity. If we want to get people to bring their best efforts to work, we need to start by understanding them at the level of their core beliefs and values, the memes that make them tick.

HUMAN BEGINNINGS

We are born a blank slate. If you hold a two-day-old infant in your arms, you will notice that it cannot even follow the movement of your hand in front of its eyes. It is not surprising, considering that for the first nine months of existence, human fetuses are an integral part of another human being. Whatever their preliminary awareness of life, it is enveloped entirely inside another. Then, when we are born, we are utterly dependent on others for sustenance. We begin a three- to six-month process of becoming aware of our individuality—that we are separate, that we are no longer totally encased in the identity of another human being, that we are "me." The genetic condition of the slate surely affects us, *and* what we write on that slate also has a huge effect.

As this awareness emerges, at least five fundamental questions arise. They are not conscious questions, but they represent issues that must be resolved one way or another. Their answers begin to shape our sense of individuality, our sense of our place in the world, and our fundamental stance in it. The questions are

1. When I'm cold, will I be made warm?
2. When I'm hungry, will I be fed?
3. When I'm wet, will I be made dry?
4. When I'm afraid, will I be comforted?
5. When I'm alone, will I be loved?

If these questions are answered affirmatively, we tend to feel (rather than think) that we are cared for, that we have a place in the world, and that life, and more particularly, the key people in it, is supportive, confirming, and comfortable. We begin to learn that although "we" are not "they," "they" are good. We begin to ascribe to the objects of our attention, our parents, and attributes of caring, concern, and dependability, which we generalize to other objects or people in life.[10]

If we get insufficient answers to these questions, we tend to develop different feelings—that we are not cared for (as much as we want/need), that we may not have a place in the world (as much

---

[9] Mihalyi Csikszentmihalyi, *The Evolving Self* (New York: Harper Perennial, 1993).

[10] For more detail on the object relations theory of human mental development, see N. Gregory Hamilton, *The Self and the Ego in Psychotherapy* (Northvale, NJ: Jason Aronson, Inc., 1996); and Jill Savege Scharff and David E. Scharff, *The Primer of Object Relations Theory* (Northvale, NJ: Jason Aronson, Inc., 1995).

as we want/need), and that life and others in the world are not supportive, confirming, or comfortable (as much as we want/need). Of course, no parent is able to be there all the time. Sometimes when we are cold, hungry, wet, afraid, or alone, mother does not come. The subsequent uncertainty can lead us to question the security of the world around us.

If the questions are answered insufficiently too often, we begin to develop "holes" in our personalities, or uncertainties, even fears, about our place in the world. Sometimes these holes are small; sometimes they are quite large. Studies of chimpanzees in France, for example, showed that if a baby chimpanzee was left alone without motherly comfort, yet supplied with more than enough shelter, warmth, light, food, and water, the baby eventually would die. In humans, too many negative responses to their basic, but deeply felt needs may lead children to a feeling of uncertainty or even betrayal. The noted English psychologist Melanie Klein calls it the "good breast/bad breast" phenomenon: part of the time I get what I want; some of the time, I don't, and that makes me angry with the very person who bore me. It can become a big psychological dilemma for a person, especially if the negative responses outweigh the positive ones.

These "holes" in our personalities can be influential in our lives. If they are large enough, they can persist, perhaps even dominating our adult activities for decades, even our whole lives. Let me give you an example. One day a student came to see me. She came in, shut the door, sat down, and began sobbing. I said, "What's the matter?" She said that she had just gotten the job of her dreams, making more money than she thought she could make, with the very company she had always wanted to work for. "Hmm," I said, "what's the problem?"

She had called her mother and reported her success to her mom, and within 15 seconds the conversation had turned to her mother's charity work, her latest accomplishments, what she was working on, how many accolades she had received lately, and so on. Then, this student said to me, "You know, it's been that way my *whole* life. Every time I've tried to talk to her about me, it quickly turns to being about her!"

This example shows two apparent emotional holes: one in the student and one in the mother. Consider what would cause a mother to behave in such a way at the moment of her daughter's highest professional achievement to date. It may well have been that this mother, when she was a child, did not get sufficient positive responses to the five fundamental questions mentioned earlier. When she needed comforting, she didn't get it. When she needed loving, she didn't get enough of it. With that hole inside her personality, she began searching for ways to "fill it in" through achievements and, later, relationships in life, trying to find ways to get the love, affirmation, and comforting that she did not get as a child.

Then, when she became a mother, her child became another means of filling in those holes. Unwittingly, she may have used her infant to love her and to affirm her importance. Instead of telling her daughter that she loved her, she may have said things like, "If you loved your mommy, you'd stop crying so I could get some sleep." Or "If you loved your mommy, you'd toilet train sooner, so I didn't have to deal with this mess." How many times a day does a mother interact with her infant or toddler children? The repetitive nature of these patterns can have a deep and long-lasting effect. In the process, the child did not get what she needed. So she grew up with a hole in her personality, such a big hole that when she was most happy and successful, her first thought was to call her mother and seek, one more time, recognition of her existence—and got, one more time, just the opposite.

Her mother was unable to focus on her daughter's achievement even later in life, and the daughter was unable to allow the reality of her success to be enough—she had to seek it from her mom. The danger, of course, is that the daughter will marry, become a mother, and repeat the process over again. In this way, these holes get passed from generation to generation.

We can observe elsewhere in adult life the behavioral result of these "holes" developed in infancy. When you meet someone at a cocktail party and the entire conversation revolves around their life, interests, hobbies, and goals, you might begin to wonder whether they aren't trying to fill in a hole, by now a habitual behavior, by keeping the spotlight of attention on themselves. Maybe you have had situations where you are in a conversation with a small group and another person comes up and somehow changes the topic of conversation (regardless of what the group was talking about) to his or her own agenda. Why do people engage in this kind of behavior? Often it is because they did not get what they needed as a small infant, and unknowingly they spend the rest of their lives trying to fill in that gap, trying to get the attention and affirmation that they did not get as a child. Melanie Klein[11] and Alice Miller[12] describe this as a "gift" that parents pass on to their children. This "gift" is the way that children learn to deal with the natural conflicts, small or large, inherent in going from being totally and completely cared for (as a fetus) to a world in which even those closest to us are inconsistent in their love and caring.

The problem is that we cannot fill in these holes later in life. The attempt to do so is an unending source of frustration and emotional anguish. Miller makes this point, as does Gail Sheehy.[13] However many achievements we may attain, however much money we make, however many buildings we may build, however many accolades and awards and prizes we may win, they will not fill in these holes left by parents who could not give what we needed at the time of infancy.

We can, however, recognize these holes and where they came from and, in that recognition, begin the necessary work of letting go of the desire to fill the hole. We can grieve the fact, if necessary, that we didn't get what we wanted or needed, and move on by learning to accept ourselves and our right as human beings to take up space in the world. In Klein's terms, we have to come to terms with the "good breast/bad breast" dilemma and reach reparation of the conflict by acknowledging this reality, perhaps grieving at the recognition and then move on. In Csikszentmihalyi's terms, we need to learn to transcend our inherited holes and rise above them.[14]

These fundamental five questions, however, imply a sixth leadership-related question that lingers throughout our lives: How can I get other people to do what I want? As we gain positions of influence, we develop strategies for influencing others holistically or "hole-listically." Perhaps we learned early on that bullying worked most of the time. Perhaps we learned that pretending to be pitiful elicited the desired results. Perhaps we learned that being the best at anything would get us the adoration we craved internally. These and other strategies all have pros and cons associated with them.

SOLIDIFYING THE TENDENCIES

Although much of this "drama," as Alice Miller calls it, takes place in the first three months to three years of life, the early tendencies, some say, tend to gel or set sometime in the first decade of life. Morris Massey[15] hypothesized that "what you were when you were ten years old" pretty much determined the basic values of your life that would shape your behavior. By then, the basic answers to the five questions have been repeated so many times that one has come to understand the world in terms of those answers. A personal example may help to explain. My father grew up in the Great Depression in the 1930s. His family grew vegetables in a small plot of vacant ground

---

[11] Melanie Klein, *Love, Hate and Reparation* (New York: Norton, 1964).
[12] Alice Miller, *The Drama of the Gifted Child* (New York: Basic Books, 1997, 1979).
[13] Gail Sheehy, *Necessary Passages* (New York: Bantam, 1984).
[14] Mihalyi Csikszentmihalyi, *The Evolving Self: A Psychology for the Third Millennium* (New York: HarperCollins, 1993).
[15] Morris Massey, *The People Puzzle* (Reston, VA: Reston Publishing, 1979).

to have food to eat. Later in life, though, he made a small fortune building large motor hotels in Idaho. When we would go to visit him as adults, his idea of taking us out to dinner was "all you can eat for $4.99." Even though he could afford to eat at any restaurant in the city without blinking an eye, he could not let go of this core value imbued upon his personality in those early formative years. Perhaps you observed this kind of behavior in your own extended family, where a person hangs on to values that seem to have been imprinted about age 10 or earlier, yet no longer seem relevant to the present situation.

Recognizing the Similarities and Differences

This same phenomenon is commonly portrayed in the popular press by references to Generation This or Generation That (Baby Boomers, Generation X, Generation Y, etc.). The hypothesis is that the current generation (however difficult it is to define when one begins and another ends) has some common core tendencies of which we, business and political leaders, should be aware. To the extent that broad societal influences can imprint themselves on young (about 10 years old), impressionable minds, these portrayals may hold some truth. The question then is, How, if at all, can we begin to see categories of humans and how they might be influenced by leadership? When we think about why people behave the way they do, we might note at least seven levels of similarity and dissimilarity.

In some ways, every human is like every other human, and in some ways, every human is unlike every other human.

---

   1. *Humankind:* Some human characteristics are universal. In addition to our DNA, our bodily shapes, and the fundamentals of breathing, drinking, eating, and reproducing, other characteristics seem to mark all people: humor, smiling, laughing, socializing, playing, and so on. William Glasser postulated that we all have five basic needs: survival, love and inclusion, power, freedom, and fun.[16]

   2. *Regional culture:* In distinct ways, Scandinavians, for instance, are different from Northern Europeans in predictable patterns and Latin Americans are different from North Americans.

   3. *National culture:* People from ethnically similar "regions" learned over the years to behave in some dissimilar ways. For example, among Scandinavians (global region), Norwegians do things one way whereas Swedes choose another; among Latin Americans (global region), Mexicans can be differentiated clearly from Colombians in some ways.

   4. *Subnational culture:* Inside most nations, regional units of similarity are different from other subnational regions. In the United States, for example, Southerners do many things differently from Northerners or Westerners.

   5. *Organizational culture:* Corporations also develop cultures. The predictable ways that employees of one company behave can often be contrasted with the predictable ways that employees of other companies behave.

---

[16] William Glasser, *Choice Theory* (New York: HarperCollins, 1998).

6. *Family culture:* Regardless of where you live, your behavior is surely influenced by your family upbringing and principles. Some people litter whereas others don't, which is, for example, largely based on their familial training.

7. *Individuality:* We know from studies of twins that even with the same genetic endowment and environmental upbringing, people will vary and will differentiate themselves. Some features about each person are unique.

Leaders must take into account all of these levels of similarity and dissimilarity, whether one is opening a new plant overseas or trying to motivate an underperforming employee to do better. On some levels, we can treat all humans the same way, yet in others we must treat every individual differently—whether an employee in our own company or a business associate from another nation or global region. Every human being has a familial and a personal heritage that shapes what he or she says and does.

Sorting out the differences and similarities between these seven levels becomes a leadership dilemma. Can I influence every Saudi the same way? Can I treat every Southerner the same way—and expect strong followership behavior? Can I assume that all humans will work for money or for praise—and hope to get their best efforts? Unfortunately, many would-be leaders assume that their own set of values mirror those of others, and they fall back on their own view of the world in their attempts to lead and influence others. It is one of the most persistent problems in leadership roles worldwide. This assumption, and others related to it, falls into the category of assumptions we make about how to lead and manage others.

MOTIVATION

The vanilla-flavored leader's view of motivation generally includes two ideas—rewards and punishments. We hold a "carrot" out in front of people and expect that they will move ahead in order to get the carrot. If that doesn't work, then we stand behind and beat their backsides with a whip. If that doesn't work, we often throw our hands up in dismay and exclaim, "I just don't know how to get these people moving!" As Harry Levinson[17] pointed out, when we use the carrot-and-stick model of motivating others, what we really mean, given the image of what stands in between the carrot and the whip, is, "I just don't know how to get these jackasses moving." But we deceive ourselves if we conclude that people are, like jackasses, necessarily unmotivated, lazy, stupid, or stubborn just because they won't do what seems so eminently rational to *us*.

One reason that the reward/punishment model does not always explain human behavior well is that one person's reward may be another person's punishment. When we extend the same carrot to everyone in the organization, only those who value that reward will respond. When we use the same whips (threats) on everyone in the organization, not everyone responds. Clearly, a person's values greatly influence the effectiveness of any particular carrot or stick. If the person doesn't value the carrot or fear the stick, he or she is not likely to respond to its use. Expectancy Theory gives us a partial answer to this question by suggesting that people are motivated to do things that they expect they can do and when they can expect to receive a reward that they value, but are not motivated if they do not value the reward.[18]

---

[17] Harry Levinson, *The Great Jackass Fallacy* (Boston, MA: Harvard Business School Press, 1973).
[18] David A. Nadler and Edward E. Lawler III, "Motivation: A Diagnostic Approach," in J. R. Hackman and E. E. Lawler (eds.), *Perspectives on Behavior in Organizations* (New York: McGraw-Hill, 1977).

We return again to the question of Level One versus Levels Two and Three. Many leaders say that we should not concern ourselves with what goes on *inside* a person because we cannot observe it or manage it. These followers of B. F. Skinner subscribe, knowingly or not, to the notion of behavior modification.[19] Because thoughts, feelings, and values cannot be seen, these followers argue, they cannot be managed, or if so, only poorly. People who attempt to understand or explain such unobservable things are thought to be charlatans and speculators. Rather, they say, managers should focus on the external behavior and then try to shape that behavior by rewarding the desired behavior and punishing the undesirable behavior. In one management seminar, the instructor suggested that managers should not be managing people but rather the inputs to and outputs of people, making sure that the desirable outputs were being rewarded and the undesirable outputs were being ignored or punished. This style is clearly the behavioral, Level One approach, susceptible to creating significant loss of energy.

Most people who change jobs, leave corporations, or withdraw from involvement in their work/organizations do so in large measure because their talents, interests, and abilities are being ignored and wasted. They see large gaps between who they are, what they want to be and can become, and what the organization asks of them. The suggestion that managers should focus on the outputs rather than the people who create them only further alienates them from organizational life and productivity. The view of humans as merely resources continues the corporate tendency to dehumanize the work experience—and perpetuates a meme that says, "People are homogeneous, predictable, replaceable parts. If one doesn't work, get another." Frederick Taylor and others who subscribed to scientific management principles unleashed this meme on the world.[20] People have proved to be much more complex than the principles of simple Level One reward and punishment would suggest. And yet, again, most managers seem to subscribe to this common meme, that as managers they are in control of their associates' behavior.

THE FREEDOM OF CHOICE

As a leader, how much of your employees' behavior do you want to control? Think about it. On a scale from 0 to 100 percent, how much of your employees' behavior would you like to control? Ninety percent? Why? Ten percent? Why? Consider also, the consequences, pros and cons, of the level of desired control that you chose Figure 10-1.

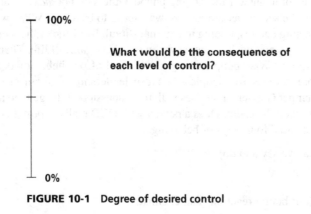

FIGURE 10-1   Degree of desired control

TABLE 10-1	Principles of Control Theory

1. I know what's right for you.
2. I have a right to tell you what's right for you.
3. I have a right to punish you if you don't do what's right for you.

William Glasser[21] clarified this *control theory.* Every child born into the world is utterly dependent on its parents for survival, which is the condition in which the memes of control theory thrive. Most parents, regardless of where they are in the world, subscribe to the three central principles of "control theory," namely, that (1) I know what's right for you, (2) I have a right to tell you what's right for you, and (3) I have a right to punish you if you don't do what I think is right for you. See Table 10-1.

When children reach their teens, many of them begin to rebel against the principles of control theory. Oddly, though, many, if not most, of them never reject those principles; they simply move to the other side of the fence and become promulgators of the control theory memes rather than recipients.

The alternative, of course, is *choice* theory. The central principles of choice theory are (1) every person knows what's right for him- or herself; (2) no one has a right to tell other people what's right for them; and (3) you should not punish people for doing the harmless things they choose to do. These memes, or VABEs, are at the heart of much of human behavior. Issues from the struggle between democracy and autocracy, between capitalism and planned economies, and between dictatorial leadership and participative leadership revolve around these central memes and how they play out in life and society.

Many people subscribe, perhaps unwittingly, to control theory when they believe that they can only respond to external stimuli (rather than choosing to respond or not), they can make other people do what they want them to, and it is their right or responsibility to reward or punish others depend zng on whether they do what one wants them to do. This meme cluster carries with it many dysfunctional consequences, including the central one of drastically one's range of choices in the world.

In the view of choice theory, *everything* you do is a choice—whether you recognize it or not. You can choose not to answer the ringing phone. Others do not *make* us angry when they do not do what we say (the second assumption)—we *choose* to be angry. When we lose sight of our own volition in selecting and responding to external stimuli by virtue of the memes within us, our range of options narrows and we become pawns in the chess game of life. Then, we begin to lose our intrinsic motivation. Wise people recognize that all of our behavior is chosen—and that leaders create more choices for people—because leadership is about creating a voluntary response. We can temper Glasser's premises with the discussion of the genetic influences on brain chemistry and subsequent behavior. Does a person with OCD really *choose* to obsess?

Glasser also posited four ways of behaving:

1. Activity (what we say and do)
2. Thinking
3. Feeling
4. Physiology (our bodily reactions and chemistry)

[21] William Glasser, *Choice Theory* (New York: HarperCollins, 1998).

Total behavior, therefore, comprises of all four components. These components are, not surprisingly, remarkably consistent with our general model of the levels of human behavior and leadership. The key point, he argued, is that we all *choose* how we behave in each arena, including the emotional one. If a loved one dies, for example, most people would say that we have no choice but to be depressed. Glasser argues that "depressed" is a choice, too. With a different perspective, we might find contentment, peace, and even harmony and happiness at this time. Glasser clarified the insight of the Roman stoic philosophers: it's not events that affect people, rather it's the view that people take of those events that affects them. Events do not control us, really; neither do other people. We choose to allow them to control us and our reactions. The truth is we *choose* our responses to the world—based on our memes or VABEs. Understanding this concept deeply is enormously freeing for most people.

Csikszentmihalyi argued that the way we get to this freedom is to pause and review our memes or VABEs when we're old enough and mature enough to do so. In fact, he'd argue that the ability to reflect on, review, and refine our core memes or VABEs is a good definition of maturity. As children, we have no choice—we inherit the memes given us. As adults, we have a choice—if we choose to take it. As adults we can become aware of our memes and our personality holes, and exercising courage, we begin to pick and choose which ones we would like to retain and utilize. In that process, we become freer, more mature, more autonomous, and more authentic. When others encourage that process in us, we thrive.

The lesson for leaders-to-be is that finding ways to support the autonomy of others engenders powerful followership, whereas persisting in the core beliefs of control theory weakens our ability to influence others. People want to be autonomous and free. They want to feel as though they are in charge of their lives, and if you want to get the most out of them as a leader, you'll not overlook this reality.

We stated earlier in this book that *the* fundamental question in life is, Will you ever be anything more than a vessel transmitting the genes and memes of previous generations on to the next? We also stated that for most people the answer to this question is no. For people who want to be leaders, the question is, Are you able to learn anything about being a more effective leader, or are you of the mind-set that you are who you are and that's just the way it is? If you're willing to learn more, then Chapter 11 will introduce to you a model of human behavior that consolidates much of what was introduced here and provides a way of thinking about how to influence others at all three levels.

Concepts Introduced in This Chapter

1. We all have genetic and memetic legacies.
2. Genes seem to determine more behavior than we previously thought, possibly including leadership.
3. The biochemical balances of the brain often cause "shadow syndromes" (ADD, BPD, SAD, OCD, etc.), which in varying degrees can significantly affect behavior.
4. Three different kinds of memes or VABEs include distinction, strategy, and association.
5. Maturity is about being able to recognize and review our legacies and inheritances as adults—no longer as defenseless children.

6. The principles of control theory include (1) I know what's right for you, (2) I have a right to tell you what's right for you, and (3) I have a right to punish you if you don't do what I think is right for you.
7. The central principles of choice theory are (1) every person knows what's right for him- or herself, (2) no one has a right to tell other people what's right for them, and (3) you should not punish people for doing the harmless things they choose to do.

Questions for Personal Reflection

1. What genetic tendencies do you have? What can you do about them?
2. Do you believe that leadership is inherited? Why?
3. How and where have you experienced shadow syndromes in life? Which ones? How were they manifest in you? What did you do about them?
4. What were the five most important memes your parents taught you? What do you think of them today?
5. How often do you feel compelled to behave in a certain way? Why?
6. How would you relate the discussion here of control theory and choice theory to the earlier discussion of living inside-out or outside-in?
7. In your business, how much of your employees' behavior would you want to control? Why? What would the consequences be?
8. What memetic or genetic tendencies have you recognized and overcome so far in life? What was that like?

CASELET FOR DISCUSSION

Bob's behavior was perplexing Mary, his boss. She was concerned because although he had lots of energy and creativity, he seldom seemed to finish projects he began. He often seemed distracted in meetings and would often blurt out during discussions, interrupting others. Sometimes, he had a very strong temper and would criticize others sharply and then, five minutes later, wonder why everyone seemed so sullen. Further, Bob's work was characterized by flashes of brilliance interspersed with periods of seeming disengagement and inattention. Last month, Bob had come to Mary and asked for an advance on next month's pay check. Mary had been observing all of this and was wondering what to do with Bob.

CONTRIBUTING YOUR OWN CASELETS

Have you seen or experienced a situation involving the concepts introduced in this chapter? If so, and if you'd like to contribute your experience/situation to our case data bank, please visit http://faculty.darden.virginia.edu/clawsonj/ and click on the "Contribute new caselets" button.

11 | THE REB MODEL

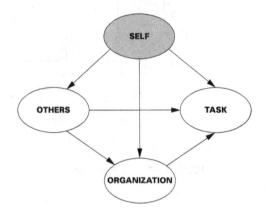

As a human, you have four basic processes, all indispensable to your survival and happiness: (1) You perceive or sense— see, taste, smell, feel, hear. (2) You feel or emote—love, hate, fear, feel guilty or depressed. (3) You move or act—walk, eat, swim, climb, and so forth. (4) You reason or think— remember, imagine, hypothesize, conclude, solve problems. Ordinarily, you experience none of these four basic processes in isolation.

—ALBERT ELLIS

Given the complexity of human behavior at Levels One, Two, and Three, leaders need a general model of human behavior that will help them get the kind of energetic behavior they want from their people. This model of human behavior must take into account genetic and memetic endowments and nurtured tendencies in order to explain why people behave the way they do and give us some practical tools to begin thinking about how to work with, how to communicate with, and

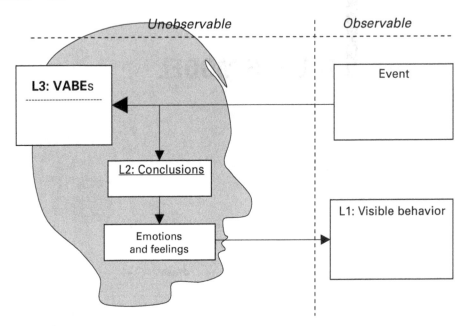

FIGURE 11-1   The REB model

how to lead others. This approach implies a model that recognizes thoughts and feelings along with behavior.

The work of Albert Ellis[1] and other "rational emotive" researchers provides such a foundation. The rational-emotive-behavior (REB) model shown in Figure 11-1 builds on Ellis's work and provides practicing managers a way of digging deeper, getting below the surface of human behavior, understanding human behavior and its motivations, and leading more effectively. The REB model includes several elements: events and our perceptions of them, values and assumptions we have about the way the world *should* be, conclusions or judgments about the present situation, feelings, and behavior ("activity" in Glasser's terms).

EVENTS

To paraphrase the common street meme, "Things happen." People speak to us. Or don't. Doors open. Or close. We get feedback on our behavior. Or we don't. It rains. Or it doesn't. All of these things are "events." We observe some of them, whereas we ignore others or don't see enough to pay conscious attention to. What we see when we observe makes a big difference—as already discussed in the earlier definition of the Leadership Point of View. Two people watching the same event may come away with different perceptions and conclusions. We can see what people do and hear what they say. How we interpret those events makes a big difference in our behavior. What a camera and microphone might capture may not be the same as what we perceive.

---

[1] Albert Ellis and Robert A. Harper, *A New Guide to Rational Living* (Hollywood, CA: Melvin Powers Wilshire Book Company, 1961, 1975, 1997).

PERCEPTIONS AND OBSERVATIONS

Observations and perceptions are not the same thing. An observation, as we use it here, means simply what would be visible to an impersonal, unemotional camera's eye. An observation is a *description* as opposed to a *judgment*. An observation would be, "John came in at 8:15 today." A perception, on the other hand, is a subset of what we might observe; it is what is left to our awareness after we've filtered out whatever it is that we filter out. Maybe we didn't notice what time John came in today at all. Maybe we didn't notice whether John was even at work today. So whereas a camera might record, without filtering, a series of events, we are constantly filtering and selecting what we will "see" or perceive. Whatever it is that comes in through our perceptual filters is what we see, even though it may be a small part of what happened.

VABEs

When we observe something, we immediately compare that event with our personal set of values, assumptions, beliefs, and expectations (VABEs) about the way the world is or should be. Any gap between what we observe and what we expect creates a problem. If no gap is noted, things are as they should be and we carry on without concern. VABEs are the beliefs we hold about the way the world should be or the way other people should behave. We can even have VABEs about our own behavior—and consequently judge ourselves by them. These "shoulds" and "oughts" make up our value systems. When we say that a person *should* do this or *should* do that, we are expressing one of our VABEs.

Our VABEs develop early and over many years, as discussed in preceding chapters. We learn them from our parents, our friends, our teachers, and our experiences. Proponents of transactional analysis (TA) call them our parental tapes or "scripts," the little messages that remind us of what our parents told us was right and wrong.[2] Our VABEs include more than just what others taught us, however; they also include our own conclusions about the way the world and the people in it operate.

For instance, one person watching the people around him work diligently to further their own fortunes might conclude at some point, "People are greedy." If this person continues to see this kind of behavior generally, he might begin to hold this conclusion as a relatively central assumption about why people behave the way they do. This assumption would be even further solidified if the person behaved that way himself. Table 11-1 lists examples of some common assumptions. Clearly, widely held VABEs will vary from culture to culture along the seven levels introduced in Chapter 10. Some of these examples may seem normal to you, others may seem foreign. That will depend on your culture, your upbringing, and your current set of VABEs.

The major thesis of this book is that an understanding of VABEs and how they shape behavior is essential to effective leadership. Some call it values-based leadership;[3] we call it Level Three Leadership. If you can understand a person's constellation of VABEs, you will have a much deeper understanding about why they behave the way they do—and therefore be much better prepared to lead them.

VABEs have certain characteristics that are important to remember:

1. *VABEs vary in strength.* Some of our basic beliefs are especially important to us. We put these beliefs at the core of our personalities. We all try to protect our core assumptions carefully. Peripheral assumptions, the ones that are less important to us, are more easily

---

[2] See, for example, Eric Berne, *Games People Play* (New York: Ballantine, 1964).
[3] Gilbert W. Fairholm, *Values Leadership* (New York: Praeger, 1991).

TABLE 11-1   Sample VABEs

1. Always clean your plate.
2. Always cross at the crosswalk.
3. Submit your will to that of the group.
4. The next life is more important than this one.
5. There is no next life.
6. Kindness is good.
7. Kindness is foolish.
8. You can't trust a _____.
9. A good father would have _____.
10. Always obey the boss.
11. Question authority.
12. People should give their best efforts to the company.
13. People should save their best efforts for their personal lives.
14. If you want it done right, do it yourself.
15. If you want it done right, find the right team.
16. Professional people should wear suits and ties.
17. You should always call your boss by his/her _____ name.
18. Never give a sucker an even break.
19. Always give the boss what he/she wants.
20. (Write in one or two that come to mind for you.)

changed than the core assumptions. Figure 11-2 shows a simple diagram depicting the concept that core VABEs are the ones that are likely to shape our behavior more powerfully than those at the periphery.

2. *VABEs vary considerably from person to person.* Although one person may believe that "a person should clean up her plate after dinner," the next person may not believe that at all. Some broadly held societal values and assumptions are shared by many within a culture. In fact, it is how we define a culture at one of the seven levels introduced in Chapter 6. If, however, you accept the notion that assumptions vary from person to person, then it follows that in order to understand why a person behaves the way he or she does, you have to understand something about that person's assumptions, not just about your own or about what you think the broader culture's assumptions are. Some authors call this way of thinking the "arrogance" of the Golden Rule: Why should we presume that others want to be

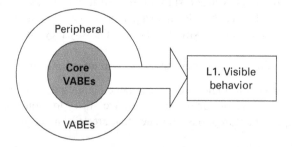

FIGURE 11-2   The importance of core VABEs

treated the way we want to be treated? They argue that the Platinum Rule would be "Treat others as they want to be treated." It is something that the human race has not been very good at since the beginning of recorded history.

3. *People have VABEs both about the way other people should behave (the external view) and about the way they themselves should behave (the internal view).* Humans have a unique capacity to judge themselves. In addition to being able to observe the behavior of others, we can observe our own behavior. We have developed VABEs that describe a "good" self. We might call this internal perspective of our VABEs the "ideal self." Our ideal self is our vision of how we "should" be. Some parts of this ideal self are more important than other parts—the important parts we defend vigorously.

Inside us all, hidden from view, are vast arrays of connected VABEs. Some we hold strongly; some we exchange for others rather readily depending on the evidence and where we got them. Some we use to judge external events, and some we use to judge ourselves. And, if we are wise, we will notice that our own VABEs do not necessarily match the VABEs of the person sitting next to us. This awareness opens a huge door of fascination and inquiry in life as we wonder, Why does that person behave the way he or she does? and, How might I best influence him or her? Part of the answer lies in the connection between the observed event and one's VABEs.

JUMPING TO CONCLUSIONS—CAREFULLY

The key to understanding why people behave the way they do is in the comparison between what they see and what they believe ought to be—the comparison between one's perceptions and one's VABEs. It is not events that take place around us that determine what we do; rather, it is the comparison we make between what takes place around us and our personal, basic assumptions about what ought to be taking place that motivates our activity. Notice in Figure 11-1 that the line to Conclusions comes out of the comparison between Events and VABEs, not directly from one or the other.

Consider a simple example. Suppose that you and a friend are playing golf together. You both hit off the tee, and you both drive into the woods. You believe that given who you are and your skill level, you should not drive out of bounds. You compare this perception to what just happened and realize a gap exists between the two. This gap is disturbing. At this point, another of your basic assumptions comes into play: you believe it is not becoming to a professional person to throw a temper tantrum, so you stifle your curse, work hard to control yourself, and keep the anger in. Yet you experience anger; your face may even grow flush, but you keep silent in order to maintain some vestige of control.

Your friend, on the other hand, compares his basic assumption, "We all make mistakes. No one is perfect all the time, especially in golf," with his perception of his errant drive and walks calmly off the tee trying to figure out what he did wrong. The events were the same, but the experiencing and the behavior were not. The comparison of similar events with different personal assumptions generated different behavior.

When we see something, we immediately—in a nanosecond—compare it with our VABEs. This comparison yields a number of options. If what we observe matches our expectations, then all is right with the world, and we go on. A mismatch between what we expect to see and what we see signals a problem. We can ignore the gap (between what we saw and what we expected to see) and go on as if nothing occurred. We can fret and stew about the event and try to change it.

Malcolm Gladwell explored this concept of instantaneous judgments or decision making based on core values in his bestselling book *Blink*.[4] We all make judgments in the blink of an eye. Sometimes those quick judgments or conclusions are effective; sometimes they are biased and dysfunctional because they don't fit the world around us. Effective leaders will have enough self-reflection to be able to review and revisit their underlying assumptions, whereas those who are going to be nothing more than vessels passing on the genes and memes of previous generations to the next persist in their Level One approaches. Unless we can reflect on our underlying VABEs and consider changing them to match our observations, we will fall into same trap. In this way, we are all scientists—we all can make observations about our reaction to events and consider the nature of the underlying VABE that must be in place in order to react that way.

In any event, in the fraction of a second that it takes to do this comparison, we reach a conclusion. We often reach or jump to the *judgments* we make about the situation, the people, and ourselves in an instant. A person says, "Well, a refined person would never do a thing like that." We immediately react—perhaps with anger and retaliation. It is important to note that the other person did not *make* us angry. If we are accurate, we'll note that we *chose* to be angry about his or her comment. If we could adjust or refine our underlying VABE (in this case probably something like "people shouldn't be condescending"), then we might hear this comment and not be upset about it. Gladwell points out that these kinds of snap judgments can have disastrous effects, for example, among juries in court or police officers on the street.

One reason we jump to conclusions is that we tend to project our own meanings onto situations.[5] This is natural and normal because we can *only* project meanings that grow out of our own experience and our own assumptions about the way the world operates. It is where the old saying "What Peter says about Paul tells you more about Peter than about Paul" comes from. This tendency to project our own meanings on the world highlights again the usefulness of learning more about *our* assumptions as well as the assumptions of others. When a person "jumps to conclusions," we can learn, if we are attentive, more about that person's basic VABEs, which will help us greatly in our attempts to manage our relationship with that person.

INTERNAL CONCLUSIONS

Humans also have the capacity to observe and judge themselves. We can call the observations we make about ourselves our *self-image*. We make self-judgments or conclusions by comparing what we believe we should be with what we see ourselves doing—that we are good parents, good golfers, poor drivers, terrible poets, and so on. These conclusions can affect our behavior in a number of ways. We may become so convinced that we *are* or *are not* something that we stop trying to do anything differently. For example, we may assume that "People who are good at something are good at it on the first try." If we try something and perform poorly, we may never try it again, which could be a significant loss for ourselves and others. These self-fulfilling prophecies represent an internally directed, negative Pygmalion effect.[6] Also, our conclusions, external or internal, often cause powerful emotions within us. Figure 11-3 shows the relationship between these external and internal conclusions in the REB model.

---

[4] Malcolm Gladwell, *Blink: The Power of Thinking without Thinking* (New York: Little, Brown and Company, 2005).
[5] P. Berger and T. Luckman, *The Social Construction of Reality* (New York: Anchor, 1967).
[6] Sterling Livingston, "Pygmalion in Management," *Harvard Business Review*, September 01, 2002, 1768.

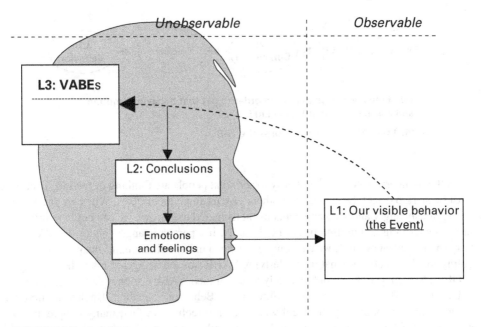

FIGURE 11-3 Judging ourselves

EMOTIONS AND FEELINGS

Whether our conclusions are internal (about ourselves) or external (about others), they tend to generate emotions. If we believe that people should tell the truth and we observe a person lying, then we conclude that this person is a liar and we become angry. If we believe we should be kind and we observe ourselves passing a homeless person by, we may conclude that we are not as kind as we should be and we feel guilty. The next person, who believes that people should make their own luck, might pass the homeless person by, feeling nothing. Clearly, emotions are a big part of human behavior.

When our conclusions reflect a match between our observations and our assumptions, we usually experience positive feelings—happiness, contentment, satisfaction, pride. When our observations violate or disconfirm our assumptions about either others or ourselves, we conclude that things or we are not right, and we tend to experience negative feelings—sadness, discontent, anger, jealousy, disappointment. To an interested observer or would-be leader, these feelings open windows of understanding into the question of why people behave the way they do; that is, they open a window to the person's VABEs.

Often, what we observe in others is their emotionally laden behavior. The REB model gives us a way of working backward to infer any underlying VABEs that must be in place for a particular event to produce a particular emotional reaction. In this way, the REB model has the structure of an equation with one missing variable: the VABE that underlies emotional behavior. If we can understand all of the parts of this comparison dynamic—that is, the observations (What did you see?), the VABEs (What do you believe?), the conclusions (What judgments do you draw from that?), and the feelings (How does that make you feel?)—we can begin to understand why a person does what he or she does. Figure 11-4 depicts this missing variable structure.

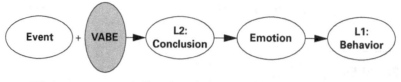

What must a person believe in order to get that behavior, emotion,
and conclusion out of that event?

FIGURE 11-4 The missing variable—the VABE

As the Skinnerians note, it is not easy to see what people are thinking or feeling. Therefore, we must be alert to detect the signals that others give us about themselves. When we see a person who is obviously angry and we know what event triggered that anger, we can begin to infer what his or her underlying assumption might be. Usually, if a person is angry, his or her VABEs are contrary to the current event. If we care enough and can listen well enough,[7] the person may even be willing to tell us outright what the underlying VABE was that triggered his or her feelings.

Often, though, people are only vaguely aware of their VABEs, so they cannot describe their own "Event + VABE → Conclusion → Emotion → Behavior" equation. Unclear assumptions leave them unclear about why they feel what they are feeling. In fact, many people are quite unaware of their feelings, period. For simple issues, talking with a person may begin to reveal to both of you what the underlying assumptions and conclusions and emotions are. For more difficult issues, it may take someone more qualified, such as a psychologist, counselor, or trained facilitator, to help understand the source of the feelings. Being able to identify accurately the underlying assumption—which, in comparison with an observation, caused a conclusion that generated a feeling—leads to major insights into why people behave the way they do.

Note that all behavior does not spring from the chain of events described by the REB model. The discussion on intelligences in Chapter 9 explores how some human behavior bypasses the rational loop altogether. If signals depicting external stimuli are sent directly to an ancient part of the brain called the amygdala, we may "jump without thinking," literally. This behavior falls in another class of behavior, emotional intelligence, which is discussed in greater detail later.

VISIBLE BEHAVIOR

Level One behavior is another result of the comparisons we make between events and our VABEs. Visible behavior is simply what people say and do that you could capture on camera. It includes what people say, their gestures, their facial expressions, and their eye movements, as well as their major motor movements such as walking and running. When we see the behavior of another, we reach conclusions about whether the person is behaving appropriately. In other words, the behavior of others becomes an "event" for us. The word *appropriately* implies that we use a judgmental filter, our VABEs, to determine what is appropriate and what is not. In trying to understand and influence others, if we ignore what lies behind their behavior, the Event → VABEs connections they see, we are ignoring the basic causes of that behavior and, in so doing, ignore a powerful tool for understanding and working with that person.

---

[7] The skill of active or reflective listening is a big help here. It provides a means of enlarging the window onto a person's VABEs. See, for example, "Active Listening," UVA-OB-341 (a technical note available from Darden Business Publishing).

AN EXAMPLE

With the basic elements of the REB model in place, let's try an example to explain why people behave the way they do. Consider this short episode:

> Georgia was coming out of the company's headquarters with an important guest when she saw Bill, one of her peer's subordinates. Bill was clearly in a hurry, on his way out. As he passed through the lobby, Bill cursed at the receptionist for not having his taxi waiting and stormed out the front door. Georgia's client turned to Georgia and remarked, "He's an interesting duck. How many more like him do you have around here?"

It's a small incident, one of hundreds we live through each day. If you were in Georgia's shoes, what would you do? Before you read on, think about it for a moment and decide what you would do or say. Interestingly, most groups will give a variety of answers, including the following:

1. Laugh it off and do nothing.
2. Go see Bill the next day and chew him out for behaving unprofessionally.
3. Chase Bill and demand an apology.
4. Go see Bill's boss the next day and demand that Bill be reprimanded.
5. Offer an explanation to the guest (What explanation would you offer?).
6. Reply, "Oh, he's not one of ours, I can assure you."
7. Wait for a while to see if Bill will come to apologize. If not, go see him.

Perhaps you would even do something different from this list. Where do all these responses come from? After all, it was a single incident. If we use the REB model, we can begin to understand what is going on behind each of these alternative action plans. Table 11-2 lists the behaviors and then provides a logical inference as to what the underlying VABE must be in order for that behavior to have emerged.

TABLE 11-2 Possible Behaviors and Underlying VABEs

Observed Behavior	Inferred VABE
Laugh it off and do nothing.	Cursing at secretaries is no big deal, and important people understand this behavior.
Go see Bill the next day and chew him out for behaving unprofessionally.	You shouldn't reprimand your people in front of clients; and cursing at secretaries is unprofessional and unacceptable.
Chase Bill and demand an apology.	You should reprimand people on the spot to obtain real results.
Go see Bill's boss the next day and demand that Bill be reprimanded.	Only a boss should reprimand a person.
Offer an explanation to the guest (What explanation would you offer?).	Others, including clients, demand an explanation of poor behavior.
Reply, "Oh, he's not one of ours, I can assure you."	Lying to cover up one's shortcomings is an acceptable way to maintain "face" or reputation.
Wait for a while to see if Bill will come to apologize. If not, go see him.	Most people recognize when they do bad things and if you leave them alone they will rectify the situation. We should give a person a chance to do well.

You can see that these VABEs are quite different and with some variation could "mutate" from person to person. The challenge is not to force people to all have the same VABEs; rather from a leader's point of view, one wants to understand the VABEs of one's co-workers.

MEANING CHAINS

The point is not so much which action plan is "right." All of the behavioral alternatives in Table 11-2 are right for the person who believes the VABE that leads to them. Rather, the challenge is first to be able to describe this linkage between Event + VABE → Conclusion → Emotion → Behavior. We can call this linkage the meaning chain because it lays out the essential links between an event, the meaning that a person makes of that event, and a person's behavior. Meaning chains are like the value chains we use in strategic analysis. One must work to identify the chain and to assess the characteristics of each link, especially if we are trying to influence someone. Pausing to tease out another person's meaning chain does not require you to become a psychologist, but it does ask you to be more careful about judging why people behave the way they do.

THE REB MODEL AND LEADING CHANGE

If we try to change a person's behavior by looking only at the behavior, we are guessing, really groping around in the dark. For example, if you offer a subordinate more money (a carrot) if he will increase his sales, you are assuming that your subordinate wants more money strongly enough to change his behavior to get it. This assumption is often true, but a person can only use so much money. Believe it or not, some people value working relationships, the challenge of the work, the variety involved, and other features of their work more than they do the monetary compensations it brings. Indeed, a series of studies showed that people, in general, lose motivation when they are paid to do something.[8] For example, volunteer organizations regularly experience much higher levels of motivation and commitment than for-profit institutions.

So, if offering a monetary reward doesn't seem to work to motivate someone, you might say, "If your sales aren't up by the end of the quarter, you're fired" (a stick). This approach can lead to compliant behavior, obedience for the sake of avoiding punishment, begrudging compliance, or even passive aggressive sabotage. The individual may compare the possibility of having to find new work with the cost of having to change behavior and conclude that he would rather find new work. Trying to change behavior in this way is like trying to move the tip of an iceberg without realizing that nine-tenths of the iceberg is under the water where you can't see it. A person's VABEs are also mostly under the surface. With people, as with icebergs, a little informed exploration will often reveal the nature of the part beneath the surface.

Suppose you are interviewing a moderate performer in your sales organization. After some conversation, it becomes apparent that this person believes that "people should not be pushy." Maybe this person had bad experiences with pushy people, perhaps even had pushy parents and is rebelling against the model of interpersonal style. Simply telling this person to be more assertive is not likely to change a behavior. Unless you can help this person clarify the

---

[8] Edward Deci, *Why People Do What They Do* (New York: Penguin, 1995). See also Alfie Kohn, *Punished by Rewards: The Trouble with Gold Stars, Incentive Plans, A's, Praise, and Other Bribes* (New York: Mariner, 1999).

underlying VABE and compare the utility of that VABE with the demands of the job at hand, you are not likely to make much progress. It may be that the person is willing to reexamine the VABE and work to change. If not, you both would be better off finding a different job fit for this person. Dealing with negative feedback is difficult for most of us.

THE SELF-CONCEPT

We tend to deny, discount, distort, or ignore negative feedback because we all want to conclude positive things about ourselves. In fact, it may be the most fundamental human motivation of all. A well-known social scientist, S. I. Hayakawa, once noted,

> The basic purpose of all human activity is the protection, the maintenance, and the enhancement, not of the self, but of the self-concept or symbolic self.[9]

What is symbolic self? Our self-concept can be usefully explained in three parts. First, the inward-looking set of assumptions about who we think we should be is the ideal self. Second, the inward-looking view of who we are is the self-image. Instead of observing an external event, we "see" our own behavior, which becomes the input to our VABE comparison. See again Figure 11-3. Third, when a gap occurs between our ideal self (self-oriented VABEs) and our self-image and when we behave in ways that we don't think we should, we reach a negative conclusion about ourselves, and our feelings about ourselves, our self-esteem, goes down, as illustrated in Figure 11-5. In other words, we can apply the REB model not only to external events, but also to ourselves. The more our self-image overlaps our ideal self, the better we feel about ourselves. The more distant our self-image is from our ideal self (either because the goals are too high or because the behavior is too meager), the worse we are likely to feel about ourselves.

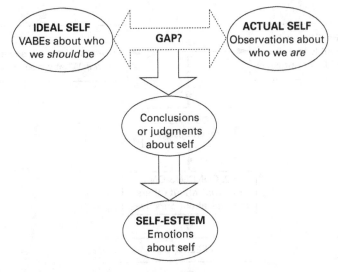

FIGURE 11-5   The self-concept

---

[9] S. Hayakawa, *Symbol, Status, and Personality* (New York: Harvest/HBJ, 1966), 37.

DEFENSE MECHANISMS

Generally speaking, we don't like seeing gaps between who we want to be and who we are. So we figure out ways to protect ourselves from the psychological pain that comes with being aware of those gaps. The fact is that we all try to protect our conclusions about ourselves, and so we develop defense mechanisms. Some are productive and motivate us to do something about the gaps. Other defense mechanisms are not so healthy or productive; we cover up the gaps or ignore them or try to make others' gaps bigger so ours won't seem so onerous. Healthy defense mechanisms include humor, reality checking, perspective enlargement, soliciting counsel, goal setting and follow-up, and doing things for others. Less healthy defense mechanisms include suppression, dissociation (ignoring), denial, acquiescence and self-loathing, and transferring feelings like anger to others. As mentioned before, brain chemistry can also affect one's "choice" of defense mechanism.

These mechanisms may be so strong that they let us be aware of only those perceptions that match our basic assumptions and, therefore, allow us to draw favorable conclusions about ourselves. In the extreme case of abused children, some will even develop multiple personalities (enormous "holes") in order to have someone inside whom they can "like."

We naturally activate our defense mechanisms when we are threatened. We experience feeling threatened regularly in life, and this is appropriate because it keeps us alive and protected from responding to every little vacillation in feedback that comes along. The absence or presence of healthy defense mechanisms is a major difference between the incapacitated psychotic and the normal, functioning adult. It is important to note that when a person's defense mechanisms are operating (or "up," we might say), the person is not likely to hear what you are trying to communicate. In coaching, teaching, or persuasion situations, you must learn to talk with others in ways that will tend to keep their defenses relaxed rather than activated. A summary of how defense mechanisms fit into the REB model appears in Figure 11-6.

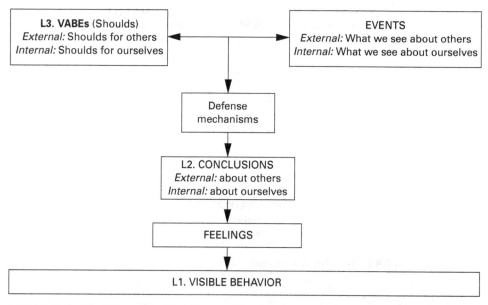

FIGURE 11-6   The REB model with defense mechanisms

IMPLICATIONS FOR LEADERS

This line of reasoning suggests a number of implications for leaders:

- One should be attentive to one's own motivations and memetic endowment. The ability to reflect on and be aware of one's own assumptions about how to lead and what motivates people is a critical leadership skill.[10] The simple statistics on the high failure rate of most so-called mega-mergers suggests that something far beyond financial expectation is going on. If one intends to build, merge, or expand in the misguided attempt to fill some personal psychological hole, the consequences can extend farther than we anticipate.

- In order to be more effective in dealing with, working with, and managing other people, one must be alert to the little tips (Level One visible behavior) of the psychological icebergs (Level Three VABEs) that we all carry around. They give us insight into why people behave the way they do.

- Unless we understand the core VABEs of people, we are not likely to be successful in guiding them through a change process. Once a manager learns something of the central VABEs of a co-worker or subordinate (by listening, observing, or testing), the manager can assess whether the assumptions provide a basis for behavior that aligns with the objectives of the organization. If a person's VABEs don't match those of the organization culture, it could mean an extended coaching or mentoring period or it could mean looking for a better alignment in another organization.

- In smaller performance-management settings, if a manager concludes that another's inappropriate behavior is based on assumptions that are fundamental to the individual's personality, the manager may begin thinking about alternative assignments for the individual because core values are not likely to change quickly. On the other hand, if the underlying assumption seems to be a peripheral one, the manager might hope to work with the individual to explore the usefulness of the assumption and its resulting behavior and perhaps initiate a change in the assumption and the behavior that grows from it. A manager who ignores the VABEs that shape and generate behavior will be negating the human side of individuals and, worse, guessing at why others behave the way they do. Guessing is not managing.

From these implications emerges a simple but powerful model for coaching—as will be discussed in more detail in Chapter 24 on leading change. The model includes the following steps:

1. *Try to see the VABEs of the other person.* Can you describe them on paper? (This exercise provides a wonderful discipline for sharpening your thinking—many people think they understand something until they begin to write it down and discover that it's not so clear to them after all.)

2. *Confirm your assessment with the individual.* Can you in informal conversations clarify and focus your tentative insights? "Gee, John, it seems to me that you seem to believe that if you want it done right, you have to do it yourself. Is that right?" And if he confirms your observation, you can check that one off as accurate and go on to the next one.

3. *Set a timeframe during which you are willing to work on this task.* What are you willing to give this change effort? Six months? Two years? You may or may not reveal this goal to the

---

[10] See, for example, Henry Mintzberg, Managers, Not MBAs: A Hard Look at the Soft Practice of Managing and Management Development (New York: Berrett-Kohler, 2004).

person you are working with, but in your mind, this timeframe relates to the slack you have both in the business and in your own patience.

4. *Begin coaching.* This step requires that you actively meet with and discuss the functionality of the agreed-upon VABEs. "If you want it done right, do it yourself" is not a very functional managerial or leadership VABE. Is "John" willing to discuss this? Are you very adept at managing the conversation? Can you guide him to see voluntarily how another approach might be more functional? This may take more time on your part. If you don't have the time to spend with this person to coach him/her on his/her dysfunctional VABEs, why would you presume to manage or lead this person? Is your model, "I speak and they respond"?

5. *Assess whether you are making progress.* At the end of the probationary period you established in step 3, if you don't see progress, you may need a different approach. If you do see progress, perhaps you can continue your coaching with the hope that things will continue to improve. Simply telling someone to delegate more, though, is not likely to produce a change. Two possible reasons might explain why you haven't been able to make progress: the person may not be willing to change the VABE in question, or you may not be a good enough coach to help facilitate this process. In either event, you're likely faced with moving the person to something else.

Conclusions

Human behavior is a complex topic. Leaders need a four-wheel-drive model that will allow them to navigate the terrain of motivation and inspiration with some dependability. The REB model is one durable, functional model. With it, you can understand the major reasons why such people do what they do and see how best to influence them. With the REB model in hand, you can begin to become a Level Three Leader, someone who can move people's hearts and not just their heads and hands.

For this task, though, you'll need to be aware of your own Level Three activity, your own VABEs, and the implications they have for your behavior. Without the ability to reflect on your own underlying assumptions, you may be using some dysfunctional ones that will get in the way. So, in the end, the true Level Three Leader is thinking about not only leading others, but also leading the self. The Level Three Leader has a chance of becoming a mature adult, the kind of person who can, by reflective effort, transcend his or her genetic and memetic legacies. That kind of leader has the potential to move others at Level Three—indeed, to inspire them.

Concepts Introduced in This Chapter

1. The REB model includes many aspects of human behavior described in the previous chapter.
2. Leaders can use the REB model to understand human behavior, including their own behavior.
3. Leaders are good, descriptive observers of events around them; they see things.
4. We all compare events around us with our VABEs and reach conclusions based on those comparisons.
5. Our conclusions stimulate emotions within us.

6. Our conclusions and our emotions shape our behavior, but our conclusions and our emotions are based on our VABEs.
7. The REB model explains not only external but also internal behavior—that is, self-judgment.
8. We all try to protect our self-concepts.
9. Effective leaders understand the VABEs of others and work to influence the VABEs, not just the behavior, which is the essence of Level Three Leadership.

Questions for Personal Reflection

1. How can you be more observant of the VABEs of others?
2. How attentive are you to when others say "should" or "ought"?
3. How good are you at listening and inferring what others believe?
4. What are the core VABEs of the people closest to you? Can you write them down?
5. What are the core VABEs of the people you supervise? Can you write them down?
6. Which defense mechanisms do you tend to use the most? Are these functional or dysfunctional? Why?

CASELET FOR DISCUSSION

Brandy, a newly minted MBA, was attending her first management team meeting. After five minutes of listening to her boss introduce the topic for the day, a particular customer's account, she raised her hand to ask a question. Her boss ignored her and continued on while the other members of the team glanced at her nervously. As the meeting wore on, Brandy noticed that none of the team members questioned any of the boss' assertions or facts. There were several points that Brandy thought needed clarifying or confirming, but no one seemed to pick up on these. After coughing and raising her hand twice and being ignored, she stopped trying to insert her comments into the discussion. After the meeting, two of her colleagues came up to her and asked, "What were you doing?"

CONTRIBUTING YOUR OWN CASELETS

Have you seen or experienced a situation involving the concepts introduced in this chapter? If so and if you'd like to contribute your experience/situation to our case data bank, please visit http://faculty.darden.virginia.edu/clawsonj/ and click on the "Contribute new caselets" button.

12 | LEADERSHIP AND INTELLIGENCE

> *Much evidence testifies that people who are emotionally*
> *adept—who know and manage their own feelings well, and*
> *who read and deal effectively with other people's feelings—*
> *are at an advantage in any domain of life, whether romance*
> *and intimate relationships or picking up the unspoken rules*
> *that govern success in organizational politics.*
>
> —DANIEL GOLEMAN

Smart people are generally considered to have the best potential for being the leaders of industry, nations, and institutions. Interestingly, a study of high-school valedictorians indicates that after 20 years, most of them are working for their classmates.[1] This counterintuitive result causes us to rethink our beliefs about intelligence and its relationship to effective leadership.

---

[1] See Daniel Goleman, *Emotional Intelligence* (New York: Bantam, 1995), for more data. Many of the concepts in this chapter come from this excellent book.

For more than a century, business leaders mostly tried to downplay emotions in business as unprofessional, undisciplined, and unrelated to good decision making. This tendency stems in part from the philosophy of the Age of Enlightenment in Western civilization. Knowledge, said Sir Francis Bacon, is power. Like the other philosophers of the Enlightenment, Bacon saw knowledge as the pathway to universal liberation and emotions and passions as obstacles to knowledge. This meme has been perpetuated in the corporate halls around the globe ever since. Indeed, today, many of the leadership models taught in business schools focus on rational analytic decision making in which emotions are viewed as detriments or obstacles to making good decisions. Students are taught to search for the "right answer" and to do so in a rigorous, analytic, and logical way.

Further, school systems throughout the industrialized world focus on the notion of rational intelligence in striving to educate millions of children. In this effort, the concept of intelligence quotient (IQ) has been the most prominent measure of intelligence. School systems designed curricula with the intent of utilizing more of students' IQs, if not increasing them. Although the validity of IQ tests and the general intelligence or aptitude substitutes have come into question in recent years,[2] tests of purely rational thinking, such as the Scholastic Aptitude Test (SAT) and the General Management Aptitude Test (GMAT), still wield a great deal of influence over individual academic opportunities.

Recently, however, some startling conclusions about the nature of intelligence, many of them directly at odds with old assumptions, have begun to emerge. Daniel Goleman points out three important inferences we can draw from recent studies:

1. Existing standardized intelligence tests fail to predict success in life or in business because they do not tell the whole story. Intelligence is not singular; rather it comes in a number of forms. Among *multiple intelligences*, intellectual intelligence, the kind measured by IQ tests, is only one kind.
2. Emotion, although it can sometimes sabotage clearheaded thought, has been scientifically shown to be an indispensable contributor to rational thinking and decision making. As oxymoronic as it would have seemed to Sir Francis Bacon, a range of intelligence that can be called "emotional" is important for aspiring business leaders to understand and employ more effectively.
3. Despite traditional views that IQ was inherited and that one could not do much to change it, the newly recognized various intelligences seem to be, to a large extent, learned.

NOT ONE INTELLIGENCE, BUT MANY: GARDNER'S RESEARCH

Goleman draws on the work of several researchers to demonstrate the existence of multiple intelligences. Howard Gardner, a psychologist at the Harvard School of Education, found the

---

[2] Harvard Business School, for instance, discontinued the use of the GMAT in making admissions decisions after concluding that they were not highly correlated with graduate success. *Time* magazine also published a cover article in March 2001, questioning the value of the long-used SAT tests.

long-standing notion of a single kind of intelligence both wrongheaded and injurious. He blamed this belief largely on the IQ test itself—calling it, in fact, the "IQ way of thinking": that people are either "smart or not," or "born that way," that "there's nothing much you can do about it," and that "tests can tell you if you are one of the smart ones." The American SAT for college admissions is based on the same notion of a single kind of aptitude that determines an individual's future. This way of thinking permeates much of global society.[3] Statistically speaking, though, IQ measurements, SAT scores, and grades turn out to be relatively poor predictors of who will succeed in life and who will not. (Goleman puts the contribution of IQ to a person's success at about 20 percent.)

Howard Gardner's groundbreaking *Frames of Mind* repudiated the idea of one kind of intelligence and the IQ way of thinking by positing a wide array of intelligences. Gardner identified seven:

1. Verbal
2. Mathematical-logical
3. Spatial (as demonstrated by painters or pilots)
4. Kinesthetic (as seen in the physical grace of a dancer or athlete)
5. Musical
6. Interpersonal (upon which a therapist or a diplomat might rely)
7. Intrapersonal intelligence (something akin to self-awareness)

Gardner's perspective explained why traditional tests were ineffective in predicting success: they measured only one or two of many necessary and important kinds of intelligence. Others have posited multiple kinds of intelligence. Sternberg suggested three: analytical, creative, and practical.[4] He noted that IQ was "inert" in that it may not have to do with any kind of practical intelligence for getting things done. He also noted that what was considered intelligent in one culture might not be intelligent in another culture with a different emphasis.

Goleman took Gardner's interpersonal and the intrapersonal types of intelligence and cited hundreds of studies to create a story that described something he called "emotional intelligence," or emotional quotient (EQ). Goleman asserted that EQ was just as important as IQ in helping people become effective leaders. Gardner pointed out that people of higher IQ often work for people of lower IQ demonstrating that being "smart" is neither the only nor even the most essential criteria for business success.

It's a compelling argument. Let's examine some various kinds of intelligence more closely.

INTELLIGENCE QUOTIENT

Intelligence quotient (which we will use as an indicator of mental capacity in general) is largely genetic but can be honed or made more manifest by curiosity, by discipline in studying, and by adding a range of experiences to a person's life. You may not be able to change your IQ score much, but you can learn to do more with what you have been given. If you don't know your IQ, don't worry about it, because, broadly speaking, even though standardized tests have some predictive power (those with low IQs often end up making little money and those with

---

[3] Howard Gardner, *Frames of Mind* (New York: Basic Books, 1993).
[4] Robert J. Sternberg, *Successful Intelligence: How Practical and Creative Intelligence Determine Success in Life* (New York: Plume, 1997).

TABLE 12-1	Intellectual Intelligence

- Genetic endowment
- Environmental encouragement
- Focus of most school work
- Processing power
- Curiosity
- Discipline

high IQs frequently take demanding, high-powered, better-paying jobs), IQ tests reflect only one kind of intelligence. Other kinds are equally, if not more, important to being successful and to developing leadership influence. Table 12-1 shows some of the characteristics related to intellectual intelligence.

EMOTIONAL QUOTIENT

Emotional intelligence, as introduced by Goleman, is basically the ability to manage your own emotions. It begins with the ability to *recognize* your emotions, then to understand them, and finally to manage yourself out of what Goleman calls "emotional hijackings." In this view, IQ is your brain power whereas EQ is your emotional control power. (This sequence follows exactly the discussion of the Leadership Point of View.)

The first step to developing your EQ, as shown in Table 12-2, is to learn to recognize your emotions. Many people are not highly aware of their emotions, even though they often say they are. Have you ever talked with someone who seemed visibly upset, whose neck veins were bulging, whose face was red, whose voice was raised, and yet when you asked them to calm down, they screamed, "I AM calm!" Such a person is not in touch with his or her own emotional reality or experience. Another manifestation of the difficulty people have in recognizing their emotions appears when you ask people how they are feeling; they often will describe behaviors or thoughts. Many are not skilled in recognizing and paying attention to their own emotional state. Many of these people learned that the emotional world is not legitimate, and after years of practicing to suppress or subdue their emotions, they lost touch with how they feel. Few talented, practicing managers and leaders are actually able to identify and talk about their emotions.

Aware of them or not, people can often become prisoners of their emotions. In Goleman's terms, they get *hijacked* by their emotions and lose control of their rational processes. An emotional hijacking occurs when a person begins with a little emotion and then it builds and builds in intensity until the person is not thinking clearly and is overwhelmed by the emotion. The most common emotional hijackings are related to anger, fear, and depression. A person hijacked by anger, for instance, may be a little irritated at first, but as time passes, becomes more and more angry until

TABLE 12-2	Emotional Quotient

- Recognizing your own emotions
- Managing your emotions
- Self-talk to get out of emotional hijackings
- Paying attention/Concentration

he or she is bursting at the seams and acting openly hostile, whether the situation calls for such behavior or not. People with a low EQ when become angry, afraid, or depressed find themselves in an ever-widening spiral of emotions to the point where they are unable to think clearly or to make good decisions.

Consider a hijacking by fear. Modern equipment gives us greater insight into how this hijacking occurs, because we can trace with increasing accuracy the electrical impulses that course through the brain during different events. We used to think that when a person saw something dangerous like a snake, the eye would send a signal to the thinking part of the brain, the brain would consciously register danger and send signals to the muscles to move quickly, and we would jump. In effect, every Level One behavior was a rational choice. In fact, we've learned that a "short circuit" bypasses the thinking part of the brain and transmits danger signals directly to a small, almond-sized structure called the "amygdala" that sits atop the human brain stem.

The amygdala is an old structure in terms of the development of the human brain; it evolved earlier than the neocortex (the area above the amygdala that handles conscious thought), and its functioning is largely beyond the control of the thinking brain. When the amygdala receives a short circuit signal from the optic nerve that you've seen a snake, it immediately begins a complex chemical process that pumps muscle stimulants into the blood stream, and you literally jump *without* thinking. If your ability to manage these chemical outbursts is underdeveloped, it can create a growing whirlpool of fear so strong that you could jump when you should hold still or be paralyzed by the fear when you should jump. When you're so enraged that you can't "think straight" or "so blue in the face that you can't function," you could blame your amygdala and its partners in the limbic system.

Dr. Antonio Damasio, a neurologist at the University of Iowa, studied patients with damage to the circuits between the amygdala and the brain's memory center. These patients showed no IQ deterioration at all, and yet their decision-making skills were amazingly poor. They made disastrous choices in their careers and personal lives, and the most mundane decisions (e.g., white bread or wheat?) often left them paralyzed with confusion. Damasio concluded that their decision making was impaired because they had no access to their *emotional* learning. Searching their memories for the last time they were in the present situation, they didn't remember how they *felt* about the outcome because the emotional lessons, stored in or regulated by the amygdala, apparently were out of reach.

Damasio's research (and other similar research) suggests that the conventional wisdom imparted to us by the Age of Reason philosophers and the intervening years of scientific and business experience was wrong at least part of the time: emotions are in fact *essential* for rational decisions. Memories of ecstatic successes and painful failures help steer the decisions we make every day.

By contrast, people who have a strong connection between the amygdala and the neocortex seem to be better equipped to make good decisions, decisions based on a balancing of rational and emotional input rather than one without the other. It seems clear that people who learned over the years to manage their emotions also learned to manage their behavior better and their relationships better, which translates into more success in the social world of business.

To a certain extent, just like IQ, we're stuck with the emotional cards we're dealt at birth: depression, for instance, has been shown to have a hereditary component as we described in Chapter 10 on why people behave the way they do. The good news is that EQ seems to be more responsive to learning activities than IQ. You can develop emotional skills, which will help enrich both your personal and your professional life. Following the outline in Table 12-2, let's explore some ways individuals can improve their EQ.

RECOGNIZING YOUR OWN EMOTIONS

The first step toward building your EQ, of course, is recognizing or being *aware* of your emotions. It may seem to you a simple task—that your feelings are self-evident, so this point is hardly worth making—but closer examination reveals otherwise.

We all sometimes lose sight of our emotions. Goleman offers examples of situations we all recognize, "getting up on the wrong side of the bed," and being grouchy all day long. What we would call "getting up on the wrong side of the bed" might actually have stemmed from kicking your toe on the bathroom door, from a curt exchange with your significant other, bad news on the radio, or a bad night's sleep caused by a heavy dinner or some modest chemical imbalance. Perhaps it related really to rainy weather. Whatever the source, with this initial emotional set, many people are unaware that they are behaving crossly or are seemingly depressed or "down" throughout their workday.

Being aware of emotions requires reflection. If one learns to pause, to focus inward, and to seek one's emotions, one can become more aware of them. You might begin asking yourself several times during a normal day, what am I feeling now? If you question yourself frequently for a week, you will probably be able to notice what you feel more readily. Then the challenge—one accepted by people with high EQs—is to manage those emotions in a more positive way. People who develop a high EQ do not yield to their emotions easily—rather they seek to manage them.

Some of you may be thinking, "Yes, but in the rational business world, I don't need to be aware of my feelings." Let's challenge this mind-set for a second. Doug Newburg, whom you'll learn more about later, uncovered an important question, Does how you feel affect your performance? Virtually everyone will answer yes to this question. Then, ask how many times you have thought about or been asked by your supervisor, How do you *want* to feel today? The answer to that question is probably close to zero. So consider how paying attention to and being aware of your emotions is critical to becoming an effective Level Three Leader, first in yourself and then in those around you. Many suppress their emotions because their work is unfulfilling. To deal with this situation, like learning to live in bad marriages, they learn to push their feelings down and just go about their work. This behavior, again, is a formula for mediocrity.

MANAGING YOUR EMOTIONS

Can a person manage his or her emotions? If you wake up grouchy, can you change how you feel? Maybe the thought of managing your emotions is too "rational" for you, or too "contrived." Perhaps you prefer to allow your emotions to ebb and flow and you like the spontaneity of them. That's fine, but the data seem to suggest that if you manage your emotions by becoming more aware of them and dealing with them, not just suppressing and ignoring them, you are more likely to have a positive impact on yourself and the people around you at work or elsewhere. This positive effect is particularly important in the case of the potentially debilitating emotions of anger, fear, and depression. We look later how this principle might apply to the more positive emotions of resonance and high performance.

To a person with low EQ, an emotional hijacking may seem like an irresistible call to action: anger leads to shouting, fear leads to fleeing, and depression leads to crying or withdrawal. With practice, however, the urgings of the amygdala can be overcome through what

Goleman calls productive "self-talk."[5] With this potential in mind, we come back again to Csikszentmihalyi's central question, Will you ever be anything more than a vessel transmitting the memes and genes of previous generations on to the next? Unless one can transcend or rise above one's unmanaged emotional tendencies, the odds are probably not. In other words, when someone cuts you off on the highway, you don't have to respond by yelling, pounding on the steering wheel, and clenching your jaw and arm muscles. You have options.

To manage your emotions, you must first decide that you want to be in control of them. Making such a decision does not mean that you can, by willpower alone, manage emotions, but unless you decide to do so, you are not likely to increase your EQ. If you say to yourself, "I want to learn how to not be angry so often, or not to be depressed so often, or to be more courageous," it is a start.

The next step is to develop productive self-talk. Recognize your emotions and then pause to "talk to yourself" and examine the perhaps irrational links that you make between an external event and your emotional reactions to it. Consider the rude driver again. If you imagine that maybe, just maybe, the driver who cut you off is in a hurry to get to the hospital, there suddenly seems to be less to get angry about. Even if you conclude that the driver is just being self-centered and rude, you can still say to yourself, "Well, I may wish that he weren't that way, and I cannot control the behavior of others, so why should I let a complete stranger ruin my moment or day?"

PAYING ATTENTION/CONCENTRATING

In the case of anxiety, the analytical thought process is itself often the source of trouble: some people can worry about almost anything. (And for some, this issue is a biochemical one that is not easily dealt with behaviorally.) If you choose, however, to look at your pessimistic assumptions critically ("Is this bad outcome really inevitable? What other possible outcomes are there? What constructive thing could I do to improve my chances for a favorable outcome? or more simply, Do I really want to be depressed today?"), you may be able to gradually break them down. People with high EQs learned over the years how to do this critical examination. Sometimes they use productive self-talk; other times they might even use physical relaxation methods, such as martial arts, meditation, or prayer, as means to stem the onset of anxiety, once it is recognized.[6]

Managing emotions is a personal challenge. Would you like to be able to manage your emotions? Are you willing to test your abilities to do so? If you can, not only will you feel better about your life, you'll be better able to manage your relationships and you'll become a better leader.

Although Goleman lumped the personal and interpersonal aspects of EQ into one concept, the next section separates them for clarity's sake.

---

[5] Much of Goleman's approach here is similar to rational emotive behavior therapy developed by Albert Ellis, in which one learns to talk one's self out of dysfunctional conclusions and thoughts. See, for example, A. Ellis, *A New Guide to Rational Living* (Los Angeles, CA: Wilshire Book Company, 1975); or Gerald Kranzler, *You Can Change How You Feel* (Eugene, OR: University of Oregon, 1974).
[6] Relaxation techniques are a central part of many religious and health perspectives. See, for instance, Dr. Dean Ornish's well-known techniques for reducing risk of heart disease in *Dr. Dean Ornish's Program for Reversing Heart Disease* (New York: Ballantine Books, 1990).

SOCIAL QUOTIENT

Goleman asserted that a high EQ has a positive impact on an individual's relationships. If EQ is the ability to manage emotions, then social quotient (SQ) has to do with recognizing and managing the emotions in interpersonal relationships.[7] SQ skills are similar to those used in EQ but are directed toward others in relationships. Like EQ, SQ can in large part be learned, and in an organizational world that places a premium on interpersonal skills in which you can't fax or e-mail a handshake, a well-developed SQ can take you places IQ by itself cannot. Similar to EQ, the SQ skills include recognizing emotions in others, developing a concern or caring about the emotional state of others, and being able to help them manage their emotional states, as outlined in Table 12-3.[8]

Recognizing the Emotions of Others

This SQ skill is the interpersonal corollary to the EQ skill of recognizing your own emotions. The better you are at understanding your own emotions, the more likely you are to be adept at noticing the feelings of others. The difficulty with tuning in to the emotional state of another, of course, is that people don't usually put their emotions into words. More often, they express them nonverbally through Level One cues, such as tone of voice, facial expression, gesture, and other forms of body language. Some research suggests that, in general, women are better than men at this kind of attunement; however, the ability to see emotions in others is something that anyone, with some attention and effort, can learn.

In the organizational environment, opportunities for this kind of learning are plentiful. In meetings, sales presentations, and chance exchanges with subordinates and superiors, attention to nonverbal cues can yield sharp insights into what another person is experiencing emotionally. Knowing how to read these signs is a valuable interpersonal skill. Practice in your conversations, in your meetings, and in group settings. While you listen, see if you can identify the emotions of the people you're talking with. At first, this dual task may be confusing to you; however, if you practice, it will become second nature and you will learn to listen more completely.

Listening

Many people pay lip service to the concept of listening as an important leadership skill. Yet many don't listen well because they focus only on content or their own agendas. "Listening" as it applies to SQ means more than just letting someone else speak. It means listening *attentively*,

---

TABLE 12-3 Social Quotient
• Recognizing the emotions of others
• Empathizing with others' feelings
• Caring
• Listening
• Resolving conflicts

---

[7] Since the first edition of this book, Daniel Goleman has published a book that recognizes the difference between EQ and SQ, *Social Intelligence* (New York: Bantam, 2007).

[8] Please note that SQ here means "social quotient" or "social intelligence." Another recent publication titled SQ explores spiritual intelligence. See Danah Zohar and Dr. Ian Marshall, *SQ, Spiritual Intelligence, the Ultimate Intelligence* (New York: Bloomsbury, 2000).

with an ear and an eye toward recognizing emotion in addition to content. It means putting out of your mind, for a moment at least, what you plan to say when it's your turn to respond. It means seeing whether you can register what the other person's heart, not just mouth, is saying. The challenge is to be conscious of the emotions the other person is experiencing. If you're able to see what the other is feeling, then the question is, do you care?

Empathizing and Caring

When you become open to and aware of the feelings of others, you become able to empathize, to tune in to their emotional experience. Empathy and caring for another's well-being usually, but not always, results in Level Three connections that bind us in our personal lives and strengthens our attempts at leadership. When we can see what others feel and when we care about those feelings, we experience a major opportunity to influence and to be influenced. If you are able to help others manage their emotions, you can be a Level Three Leader.

Helping Others Manage Their Emotions

If you see the emotions of others, if you care about that emotional reality for them, and if you have the skills that allow you to help them manage their emotions, you will have the opportunity to influence others. It is a powerful form of leadership. If you can strengthen the emotions that are functional and diminish the emotions that are dysfunctional, you can have enormous impact on people.

In some cases, you may help others manage their internal emotions, to help them out of emotional hijackings. Consider this example of an eight-year-old girl. Although she was very talented and energetic, she had a tendency to become overwhelmed by daily events. When she was feeling this way, she could talk herself into a dither until she wound up a sobbing heap on the couch or in her bed. Her parents could see this emotional storm developing, almost as clearly as the gathering rain clouds on the horizon outside. Armed with Goleman's insights, they tried to help her manage her emotions by talking with her and helping her to see that (1) she could get control of her feelings and could stop the downward spiral, (2) she could focus on only one thing that needed to be done and do it without worrying about the others, and (3) she could begin to feel good about herself not only for doing that one thing but also for managing her feelings. Several years later, now, she has become much more adept at seeing her own emotions and at managing them. Perhaps it was just the passage of time, but for many, the passage of time does nothing more than reinforce their earlier behavior. If biochemical imbalances are in play as well, the challenge is even greater.

Co-workers in business are similar. You can help some of them learn to manage their emotions more effectively. To begin, try to find out why they are feeling what they feel. Often, emotions are based on a comparison between an event and an underlying VABE (value, assumption, belief, or expectation) as we explained in Chapter 11. If you ask yourself or them, why are you feeling this way? you can begin to get insight into their basic values and assumptions. If you can understand those, you can see more clearly how they respond to the world around them. Then you may begin to help the person reexamine those assumptions. Many managers feel ill at ease with this approach, but those with some skill at it are able to have a profound impact on colleagues.

Social quotient (SQ) also can come into play in helping others manage their emotions in relationships. One of the most valuable skills in the organizational environment and one of the most striking examples of SQ in action lies in resolving conflicts and disputes. Conflicts arise frequently in the business world, sometimes accompanied by heated feelings and accusations. All too often, "solutions" are handed down from above, and emotionally speaking, they are solutions in name only: business goes on, but someone inevitably comes away feeling wronged, resentful, and perhaps in search of payback. In the long run, as morale and cohesiveness break down, the organization as a whole will suffer.

Developing skill in managing emotionally charged conflict situations is a valuable personal asset. When people have low EQs and SQs, they can let their emotions get the better of them. When you are skilled at recognizing emotions and at managing them in yourself and in your relationships, you can help balance the rational content and the emotional content and influence people to make better decisions. Not only are good mediators smart, they have strong EQ and SQ skills.

Here's a simple example. An employee reacts to a co-worker's criticism, gets hijacked, and launches a volley of defensive remarks, making matters more volatile and charged. A person with high EQ skills would have instead turned to self-talk, interpreting the criticism judiciously in order to keep destructive emotions in check. In much the same way, a high-SQ mediator can explain to the injured party that the remarks may not have been intended to wound, and at any rate, the comments are only data and not necessarily fact and need not be internalized unless one *chooses* to do so. The mediator might then explain to the critic better words have to be chosen, if one wants to influence others.

"Common sense!" you say? Yes, common for people with high SQs, but maybe not so common for people with lower SQs. One person gifted in SQ can help offset the EQ deficiencies of many others and, in so doing, is likely to be seen by co-workers as an extraordinary kind of person, a person worthy of leadership. Needless to say, organizations find such mediators and leaders extremely valuable. Conflict resolution skills, the skills of SQ, as any diplomat or marriage counselor will tell you, can be learned.

CHANGE QUOTIENT

Another kind of intelligence should be introduced at this point. Although not one that Gardner or Goleman identified explicitly, it has a big impact on leadership and the ability to lead and is called *change quotient*, or CQ. People seem to vary in their change intelligence, which is their ability to recognize the need for change, their comfort in managing change, and their understanding and mastery of the change process (Table 12-4).

High-CQ people are lifelong learners who adapt to rapidly changing business environments much better than their more stubborn counterparts. When high-CQ people look at challenges, they see opportunities rather than threats. They are willing to learn whatever skills a situation calls for rather than look for ways to reapply what they already know. What follows are a few ideas for managing your development in CQ.

TABLE 12-4 Change Quotient

- Recognizing the need to change
- Being emotionally comfortable with change
- Mastering the change process

Recognizing the Need to Change

Many people find it difficult to recognize signals of change that surround them in the environment. Maybe the signals are coming from customers, significant others, employees, the financial indicators, or colleagues and peers. E. C. Zeeman, an English researcher, made an interesting observation in this regard. He noted that drunk drivers are particularly dangerous because they begin to steer off the road, see a tree, overcorrect, see oncoming headlights, and overcorrect again, perhaps plowing into the next set of trees. Then he noted that, paradoxically, sober drivers behave the same way. They never drive perfectly straight; they see disconfirming data coming in (gradually approaching the side of the road) and make a small midcourse correction. The difference is that the drunk driver's ability to *see* the disconfirming data is impaired and he or she waits until too late to make the appropriate correction. Of course, the opposite is equally dangerous; people who are hypersensitive to incoming data may get so overloaded with minute variations in their course that they become paralyzed.[9]

We can apply the same reasoning to business leaders. Effective leaders will have a high CQ; that is, they will be able to recognize the need for change before it's too late. In fact, Jack Welch, CEO of General Electric for the last two decades of the twentieth century, takes as one of his six core leadership maxims, "Change before you have to."[10] The ability to sift from among a multitude of signals and pick out the ones that are important, combined with a willingness to change, to consider new ways of doing things, and the mastery or skill of implementing new changes are critical for leaders-to-be.

Understanding and Mastering The Change Process

Many people are afraid of things they don't understand. The more we understand and become competent at something, the less frightening it becomes. Change is no different. Some predictable patterns and reactions to change can be described and understood. One can practice managing small change efforts and in so doing become more adept at managing larger ones. A general change process and ways of managing it are presented in Chapter 16.

Emotional Comfort with Change

For many of us, little about change is comforting, in and of itself. By definition, *change* means getting out of our comfort zone and experiencing different things. Although some people enjoy and seek out-of-the-comfort-zone experiences, most of us seek comfort and solace in the things we know well. We like our habits, which can actually account for as much as 70 to 95 percent of our behavior.

One sign of a high CQ is a positive emotional attitude toward regular change: the feeling that change will be for the better and ought to be embraced. In one management seminar, a participant, describing one of his core leadership principles, said, "Pain is your friend." He meant that learning is almost always the result of something that is uncomfortable or in some way, even a small way, painful, and that learning is good because it helps enhance your competitive advantage, and hence, pain is your friend.

---

[9] See E. C. Zeeman, "Catastrophe Theory," *Scientific American*, 234 (April 1976): 65–83.
[10] See Noel Tichy and Stratford Sherman, *Control Your Destiny or Someone Else Will* (New York: HarperBusiness, 1993).

This idea is consistent with the theme of *The Road Less Traveled* by Scott Peck.[11] Peck argues that most people take the comfortable road, the one they know, but that the person who learns, grows, and contributes more takes the road less traveled, the one with a little discomfort, a little pain, a little learning in it. He notes that taking this path usually means a little extra effort. And it usually results in someone who is better adapted to the world around him or her and more influential in it.

Conclusions

In *Emotional Intelligence*, Goleman uses the metaphor of a journey to underscore the idea that emotional learning is not a single lesson but a course of study: "In this book I serve as a guide in a journey through these scientific insights into the emotions, a voyage aimed at bringing greater understanding to some of the most perplexing moments in our own lives and in the world around us."[12] This purpose is consistent with the concept of clarifying, introduced in Chapter 8.

As with most journeys, a guide can only take you so far. In the end, each traveler must personally make the effort to get from one place to another. The challenge/invitation presented in this chapter to each of us is to assess our emotional preparedness for leadership and to invest in our abilities to improve that kind of intelligence. This assessment requires viewing intelligence in a broader context, one that includes not only IQ, but also EQ, SQ, and CQ.

Concepts Introduced in This Chapter

1. Intelligence is often associated with good leaders, but recent research suggests that effective leaders have many kinds of intelligence.
2. Effective leaders have a high EQ and are able to manage their emotions appropriately.
3. Effective leaders also have a high SQ in that they are able to recognize and help manage emotions in others.
4. Effective leaders demonstrate a high CQ, the ability to recognize the need for change, and some comfort and skill in understanding and managing the change process.

Questions for Personal Reflection

1. How well do you manage your emotions? If you'd like help assessing your EQ, you can search the Web for ways of measuring it.
2. How well can you discern the emotional states of the people you work with on a daily basis? Do you ever check with them to confirm or disconfirm your views? What emotions did you observe at work this past week?
3. When did you last help someone else manage their emotions? What did you do? How did it go? What could you have done better?
4. How is high EQ different from stuffing or ignoring emotions? What is the consequence of each approach?
5. List the major changes you've made in your life. How well did you navigate them? What did you

[11] Scott Peck, *The Road Less Traveled* (New York: Touchstone, 1978).
[12] Daniel Goleman, *Emotional Intelligence* (New York: Bantam, 1995).

learn from them? What feelings were associated with those changes?

6. What signals for change do you see around you today? What kinds of changes are these signals asking you make? How do you feel about them? Do you anticipate making changes or avoiding them?

CASELET FOR DISCUSSION

Ellen was assigned to lead a team of internal consultants charged with discovering inefficient processes in her company and then designing and recommending new processes to replace them. She had five people on her team. Bob was very smart and socially inept in that he often criticized others' thoughts as being stupid or not well thought out. Mary was hard working and willing to do whatever Ellen wanted. Xiwen was also very bright and very respectful. He played three musical instruments and spoke four languages. He often confided to Ellen in private that he thought the team needed to work together better. George was a former athlete, very hard working, and ambitious. He always made it a habit to meet and chat with each team member before each meeting. Lakisha was the only other person with a master's degree. Her field was

technology and science, and she was very good at designing research studies. As Ellen thought about the challenges facing her team in developing reasonable efficiency-enhancing suggestions for the company, she was also concerned about how to help her team work efficiently. She had just been given a new assignment to assess one of her company's divisions and wondered how she should best organize their efforts.

WORKBOOK

There is a simple instrument designed to help you self-assess on intelligence on page 363 of Workbook. Complete the exercise and then make some notes about how you'd like to develop your various kinds of intelligence.

CONTRIBUTING YOUR OWN CASELETS

Have you seen or experienced a situation involving the concepts introduced in this chapter? If so and if you'd like to contribute your experience/situation to our case data bank, please visit http://faculty.darden. virginia.edu/clawsonj/ and click on the "Contribute new caselets" button.

13 | RESONANCE, LEADERSHIP, AND THE PURPOSE OF LIFE

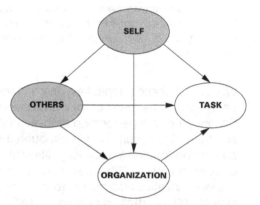

I've always been interested in the mountains. The first time I went to Switzerland, I saw the mountains, and I said, 'This is where I've got to be.' I dropped everything and found a mountain-climbing school and spent a couple of weeks in Switzerland and learned some basics of climbing, how to cut ice steps in glaciers and basic mountaineering. I really liked that. Clearly, in technical climbing you get in situations where, if you slip, you are dead. You don't consciously seek those situations, but you reach dicey points where you basically can only go forward rather than back. And the level of concentration and thrill of operating at that level is just . . . you are alive then, and it's almost like your sense of . . . your visual acuity and sensual acuity dial up tenfold, and you can see things and you are aware

> *of things that you are not aware of in everyday life. That is the part of*
> *rock climbing that I really enjoy.*

—TOM CURREN,

Former senior vice president of strategic
planning, Marriott Corporation

A world-renowned musician performs in concerts all over the globe.

The world-record holder in a swimming event wins the gold medal at the Olympics.

The CEO of a consumer electronics firm reports annualized growth of 40 percent per year for the last 10 years.

The head of thoracic surgery at a major teaching hospital performs a coronary bypass operation on his 400th patient.

What do all these people have in common? First, and most obviously, they are performing at the peak of their professions and probably at the peak of their abilities. Second, they are performing at these high levels repeatedly, not just on occasion here and there. Third, surprisingly, although they come from radically different backgrounds and are performing in distinctly different careers, they seem to be following a consistent pattern. What seems to work in music also seems to work in surgery; what works in athletics also seems to work in business. Each of the people described and almost 500 world-class performers (WCPs) like them, as noted in a study conducted by Doug Newburg,[1] seem to be following a pattern of thinking and behaving that is remarkably consistent. From interviews with these WCPs in various professions, Newburg[2] developed a powerful model of world-class performance. The concepts in this model relate directly to our discussion of how leadership is about managing energy, first in one's self and then in others. This resonance model could help you learn how to perform better, be happier in your work, and even engage a simple but powerful definition of the meaning of life and therefore become a more powerful, centered Level Three Leader.

WCPs are people who are performing at the pinnacle of their professions. The people in Newburg's study include, for example, a world-record holder and Olympic gold medalist in the 100-meter backstroke, a two-time NCAA basketball player of the year, an internationally known jazz musician, the director of training in the thoracic surgery department of a major university medical center, military personnel responsible for the lives of highly trained pilots and their equipment, and the CEO of a high-tech retail chain that has grown at double digits for the last 15 years.

---

[1] Newburg received his Ph.D. in sports psychology from the University of Virginia, where he studied under Bob Rotella. As of this writing, he was employed by the University of Florida medical school thoracic surgery department, where he worked as a performance counselor with thoracic surgery residents.

[2] At other institutions, Mr. Newburg might be called Dr. Newburg; however, the convention at the University of Virginia is that all faculty are referred to by Mr. or Ms. out of respect for the remarkable talents of the university's founder, Thomas Jefferson, who, although never sat for a doctorate, is recognized to be one of the brightest men of our era. In this way, University of Virginia faculty do not presume superior title or capacity to Mr. Jefferson's.

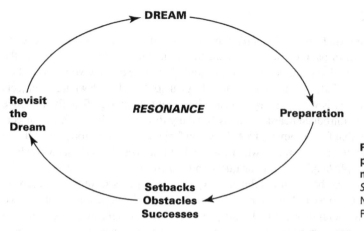

FIGURE 13-1 World-class performance: the resonance model
Source: Based on Doug Newburg, University of Florida

The model that Newburg saw in his interviews consists of the following: consistent high performers have an *experiential* dream; they are willing to work very hard for what they want; they feel a strong sense of personal responsibility for creating the freedoms they wish to enjoy; they all encountered significant obstacles; they managed their own energy and mental state by staying in touch with their experiential dreams; and when they were performing at their best, they reported an experience of harmony or wholeness, which Newburg calls *resonance*. The resonance model Newburg developed is shown in Figure 13-1.

DREAMS

The WCPs in Newburg's sample described two kinds of dreams. The first was the kind of dream that most people are familiar with, the thing they wanted to do or be when they grew up. This do/be aspect might be phrased as "a doctor," "a musician," "an Olympic gold medalist," "a CEO of a rapidly growing company," or "a world-record holder." Typically, the WCPs referred to these aspects as *goals*. Most of us have had fleeting thoughts about this kind of dream, which we will refer to as an "external dream," or D*ext*. We dream of being pilots or lawyers or presidents or senators. Some of us may achieve those dreams; some may not. One thing is clear from this research, though—fulfilling your dreams requires much more than acquiring a title or accomplishing an achievement.

Newburg's WCPs went further and included in their comments an unusual description, a description of an experiential dream—a feeling really—that characterized what was going on inside of them when they were performing at their best and enjoying it the most. A two-time NCAA player of the year in basketball said, "Look, it's not about winning the gold medal. That's our goal, sure. But that's not why I play. My dream is to play to win at the highest level for as long as I can." An Olympic gold medalist in swimming said his dream was "easy speed," the harmony he felt in the water when he tried about 85 percent but got 100 percent of his speed. These sample definitions are "experiential" in that they describe feelings that people have when they are performing at their best, quite apart from what they are doing or what they are accomplishing.

INTERNAL DREAMS

Experiential dreams, or "internal dreams" (D*int*), have to do with how one wants to feel. As discussed in Chapter 12, most of us in life are systematically trained to ignore how we feel at the expense of what we are doing. "No pain, no gain," we're told. "I don't care how you feel, just do your job and deliver those results!" "Stop whining and do your job!" What Newburg's subjects reported, though, is that not only is what's going on inside important, it can significantly influence results. In other words, as we introduced earlier, and as Newburg discovered, how you feel affects your performance. Consider that for a moment: Does how you feel affect your performance? If you say "yes" as most people do, then ask yourself when was the last time your "boss" asked you how you *wanted* to feel. Most people laugh because the question is so absurd, and say "never."

Precedent for this balance between results and experience appears in other research on business management. The Ohio State Leadership Studies, for example, concluded that the two main factors in effective leadership were task and process. The managerial grid developed by Blake and Mouton was one summary of these findings that encouraged managers to pay attention not only to getting the job done, but also to how they did it.[3] It isn't enough to get good numbers; one must also develop relationships along the way. This dichotomy of task and process also emerged in Lawrence and Lorsch's groundbreaking study of organizational design, when they noted that differentiation by task and integration across organizational boundaries was complementary and a necessary force in effective organizational designs.[4]

More recently, Mike Beer and Nitin Nohria at the Harvard Business School explored ways in which leaders of change efforts cluster into one of three categories: those who focus on economic results (task), those who focus on organizational processes (process), and those who focus on both.[5] Further, Jack Welch, during his extraordinary tenure as CEO at General Electric, used a 2×2 grid to plot the talents of his senior executives: one axis was labeled results, and the other was labeled process.

Even though this recognition of the need for balance between task and process is not new, Newburg's subjects clarified the distinction more sharply than many managers do: there are two kinds of dreams. One kind of dream is about achievement, and the other is about experience and feeling.

For most people, this second kind of dream, the internal dream, or D*int*, is a difficult concept to grasp. In part it relates to our earlier discussion of emotional intelligence and the low capacity many have for recognizing their own emotions and emotional experience. Most people are not skilled at this discernment. The basic question related to the internal dream is, how do you want to feel today? Most people never think about this question and would probably find it, at first blush, irrelevant. "It's not about how you feel," they argue, "it's about what you do." It turns out that how you feel can have a big impact on your performance. When Doug first asked me this question, I was stumped. No one had ever asked me this question—not my mother, not my dad, not my professors, not my employers.

The dream portrayed in the resonance model is the internal dream, or D*int*. To begin thinking about your D*int*, you need to distinguish it from your D*ext*, or external dream (of doing or becoming something). What is your emotional life's dream? That is, how do you want to feel on a daily basis? A good place to start is to reflect on how you feel when you are performing at your best. Can you describe it? Can you put into words the inner experience when you are at the peak of

---

[3] Robert Blake and Jane Mouton, *The Managerial Grid* (Houston, TX: Gulf Publishing, 1969).

[4] Paul Lawrence and Jay Lorsch, *Organization and Environment* (Homewood, IL: Irwin, 1969).

[5] Mike Beer and Nitin Nohria, "Cracking the Code of Change," *Harvard Business Review,* May–June 2000.

your capacities? We included a brief exercise in Workbook in Chapter 26 on page 369 to help you begin to identify your D*int*. Some additional concepts will help illustrate this idea of D*int*.

FLOW AND RESONANCE

Mihalyi Csikszentmihalyi, former chair of the department of psychology at the University of Chicago, spent his career studying a phenomenon he called *flow*.[6] He became interested in this concept as a small boy in a Nazi concentration camp when he noticed how some prisoners found a way to tolerate and even magnify their existence whereas others seemed to give up easily and die quickly. Later, he found people in many walks of life who exhibited this ebullient energy he eventually dubbed flow. In the book by the same title, he said that flow had several characteristics (Table 13-1).

1. *Time warps.* To a person in flow, time either speeds up or slows down. If it speeds up, one becomes unaware of the passage of time and suddenly at some point observes, "Wow, where did the time go?" If it slows down, one becomes aware of minute detail as if life were passing by in a slow-motion film. Ted Williams once said he could see the seams on the baseball as it flew toward the plate—as if it were in slow motion. The epigraph of this chapter reflects a time-warp slowdown phenomenon for a technical rock climber.
2. *People in flow lose their self-consciousness.* They are no longer worried about how they appear to others. In flow, they are living inside-out instead of outside-in. Concerns about hair, clothing, language, and so on melt away.
3. *People in flow experience intense focus on the task at hand.*
4. *People in flow perform at their peak, at the limit of their capabilities. . .*
5. *. . . Yet it seems effortless, as if the performance was just "flowing" out of them.* Athletes sometimes talk about this sensation, not straining and struggling, yet they are performing at their best. Mathematicians sometimes say the same, at that moment when the pathway to a solution appears almost effortlessly.
6. *Being in flow is intensely satisfying.* People in flow thoroughly enjoy it. It's a powerful psychological experience.
7. *A larger sense of self is the result.* When a flow experience is over, one feels enlarged, more capable, and more grounded in the world and able to deal with its ups and downs. There is a sensation of growth and development.

TABLE 13-1 Characteristics of Flow

- Time warps (slow or fast)
- Lose sense of self
- Intense focus
- Perform at highest level
- Seems effortless (flow)
- Internally satisfying
- Regain larger sense of self

Source: Adapted from Mihalyi Csikszentmihalyi, *Flow: The Psychology of Optimal Experience* (New York: Harper & Row, 1990).

---

[6] See Mihalyi Csikszentmihalyi, *Flow: The Psychology of Optimal Experience* (New York: Harper & Row, 1990).

Csikszentmihalyi referred to this phenomenon as *flow*. Basketball players call it "being in the zone." Eastern religions and languages refer to it as "wa,"[7] or being in harmony with one's surroundings. Newburg called it resonance. Resonance is the experience of being in harmony with the situation and the events in which one is performing to such an extent that one is able to influence those events masterfully, effortlessly, and with great psychic reward.[8]

So what is your internal life's dream? Is it "to play to win at the highest level," "easy speed," or "light, unhurried, and engaged"? If you cannot answer this question immediately, don't despair. It seems like such a simple task. The first time I heard Newburg speak and describe this phenomenon, I went home and couldn't sleep that night. It took me two years to figure mine out. Perhaps you'll be faster than I was. As you try to identify your D*int*, you might perhaps begin with reflection on the times in your life when you've felt "flow." Virtually everyone has experienced flow or resonance at some point in their life. What were you doing when you felt it? Where were you? What were the circumstances? How did you feel?

When executive groups are asked when they felt flow, the room typically fills with energy and enthusiasm, with much smiling and hand waving as people describe where they were and what they were doing. Some people will mention running, others childbirth, others skiing, some writing computer code, some even calculus![9] (We acknowledge that some will note that sex seems to have all of the characteristics of resonance, but we leave it out for propriety's sake.) Resonance comes to people from different sources.

Transporting Flow

Living your D*int* is not just about playing basketball all day or quitting work to go fishing. Some people will say, "Well, I get flow when I run, but not at work. How can I get that at work?" This question is significant. First, note that the activity and experiencing the activity are not the same. Clearly the activity and the experience are related as we have tried to illustrate in Figure 13-2.

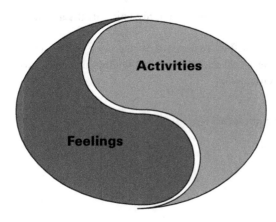

FIGURE 13-2   The interconnectedness between Dints and Dexts

---

[7] In Japanese, pronounced *wah*, which is the *on* or Chinese reading for a character meaning harmony, depicted as a sheaf of rice next to a mouth—a condition of "harmony."

[8] See also Ryan W. Quinn, "Flow in Knowledge Work: High Performance Experience in the Design of National Security Technology," *Administrative Science Quarterly*, 50 (2005): 610–641, for a more academic and slightly different take on this phenomenon.

[9] Yes, calculus. A participant in one executive program described how he had taken an advanced calculus class, aced all of the preexams, took the final exam even though he didn't have to, for the sheer joy of it, and then took all the makeup exams.

What if you could transport your experience of flow in one activity to another? Can a person move the experience to an activity that might not, at first blush, seem a likely candidate? The answer is yes. In other words, one can learn to bring the resonance of basketball, fishing, music, or swimming, for example, to another setting. Think about Csikszentmihalyi's experience as a teenager watching people in the concentration camps. If one could observe flow there amid horrible conditions, why not be able to take flow with you from one activity to another?

When I was a young assistant professor, a senior colleague who was famous for his teaching skills took me under his wing. I asked him one day if he would observe me teach. He agreed, and I prepared late the night before, tried my hardest in class, and ran to his office afterward for feedback. His summary: "You're boring!" Ouch! Then he said, "I notice that you play basketball at lunch with the doctoral students." "Yes," I said, "I love basketball." "It's apparent," he replied, "when you come back, your face is glowing, you are floating down the hall, exuding energy! You've got to figure out how to play basketball in the classroom!" When I heard this, I thought, "Hmm, that's dumb. You can't play basketball in the classroom. Teaching is work, and basketball is play." As I reflected on this, the awareness gradually dawned on me that yes, one can play basketball in the classroom. There's a tip off. One passes the "ball." Some people fumble it, some make fancy dribbles and fancy shots, everyone oohs and aahs, and then we race down "court" in the other direction. The point is that resonant experiences are transportable and those who learn that skill of transporting significantly improve their performance in a variety of activities. The first challenge, though, is to recognize the sources of your resonance and what it is when it occurs so that you are able to recognize it and describe it.

Re-creating Flow

Regardless of where their flow came from, most people conclude that experiencing resonance is a fleeting thing that comes and goes and cannot be re-created. One of the central and most powerful implications of Newburg's research is that many people out there are aware of this phenomenon and are working to re-create it, whether it be in sports, in music, in the operating room (OR), or the boardroom, on a regular basis. A number of professions require excellent performance on a daily basis, where if you mess up, people die or the mediocrity is devastating. If you're the landing officer on an aircraft carrier and you cannot communicate well with the pilots coming down, it's a big problem. If you're an Olympic athlete, you can't be missing the sound of the gun or saving something for tomorrow. If you're a heart surgeon or a performing musician, when the time comes, you cannot be wondering whether you'll be on today; you need "it" to happen regularly and on cue. You may never get to the point where you can "make it happen" every time; however, at least 500 people in the world are ramping up their percentages dramatically.

Some people seem to know immediately what their D*int* is. Others struggle for some time trying to identify it. Perhaps you had a natural awareness of your peak emotional experiences. If not, you may have to work at it for a while before you can identify and feel confident that you've identified what it is that you would like to re-create on a regular basis in your life. An exercise in Chapter 26 can help you work through this question—What is your internal life's dream?

The Universal Search for Resonance

A case can be made that much of human activity is directed at the search for resonance. WCPs recognize it, find a field in which they can experience it, and invest heavily in re-creating it as much as they can in their lives. Average people, too, seem to be searching constantly for resonance. Look at small children. Their curiosity and inquisitiveness are infectious. At play, they are completely engaged, absorbed in the moment, learning, growing, stretching their boundaries. Somehow, as they grow older, this "magic" seems to evaporate from the lives of many. Robert MacCammon, in *Boy's Life*, described this magic as something that gets pounded out of us by family, school, church, and other forms of cultural tradition reinforcement.

As you look around you, how many people do you see who are just going through the motions? How many people do you know who have lost their magic? Conversely, how many people do you know who love their work and seem energized and uplifted by it? Scores of executive education groups usually guesstimate that in their experience somewhere between 10 and 40 percent of people seem engaged at work. Most people are knowingly or unknowingly searching for this resonance phenomenon, but often in the wrong places. Consider the modern addictions—drugs, alcohol, gambling, promiscuity, and thrill seeking—they all seem to be manifestations of this innate human drive for resonance and flow. People naturally want to feel good, to feel productive in the use of their talents, and to do that in an effortless, flowing way. The problem with these addictions, though, is that they are shortcuts to resonance and therefore are false. They miss the seventh characteristic of flow, a sense of growth and expanded capacity. When one gets high on alcohol, drugs, sex, or even the sterile experience of roller coasters and bungee jumping, it is always followed by "the morning after," when one realizes that the high was a false one in that there was no growth involved.

Unless the individual worked to make the resonance experience happen, it becomes nothing more than a short-term engineered artificial experience manufactured by someone else. False resonance doesn't add to your skills, your strength, or your capacity. In short, you haven't grown, so the attempts to take shortcuts to resonance don't work; false resonance doesn't provide the real growth upon which one can build regular resonant experiences. This place in the resonance model forces us to address the topic of working for what we want.

PREPARATION

People who eventually performed at the world-class level moved from the formation of a life's dream (D*int*) to intense, sometimes extended periods of preparation. Preparation is the work necessary to realize a dream. Preparation may include schooling, training, practicing, studying, scheduling different experiences, traveling, making appointments with experts, reading, and changing one's lifestyle or structure. The central goal in each of these activities is gaining mental, emotional, physical, and even cosmological mastery in one's chosen arena. The central question here is, What activities will help you experience your internal dream?

Preparation can take months, years, or even decades. A well-known jazz musician told of renting a remote farm with a small barn behind the house in his early years. For more than a year, he would spend 8 to 10 hours a day in this shed, playing scales on a baby grand piano. His new wife said it was not a very pleasant time. He seldom bathed, changed his clothes, or got a haircut. About halfway through his 15-month "shedding" period, he decided to learn to play with "both" hands, so he crossed his hands and began his self-invoked training regimen again. Co-performers who observed him on stage reverse hands and continue without missing a note were flabbergasted at his virtuosity. So by virtue of his preparation, when he emerged from the shed, he had developed a complete freedom of expression. He could express freely through his fingers on the keyboard what he was feeling inside. It did take 15 months of concentrated effort on top of years of study and practice.

The time spent in preparation to excel becomes irrelevant, though, if the preparation isn't on target and in line with the realization of one's life's dream. Participants resonate because they love the thing itself. To a resonating musician or artist, selling one's work is secondary—experiencing the joy of doing it is primary. To understand this concept, one must remember that the internal dream, the resonance, is different from the external dream, the goal. Good preparation provides momentary glimpses of resonance and how it might be during the real thing. Additional preparation, then, is the work required to lengthen those experiences and to make them more frequent, to increase the probability of making them happen again, and to increase the glimpses of resonance to a designed recurring lifestyle in which resonance is a regular experience. What does it take to prepare that diligently? How does someone become so dedicated to excellence that he or she can work that hard?

THE ENERGY CYCLE

The answer lies in how they manage their energy. We go back to the opening definition of leadership: managing energy, first in yourself and then in those around you. Most people focus on time management, but WCPs focus on managing their energy. What kind of energy would it take for you to become world class at something? Most people give up along the way because the preparation is too intense and demanding. Olympic athletes will train for months and years, over and over again at the same thing, in order to become excellent. One colleague says that "excellence is a neurotic lifestyle," and he's right. To become world class, you must have the energy to devote your time and talent to one thing. Most people don't seem to have this energy—perhaps because they think too much about the end result and not enough about how they love doing the thing itself. If you're doing something because of some future hoped-for result and not because you love it, you won't have the energy required to sustain this kind of intense preparation. "Having to practice more" won't cut it.

WCPs do things out of choice, not obligation. When you move into the realm of obligation, you actually create a drain on your own energy. Consider this quote from Dave Scott, six-time winner of the Hawaii Ironman Triathlon, which consists of a 2.2-mile swim in open ocean water, a 112-mile bicycle race, and a 26.4-mile marathon running, all back to back:

> During a race, I never wear a wristwatch, and my bike doesn't have a speedometer. They're distractions. All I work on is finding a rhythm that feels strong and sticking to it.[10]

What Scott has realized is that even if you set your own goals, they become outside-in, and the sense of duty or obligation ("I *have* to go faster") actually drains rather than enhances energy.

Several aspects of developing energy are required to get to world-class performance. First, the WCPs in Newburg's study talked a lot about freedom. Freedom, it turns out, is important to them. Those in Newburg's sample, in their various ways, talked about the need to feel free, to be free, and to behave freely. They talked about *freedoms of*, *freedoms to*, and *freedoms from*. Although these freedoms are similar, we can see some nuances in the way WCPs talked about their freedoms.

"Freedom of" has to do with freedom of expression. It is a kind of release from the inability to perform. Freedom of expression for an artist or musician, for example, has to do with a developed capacity to put on canvas or into notes an accurate representation of what one

---

[10] *Outside Magazine*, September 2003, 122.

sees, feels, and experiences inside. *Freedom of* has to do with a developed capacity for performing, with the discipline of competency. A freedom of performance resides in an athlete who can jump high enough to stuff a basketball in the hoop or who can swish the ball consistently from 30 feet (as Newburg can). A freedom of performance resides with a surgeon who has done repeatedly and successfully what the body in front of him or her on the operating table needs to have done. Those of us who wrestle with our abilities to perform, whether it's at work, in conversation, in writing, in conducting a meeting, or in coordinating a complex project, are still developing our *freedoms of. Freedom of* is a freedom of performance or expression developed by the discipline of intense practice or preparation.

"Freedom to," on the other hand, means overcoming and moving beyond the parameters and constraints that inhibit us from performing what we know how to do. We may have the ability internal to us, that is, the freedom of performing, but if we aren't invited to the key meeting or if we are restricted from the big tournament or if we are unable to see patients, we may not have the freedom to do what we know we can do. Organizational regulations, customs, traditions, expectations of others, financial constraints, legal guidelines, and other external factors all can prevent us from doing what we are able and limit our freedom to. Unless we have developed a set of *freedoms to* related to managing our external environment, we may not have the freedoms to be in situations where our *freedom of*s can be exercised. One well-known musician, for instance, says that he puts up with and is paid a lot of money for the hassles of traveling from city to city, wrestling with agents, airlines, motels, and difficult schedules—all just so he can be free to perform when the lights go down and the spots come up on stage. What he does then, he says, is for free. He has, inside him, the freedom of expression—and he puts up with lots of inconvenience imposed by the outside world in order to have *freedom to.*

"Freedoms from" relate to conditions or states of mind that keep one from performing at the highest level. These conditions might include lack of confidence, depression, a sense of mediocrity or anonymity, ignorance, or lack of motivation. *Freedoms from* are in one sense enablers of *freedoms of.* If one is free from doubt, free from fear, free from analysis paralysis, one may develop freedom of expression.

The key thing about the WCPs' view of freedom is that they accepted, fully and deeply, the responsibility for their own outcomes. No sense of entitlement came out of the interviews. Rather, these WCPs were aware that it was their responsibility to learn new ways to prepare (practice) and to develop the determination to see that preparation through. This awareness of the freedom–responsibility link stimulated an intense desire to learn, to search for new ideas about how to expand their freedoms.

The Search for Ideas

When a person identifies freedoms that he or she wants to achieve and accepts the responsibilities that come with winning that freedom, he or she begins exploring. This exploration may mean reading, taking courses, creating new experiences, building new relationships, or going different places. Implicit in this exploration is the understanding that, as Alcoholics Anonymous says, "Insanity is expecting different results while continuing to do the same thing." WCPs understand that they need to find, learn, and do something different in order to get from where they are to where they want to be. They realize the connection between freedoms and responsibilities. This exploration leads to lots of new ideas.

The new ideas may come from conversations, films, readings, research, taking classes, new experiences in new places, or reframing old experiences in new ways and places. WCPs are open to and are always searching for new ways of framing who they are, what they want to do, and how they can go about doing it. In a sense, this search for new ideas is developing a freedom from ignorance, ignorance from not knowing who one is, what one wants to do, and what one enjoys doing.

We all, to some degree, engage in this search. In fact, one way of thinking of career development is as a series of explorations down alleys, some of them blind, in which we try things, reject the ones we don't like, and pursue the ones we do like. WCPs explore these various possibilities with a passion in the search for answers that will help them reach their dreams. Many of us unfortunately have given up on the possibility that we could experience regularly the kind of internal thrill we've had when we've been in flow.

Managing Your Energy

The second main issue in the energy cycle is becoming aware of and managing energy enhancers and energy drainers. Time management specialists focus on the hours spent on various activities and talk about balance. Heart surgeons working 100-hour weeks cannot afford the luxury of balancing time. One colleague in surgery focuses much more heavily on managing his energy. He pays attention to the things that drain his energy and the things that enhance his energy. He tells a story, for example, of choosing how to walk from his office to the OR. The direct route is the "back way" through a narrow, bare hallway, often stacked with boxes and other storage items. It's dirty, dusty, and dark, but faster. The alternative route is more circuitous, around a carpeted hallway, and then across a balcony that overlooks the large foyer that includes patients coming and going, and occasionally someone playing the baby grand piano there. By careful self-observation, he noticed that when he took the direct route, his mood and energy somewhat declined by the time he got to the OR. When he took the slightly longer route, he was more upbeat and encouraged, his spirits were higher, and his energy was enhanced.

This same surgeon has paid careful attention to how he feels after he eats. Step by step, he eliminated from his diet those things that drained his energy and retained those foods that enhanced it.[11] If you were facing open chest surgery in a life-or-death situation, what kind of surgeon would you want working on you? No one wants to go into the OR wondering whether the surgeon is feeling "in the zone" that day.

A brief exercise in Chapter 26 on page 364 will help you begin thinking about how you manage your energy. This exercise will help you clarify the things in your life that drain your energy and the things that enhance your energy—and to begin thinking carefully about managing those to your advantage. Note that this self-awareness concept is an extension of the discussion on emotional intelligence introduced in Chapter 12. Most people don't pay attention to how they feel and what causes those feelings. The surgeon just described is a man who pays careful attention to his energy and what influences it. You could be that self-aware too, and if you were, you'd be a big step ahead in managing energy, first in yourself.

The fundamental question related to the energy cycle is, what are you willing to work for? The word "willing" covers a lot of territory. By "willing" I mean that you understand that your freedom in this area depends on you and you alone taking responsibility to make it happen, that you are intensely interested in learning whatever you can about how to perform in this area, and that you are willing to manage your energy to make it happen. We come again to the definition of leadership as "managing energy, first in yourself, and then in those around you." If, indeed,

---

[11] If you'd like to learn more about this kind of dietary journaling, see Kathleen DesMaisons, *The Sugar Addict's Total Recovery Program* (New York: Ballantine, 2000).

leadership is about engendering a voluntary response in followers, then how can you manage a voluntary response in your self-leadership? How can you, like Dave Scott, avoid the common misguided myth of slipping into an obligatory mind-set (telling yourself that you have to do whatever) and stay in the realm of choice and high energy?

These three components of the energy cycle feed into each of the four steps in the resonance model. It takes energy to define and clarify your dream, it takes energy to practice over and over again until you can do something, it takes energy to overcome obstacles, and it takes energy to develop the mental focus that allows you to revisit your dream without external inducement.

Most of us dream about the various freedoms already discussed. We think, Wouldn't it be nice if I had Tiger Woods' endorsement contracts or if I could sing like Bette Midler or if I could manage a business like Jack Welch or Jeff Immelt? In truth, though, most of us, compared with the WCPs, have a shallower understanding of the connection between freedoms and responsibilities. We may be envious or even frustrated because someone else has won their freedom and we haven't. What we lose sight of is that WCPs have worked years—maybe decades—to win their freedoms. Again, we come back to the central question in this section, what are you willing to work for?

In truth, though, most of us, compared with the WCPs, have a shallower understanding of the connection between freedoms and responsibilities.

Maybe you recognize the connection between freedom and responsibility and made a conscious choice that you are not willing to pay the price for developing those freedoms. In this case, you may not be frustrated, you have just chosen a simpler, gentler, easier path, and if you are honest with yourself, you will admit that you are content with the consequences—not performing at the further reaches of your potential and living with limited freedoms. It is a choice. It is, in contrast to Scott Peck's *The Road Less Traveled*, the road more commonly traveled.

Alex Horniman says, "Excellence is a neurotic lifestyle." Many find this statement irritating and uncomfortable. It may only be so to those who have lost an understanding of the connection between freedoms and responsibilities. What Horniman means by this statement is that to perform at one's highest level, one must dedicate a significant portion of one's life to developing that "freedom of." Michael Jordan, for instance, was cut from his school's basketball team in his early high-school years, but became so dedicated to improving himself that he began cutting school classes in order to play basketball. Surgeons spend years and years of rigorous schedules, developing almost obsessive study habits in order to get through medical school and then surgery residencies in order to be able to perform in the OR. Successful chief executives in the private sector often spend longer hours at the office than most of their colleagues, working evenings and weekends. To some, it seems that they are obsessed with their work. To the extent that a neurosis is a fixation on a particular aspect of life, a striking similarity arises between what "normals" might call neurotic behavior and the focused existence in which WCPs live.

In many respects, this level of commitment is similar to that of effective leaders, regardless of their profession or career. One simple, powerful definition of leadership, again from Alex Horniman,[12] is "Leadership is an act of engagement." That is, when a person becomes really

---

[12] Mr. Horniman is a full professor at the Darden Graduate School of Business Administration and teaches a variety of programs at the school and worldwide. Trained at Harvard University, he works in organizational behavior, leadership, managing change, and creating high-performance workplaces.

deeply engaged in a cause, an issue, an activity, or a theme, people begin to notice and to respond even if the person is doing nothing intentionally to lead others. The commitment becomes infectious and leadership happens. Likewise, when WCPs become committed to developing a freedom, they begin to work diligently on the responsibilities associated with achieving that freedom. Pretty soon they develop freedom of and then freedom to and then experience freedom from. Usually, however, the aspiring WCP runs into a wall.

SETBACKS, OBSTACLES, AND ALTERNATE SUCCESSES

Unfortunately, lengthy and intense preparation does not guarantee realization of one's dreams or goals. Many prepare hard and then encounter major setbacks. Perhaps the preparation and training doesn't produce the result one hopes for, but an injury instead. Or the research study doesn't yield new insight, but disappointing statistics. Or traveling to a performance site creates fatigue rather than energy—maybe the experts who were consulted didn't lend much insight. Or the hard workouts don't produce more speed or better accuracy. Or the team meetings produced nothing but heat and friction among the members.

What often happens at this stage, according to Newburg's subjects, is that they believed that if only they could work harder, they could win. Then they began to cycle back and forth between Preparation and Setbacks as illustrated in Figure 13-3. Running into an obstacle, they felt it "necessary" to redouble their efforts and worked harder. Frequently this process created a sort of vicious cycle, work harder, setback, work harder, setback. In the course of this repetitive ping-ponging, the energy, the commitment, and the motivation for the dream became faded, fuzzy, or even lost. When the practice becomes mechanical, the study becomes drudgery, the exploration becomes a task, a chore, and loses its energy, and one is on the path to mediocrity. We call this the "obligatory" or "duty cycle" because the language a person uses in this phase is usually sprinkled with "I *have* to go do this" or "I *gotta* go practice." Whenever you hear yourself using duty-cycle language, obligatory language, beware! It's a good indicator that you're caught in this ping-pong phase and that your energy is draining. It's neither the way to world-class performance nor the way to world-class leadership.

Many people, it seems, become trapped in this preparation–setback cycle, lose heart, and begin exploring other ways of making their way in the world. The aspiring actor or actress becomes a waiter, then a maitre d', and buys a car and slowly becomes a prisoner of obligations, and paradoxically of the ancillary, diverting small successes into areas other than the dream's. When one experiences some small positive feedback in other areas, the temptation to divert

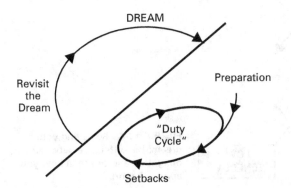

FIGURE 13-3 The obligatory duty cycle
Source: Based on concepts created by Douglas S. Newburg, University of Florida

energy from one's dream and into the alternative activity grows slowly and insidiously. Then one day in a moment of clarity, you wonder how you got where you are and how you let go of your dream. Maybe you never realize the loss, and never ask. The key question related to setbacks and obstacles is, What keeps you from experiencing your internal dream daily?

The Paradoxical Obstacle of Success

In another way, paradoxically, succeeding at one's external dream can lead to alienation from one's internal dream. Often, people who succeed in their external dream are promoted, which may be a good thing or a bad thing. Golfers who win tournaments, for example, are suddenly put upon for corporate outings, endorsement meetings, requests to design courses, invitations to appear on late-night television shows, and so on. If they are not careful, they find themselves playing less often and less well. Perhaps they realize their D*ext*, but they may be losing sight of their D*int*—the feeling they get when they play well. Only if they do what the WCPs in Newburg's study reported as a common means of breaking through the setback/obstacle/success barrier can they be assured of continuing to live their internal dream.

REVISITING THE DREAM

When Newburg's WCPs lost sight of their dreams, their efforts became mechanical and something less than world class. Perhaps they did "well enough" to make a living or to continue on in their chosen profession, but at a more mediocre level. On the other hand, when they were able to remember and focus on their internal dream, the way they wanted to feel, they were able to move ahead with a sense of clarity, purpose, and commitment. Distractions became less enervating, obstacles became less formidable, and setbacks became less depressing. The difference is that the WCPs came back to the hard work, the preparation from the dream side instead of the obstacle/setback side, as illustrated in Figure 13-4. It's much easier to work hard when you are mentally and emotionally connected with how you want to feel—with your vision of what you're seeking—than from the disappointment of another setback.

A mental or perhaps an emotional discipline defines the picture here. It may be an aspect of emotional intelligence. It is not easy to consciously change your mind-set, to refocus on your

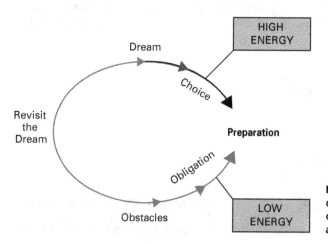

FIGURE 13-4 Revisiting your dream: the difference between obligation and choice in how you approach work

external and internal dreams and find renewed energy for preparation/practice/work. Nevertheless, people who do refocus report an infusion of enthusiasm, a more relaxed approach, and a certain letting go that allows them to perform better. One Olympic swimmer who had previously set a world record listened to the media and became convinced that unless he won the gold medal, his career would be lacking. In his final heat at the Olympics, he tried hard to win the medal and ended up losing by 0.06 seconds. Even though the silver medal is nothing to sneeze at, he was very disappointed. The next day, he was scheduled to swim the lead leg as an underdog in the 4×100 medley relay. He said he felt so tired he wasn't sure he could swim at all. Just before the race, a teammate reminded him, "You should go swim the way you did to get here; don't worry about winning." At that point, he said he determined to focus on how he felt in the water, the "easy speed" he had enjoyed frequently while training, and not to focus on winning. A few moments later, less than 24 hours after losing the day before, he broke his own world record on his leg of the medley and his team won the gold medal. This example demonstrates the way in which revisiting one's D*int* can have a better influence on performance than focusing on one's D*ext*.

When the preparation doesn't seem to be working and the setbacks and obstacles seem insurmountable, WCPs are able to break through the barrier consistently by revisiting their internal dreams. It means pausing, getting out of the vicious failure–I-have-to-try-harder duty cycle, revisiting one's definition of the internal dream, refocusing one's mind and attention on the joy that the dream brings, and letting go of the outcome. Paradoxically, by stepping back in this way, one performs better. Golfers often recognize this concept. If you try too hard to do all the things that you must do to hit the ball well, you become paralyzed. George Plimpton, a writer for *Sports Illustrated*, was once allowed to play three PGA tour events as research for a story and later a book. In his book he describes the paralyzing feeling he had standing over the ball on the first tee. It felt, he noted, like his brain was the captain of an old aircraft carrier shouting messages through air tubes to the engineers below. Keep your arm straight! Flex your knees! Don't bow your wrist. Low and slow. Tuck your right elbow in. Roll your wrists. Push off your right ankle. And so on. His account was hilarious and pointed out that focusing on the outcome and trying harder often leads to disastrous results.

What Plimpton is making beautifully and hilariously clear is that when we try to *manage* our body's behavior, we often fail. The challenge is to let go and engage the experience we seek, the *Dint*. Preparation is essential *and* it can be like a well-used battery: eventually it runs down. Without a way of reenergizing one's efforts, the obstacles begin to have more power than the dream, and they win. Take, for example, the experienced heart surgeon who one afternoon has his 403rd operation scheduled. That morning he lost a patient. Does the 403rd patient understand the frame of mind the surgeon is in just before her operation? If the surgeon is not able to get past the setback experienced earlier in the day, he may not be able to perform at the world-class level that afternoon, something that the 403rd patient would like to know in advance. If the surgeon has a means, external or internal, of revisiting his internal dream, he may be able to revitalize his emotional, mental, and physical self before the 403rd operation. In this case, when the patient died, a call went out to Newburg, who came in and interviewed the surgeon. The basic question was, why did you become a heart surgeon? At first, it is an unpleasant, uncomfortable conversation.

Many people find this line of reasoning too touchy-feely or too soft, but in the end, it's about enhancing performance. The key question related to revisiting the dream is, what will it take to regain your dream?

Pushing back in time with Newburg's nudging, eventually the surgeon recalled his original dream. As a six-year-old boy, he said, he heard a commotion in the house during the night and ran to the living room. There, standing in the doorway, he watched his grandfather die of a heart attack. The boy felt helpless and vowed he'd prepare himself so that would never happen again. That's why, he said, he became a surgeon.

At that point, he reconnected with an emotional experience that shaped his career. The experience of revisiting his dream gave him a new mind-set. Then the two of them, the performance counselor and the surgeon, went to visit the patient, one in a long line of patients. After several minutes of inquiry, also viewed skeptically at first, about why the 65-year-old woman wanted to live longer, she paused and said that she had two grandchildren and that she wanted to go swimming with them. The surgeon at this point was able to connect his internal dream with her dream and in the process was energized.

As it turned out, the surgeon reported later that during surgery he felt as if he were having an out-of-body experience—he could see his hands tying the sutures, flying nimbly, yet it didn't feel like his own. It was as if he were watching himself from above. The four-hour surgery seemed like minutes. He had a resonance experience, most importantly one that he had engineered.

The patient survived the operation and several months later sent him a picture of herself swimming with her grandchildren. After several iterations of this experience, the surgeon learned to manage his own reconnection with his D*int*. He keeps a drawer full of pictures of people with whom he's connected his dream and who have gone on to connect with theirs. When he's down or in an obligatory duty cycle, he pulls out the drawer and looks at one or two pictures and reconnects with his internal dream, the emotional reason why he's doing what he's doing. It is a powerful motivator—in short, an energizer.

By revisiting the D*int* first, the WCP can approach Preparation with a renewed vigor and sense of purpose and, more importantly, enjoyment as indicated in Figure 13-4. By developing the internal capacity to reconnect with the joy of fulfilling one's D*int*, WCPs bring energy, enthusiasm, and the freedom of together in ways that allow them to perform at their best.

The same is true, too, of people who go to work in the work-a-day world where we might not often think about world-class performance. Whenever we begin to think that our work is a drudgery and that our energy is lost, we can revitalize our efforts if we pause and revisit the choices we made that got us to where we are and, more particularly, *how we want to feel* as we are engaged in that activity. Fundamentally, if we understand and use the principles of the energy cycle, we realize that we chose to be where we are.[13] If we allow ourselves to stay in the drudgery mode, the duty cycle, we will not do our best and our opportunities will shrink. If, on the other hand, we are able to reenergize each day by revisiting and remembering that, of all the choices before us, we chose this path, this work, and the way that it makes us feel inside, then we can invigorate ourselves and our work. When we do, when we remember how we are working toward a way of feeling and being, something special happens.

That something special is resonance: the sense of seamless harmony with one's surroundings so that internal experience and external experience are one—the fulfillment of the desire to perform at your best without strain. "Happiness is when what you think, what you say, and what you do are in harmony," said Gandhi. Phil Jackson, award-winning coach of the Chicago Bulls and the Los Angeles Lakers basketball teams, noted, "Winning is important to me, but what brings me real joy is the experience of being fully engaged in whatever I'm doing." When we call this insight, tritely, the "journey not the train station," we underestimate the power of this concept. When we realize the importance of giving at least equal time and attention to our experience as to our attempts to achievement, we begin to see the value of this idea.

---

[13] See William Glasser, *Choice Theory* (New York: HarperCollins, 1998), for more details on the power of this fundamental concept.

Conclusions

The concept of resonance and how to develop it is so valuable, in fact, that it gives us a powerful answer to one of life's fundamental questions: What is the purpose of life? The resonance answer to this question is fourfold: (1) to find your resonance before you die, (2) to invest in the ability to create that resonance, (3) to realize that when resonance occurs, life doesn't get much better, and then (4) to help others find their resonance. Table 13-2 summarizes this view.

The first question is, Can you, before you die, figure out what it is for you that creates this flow or resonance experience? Sadly, many people never figure it out. Second, if you discover your resonance, do you have the energy and determination to invest in your capacity to re-create it on a regular basis? Third, when resonance occurs, will you have the presence of mind to recognize it and acknowledge that life doesn't get better than this? By definition, if you are focused, performing at your best effortlessly, enjoying it, and learning and growing at the same time, what more could one ask for? And fourth, if you can help others discover and re-create their resonance—at home, at work, at play, wherever—what a wonderful kind of leadership that would be in the world!

Some may be concerned that this resonance model is a selfish concept. Consider then that one may resonate as Mother Theresa did in the service of others. Further, if one is helping others find ways to experience resonance repeatedly, how could it be a selfish thing? Others may note that it is a religious view of the world that somehow, it negates deity. If one resonates teaching the gospel or in doing missionary work, go ahead, serve missions, and teach the gospel. The key is, Can you figure out what it is for you that produces this resonance before you die? And if you are lucky enough to do so, are you willing to work for the freedom of re-creating it regularly? The resonance model clearly allows for religious experience as well as scientific focus, fine arts expression, and business achievement.

Sadly, it seems, too many go through life and never identify what resonates for them, never find the endeavor that engages them and calls on their best efforts, never experience in more than fleeting ways the deeply satisfying experience of resonance. What more positive cause could there be for aspiring leaders than to find resonance in their own experience, invest in the capacity to re-create it, to enjoy it when it happens, and then to help others find theirs?

One final question: What about people who have a dream but seem destined never to achieve it? Take, for instance, basketball players who never make the NBA, students who never get to medical school, or managers who never become CEOs. In some cases, we observe almost pitiful attempts to carry on in spite of clear evidence that the dream will not happen. First, in such instances, many of these people are following a D*ext* not a D*int*. They are concerned about becoming somebody or something *instead of* focusing on how much they enjoy their work. Who's to say that the former collegiate basketball star playing in Italy is not enjoying his work? Who's to say that the pharmacist who once wanted to be a doctor is not engaged in helping others improve their health? Who's to say that the

---

TABLE 13-2   The Purpose of Life from a Resonance Perspective

1. Find your resonance
2. Invest in your resonance
3. Enjoy your resonance
4. Help others find their resonance

middle manager frustrated in her attempts to be promoted cannot enjoy her work with her present subordinates or seek a larger job in another company? Who's to say that the writer or the artist who struggles to make ends meet (the external measures of success) is not resonating in his or her work? The difference lies in where we place our attention, Dext or Dint. (An exercise in Chapter 26 is designed to help you work through the key questions related to Dints and Dexts introduced throughout this chapter.)

Sometimes, though, we have to revise our dreams to deal with reality. Clinging to an unrealistic Dext is, in a way, one's own loss of freedom and avoidance of the responsibilities that come with seeking freedom. Finding resonance is also about finding what we can do and doing it to the best of our abilities. When that happens, life is enormously rewarding. If we have felt that resonance ourselves and are investing to re-create it more frequently in our lives, perhaps we can understand why some who seem to be at the end of their careers hang on for a little longer, seeking out of their lives that last ounce of resonance.

Principles Introduced in This Chapter

1. Flow or resonance is found where people perform at their best in an effortless, fulfilling way in harmony with their surroundings.
2. Most people have experienced resonance or flow or "the zone" at one time or another in their lives.
3. Despite common belief, flow or resonance can be enhanced and repeated.
4. World-class performers have dreams.
5. The two kinds of dreams in the world are internal dreams (Dint) and external dreams (Dext). We need to pay attention to both.
6. Some people have a natural dream, others have dreams given to them by their parents or churches, and some people have to rediscover or build their dreams.
7. World-class performers work hard to create their dreams.
8. World-class performers manage their energy as much as or more than their time.
9. World-class performers are especially aware of the relationship between freedoms, responsibilities, ideas, and learning.
10. All aspiring world-class performers have setbacks, run into obstacles, and experience alternative successes that get in the way of living their dreams.
11. The way world-class performers get past their obstacles is to revisit their dreams, particularly their Dints.
12. Leaders who resonate and can help others resonate can produce extraordinary results.
13. One way to define the purpose of life is to suggest that people should find their resonance before they die, invest in their capacity to re-create that resonance, enjoy it when it happens, and help others find their resonance.

Questions for Personal Reflection

1. When have you resonated? What were you doing? How did it feel? How might you re-create it in your work?
2. What is your internal life's dream? (See exercise in Chapter 26 on page 369.)
3. What are you willing to work for?
4. What helps you realize your Dint?
5. What keeps you from realizing your Dint?
6. How can you reconnect regularly with your Dint?
7. What drains your energy?
8. What renews your energy?
9. What would happen in your work group if everyone were resonating regularly?
10. How might you take the lead in moving toward resonance in your work group?

CASELET FOR DISCUSSION

A retired CEO with tens of millions of dollars in the bank was wondering what to do with his life. He was separating from his wife, had seen his children marry, and, although under 60, had already had open chest heart surgery. He'd bought and sold a Ferrari. He'd lived in most parts of the world. He was 30+ pounds overweight. And wondering what to do with the last years of his life. What advice would you give him?

WORKBOOK

Complete the Life's Dream exercise at the end of the book on page 367. Try to write your internal Life's Dream, that is, answer the question, how do you want to feel? Also complete the Energy Management exercise in Workbook on page 365.

CONTRIBUTING YOUR OWN CASELETS

Have you seen or experienced a situation involving the concepts introduced in this chapter? If so and if you'd like to contribute your experience/situation to our case data bank, please visit http://faculty.darden.virginia.edu/clawsonj/ and click on the "Contribute new caselets" button.

14 | THE GLOBAL BUSINESS LEADER

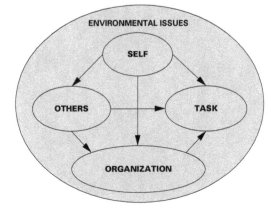

Should we not then be encouraging our managers to be more worldly, more experienced in life, in sophisticated and practical ways?

—HENRY MINTZBERG

In order to succeed in today's global economy, the "flat world,"[1] one will likely be doing business in all corners of the earth. The implications are obvious. How then does one learn to conduct business effectively across regional, national, and subnational boundaries? Without this knowledge and skill, the global economy would not exist. And whereas international business in the latter half of the twentieth century was a small and growing segment, in the twenty-first century we have already created a global economy that affects virtually every

---

[1] Thomas Friedman, *The World is Flat: A Brief History of the Twenty-First Century* (New York: Giraud, Strauss and Giroux, 2006).

human being on the planet. You cannot escape the reality that you live and participate in a global economy. You may be doing business quietly in your home country and then wake up one day to find out that your company is the target of a takeover by a foreign firm. If you check the labels on most of the products in your home, you're likely to find that the majority of them come from international or global firms. Even your wages are affected by the global marketplace and its benchmarks.

We used to think of firms as being primarily domestic, international, regional, or global firms. Domestic firms did business completely within the boundaries of their home country, using local suppliers and serving local customers. International businesses had established offices overseas either for procuring materials or goods or for enhancing sales. These were not truly global firms because their managements were predominantly local and parochial in perspective. Regional firms primarily operated in global regions and reflected the VABEs (values, assumptions, beliefs, and expectations about the way the world is or should be) of that region. These companies might have suppliers and customers across several national boundaries but were contained primarily in the European, North American, African, or Asian regions. Global businesses have operations, partners, alliances, and most importantly, senior managers from all over the world representing virtually every global region. Many will have more than one "headquarter," signaling the diversity of their thinking and perspective.

CULTURES ARE COLLECTIONS OF VABEs

A *culture* is a group of people who share a set of significant VABEs. In fact, shared VABEs define group identities. As you think about your affiliations, how do you "define" yourself? Consider the list in Table 14-1. Rank order your top three identifications. That is, how do you think of yourself in the main?

Global business leaders must work across all of these categories, and to do so effectively requires the ability to respect the identities and affiliations of others. Some people can do that, many or most cannot. We've described these differences earlier in the book. Of course, geographic boundaries are not the only ones. There are ethnic, religious, and racial boundaries. Global leaders must navigate these as well.

TABLE 14-1 Geographic Identity Categories

1. Human
2. Global region
3. Nation
4. National region
5. City
6. Neighborhood
7. Family
8. Individual

The Single Most Destructive VABE

The VABE most destructive to effective global business leaders is this: IR, AYAW. "I'm Right, and You Are Wrong!" As long as any individual holds on to this assumption, the ability to negotiate, to do business across boundaries, and to live in a peaceful world is compromised. This assumption (I say) has caused more pain and death in the world than any other. I can hear your mind spinning clear across space and time. "NO!" you may say. "If that were true, then it's just a relative world and anyone could believe anything they wanted and the world would be in chaos!" Hold on. My assertion is not to say that all the world is relative and that anyone can believe anything they want to. It is to say that when individuals or groups of people or nations assume that they are right and others are wrong, this leads to prejudice, arrogance, condescension, bias, conflict, war, and death on massive scales. In discussing national or global politics and history, this seems obvious. At the level of doing global business, the connections may not be so clear.

People who approach business opportunities with a deep-seated belief that they are right (and/or "righteous"), and others are not-so-much-so, will find it more difficult to consummate a deal. Others will sense their condescension and be put off. Short of conquering the other, though (and that's been a persistent strategy throughout history), this mind-set creates ill-will and disharmony. There are alternative ways of thinking.

One is to think, "I like my way of living, and I allow you to live the way you want, and in fact, I find it interesting to learn about your way of living." Take a simple thing like taking a bath. Growing up in rural Idaho, we took a bath weekly whether we needed it or not. I can remember my mother instructing me to clean the tub when I got out by washing it down and removing the scum ring that had collected where the water line was. Then as a young 19 year old, I went to live in Japan for two years and once, about to climb into a tub of hot water, was accosted by my host, "No, No, No!" You bathe before you get into the water. And for that purpose there was a little wooden stool, some spigots on the wall, a small wooden bucket, some soap, and a short, thin "hand towel." I learned that in Japan you wash yourself thoroughly, including shampooing and shaving, while squatting on this tiny wooden stool and facing the wall and the water spigots. You filled the bucket with water and doused yourself to rinse. After you were spic-and-span, you could get into the water. Why? Because other people were going to use the water after you. Why? Because it cost money to heat the water, and fuel and energy and money were scarce resources, so you conserved them. So which way is "right"?

Of course, the conversation gets more complicated when one considers religion, politics, ethnicity, and race. That said, consider this: if you and I were born in Northern Pakistan or Central Africa or Northern Ireland or South America, would our worldviews be different? If we were born with a different skin color than the one we have now, would we have a different world-view? Of course the answer is yes. Then, how do we get from there to, "I'm Right, and You're Wrong!" Historically, the path has been power and conquering. The global business leader moves beyond that approach to a more mutually respectful one. I have come to believe, given the strength with which most religious leaders and political leaders seem to believe that they are right and others are wrong, that the future of a peaceful globe lies in the hands of global business leaders. This assertion puts a much larger challenge and potential burden on the shoulders of global business leaders. It's more than providing products and services. The ancillary but more important by-product is nothing less than world peace. And when you throw the issues of the environment and sustainability, and the ability to do business in a recyclable world, the burden on global business leaders is enormous and extraordinarily important. So how does one learn to become a better global business leader?

CHARACTERISTICS OF EFFECTIVE GLOBAL LEADERS

Morgan McCall conducted a study of global executives that identified 11 key characteristics that would tend to predict success in global business.[2] These included willingness to learn, integrity, cultural sensitivity, focus on impact, and a broad perspective.

McCall's dimensions come from a study of 838 managers working in six different international corporations. It's a lengthy list. With a little consolidation, though, perhaps we can make it more manageable without oversimplifying. Combining these dimensions with the reflective advice of some successful business people in their own right, we can identify a handful of key characteristics of the modern global manager—as seen from a distinctly Western point of view. We also already know that trait theories of leadership have many difficulties associated with them. That said, we can use this profile as a starting point for a discussion about what one needs to do to become an accomplished global leader.

Overseas Experience

Global executives understand the global economy and what it's like to do business in a flat world because they've lived overseas, sometimes for decades at a time. For some, these experiences are limited to one country or region, and to that extent, their ability to grasp a global perspective is limited. It helps enormously to live in more than one country and in more than one region of the globe. These diverse overseas living experiences usually lead to the ability to speak additional languages, but not necessarily. What's key is learning how business is done in each region and how to play in those different contexts. What's death to a global perspective is constantly wishing to go back home, comparing the local environment unfavorably to home, and living in isolation from the executive ranks in that country or region.

If you haven't lived overseas already or are not eager to do so, it will be difficult to get beyond, to transcend, your own cultural history and perspective. Take the example of Robert Johnson, former CEO of Honeywell Aerospace and later founding CEO of Dubai Aerospace Enterprises (DAE). Johnson in his work with General Electric and later Honeywell had assignments in Europe and Singapore as well as Kansas and New York and Phoenix. As of this writing, he's living in Dubai. Moving from place to place, Johnson maintained a vibrant enthusiasm for learning about each new culture in which he found himself.[3]

Deep Self-Awareness

David Newkirk, a senior international consultant who was born and educated in the United Kingdom and then later worked all over the world and now lives in the United States, noted that "deep self-awareness" that would allow one to understand one's own beliefs and see where they would differ from others' is critical to global executive success.[4] Henry Mintzberg of McGill University in Montreal, Canada, agrees with this as he includes self-awareness as one of his five key executive skill sets.[5] Essentially, what Mintzberg is suggesting is that unless an individual understands his or her own VABEs deeply enough to know when others will differ with them on

---

[2] Morgan McCall, Jr., *High Flyers: Developing the Next Generation of Leaders* (Boston, MA: Harvard Business School Press, 1998).

[3] James Clawson, "The Life and Career of a Divisional CEO: Bob Johnson at Honeywell Aerospace," Darden Publishing, Case UVA-OB-0872, 2006.

[4] David Newkirk, "One Market, *Many* Cheeses," *strategy+business*, issue 29.

[5] Henry Mintzberg, "The Five Managerial Mind-sets," *Harvard Business Review,* November 1, 2003.

those issues, the individual won't be able to see and, therefore, adapt to and tolerate or embrace the deep-seated beliefs of others. One must be aware of one's own beliefs in order to see and appreciate the beliefs of others. Without that, one becomes judgmental and condescending—and opportunities for business evaporate.

Culturally Diverse

It's easy to say that a global executive needs to be culturally diverse, but much more difficult to live it. Are you willing to eat raw fish? Snake? Raw monkey brains? Or to adjust your eating and sleeping habits to match the local executives' routines and patterns? Have you thought to bring gifts to your counterparts? Do you realize how little things can be off-putting, such as sticking your chopsticks in your rice or showing the bottom of your foot to another or touching them with your left hand? Much of this insight comes from experience; hence, our first suggestion is to live abroad, but much can be gained from preparation and reading and from curiosity. I once traveled with a senior executive who had been to a particular foreign country 17 times and never seen anything, by his account, but the inside of the limo and the office. At the other end of the scale, Sir Richard Burton was one of the most energetic cultural explorers during the nineteenth century. Renowned for his determination to find, explore, and live among new cultures around the globe, he once noted, when asked why he did this, "the Devil drives."[6] Do you have a similarly intense interest in the lives and cultures of others? Or is your usual way of thinking that your culture and background are, inherently, superior?

Humility

To be interested in other cultures and how they do things, especially business, implies a certain humility. Since Jim Collins's book *Good to Great*, and his description therein of "Level Five Leadership," humility has taken on a new energy in discussions of leadership. Whereas Collins's description of humility focuses on a lack of self-aggrandizement and egocentricity, humility here focuses more on a belief that other lands and cultures have figured out very interesting answers to life's problems and a good international business person will be open to and fascinated by those answers. By humility, I don't mean discomfort in the company of power and wealth—far from it. Rather, an underlying engagement in learning with genuine interest how others do things. This humility includes the willingness and ability to listen well and with real intent to understand the workings of another way of doing things.

Lifelong Learning And Curiosity

This characteristic is related to humility in that learning has to do with the humble awareness that one has more to learn and that what one "knows" is not enough. Eric Hoffer is reputed to have said that "the learners shall inherit the earth while the learned shall find themselves increasingly suited for a world that no longer exists." It's a powerful concept—that to be "learned" is a dangerous thing. Mick McGill at Southern Methodist University points out the importance of recognizing how your "learnedness" can be self-limiting and self-defeating.[7] The world is changing and moving too rapidly. Without an intense curiosity and desire to learn, the would-be global executive will be left behind and increasingly unable to converse with, much less, keep up with his or her peers.

---

[6] Fawn Brodie, *The Devil Drives: A Life of Sir Richard Burton* (New York: W. W. Norton & Company, 1984).

[7] Mick McGill and John Slocum, "Unlearning the Organization," *Organizational Dynamics,* Autumn, 1993.

Honesty

Despite what many Americans may say about how dishonest other business cultures are (and based on what foundation given Tyco, Enron, World Com, and others?), honesty and integrity are essential characteristics of the executive doing business across international borders. Global business executives must follow through on their promises and deliver what they say they will. Anything short of that and their reputations will suffer in the networking of the political and economic powerful. This is a very interesting and engaging topic. You'd think that "honesty" or "integrity" would be a straightforward issue—either you tell the truth or you don't. It turns out that for virtually every international managerial or executive group I've worked with, the definitions of *honesty* and *integrity* vary widely. Do they mean to tell the truth? The whole truth? Only the truth that you think the other person needs to know? Only the truth that they expect to hear? Only the truth that allows one to do business in one arena and not another? Many of these issues are discussed in greater detail in the chapter on ethics and morality.

But consider this example. I was having dinner one evening with a CEO, an international executive, and the head of his own large business. We were talking about politics and honesty and the Clinton Administration. I quoted him a statement Stephen Covey had mentioned to our class way back in the day: "If a man would cheat on his wife, he'd cheat on his partners in business." This CEO declared that that was absolutely not true, that he knew many executives who regularly cheated on their wives and he would trust them any day in a business deal. In other words, can you compartmentalize honesty? I've been in executive sessions with people shouting at each other about the pros and cons of an issue. Despite all of that and however you personally design your life's ethics and morality, in global business settings, executives need to know when they can count on you. If you don't deliver on your business promises, your reputation will suffer.

Globally Strategic

Global executives have a global perspective, and they can think strategically about managing businesses using the best people they can find from all over the world. The abovementioned Robert Johnson, CEO of DAE, developed a global aerospace business in Dubai using managers from Europe, Africa, the Middle East, India, and the United States and, in less than a year, built an 8-billion-dollar industry with operations all over the world—based on his globally strategic thinking. Much of one's ability to do this comes from a lifetime of networking at the highest levels in boardrooms all over the world, of course. And the ability to see how the various pieces of global industries play out all over the world. Where are the best suppliers? Raw materials? Labor rates? Economically favorable conditions? Opportunities for creating value with better management? Opportunities for adding new technology and realizing greater efficiencies and margins?

Patiently Impatient

At the same time, Johnson notes that one must be patiently impatient. It's easy to see how one might need to be patient in learning to do business in another environment where relationships, history, cultural guidelines, and a sense of timing are different. But how does one become patiently impatient? The implication is that one must be in a hurry and yet patient enough to allow the local and regional processes to unfold as they do. You cannot force a blossom to bloom before its time. Actually, there's a similar principle in aikido, the Japanese defensive martial art.[8]

---

[8] James Clawson and Jon Doner, "Teaching Leadership Through Aikido," *Journal of Management Education,* 1996, 20, no. 2: 182–205.

Well Spoken

Given the challenges of working through interpreters or fumbling with conversational abilities in more than one language, the ability to say clearly what you mean is a key global business skill. If your sentences ramble, if your thoughts are unclear, if you cannot find the words, it will be hard to succeed in business. A friend recently told me of an uncle who could speak seven languages and couldn't be understood in any of them. If you can converse with others in their native tongue, you usually get lots of brownie points for this—however, if what you have to say is so obscure, obtuse, or unintelligible, you'll quickly be in a deficit balance. Communicating clearly is a key leadership skill as we've described elsewhere, and it plays out even more powerfully on the global stage.

Good Negotiators

Doing business across ethnic, national, and regional boundaries requires strong negotiating skills. Some people seem to enjoy the negotiating process much more than others. If one is worried about "taking care of the other" or "not being too aggressive" or "not imposing on others," it's difficult to be a good and strong negotiator. Many business schools teach courses in bargaining and negotiating (often very popular) in the attempt to enhance students' skills in this arena. And there are many techniques and skills that one can pick up by taking these courses. Numerous books are also available to help one think, at least at Level Two, through the principles of effective negotiating.[9] If one can add these skills to an innate enjoyment of the gamesmanship involved in negotiating, one can become quite good at it. Of course, you may be competing with or negotiating with people who come from cultures where negotiating is a part of daily life from the time one is a small child, cultures in which prices are seldom "set," and where everything can be and is negotiated.

Human

This may seem like an odd characteristic. By *human* I mean that one has a strong sense of his or her membership in the global human community, that we are all more alike than we are different. It goes back to our earlier discussion of geographic differences ranging from human to global region and the like down to the individual. Many if not the vast majority of humans tend to identify more strongly with their local groups and cliques than with the human race. The power of this identification process is manifest in the number of religious, ethnic, racial, and other superficial conflicts that continue to rage worldwide. The global business leader may maintain a sense of history, background, and national or ethnic pride; however, their sense of membership in the human group is stronger and dominates their visible behavior. This sense of common identity allows one to negotiate with people from very different backgrounds—something that again most people cannot do. The sense of "We are in this together" and "We should put aside our differences and focus on our commonalities for the sake of doing a deal" is more important to the global leader than uncompromising commitments to religious or ethnic background.

---

[9] See, for example, Roger Fisher, Bruce M. Patton, and William L. Ury, *Getting to Yes: Negotiating Agreement Without Giving In* (Boston, MA: Houghton Mifflin Company, 1992).

Presence

Does presence make a difference in the global arena? Global managers and observers say that it does. Presence comes from different things. One may or may not be large in stature or endlessly energetic by nature (it's an advantage if you are), so it's a challenge to consider consciously and intentionally how you present yourself might influence others. The story is told that Lyndon Johnson, later to be president of the United States, went to Washington, D.C., first as a congressional aide and that when he arrived in the aides' dormitory, he made several trips morning and evening to the common washroom to "brush his teeth." In fact, he was creating opportunities to meet people and begin to gauge them and to practice discussions with them. Later, Johnson was notorious for his ability to cajole and persuade others by sheer size and mannerisms— like bending over and looking another straight in the eye and nose-to-nose demanding his point of view. You've heard of people who, when they enter a room, immediately command, somehow, the attention of everyone else. There's a charisma that surrounds the influential global leader. Part of it, but only part of it, is position or title. By far the bigger portion is dress, self-confidence, energy level, interest in other people, and comfort with the challenges at hand. We may not like to believe that size, dress, speech, energy, and interest in others make a difference—but they do.

Conclusions

Global business leaders are high-energy individuals who are determined to make things happen across national boundaries. To do so requires patience and impatience, a certain humility defined as a respect for the differences across those boundaries, a sense of the commonalities of all humans, and poiseful presence. Many of these things can be learned—some get them naturally and by dint of their genetic inheritances. Living abroad alone won't guarantee the development of an international presence, but it helps a lot. Living abroad with the respect for others and curiosity and determination outlined above will accelerate the process.

Principles Introduced in This Chapter

1. We can view human behavior as collections of agreed-upon VABEs at the human, global regional, national, national regional, city, neighborhood, family, and individual levels.
2. Collections of VABEs also exist across geographic boundaries by race, religion, or ethnic background.
3. Level Three Leadership is very important for the global business leader because cultural differences are differences in collectively-agreed-upon VABEs. Unless one is comfortable recognizing, understanding, and dealing with Level Three

VABEs, it will be difficult to be an effective global leader.
4. The central assumption of "I'm right, and you are wrong" persists in virtually all strong cultures regardless of location or history or origin.
5. Successful global business leaders tend to be less judgmental of the VABEs of other cultures, to be open minded, to have a good sense of humor, to be dedicated to their work, to enjoy seeing and living in different parts of the globe, and to be patient with those who think or believe differently than they do.

Questions for Personal Reflection

1. What group are you most intolerant of or most critical of? Why is that? Would you be able to do business with a person or people from this group? Would you trust a person or people from this group?
2. How many different countries have you lived in for six months or more? What did you learn from your experiences there? What VABEs that you held before you went were challenged by your living abroad?
3. How many different languages do you speak? How does this help or hinder your ability to do business in the global marketplace?
4. List the countries in which you'd be willing to live for two years or more. Why not the countries you didn't list?
5. Would you be willing to eat or drink the "special" cuisine of the following countries? What do you imagine these special cuisines to be/include? Indonesia, Japan, China, Nigeria, South Africa, Egypt, Lebanon, Greece, Germany, Russia, India, Pakistan, Uzbekistan?
6. What characteristics (based on what underlying VABEs) do stereotypical American business people tend to exhibit when they do business abroad? How do these affect business people in other cultures?

CASELET FOR DISCUSSION

As a junior member of an international traveling team preparing for an upcoming two-week trip to Asia, you are told by the CEO a week before traveling that he does not carry bags or credit cards and then he walks off. After checking out of an expensive Tokyo hotel, you get a call from your spouse saying that the credit card is maxed out and he or she cannot buy groceries. That weekend you are to meet with the CEO of a Japanese firm, but your CEO refuses to change into a suit because it's the weekend. Your counterpart meets you at the station, and you can see his face drain of all blood as he realizes that your CEO wearing an open-collared shirt and khakis is about to meet his CEO and his entourage wearing a suit. Your counterpart whispers to you that you cannot allow this to happen, so you urge your CEO into a tiny bathroom about 4´ by 4´ with his suitcase and ask him to change. At the beginning of the luncheon, the host CEO presents his card and some gifts for each team member and waits. At the luncheon, the first course includes raw fish and seaweed and soup with raw fish eggs floating around.

WORKBOOK

Review the list in Table 14-1 and rate yourself high, medium, or low on each of the dimensions listed there. Then, consider how you'd need to develop your skills or personal profile if you wanted to be an effective global leader.

CONTRIBUTING YOUR OWN CASELETS

Have you seen or experienced a situation involving the concepts introduced in this chapter? If so, and you'd like to contribute your experience/situation to our case data bank, please visit http://faculty.darden.virginia.edu/clawsonj/ and click on the "Contribute new caselets" button.

SECTION IV

LEADING OTHERS

15 | POWER AND LEADERSHIP: LEADING OTHERS

You have to look at leadership through the eyes of the followers and you have to live the message. What I have learned is that people become motivated when you guide them to the source of their own power.

—ANITA RODDICK,
Body and Soul, 214

Leadership eventually comes down to influencing others. Even with a strategic vision and skills in managing change, leaders must know how—and be willing—to influence others. This chapter deals with the north–west axis of our basic leadership model, the relationship between leaders and followers. Our earlier definitions of power and leadership (highlighted in this page), along with the discussion of levels of influence (behavior, conscious thought, and VABEs (values, assumptions, beliefs, and expectations)), compel us to consider how we might think about influencing others at Level Three.

> **Power** is the ability to get others to do what you want them to do.
> **Leadership** is the ability to influence others and the willingness to influence others so that they respond voluntarily.

Historically, leadership was associated with title or position. Later, in the mid-twentieth century, leadership was described in formulaic fashion, often as planning, organizing, motivating, and controlling (POMC), or knowledge, attitude, skills, and habits (KASH). These approaches were designed to get others to do what the leader wanted them to do, our definition of power.

The widely read and quoted classical view of power comes from French and Raven,[1] who concluded that people influence others by using one or more of five fundamental sources of power: legitimate authority, coercion, reward, expertise, and reference. Legitimate influence is based on the follower's recognition of the legal authority of the title of the leader. If the follower believes that people should obey their bosses (or the teacher, the duke, the coach, or whatever title is presented), then the follower will allow those people to influence him or her, in effect giving them power. This legitimacy may be because of nobility, organizational title, rank in an organization, or some socially defined right to respect, such as age or seniority. We say that the CEO of a company has a legitimate right to tell others what to do by virtue of his or her title. Police have a legitimate right to tell citizens what to do.

SOURCES OF POWER

1. Legitimate authority
2. Coercion
3. Reward
4. Expertise
5. Personal reference

Coercion, of course, is based on fear. Coerced followers are afraid of the consequences if they do not do what the leader wants them to do. These consequences could be physical, emotional, social, or professional, such as losing one's job or having private or secret information publicly exposed. Sometimes, coercion is nothing more than force of personality, the ability to intimidate a person by fixed stares, glowers, or other facial expressions and intimations.

Reward power comes into play when the leader influences others by offering them something in return for their conformity. These relationships are usually if-then relationships (e.g., "If you do this for me, then I'll do that for you"). Reward power is based on the leader's ability to exchange something of value to the follower, which may often involve money, access to business deals or people, positive evaluations, and so on.

Expertise influence comes about when one person knows more about a critical issue than another. If the job, for instance, is to build a bridge, and the group includes only one civil engineer, this engineer is likely to exert the most influence and become the leader of the group.

---

[1] Based on the classic article by John R. P. French Jr. and Bertram H. Raven, "The Bases of Social Power," in D. Cartwright (ed.) *Studies in Social Power* (Ann Arbor: University of Michigan, Institute for Social Research, 1959), 150–167.

In another group or relating to another goal, of course, the engineer might have no influence. Expertise power depends largely on the task at hand and on followers' perceptions of the relevance of the leader's skills.

Finally, referent power relates to the ability to influence others because they admire, respect, and want to be like the leader. People who want to emulate a person's style will be influenced by that style. People who want to join a club will be open to influence by those who control admission to the club. Referent power is the source of what society often calls "wannabes," those "groupies" who follow celebrities around with the desire to be closer to them and more like them, to be included in their inner circles.

SOURCES OF INFLUENCE AND LEVELS OF LEADERSHIP

People can and do draw upon all of these sources of influence in any given situation. No one uses one source of influence exclusively. Not all sources of power are equally useful, though, depending on the situation, the people involved, and expectations for the future. In the view of leadership described here, reward, expertise, and referent power are all more effective in the long run than legitimate and coercive power. The reason is that legitimate power and coercive power diminish the possibility of a voluntary response, and followers' voluntary response is a defining aspect of leadership.

In the long run, all enduring and effective relationships, leader–follower relationships included, are voluntary and reciprocal in nature.

Legitimate power relies on title rather than on expertise or willingness to exchange rewards. Data from around the world show that the level of respect middle managers have for their senior executives is low, which suggests that legitimate power is not the basis for excellent leadership. Further, legitimate power and coercion often go hand in hand. Coercion may get people to comply in the short run, but it will not have the staying power of the more respectful sources of influence. Coercion is a Level One source of influence: "You do what I say or you'll be punished, and I don't care what you think or feel about it." Using coercion or legitimate power as a basis for getting things done is a formula for mediocrity, not world-class performance.

Expertise power that relies largely on skills and judgments and reward power that relies on mutual exchanges can both be considered rational or Level Two sources of influence. In these uses of power, one person tries to change the thinking of the other person, to persuade the other. The Level Three values of the followers come into play when they consider whether the rewards offered by the leader are attractive, but the target focus is on logical persuasion.

Finally, when someone follows because they want to emulate the leader, they are responding at a VABE level or Level Three. Our identities—who we think we are and who we want to be—are a significant part of a referent response. For this reason, labels and memberships are important in the world, in general, and in leadership roles, in particular. When we say, "I am a Christian" or "I am a Muslim" or "I am a Delta Tau" or "I want to be like John Kennedy," we declare to the world something about our core values and beliefs. Religious leaders, leaders of not-for-profits, political leaders, national leaders, regional leaders, cult leaders, and some business leaders all recognize the power of a Level Three referent approach. Those who ignore it may well have significant influence using the other bases of power, but they "leave something on the table" in terms of their potential for influence.

Furthermore, given our definition of leadership, any source of power that gets people to respond involuntarily is something other than leadership. In this view, coercion moves a person out of the realm of leadership. Individuals may be exerting power and people may be responding, at least in the short run at Level One, but if they aren't responding willingly, then it is not leadership.

Clearly, legitimate power and coercion are common sources of influence used by people in positions of power today. Many people respond to the wishes of others either because they assume that the "boss" has the right to ask, has all the answers, or has the power to hurt them in some way. These approaches are common and well recognized as a means of getting things done,[2] but they are not leadership. Stephen Covey once asserted that when you use your title as a means to get something done (e.g., "I'm the vice president, so you need to do what I ask!"), you're using a crutch. Similar to a walking crutch, a leadership/power crutch is unwieldy and doesn't contribute much to world-class performance. Therefore, even if you have positional power or the means to coerce others, if you use it, you're undermining your own ability to lead.

One way to test this concept is to ask a central leadership question, Are these people doing this work because I told them to or because they understand why we need to do it and voluntarily agree that it's the right thing to do? If the answer is "Because they understand and agree," then you're on the road to becoming an effective Level Three Leader. If the answer is "Because you told them to," then you might rethink the long-term consequences of your approach to influencing others. In the long run, all enduring and effective relationships, leader–follower relationships included, are voluntary and reciprocal in nature.

BRADFORD AND COHEN'S PRINCIPLES OF INFLUENCE WITHOUT AUTHORITY THROUGH EXCHANGE THEORY

1. See others as potential allies.
2. Clarify your goals—what you want.
3. Determine what the other person wants.
4. Determine what of value you can give to the other.
5. Determine whether you have a relationship foundation for exchange.
6. Select a basis for exchange and begin exchanging until it is reciprocal.

BUY-IN

The purpose of any attempt to influence others, of course, is to generate energy in their responses. That is, leaders want to get "buy-in" for their ideas. "Buy-In" is a term that practicing managers and management students alike use frequently. They may say something like, "I'd talk to the boss (or my employees) and make my case and get their buy-in and then go on from there." Many seem to assume in this equation that buy-in is a binary thing, something you either have or you don't.

Buy-in is not really a binary construct. And it's more complex than "positive, neutral, or negative." Consider the analog scale shown in Table 15-1. There are at least seven different levels

---

[2] See, for example, the chapter on coercion in Edwin C. Nevis, Joan Lancourt, and Helen G. Vassallo, *Intentional Revolutions* (San Francisco, CA: Jossey-Bass, 1996).

TABLE 15-1	Levels of Buy-In

1. Passion
2. Engagement
3. Agreement
4. Compliance
5. Apathy
6. Passive resistance
7. Active resistance

of buy-in or commitment to leadership that we might consider. The first level of response to attempt by others to lead is active resistance. This is when the intended followers actively fight against what the leader(s) want. Forms of active resistance might include sabotage, revolt, rebellion, and striking.

Passive resistance is a step above active resistance but it's nothing to be proud of. People who resist passively wouldn't think of themselves as revolutionaries, but as opposed to leadership initiatives and willing to be resistant without being recognized. Passive resistance includes slowing down work, making "inadvertent" mistakes, doing only what's asked, and emphasizing leadership faults in conversations.

Apathy is when employees just don't care one way or the other about what management says. These employees show up, ignore leadership, and after going through the motions, go home. What they care about is not what's happening at work.

Compliance is doing just what one is supposed to do in order to obey. Compliance is "going through the motions," obeying the letter of law or policy or instruction without any consideration of the intent.

Agreement is when employees will say, "I agree to do that," but they don't have any personal energy or engagement in the task. Agreement is, at least, positive and not negative in nature. Employees operating out of agreement are more positively motivated than those in compliance.

Engagement is when employees say not only "I will do that," but "I want to do that." Most leaders would be happy to have this level of buy-in, in that it reflects an internal commitment beyond obedience that augurs well for performance and results. Engaged employees are eager to get to work and eager to engage in the content of their work. They tend to go the extra mile, to think beyond what they're asked to do, and to apply their best efforts while at work.

Passion is a step above engagement in that passionate people put their work as first priority in their lives. Everything else is subservient and secondary to their professional activities. You may think this definition extreme, and in some ways it is. To the extent that excellence is a neurotic lifestyle, it takes passion for the work to organize everything else in life around it. People with passion tend to have few ancillary or alternative interests. They are driven. They may become workaholics. Consider for example, John Steinbeck, the Nobel Prize–winning author of *The Grapes of Wrath*. While he was writing the book, he kept a diary. Part way through the writing, he was fussing with his wife and noted in his diary that if a man is a writer and he has a wife and he cannot write, he should get a new wife. This is shocking to many who believe that family should come first. In Steinbeck's case, his professional activities came first and all else was organized around it. He's not alone. Many world-class performers throughout history have done the same thing out of passion for their work.

One set of questions arises at the individual level as we consider this continuum of buy-in. Any leader or coach or supervisor might ask him- or herself what level of buy-in or motivation are they getting from each individual employee. One might also ask the group-level questions about one's team or department. One could also ask the same buy-in questions with regard to an organization. Consider, for example, issues of environmental friendliness and sustainability. Does an individual "buy-in" to the idea that we need to develop environmentally friendly ways of conducting business? What about the department in general? Finally, does the organization as a whole comply with the laws in this regard, agree with them, engage the concepts, or lead passionately in its industry to implement sustainable concepts because they are the right thing to do?

Additionally, we may ask, What kinds of leadership techniques and approaches tend to lead to higher levels of buy-in? This will be the focal point of the next three chapters as we explore the kinds of reactions that Level One, Level Two, and Level Three techniques tend to produce in others. In these chapters, we'll identify what those various techniques might be and how they tend to influence others on average. In the meantime, we note that many managers rely on their title, their "legitimate" authority, to get others to do what they want them to do. Our buy-in continuum suggests, however, that followers will choose how to respond to all attempts to lead them. Just because a person in authority, an "authoritor," says they should do something doesn't necessarily mean they will do it, or if they do, it will be without any vigor or energy.

THE CURRENCY OF RECIPROCITY

Allan Cohen and David Bradford[3] take this fundamental insight several steps further and argue that relationships in which influence—with or without authority—occurs are based on reciprocal exchanges and that the currencies of these exchanges can be identified and managed. These currencies are not monetary currencies, but psychological ones in which people will exchange, for instance, effort for praise, work for recognition, and compromise for inclusion. Cohen and Bradford assert that this exchange model implies the following logical sequence to developing influence with others:

1. Assume the other persons are *potential allies* in accomplishing your purposes. If you can't make that connection, it will be difficult to consider giving them something they want in exchange for something you want from them. This perspective aligns with the view—the six steps to effective leadership—that a key leadership skill is to clarify what others can contribute to your cause.

2. Clarify your goals so that you know what you want. This step is consistent with our principle of clarifying your vision. If you are unclear about what you want, how can you assess whether others can contribute and how to begin to invite them?

3. Build on Kotter and Gabarro's famous article on managing your boss[4] by carefully assessing the other person's world in order to understand their concerns, their priorities and goals, and their immediate needs. Unless you make this type of assessment, you are unlikely to be able to offer them something they want in return for giving you something you want.

---

[3] Allan R. Cohen and David L. Bradford, *Influence without Authority* (New York: John Wiley & Sons, 1991).
[4] John Gabarro and John Kotter, "Managing Your Boss," *Harvard Business Review*, R0501J.

4. Assess your resources to determine what you can give that they want or need. Sometimes you must evaluate your own willingness to give recognition or praise or other forms of interpersonal currency where you otherwise might not do so.

5. Diagnose your relationship with the other person to see whether the underlying foundation supports a series of exchanges. This step is similar to the need to have the moral rock or moral foundation in place before you begin trying tools and techniques of leadership influence. If the foundations of trust and respect are not in place, developing influence on an exchange basis will be difficult.

6. Select a basis for exchange and start making exchanges in the relationship until it begins to be a comfortable and ongoing reciprocally rewarding relationship, much like a business relationship. If you haven't established a relationship with the other that will support exchanges of mutually valuable currencies, trades or interactions are not likely to occur.

The focus in the Cohen and Bradford model is on the medium of exchange between people, a set of various kinds of psychosocial currencies that are ethereal but very real. People value these currencies differently. If you are skilled in identifying them, identifying which ones a person values, and in exchanging them, you can significantly enhance your ability to influence regardless of your title or authority. Cohen and Bradford identify several currencies in which people can trade influence: inspiration-based currencies, task-related currencies, position-related currencies, relationship-based currencies, and personal-related currencies.

Inspiration-based currencies include vision, excellence, and moral correctness. When you have a vision with larger significance for your department, organization, community, or society, the other person may wish to be a part of it and will do what you ask in exchange for being included. If you are part of a team that is recognized for being outstanding at what you do, the other person may be open to influence in order to associate in some way with this reputation for quality. Alternatively, the other may be inspired by the moral rectitude of your activity and wish to participate in it. The inspiration currencies that the leader exchanges for followership are a new view of where to go, of how good it could be, and of how right it is.

Task-related currencies include new resources, opportunities to learn, home job support, rapid response, and information. If you can offer others additional resources such as money, personnel, or facilities, they may be open to your requests. If you can offer them an opportunity to learn something new, they may respond. If you can lend them support for their work, they may be willing to support yours. If you can promise them quicker response times in your relationship, they may be willing to adjust the way they do things. If you can give them better access to key information that they need, they may be willing to follow your lead.

Position-based currencies are recognition, visibility, reputation, insider importance, and network contacts. If your recognition of their good work, even if they don't work directly for you, could be influential in their world, you could exchange such recognition for their help on your work. If you have access to people who are viewed by others as important, you could trade introductions to these people (visibility) for response. If your comments on the social network of your organization have an impact on one's reputation in the firm, you could exchange reputation-enhancing comments for another's willingness to help. If you are a member of an "inside" group and the other person values membership in that group, you could trade this sense of belonging by including that person. Moreover, if you know people who could benefit the other, you could exchange your introductions as a means of expanding the other person's networks in return for helping you out.

Relationship-based currencies are those that are related to the quality of your relationship with the other person and include understanding, acceptance, and personal support. If you are willing to take the time and emotional energy and have the skills of reflective listening and empathy, you can exchange your willingness to attend to and understand the other person's point of view or situation for their willingness to assist you in meeting your goals. Further, if you can genuinely express a sense of acceptance and friendship with the other person, you will likely have more influence on them than if you cannot. If you can extend your friendship to include personal and emotional support in times of need for the other person, they are more likely to help you when you need it.

Finally, Cohen and Bradford identify personal-related currencies such as gratitude, ownership, self-concept building, and comfort levels as means of influencing others through exchange. When you express your gratitude to others, they often feel closer to you and more bonded so that when you need help, they are more likely to help. If you can acknowledge the ways in which others might "own" or be the key figure in a project, they are likely to be open to your influence. If you can honestly affirm their personal values, their sense of self, or their definition of who they are, they are likely to be more responsive to your requests. Finally, if you can manage your relationship in a way that minimizes the hassles experienced by others, you are more likely to get their attention and willingness to respond.

As you read down through these influence currencies, you probably thought that they could be used in many, perhaps manipulative, ways to get others to respond when your own feelings might not be genuine. A word of caution here: although it may work in the short run, unless you have the moral foundation in place to begin with, using any technique of influence to manipulate will eventually be perceived and your ability to influence greatly eroded. Giving praise to someone who wants it but doing so insincerely will most likely be exposed as fake and your ability to influence at that point will be undermined.

After every exchange, ask yourself, As a result of this encounter, am I viewed as an adversary or an ally? If the answer is "Adversary," your influence declined; if the answer is "Ally," your influence increased (Figure 15-1).

One major advantage of an exchange model is that it helps us to consider how we might manage our bosses or others with whom we have no formal authority. The steps outlined here include searching for the basis for alliances. Many people approach relationships with a strong, though sometimes well-masked, intention of changing the other person. Even if a person says, "My boss is doing the wrong thing, but I need to go in and learn his way of seeing things," they will typically begin trying to change the boss's mind within minutes. Usually with this tone and subsequent conclusion of the meeting, the person is viewed by the boss as more of an adversary than an ally. The challenge is to present yourself as an ally to the other person's goals and aspirations. Unless you can do that, you will be perceived as something of a hindrance rather than a help.

Of course, the first challenge in this approach is to assess and understand the goals, challenges, visions, dreams, and motivations of the other person. If through careful listening

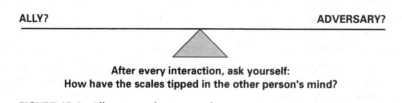

FIGURE 15-1   Ally →←— adversary scale

and observation you can make this assessment, then the challenge is to discover how to help that person achieve what he or she wants to accomplish. This simple construct is the basis for the highly successful careers of many people.[5] If you cannot in good conscience align yourself with the goals of another, then you may not be able to influence them using Level Three approaches.

A major, potentially negative aspect of exchange models is that they can create resentment in people who sense that someone is doing favors primarily to establish influence rather than out of a genuine concern for the well-being of the recipient. In this case, recipients feel "beholden" or obligated to respond in kind. They may meet those obligations in order to relieve their sense of indebtedness, but this effort is not likely to be of the quality or long-term consequence that an aspiring Level Three Leader would hope for. Recall from the earlier discussion of inside-out versus outside-in living that a person who feels an obligation to another, rather than a choice to serve, is not likely to feel great motivation and energy.

The primary solution for this dilemma is to have a deep, honest, and genuine interest in the well-being of others and in helping them achieve their goals. Without it, leadership will eventually be seen for what it is—self-serving and uncaring—a perception that is disastrous to your ability to influence. You may say that you don't particularly like the people you work with or that you really don't have a lot of respect for the people who work for you. In such a case, you may have to settle for Level Two Leadership or even Level One Leadership. Remember then, of course, that if you compete against an organization with a Level Three Leader, you may have a difficult time keeping up.

THE ROLE OF TRUST AND RESPECT

When mutually rewarding relationships are built upon a moral foundation, trust and respect develop and influence the willingness of potential followers. In a study of superior–subordinate pairs in a large insurance company, the level of trust and respect in the relationships accounted for more than 75 percent of the perceived learning that the subordinate experienced. To the extent that learning is a substitute for openness to influence from another, trust and respect are essential in establishing a strong leader–follower relationship.[6]

Sometimes people resist the notion of looking at relationships as a series of trades or exchanges. It seems too commercial to them. Yet substantial momentum behind this view bears consideration. Stephen Covey, in *Seven Habits of Highly Effective People*,[7] compares relationships to the accounts that bookkeepers use to keep track of a company's finances. Covey argues persuasively that we have "accounts" with other people. When we do something for them that they value, we make a deposit into our mutual account, and when we ask them to do something for us, we make a withdrawal. Likewise in reverse, if they do something for us, they make a deposit in our account, and we are likely to be responsive to them in the future because of this "credit balance." If we ask them to do more for us than we have done for them, we may use up our credit with them and perhaps even overdraw the account to the point where they feel that they have been carrying us in the relationship. If they trust us, they may let us carry an overdrawn account in the

[5] See, for example, Zig Ziglar, *On the Top* (Nashville, TN: Thomas Nelson Publishers, 1994), in which a central point is that if one can help others get what they want, one has a lifetime of success ahead. Likewise, Stephen Covey's principle, "Seek First to Understand, Then to Be Understood," conveys the same message.
[6] James G. Clawson and Michael Blank, "The Role of Interpersonal Respect and Trust in Developmental Relationships," *International Journal of Mentoring*, Spring 1990.
[7] Stephen R. Covey, *Seven Habits of Highly Effective People* (New York: Simon & Schuster, 1989).

short run, but this situation is unstable and probably won't last long. The challenge in managing our relationships and our ability to influence others is to maintain at least a balanced relationship account and, if we want to have more influence in the future, to build a large credit balance.

Further, the exchange model system of credits and debits in relationships has been used in many societies and formalized in some. In published accounts of the Mafia, for instance, or in the nation of Japan, clear rules about exchange of favors have been established. In Japan, members of society are taught to watch carefully the balance between *on* (pronounced *own*), or bestowed benevolence, and *giri* (pronounced *gee-dee*), which means duty or obligation. People will manage their obligations so carefully that they may not accept a random act of kindness from a stranger for fear of generating more responsibilities than they feel they can manage in the future.

GENERAL APPROACH TO INFLUENCE

If we consolidate the classic and exchange models of influence introduced here, we can create a general approach to influencing others. In this approach, unless you (1) have a clear purpose, (2) are able to communicate that purpose clearly and inspirationally, (3) can garner the support of others by showing them how the purpose and your relationship benefits them, (4) can manage reciprocal exchanges with others, and (5) can manage progress toward the purpose, you won't have a lasting influence on others.

Purpose

Most leadership fails because of an ill-defined or weak purpose. The leader has no strategic story to tell; the north–east axis of the general model of leadership is broken. If you aren't clear on who you are and what you want to do, you will be unable to inspire superior effort in yourself and in others. It is essential that you clarify what you want to do and commit your professional efforts, if not your life, to this purpose, mission, or dream. Earlier chapters discussed various perspectives on developing a strategic vision, a charter, and of creating a personal dream. Unless you can clarify these things to yourself, you won't be able to engage others.

LEVEL THREE INFLUENCE

Given an understanding of the sources of social power, of exchange theory in relationships, and of the power of the language of leadership, we are confronted with how to use these in developing influence on the VABEs, and hence the thoughts and behavior of others. Effective Level Three Leaders understand, either intuitively or explicitly, the following basic principles: clarify what you want, observe the VABEs of others, confirm the VABEs of others, set a probationary period, and utilize your influence to invite reexamination and modification of VABEs. These principles represent a consolidation of the research and insights introduced in this chapter.

The first challenge is to be clear about what you want. Your life's dream, your mission in life, your ambitions, your definitions of success, and your short-term goals are all a part of what drive your behavior daily. Unless you're clear about these definitions, it will be difficult for you to have influence on others. You won't know how you can trade with others. You will probably be unclear as to what you ask of others.

Second, with a somewhat trained eye you can observe the apparent VABEs of others and gain powerful insight into why they behave the way they do. We devoted Chapter 6 to this phenomenon. Every time someone says, "I should do this" or "People should do that," they are revealing to you part of their core VABE system. If you keep notes—preferably on paper because thoughts are so ethereal and imprecise—you can begin to develop a profile of a person's Level Three motivations.

Observations are only observations—they don't necessarily reflect fact. So, the third step in a Level Three influence model is to confirm your observations. By talking with the people, you can confirm whether your observations are accurate. Politicians do it all the time to try to get the "pulse of the country." Of course, one may interpret the data in self-serving ways. Nevertheless, it is important to confirm whether your inferences are, in fact, accurate. You might meet with a person you're hoping to coach or train and note, "You know, it seems to me from watching you that you really value getting positive feedback. Is that true?" Or, "From watching you, it seems that you believe if you want it done right, you have to do it yourself. Is that right?" You'll find out quickly whether your inferences were on target or off base.

Fourth, most leaders set time frames of some kind. They ask themselves, how long am I willing to give to this effort? In the case of influencing others, in singles, pairs, groups, or organizations, leaders make the same assessment. They may announce their time frames. Often it is better not to. Announced deadlines, particularly in change efforts, can come back to embarrass you. If you want to coach a person toward changing their behavior, you might declare to yourself, "I'm going to give this effort six months." Then, at the end of your "probationary time," you can reassess and determine whether it's worth it to carry on.

Fifth, with a clear goal in mind, a clear understanding of the other's VABEs or Level Three realities, and a bounded time reference, you can begin "coaching" or influencing. This coaching could take any number of forms including speeches (to larger audiences), one-on-one counseling sessions, debriefings of performance, supervision of practice sessions, and so on. Your effort may bring to bear all of your best skills as a leader and a coach. You may learn this process along the way by reading or seeking your own counsel from other experts.

At the end of your probationary period, you can then pause and assess how the effort is going. Is the person making progress? Have you established a stronger relationship? Are you making more effective exchanges? Is the performance improving? If the answer is yes to these questions, then you can, with a certain sense of satisfaction, acknowledge your developing skills as a Level Three Leader, one who is influencing the basic VABEs of others and doing so in a respectful way with voluntary responses. If, on the other hand, little or no change is made, you may necessarily conclude that the effort is not working out.

Two basic reasons explain why you might have negative results. Either your skills as a coach are insufficient to have impact on the other or the other's CQ, or change quotient, is too low. In either case, you may stop the effort and reassign either yourself or your counterpart(s) so you both can move on to more productive efforts. Again, this process happens in every walk in life, in politics, in the military, in athletics, and every day in business organizations.

Conclusions

Leading and influencing others is a complex task. You can go about trying to lead in many different ways. If you choose to influence others using power as a base and the tools of coercion, manipulation, and force, you will get a Level One response; the body may move, but the head and the heart will be unfazed. If, on the other hand, you choose to work a bit harder on the front end to clarify your wants and the other person's VABEs, and learn how to speak in ways that are clear, respectful, stimulating, and congruent and if you use that language ability to extend invitations to others, you are likely to get favorable responses, not only behaviorally, but also at Level Two and Level Three.

This approach implies that the ability to influence others, and to influence them deeply, is as much about attitude, philosophy, and motive—*your* attitude, *your* philosophy, and *your* motive—as it is about learning specific techniques and tips of leadership skills. If you truly want to be more effective in leading others, then we invite you to consider the principles introduced here and focus on your purpose, your language, and your ability to deliver what we might call Class Five invitations—those that invite world-class performance at the upper end of the 1 to 5 performance distribution introduced in Chapter 13.

Concepts Introduced in This Chapter

1. In general, we use our titles, coercion, rewards, our expertise, or our group membership to influence others.
2. People respond to our attempts to influence others in a variety of ways. Their "buy-in" can be arrayed on a continuum ranging from active resistance to passive resistance to apathy to compliance to agreement to engagement to passion.
3. Virtually all relationships are based on exchanges, which must be mutual and approximately equal if the relationship is to endure.
4. Language is one of the most powerful tools of the effective leader. The language of leadership is clear, respectful, stimulating, and congruent.

5. Effective efforts to influence others respect the goals of the other and present one's self as an ally to the achievement of the other's goals.
6. Effective leaders know how to issue world-class invitations that get voluntary responses from the people they wish to influence.
7. Level Three Leaders are clear on their wants, observe others to infer their VABEs (wants), confirm those VABEs, and set time limits for their change efforts. They coach as well as they can as an ally, using respect, invitations, and exchanges, and then assess and either stop or move on.

Questions for Personal Reflection

1. How do you most often try to influence others? What sources of influence do you use most frequently?
2. When you influence people, are you aware of how they are responding on the buy-in scale? How can you tell?
3. What are the personal goals of the people you'd like to influence? If you can't think of them, how can you present yourself as an ally? If you can't list them, how could you find them out?
4. Make a list of the people or groups of people you'd like to influence. Next to each person or group, note whether you've been trying to influence them at Level One, Level Two, or Level Three. If you've been trying at Level One, consider the consequence of your efforts and the results you're getting. If you've been trying at Level Three, consider how you might make those efforts more effective.
5. The next five times you try to influence someone, listen to yourself speak and search for the invitation that is clear, respectful, stimulating, and congruent in

what you say. Think about how you might improve your invitations. And compare your language with the kind of buy-in you get in return.

CASELET FOR DISCUSSION

Greg struggled with his relationship with his boss, Barbara. Greg was a planner and liked to have things sorted out in advance. In Myers–Briggs terms, he was strong J. Barbara, on the other hand, was strong P. She tended to like to explore all the options and delay decisions, whereas Greg wanted to find an acceptable answer and move forward. Both were very active contributors to their organization and made valuable additions in several different arenas. Recently, Greg had worked hard on two projects. Both had sat on Barbara's desk for months. At a team meeting, she announced that times had changed and she wanted to start over on each project. Greg felt frustrated, deflated, and resolved to disengage from Barbara's leadership.

WORKBOOK

There are several exercises in Workbook that you can use to sharpen your interpersonal influence skills. We invite you to complete the Leadership Steps Assessment, the Life's Story Assignment, and the Assessing the Moral Foundation of Your Leadership exercises. We've also included a Team Assessment Exercise that you may find useful.

CONTRIBUTING YOUR OWN CASELETS

Have you seen or experienced a situation involving the concepts introduced in this chapter? If so, and you'd like to contribute your experience/situation to our case data bank, please visit http://faculty.darden.virginia. edu/clawsonj/ and click on the "Contribute new caselets" button.

16 | THE HISTORICAL STRENGTH AND MODERN APPEAL OF LEVEL ONE LEADERSHIP

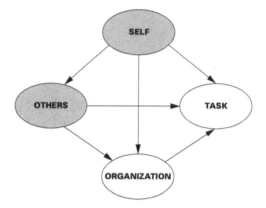

The COO looked at Lisa blankly and told her she had never studied leadership, didn't know anything about it, and had no desire to learn. Lisa was stunned. In questioning her further, Lisa learned that the COO's management philosophy was simple: people need to do what they are told and not whine.

—REPORT OF AN ANONYMOUS EMPLOYEE
IN A LARGE ENGINEERING FIRM

To achieve and maintain the relationships we need, we must stop choosing to coerce, force, compel, punish, reward, manipulate, boss, motivate, criticize, blame, complain, nag, badger, rank, rate, and withdraw. We must replace these destructive behaviors with choosing to care, listen, support, negotiate, encourage, love, befriend, trust, accepts, welcome, and esteem. These words define the difference between external control psychology and choice theory.

—WILLIAM GLASSER[1]

Level One Leadership, leadership that focuses on influencing visible behavior primarily, has been the dominant leadership model throughout history. This in all likelihood began with the hunter–gatherer era described earlier and has extended well into the modern era. In early human societies in which we presume authority was determined by force and power, a focus on controlling visible behavior would have been a natural outgrowth of taking or assuming positions of authority. If you fought to gain control, you fought to maintain it. More recently, most people in leadership positions (let's call them "authoritors" so we can distinguish between good leaders and ineffective leaders in positions of authority) over the last 200 years of the Industrial Era have also subscribed to a Level One approach to leadership. There are a number of reasons for this. Level One Leadership seems to be simpler, faster, more efficient, and to some more "moral."

Level One Leadership is "simpler" because one doesn't have to think about or worry about what the others are thinking or feeling/believing. You tell someone to do something, and either they do it or they don't. And you can see that. You can measure what they do. You may note whether they do it with enthusiasm and energy or as if they are stuck in molasses, but that is a side consideration that's attributable to "their personality." Level One Leadership is indeed simpler—unless you take into account how much you have to super- vise others when you use a Level One approach. Consider conscripts in the armies of the earlier millennia. If, during the invasion of Greece, the Persians were right behind their Asia Minor draftees with spears, the conscripts would have bolted for home. Likewise, if a modern Level One Leader leaves the room, "follower" performance typically drops off dramatically.

Level One Leadership is "faster" in that all an authoritor has to do is specify carefully the behaviors he or she wants to see and step back, and it either happens or doesn't. No lengthy conversations are required, no in-depth analyses, just clear, specific instructions. Clarity of communication is an important skill for the Level One Leader. And problems with results are often attributed to lack of clear directions or listening or employee motivation.

Level One Leadership also often seems to many to be more efficient, that is, you can get things done faster. Giving orders, dictating, compelling, and threatening can make things happen immediately. The time from issuing a command to seeing someone move is often shorter with Level One techniques. This gives rise to the old saying, "When I say jump, you should be asking how high on the way up!" The problem is that this apparent efficiency is not real. The underlying buy-in is usually low on our scale and people begin to slow down, to lose energy, and to procrastinate. This leads to an overall lower level of efficiency over time.

Level One Leadership is also seen by some to be more "moral." These people are uncomfortable with "tinkering" with a person's mind or personality and believe it a matter of ethics to focus only on visible behavior. For them, the carrot-and-stick approach is tried and true: entice your followers with carrots and if they don't respond, beat them with sticks. In this distinctly Skinnerian approach, human thoughts and values are like the indiscernible contents of a hidden box and, therefore, irrelevant to the goals of a leader. The often-overlooked implication of the carrot-and-stick approach (which, by the way, implies that the object of

---

[1] William Glasser, *Control Theory: A New Psychology of Personal Freedom* (New York: HarperCollins 1998).

attention in the middle is a mule)[2] is that one must begin to take into account what is happening inside the person in addition to observing the person's external behavior; if you don't, how can you know which carrots and which sticks will work? Level One Leaders sidestep that issue by assuming that everyone is motivated by money.

The carrot-and-stick approach, though, requires an explicit or implied link between the carrot and one's internal values—if I don't like carrots, I'm not motivated to move. Although it makes sense to reward people for desirable behavior, it is folly to hope for one behavior while intentionally or unintentionally rewarding another.[3] If you don't know what people value, how can you design an effective reward system? And it is clear that different people value different rewards. Extra pay to one person is an incentive, whereas job fulfillment to another is a stronger incentive. People will indeed exchange time and some effort for financial return—in some cases for a pitifully small financial return.

Much of the research about operant conditioning in psychology and about its cousin, expectancy theory in management, attempts to clarify the connections between reward and behavior. Expectancy theory—which asserts that motivation to effort, in general, is a function of a person's belief that they can do a task, multiplied by their belief that they will be rewarded for doing that task, multiplied by the value of that reward to them—begins to question the strictly Skinnerian view. If a person doesn't value the reward, expectancy theorists would note, the motivation of the individual declines rapidly. Expectancy theorists, therefore, want to know what rewards people value (Level Three) and why. That inquiry leads us to a decidedly non-Skinnerian viewpoint that leaders must understand and work with more than visible behavior—that effective leaders must work at Levels Two and Three.

LEVEL ONE LEADERSHIP ASSUMES CONSISTENCY ACROSS INDIVIDUALS

One of the underlying assumptions of Level One Leadership is that people can be thought of as interchangeable machine parts. Perhaps this is normal given the growing size of organizations (so that it's hard to meet and know every individual) and the pervasive thinking of engineers following the invention of mass-production techniques. Leaders for at least 100 years took a mechanistic view of organizations. But people are different from machines in many ways. Our abilities to think and to value one thing above another—different from our neighbors—set us apart from machines, and other mammals, with which we expect behavior to be consistent across individual units: every robot should, and does, behave the same way.

The assertion of this book is that because human behavior is so closely connected to both conscious thoughts and VABEs, if we hope to understand why people behave the way they do, we must understand something about their thought processes, their hierarchies of values, and basic assumptions about the way they think the world is or *ought* to be. And if we want to lead those people we need to understand why they behave the way they do.

Our definition of leadership (the ability and the willingness to influence people so that they respond voluntarily—essentially managing energy first in yourself and then in those around you)

---

[2] Harry Levinson, *The Great Jackass Fallacy* (Boston, MA: Harvard University Press, 1973).
[3] See Steven Kerr's classic article, "On the Folly of Rewarding A While Hoping for B," *Academy of Management Journal* 18 (1975): 769–783.

implies that in true leader–follower situations, the *willingness* of the followers is essential to effective leadership. Unwilling followers, or obligated followers, are low-energy followers. If we want to get enthusiastic high-energy followers, we must attend to the issue of energy—which is a function of a person's thoughts and their VABEs. We must pay attention to whether we are forcing people to obey or whether they are choosing to do our bidding. That means, we must be concerned with what people think and feel. If the authoritors leave the vicinity, what do the followers do and why? If the rewards offered by the authoritor go away, what do the followers do and why? Do they choose to continue doing as they were asked? If so, perhaps leadership is truly occurring. If not, perhaps what was happening was not leadership but some other form of power-based relationship.

LEVEL ONE LEADERSHIP TECHNIQUES

Level One Leadership focuses primarily, if not exclusively, on visible behavior. The Level One Leader is not concerned about what people think or feel, but only what they do. By ignoring what people think or feel, the Level One Leader has the luxury of just giving directions or orders to the followers and of expecting them to obey or comply. The common tools of the Level One Leader, therefore, are giving directions, giving commands, giving instructions, telling people what to do, demanding results, demanding reports, and meting out punishment when results are not achieved. One of the problems with this approach, though, is that the followers often find it offensive and demeaning.

COMMON LEVEL ONE LEADERSHIP TECHNIQUES

Orders
Commands
Directions
Intimidation
Threats
Coercion
Incentives
Rewards
Manipulation
Goal Setting

Bob Sutton of Stanford University, in his *The No Asshole Rule*,[4] describes obnoxious jerks who get to positions of leadership often in large part because of their ability to intimidate others. These people yell, shout, curse, throw things, pound the table, jump up and down, foam at the mouth, scream, and otherwise seek to bully their way through their managerial careers.

---

[4] Robert Sutton, *The No Asshole Rule: Building a Civilized Workplace and Surviving One That Isn't* (New York: Warner Business Books, 2007).

Clearly they don't care about what others think or feel; they only want to control the others' visible behaviors.[5]

A more modest but equally insidious aspect of Level One Leadership is a slavish attention to results and goal achievement. Here, Level One Leaders focus so heavily on goal setting and achievement that they begin to assume and to promulgate what I believe has become the single most energy-sapping managerial assumption of the past 100 years:

PWD WTHTD ROHTF

It's an assumption that many equate even with maturity and adulthood, and in my view, it's a two-headed monster that saps energy from employees in most organizations. The assumption (VABE) is this:

Professionals will do what they have to do regardless of how they feel.

Many, if not virtually all, managers seem to believe this. Many, in fact, would argue that this assumption is the basis of "adulthood." Children do what they want based on how they feel; adults learn to sacrifice choice and feel for the sake of performance. Consider, though, that when you put employees in an obligatory mind-set and put aside how they feel, you negate the very things that create energy, enthusiasm, and creativity: choice and enjoyment.

So intimidation, threats, commands, dictation, overattention to goals at the expense of experience, and coercion or manipulation in any form are Level One tactics and they all have a big downside.

THE DE-ENERGIZING IMPACT OF LEVEL ONE LEADERSHIP

Level One Leadership has been, as noted above, the dominant model in history: the strong controlled the weak. Yet such behavior is not exactly powerful; indeed, by our definition, it is not even leadership (unless the response is not voluntary). When we focus only on the visible behavior of others and ignore and downplay an understanding of what they are thinking, believing, and feeling, we retreat from leadership as influencing others to respond willingly and move toward a coercion-based relationship. Were the kings of medieval Europe leaders or dictators? Did people do what they bid because they feared for their lives or because they shared a common value set? In power-based dominance relationships in business, employees are frequently aware that managers, the self-proclaimed leaders, are not interested in them as people, only as cogs in the bureaucratic machinery or as means to a goal. In other words, they take a Level One approach to leadership. And that awareness alone, that the managers don't really care about us, but only for the jobs we do, is in itself de-energizing.

So when you begin with a lack of caring, expectations of undeviating consistency across individuals, and a focus on external results only, and you add obligation instead of choice to the mix, you get low-energy, unengaged "followers." If and when this kind of relationship is tested by events or situations that hit at or question what the employees think or believe, their loyalty to the Level One Leader will be severely threatened. Their stamina for continuing as asked will

---

[5] We continue to refer to "visible behavior" to help you see that "controlling behavior" is really a misnomer in that one is only able in any way to control *visible behavior*—brainwashing and cult creation aside for the moment. When we refer to "behavior," we must consider more than just visible behavior.

seep away, along with their willingness to contribute creative thought and passionate effort. If treated in this manner for an extended time, employees will become what the system encouraged them to become—mentally and emotionally disengaged from their work, bringing their bodies to the job, but leaving their minds and hearts at the entrance, out of gear and idling in neutral.

This chain reaction creates the next link in the chain, a strong and central interest in "motivation." Managers have asked themselves repeatedly over the last 100 years how can they better motivate their employees. No textbook on management is complete now without extensive chapters on motivation. How do you get employees to do what you want them to do? The usual answer has to do with incentives. We go to great lengths to avoid thinking about employees' conscious thoughts and underlying VABEs and to design incentive systems that work momentarily and then slump back down into the lukewarm pool of tepid followership. If managers paid more attention to followership as needing to be voluntary and to the dynamics of Levels Two and Three of human behavior, the issue of motivation would be much less critical.

Nevertheless, for a long period of time, Level One Leadership, the traditional approach, worked remarkably well. Worldwide economies were expanding, labor was relatively inexpensive and easy to find, and the relative stability of domestic markets allowed managements to view labor as a commodity like plant and equipment. In this light, the formation of labor unions can be seen as a large-scale, organized reaction to the impersonal approach of Level One Leadership. Nevertheless, the system "worked," and companies grew and were profitable.

Today, though, with the environment changing so dramatically and competition growing even more fierce, management teams can no longer compete successfully with that kind of mercenary, Level One relationship with their employees.[6] Getting one-half to two-thirds of employees' energy is no longer good enough. Everywhere now, people are looking for ways to create high-performance workplaces. Unfortunately, many managers attempt to retain their old management principles and at the same time apply the new, emerging leadership techniques superficially, at Level One. This type of disconnect can be observed in the application of the latest management fad—whether it be Total Quality Management (TQM), empowerment, or self-directed work teams—without concomitant changes in the other aspects of the organizational reality, like reward systems, promotion systems, training, structures, operating cultures, and leadership approach. The difference between espoused theories of leadership and leadership behavior creates in the minds of the employees a credibility gap. "Leaders" say one thing and do another, or fail to "walk the talk." This credibility gap saps employee energy to obey or comply. It need not be this way and it is, because although research has uncovered many of these issues in the last 50 years, the "world" knows more than what most managers do. This gap is also known as the "knowing–doing gap." The credibility gap and the knowing–doing gap leave many, if not most, employees disheartened by their authoritors' behaviors.

Many of the new management systems attempt to deal at Levels Two and Three. If they are applied in a Level One way, though, they often fail, and those Level One Leaders who tried say, "See, I told you. This won't work." A Level One Leader attempting to implement a Level Three program is likely only to create more cynicism among employees. The observance of the gap between new programs and old persistent styles of managing breeds alienation in the workforce.

---

[6] The relationship between Employees and Organization is represented by the south–west axis of our basic Diamond Leadership Model illustrated in Figure 3-4.

Conclusions

Level One Leadership has been pervasive throughout history. On the surface, it seems to be more efficient and effective. Those results tend to show up only in the short run. Over time, leaders will get higher levels of buy-in from using Level Two and Level Three techniques. We'll explore Level Two techniques in the next chapter.

Concepts Introduced in This Chapter

1. Level One Leadership is leadership that focuses primarily if not exclusively on controlling visible behavior.
2. Level One Leadership has been the dominant model throughout human history probably because in history the strong controlled the visible behavior of the weak.
3. The dominant assumption of the Level One Leader is PWD WTHTD ROHTF.
4. Level One Leadership techniques include force, intimidation, coercion, threats, manipulation, commands, and punishments.
5. Level One Leadership is inherently de-energizing.
6. Level One Leadership persists because it grows out of historical power structures and is seen as simpler, faster, more efficient, and more "moral."

Questions for Personal Reflection

1. Pay attention during the course of a week and note on paper or in a journal the number of times you observe Level One Leadership occurring around you. Note the circumstance and the specific behavior that you observed.
2. Note during the course of a week how many times you tell someone to do something without concern for how they think or feel.
3. Reflect on your personal history and note in your journal incidents in which you were commanded to do something regardless of what you thought or how you felt. Note how you felt during those incidents.

CASELETS FOR DISCUSSION

Caselet 1

An analyst for a Wall Street brokerage was planning an extended weekend vacation to the Caribbean with his fiancé. He'd informed his supervisor about this months in advance and was caught up on his work. On the

Thursday before the planned Friday departure, the boss told the analyst that they had a high-powered meeting scheduled for Monday morning at 8:00 and that he needed the analyst to stay home and work through the weekend to get the analysis and data package for the meeting ready. The analyst protested but was told, "Either you stay and do the work or you're fired." The analyst canceled all of his arrangements and worked through the weekend, including an all-nighter on Saturday. He put the report on his boss' desk at 7:30, Monday morning. As he went by his boss' secretary's desk, he asked her about the meeting. She replied that there was no such meeting scheduled.

Caselet 2

The director of a leadership development program was concerned about one of the participant teams in her latest program. The three team members were not getting along, and although they had a final presentation to the CEO due in six weeks, they had not been able to agree on the project focus, research methodology, and milestones. At last, the program director went in, threatened the group with embarrassing themselves in front of the CEO, and told them to "grow up." Six weeks later, the team made a successful presentation. Two of the three sent in essays on what they'd learned from the project; the third member did not.

WORKBOOK

If you haven't already, complete the Leadership Levels Assessment to get a rough indication of your profile on the three levels.

CONTRIBUTING YOUR OWN CASELETS

Have you seen or experienced a situation involving the concepts introduced in this chapter? If so and if you'd like to contribute your experience/situation to our case data bank, please visit http://faculty.darden.virginia.edu/clawsonj/ and click on the "Contribute new caselets" button.

17 | THE CHALLENGES OF LEVEL TWO LEADERSHIP

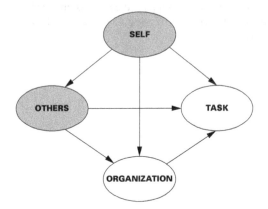

There has never been any doubt that, under certain circumstance, emotion disrupts reasoning.

—Tony Damasio[1]

Level Two Leadership is leadership that attempts to influence the way others think. This approach assumes that a person's thinking affects their visible behavior, and therefore the way to affect visible behavior is to alter the way the other person *thinks and decides.* Level Two Leadership is all about rationality, gathering information, data, rationale, arguments, and using those things to persuade others. Level Two Leadership assumes that others are "mature, rational adults" and will be persuaded by superior arguments and data.

Level Two Leadership became much more popular with the Renaissance and the rise of reason and science. Before that, certain institutions held control of truth and defined what was acceptable and not acceptable. With the Renaissance and then the Industrial Revolution,

---

[1] Antonio R. Damasio, *Descartes' Error: Emotion, Reason, and the Human Brain* (New York: Avon, 1994).

mankind became more susceptible to reasoning and data-based arguments than before. If Level One Leadership is about the body, Level Two Leadership is about the head or the brain and specifically, the cortex.

THE HUMAN BRAIN

Because Level Two Leadership is concerned with influencing the way people think, we should explore something about how that happens—that is, how people think. The "science of the mind" is evolving rapidly so that what we know now will likely be expanded and perhaps superseded in the near future. Most researchers today acknowledge that the human brain is comprised of three main sections: the brain stem, the limbic system, and the cortex.

The brain stem sits physically atop the spinal cord and seems to be, in structure and function, an evolutionary residual of reptilian ancestors. Scientists refer to the brain stem as the "reptilian brain." It controls relatively primitive activities such as hunting, roaming, mating, territorialism, and fighting.[2] We might wonder how the influence of our reptilian brain stem serves us in a modern global society where interconnectedness, cooperation, collaboration, and partnering are much more valuable and essential than in the distant past. How much of human behavior today is driven by reptilian instincts compared with higher level motivations? How can we encourage one and not the other? How much can any individual control those basic instincts?

The limbic system lies above the brain stem. This set of structures is generally related to the development of mammals in the evolutionary chain. This region contains modules and segments that control emotions, including interest in play, happiness, sadness, and, it turns out, preferences. Disturbances in the limbic system can affect a person's enjoyment of things and perhaps lead to oscillations in mood and the variations in feeling that give variety and color to life.

The cortex is the "third brain" and the most highly developed. In it reside the capacities to think, to problem solve, to recognize, to connect symbols to concepts, to remember, to sense time, and to evaluate options. The cortex is what makes us human in some sense. With a cortex, we can see and express concern for others, for humanity, and for the future, interpret the past, and attempt to lead ourselves—the subject of another chapter. The cortex itself is, in science, divided into several regions or lobes. Each of the various lobes seems to have specific functions, yet the degree of interconnectedness and, in some cases, overlap is substantial.

Eric Kandel, Nobel Prize–winning scientist of the mind, for example notes, "The new biology of the mind is potentially more disturbing because it suggests that not only the body, but also the mind and the specific molecules that underlie our highest mental processes—consciousness of self and of others, consciousness of the past and the future—have evolved from our animal ancestors. Furthermore, the new biology posits that consciousness is a biological process that will eventually be explained in terms of molecular signaling pathways used by interacting populations of nerve cells."[3]

Consider for a moment the development of the human brain at birth. Evidence suggests that the human brain is proliferating at the rate of 250,000 cells per minute at birth up until the point that it reaches a complete complement of some hundred billion neurons. And each of these neurons has the capacity to make 10,000 connections to other cells. These are astronomical numbers.

---

[2] Richard Restak, *The Brain* (New York: Bantam, 1984), 136.
[3] Eric R. Kandel, *In Search of Memory: The Emergence of a New Science of the Mind* (New York: Norton, 2006).

Each brain cell, or neuron, has a nucleus contained within a cell body, an axon or long spindly section, and a series of dendrites or branches that can look like the branches of a tree. Some neurons have dendrites at both ends, some just at one end. Some axons can be as much as one meter in length, phenomenal length given their tiny size.

The tips of the dendrites connect to other cells, neurons, or muscles. But they don't really "connect" in that there is a tiny gap or *synapse* that separates the two physical entities. Brain researches have learned a lot about these tiny gaps and the amazingly complex series of chemical and electrical processes that occur there. If these minute synaptic processes are deviated or disturbed in any way, the results can be enormous for the individual's living and experiencing.

One major observation here is that the cell-to-cell connections or pathways that are used more repetitiously become stronger. That is, they develop more dendritic connections, and the process becomes "easier" for the organism. The more you practice writing with your right hand, the more neuron-to-neuron and neuron-to-muscle connections are created and the easier it is for you to be "right handed." This capacity for dendritic development apparently continues throughout one's life. In other words, if you practice a thing repetitively, regardless of age,[4] you can improve your skill and comfort with doing that thing. By the same token, if you do not practice a thing, your capacity to do it, on the whole, deteriorates—that is, your physical dendritic connections begin to disappear.

Child developmental psychology suggests that children develop cell-to-cell connections rapidly during the first 6 to 10 years of life. The habits of speech, language, physical play, handedness, and hundreds of other routines become "gelled" during that period. By *gelled* I mean the dendritic connections that support the comfort and ability in doing something develop or don't. And those that don't are apparently resorbed back into the body—that is, disappear. This physiological discussion makes it easier to understand how habits form and how hard they might be to change, as discussed earlier. Consider, for example, habitual ways of thinking.

FORMULAE AND DEDUCTIVE REASONING

You are aware that you think and of your own presence. Deviations in the development of the brain may lead to the two main categories of mental dysfunctionality noted today: mood disorders and thought disorders. Mood disorders (such as bipolar disorder) may be more related to the limbic system, whereas thought disorders (such as schizophrenia) may be more associated with the cortex. In normal development, as one learns and then goes to school, cell-to-cell connections are made in ways that we don't completely understand yet so that one develops patterns of thought. We can speak, for example, of inductive reasoning and deductive reasoning and note that some people find one more comfortable than the other.

Many people are more comfortable with deductive reasoning. *Deductive reasoning* is thinking that begins with a principle and then applies that principle to experience in the world. Formulae represent principles that deductive reasoners can use to apply to the world. Told that "force equals mass times acceleration," a novice physics student can begin to measure the mass of an object and its motion and calculate the force. Told that "assets equal liabilities and equity," business students can begin to calculate the capital structure of a corporation.

---

[4] Recent evidence suggests that even in cases of severe trauma it is possible for "neurogenesis" to occur. Some severed nerves can with persistent effort (months or years) regenerate. For more information, see Norman Doidge's book, *The Brain That Changes Itself* (New York: Penguin, 2007).

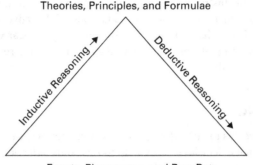

Theories, Principles, and Formulae

Events, Phenomena, and Raw Data

FIGURE 17-1 Induction and deduction

But where do the formulae that deduction requires come from? They come from those who have thought inductively over the millennia. Induction is the reverse of deduction in that one begins with phenomenological experience, that is, with things that happen. By watching them carefully, one can begin to describe the patterns, and then create the principles that describe why those events happened. Newton was using induction as he observed heavenly and terrestrial bodies and wrote his laws of physics. So too were the early shaman and religious leaders, who observed various phenomena and created a "pattern" to explain them. We can think of induction and deduction as opposite slopes on a mountain of knowledge, induction rising on the left and deduction descending on the right, as shown in Figure 17-1.

This distinction is important to note in connection with a discussion about leadership, because formulae abound in the business world. Researchers and writers over the centuries have given us formula upon formula in economics, accounting, finance, marketing, and operations. And as the years have gone by, the formulae have proliferated. One result of this is that business education has become largely the attempt to pass on to the next generation of students the capacity to remember and use all of these formulae.

There are, however, several problems with this. One is that business, the processes of exchanging value between humans, is dynamic not static—that is the processes change from time to time, sometimes rapidly. In this environment, the ability to see patterns in raw events, to infer principles in those patterns, and then to apply them in high-stakes situations with relatively immediate results becomes a critical set of skills. Yet although business students need to develop these inductive logic skills, their business education is largely comprised of deductive exercises. This is a major dilemma. How does one decide how much of the insight of previous thinkers new students should learn in proportion to developing their own skills in pattern recognition in the chaotic marshes of raw data? On the one hand, we don't want students or employees to take too much time and effort in reinventing wheels that have already been discovered. On the other hand, we don't want them to lose their mental capacities to invent "wheels" that are emerging and evolving.

Neurolinguistic Programming (NLP) represents a line of reasoning that suggests that as people learn to learn, they develop practiced pathways of the mind that lead to characteristic patterns in their thinking. Proponents of NLP will argue, for example, that some people prefer to see things in order to learn better (visual types), some people prefer to hear things in order to learn well (audial types), and some people prefer to be physically engaged in order to learn (kinesthetic types). Given our earlier discussion of the brain and its neural nets, there's a well-founded rationale for this basic premise. Some neuron-to-neuron pathways may favor the visual linkages, whereas others may favor the audial ones. NLP advocates will argue that you may hear a visual say, "I see what you mean" and audials say, "I hear you." But all of this is to suggest that people develop patterns in the way they think as they repetitively use one set of neural pathways and not another.

DECISION MAKING

We use our thought processes to make decisions. Or not. Sometimes we get paralyzed by analysis. Leaders, though, must make decisions. They help us determine whether to go left or right. Up or down. In or out. And formulae help us to do that.

Take for example the time value of money. Would you like to receive $100 now or $120 next year? It's a deceptive question. On the surface, it seems simple if one is aware of the formulae associated with calculating the time value of money. First, we have to know the prevailing interest rate in question. If the interest rate is 10%, then we'd be delighted to get $120 next year because we could reasonably be assured of getting only $110 next year if we got our $100 today and invested it.

Or would we? Is there any risk associated with getting that $120? Is it a "sure" thing? Is there such a thing as a "sure" thing? What if interest rates went up during the year? What if the organization promising me the $120 next year went bankrupt in the meantime or was nationalized by its local government? How could I assess those probabilities if at all?

But review the question again: Would you like to receive $100 now or $120 next year? The rational answer might be determined as we outlined in the previous two paragraphs. But what if you were facing eviction and needed the money today regardless of your investment opportunities in the future? What if you wanted to establish a relationship in a country where for political or other reasons you weren't concerned about the return on investment? What if you were trying to show a tax loss? Then what you like becomes a critical part of the discussion. And it turns out, the decisions made in business are not always (who knows what the proportion is?) the most rational. Yet at some point someone must make a decision and act.

COMMON LEVEL TWO LEADERSHIP TOOLS AND TECHNIQUES

Logic
Data
Reasoning
Analysis
Charts
Argument
Debate
Goals
Discussion
Formulae
Evidence
History

Goal Setting. There is one more major area of discussion we need to introduce here: goal setting. While this discussion might have been introduced in Chapter 10, we introduce it here because it is a distinctively cognitive activity. Scholars have long debated why people are motivated to do one thing and not another. As mentioned before, Norhia and Lawrence's book *Driven* posits four fundamental human drives: to acquire, to protect, to procreate, and to create. That drive to acquire—to add a little bit more no matter how much we have—leads us to a discussion of the role of goal setting in human behavior. Humans set goals for themselves and others. In fact, setting goals is a major means of influencing behavior both in self and in others. Research suggests that humans expend more energy on a goal when it's specific rather than general, when they believe they can accomplish it, and when they are committed to it.[5] Clearly one person's goals are not the same as the next person's, and further, some people have many more goals than others. Effective leaders will learn how to manage the processes of setting goals for themselves (self-leadership) and for others. If the leader's goals don't match the followers' goals and/or the follower's don't believe they can achieve the leader's goals, motivation—that is, energy toward the goal—will likely go down. We'll use the importance of proper goal setting as a segue into the topic of how to convince others logically, that is, at Level Two, of what you want them to do.

LEVEL TWO TOOLS AND TECHNIQUES

Level Two Leadership's main tools are logic and data. One needs both to make a strong and robust argument. If you want to persuade someone to your point of view, you'll need, for the rational parts of the effort, good logic and good data. Many decision makers ignore logic and rely on their gut feel or their personal preferences (VABEs) to make decisions. We'll come to that later. For now, though, consider the attempt to convince someone else of your conclusion using rationality. How does one make a good Level Two argument?

To be effective at convincing one rationally, the sequencing of your logic must be clear, impeccable, and powerful. This (as well as the rudiments of neuroscience introduced earlier in this chapter) is the subject of books and whole departments in universities so we won't try to re-create all of that here, but we can suggest some beginning tips. The first would be to get some good books on logic and read them. Essentially, what they will assert are the same principles one uses in good science. These principles include the following:

1. *Clarify your concept.* What is it exactly that you want to get across? If you cannot state your conclusion or your premise succinctly, you probably haven't thought through it carefully enough. You may have studied this notion in your composition classes in school. That principle is important in leadership as well: what's your point?
2. *Avoid non-sequitur assumptions in each step of your logic.* Ensure that each step in your logical analysis and progression is built carefully on the previous one. Avoid interjecting wishes or hopes or dreams or sidesteps in the development of your arguments.
3. *Present your supporting data and analysis transparently.* The data you present should be representative, unbiased, and complete. Don't omit contradictory evidence. Make sure your analysis fits the problem and that you're not using an outdated or refuted technique.

---

[5] Edwin A. Locke and Gary P. Lathan, "Building a Practically Useful Theory of Goal Setting and Task Motivation," *American Psychologist,* 57, 9 (September 2002): 705–717.

Make sure your data are well selected using proper principles of sampling. Be transparent about every step of the process. Let your listener "see" your logical steps and the conclusions you reached.

4. *Make sure you're dealing with similar concepts.* Don't mix apples and oranges. Stick to the central concept.

5. *Avoid tautologies.* Beware of circular reasoning. Robust logic has a beginning and an end, not an end that is the beginning. We discuss the notion of causal maps elsewhere in the book.

6. *Present your conclusions based on the analysis and data.* Avoid allowing preferences, wishes, hopes, and other illogical and extraneous issues and comments to creep in.

7. *Protect yourself against your own biases.* Retain a desire to find out the "truth," that is, the way things are and the way they work. Try to acknowledge your own biases (hard to do) and focus on the facts and data at hand.

8. *Find allies.* Many executive decision makers respond to the "weight" of advice. If you can find several people, especially those who are respected by the executive, to agree in advance with your rationale, you raise the probability that your arguments will be listened to.

9. *Cross-check.* Check your reasoning with intelligent and experienced others to ensure you're not overlooking something. Have you considered all the forces at play? Have you left something out? Does your sounding board agree with your logic step by step? And your conclusions?

Using these principles, you will able to develop logical arguments. Whether they are convincing and compelling, of course, will depend on several things. Did you deliver the conclusions in a way that the boss could get it?[6] Did you "borrow authority" by citing other well-known authorities who agree with you? Did you take into account your boss' Level Two cognitive habits? That is, if he is a visual (see the NLP discussion earlier in this chapter), did you include charts and diagrams in your presentation, or did you assume that he or she would adapt to *your* preferred style? Even if you did, even if your logic is clear, robust, well buttressed with good data, and includes a comprehensive citation of related authorities, the other may not agree with you and may not accept your recommendations. It happens all the time.

THE PROBLEM WITH LEVEL TWO LEADERSHIP

The problem with Level Two Leadership is that virtually every formula contains or is built upon multiple assumptions, some of which may or may not be true or consistent. Newton assumed that time and space were consistent and unchanging. Einstein relaxed that assumption and the whole theory of relativity, which is a better explanation of the way things work, came into being. Economists often make assumptions, ceteris paribus (all other things remaining equal), to assert their theories. The problem is that all other things are not equal and unchanging. What's worse, lots of people, even most people, hold VABEs about the way the world is or should be that don't match the data or the logic. When these two come into conflict, it's not clear which will win out. It's a daily battle in the minds of every human being: Do I accept this new information and data, or do I reject it because my old way of thinking is more comfortable for me? Of course, they don't think that necessarily at Level Two; they may only experience that at the semi- or preconscious Level Three.

---

[6] Here are two excellent accounts: Restak, op cit., 147–156; and Damasio, op cit., 1–19.

Not everyone makes rational decisions. In fact, we might argue that no one makes completely rational decisions, that every decision has a distinctly irrational, value-laden (read "Level Three") component to it. Many decisions are based purely on desire or preference. You may win the argument and still lose the decision. There are many reasons for this: personal preference, saving face, pride, investment in the past, avoidance of risk so going with the "safe," and so on.

Let me state it more bluntly: Without your Level Three VABEs, you cannot make a decision regardless of the quality of your logic and your data. Perhaps you've heard the story of Phineas Gage.[7]

Gage was working on a railroad in Vermont in 1848. His job was to tamp down the gun powder in holes drilled in granite to blast the path for the railroad. One day he made a little mistake, the metal tool he used for this tamping caused a spark, and the gunpowder went off and shot out of the hole and up through Gage's head and out the top of his brain. Long story short, Gage amazingly survived this event, but the tool had surgically removed portions of his brain that controlled his emotions and preferences. Subsequently, Gage was studied extensively given the oddity of his survival. He was later able to manipulate numbers by adding and subtracting and the like, but he couldn't make the simplest of decisions like what color socks to wear, when to meet with his therapist, and so on. Although he could calculate, he couldn't decide because along with specific parts of his brain, he'd lost all preference. Without your VABEs, you become little more than an organic computer. This is why learning to influence people at Level Three is so important. Rationale alone is not enough.

There is a huge collision daily in the minds of business leaders worldwide. This collision occurs as these executives experience the impact of visible behavior, conscious thought, and underlying VABEs about the way the world is or should be. People do things the executives don't want them to. So, executives try to control employees' "behavior." And in those efforts, they often use logic to be persuasive and compelling. But in the end, both Level One Leadership and Level Two Leadership behaviors boil down to a need to examine and understand the underlying assumptions upon which the "higher" level conclusions and formula are built. This leads us to Level Three.

Conclusions

Since we developed a more complex brain, we humans have been using that brain to try to convince others of the correctness of our thinking. Since the Renaissance and the development of scientific methods, we have tried to rely more and more on logic, reason, data, and analysis and less and less on feelings and beliefs. Many have gone overboard in this attempt and stopped recognizing the importance and impact of people's less rational beliefs and feelings. Rational debate and argument will only take you so far. To be a complete leader, you need to learn how to function at Level Three.

Concepts Introduced in This Chapter

1. With the Renaissance and the age of reason, mankind's interest in rational leadership grew dramatically.

2. The tools of Level Two Leadership are reason, rationale, logic, data, persuasion, and argument.

3. The human brain contains reptilian, mammalian, and "human" elements developed over millions of years of evolution. Each of these has significant influence on our Level One visible behavior.

[7] Michael Lewis, *Moneyball: The Art of Winning an Unfair Game* (New York: Norton, 2004).

4. Goal setting is a primary means by which humans consciously drive their own behavior. Effective leaders learn how to set specific, doable goals that are aligned with those of their employees.

5. Level Two Leadership is concerned with authoritors' attempts to influence the way people think, especially how they make decisions.

6. Decisions, however, are affected not only by reason and logic but also by preference and emotion.

7. Level Two Leaders must consider not only the strength of their arguments but also the open-mindedness and mature rationality of their targets in order to be effective.

8. Effective Level Two Leadership approaches are typically characterized by sound logic, robust data, and excellent and sensitive delivery.

9. In the end, even the most sound and robust arguments may not be enough to sway another's thinking or decision making. This leads us to Level Three, the realm of VABEs.

Questions for Personal Reflection

1. When you try to influence another, how often and well do you use logic and data to make your points?

2. Do you assume that others are mature, rational, logical people and that they should agree with the strength of your logical arguments?

3. When another tries to influence you, do you ever ask, what data make you reach that conclusion? or how did you reach your conclusion? in the attempt to uncover their logic and their supporting data?

4. Consider all of the people you've met thus far in life. In your estimation, what proportion of them respond to sound logic and robust data?

5. In what areas of life do you observe lower levels of logic and data than in others? What about business and business-related decisions?

6. Consider all of the business decisions that you've come in contact with thus far in life. What proportion of them were made on the basis of sound logic and robust databases? Why?

CASELET FOR DISCUSSION

Caselet 1

Johanna, a recently graduated MBA, was asked by her boss to prepare an analysis of whether her company, a global manufacturing firm, should purchase a small company in a foreign country with ancillary markets and competencies. Johanna was thrilled to be using her education and set about assembling a small team and then gathering, analyzing, and compiling her data. She gathered information on the economy of the country, including interest rates, exchange rates, political trends, and privatization history, the financial history of the firm, including its revenues, profits and debt structure, nature of the labor market, technology base, and fit with the parent company's stated strategy. At the appointed time, after an enormous, challenging but satisfying effort, she and her team came into the executive conference room to report. Johanna was confident in her findings and the quality of her thinking and data. She was eager to present her findings. She laid out her decision, which was not to buy the firm, and her rationale and data. The executives listening waited patiently until she had finished. Then she was asked to return to her desk and find another answer to the question.

Caselet 2

Read *Moneyball* and explain the nature of decision making in Major League Baseball in the United States. Is it rational or something else? Be prepared to describe a time when you won the argument based on your data and logical analysis and "lost the war."

CONTRIBUTING YOUR OWN CASELETS

Have you seen or experienced a situation involving the concepts introduced in this chapter? If so and if you'd like to contribute your experience/situation to our case data bank, please visit http://faculty.darden.virginia.edu/clawsonj/ and click on the "Contribute new caselets" button.

18 | THE FOCUS AND IMPACT OF LEVEL THREE LEADERSHIP

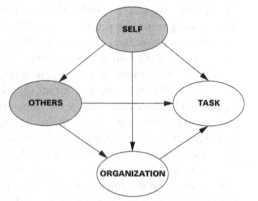

Without exception, men and women of all ages, of all cultures, of all levels of education, and of all walks of economic life have emotions, are mindful of the emotions of others, cultivate pastimes that manipulate their emotions, and govern their lives in no small part by the pursuit of one emotion, happiness, and the avoidance of unpleasant emotions.

—TONY DAMASIO,
The Feeling of What Happens, 35

Level Two and Level Three Leadership is leadership that recognizes the importance of the thoughts and values of potential followers. Level Three Leadership is the ability to influence people's hearts, that is, their basic values, assumptions, beliefs, and expectations (VABEs) about the way the world is or should be. Whereas Level One Leadership focuses on getting compliant visible physical movement out of people, Level Three Leadership seeks to get deep-seated engagement or even passion. Level Three Leadership recognizes that workers of today's generation are looking for more than a monthly paycheck; they want meaningful work that is worthy of not only their time and talent but also of their creativity and commitment. Because of how they are treated, many employees worldwide end up believing, at Level Three, that work and engagement are incompatible.

Level Three Leadership recognizes that in service-oriented economies, unless one can engage people at Level Three, they cannot and will not deliver superior customer satisfaction, much less delight. In a Level One Leadership organization, the myriad "moments of truth," when service or product is delivered to the customer, will be experienced by the customer as unsatisfying and irritating.[1] The fast-food drive-through window employee operating at Level One delivers the sack of food with a fake smile and no eye contact; when questioned about the four missing items, the employee says, "I put them in there, you must not be seeing them" and then gives an impatient look because you are holding up the line. This kind of Level One employee is going through the motions. In a world where competition is growing and some companies are learning how to organize large numbers of employees to care about what the customer thinks and feels, the alternatives will be more attractive to customers who are tired of dealing with employees who are only operating at Level One.

Level Three Leadership seeks to understand the basic assumptions and values of employees and to match them or educate them toward harmony with the goals and strategic directions of the firm. This relationship is represented by the east–west axis of our basic leadership model. Level Three Leadership recognizes the importance of dealing with people at this level and rejects the basic assumption that leaders don't need to know what people are thinking and feeling and only need to focus on people's behavior. Level Three Leadership assumes that employees' behavior is closely intertwined with their thoughts and feelings.

Clearly, Level Three Leadership requires potential leaders to have a different perspective than the historically dominant Level One approach described earlier. Level Three Leadership also goes beyond the rational human/scientific data-driven model to acknowledge that people often choose their commitments for "nonrational" reasons. Would-be Level Three Leaders must develop new skills, including the ability to infer what people are thinking and feeling. One of the central invitations of this book is to develop these skills so you can begin to influence at Levels Two and Three. Are you willing to learn how to engage people not only in their visible behavior, but also in their minds and hearts? If you find yourself thinking, "I don't care what they think or feel, I just want a good day's work for a good day's wages," we invite you to pause and reflect on the consequences of your approach. Will you be able to organize a high-performance workplace with a series of exchange-based, superficial mercenary relationships? Will you be able to develop an organizational culture of excellence and quality if your management team is constantly worried about controlling and guiding employees' behavior when the supervisors are not there? Can you expect to create an organization characterized by extraordinary performance if you only work at Level One? What does it take to get extraordinary performance?

You may be thinking that lots of people out there don't want to be engaged in their work and that they only want to work a day, collect their paycheck, and go home. I've observed the same. And I wonder how many of those employees were trained or conditioned by their

---

[1] See Jan Carlzon, *Moments of Truth* (New York: HarperCollins, 1987), for a nice discussion of the importance of moments of truth in service industries.

educational and work experiences to behave that way. At any rate, this is Level One thinking and it's a formula for mediocrity.

A Level Two or Level Three question might be to ask yourself, "Go home to what? What is it that motivates these people? Do they drudge through work and then go home and begin yelling enthusiastically during the match at their local bowling or softball league?" If so, a Level Three Leader would be asking, "How can I get some of that latent energy to emerge at work? How can I get them to play softball at work?" If you followed your employees around before and after work, would you ever find them working hard, even passionately, to accomplish some personal goal? What would that goal be? If you can imagine them doing something with passion, you might ask yourself, "How can I get some of that passion here at work?" Maybe some of them go home to nothing.

Maybe some employers' level of activity at home is even lower than at work in a Level One organization. In this case, the odds are you aren't going to be able to make a significant change in their lives. Perhaps then you need to consider reexamining and perhaps redesigning the recruiting system that invited these people to work in your organization in the first place.

If, on the other hand, you have accepted the premise that attempting to lead at Level Three is a much more powerful proposition than leading at Level One, you may be wondering how.

LEVEL THREE TECHNIQUES

How does one begin to influence people at Level Three? There is perhaps no single recipe that will accomplish this, and surely even if there were, it could not be faked unless the leader were authentically engaged in its steps. We offer one set of guidelines in Chapter 19, but it is not the exhaustive and definitive set of Level Three techniques. In general, though, we invite your consideration of these behaviors. Can you call them "techniques"? Probably not, because unless you live them, they probably won't work. Can you learn to do them? My experience in 30 years of teaching and consulting says "yes." The first set of behaviors has to do with your orientation to others: Is it respectful or not? The second set of behaviors has to do with what you can do to impact another's VABEs.

Techniques for Showing Respect

The basic premise here is that if you don't feel and demonstrate respect for others (remember our moral foundation of leadership introduced in Chapter 6), they won't engage your agenda at Level Three. There are many things you can do, or not do, that will show the respect you have or don't have for others. Perhaps the first is the quality of your listening. To listen to someone is to believe that they have something to say. To ignore them is tantamount to saying, "Your opinion doesn't matter to me." So to demonstrate your respect for others, the first and perhaps the most powerful thing you can do is to listen well to them. Listening is a skill that can be developed. I took a three-month-long course in listening during my doctoral studies at Harvard. I would never have guessed the topic could be so involved. And although my wife and children might say I should have failed the course, I did learn a lot about what a poor listener I'd been to that point.

Quality listening, for example, means that you're not multitasking. If you're reading the paper, eating, petting the dog, and listening, the message is that the listening is not that important. Respectful listening is a singular focus in which you attend completely to the speaker and nothing else. People who like to multitask find this very difficult to do. It takes skill, interest, patience, and significant amounts of respect to let go of everything else and listen. The skill, you can learn; the patience and interest and respect, you have to find within yourself.

Quality listening also means you're *attending* to the other. And attending not just to what they're saying, but also to the other communication channels on which we send and receive signals: facial expressions, eye movements (which requires some eye contact), hand gestures, other forms of body language, tone, pace, pitch, speed, and many more dimensions of how the individual is communicating to you. If you listen with *attention*, you'll begin to pick more and more information about their emotional state, their unspoken concerns, their fears, their hopes, and so on. Level One Leaders either by lack of skill or by lack of intent simply ignore most of that data.

One also shows respect to others by leaving them with *choices*. By this I mean Level Three Leaders use *invitations* rather than commands. If you tell someone to do something, you are removing their choices and your relationship has devolved to a physical or legitimate power relationship. In these relationships, fear is often the major motivator. And fear, I assert, is not the basis for world-class performance. Consider the difference between being asked to do something and being told to do something, that is, when you are moved from choice to obligation. How do you respond inside? What's the impact on your motivational level? Making powerful invitations means asking with a reason (Level Two) and a purpose (Level Three) rather than telling with an expectation of obedience (Level One).

Sometimes we disrespect others without being aware of it. This occurs when we use habits of speech that create defensiveness and resentment. Chapter 20 goes into this in more detail, so I'll leave the discussion for there. The point is that we use habits of speech, semantics you might say, that undermine our ability to lead at Level Three.

Another way we show respect for others is through *disclosing* personal information. We withhold information from others because we don't trust them or don't want to invite them into our personal circle. Withholding is a way of saying, "You're not good enough or close enough to me to be worthy of this information." Though Chapter 20 explores this further, note at the moment the impact of social distance from the other on your ability to influence. The farther you are from another person (socially), the less likely they are to follow you with heartfelt enthusiasm. Whereas the old saw goes, "Familiarity breeds contempt" (and I wonder if this wasn't first uttered by a Level One Leader), the opposite is often true: "Distance erodes commitment."

Finally, the ability and willingness to *explain*, to the satisfaction of the other, one's reasons and rationale shows respect to the other. If you don't explain, the underlying assumption must be, "You wouldn't understand" or "You're not worthy of an explanation, just do your job." Sometimes authoritors will "explain" things, giving minimal information and offering a superficial rationale for their behavior. This leads to mistrust and suspicion. Explaining to satisfaction means you respect the other enough to continue the discussion until their honest questions are satisfied.

Techniques for Influencing Vabes

Showing respect is a way of building a foundation for influencing others' VABEs. If you have that foundation in place, what comes next? Given that Level Three commitment is based on a congruency of belief, Level Three Leaders must have a *clear vision* of what they're trying to do. The ability to clarify where you want the organization to go is fundamental to inviting others to follow. If they cannot see where you want to go, how can they commit to follow? More about this in Chapter 19.

LEVEL THREE LEADERSHIP TOOLS AND TECHNIQUES

Self-disclosure
Story telling
Visioning
Honest conversation
Active listening
Protecting confidentiality
Candor
Modeling
Caring
Serving others
Invitations
Respecting others

Assertion is another key Level Three skill. Can you *clarify what you want*, invite others to participate, and then assert why they should want to join your venture? In reality, no leader knows for sure the outcomes of a future endeavor. But you can assert what you believe. And you can explain why you believe what you believe.

If you are *authentic* in those efforts at clarifying, explaining, visioning, and asserting, others will sense the consistency in your talk and your walk (behavior). You can't fake this for very long. So the willingness to be transparent in a sense, so that others conclude, "What you see is what you get" without deception or manipulation, goes a long way to touching people at Level Three.

It also helps to avoid superficiality. You could spend your time in superficial chitchat, discussing the weather and avoiding the difficult conversations. In my experience, effective leaders are eager to get to the core of the discussion and impatient with the superficial packaging or the vagueness of fuzzy logic. They want to know what you think about the core issues. And they ask. Some people find such conversation too intense or too invasive. Those thinking and working at Level Three find everything else superficial and mostly a waste of time.

A big part of convincing others that you mean what you say is *modeling*. By this, I mean practicing what you preach. Because we have so many habits that shape our lives, most people need to see and experience alternative ways of doing things before they can even understand what the alternatives might look like. When you behave in ways that cause others to pause and look again, you're disrupting their expectations about the way the world is or should be and, for a moment, have a little window into getting them to consider a different way of doing things. You might either consider this eccentricity or oddity or consider it an opportunity to see a different way of doing things. If you think you have a better way, and you can model it for others to see, and you get good results, they might be willing to learn more.

One of the hardest things for many authoritors to model is *flexibility*. People who have gotten to powerful or successful positions often believe that they got there because of how they were and how they behaved, so that their expectations become that others should adapt to them rather than the other way around. Business managers often *talk* about how important it is to be flexible, yet often this flexibility is not evident in their *behavior*. It's one thing to ask others to change the way they do things; it's quite another to be willing to change the way *you* do things in order to grow, model, and be authentic.

Storytelling is an effective Level Three technique as well. Clearly, in prehistoric times, all humans had as a means of transmitting learning was the oral tradition. Even in modern times nothing is quite so gripping to humans as a good, powerful story. Powerful Level Three Leaders will use stories and vignettes as ways of clarifying their points and making them more memorable. Surprisingly, most people don't think to use their *own* histories, their *own* life's stories, to help them convey what they're trying to say. Yet the most powerful lessons one learns in life, by definition, comes from one's own story. There's an exercise in the Workbook (Chapter 26, The Life's Story Exercise) that is designed to help you clarify the key incidents in your life's story and then to translate those into ministries that you can use to influence others. Remember here, authenticity is paramount. Don't go making up stories, as some have, for the sake of impact. Eventually, that comes back to haunt.

These ideas about what it takes to influence others at Level Three may help you begin to be more influential in your leadership roles. I assert that Level Three Leadership is more powerful than Level One or Level Two Leadership. But there's a dark side to Level Three Leadership that you should also be aware of.

THE DARK SIDE POTENTIAL OF LEVEL THREE LEADERSHIP AND ENGAGEMENT

When people work on something that they believe in and value, often they work especially hard. This is a good thing. This is the energy and engagement that we're looking for when we assert Level Three Leadership. On the other hand, be aware in that when people work on something that they believe in deeply, they can work so hard that they begin to do damage to themselves and others. They may work excessively or obsessively and eventually burn out. This intensity can extend to others, to co-workers and subordinates, who are asked to do more than they can or should. More and more literature describes this phenomenon, and it is likely to grow as the pace of the world, the volume of information available to us, and the pressures of stiffened competition continue. If you're interested in this topic, you might read *Workaholics* by Marilyn Machlowitz, *Working Ourselves to Death* by Diane Fassel, or *The Addictive Organization* by Anne Wilson Schaef and Diane Fassel. Robert Reich's book, *The Future of Success*, makes a similar point that people work harder and longer today than a decade ago but for less time off and even for relatively less wages.[2] Diane Fassel describes a progressive path toward workaholism beginning with constant busy-ness and making lists and ending, sadly and surprisingly, in death.

Even though Level Three Leadership can lead to extraordinary results and deeply committed relationships between individuals and their employers, it can also lead to burnout and exhaustion.[3] Bob Johnson, former CEO of Honeywell Aerospace and Dubai Aerospace, once noted that he got so excited about new assignments that he'd work through lunch and deep into the night. In the process, his exercise, and health, declined.[4]

Those who create cults are typically very effective Level Three Leaders. They are able to clarify a set of visions, principles, and values that engage others. If the followers are living too

---

[2] Some scholars may find this terminology weak, yet over a dozen years, it has proved effective in executive education settings as a means for consolidating several ideas and making them memorable.

[3] See B. F. Skinner, *Beyond Freedom and Dignity* (New York: Bantam, 1971).

[4] "Bob Johnson at Honeywell Aerospace," UVA-OB-0872 and related video interview clips.

much outside-in, a cult can form in which the leader is the central force. To the extent these leaders have removed choice from the lives of their followers, though, they have probably sacrificed respect for others for their own power and influence so that while they may be effective, we could not call them "good."

Working with people at Levels Two and Three initially requires more effort and more involvement on the leader's part, but it promises a more committed group of followers and higher quality of production. When the work group gets to the point that it can function without the boss's oversight at a high level of productivity with high levels of quality, the need for leadership involvement or oversight begins to diminish. Level Three Leadership is front-end loaded; you make a significant investment in up-front learning and focusing on co-workers' Level Three values, but when you understand them and can align those values with the work, your need to monitor and manage later on drops significantly.

ORGANIZATIONAL IMPLICATIONS

So far, we have looked at Level Three Leadership primarily from individual and interpersonal perspectives. We can also speak of three levels of activity in a broader, organizational sense. We'll have more to say later in Chapter 22, the chapter on organizational design, but for now, just note that all three levels appear in organizations as well as in individuals and relationships. A Level One or superficial focus in organizational leadership is reflected in the application of the latest fads or techniques. Level One Leaders read about the latest technique in the literature and try to apply these techniques over the top of their existing organizations without considering how these new techniques affect other interrelated systems and the structures and cultures of the organization. Sometimes it manifests itself in commissioning expensive educational programs, but then never attending personally or practicing the concepts taught. Other Level One elements in the organization include the physical plant and equipment the organization maintains. These physical manifestations of an organization reveal much about what lies beneath.

Level Two at the organizational level refers to the rules, processes, guidelines, and routine behaviors that they produce. In anthropological terms, it is the rituals that organizations perform. Although we cannot observe them after the fact, if we are on site at the right time, we can watch these collective habits unfold. These might include morning exercises in a Japanese organization, a coffee break in an American company, or the month of August off in a French company. People do these things consciously, but why?

Every Level One building and every Level Two ritual or process is based on some set of underlying beliefs. The challenge is to interpret the things you see at Levels One and Two accurately, so that you can get a clear picture of what people must be believing. This is not always easy because there are many factors involved. In Chapter 22, you'll learn more about how background factors, leadership VABEs, and organizational-design decisions combine to produce an organizational culture—which in turn produces organizational results. Level Three in the organization includes the organizational culture, the set of commonly held values and operating principles that people take for granted as the "way we do things around here." These cultural realities may or may not line up with the formal organization and its subordinate designs. When they don't, "unintended consequences" are the result.

Level Three in the organization, as in the individual, is semiconscious. Some employees may be able to talk about aspects of the extant culture; others may not be clear

TABLE 18-1   Levels in Personal and Organizational Analyses

Level	Personal	Organizational
One	Visible behavior	Artifacts, buildings, physical things
Two	Conscious thoughts	Espoused theories, the "talk," rituals, ceremonies, fads
Three	Values, assumptions, beliefs, and expectations	Theories in action, the "walk" and the underlying assumptions

enough about it to articulate it, although they behave it. Using Chris Argyris's terms, Level Two is the "espoused theory" of the organization, whereas Level Three is the theory in action.[5] These elements are shown in Table 18-1. They differ somewhat from Ed Schein's characterization, yet they illustrate the point that what managers do (trying to apply the latest fad in the literature), how they think about the organization (its structure and processes), and what they believe deeply about how to manage and organize are all potentially quite different things.

APPLYING LEVEL THREE LEADERSHIP AT BOTH THE INDIVIDUAL AND ORGANIZATIONAL LEVELS

Level Three Leadership is leadership that influences Level Three in both individual relationships and in the management of the organization. In both instances, it assumes that high performance comes when the central features of Levels One, Two, and Three are all aligned. Variations between the directions and main thrusts across these three levels—between what people or organizations do, think, and feel—introduce inefficiencies and diffuse the effectiveness of leadership and the energies of their members.

Increasingly, in today's turbulent world, leaders must learn to influence people at Level Three if they want to be effective. The titular power bases of bureaucracies continue to melt, and personal influence grows increasingly more important. Although Level One is seemingly faster and two centuries of momentum "support" dealing with people at Level One, Level One Leadership is becoming increasingly dysfunctional. The increasing importance of customer service moments of truth and the explosion in competition worldwide demand that employees participate more and more deeply in strategic decision making. World-class efforts based on high levels of engagement at all levels are increasingly critical if the organization is to survive and thrive. Although the up-front costs of learning to influence people at Level Three may be more time consuming than operating at Level One, the long-term benefits include more deeply committed employees, higher quality work, more satisfied customers, and a higher probability of surviving.

The downside is that Level Three Leaders must learn to recognize and manage in themselves and others the dangers of overwork and burnout. This observation leads us to a consideration of the moral aspects of Level Three Leadership, which is addressed in Chapter 19.

---

[5] See Frederick W. Taylor, *The Principles of Scientific Management* (New York: Harper & Brothers, 1911).

Conclusions

Most authoritors use a combination of Level One, Two, and Three techniques as described in this and the last two chapters. Each of these approaches has strengths and weaknesses. Level One techniques are faster and simpler, but they tend to engender superficial and half-hearted responses. Level Two techniques are logical and yield to solid reasoning, but they are often trumped by underlying beliefs and irrational behavior. And Level Three techniques can be very powerful and energizing, but they often take longer to develop and can be misused to create cults and may lead to burn out. Surely no leader uses only one set of techniques exclusively. The difference between leaders lies in the balance of techniques that they use. As you consider your own efforts to lead others, what balance do you demonstrate by your behavior? Do you favor Level One? Do you rely heavily on Level Two logical and rationale? Whereas we are not prepared to say what the "right" balance would be for any particular job, clearly it would change from organization to organization. It probably varies more by personal bent, though, that goodness of fit with the task at hand. And, I assert, more business authoritors emphasize Level One than the other two. And this tends to lead to de-energized employees and organizational cultures. What's your personal profile across these three levels?

Concepts Introduced in This Chapter

1. Level One Leadership that focuses only on behavior ignores two major sources of motivation for most people: what they think and what they believe and feel.
2. Level Three Leadership is leadership that attempts to influence people's VABEs as individuals or organizations.
3. Level Three Leadership techniques are based on the development of respect and the willingness to assert while retaining choice. These techniques include listening, explaining, disclosing, inviting, asserting, visioning, attending, storytelling, and others.
4. Level Three Leadership often takes more time up front than Level One Leadership, but tends to be more powerful in the long run.
5. Most leaders use a combination of Level One, Two, and Three techniques. The difference is in the balance among these techniques.

Questions for Personal Reflection

1. Use the Levels of Leadership Assessment worksheet on page 344 in Workbook to assess your Leadership Level profile. What are the implications for followers of your profile? What do you think people who know you well would say your profile is?
2. Identify some people in your history who were Level One, Two, or Three influences on you. Which ones did you respect the most? What did you learn from them? What about them would you like to emulate? Or do the opposite of?
3. How would you characterize your parents' style of influencing you, Level One, Two, or Three? What examples can you cite? How do you suppose this experience has shaped your leadership style?
4. What organization or institution do you believe the most in? Why? What about that institution that touches you so deeply? What would you be willing to do for this institution? What would you not be willing to do? Why?
5. Identify some times or incidents when you tried to influence others. How did you go about it? Were your efforts dominantly Level One, Two, or Three? What makes you think so? What was the result?
6. What Level Three techniques would you like to become more proficient at? How would you plan to accomplish that?

CASELET FOR DISCUSSION

After a comprehensive reorganization, the communications group of a large technical company received word they would have a new director. When the new director was announced, it was not met with excitement. First, her last job ended in disgrace because of her ineffective and Draconian management style; second, she was good friends with a company executive, so her appointment was seen as cronyism; and third, she had no formal training in communications—she was an industrial engineer.

The new director decided to create a new management position to help lead her change efforts. Unbeknownst to her, one of her managers shared with employees that she had already chosen the person to fill the position—an astrophysicist. The communications professionals felt hurt because the new director did not see the need for true communications practitioners.

The director's first all-hands meeting attempted to rally support and get employees excited about the new direction of the communications group. She began by admitting she was not trained in communications but she had given many presentations, so she felt she was experienced. Then she announced the new management position, stating she would "cast a net far and wide" to find the right person for the job (she didn't know we already knew she had chosen someone). She ended with an interesting directive: we were forbidden from discussing the changes. She added that she did not want to hear of anyone discussing the changes and that she would be unhappy if she found out that employees were talking. She added that if anyone had questions, she wanted them to come to her.

CONTRIBUTING YOUR OWN CASELETS

Have you seen or experienced a situation involving the concepts introduced in this chapter? If so and if you'd like to contribute your experience/situation to our case data bank, please visit http://faculty.darden.virginia.edu/clawsonj/ and click on the "Contribute new caselets" button.

19 | SIX STEPS TO EFFECTIVE LEADERSHIP

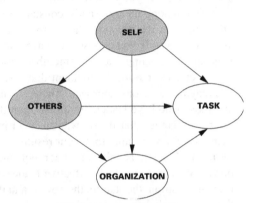

Not much happens without a dream. And for something great to happen, there must be a great dream. Behind every great achievement is a dreamer of great dreams. Much more than a dreamer is required to bring it to reality; but the dream must be there first.

—ROBERT GREENLEAF,
Servant Leadership, 16

The choice to lead can be a complex one. Sometimes leadership responsibility is thrust upon one without application. Sometimes leadership is something sought from youth. Others argue that it may be a genetic drive. However you come to a position of authority, you'll need to begin somewhere. At that point in time, it will be too late to run out and buy another book on leadership. The leadership-related VABEs that you have inside you at the time, for better or worse, will be the platform for your leadership efforts. It's hard to know what those leadership opportunities might be, so it's hard to prepare for all the contingencies. In this chapter, though, we offer a general prescription for effective leadership that should serve you well regardless of the situation.

First, I assert that you can make a difference. The world may seem big and overwhelming at times, and you may never get to influence thousands or millions. Yet in your neighborhood, department, division, or region, you may well have the chance to lead. My hope is that you'll be well prepared for the time.

Leadership has a big impact on lifestyle. Making ever-larger decisions that influence more and more people requires mental, emotional, social, intellectual, and moral growth. Whether you want or choose to lead in some fashion is up to you. How large a difference over how large a circle of influence is also up to you. You can choose whether to influence one other, ten others, or millions of others and in what way. Of course, each choice carries with it demands and consequences. If you choose to influence thousands, your choice will require that you spend your time among the thousands, constantly working to gain their followership. This lifestyle is different from the lifestyle chosen by a person who wishes to influence only a few or none. Whatever lifestyle you choose will have consequences for you and those around you, including your family. It is important to remember, though, that the choice is yours.

Let's assume for the moment that you want to influence others, to be a leader. Time out: this may be the wrong approach. There are at least two kinds of leaders, those who want to lead and those who have leadership thrust upon them. If you *want* to be a leader, ask yourself why. There's a danger that if you want to lead in some generic sense, you'll focus on the accoutrements of power rather than your results. You may have put the cart before the horse, and your results are likely to be mixed or inconsequential as you focus on establishing and protecting your power. We argue that truly effective leaders don't start out wishing to be leaders and that the title, the position, the stature, the power, and the accoutrements of leadership do not wear well on those who seek them as the primary goal.

Rather you may better ask yourself, "What value do I want to add to society (my community)?" Or, "What changes do I believe deep down are necessary to improve my organization, our world, or my community?" I believe that truly effective and morally grounded leaders begin with a cause, a purpose, a goal that serves fellow citizens—and not with the goal of being the leader because it appears attractive, powerful, respected, and well paid. Ultimately, "leaders" who sought the positions mostly for the position's sake end up being caretakers who do little and are not long remembered.

Consider people you know who set goals to gain some title and made it. What did they do once they became the leader? Were their administrations focused and productive or unfocussed and unproductive? Why? There's a rationale that would say behaving as and becoming an effective leader is a secondary by-product of an intense commitment to a purpose that serves others.

Behaving as and becoming an effective leader is a secondary by-product of an intense commitment to a purpose.

So we begin with the premise that the morally grounded, effective leader begins with a powerful purpose or cause. In the relentless desire to accomplish that purpose, that individual becomes a leader as a necessary stepping stone to influence others to join voluntarily in that purpose. Without this purposeful base, so-called leaders are little more than self-serving caretakers—managers who maintain and protect the past. They tend to seek title and prestige for their own gratification rather than to serve or improve those around them. Does this assessment seem too harsh to you? Or perhaps too idealistic? Clearly thousands of people in the world are powerful and wealthy—and narcissistically so. This book, however, is not about how to get rich and powerful—though for the Level Three Leader, influence and wealth often come.

As Nigel Nicholson points out, some seem "born to lead."[1] Clearly many want to be rich and powerful. Others want to fix things, to make the world a better place. So, whether you feel the need to lead, desire to be wealthy and powerful, or want to improve your leadership skills in order to make a positive difference, we come to the question, "If you want to enhance your ability to influence others, how can you proceed?"

"Steps-to-Leadership" recipes are dangerous. With so many leadership formulae in the world,[2] some aspiring leaders are simply looking for the shortcut to power, overlooking the importance of incorporating the underlying principles of such recipes in their world view at Level Three. But when it comes to developing deep influence on others, pasted on Band-Aid approaches won't work. Beware of the temptation to find a favorite recipe and try to slip it on like a jacket. Unless you build a personal leadership style on your core VABEs, your efforts to influence are likely to be viewed with skepticism and confusion. In the end, you can only effectively lead at Level Three if your efforts to influence are based on the authentic you. As mentioned at the outset, one of the invitations of this book is to explore leadership concepts widely and then integrate the pieces that work for you into your unique leadership style.

For that reason, the recipe offered here begins with clarifying your Level Three assumptions about leadership. We then go on to suggest five other "steps" or processes that you can take or learn, with the belief that if you pursue them authentically and vigorously, they can help make you a more effective, powerful leader (Table 19-1).

You will notice that all the steps introduced in this chapter are presented with the present participle form of the verbs, the -ing forms. This presentation is intentional in order to communicate the idea that none of these steps is a binary process (you don't either do it or not do it). You also don't do it once and then are done with it. Rather, each is a process that involves a lifelong commitment to continuous improvement, constant polishing, revisiting, and adjusting and growing along continua. These six steps become a way of life, not something you put on for a few moments to impress others or something that, once achieved, are fixed forever.

TABLE 19-1 Six Steps to Effective Leadership
1. Clarifying your center
2. Clarifying what's possible
3. Clarifying what others can contribute
4. Supporting others so they can contribute
5. Being relentless
6. Measuring and celebrating progress

[1] Nigel Nicholson, *Executive Instinct* (New York: Crown Business, 2000).
[2] See, for example, James Kouzes and Barry Posner, *The Leadership Challenge* (San Francisco, CA: Jossey-Bass, 1987), for one of the best and most widely used formulas. Kouzes and Posner's model is based on interviews and surveys done with thousands of practicing managers and consists of 10 skills arranged in five clusters. See the Leadership Theories Appendix for the list.

CLARIFYING YOUR CENTER

James Allen once noted, "As a man thinketh, so is he."[3] Although Allen's statement fits more at Level Two than at Level Three, it does imply that who you are inside will manifest itself at Level One in how you deal with others. "Who are you?" and "How does that core affect your leadership?" are critical issues for the would-be leader. Your center or core and its content are crucial to your ability to lead. When your center is clear and focused, you are more likely to have a powerful influence on others. When your center is foggy and diffuse, you are less likely to be able to move others. Physically, emotionally, socially, and organizationally, you will be off balance and unable to provide dependable anchor points to others.

Students of the martial arts, for instance, learn to stand in a stable manner and in balance. They focus on their physical center of gravity, in aikido called the "one-point," a physical metaphor for the VABE-related concept of "center." A person who is physically or emotionally centered is difficult to move. You can push and shove, and this person stands firmly without moving. The same is true of people who are centered socially and, in general, in life—they have "mass."

When you understand that when you are centered, opposing forces, shifting currents of approval or disapproval, unstable foundations, and even censure by those you love will not unsettle or dissuade you or knock you off balance, you will begin to develop a desire to clarify your center. As you do so, you will become calmer, more purposeful, and more stable in the midst of turbulence around you. Although practice in some physical techniques will help you develop this capacity, clarifying your emotional center is about clarifying what you believe in and value. Centering, therefore, is often a reflective, meditative exercise.

Centering is also about learning to live inside-out as opposed to outside-in. If you are constantly worried about what others will think or how they will react to your behavior, it will be difficult to calm your heart and become centered. You must be able, in large part, to let go of the importance of others' evaluations of you. Only when you are the final judge of your behavior can you have the confidence to be who you are and not stress about the judgments of others.

It may be that one can never fully clarify one's center. The reason is that we can never fully experience all of life, and life will constantly impact and force us to revisit and perhaps polish, if not remold, our core values. We may think we know what we would do in a given, perhaps challenging, situation. We may hope so, but the truth is we will never really know for sure what we would do until we encounter that situation at least once—probably several times—and see how we respond.

Here's an extreme, but poignant, example. In Mark Baker's book *Nam*—a compilation of firsthand, eyewitness accounts of what it was like to prepare for, go to, fight in, and return from Vietnam[4]—one account is of a platoon of young Americans, days into a patrol in a free-fire zone; they were tired, hungry, scared, and pumped full of adrenaline, on a keen edge. At one point, they spotted an elderly Vietnamese man and a young woman on a motor scooter. They stopped the two, searched their bags, and found American canned fruit. They accused the man of stealing the fruit from American soldiers. The old man protested. As he did, two of the soldiers took the young woman, his granddaughter, out into the rice paddy and raped her. The rest of the platoon lined up. When the old man protested, someone shot him almost in half with automatic weapons fire. When they were all done with the girl, they killed her.

[3] James Allen, *As a Man Thinketh* (New York: Crowell, 1913).
[4] Mark Baker, *Nam* (New York: Marrow, 1981).

Most of us find this story appalling and disgusting. Most of us would like to think we know what we would do if we had been members of that platoon. We can imagine ourselves, at age 19, standing up to our platoon mates, saying, "Don't do this!" or "This won't happen here!" Perhaps we can imagine ourselves even being willing to lose our lives to not participate in or silently support the episode. Yet, truthfully, it is not really clear what we would do if threatened with death by our "friends," people with whom we'd trained, ate, slept, saved, and been saved by. If we'd been attacked by women and children with rifles and grenades before, if we were hungry and not thinking clearly, or if we for any reason were unable to see a grandfather and his granddaughter as individuals worthy of respect, we might not have done what we think we'd do as we contemplate the situation from the comfort of our living rooms or classrooms. Thus, life requires us to constantly clarify our centers, and think about, practice, and behave our basic values.

We can explore and polish our centers, and we can resolve and reinforce our core resolves from time to time. If we have a desire to deal with life's various situations one way rather than another, it behooves us to constantly explore, examine, and refine our centers and to be as clear as we can be about what's there and how we will implement its content as we live.

Matsushita Seikei Juku is a leadership institute established in Kanagawa, Japan, by Konosuke Matsushita, the founder of Matsushita Electric Company. A truly remarkable individual, Matsushita and his leadership style have been the subject of several books.[5] His school of leadership was no less remarkable. In 1993, from more than 250 applications to the school, only five individuals were admitted to study, an application-to-admission ratio of 50 to 1. The program of study is for five years. The first year of study has no faculty and no courses. At the end of the first year, students complete a one-question examination. If you fail, you're out. The question is, "What is your life's purpose?" First-year students are given the *year* to determine their life mission. The underlying assumption is that to qualify for leadership one must know one's life mission; otherwise, how could one purport to lead others? It's a simple but powerful tenet.

Are you clear on what your life mission is? Are you clear about what's at your center? Do you know what you stand for? Do you know what you would do and would not do? If not, it will be difficult to lead. Are you willing to spend some time wrestling with this issue? If you were at the Matsushita's leadership institute, you'd have a whole year with no other distractions to explore that single question. Are you willing to spend something less than a year answering it? Chapter 8 on charters and Chapter 13 on resonance are designed in large part to help you think about this fundamental question. Here are some additional suggestions for how you can begin to clarify your center.

Clarifying Your Center

Many people go through life never clarifying their centers. They live and die having never tested their inner beliefs to see if and how they hold up under fire. In that way, they avoid leadership roles that will call one's center into activity and hence never became leaders. One way to begin clarifying your center is to identify what engages you. *Engage* means more than what interests you, or as Stephen Covey would say, what "concerns" you.[6] What is it that

---

[5] See, for example, Konosuke Matsushita, *As I See It* (Tokyo: PHP Institute, 1989).
[6] Stephen Covey speaks of Circles of Concern and Circles of Influence in *The Seven Habits of Highly Effective People* (New York: Simon & Schuster, 1989).

captures your imagination, your leisure thinking moments, and your dreams? What is it that causes you to smile spontaneously, to increase your pulse, and to speak animatedly with others? What is it that motivates you and prepares you to expend tremendous energy, mental and physical, as you anticipate participating? We have included an exercise on your personal engagement planning in the Workbook (Chapter 26, Life's Dream Exercise).

These things begin to constitute your core. As Alex Horniman, professor at Darden Graduate School of Business Administration, is fond of saying, "Leadership is an act of engagement." When we are truly engaged in something, we begin to influence others even without trying. They begin to notice the energy and excellence with which we pursue our engagement, they begin to hear the animation in our voices, they begin to see our motivation, all of which rubs off on them—they begin to want to be a part of it. In effect, we begin to lead without ever being cognizant of or claiming a desire to be a leader. When we are truly engaged, leadership happens. Engagement is contagious; like a virus, it spreads, and others begin to feel it and to be swept into it.

LEADERSHIP IS AN ACT OF ENGAGEMENT.

—ALEXANDER HORNIMAN

Identifying and examining your central engagements can help clarify the content of your center. This centering process is critical to your becoming more influential because it strengthens your ability to live inside-out. Obviously, centering is not something you can do in an afternoon. Nor can you seek to see someone else's center simply by asking them where they are coming from. Clarifying your center is a lifelong process. Reviewing and refining your engagements will cause you to be constantly polishing your definition of who you are. The next step in that process requires looking at the process values that you hold, looking at the how of getting to the realization of your core engagements.

Developing Character: Ends Versus Means

A person's character is the sum of his or her choices: choices of goals and choices about how to achieve those goals. The way a person makes those choices underscores the moral dimension to leadership already discussed. One way to check the moral level of your leadership with regard to your respect for the followers is to ask yourself, given your behavior toward the other person, whether you would be willing to trade places with them immediately. If not, you might begin to ask yourself if you're behaving with respect for the individual—as outlined in Chapter 5.

A second method, commonly used, is to imagine that your dealings with this person suddenly made the headlines on the front page of a national newspaper. Would you be proud to have the story out in the public light for all to see? Or would you find yourself leaving out certain conversations, side deals, or actions in hopes of being better received? If you hesitate with either of these tests, we suggest you not only rethink your attempts to influence the others, but also to reflect on what this hesitation might mean in terms of clarifying your center.

Various Forms of Meditation

A third method for clarifying your center is more metaphysical and involves various forms of meditation. People often find increasing clarity in their centers by praying, meditating, or practicing stress-reducing exercises. Physically centering, as one does in martial-arts training, can also help. Interestingly, the physical practice of centering can help you strengthen your view of your center and of how to manage your life. The experience of studying aikido or taekwondo, for instance, can be helpful in seeing new ways of thinking about life and about relationships. If you learn to sit or stand quietly for several moments, to focus your mind on your breathing, and to let all other thoughts leave your mind, you will find that you have a remarkable sense of calm and peace. This physical/mental exercise will help you see more clearly what you believe and feel.

Because one is never finished clarifying one's center, it doesn't make sense, then, to wait to influence others until the center is completely clear. We still have to carry on with our lives even if we haven't reached a final realization or don't have a crystal clear picture.

The strategic corollary to clarifying your center is clarifying what's possible for you and your work group, organization, or society. If you clarify your center, but have no view of what could be for those around you, not much will happen. Clarifying your center, by itself, is inherently passive. So, the second step to effective leadership is clarifying what's possible.

CLARIFYING WHAT IS POSSIBLE

If clarifying your center involves looking inward to the core, clarifying what's possible involves looking outward to the extreme—as far as you can see. For most of us, clarifying what's possible involves stretching our horizons beyond what we usually see and apprehend. To clarify what is possible is to imagine in sharp detail what can and should happen for an individual or an institution in the future. In essence, it is strategic thinking. Chapter 4 is devoted to that topic, but we can make some general comments at the moment.

Stan Davis, in *Future Perfect*, claims that leaders think in the future perfect tense; that is, they have seen what they want to accomplish so clearly and understand the steps to that dream so thoroughly that they literally speak in the future perfect tense.[7] For instance, they note, "When we have achieved our dream, we will have done A, B, and C." It's as if the leader is working backward having seen, as Martin Luther King put it, the Promised Land. Most of us don't see the Promised Land or even the quadrant of the future in which it lies. Effective leaders work hard to figure out where they are going. They have "seen" a future they desire and therefore know where they're trying to go. Robert Fritz asks the question, "What do you want to create?"[8] To answer that question, one must know what he or she wants. You can call it strategic thinking or visioning or whatever you want, but effective leaders have an idea in their minds about what they are trying to do. Their job is to clarify that for others.

Clarifying Mental Images of What Can Be

Clarifying your mental images of what you and your organization can become is not easy. It requires getting out of present mental boxes, relaxing present mental constraints (assumptions), and vigorously pursuing a mental mural painstakingly put together with thousands of mosaic

---

[7] See Stan Davis, *Future Perfect* (Reading, MA: Addison-Wesley, 1987).
[8] Robert Fritz, *The Path of Least Resistance* (New York: Ballantyne, 1989).

thought and data tiles. Some may find this task easy when it comes to imagining a romantic liaison, playing a Major League baseball game, or driving to a world championship on the Formula One circuit. With these exciting pursuits in mind, we can imagine tiny details of how we would behave in those situations. Effective leaders possess this same energy about their personal and organizational dreams and visions. To become an effective leader, one needs to develop this skill.

One of the biggest difficulties in developing mental pictures of the future is allocating time to the process. Most of us don't turn off the phone, close the door, and put our feet up and simply think hard about where we're going and how we're going to get there. In the rush to respond to the daily press of mail, phone messages, meetings, and emergencies, we spend our working lives, as Covey puts it, in Quadrant I[9]—working on high-priority items that have become urgent—in crisis mode. We lose sight of, and even the desire to gain sight of, the long view.

Another difficulty is keeping these future-oriented images current in our minds. We often get a glimpse of the future and then lose sight of it in our daily routines. For instance, how often in the last month have you thought out 10, 20, or 30 years into the future? Our tendency is to focus so much on the pressures of the moment that we lose track of our direction. If you can't keep these images in your mind, it will be difficult to allow them to influence your thinking, much less the thinking of the people you interact with daily.

Can you see clearly where you think your organization or work group should be in 5, 10, 20, 50, or 100 years? You may find these questions silly, particularly given the rapid change that characterizes the infocratic era. Many participants in executive education classes wrestle, they say, with 30- and 90-day horizons, maybe a 360-day horizon, but argue they can't see what's going to happen, especially in this increasingly turbulent world, months down the road, much less years.

Konosuke Matsushita, again, provides an interesting counterpoint. Asked in the late 1980s whether he was concerned about the recent losses his firm, Matsushita Denki (Panasonic Electronics), was sustaining, he said, "No, everything was on schedule." When asked how long his schedule extended, he replied, "250 years!" He had a vision of his firm, the firm he founded, that extended through ten 25-year periods. Each period had a set of goals and objectives and things that had to be accomplished in order to reach his view of what could be— of what was possible—two and a half centuries past the dark curtain of the future. Although his firm was experiencing some short-term losses, the basic elements of that first 25-year period were on schedule and moving as planned. Surely he was interested in a profitable company, yet his primary focus was not on steadily increasing profits, but on the underlying elements and strategic pillars that would generate those profits over the long haul. In the meantime, Matsushita Denki moved into the second 25-year period, having completed the goals of the first period.

We urge you to begin now developing the habit of allocating time regularly to discipline your mind to think into the future, to imagine what could be, to play with the details, to follow the thin threads of reasoning that describe how those images could be brought to pass. This skill will not come to you in a flash. Like physical tone, your mental strategic imagining tone will come from repeated and vigorous effort. Chapter 5 will provide you some additional guidance on how to go about this effort.

Reading is a great way to increase your stockpile of ideas. If you read widely, not just in your field, you'll begin to see connections among, and between, different disciplines and industries. Be willing to read in other fields so you can begin to identify trends and events that will

---

[9] Covey's four-quadrant model depicts our attention to things important or not and things urgent or not. Quadrant I refers to things both urgent and important, the so-called Crisis Zone.

impact your field. Recently, one participant in an executive program reported that he read two books a night. Yes, two books a night! He began to develop this skill many years ago when in the desire to take a class from a favorite high-school instructor, he signed up for remedial reading because it was the only class this instructor was offering that term. Although our friend was a normal reader, he learned techniques and insights into the reading process that now, after years of practice, leave him able to consume and understand close to 600 books a year. Can you imagine how this kind of input would inform and stimulate your mind in seeing the future and what could be? I'll admit this man was a nuclear physicist and therefore smarter than the average bear; however, if he can train himself to be able to learn rapidly, so can you.

We also encourage you to begin developing scenarios that will inform the paths you might take to your dreams. Peter Schwartz, in *The Art of the Long View*, describes this process well. It is different from strategic planning and corporate planning. This process will be described more in the chapter on strategic thinking.

CLARIFYING WHAT OTHERS CAN CONTRIBUTE

One of the fundamental issues a potential leader faces is clarifying one's own view of what the others, the potential followers, can do. Unless you can develop a view of what others can do and how they can contribute to your objectives and vision, it's not likely that you'll be able to get their commitment. The breadth of your view of what others can contribute can make a big difference in your effectiveness as a leader. Some take a narrow view of what others can add, whereas others see a wide range of possibilities. Two factors are critical in clarifying what others can contribute: (1) your basic underlying assumptions about others and (2) clarity in identifying the critical skills you will need to reach your vision.

Basic Assumptions About Others

One common and dangerous outcome of the bureaucratic Industrial Era has been that many managers think of their people in terms of job descriptions. The corollary is thinking about people in terms of the job descriptions that you'd like them to fill. This perspective constrains one from thinking about the talents of the individual and imagining what they might contribute to a particular goal or agenda. Such bureaucratic thinking—based on the assumptions that we need to find people to fit into particular job descriptions and that the management task is to minimize variance from the performance of that task—can be devastating to highly talented individuals. It is a Level One way of thinking about what people might contribute to an effort. Jim Collins argued forcefully in *Good to Great*[10] that those who do the hiring would do better to hire the talented person and let them figure out what to do.

As argued earlier, the bureaucratic approach assumes management knows exactly what needs to be done, that people can behave in that robotic way, and that the environment will be stable enough to avoid the need for quick response time and creative employees. Clearly, this description is not always valid in today's world.

A more powerful leadership approach is to assume that people have talents, can learn new ones, and have a basic desire to do well. Of course, these skills vary from person to person, and it will always be important to monitor behavior. If one views, hires, trains, and manages people with an eye

---

[10] Jim Collins, *Good to Great* (New York: HarperBusiness, 2001).

to developing their skills and judgment, however, one is increasingly able to rely on their abilities at work rather than on their job descriptions. Further, their insights into the job may, especially in turbulent times, be more informed and accurate than management's, several layers up the organization.

This whole process of working with people's talents and willingness to accept responsibilities for outcomes has been termed *empowering*, which has become somewhat trite, in part because many in management pay lip service to it but don't really believe its underlying assumptions. Empowerment is not really a binary concept; rather, like most things, it lies on a continuum. We can think of empowerment in terms of who gets to make the following decisions:

1. What are the problems here?
2. What are the sources of these problems?
3. What alternative solutions are available to us?
4. What are the benefits of the various solutions?
5. Who will choose the alternative we will use?
6. Who will implement the alternative we chose?
7. Who will evaluate the results of the experiment we did with the alternative we chose?

Too often, so-called empowered workforces are not permitted to do anything more than numbers 1, 2, 3, and 4. The "higher" level decisions are reserved for management. So a workforce is not either empowered or not, but sits somewhere on this scale with relative empowerment or not.

In a sense, clarifying what others could contribute by examining your own deep assumptions about the value that others bring to work is a part of clarifying your center. If your basic assumptions about what others can do are limited, then your ability to clarify what others can contribute will be limited as well. If you are able to imagine and perceive people as growing, learning, developing beings and are willing to invest in that growth, you can get a different kind of response. What you see about people certainly helps to determine how they will respond. If we treat people like robots, they will begin to behave like robots. If we treat people with expectations of higher contributions, they will begin to make higher contributions.

Identifying the Critical Skills

Another challenge to reframing how we look at people and conceive of what they have to offer is being aware of what we need to accomplish our purposes. Most companies look primarily at technical skills when assessing a fit between a job and a candidate, which is Level One thinking. Consider a different approach.

The FMC nee BAE plant in Aberdeen, South Dakota, built missile-launching canisters for the U.S. Navy. This facility was organized by an unusual and effective leader, Bob Lancaster, who worked hard to develop a different kind of working environment in the facility. When the facility needed a new welder, management used the basic assumptions of their new organization rather than a traditional approach to find the next new employee. The traditional approach, the Level One approach, would be that a company would advertise for a welder, accept applications with resumes summarizing experience, and then pick the most qualified welder based on experience, references, and maybe an interview.

At Aberdeen, though, there was a different set of underlying assumptions and, correspondingly, a different set of identified critical skills.[11] The first new basic assumption was that the process of the organization was more important than the technical skills in the organization.

---

[11] See "The Aberdeen Experiment," UVA-OB-0998, a business case.

According to this logic, a collection of highly qualified people who couldn't work together would be less effective than a group of moderately talented people who could work together well.

The second assumption was that social skills were harder to teach than technical skills—it was easier to teach welding than it was to teach teamwork, learning, self-esteem, and other related interpersonal talents. The third assumption was that people who were trained in a specific technical way that was reinforced by a union experience that encouraged focusing on a narrow range of skills would have difficulty learning new ways of organizing their work.

With these three assumptions in mind, the management of Aberdeen realized that the critical skills they needed were self-esteem (so one was able to receive feedback without getting defensive), a learning attitude (so one was interested and even eager to learn new skills and techniques), team spirit (so one was willing to share in the work and responsibility for results), and a pride in quality (so one was eager to find ways to improve results). Consequently, they developed a recruiting/screening process that lasted four hours and focused on these principles, rather than on the technical skills of welding.

After using this process, they screened out virtually all of the experienced welders who applied for the job and ended up hiring a woman who had never welded before. They chose her because she was bright, interested in learning, socially well adjusted, willing to take feedback, and clearly a team player. As it turned out, she became a master welder within a short period of time and then went on to learn a wide variety of the technical skills listed in the plant's pay-for-skill compensation system. Management was convinced that had they hired a skilled welder, maybe with union experience, they would have had difficulty teaching the person new, more important social skills and a wider range of technical skills. Although it took several weeks before the new hire could weld proficiently, within the first year the value added to the firm was far beyond what it would have been had they hired a welder.

A big part of why this situation worked out the way it did was in the philosophy that was central to the founding of the plant. Another part lay in the innovative ways that Aberdeen organized its critical human resources. And a big part had to do with its leadership: first, Bob Lancaster, then Jeff Bust, Roger Campbell, and later, Sarah Mann. These people understood the importance of building an organization that supported people so that they could do their best. A central part of that organization relied on determining the critical skills necessary to create the kind of workplace they wanted. In this case, many of those skills were the so-called softer skills of giving and receiving feedback, learning, team play, flexibility, and interpersonal relationships.

The point is that unless you can clarify what you want others to do and your assumptions about who can do it, you may be inadvertently hiring, relying on, or trusting the wrong people. Effective leaders get below the superficial assessment of technical credentials to the Level Three VABEs that people bring to their work.

SUPPORTING OTHERS SO THEY CAN CONTRIBUTE

The traditional leadership assumption mentioned earlier, namely that people should fit into job descriptions, limits what management can expect from people. This same assumption also limits the structure, systems, and culture of organizations. Increasingly, in changing environments, organizations have to find new, nontraditional ways of organizing and managing their people. Chapter 22 covers more on this topic, but we offer some preliminary insights here.

Two forces are shaping this redesign: (1) the explosion of information technology and (2) the constantly burgeoning press of people to be in control of their lives. Both forces are "empowering" the workforce, whether management wants to or not. Both forces demand that effective leaders find ways of supporting their people by designing new organizational forms that no longer hinder people's creativity and sense of responsibility for results, but encourage it.

Information Age Organizational Structures

Perhaps nothing has been more influential in the organizational redesign wave that has hit the world than the explosion in new information technologies. As introduced earlier, the growing widespread availability of accurate, voluminous, and timely data about business activity has begun to literally transform the shape of modern organizations. Colocating becomes less and less of an issue as simultaneous databases, videoconferencing, Web-based meetings, and e-mail become more prevalent and inexpensive. Cheap, distributed computing power for analysis and communications means that people at all levels of organizations can gather, analyze, decide, and communicate with people at all levels of other organizations, if they are allowed to. The need for vertical hierarchies to make good decisions is rapidly evaporating. In fact, in many cases, better decisions are being made by people who are closer to the data and the customer than those several layers up. And the layers are disappearing in organizations as management recognizes this latent power.

The new, emerging infocracies look a bit like what we used to call the informal or organic organization. In older cities like Boston, streets eventually grew out of meandering cow paths; likewise in organizations, new lines of authority and influence are developing out of informal lines of communication where the data are fast and accurate. In some cases, organizational control is quickly being shifted away from vertical hierarchies toward information-based networks. Take, for instance, a chapter in the history of (formerly) BancOne in the Midwest.

BancOne was a large and growing regional bank that had taken a different and exciting approach to managing its growth. Unlike some other growing regional banks that acquired new subsidiaries, repainted the buildings, added new signs, and delivered volumes of new operating procedures in an attempt to get the new affiliates to do things "our way," BancOne used information technology to manage its new partners.

First, being clear on their goals, BancOne management identified 47 key indicators of the kind of performance they wanted to see. Then, they developed an information system that allowed them to tie new affiliates in quickly. Next, they designed the information system to give almost instantaneous feedback on results from data collected. Management also shared the results with those managing the more than 50 banks in their system rather than keeping it close to their chests. All these features are dramatic departures from the traditional methods of planning, organizing, motivating, and controlling that grew out of the bureaucratic mind-set.[12]

With this system, presidents of newly acquired banks in the BancOne system suddenly found themselves receiving on a weekly basis a ranked listing of all of the banks in the system on each of the 47 key indicators. In other words, the president of a bank that had been acquired the month before began getting Monday printouts showing how the bank ranked among the other subsidiaries on each of the 47 indicators.

Now, what do you suppose happened next? If you assume that people don't care about their performance (a commonly held bureaucratic assumption that limits one's thinking), then you might think not much would happen. On the other hand, if you believe that people want to think well of themselves and want to do well among their peers, then you might expect something else to happen.

---

[12] See the case "BancOne Diversified Services," UVA-BP-0335.

What happened was that bank presidents looked quickly to see how their bank was doing compared with the others in the system. When they saw that they weren't doing so well on a particular indicator, they looked to see who was doing well, which led the acquired bank president to a critical point. If the bank president was proud and lacking in the learning spirit, that president might stonewall for a while and avoid learning from others in the system.

More often than not, however, the process created a new and emerging culture. The bank presidents began to call one another, completely bypassing corporate management, to find out how they got such good results. Quickly—much more quickly than corporate training or quarterly review meetings could hope to accomplish it—the best practices of the organization were not filtering, but flowing from one part of the system to the next. Week by week, each of the decision makers, the small "l" leaders throughout the organization, got timely data, compared their results with others, and sought to improve their standing. Each implemented the suggestions of others in ways that fit their organizations and people; each adjusted, modified, and recast the suggestions they got to match what they thought they could do and their current priorities. In the process, they created a much stronger learning organizational culture.

Then, the following week, each bank received another current listing of what was happening among the other banks in the system, and each leader was confronted again with the consequences and emergent results of whatever steps they had taken the previous week. All these things happened without negative organizational politics and without the time delays involved in waiting for senior-management analysis, decision making, training programs, and coordination. It would all have been impossible without superb information technology and a senior-management philosophy that utilized it efficiently. Of course, the selection of the 47 indicators was a critical part of this system. One could argue that no leader could keep track of 47 "key" indicators; however, if you're well organized, why can't?

This example shows how effective leadership can redesign organizational systems to support others/followers and make it easier to release their potential contributions to the organization. Effective leaders are able to clarify not only what potential followers have to contribute, but also how the work systems in which they operate can be reorganized to realize workers' potential.

Empowering Systems Design

The BancOne organization also provides an example of a system that empowers people. Its tacit assumption was that the bank managers all wanted to do well, that they knew their banks better than anyone else, and that they would do what they could within their historical tradition and operating environment to move toward improving in the key indicators. Little was said to them about what they had to do or not do. Senior management assumed that the managers would know what to do if they had the right information and could see the direction the company wanted to go. (To be fair to Skinnerians, given our earlier discussion, this fundamentally Skinnerian system focused on inputs and outputs and gave little attention to Levels Two and Three at the presidential level.)

Often, our organizational structures, systems, and cultures inhibit rather than encourage people to use their full talents. Too many workers hear too often, "That's on a need-to-know basis only" or "Don't ask questions, just do it!" or "You're not paid to think; you're paid to do what you're told" or "My job is to think; your job is to do" or some other similar comment.

Although this kind of language[13] and the assumptions upon which the language was based formed the foundation of the bureaucratic mind-set, the newly emerging postbureaucratic organizations or infocracies will be characterized by different kinds of language based on a different set of assumptions.

One of the changes occurring in the new, emerging infocracies is a movement away from the assumption that people should fit into the organization ("Here's my organization chart, now let's figure out who fits into it and where") and toward the assumption that we give talented people current information and let them organize their work to meet customers' needs ("Here are my people, let's figure out how to organize for the moment to meet the customer's needs"). What this shift means is that, as Peter Senge has written, leaders are increasingly becoming designers of new kinds of organizational forms.[14] Many of these organizations are built around circles or networks rather than pyramidal bureaucracies. Who has what authority is becoming less and less the organizing principle, whereas who has the right information and insight is becoming more and more the basis for the forms of the new organizations.

So effective leadership means, in part, casting away the bureaucratic assumptions taught in business schools for decades and perpetuated by corporations; instead it means searching for and creating new organizing principles that promote the rapid use of good information and the multiple talents of the people employed.

BEING RELENTLESS

Effective leaders are relentless. They exhibit stamina often in enormous volumes. Jim Collins calls this characteristic "will."[15] When a person has a purpose and a vision and wants to achieve both, it is difficult to push him or her off that chosen track. If commitment to the purpose and vision is weak, that person can be diverted, making the person less effective with others and more confused even to him- or herself. Just as it is difficult to know what values we truly hold until they are field-tested among our peers and in high-stakes situations where our true (operating) basic assumptions and priorities will be manifest, the same is true of our commitment to our purpose. We often learn about how committed we are to an endeavor by watching ourselves in our commitment to that endeavor. Like the steps introduced earlier, this principle is both a reflection and a means of clarifying our centers. We learn how much stamina we have by watching our own commitment to our goals. We clarify our centers by learning from that observation.

Life as a Motorboat or a Wood Chip

One way to think of the commitment-building or stamina-building process is to compare life and business to an ocean—vast, inviting, constantly changing, open, available, and inviting to the skilled sailor. At the same time, life's sea has currents, winds, storms, denizens of the deep, and the possibility of total destruction. Some people launch into life without a purpose or direction, seeking in their naiveté to experience all of life as quickly as they can. Not thinking beyond the bows of their ships, they push off from shore with no motor, no sail, and no rudder and become a chip upon the tide, floating aimlessly without destination. It is true that sometimes such chips

---

[13] Chic Thompson, *What a Great Idea!* (New York: Harper Perennial, 1992), calls them "killer phrases"—phrases that kill motivation and creativity.

[14] See Peter Senge, *The Fifth Discipline* (New York: Doubleday Currency, 1990).

[15] Jim Collins, op cit.

end up, by luck and the wind, ashore on favorable beaches and enjoying the finer things in life. Most, however, never get anywhere and sink before they realize that it could have been different.

Leaders have a purpose, one to which they are committed. These purposes provide the charts by which they sail. Their stamina becomes the large sails, and their center acts as the compass to help them move ahead. When the winds of fate blow, they adjust the trim and the rudder to utilize whatever life brings them to keep them headed toward their destination. Leaders also have internal motors that keep them moving when the external winds are calm or blowing against them. Leaders have fuel to burn and reserve bunkers to feed their motors when the going gets tough and the waves mount. Leaders are not easily blown off course.[16]

This relentlessness, the drive to get up when you've been knocked down, to right yourself when capsized, is essential to achieving important goals. Without it, leaders-to-be will become followers. This kind of behavior may seem to be stubbornness, but relentlessness is different from stubbornness. Relentless leaders can still be willing to listen, willing to understand and utilize any fact, truth, valuable information, or alliance that will move them toward their envisioned goal. Stubborn people stick to the original vision or strategic means selected without modification regardless of what's happening around them. Relentlessness requires a different kind of commitment.

Developing Commitment

Easily chosen goals do not lead to deep commitment. Constancy of commitment is a function of careful thought, sometimes-painful scrutiny of the purpose and vision—often stimulated by the criticism of others—and an ever-clarifying sense of one's center. Commitment grows out of knowing yourself. If you know what you want and why you operate the way you do and you are willing to change your ways of operating in order to get what you want, you will be able to develop commitment. The more commitment you develop, the more relentless you will become.

Relentlessness is also born of confidence in one's self. If you don't believe in your goals or in your ability to achieve them, it will be easy to push you aside. One of the most dramatic examples of relentlessness was Thomas Edison, the inventor of the light bulb. He tried over a thousand configurations before he found the one that produced light from electricity. Can you imagine how you would feel working on your goal and having just failed the 200th time? The 600th time? The 900th time? Would you have the commitment to carry on? This kind of relentlessness requires a high level of confidence in the value of your purpose and in your contribution to achieving it.

MEASURING AND CELEBRATING PROGRESS

Few of us can carry on without some positive feedback. We all need some data that say to us, one way or another, "Okay, you're getting there! You're making progress!" Without this encouragement, our sense of forward movement, our sense of value added, our sense of the possibilities, and hence our motivation and hope begin to wither. Effective leaders recognize this principle in the way they deal with themselves and others.

---

[16] If you find the sailing analogy of interest, you may enjoy reading Richard Bode, *First You Have to Row a Small Boat* (New York: Warner, 1995), which describes learning life's lessons through sailing.

Focusing on the Right Measures

As the BancOne example demonstrated, a key leadership skill is focusing on the right measure. Steve Kerr's article "On the Folly of Hoping for A While Rewarding B"[17] made a strong point that we can't realistically expect to get results A whereas we model and reward behavior that leads people to an entirely different outcome, B. Yet, he notes, many managers and management systems get caught up in that very misconception. Operating on the basic principle "the boss knows best," bureaucratic organizations too often make decisions that later actually make the problem they are trying to solve worse. We often refer to these results as unintended consequences.

Unintended consequences come from not seeing ahead clearly and not understanding the people with whom we're dealing. A good example lies in the air pollution problem of Mexico City, one of the largest cities in the world. Lying as it does in a geographical bowl of mountains, Mexico City often has intense air pollution caused mostly by the huge number of automobiles there. In the attempt to alleviate this problem, city officials once conferred and came up with a plan to dramatically reduce the number of cars on the roads and hence, they hoped, the air pollution.

They decided that every person should not be allowed to use his or her car at least one day a week. This regulation, they thought, would stimulate carpooling and reduce the number of cars on the roads. The simple way to proceed with this plan, they thought, was to assign a day of the week to the last digit of license plates. If your license plate number ended in 1, you could not drive your car on Monday, and so on. They expected to reduce air pollution by 15 percent immediately. Instead, the unintended consequences were that most people bought an older, used car with the last digit of license place differing from that of the already owned car, most of them with less efficient engines and exhaust systems and drove that car on the restricted day, so that rather than reducing the air pollution problem, the law actually worsened the problem—almost doubled it!

The ability to focus on the right measures is a key leadership skill.[18] If people begin to believe that they are working to create results that are trivial or diversionary from the basic goal or purpose, they will lose heart and become weak followers. On the other hand, if the leader can home in on a small set of key indicators and is able to show how those indicators relate to the purpose and the vision, people will be focused and clear on what they are working for. If you choose the wrong measures, you can divert enormous amounts of human energy in unproductive directions.

One example of focusing on a diversionary goal is often found in monthly or quarterly profit figures. Everyone, especially investors, wants to see stable, steadily increasing profits. If that focus is the primary one, however, it can have unintended consequences among followers as described earlier in Chapter 8.

Focusing on the Glass Half Full

Another common measurement-related residue of the bureaucratic mind-set is variance management. This practice is the willingness to let things go until a variance from the organization's plan occurs, at which time management's job is to step in and get things back on track. Fundamentally, this approach negatively affects the motivation of the people involved.

---

[17] Steve Kerr, "On the Folly of Rewarding A While Hoping for B," *Academy of Management Journal*, August 15 (1988): 298.
[18] See Tim Gallwey, *The Inner Game of Work* (New York: Random House, 1999).

First, who knows whether the plan was accurate and right for the current business conditions? As business conditions change rapidly, business plans grow obsolete and out of touch. More and more companies are developing flexible plans that respond more quickly than the traditional semiannual or annual reporting and management cycles. Second, if management's primary communication with the employees revolves around criticism when things aren't going well, how can employees be expected to be enthusiastic followers and coordinate their efforts smoothly with management? This formula manages the downside, not the upside. Determining the right measures and developing a positive philosophy about how to administer them makes the difference between an average organization and a vibrant, leading one.

Effective leaders watch for progress on key indicators and celebrate the positive with their people. Rather than looking for how the glass is half empty—the mistakes and faults of the organization—they look for ways that the glass is half full and how to fill it further. They build on the successes rather than railing on the failures. Sure, yelling may get short-term, Level One results, but if the leader leaves for a while, have the employees learned how to carry on? Probably not. Rather, they've learned an insidious, unintended dependence on the manager on matters of performance and quality. The employees who've worked with a leader know when they're doing the right thing because they are celebrated. They begin to look for other ways to get positive feedback. Celebrations of forward progress bring the work up out of the mundane and routine and present it as it is, on the track of the organization's purpose and in line with the vision of what can be.

Conclusions

Personal leadership characteristics are only part of what is necessary for effective leadership to occur. Nevertheless, who you are and what you do as an individual contribute a major portion of a positive leadership outcome. This chapter presented six things you can do to improve your personal leadership effectiveness. Each step is an ongoing process, not something that one can do or learn once and for all. Leadership requires a long-term commitment to personal exploration and to personal visions. Without that level of engagement, leadership is not likely to happen.

Concepts Introduced in This Chapter

1. Effective leaders are centered; that is, they know who they are, what they believe in, and what they want to accomplish in their lives.
2. Effective leaders have a clear view of what's possible for the organization; they have created a vision of where to go.
3. Effective leaders can see what others can contribute in their unique ways and with their unique talents in accomplishing the vision.
4. Effective leaders are good organizational designers; they reshape the organization to support talented people as they work toward the vision, creating an organization that helps rather than hinders the people working in it.
5. Effective leaders are relentless. They don't give up, and they are flexible enough to take different routes to their goals.
6. Effective leaders recognize progress and praise those who make it.

Questions for Personal Reflection

1. What are your core leadership principles? If you were asked to take charge of an organization, what have you learned/concluded thus far in life about the way you would approach the task of leading?

2. What is the purpose of your organization? Can you write it succinctly and immediately? Are you engaged in that purpose? Why or why not?

3. What do all of your co-workers contribute to this purpose? Can you identify contributions that each makes?

4. How would you reorganize your organization to make it more effective? How could you make your ideas happen?

5. What things in life are you relentlessly committed to? What, if anything, are you willing to spend 10 years working on? What does this commitment have to do with your ability to lead?

CASELET FOR DISCUSSION

A newly appointed middle manager of a communications group insisted on having a lengthy staff meeting each Monday morning. It was obvious from the start that he had little or no managerial experience and knew nothing about meeting management. He had gotten the job by default and soon was being called by members of the group "Peter" after the Peter Principle.

Participants spent most of the Monday morning meeting time listening to the manager, because his style was one-way communication. He had even made the statement that he could discuss whatever he wanted because it was *his* meeting. Employees were "floored" (surprised, shocked, and confused).

After each Monday meeting, he would send out lengthy summaries with action items. Throughout the week, he would update summaries and inundate employees with lengthy and duplicate e-mails. The employees, who were rather close, began comparing notes and discovered "Peter" was sending out several sets of e-mails to different employees of the same group. In addition, he would blind copy numerous managers and co-workers.

One day, "Peter" stopped by one of his employee's office and asked if the employee thought trust was an issue in the group because he had felt negative "vibes" from certain employees. The employee told him trust was indeed an issue and that his first step should be to denounce the use of blind copies. His face turned bright red, and he quickly left the employee's office.

WORKBOOK

Complete the Leadership Steps Assessment on page 379 in Workbook. This instrument is also available online at www.CareerNextStep.com.

CONTRIBUTING YOUR OWN CASELETS

Have you seen or experienced a situation involving the concepts introduced in this chapter? If so and if you'd like to contribute your experience/situation to our case data bank, please visit http://faculty.darden. virginia.edu/clawsonj/ and click on the "Contribute new caselets" button.

20 | THE LANGUAGE OF LEADERSHIP

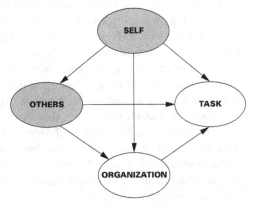

Use what language you will, you can never say anything but what you are.

—Ralph Waldo Emerson

Language is the primary implementation tool of leaders. If you lack the ability to communicate and convey your vision and strategy, others cannot know who you are and what you stand for. If your language is fuzzy, illogical, uninspiring, or diffuse, the odds are you won't be able to inspire, motivate, or energize others.

At least four basic attributes seem to govern effective leadership communications: clarity, stimulation, congruency, and respect. Let's consider them one at a time, and then consider some principles for using them.

CLARITY

Clarity is essential in leadership communications. You must be clear on your purpose and on the role that others can play in that purpose. If either of these two elements is fuzzy to you, it is likely to be fuzzy to others and your attempts to influence them will be fuzzy. If you can describe with focus what you're trying to do, why others also should want to do it, and how they could help make it happen, you have taken major steps toward enlisting others in your enterprise. For example, in your experience, how many management meetings have you attended and come away wondering what they were about? That percentage, whatever it is, is a measure of the fuzziness of the leadership of the people conducting the meetings. When I ask executives if they've ever been in a business meeting after which they couldn't figure out the purpose of the meeting, every hand in the room goes up. Such a meeting is a huge waste of time and effort.

One of the challenges in speaking clearly involves making two translations, one from Level Three to Level Two and one from Level Two to Level One. The first translation involves becoming more aware of our experiences. The chapter on global leadership explores this concept more completely, but the basic concept is that many of us live our lives and aren't really aware of what's happening around us. People have experiences—sometimes they are vague feelings or emotions—and aren't sure where they come from or why they're there. To become aware of one's experiences and emotions is the job of the first translation as shown in Figure 20-1. This is the essence of living mindfully rather than mindlessly, the subject of Ellen Langer's career-long research stream at Harvard.[1] People develop filters over the course of their lives that may inhibit the first translation; that is, people may become habitually unaware of how they're feeling, that is what they're experiencing.

Once a person has become able to *think* about his or her emotions and experiences, there comes the challenge of creating words and language that will convey those thoughts to

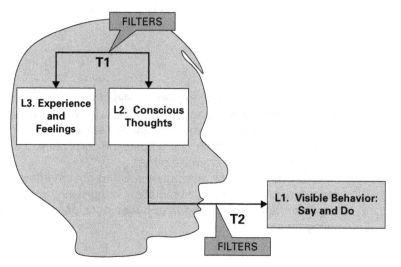

FIGURE 20-1 Two key Translations: Making Sense of our Experiences

---

[1] See Ellen J. Langer's books, *Mindfulness* (New York: de Capo, 1990) and *Counterclockwise: Mindful Health and the Power of Possibility* (New York: Ballantine, 2009).

others. This is the work of the second translation. Have you ever thought to yourself or said, "I know what I'm trying to say, but I cannot find the words"? This would be a symptom of the second translation process. If you find yourself stumbling on your attempts to understand or to describe your thoughts or feelings, I encourage you to find ways to practice both of these translations.

There are linguists who point out the benefits of using language that is vague and nonspecific.[2] These benefits include allowing the listener greater room to make their own interpretations, reducing the defensiveness in the listener, allowing the speaker to be less specific about their thoughts and beliefs, smoothing social interactions among those of different points of view, and putting some "ease" in the fabric of daily interactions. Too much clarity, they argue, would add too much grit and abrasion to conversations. They might say, "Give me the salt!" is too sharp whereas "If you're not too busy, would you mind passing the salt?" is less so. In some sense these are extremes. One could say, for example, "Please pass the salt" without being overly abrasive or vague.

We observe many in society who use intentional vagueness in language to their advantage. These include politicians, clergy, journalists, advertisers, and media announcers. On the other hand, it seems to me that people tend to err on the side of vagueness more than they do on the side of clarity. Speaking without being clear on what you're trying to say is more likely to become a habit in society and in business settings than the opposite. So although intentional vagueness may serve its purposes in greasing daily conversation, we need more clarity than we do more vagueness in business leadership roles.

STIMULATING AND MEMORABLE

Effective leadership language is also stimulating. Even if we are clear, if we don't deliver our message in powerful, inspiring, dramatic ways, others may not see the significance or appreciate the urgency of what we propose—or worse yet, even remember what we've said. Effective speakers find ways to present data in poignant ways, to make provocative statements that jar and cause listeners to pay attention and to think, and to dramatize their points with stories, nuances of speech, and emotional connections. If the others can't remember what you say, how can they be galvanized by your strategy or sincerity?

Many potential leaders feel uncomfortable thinking about—much less working on—improving their delivery style. They believe that the content of their message should carry the day. The reality is that many stimulating messages with weaker content can and do carry the day in innumerable human endeavors. Consider all of the less-than-leading-edge products that dominated their market segments because of superior marketing. Better yet, think of the speeches and leadership invitations you can remember. What made them memorable? Why did you respond? Perhaps it was because, in no small part, of the *way* in which the content was delivered.

Consider the simple eloquence and inspiring nature, for instance, of Gandhi's march to the sea to make salt, which was prohibited by the British government at the time. Gandhi's simple, stimulating act—declaring his intention to walk from the interior to the sea and make salt, and then doing so—captured the attention of millions of people and presented an extraordinary challenge to the government. When you want to influence, consider carefully how you can make your message stimulating.

---

[2] For example, Steven Pinker, *The Stuff of Thought* (New York: Viking, 2007).

Here's an example that I use. Sometimes in discussions about how corporate life can be overwhelming and discouraging to people, we talk about the importance of protecting your mental, ethical, and physical being. If people compromise too many times what they believe, they can eventually become inured to events that previously might have spurred them to action. To illustrate this point, I ask if participants have seen the film *Hannibal.* This is a film about a serial killer who eats his victims. It's a grisly thought—and right away their attention is riveted. There's a scene in this film where the protagonist has brought a "bad" guy home "for dinner." He's taped this man's arms and legs to the chair and then sawed off the top of the guy's head so his brain is exposed to the air. He's slowly slicing off pieces of his cortex and sautéing them in a fry pan by the table—and feeding them to him. Again, a grisly scene. But what's interesting, I note, is that with each slice (compromise) the man's ability to speak erodes so that his speech patterns go back in time to college, to high school, to middle school, and to elementary school, and eventually, he's reduced to childlike communications. The point being that sometimes corporate life can do this to us: we're asked to compromise our values and beliefs, and if we give in too many times, we may find ourselves one day unable to act for ourselves and to do what we once thought was right. During this discussion, some participants will grimace, some will cringe, some will sigh or groan—and *none* of them forget the story and that's the point.

CONGRUENT AUTHENTICITY

Congruency is another principle that many would-be leaders violate, and as a result, their efforts to lead fail. Congruency means that you walk your talk; that is, you do what you say you will do. Congruency is about being authentic—that is, showing who you are inside and out. As was discussed earlier in the chapter on the moral foundation of leadership (Chapter 6), you don't make promises that you cannot keep—and still expect people to be eager to follow you. Effective leaders understand deeply that unless they are willing to live what they are asking others to do, they will not be able to sustain their influence. If we ask employees to endure cost cutting and yet take a big salary increase, our ability to influence employees is greatly undermined. If we ask people to be creative and then hammer, punish, or ridicule those who try it, they learn that we speak with a forked tongue. To be an effective leader means to be at one in our speech and in our actions. So the principle here would be "When you speak to others, be yourself." Don't promise things you cannot deliver. Don't try to pretend to be something you're not. And if you can't do what you're asking, don't say it. If you do, you'll just be undermining how others see you. If they cannot trust what you say because your behavior seems different, their trust in you will be undermined.

Effective leadership communication is also respectful of others. This respect can take several forms. In general, leaders who engender trust in others and as a result energize them are not condescending or disparaging. Rather, effective leaders imply by their speech the value that others have toward the leader's goals. Consider U.S. president John Kennedy's famous remark during his inauguration, "Ask not what your country can do for you; ask what you can do for your country." On the surface, this comment might seem discouraging to listeners in that it seems like a demand, but if we consider the implied message, namely that "you have talents and abilities and your country *needs* you; let's find a way for you to make your best contributions," the statement becomes a powerful communicator of respect. It doesn't convey a sense of manipulating the rubes, of fooling some of the people some of the time, or of getting the masses to do what we want them to do. Rather, the implication is one of profound respect for people, respect that if they would choose to do so, they could make an enormous difference in the quality of their lives, others' lives, and the realities facing our nation. When you communicate respect to others for their views, for their concerns, and for their talents, you are much more likely to get a positive response.

RESPECTFUL

Invitations

One reason people don't do what we'd like them to do is that we don't ask them properly. Effective leaders know how to frame and extend powerful invitations rather than demeaning commands or orders. Of course, unless an invitation is based on clear purpose, clear reward, clear roles, and respect for others and is delivered with stimulation and congruency, it may not be accepted. Effective leaders, though, don't shrink from asking. If they learn how to ask powerfully, to frame the invitation in a way that is attractive and engaging to others, their probability of getting favorable—and voluntary—responses goes way up. The concept of Level Three Leadership—extending invitations rather than demands, commands, or instructions—implies a different attitude toward leadership than most people in positions of power take.

Invitations are respectful because they leave the other with *choice*. An invitation is consistent with our basic definition of leadership that includes a voluntary response from others. When you invite someone to do something, you acknowledge that unless you have done your homework and can present the invitation in a powerful way, he or she may say no.

For many, this whole concept of leading by "invitation" is bizarre and out of step. If you conclude at the moment that invitations and leadership are incompatible, then your language with others will revolve around giving instructions, commands, guidelines, and demands, and although the others' mouths may say yes, inside—at Level Two and Level Three—they may well be saying no. Given this, I invite you to consider how able you are to frame and offer compelling invitations. These are not, as Marlon Brando in *The Godfather* said, "making an offer he can't refuse." That's the same as coercion, and no real choice is involved. Consider the effect your attempts to lead would have if you could find ways to frame and deliver powerful and deep-seated (Level Three) invitations.

Rules of the Interpersonal "Dance"

If you accept the premise that language is a critical tool of the effective leader, then you may wish to pay attention to the little habits of communication that can undermine one's ability to influence others. These seemingly innocuous habits erode our ability to influence in subtle ways we seldom recognize. I offer here tips for effective leadership communication based on years of observation and experience. I invite you to consider incorporating them into your daily language and practice. I expect if you do so, you will notice that your accuracy in communication and your influence have grown.

1. *Replace "but" with "and."* Or put more directly, "lose your buts." This is one of the most common and confounding usages in modern language. Consider the meaning of this sentence fragment, "Mary, I agree with everything you've said, but. . ." What's the immediate reaction? What's the actual meaning? The word "but" discounts all that came before it. In other words, "Mary, I *don't* agree with everything you've said." In this instant, the listener becomes aware in a microway that you are telling a little lie and the other shoe is about to fall. This construction, this habit of speech, creates little concerns about the speaker's accuracy, honesty, and style of speech.

A better alternative is to use the word "and." "And" is more *accurate* in that it allows room for consideration of both the other's point of view and your point of view. This "larger container" is a concept much discussed in the learning-organization research that tends to be more inclusive of other points of view and therefore to engender trust, commitment, and engagement. Using "and" can help create a win–win climate, whereas "but" tends to create a win–lose climate. Using "and" instead of "but" can help both parties to feel like they are solving the issue at hand together rather than competing for the solution.

Because this Level One habit is so common and so pervasive, I invite you to begin in a small way. Can you just pay attention to how many times others use "but" in their speech and each time, think for a second or two, "What was the impact of that single, tiny, three-letter word?" Next, you can begin to be aware of how often *you* use the term. I hope that from now on, your "Clawson but radar" will go "beep, beep, beep" every time you hear yourself or someone else use "but." And I hope that this awareness will gradually move you to change your speech habits to include more "ands" and fewer "buts." If you can do this, I think you'll find your relationships and communications improve significantly. It's a tiny thing (habit) with a bit impact.

2. Use "I" statements. Your high-school English or language teacher may scream at this one. I invite you to speak in the first-person singular to describe your own data—conclusion connections and emotions rather than imputing absolute truth to your statements. For example, say "I believe. . ." instead of "It is. . ." Which is more accurate? What do you know for *sure*? If, when you speak, you speak in absolutes, where is there room for others to participate in the discussion or in your vision? Using a variation of "I see . . ." is a more accurate statement of what "is." Do you realize that your "truth" may not be what others see or believe?

Using the second person, "You" (e.g., "You have a problem. . ."), tends to create immediate, if subtle, defensiveness in others. Much of communication theory argues the opposite, that one should avoid saying or writing "I" too much as it is too "self-centered." The challenge, however, is to be accurate, to say what you mean and mean what you say. This does not mean that you start each sentence or each paragraph with "I," but it does mean that you acknowledge your opinions and perspectives as that—and don't state them as "fact." It also means that you don't attribute problems to others when they really belong with you. Using the second person "you" can very quickly create defensiveness and resistance. "I," although it may not make your language teacher happy, is more accurate and less imposing on others. In short, it's more "respectful."

3. Don't disguise your opinions as questions. The most common manifestation of this principle is the oft-used "Don't you think that. . .?" construction. This common construction shifts the spotlight of attention from the speaker to the listener—which tends to create defensiveness and is a subtle means of avoiding responsibility for one's own beliefs and conclusions. The "Don't you think. . .?" form tends to paint people into corners. When a listener hears this, they immediately begin thinking about whether or not they're being led to a conclusion they don't want to reach and whether they're being manipulated in the conversation. This "awareness" may not drift up into consciousness at Level Two, and most people when asked can describe what it feels like to be "nudged" in this way.

A more influential, courageous, and respectful leadership-language approach would be to acknowledge one's point of view by stating it: "My belief is. . ." or "I believe. . ." There is a big difference between the kinds of responses these two approaches elicit. One creates defensiveness, and the other respects the listener's point of view and allows him or her to speak it as they choose.

Listen for the next time you say, "Don't you think that. . .?" and watch for the immediate and perhaps fleeting reaction in the person you're talking with. When someone else begins his or her thought to you in this way, what's *your* immediate reaction? I've become sensitized to this, so that when people begin their comments to me with, "Don't you think that. . ." I immediately interrupt and ask whether they're asking a question or stating an opinion. They usually think for a second and then admit they're stating an opinion. "So," I say, "then state it as such and let me respond without you putting me on the spot." It works.

4. *Seek to understand* **before** *seeking to be understood.* Be able to restate what the previous speaker has said to his or her satisfaction especially if it is creative/unusual. Although Stephen Covey popularized this principle in his book *Seven Habits of Highly Effective People*, it is a concept that was established by Carl Rogers, a well-known now-deceased psychologist. People who do not feel "heard" are much less open to influence. If you show respect to people by listening to them until they feel completely and fully heard and understood, you are more likely to get a Level Three listening ear when you speak. Try confirming what you heard (e.g., "I heard you say. . .") before you try to make your point (e.g., "Yeah, here's what I want you to do. . ."). This *active listening* is much talked about and not so commonly practiced. In my experience, powerful Level Three Leaders are very intense listeners. Their genuine desire to *know* what you think is at once stimulating, rare, energizing, clarifying, and respectful.

5. *Affirm your right to your conclusions, ideas, opinions, and emotions by not discounting them, especially if they are creative.* How many times have you heard someone begin his or her comment with, "This may not be right, but . . ." This initial discounting of one's own beliefs, values, or conclusions tends to minimize one's influence. A more powerful way of acknowledging that we may not know some kind of absolute truth is to begin with "I believe. . ." rather than "I don't know much about this but . . ." Don't discount yourself or your ideas before you've even expressed them. The repeated use of this construction may be a Level One manifestation of an underlying outside-in stance toward the world. I invite you to review the discussion on inside-out and outside-in in Chapter 1 and reflect on how your speech habits reflect that orientation.

6. *Support your conclusions with data first, then emotion.* Recognize the difference between logic and emotion, and be able to use both appropriately. Some people believe that if they press their point with more emotion, this will make up for a lack of supporting data. In fact, though, pounding the table and shouting does not change your logic. At the other end of the spectrum, some believe that if you have the facts, you don't need emotion or dramatics to make your point—logic will carry the day. From our point of view, both style and substance are necessary. What are the facts—as you see them? Cite your data and let others reach the same conclusions you have—IF there are logical links, they'll likely see them.

When can you be passionate about your facts? If you can state your case logically and based on evidence, then let your emotions dramatize the conclusion. Neither emotions nor cold data alone will carry the day. The considered and engaged use of both makes a much more powerful and memorable (the result of "stimulating") presentation or conversation.

7. *Be descriptive, not judgmental.* Judgments, conclusions about others, tend to create defensiveness. Learn the difference between describing facts and jumping to conclusions. "John, you're lazy" is quite different from "John, I noticed your last two assignments were late." The more objective and descriptive you can be, the better you will be equipped to influence others. Practice observing and describing what goes on around you. (Again, Ellen Langer's work is very informative here.) Can you describe another's point of view or underlying logic or even better, the underlying set of VABEs, upon which his or her communication is based? If you can do this well, you'll be a powerful negotiator and a much better communicator.

8. *Think creatively*. Many of us have learned to think critically. Although this is a good skill, without *restraint*, it keeps us from recognizing new and unusual ideas that don't match our current VABE's. People who have a habitually critical view of the world tend not to be open to possibilities for changing it. Part of the reason is that they have learned, habitually, to listen for *conformity*. It's one thing to listen for conformity to what you already believe; it's quite another thing to listen with an open mind for the possibilities. Review Chapter 7 on innovation for more suggestions about how to improve your ability to think creatively. Learn to think first about why another's ideas might work rather than why they might not. If after lengthy consideration you disagree, be sure to use Principle #6 above and use the term "and" to describe why you have reached the conclusion you did.

9. *If you don't understand, assume that others don't as well.* Don't discount your own abilities or experience by not asking the dumb question. Be willing to be a bit vulnerable in order to learn. If you don't understand something, assume that others don't as well, and be willing to be their voice and get the confusion sorted out. Take responsibility for your own outcomes. Again, the ability to do this rests on a strong self-confidence, the ability to live more inside-out, and a determination to satisfy your curiosity—even at the marginal expense of your perceived reputation among others (most of whom you don't know, right?)

10. *Accept responsibility for the content, process, and outcomes of every situation you are a part of.* If you don't like it, change it. If you can't change it, make it work. Choose to be happy if not content. Ask yourself, "How have I contributed to this situation? How can I improve it? If a meeting is not going well, do something to improve it." Be assertive. This is a key principle—akin to Covey's "Be proactive," the first of his seven habits.

May I give you a short anecdote? I was invited once by a good friend of mine to play in a member-guest golf tournament at his club. This was a very nice club with many well-to-do members. As it turned out, we'd won our flight, so we were attending the awards banquet and happened to be seated with four other people we didn't know. One of them was an elderly gentleman, who by his relaxed demeanor I took to be a member of the club. The dinner service was slow, so it looked like it might be a two-hour dinner before the ceremonies even began. And this elderly gentleman across the way had nodded off and was snoring. I'm thinking—I'm sure not alone—that this was going to be a long and boring evening despite the fun of winning something.

I decided to take responsibility for my own evening. You tell me what you think: too overbearing? I'd learned, despite being quite introverted growing up (something one learns to do in an alcoholic environment), that a good way to stimulate conversation at receptions is to ask about others and stop worrying about yourself. So, I hemmed a bit and asked this gentleman, "Excuse me, sir!" He harrumphed and woke up. "What?" "First, I just wanted to thank you and your club for organizing this member-guest tournament. It's been a delightful time. And as a professor of business who teaches among other things, career management, I'm always curious about what people have learned over the course of their lives. You look to be very successful. May I ask what you do or did for your career?" He said he'd been a manager for a very large Fortune 20 company for over 35 years. "Hmm," I said, "may I ask, given that I teach a lot of young and eager MBAs, what would you say are the two or three most important things you've learned in life?" Harrumph. He thought for a while and then said, brusquely, "Work hard." And nodded off again. Wow. That was the summum bonum of his lifelong work. I could see that his wife had perked up at this conversation and had been eagerly awaiting her husband's reply. She seemed a little disappointed at his response, and as soon as he'd nodded off again, she with a twinkle in her eye said, "Hmm, well I learned that sex is wonderful!" You could have knocked us all of our chairs with a feather! We were flabbergasted! And she was all aglow, eyes twinkling. And we're thinking, "With *him*?" The conversation went on from there, and we had a delightful evening. My point is simply this: take responsibility for your own outcomes. If you're bored, do something about it. Be respectful of others, and then take accountability so that when you return home, you can say, "Wow! That was a wonderful time."

Listening

An often overlooked aspect of leadership communication is that of listening. Many leaders believe their job is to tell not listen. Yet effective leaders, especially Level Three leaders, are masters of active listening. By active listening I mean the ability to attend genuinely to two things, *what* is being said and the *emotion* beneath what is being said. This is not as easy as it may sound. Most Western leaders assume (a VABE) that the job of the leader is to guide, instruct, coach, direct, command, and tell. Many Eastern leaders assume the opposite, that their job is to listen carefully to what's being said before making a decision. Both Western and Eastern leaders in my experience can be very egocentric and controlling—but the cultural norms (VABEs) about how to do that vary widely.

Steve Covey popularized the concept "Seek First to Understand, *Then* to Be Understood."[3] It is a powerful principle. Those who strive to enhance their ability to communicate will include in their efforts practice at listening more intently, more completely, and more deeply. It is in fact through careful listening that one picks up signals about the other person's buy-in level as previously discussed.

Sometimes listening is a great service to another who is using the conversation to clarify his or her own thoughts. Practice learning to listen to people's thoughts completely before (a) assuming you know what they are going to say or (b) interrupting them to say it for them or dismiss it altogether. If you do, you may find new nuggets in their thoughts, *and* your willingness to listen will tend to build bonds between you because listening sends several important underlying messages including "I value you," "I value what you have to say," and "I have the time to give to you." Poor listeners tend to send the opposite messages and that undermines their ability to lead. If you want to learn more about how to listen effectively, you might get a copy of "Active Listening" (UVA-OB-0341, one of the most requested technical notes from Darden Business Publishing).

Conclusions

Language is one of, if not *the* major tool of the effective leader. Many authoritors struggle with language and with making themselves clearly and memorably understood. And yet, of all the leadership skills, language is one of the most trainable and manageable. You can learn to be clearer, more stimulating, more authentic, and more respectful in your daily conversations. It takes clear theory and lots of practice, but the good news is there are lots of sources and lots of opportunity to practice. Although I stuttered badly in high school, with good instructors and theory and lots of practice (in the shower, in the car, jogging, in all kinds of places), I've learned to speak much more effectively. You can, too. The Questions for Personal Reflection at the end of the chapter may stimulate your language development thoughts.

[3] Steve Covey, *Seven Habits of Highly Effective People* (New York: Simon & Schuster, 1991).

Questions for Personal Reflection

1. Would people say you communicate clearly? Or would they say they often aren't quite sure what you're trying to say? How often do you stumble trying to find the words to express your thoughts? Keep track of how often you find yourself stumbling on the translation between your thoughts and your words. Do you read your speeches? Do you lose your place? If so, you may not have your beliefs clearly in mind.

2. How often do you practice out loud trying to find ways to express your beliefs or principles or thoughts? Where could you do this? What would keep you from doing this? If you're shy or introverted, what could be safer than practicing this when no one else is around? Are you afraid of your own judgments?

3. Is what you say memorable? Do you strive to find ways to ensure that people will remember what you've said? Can you find little stories, anecdotes, or vignettes to bring your ideas and concepts to life? Do you enjoy telling stories? Are you a good storyteller? How could you practice your storytelling abilities?

4. What do you think about authenticity? Do you prefer to hide your thoughts and feelings? Why? What is dangerous or threatening about sharing your innermost thoughts? Do you think them sacred and therefore not appropriate to share? If no one knew your most important thoughts and beliefs and feelings, how could you lead them?

5. How much do you respect others? Do you ever find yourself telling ethnic jokes? Do you tend to find humor in putting others down? Why? If people don't respect you or if you don't respect others, how likely are they to follow you?

6. Do you show your respect by the way in which you listen to others? Do you listen for both content and emotion? Are you able to read the buy-in signals that people send when they speak?

7. Keep track of how often you hear the word "but" in a single day. Note the impact of these events and then reflect on how often you say the word and how it affects your ability to influence others.

8. How could you practice becoming more articulate? Where? When? What would you "talk" about?

CASELET FOR DISCUSSION

The speechwriter for the CEO of a company was asked each year to ghostwrite his electronic messages for companywide distribution. One year, the speechwriter, as usual, wrote the annual holiday message to all employees. The speechwriter included the phrase "the women and men of the company . . ." The CEO approved the message and it was sent out. Afterward, the speechwriter received a censure from her direct supervisor for writing "women and men" rather than "men and women." At first, she thought he was joking, but she soon discovered he was not. Her supervisor then proclaimed a policy that we would only use "men and women," arguing that to change the order drew attention to the gender issue rather than the central issue of the message. Was this a syntax issue or gender issue? The supervisor sent around an e-mail saying, "As a matter of policy, we will use the following construction: 'men and women' rather than 'women and men.' Along the same lines and strictly as an example, we will say, 'Ladies and gentlemen' rather than 'gentlemen and ladies.' To switch the order in the construction of these phrases draws attention to the phrases themselves not the content of the note." The speechwriter wondered what to do.

WORKBOOK

Complete the Leadership Language exercise in Workbook on page 378 by noting how you'd like to improve your language as you try to influence others.

CONTRIBUTING YOUR OWN CASELETS

Have you seen or experienced a situation involving the concepts introduced in this chapter? If so, and you'd like to contribute your experience/situation to our case data bank, please visit http://faculty.darden.virginia.edu/clawsonj/ and click on the "Contribute new caselets" button.

21 | LEADING TEAMS

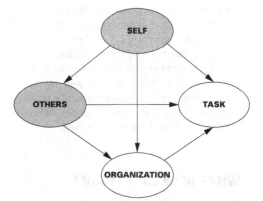

*[W]hile not ignoring or neglecting the individual, we should
devote far more thought to teams: to the selection,
development, and training of teams, to the qualifications,
experience, and achievements of teams, and above all to the
psychology, motivation, composition, and behaviour of teams.*

—Anthony Jay

*Not finance. Not strategy. Not technology. It is teamwork that
remains the ultimate competitive advantage, both because it
is so powerful and so rare. A friend of mine, the founder of a
company that grew to a billion dollars in annual revenue,
best expressed the power of teamwork when he once told me,
"If you could get all the people in an organization rowing in
the same direction, you could dominate any industry, in any
market, against any competition, at any time."*

—Patrick Lencioni,
The Five Dysfunctions of a Team, vii

An information systems project leader wrestles to organize a massive change effort in an urban municipal modernization program involving hundreds of people.

An account executive for a global financial services firm wonders how to coordinate the efforts of colleagues in eight different cities on behalf of a single global client.

A wiring harness group seeks help in making up a backlog of product a customer needs immediately.

A course head struggles to find a way to build a cohesive teaching team among colleagues teaching multiple sections of the same course.

A world-class climber tries to manage his emotions as the expedition moves up the 8,000-meter mountain despite large egos, troublesome porters, and peers jockeying for position on the summit team.

In a rapidly changing environment, the capacity of an organization to form, develop, utilize, and then re-form high-performing teams is a source of sustainable competitive advantage. Most organizations cannot do it. Each of these teams faces a common set of problems. How does one build an effective team, especially when time is short and the consequences are significant? The answers are not easy, but increasingly important as Anthony Jay pointed out above. The paradigm shift described in Chapter 4 is creating more and more team-based organizations. As a result, more and more leaders are faced with the dilemmas and challenges of managing teams—short-term teams, project teams, program teams, special-function teams, ad hoc teams, and permanent, goal-oriented, profit-motivated teams. Numerous conferences, nationally and internationally, are now designed primarily to help people learn how to lead teams more effectively.

WHAT MAKES A TEAM?

First, note that every group of individuals does not necessarily constitute a team; certain differences distinguish work groups from teams. Authors Katzenbach and Smith, first, offer a definition of what a team is and then identify differences between groups and teams. In doing so, they create a worthy target for team leaders and members alike: What must we do to make our work group an effective team? Simply meeting often will not be enough; effective team leaders will actively manage the principles of team dynamics to forge effective teams. Katzenbach and Smith's definition of team is "a small number of people with complementary skills who are committed to a common purpose, performance goals, and approach for which they hold themselves mutually accountable." This definition may seem a little dry, but in essence, teams are cohesive groups of people mobilized around a common goal.

Katzenbach and Smith also identified the following seven characteristics of effective teams that distinguish them from simple work groups.[1] These were shared leadership, joint accountability, unique purpose, joint work, inefficient open-ended meetings, collective measures, and real not made-up work.

These criteria provide the basis to assess whether a work group is a team or is on the road to becoming a team. Some of the criteria concern the internal affairs of the team (the first five), whereas others may require changes in the surrounding, supporting organizational context (the last two). The group and its members, though, can manage much of a group's future and possible destiny as a group or a team. One of the first things to note is that groups evolve over time.

---

[1] Jon R. Katzenbach and Douglas K. Smith, *The Wisdom of Teams* (New York: HarperBusiness, 1994).

TEAM LIFE CYCLES

Groups, short lived or long lived, seem to pass through a life cycle of distinct stages, each one presenting its own challenges. Perhaps, you've heard the common phrase that groups go through stages of forming, storming, norming, and performing. Based on the research on group behavior and the realities of the current paradigm shift, a slightly different predictable pattern that groups exhibit and that group leaders need to understand includes these stages: forming, norming, performing, and re-forming. This sequence is somewhat different from the classical one of forming, storming, norming, and performing.

Forming: Initiation and Orientation

When groups first come together, their members spend most of their energy getting accustomed to and assessing one another. Communication is tentative as members try to answer some key questions: Should I be here? What is the purpose of this group? Who is the leader? Team members often look for a leader to instill in the group a sense of purpose. If the membership, purpose, and leadership issues are not sorted out quickly, the group's efforts to do its work will proceed inefficiently or perhaps even flounder. If the group jumps into its "task" immediately or prematurely (the most common team-building flaw), the issues of membership, purpose, and leadership will surface later and cause disruption and confusion. This phenomenon occurs repeatedly in multiple settings including live work situations, low ropes experiential team-building exercises, and more sophisticated simulation exercises where groups typically try to jump immediately in doing their task.

Effective team leaders or even effective team members who are willing to participate in a distributed leadership pattern will work through these three fundamental issues explicitly and early enough in order to avoid inefficiencies later on. This includes clarifying the task and intended output of the team; the reason each member is there and how they might contribute to that output; and some discussion about how leadership of the team will evolve and develop.

Norming: Exploration of How We'll Do the Task

As soon as a group sorts out what they are supposed to do, who should be there, and how they will manage the leadership, it begins thinking about the how questions: How will we work together? How will we resolve disputes? How will we relate to the outside world? Disagreements over the ground rules, the scope of the group's mission, and the best course of action make the norming stage one of the most fertile, and the most trying, for leaders and group members. Members want to know where the boundaries are and how firm they are, so they test them in myriad ways. Who speaks? How do we determine who speaks? How do we make decisions? How do we revisit those decisions? How often do we meet? What do we do before and after we meet? These questions bring up only some of the issues that members need to sort out first, so they can focus more effectively on their task.

In this creative but often volatile stage, members cultivate their ability to work together. The effective leader will neither take a challenge as an invitation to rule autocratically nor take group upheaval as an excuse to micromanage. Instead, these times become opportunities to point out how the skills and abilities of each member will contribute to the whole and the achievement of the team's task. It's a time to explore the emerging values, assumptions, beliefs, and expectations (VABEs) of the group and to ensure that those VABEs are explicit, shared, and consciously chosen.

TABLE 21-1 Stages of Group Development

Task	Forming	Norming	Performing	Re-Forming
Membership	X			
Purpose	X			
Leadership	X	X		
Rules		X		
Procedures		X		
Measures		X	X	
Action			X	
Performance review			X	
Learning			X	X
Celebrating				X
Letting go				X
Moving on				X

Most groups don't manage this exploration explicitly or well; it just happens as groups develop by spending time together. In fact, that's the point. Effective leaders are aware of these developmental stages and the tasks a group faces in each stage and are able to manage the team through them explicitly. Team leaders who ignore this predictable pattern of group development may feel like they are getting ahead, but usually, the issues come up later and bog down the group. So in the long run, jumping immediately to the task and ignoring the forming and norming stages makes the group/team less effective and less efficient.

The key way a designated team leader can manage through the early stages of group development is by making the tasks of each developmental stage explicit and by talking about them. Of course, the team may decide, as time passes, that some of the earlier discussions and conclusions don't work, and they may feel that the early time was lost. Nevertheless, the more effectively a leader can help a group move through these two early stages, the sooner the group can focus on getting the work done without distraction. See Table 21-1 for a list of the tasks involved in each stage of development.

Performing: Stabilization

Eventually, if the leader has managed it well more quickly, much of the uncertainty that hung over the group at the outset evaporates and the group can get down to the actual work assigned to it. Individual roles and interpersonal relationships become clear and comfortable. Members can now look to established precedent as they draw up their plans. Members stop challenging the purpose, membership, or leadership and focus their efforts on getting the job done. As the group progresses along a collective learning curve, it can operate at increasingly higher levels of efficiency.

New dangers, however, emerge. Having drawn energy from the heady atmosphere of the exploration stage, members may begin to see stability as dull and routine. Although working with the team to ensure that efficiency is, in fact, improving, effective leaders try to maintain the sense of urgency and excitement that often characterizes the early stages.

In this ongoing dilemma, how does one reenergize long-term work groups? How does one combat the debilitating effects of day-in day-out routines at work? One answer lies in the concepts introduced in Chapter 13 on resonance. If you can help your team to identify and revisit their team dream (team D*int*) regularly, you can help them see how today's work fits into the plan to realize that dream. If you organize the structure and relationships of the team with solid foundations of trust, respect, and vision, then you can do much to revitalize the ongoing efforts. In many respects, it is the work of the team leader to find ways to remind, refocus, and rebuild the resonance that comes from doing important work in ways that are intrinsically rewarding to the team members.

One way to combat the slide into routine, mediocre behavior is to emphasize learning. Effective organizations are already managing their learning aspects in a conscious, intentional way, so that all team members, when they are ready to leave the team and move on to the next project, are aware of what they learned from the last experience and are consciously (at Level Two) ready to apply it to the next assignment.

Re-Forming: Reassessment

Stable work groups often develop deep-seated working habits and, in doing so, become an organizational subculture. The more stable a group becomes, the more difficult it will be for that group to respond to radical change. Eventually, though, some fundamental change—declining profits, a transformed marketplace, different demands on the group from above, or just finishing the original job—makes reassessment and even dissolution or re-forming unavoidable.

What makes this crossroads so difficult—indeed, life-threatening—for the group is that feelings about these fundamental changes are likely to be wildly varied among group members. Some will vehemently oppose any change in the group's mission, some will accept it enthusiastically, and some will feel betrayed by the leader, top managers, or even their customers. As discussed in Chapter 15, competitive advantage is based in part on flexibility. Unless the processes of understanding and dealing with change are built into the culture of the group, finishing the present task can easily destroy the group in a negative way. The inability to dissolve teams effectively can be a source of competitive disadvantage.

Depending on the culture of the team and the quality of its leadership, several things can happen near the end of a team's life cycle. The group may emerge from this reassessment phase revitalized and refocused, it may burst from internal dissent, it may cling to its outmoded vision and die a more protracted death, or appropriately, it may just disband with a sense of completion while the members move on to other work. Organizations that pay attention to and develop the processes of reassessing and re-forming productive work teams will realize a distinct competitive advantage over those companies that do not. Another aspect of groups/teams that unfolds over the course of a team's life is the common and predictable roles that team members play.

An additional challenge is that many managers try to jump immediately to phase 3, performing, and ignore the challenges that relate to forming and norming. The problem with this "fire, fire, fire, ready, aim" strategy is that the unresolved issues of membership, purpose, leadership, and the like come back to plague the team later on. Figure 21-1 shows concept of working through the phase 1 issues first, and then moving on to issues of phases 2 and 3.

TEAM ROLES

Every time you are invited to a new group (will it be a team?) meeting, you are likely to see a predictable pattern of roles being played by the group members. You'll see the person who tries to be the dominant, loud leader; you'll see the quiet mouse who never speaks the whole time; you'll

	1. Forming	2. Norming	3. Performing	4. Re-forming
Purpose	X			
Membership	X			
Leadership	X			
Rules		X		
Measures		X		
Task			X	
Disconnecting				X

FIGURE 21-1 Team life cycles

see the "naysayer" who disagrees with everything no matter what it is; you'll see the "joker" who tries to make a joke out of everything; and you'll see the "skeptic" who sits back with arms folded, frowning, exuding vibrations of "prove it to me!" What other roles have you seen in your group meeting experience?

Obviously, not all of these common roles are effective and helpful. From his work with executive education teams in the United Kingdom and Australia, Meredith Belbin identified a series of roles that are essential for building effective teams.[2] They include Company Worker, Chairperson, Shaper, Plant, Resource Investigator, Monitor-Evaluator, Team Worker, and Completer-Finisher. Company Workers put company ahead of self and like to organize and arrange things to suit the larger organization. Chairpersons are adept at utilizing the resources in the group to good advantage, calling on varied skills to get things done. Shapers are hard-driving, action-oriented leaders who like to get things done. Plants are introverted, clever people who tend to be technical specialists with deep expertise. Resource Investigators are networkers, constantly on the phone, walking around, always wanting to check on things, wanting to be in the know on all fronts. Monitor-Evaluators are decision makers, usually serious-minded, immune to group enthusiasm, always testing and checking assumptions and the validity of group conclusions. Team Workers are extroverts without the need to dominate, so they are willing to do what's necessary for the good of the team's efforts. Completer-Finishers are those who want to get a job done, and who tolerate creative exploration, but in the end, push to closure. Belbin identified several roles including chairman, worker, creative, shaper, resource investigator, evaluator, and finisher from a variety of studies using psychological testing and observations of executive education teams.

Effective team leaders pay attention to making sure that the jobs and tasks assigned to members fit their talents and their inclinations. Sports coaches, expedition team leaders, project team leaders, and work-group leaders all understand the value of this principle. Sometimes, the person with the talent for a job doesn't want to do it, and unless the leader can build a process that allows each member to do things he or she wants to do along the way, the

---

[2] R. Meredith Belbin, *Management Teams: Why They Succeed or Fail* (Woburn, MA: Butterworth Heinemann, 1981, 1999).

success of the whole team can be jeopardized. Yet if left alone, talented team members will often tend to find niches themselves, zeroing in on the work for which they're best suited and in which they are most interested. Several Darden alumni report that some organizations leave the assignments of new employees intentionally ambiguous in the belief that talented people will create their own best way of making a valuable contribution.

Consider four general roles that are essential in effective groups (see Table 21-1). These roles can be viewed as two pairs of polar opposites, with each member of a pair contributing in a way that holds his or her counterpart in check:

- *Task Driver.* This results-oriented member of the group is the one who keeps the group focused on the ultimate goal of completing the task. Urging his creative colleagues to get their brainchild, the Macintosh, off the drawing board and into stores, Steve Jobs played the role of task driver when he said, "Real artists *ship.*"
- *Process Facilitator.* The task driver's counterpart, this member monitors the interpersonal dynamics of the group. The quality of working relationships among group members is critical—and the process facilitator watches them carefully, working hard to help the group manage misunderstandings that arise in the course of the team's work.
- *Creative Visionary.* This member's mind is most open to creative solutions—no matter how outlandish they might sound—and is always trying to find a better way. Creative visionaries are always exploring the four basic components of creative thinking: risk-taking, considering the opposites, relying on uncertainty, and looking for multiple possibilities.[3] Sometimes, team members, particularly the task drivers, try to squelch the creative types in the name of getting things done. In doing so, they may overlook alternative ways of doing things that might, in the end, entirely reshape the team's process or product.
- *Practicality Pusher.* The counterbalance to the creative visionary is the practicality pusher. This person attends to the practical realities of getting the assigned job done. Just as overattention to practicalities in finishing a job can stifle creativity, overattention to creative alternatives can strangle a team in possibilities. Practical protectors make sure that what the team asserts to do is feasible and push for completion.

These four roles form two polar scales: creativity versus practicality and task versus process (Figure 21-2). In effective teams, these opposites are balanced and well managed. What, however, if your group doesn't naturally include these roles and in a balanced way? If team members don't naturally seem to fit these four roles, they can be assigned. Team efforts can improve dramatically by simply assigning team members to attend to and be responsible for these four roles. These invitations ask group members to become "team workers" in Belbin's terms, who are willing to do what's necessary for the group's growth and success. The recognition by all members that these roles are necessary and helpful contributes to their willingness to try and to their evolution as a team ultimately.

Effective teams exhibit certain characteristics, evolve predictably though not necessarily through stages, and include a variety of roles. Designated or would-be team leaders understand

---

[3] James Clawson, John Kotter, Victor Faux, and Charles MacArthur (eds.), "Survey of Behavioral Characteristics" in *Self Assessment and Career Development,* 3rd ed. (Upper Saddle River, NJ: Prentice Hall, 1993). Chic Thompson, *What a Great Idea!* (New York: Harper Perennial, 1992) and Roger von Oech, *A Whack on the Side of the Head* (Menlo Park, CA: Creative Think, 1983).

TABLE 21-2	Belbin's Roles in Effective Teams

1. Company Worker
2. Chair (leader)
3. Shaper (leader)
4. Plant (creative)
5. Resource Investigator (creative)
6. Monitor-Evaluator (decision)
7. Team Worker
8. Completer-Finisher

these aspects of work groups and try actively to manage them. Bill Dyer and sons have developed a popular way of putting all of this together into a way of looking at teams.[4] They assert four key "C's" of building teams: context, composition, competencies, and change management skills. In essence, to build a strong team one must consider the context in which the team will be operating, whether or not you have the right people in the room, whether or not the team has the right set of skills (might be a function of the composition), and whether or not the team can adapt as things change. Essential team competencies, they say, are (a) clear articulation of goals and measures, (b) clarity of means to achieve goals, (c) effective decision making, (d) effectiveness in giving and receiving feedback, (e) high levels of trust and commitment, and (f) ability to resolve conflict.

As a team leader, your challenge will be to recognize these aspects of effective teams and manage them well as the development of your team unfolds. But how? How do you combine all of this insight into an effective team leadership style? Warren Bennis and Patricia Biederman conducted an interesting study of seven of the most successful groups in history that helps shed light on this question.[5] Their insights, which are outlined next, provide a powerful profile of effective teams and team leadership. As we describe these lessons from seven great teams, try to link them to the frameworks already introduced. This integration exercise will strengthen your learning and mental map of what it takes to lead a team effectively.

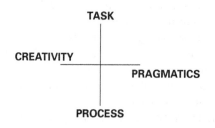

FIGURE 21-2   Essential roles in effective teams

---

[4] William Dyer, Gibb Dyer, and Jeffrey Dyer, *Team Building: Proven Strategies for Improving Team Performance*, (San Francisco, CA: Jossey Bass, 2007).
[5] Warren Bennis and Patricia Ward Biederman, *Organizing Genius: The Secrets of Creative Collaboration* (Reading, MA: Addison-Wesley, 1997).

INSPIRED VISION THAT CREATES

Bennis and Biederman found that the groups they studied shared a certain kind of leader who provided a vision that inspired the team. These leaders were able to paint this vision in such vivid and alluring color that others could see it clearly and wanted to join the enterprise in order to see it realized. For example, they cite the conversation when Steven Jobs was courting John Sculley, an executive from Pepsi, for the CEO position at Apple Computer. Jobs reportedly asked Sculley, "Do you want to spend the rest of your life selling flavored water, or do you want a chance to change the world?"

Walt Disney, as the leader of the group that produced in 1937 the world's first feature-length animated film, encountered stiff opposition to his idea, so he stood up in front of the group and acted out the entire story of Snow White and the Seven Dwarfs. The performance was convincing and ultimately, spectacularly successful. Those who will be able to galvanize the efforts of groups of people will be able to articulate a clear and powerful vision. This vision, in turn, will mobilize the resources of the team.

... A POWERFUL SENSE OF MISSION

Because of an inspiring vision, members of successful groups feel more zealous about their work than average employees. They feel like they're indispensable parts of a vitally important enterprise. A leader who hopes to get peak performance out of a group must make certain that this sense of mission is clear—and clear in a way that ties in at Level Three to the goals and aspirations of the members of the team.

Bennis and Biederman draw an instructive example from the Manhattan Project, which built the first atomic bomb during the latter half of World War II.[6] At first, the secrecy surrounding White Sands was so complete that the researchers themselves were not told exactly what they were doing or why. The secrecy led to a declining morale and real climate of anger and confusion. The group floundered—until the leader, Robert Oppenheimer, called them together, laid all the facts on the table, and told them what the project was trying to do and how each of their various pieces was important to the overall mission, and laid out in emotional terms that the survival of the free world was at stake. The project was suddenly a crusade and productivity soared.

Corporate leaders face less apocalyptic challenges, but effective ones share Oppenheimer's ability to instill in their followers a sense of mission. This ability was one of Steve Jobs's strengths at Apple. Jobs convinced his team that they were marauding rebels destined to defeat the IBM Empire—and even flew a Jolly Roger above Apple headquarters as a playful reminder of their mission.

GETTING THE RIGHT PEOPLE

Perhaps, the first step in realizing a vision is getting the right people to be a part of the team. "You can't pile together enough good people to make a great one," said Bob Taylor, one of the kingpins of Xerox Corporation's Palo Alto Research Center (PARC). Taylor looked only for great people in his recruiting efforts at PARC, which spent the early 1970s radically rethinking

---

[6] Some people find this example distasteful. I invite the reader to separate the process from the content; focus on what Oppenheimer did to build an effective team and not on the product the team was working on.

computer science. Taylor's comment points out the importance of having the right people on the team.[7]

Taylor's group of young maverick thinkers refused to let any assumption about computers go unchallenged. They were revolutionary thinkers, as outlined at the end of Chapter 15. The computer PARC created was the first to boast many features we now take for granted: for instance, a graphical user interface, a mouse, and a desktop display format with windows. Unfortunately for Xerox, the company did not share its research lab's vision, leaving the development opportunity open for a young visitor to PARC's facility. Steven Jobs was so taken by the new machine that he decided to use his small upstart company called Apple to exploit these innovations commercially.

For whom do you look when recruiting? Bennis and Biederman offer a list of attributes shared by members of successful and innovative groups: original thinking, specialized skills, fresh perspective, ability to see gaps in current thinking, good problem solving, ability to make connections across broad disciplinary gaps, and broad frames of reference. The mix of these characteristics put in the cauldron of an inspiring vision and stirred by powerful leadership has created dramatic results.

Members of a team will periodically assess their own appropriateness or worthiness to be on the team by weighing their abilities and contributions to the group against their perceptions of the abilities and contributions of the other members. A member who feels unworthy or inappropriately included will likely participate less often—out of fear of censure or lack of interest—thus damaging the group's effectiveness in the process.

Consequently, one of the first requirements of an effective group leader is to make certain the right people are on the team and, once the team is selected, to reinforce the right of each to be on the team. These tasks don't mean just including those with the best technical skills. More importantly, it often means paying attention to the social, team-related skills of each person. Further, it means that the leader/organizer should help the members of the team in its early days to solidify their sense of why they were included. One place this requirement is evident is in mountaineering expeditions. People who organize such dangerous trips, often to climb an 8,000-meter peak, take great care in choosing their teammates and in strengthening each member's view of why they were included. Lou Whittaker, renowned mountain guide and leader or member of several Himalayan expeditions, concludes after years of forming and leading teams that deal with life-and-death situations regularly, "I came back from K2 in 1975 with this understanding: The measure of a good team is not whether you make the summit, but how well you get along during the climb."[8]

DISTRIBUTED LEADERSHIP

Once membership and purpose are determined, most groups will naturally wrestle with issues related to leadership. It is a natural human tendency to try to sort out who's in charge. Effective groups have strong leadership, even though it doesn't always come from a strong leader. Increasingly, groups are led by distributed leadership rather than a designated leader. Distributed leadership is a comfortable process in which those who have the perspective, the

---

[7] As reported by Bennis and Biederman, *Organizing Genius.*
[8] Lou Whittaker with Andrea Gabbard, *Lou Whittaker: Memoirs of a Mountain Guide* (Seattle, WA: The Mountaineers, 1994), 111.

skills, and the motivation to deal with the situation of the moment step to the fore, assume—and are granted—influence on the group. For distributed leadership to happen, each team member must be comfortable with the purpose of the team and his or her role in it. Concerns about control and who is the boss must give way to a focus on the objective. This kind of process is not usually easily won but often develops because of the experience of working together as a team.

The need to develop distributed leadership is one reason why many corporate clients use "ropes courses" or "adventure challenge" courses. These team-based adventures into the woods for low events at 2–3 feet off the ground to high events at 60–90 feet help team members realize that every member of the team can contribute something of value and then to develop a repeating process. This kind of learning can transfer to business settings and can allow the team members to work together more efficiently regardless of location.

EXTRAORDINARY COORDINATION

Effective team leaders may not have the specialized technical expertise that other team members possess. Instead, they exhibit an extraordinary expertise in mobilizing and coordinating the efforts of the team. The leader's role is to provide the best possible environment for those recruits to do their work—not to do the work personally. This hurdle is a difficult one for many would-be managers and leaders to overcome. Sometimes, people are promoted into positions of leadership and struggle with letting go of the work and learning new coordinating and facilitating skills. A psychological leap must be made when you become responsible for work that you aren't doing directly.[9] Effective team leaders don't micromanage. Instead, they have a good sense of the "loose–tight" paradox that allows them to guide the group without interfering with the initiative and talents of the team members.

CREATIVE SUPPORT

Effective team leaders also buffer the team from bureaucracy and bureaucratic processes. As Bennis and Biederman observe, "Great Groups are never places where memos are the primary form of communication. They aren't places where anything is filed in triplicate. Time that can go into thinking and making is never wasted on activities, such as writing reports, that serve only some bureaucratic or corporate function outside the group."

Jewel Savadelis was confronted one day at Atari with the prospect of managing more than a dozen highly creative software programmers—people on whom the revenues from the home video game market depended. They presented her with a list of challenges, which if she could meet, would allow her to manage their team. One of the demands was that she buffers them from the paperwork of the organization. Effective team leaders figure out ways to minimize the time spent by team members in organizationally originated diversions from the primary task.[10] This incident raised for Savadelis a series of questions, some of which had clear moral and ethical overtones.

---

[9] Gene Dalton, Paul Thompson, and Raymond L. Price, "The Four Stages of Professional Careers: A New Look at Performance by Professionals," *Organizational Dynamics* (Summer 1977): 19.

[10] "Jewel Savadelis A" case, UVA-OB-0190, for more details.

MORAL FOUNDATION FOR RESPECT

Effective team leaders build their influence on the moral foundation introduced earlier: truth-telling, promise-keeping, fairness, and respect for the individual. Jewel Savadelis knew that whatever was her title, unless she could gain the respect of the programmers, she wouldn't be able to manage, much less lead, them.

Likewise, Bennis and Biederman report that Kelly Johnson, leader of the Skunk Works—the top-secret research group at Lockheed that created the U-2 spy plane, the SR-71 Blackbird, and the F-117 Stealth Fighter—was an irascible man who could scare away group members and clients alike with his temper. He, however, made up for this weakness in the immense respect he inspired in his researchers. They knew he would not build a plane he didn't believe in: once he returned millions of dollars to the Air Force rather than do exactly that.

THE RIGHT ROLES FOR THE RIGHT PEOPLE

Having the right team members and the right leadership processes doesn't ensure the creation of an effective team. Team organization that puts its members in the right roles is critical for success. Recall that "supporting others so they can contribute" is one of the six steps to effective leadership introduced in Chapter 19. Thomas Carlisle, the English philosopher, once said he did not believe in the "collective wisdom of individual ignorance," yet time and time again, team decision-making produces better decisions.[11] This effectiveness is even more probable if team members are organized to take the greatest advantage of their talents and abilities.

PARTICIPATION

Not all talented people are equally adept at collaboration. People vary in their introversion and extroversion, for example, regardless of their technical skills.[12] Some are active in the discussions that surround the team's purpose, whereas others are more reticent. Effective teams figure out ways for all team members to participate. In effect, participation is an extension of membership. If you have the right membership, everyone should be participating. If everyone is not participating, then you may not have the right membership.

Participation is not limited to the team in effective groups. Robert Kelley and Janet Caplan, in their article "How Bell Labs Creates Star Performers," summarize seven years of research into the work strategies of standouts—and their less successful peers—at AT&T's prestigious research unit. Bell engineers all agreed on nine work strategies that influenced productivity, two-thirds of which—networking, teamwork effectiveness, leadership, follower-ship, "show-and-tell," and organizational savvy—can be seen as varieties of group cooperation skills.

The importance of networking in particular became apparent when Kelley and Caplan investigated the actual work habits of average-performing and star teams. Even though both groups agreed that a network of knowledgeable colleagues was crucial to weathering a crisis on the job, much of

---

[11] For example, in the well-known survival team exercises, Desert Survival and Subarctic Survival, team decisions almost always are superior to individual choices, even when the individuals have had survival training and experience.

[12] See, for example, the Myers–Briggs Type Indicator as one way of measuring level of introversion. One place to start is David Kiersey and Marilyn Bates, *Please Understand Me* (Del Mar, CA: Prometheus Nemesis Book Company, 1978).

the star teams' success could be traced to their efforts to build networks before those crises happened. For example, a member of a mediocre team (still great by most standards) talked about being stumped by a technical problem. He painstakingly called various technical gurus and then waited, wasting valuable time while calls went unreturned and e-mail messages unanswered. Star performers, however, rarely face such situations because they do the work of building reliable networks before they actually need them.

THE RIGHT MEASURES

The more organizations are built around teams, the more old measures of performance become outdated. Traditional measurement systems often serve the top-down power structures of the Industrial Age. These are what Christopher Meyer called "results measures."[13] A *results measure* is one that gives you information about something that happened in the past as opposed to one that gives you information about what's happening at that moment. Furthermore, results measures are usually functionally based: the marketing department monitors market share, finance keeps track of costs, and so forth.

The trouble with results measures is that even though they help top managers monitor the company's or a team's past performance, they don't shed much light on the current processes that determine whether the company will achieve its goals. As Meyer says, "The fact that a program was six months late and $2 million overbudget doesn't tell anyone what went wrong or what to do next."

Results measures are especially harmful to groups because they tend to be function specific (market share is relevant to marketers, but less so to production people) and therefore undermine the advantage of group decision making in which people from different functions develop a strategic overview together. Further, they divert attention away from the ongoing processes that a team is employing to produce.

Process measures are like the gauges on an automobile dashboard. They indicate current status (so that you know before you run out of gas or before a drop in oil pressure ruins the engine).

The alternative to results measures is to use what Meyer calls "process measures": ones that track the activities throughout an organization and help reach a given goal. Process measures are real-time indicators of key processes and their central contributors. For example, rather than simply knowing that the project is behind schedule and overbudget, groups where staffing is critical could benefit from tracking staffing levels during the course of the work—a process measure that could point to corrective fine-tuning.

Process measures are like the gauges on an automobile dashboard, giving the driver and passengers current information on key processes: how much fuel is left, how far the vehicle traveled, whether the battery is charging, and how the oil pressure is doing. All these measures are indicators of current status and necessarily so; it doesn't help to know that you've run out of gas after the fact.

---

[13] Christopher Meyer, "How the Right Measures Help Teams Excel," *Harvard Business Review*, May 1994, 94305.

Meyer offers four guiding principles that may help in designing a measurement system to suit the needs of a group.

1. *The team's process measures should be designed to help the team during the process, not management after the fact.* The measures should be a warning system that alerts the group when corrective action is needed.
2. *The team should design its own process indicators.* This principle is consistent with the earlier assertion that the key process contributors, those closest to the work, know what really needs to be done. Of course, to devise the right measures, the team needs to be clear on the strategy of the firm: if the east–west connection in the basic model is flawed, the team's ability to create good measures will be undermined.
3. *The process measures should be multifunctional and focus on the whole work of the team, not just a few aspects of it.* Along with tracking receivables, for instance, the system might also gauge the percentage of new parts to be used in a product. New parts are often an "unknown quantity" and thus can raise issues across a number of functions—design, inventory, manufacturing, and assembly.
4. *Teams should keep the number of process measures down.* Meyer recommends no more than 15, or the team will become paralyzed by evaluation. The challenge is to build a dashboard for the team's metaphorical car that will keep the driver and the passengers informed about how the car is doing while they travel.

One way that some organizations are managing the "right measures" problem is by developing "dashboards." Dashboards consist of real-time measures that allow managers, and observers, to keep track of how things are going while they're going and not in retrospect. The idea is that like driving an automobile, you can't be looking in the rearview mirror the whole time; you need to be looking forward while scanning real-time indicators of key systems and results. Of course, the first challenge in creating a dashboard is to select the right measures. Too many, and the managers (drivers) lose focus. Too few, and the managers (drivers) may be blindsided by critical system failure. The second challenge is to develop the underlying information system that will allow real-time review (perhaps daily rather than minute by minute—organizations don't move so quickly as automobiles). The Virginia Department of Transportation (VDOT) has created one such dashboard that is updated daily. This dashboard captures the current process completion or compliance rates for major indicators of VDOT's activities. The dashboard is posted online for the public to view as well as for the use of managers and employees at http://dashboard.virginiadot.org/default.aspx. It's an excellent example of transparency and currency.

HOW WOULD-BE TEAMS GO AWRY

Despite all that we've learned about how to forge work groups into teams, highly functioning teams are still an elusive goal for many companies. There are many pitfalls along the way. Patrick Lencioni introduces five such pitfalls: lack of trust, fear of conflict, lack of commitment, avoidance of accountability, and inattention to results.[14]

---

[14] Patrick Lencioni, *Five Dysfunctions of a Team* (San Francisco, CA, Jossey-Bass, 2002).

Members of groups who don't trust each other will have a difficult time developing into a team. Suspicions and concerns about the motives of each person, his or her operating style, or his or her habitual foci can destroy the desire of group members to weld their efforts. Trust is, as I'm sure you know, easily broken. Violated confidentiality, talking behind one's back, not keeping promises—in essence not having the four cornerstones of the moral foundation described earlier—can destroy a group's hopes of becoming a team.

If group members are unwilling to confront and deal with disagreements and internal conflicts, the problems fester and grow. Although in the short run, facing and dealing with conflict can be unpleasant for some, it's better to do so than to let the problems get worse and have members engage in passive aggressive behaviors or to disengage. And the challenge is to confront conflicts in healthy not destructive ways. Blaming, accusing, and being unwilling to compromise while confronting others—that is, destructive conflict management—will just make matters worse.

Lack of commitment or disengagement can also sap a team's strength and energy. Coming late or not showing up, coming unprepared, not following up, and being unavailable for meetings all demonstrate a lack of commitment and willingness to help the team move along.

Weak teams avoid accountability for their actions both as individuals and as a group. Displacing responsibility on customers, suppliers, management, peers, or any other group for the lack of performance drains energy and productivity from the group. These also contribute to the final dysfunctional element, inattention to results. Groups that don't, as Collins says, "confront the brutal facts" or accept accountability for them will be unable to improve their performance.

You can see that these five elements, like most things, are interrelated. Lack of respect contributes to an unwillingness to deal with conflict, which causes disengagement, which adds to the tendency to avoid accountability, which negates the value of results. As we said earlier, if the underlying moral foundation represented in this case by the first link, respect, is not in place, it will be virtually impossible to develop strength in the other links. This is all made even more difficult, of course, by the advent of non-colocated teams in the virtual, flat world.

VIRTUAL TEAMS

In today's global marketplace, business leaders are increasingly confronted with managing virtual teams, people who have a joint purpose but are spread all over the world. Many financial services, consulting, and conglomerate organizations wrestle with the management of virtual teams. Let's be honest: it's difficult. Companies use e-mail, shared documents, faxes, telephone, videoconferencing, or other technological advances in the attempt to reduce the costs of travel and to try to bond people from all over the world into highly functioning teams.

Many obstacles exist to this objective. First, people have local objectives; they are focused on their work in their local region and, because a local objective is closer and often more pressing than the global objective, they tend to ignore the "larger" purpose. For instance, Australian members of a global account team for a well-known accounting firm may not pay attention to a major global account in Sydney because the company's presence there is small. This inattention can be frustrating to the account manager in New York who is trying to get account managers all over the world to pay attention to their joint responsibility for his client.

Second, people are dispersed. Studies of communication show that when people are more than 90 feet away, the level of their interactions drops off dramatically. Even though technological advances help in this regard, most managers agree that nothing really substitutes for personal, face-to-face interactions.

Third, team members often have allegiances to local leaders rather than global leaders, which is another manifestation of the power of personal contact. Distant virtual-team leaders must overcome or at least compensate for the influence of local "site" managers who may have different priorities and certainly have more contact with the global team members.

Despite these challenges and others, virtual-team leaders struggle to build cohesion and concerted effort among team members who are widely dispersed. A number of practices can help ease this struggle. First, face-to-face meetings with some regularity are important. Virtual-team leaders must travel often. Getting team members to understand and remember the team's charter takes lots of personal time, particularly when team membership crosses international and cultural boundaries. The well-known difficulties of communicating via e-mail are exacerbated by cultural differences.[15] New technology continues to make virtual "face-to-face" meetings more effective, but it is no substitute for leisurely conversations over dinner.

Active and frequent use of technology to overcome the distance gap is also a growing means of team management. As noted earlier, though, e-mail, telephone, fax, and shared documents cannot substitute for face-to-face meetings; they can only fill in the gaps between visits. Sometimes, the ambiguities and misunderstandings caused by technologically based communication must be addressed by personal visits.

Conferences can help weld international groups into teams. It is clearly more expensive than having the team leader travel; yet many companies use annual conferences or retreats as an effective means of networking and team building. Conferences of this type should include not only corporate-wide communications and training, but also opportunities for each virtual team to meet and renew their operating preferences (D*ints*), charters, and operating principles and goals.

Teleconferences built around creating and confirming a team charter can be an effective virtual-team management technique: for example, a team with members from three continents all got online together to work through a team charter (described in Chapter 6) in the course of a day. Team members were online for a couple of hours, then worked offline to consolidate or brainstorm, then got back online for several more hours, talking, sorting out, consolidating, and defining their common purpose, vision, values, and goals.

The research around virtual teams is thin and new. As the technology front continues to advance and as we continue to wrestle with international boundaries and cultures, we will learn more and more about managing virtual teams.

---

[15] See "Intersoft of Argentina A," Harvard Case Services, HCS 497-025, for an example of the difficulties in managing teams across cultures.

Conclusions

Leading highly effective teams is an essential skill for the modern leader. As team-based organizations become more and more common, the challenges of leading teams become more apparent. Status hierarchies continue to break down not only in team-based organizations, but also within the teams themselves. Distributed leadership becomes more important. Clarity of mission and purpose, vision, and careful attention to roles are challenges that the team leader faces. People who understand the characteristics of effective teams and how to manage them over the natural course of their development, from formation through dissolution, will become more effective leaders and better contributors to their organization's development of competitive advantage.

Concepts Introduced in This Chapter

1. Effective teams often display smooth processes of distributed leadership.
2. Groups and teams are not the same.
3. Predictable roles often appear in groups and teams: some are necessary for effectiveness, whereas others are dysfunctional.
4. Groups and teams move through stages of development. Good team leaders understand these stages and manage them.
5. Effective team leaders understand the importance of clarifying membership, purpose, and leadership processes early in a team's life cycle.
6. Effective team leaders will pay close attention to the four C's: context, composition, competencies, and change skills.
7. Effective team leaders will find ways to revisit the team's dream/vision while it is performing its task in order to keep energy and motivation high.
8. Effective team leaders understand and are able to manage the team's response to changing environmental and internal conditions and events.
9. Effective team leaders can manage the difficult reassessment and re-forming process that occurs when a team's work ends, for whatever reason.
10. Companies are exploring means of managing virtual teams as they become more common.

Questions for Personal Reflection

1. Is your current group a work group or a team? How do you know?
2. What is your present work team's mission? Can you describe it verbally with energy and passion and without reference to notes? Why or why not?
3. How can you ensure that you have the right members on your present work team? What does each member of the team contribute to the vision of the team?
4. How can you ensure that you have each team member working in a role that maximizes his or her contribution to the team's work? When the team meets, do you have a balance between task and process and between creativity and pragmatism? If not, how could you develop that balance?
5. How can you help your team periodically revisit its mission or dream and, in doing so, revitalize its energy and commitment? What contribution does the team make to the organization? What contribution does the team make to the organization's customers?
6. How do you envision the transition of the team from its present status to a new status once the team's work is done? What processes could you design that would facilitate this process? Under what conditions could you imagine the team's work being done? What would you do then?
7. How do you measure your team's work and effort? Do you have analog measures in place? What measures could you develop?

8. What roles do you commonly play in the teams of which you are a member? What other roles could you learn to play? How could you help others expand their repertoire of roles?
9. How do you manage participation in your teams? Do you ensure that every team member has a chance to contribute the value for which he or she was chosen as a team member?
10. What is the D*int* for your team?

CASELET FOR DISCUSSION

A project design team consisted of two women and four men: two African Americans and four Caucasians; two NPs and four NTs (in Myers–Briggs terms); two senior, three middle, and one junior rank. As the team worked to develop and design its intended product, tensions arose. The NPs wanted to wait until the last minute and explore all the possibilities. The NTs wanted to make decisions up front and focus on execution excellence. Meetings often ran over and seldom completed the loose agenda despite near-term deadlines. Team leadership had rotated in the past, but there was one assigned leader at the moment. Each of the members of the group had been assigned to and worked on various pieces of the product. The junior person wanted to incorporate several new changes in the design. The older senior person wanted to go with the tried and true. The middle-ranked people were concerned about turning off both. Preliminary customer feedback had been poor, but the majority of the team wanted to continue innovating in the belief that they knew what was best for the customer. The next link in the supply chain was complaining that the team's design was running over schedule and threatening delays in customer delivery. Several design decisions that had been made had never been executed. Morale was sagging.

WORKBOOK

Complete the Team Assessment exercise (page 396) and discuss with your team members.

CONTRIBUTING YOUR OWN CASELETS

Have you seen or experienced a situation involving the concepts introduced in this chapter? If so and if you'd like to contribute your experience/situation to our case data bank, please visit http://faculty.darden.virginia.edu/clawsonj/ and click on the "Contribute new caselets" button.

SECTION V

LEADERS AS DESIGNERS

22 | LEADING ORGANIZATIONAL DESIGN

> *. . . most organizational designs and management practices were not created with the current rate of change in mind. They were created to work well in a more stable, predictable world.*
>
> —Jay Galbraith and Ed Lawler[1]

Effective leaders are architects of effective organizations. The design of the context in which people work is a frequently ignored and underutilized aspect of effective leadership. Even if a leader has a clear strategic vision and is effective at communicating that vision to followers, unless the organization in which they work has been designed to facilitate their contributions, little progress is likely to be made. The north–south axis between Leader and Organization on our general model represents this aspect of leadership, designing effective organizations. Good leaders understand the nature of organizations and are insightful about how to design and shape them. Design is not the only issue, however; *fit* matters. Some people might have leadership

---

[1] Jay R. Galbraith and Edward E. Lawler III, *Organizing for the Future* (San Francisco, CA: Jossey-Bass, 1993).

styles that would allow them to function well in many kinds of organizations, whereas others will thrive only in a narrower range of organizational parameters.

Depending on your authority and power base, you may or may not have the opportunity to design or redesign an organization or parts of it. If you are wise, though, you'll recognize that you cannot get good results if the hiring, work-design, appraisal, reward, and educational systems of your organization aren't aligned with your strategic goals. As Peter Senge pointed out, leaders are designers.[2] In fact, decisions made in the designs of organizations ultimately are more powerful than subsequent decisions about allocations of resources within those designs. Further, the basic Level Three assumptions you hold about people are likely to greatly influence your design. If you trust people, you may design systems one way. If you believe people are lazy, you are likely to design systems another way. Your leadership VABEs about people will shape the organizations you create—and hence, designing organizations is, one way or another, a Level Three activity. Let's see how this process plays out in organizations.

A GENERAL MODEL OF ORGANIZATIONAL DESIGN AND ITS IMPACT ON RESULTS

Leaders scan an environment and make decisions about what they want to work on as outlined in the chapter on strategic thinking. Having selected or created goals and objectives for their business, they begin to make design decisions, some of them explicitly, others by default. These design decisions (about hiring, pay, work, benefits, promotions, information, etc.) affect the people working in the organization. The interaction between design features and the employees creates an "organizational culture." In other words, organizational culture is the result of the collision between management's design decisions and the injection of people into them. This culture, in turn, produces the results of the organization. This sequence—Background factors, Leadership philosophy, Design decisions, Culture, and Results—provides a simple but powerful way of thinking about the role of organizational design in tandem with leadership in producing results. This sequence demonstrates a rough causal linkage as shown in Figure 22-1.[3] Each of these elements contributes to the overall outcome of an organization's efforts and hence to the ability of an organization's leader(s) to make things happen. Effective leaders need to understand how they link with each other.

Background Factors

Background factors have to do with the basic building blocks of an organization, the raw materials from which one hopes to build an effective company. Sometimes they are taken for granted and ignored; other times, they are carefully examined and managed. These background factors include such things as local labor pool, local political and economic environment, relative isolation from other hierarchical influence (e.g., in the case of a new plant), history, and any other factor that will influence the company's success. These background factors are similar to the environmental factors mentioned in our general leadership model introduced earlier.

---

[2] Peter Senge, *The Fifth Discipline* (New York: Doubleday Currency, 1990).
[3] Although this viewpoint is an older one, the connections are powerful and still generally applicable. This view was adapted from Anthony G. Athos and Robert E. Coffey, *Behavior in Organizations: A Multidimensional View* (Englewood Cliffs, NJ: Prentice Hall, 1968).

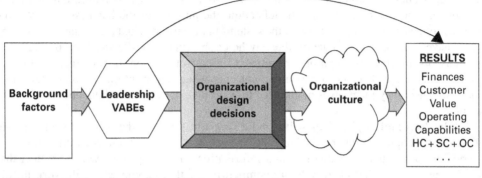

FIGURE 22-1 The indirect effect of leadership on results

Garage-based entrepreneurs may not give a lot of thought to these factors as they focus their efforts on developing an idea and getting it before the public. More sophisticated entrepreneurs, perhaps working through venture capitalists, may pay considerable attention to the best place to start their company in terms of availability and cost of labor, regulatory restrictions, and local or regional tax incentives. Steve Jobs and Steve Wozniak, for example, didn't travel the country to build their first Apple computer, but worked in their garage, albeit in technology-rich and soon-to-be "Silicon Valley," California. By contrast, General Motors, in its attempt to build a new kind of small-car manufacturing plant based on the Japanese model of high quality, lean operations, and efficient processes, searched the country before settling on relatively remote Smyrna, Tennessee, as the site for its Saturn plant. An important consideration in that decision was the relative isolation from corporate headquarters. This isolation tended to reduce the number of managers, steeped in the old way of doing things, who would come by and raise questions and inhibit innovation in process as well as product. Isolation from headquarters is a way of breaking with historic tradition.

The effective leader understands how these background factors influence attempts to create a new organization. Bob Lancaster, for instance, who was given the assignment by FMC Corporation to build a new kind of plant, chose his location carefully so that he could create a new kind of facility without a history, based on a new philosophy, and in a place where senior FMC management was not likely to interfere. Had he chosen to build the plant in Minneapolis, Minnesota, the site of company headquarters and accessible to divisional executives, he might have experienced a different outcome.[4]

Leadership Philosophy

Leaders take philosophies, their VABEs, into a context of background factors and, using what they know and believe, begin to create a business. The purpose that they define for themselves and their organizations (the north–east connection in our general model), the principles on which they operate, and the style they use in dealing with others all begin to have an effect on the organization—some intended, some not. Earlier chapters discussed the role of strategic thinking

---

[4] See "FMC Aberdeen" case (UVA-OB-0385) for a description of Lancaster and his work in establishing this plant.

and of organizational charters, including mission, vision, and values, in demonstrating a leader's philosophy. A leader's Level Three beliefs about the purpose of the business, the way one influences others, the appropriateness of the systems in the business, and the means of managing change have an enormous impact on the way he or she approaches leadership opportunities, especially organizational-design opportunities. Consequently, a significant stream of today's literature encourages leaders to reexamine not only what they want others to do, but, more importantly, how they themselves might need to reevaluate the way they think about their work and role.[5]

A leader's philosophy shapes the kind of organization that the leader designs. If one believes that people are inherently lazy and have to be supervised, the recruiting, training, supervision, performance evaluation, and information-sharing systems will all reflect that bias. If one believes that all people are competitive or that people who will work in this organization should be competitive, this belief will shape the way that leader designs the structure and reward systems in the organization. The structure and systems of an organization are Level Two intangible rituals and rules that are manifestations of those deeper Level Three beliefs. By studying an organization's major components, one can often discern many present and past leaders' Level Three beliefs about how the organization should be run.

The key issue here is that management's mind-set or philosophy about how organizations should work will be a key factor in determining how it would create a new organization, or perhaps how effectively it would be able to work with or design changes for an existing one. The result is that the north–south connection, the Leader–Organizational Design axis, becomes critical in understanding how a leadership situation will turn out. By default or by design, leaders begin making design decisions based on their VABEs that will affect how work is done and the results an organization will realize.

Organizational Design Decisions

STRUCTURE   The first place many people in positions of power look is to the organizational structure. Whether on paper or simply evolving in people's minds, the structure of an organization forms the network of intended relationships in an organization for coordinating decision making across many functions. Another way of thinking of organizational structure is as the pattern of power-based relationships that help hold an organization together. Some people, it turns out, have a strong orientation to hierarchy, whereas others are more egalitarian in their view of how organizations should be structured.[6] This orientation varies also by country. Geert Hofstede demonstrated that countries have characteristic differences in their "power distance," that is, their orientation to hierarchy.[7] This variation raises some interesting questions as one thinks about designing organizations that will operate in multiple national settings.

---

[5] See, for example, Chris Argyris, *Improving Leadership Effectiveness* (New York: Wiley, 1976); and Robert E. Quinn, *Deep Change* (San Francisco, CA: Jossey-Bass, 1997).

[6] See Jim Sidanius and Felicia Pratto, *Social Dominance: An Intergroup Theory of Social Hierarchy and Oppression* (Cambridge: Cambridge University Press, 2001). See also James Clawson and Gerry Yemen, "Orientation to Hierarchy," working paper, Darden School, 2004.

[7] See Geert Hofstede, *Culture's Consequences: Comparing Values, Behaviors, Institutions and Organizations across Nations* (Thousand Oaks, CA: Sage, 2003).

In Japan, for instance, often thought of as a more group-oriented culture where the individuality of people is minimized compared with the more individual-oriented culture of the United States, power distance is thought to be less than in the United States. That is, Hofstede measured the Japanese culture, in general, to be flatter than in the United States in the sense that hierarchy or social dominance mattered less. It's not a simple issue, however, because anyone who has lived in Japan will tell you that the Japanese have a strict sense of hierarchy going way back in history to what was essentially a caste system consisting of emperor, nobility, warriors, farmers, merchants, and untouchables. Even today, the Japanese language consists of multiple levels of politeness depending on whom you're talking to. Executives have a formalized system of exchanging business cards so you'll know the level of the person you're dealing with.

In the United States, on the other hand, things seem much less hierarchical, perhaps because of a history of democratic laws and processes and a shared belief in the value of what a person does rather than who that person's father was. Despite this lower level of power distance, however, U.S. managers are off the charts in terms of their salaries compared with front-line employees (see Figures 6-4 and 6-5). These data cause us to wonder about the difficulty of making simple statements about a country's orientation to hierarchy or social dominance. Orientations to hierarchy clearly differ in terms of the base scale. Are we talking about respect for elders (high in Asia, lower in North America and Europe)? Are we talking about voice in governance (higher in Europe with unions and mandated employee presence on boards)? Are we talking about wealth (where the United States is the high-end outlier)? Managers thinking about how to structure organizations in different cultures should pay careful attention to the differences in the base and nature of social hierarchies.[8] The kind of organizational power structure that would work in one culture might not work in another.

That said, human behavior across cultures shows more similarities than dissimilarities. When organizational designers can emphasize the similarities and downplay the differences, they are able to build global business structures. The danger is that the designers assume that all employees worldwide are like them, rather than discovering what in their own behavior is culturally based and therefore not necessarily "true" or the "right way" to do things.

When people think of organizational structure, they often think of organization charts. This perspective can create problems, because when things change, people who've become accustomed to one structure may feel betrayed or frustrated. If we accept Stan Davis's maxim that organizational structures are by definition obsolete,[9] we can look at organizational charts as we do financial balance sheets—nothing more than a snapshot picture of how things are at one instant in time—and realize that they do not reflect the dynamic nature of what's really happening in the organization over time. (In our general model, this observation suggests that the south–east relationship between Task and Organization is always going to be obsolete and that, therefore, leadership on that axis is always about managing change, the subject of Chapter 23.)

---

[8] See the Karen Leary case series (HBS case, HCS 487-020) as an example of how the nature of social hierarchies might play out even within one national culture.

[9] See Stan Davis, *Future Perfect* (Reading, MA: Addison-Wesley, 1987). His argument is that if all organizational designs follow a strategy in some sense, by the time the organization has been "built," the surrounding environmental factors have changed sufficiently enough that the strategy has shifted and the organization has become out of date. The challenge, of course, is to build organizations that will respond to environmental changes more quickly.

Yet by law and by principle of order, organizational leaders must figure out how important decisions will be made, which is the crux of the attention we pay to the distribution of power throughout some kind of structure. A number of common structures grew out of the Industrial Age.[10]

MILITARY MODEL   One of the most common models of the Industrial Age bureaucracy was the military model developed in large part by Frederick the Great.[11] This pyramid structure helped clarify who was in charge and codify who could make what decisions. It was a hierarchical model, where each officer was responsible in turn to a higher officer. Each layer had its functional specialties, which were coordinated by the authority at the next highest level. Although it was an orderly system, it featured slow decision making. In the rapidly changing environment of the 1980s and 1990s, the classic bureaucratic model became sluggish.

DIVISIONAL MODEL   As corporations grew in size, they developed broader interests and, eventually, new organizational structures. The natural outgrowth of the pyramid bureaucracy was the M-form or divisional structure, which was an association of bureaucratic pyramids loosely coordinated toward common corporate goals.[12] As in the single-pyramid organization, M-form organizations (so called because when you put two pyramids side by side, they look like an *M*) developed great efficiency skills but encountered difficulties sharing and building on skills horizontally. Redundancies in special functions such as finance, marketing, accounting, information processing, and human resources, as well as larger and larger project demands by customers, led to the formation of a hybrid organization, the matrix.

MATRIX MODELS   Originally, matrix organizations were an answer to engineering projects, such as space vehicles and defense weaponry. Typically, matrix organizations had two sides: a project-leader side and a functional-specialist side. The project-leader side included a list of project managers who handled various parts of the overall project and had budgets assigned to them for reaching their goals. The functional-specialist side included technical specialty managers who had the human resources needed to tackle the various challenges the project or program leaders faced.

Matrix organizations attacked and destroyed many widely believed bureaucratic principles, such as "one person, one boss." Employees in a matrix organization usually had at least two bosses—the project leader, to whom they were temporarily assigned and who paid their salary, and the technical specialty boss, who hired and assigned them based on their skills and availability. Matrix organizations heralded the beginning of the end for the Industrial Age functional bureaucracies.

Matrix organizations not only allowed people to be used more efficiently by moving from one project to another, but also created a wave of confusion among those who were used to the simple orderliness of bureaucratic pyramids.[13] Soon, volumes of description and counsel about how to manage matrices emerged, and many companies tried to incorporate aspects of matrix organizations in their own structures.

---

[10] For more details on various organizational forms, see the technical note, "Organizational Structure," (UVA-OB-0361).
[11] See Chapter 2 on the context of leadership, for more details.
[12] See Alfred Chandler, *Strategy and Structure* (Cambridge, MA: MIT Press, 1962), for a detailed account of how this form evolved; and William Ouchi's *The M-Form Society* (New York: Avon, 1984), for an overview.
[13] For more information on managing matrix organizations, see Stan Davis and Paul Lawrence, *Matrix* (Reading, MA: Addison-Wesley, 1977).

HYBRIDS   Following the boom of matrix organizations in the 1950s to the 1970s, organizations continued to evolve in a variety of directions. The major forces that contributed to the speed of this evolution are the Information Revolution, the increasingly global nature of modern corporations, the sheer size of modern projects, and the necessity of managing more efficiently in the face of new competition. As people become better educated and have better information available to them, they become more aware of their organization's business processes and how they work. The Internet, local area networks, and personal computing give people access to the data that are necessary for making business decisions—and better educational backgrounds help them interpret those data. As a result, the power of knowing what needs to be done in a company is rapidly dissipating downward throughout the ranks of most companies. Many senior managers are distinctly uncomfortable with this trend, but it has continued unabated for the last 30 years and likely will accelerate in the future.

This dissemination of data and the increasing reality of having to compete on a global scale put pressure on meeting customer needs, responding to increasing competition, and doing so without raising costs. Consequently, organizations around the world for the last 20 years have worked on downsizing, dissolving layers, and reengineering, in the attempt to find more adaptive, distributed, empowered organizational forms that could keep up with the rapid pace of change. These forces spawned a variety of hybrid organizations.

Charles Handy described four kinds of organizations that are emerging: the federalist, the shamrock, the doughnut, and the clan.[14] The federalist form is akin to the M-form organization but spreads across national boundaries in global settings. Each pyramidal bureaucracy is both independent and obliged to the holding company, working together like a loose federation with some common guidelines and goals. If these federalist structures were to work, leadership had to ensure that the local pressures did not overwhelm the common goals and benefits that could be gained overall by cooperating among themselves. Royal Dutch Shell, Unilever, and Johnson & Johnson are examples of federalist structures that did remarkably well in the 1990s and that continued to wrestle with the balance between competing interests in various parts of their organizations.

Shamrock organizations, so named because of the distribution of their employees, are about one-third full-time employees, one-third contract employees, and one-third part-time employees. This structure gives an organization more fluidity of talent, greater flexibility in managing human resource costs, and a manageable core of full-time, ostensibly dedicated employees. The challenge, of course, is to meld the efforts of the part-time and contract employees with those of the full-time force and still develop strong competitive advantages—from people who are only partially committed to the firm. Ethical issues also arise, as companies utilize more and more part-time employees, with the nature and allocation of benefits and the impact of lesser benefits on family structures and health.

The doughnut organization, Handy says, reflects an emerging principle in which organizations are organized around a core of key people who mobilize and organize the talents of "stringers," who operate outside and around the core. A central task of the core group is to balance the energy and activities of the core group with the outside groups. Part of that job is defining the boundaries that identify the core group and those who are suppliers, contributors, vendors, and contractors working in the surrounding space. In a sense, these doughnut organizations are extensions of the shamrock organization, where the focus is on the type of connection to the main organization.

---

[14] Charles Handy, *The Age of Paradox* (Boston, MA: Harvard Business School Press, 1994).

The clan organization emerges from what Handy calls the Chinese Contract, a philosophical approach to relationships, including business relationships, that recognizes and values not only self-interest, but also a greater common good. This Chinese Contract reminds us of our earlier discussion of the moral foundation of leadership, of the need for building a business purpose beyond profit, and of the strategic notion of a business ecosystem. A clan organization recognizes that its future is inextricably intertwined with the futures and fortunes of other organizations and visions around it and that it must fit into this broader purpose for the well-being of all.

Perhaps the extreme form of hybrid organization evolution was described by Tom Peters[15] when he wrote about a Danish CEO who became so concerned about his organization's inability to break through functional boundaries that he bulldozed the walls of the head office building, put everyone's phone, computer, and other personal effects on wheeled carts, and installed electrical and data hookups all over the floor. In this "spaghetti organization," as the CEO called it, people group together as long as they are working on a common project and then immediately move their "desk" to another group for their next assignment. This example also highlights the competitive advantage to be gained by the ability to rapidly form and re-form project teams as outlined earlier.

Despite the wide and ever-changing array of options to choose from, organizational structure is only one of several design factors with which leaders and designers need to deal. Sometimes managers rearrange the boxes and lines in their structures while ignoring the other design factors of the organization and are then perplexed when things don't change. Unless they pay attention to all of the key organizational design features, a perplexing outcome is the likely result. As a classic article once noted, "Structure is not organization."[16]

CENTRALIZATION VERSUS DECENTRALIZATION   Many organizational architects struggle with the tradeoffs between centralization and decentralization. First, it's a question of the amount of control desired. Centralized organizations are built around the desire to have more control over what happens inside the organization. Unfortunately, one cannot control what happens outside of the organization, so centralized organizations are often less adaptive to the environment. Second, it's a question of the amount of innovation and creativity desired. Decentralized organizations tend to be more creative because they are more autonomous. So one way to think of the centralize-or-not question is to think of it in terms of control versus creativity.

Clearly, one cannot have complete control over everything that happens in an organization even if one wanted to. I've had executive participants argue for "110%" control—they wanted to know what their employees were doing during evenings and on weekends. Others argue for zero control. This would mean you couldn't get accounting reports or know who was showing up for work. Neither extreme is tenable. To be an organization requires some centralized control and guidance if nothing else in order to collect performance data to report to the tax collector and investors. But how much?

Sometimes the centralize-or-not question is a geographic or political question. National regulations may require a certain amount of decentralization in the global corporation for financial, tax, or national-pride purposes. The size and scope of one's supply chain may also have an influence on the degree of centralization that is "optimal."

---

[15] See Tom Peters, *The Tom Peters Seminar* (San Francisco, CA: Vintage Books, 1994), 29.

[16] Robert Waterman, Tom Peters, and J. R. Phillips, "Structure Is Not Organization," *Business Horizons*, 23, no. 3 (June 1980): 14–26.

In general, the question of how much to centralize involves a series of tradeoffs much like the challenges facing the economy. National banks regulate interest rates in order to keep their economies neither too cool nor too hot. Similarly, organizational architects can put their foot on the gas by decentralizing to get more autonomy and the resultant creativity or their foot on the brake by centralizing to ensure more commonality in reporting contents and operating procedures. Reorganizations are not so easy to implement as changes in interest rates, though, so these tradeoffs need to be made with a longer time frame in mind. That said, many participants bemoan how many reorganizations they've gone through in the last year or two. The reality is reorganizations will continue to be a fact of life in the global business community as executives struggle to find the right balance between control, creativity, local regulations, changes in the market place, and mergers and acquisitions.

DESIGNING ORGANIZATIONAL SYSTEMS   In addition to structure, several key systems in most organizations have major effects on the organization's ability to perform. Effective leaders who understand the designer role in leadership will not ignore these systems. There are hundreds of systems in any large corporation. These include accounting systems (for purposes of information and control or governance), finance systems, information systems, procurement systems (supply-chain management), marketing systems, public relations systems, and human resource management systems, to name a few. In fact, the major disciplines of major business schools are set up to focus on the understanding, development, and management of these various systems. One of the challenges of the modern executive is to oversee and integrate these systems so that the organization works together as a whole. It's simple to say, much more difficult to do and to do well. Virtually every client I have is working hard to refine the individual systems amid competitive and cost pressures and then to integrate them well so that the whole organization functions as effectively, efficiently, and smoothly as possible. When a business cuts across industry boundaries, the challenges are even more pronounced.

I will not pursue principles of designing and managing all of these different systems, rather leave that to my colleagues in those fields. It is important to note, however, the seminal insight of my mentors at Harvard, Paul Lawrence and Jay Lorsch, in their book *Organization and Environment*, in which they outline a key principle. Their insight was that one of the central principles of organizational design is that when an organization grows in complexity or as they called it "differentiation," it must also grow in coordination or as they called it "integration."

Increasing complexity is a natural result of organizational growth. If a company does not learn how to coordinate or integrate across organizational boundaries during such a growth, however, its capacity for effective delivery of its internal capabilities will be hindered. In reality, most organizations grow faster than they are prepared for. This is why in most organizations there are problems with silos, with interdepartmental coordination, with customers having difficulty in dealing with several organizational representatives, and with finding and using talented people who already work for the company. Most organizations today continue to wrestle with these issues at the broader human capital management level and at the individual career development level. The technology available to us in the Information Age holds out the promise of making this internal coordination easier and more effective; however, in practice, again, it remains a challenge.

INFORMATION TECHNOLOGY   Information processing in the Information Age has become a strategic weapon. Yet many senior managers still think of information systems as tactical tools rather than as sources of strategic capability. Poor information systems can hamstring an organization's ability to bring its high-quality resources to bear on market issues. Superior systems can enable and facilitate the application of highly talented individuals to key issues and even create a new and powerful business model.[17] In today's environment, I assert, information systems are strategic weapons. The way we structure our information systems—gathering, sifting, disseminating, and sharing data and making decisions based on these data—will help to build, even provide a basis for, or erode our opportunities to build competitive advantage.

Increasingly, organizations are realizing how new information systems are literally transforming the structure, culture, and other systems of their organizations. Powerful information systems are flattening organizations, distributing key data to lower levels of the organization, and making the vertical decision-making chain obsolete. With access to data around the world, team members can communicate instantaneously with clients and colleagues in an up-to-date and informed way. More than anything else, the Information Revolution caused the erosion of the bureaucratic pyramid, replacing it with a range of organic, powerful, highly responsive organizational forms as described in Chapter 4.[18] Because superior information systems are both difficult to design and expensive to implement, as companies make this investment and learn how to manage the impact of these systems on their organizational cultures, they develop a competitive advantage that will take others years to duplicate. Jay Galbraith and others described extensively how this information technology is affecting the nature of organizational design.[19]

Numerous other organizational systems and processes besides the ones mentioned here include financial systems, accounting systems, marketing systems, and operating systems. One powerful definition of an organization is as "a bundle of established processes." The elements of the human resource cycle plus information systems, however, are critical ones that bear special attention. A key point is that unless all of these systems are aligned in the organization—encouraging people to think and behave in consistent ways—people will be confused, the force of the strategic intent will be dissipated, and the organization's effectiveness will be diluted.

In established organizations, the leader-as-designer work that needs to be done involves reexamining key processes and systems and if necessary redesigning them so they are consistent with each other and with the corporate intent. This kind of reengineering effort takes enormous courage, conviction, and stamina. Part of the reason is that all of these design factors do not have a direct impact on organizational outcomes. Instead, they create an environment in which people work and, as they work, develop a deep-seated set of guidelines about what is acceptable and what is not.[20] Organizational culture—the behavioral outcome of the collision between leaders' design decisions and the people who work within them—can be an enormous help or a huge hindrance in realizing strategic intent.

---

[17] See, for example, the Capital One Financial Services Corporation, whose sophisticated, intentionally designed information system provides the basis for their highly customized line of credit card products and services.

[18] See also James Clawson, "Leadership Implications of the New Infocracies," *Ivey Business Journal* (May–June 2000).

[19] See Jay R. Galbraith, *Designing Complex Organizations* (Reading, MA: Addison-Wesley, 1973); Jay R. Galbraith and Ed Lawler, *Designing the Organizations of the Future* (San Francisco, CA: Jossey-Bass, 1993); and Charles Savage, *Fifth Generation Management* (Burlington, MA: Digital Press, 1990).

[20] Michael Hammer and James Champy, *Re-engineering the Corporation* (New York: HarperBusiness, 1993).

Organizational Culture

Cultures, according to Ed Schein, develop in response to problems that confront a group of people.[21] As the group addresses, analyzes, and solves each new problem, it develops a history of acceptable ways of behaving, which becomes a part of its culture. If the group agrees to explain thunder and lightning as a manifestation of the displeasure of the gods, then this explanation becomes a part of the group's history and culture and passes from one generation to the next. If the founders of a company conclude that closed architecture is the best solution to the problem of competing with clone manufacturers (e.g., Apple Computer), then the company develops a history and a culture that shapes its behavior in the future and distinguishes it from other company cultures (e.g., IBM). *Organizational cultures, then, are the results of myriad decisions made over time that, when combined, make up the pattern of shared VABEs that distinguish one group from the next.*

These cultures, referred to in the vernacular as "the way we do things around here," may be so deeply ingrained in the way a group of people behave that they no longer recognize them as something they created, but rather as just the way things are and the way things are "supposed" to be done. It is often not until visiting another culture that a person becomes aware of how cultures differ and of how much he or she has taken for granted about the way things "should" be done.

Organizational cultures can be shaped intentionally,[22] but usually they evolve over time as decision after decision is made and the consequences are accepted and incorporated into the daily routine of doing business. The challenge to the leader-as-designer is to clearly anticipate the impact of organizational design decisions on the culture that emerges from the other side of those decisions. What many seem not to realize is that design decisions do not have a direct impact on organizational behavior. The behavior that emerges is filtered through the existing culture. A leader who pays careful attention to that fact—and includes more people who are going to be affected by the decisions in the design decision-making process—may be better armed to avoid unintended consequences.

Because organizational cultures are the results of many decisions made over time and these decisions have become so much a part of the culture, organizational cultures are often nearly-invisible to the people who work within them. Determining what your organization's operating culture is can be a frustrating effort. As Schein points out, this effort requires large amounts of courage, self-reflection, the collaboration of outsiders who can recognize things that insiders take for granted and don't even notice, and extraordinary skills of observation, abstraction, and articulation. Being able to identify some part of the present culture allows a person to be partially prepared to think about how it aligns with strategic intent and then to begin thinking about how design decisions might impact that culture in ways that would support the strategic intent. It is not easy to define what you might want the organization's culture to be and then to try to change it. Many executives who, during the 1980s and 1990s, presumed to undertake a "culture change" in their organizations, learned that the task was neither easy nor quick, nor in the end was it something that might even be feasible.

. . . all of these design factors do not have a direct impact on organizational outcomes. Instead, they create an environment in which people work and, as they work, develop a deep-seated set of guidelines about what is acceptable and what is not.

---

[21] See Edgar Schein, *Organizational Culture and Leadership*, 2nd ed. (San Francisco, CA: Jossey-Bass, 1992).
[22] See again, for example, the FMC Aberdeen case (UVA-OB-0385), which describes the intentional construction of a relatively unique organizational culture by an extraordinary leader.

Jack Welch, for instance, undertook what amounted to a major culture change at General Electric (GE), with his "Work Out" effort in the late 1980s and early 1990s. His goals were to reduce bureaucracy, to increase initiative and decision making among middle and upper-middle managers, and to ingrain a new set of operating principles (speed, simplicity, and self-confidence) in the company's multiple divisions. The well-publicized Work Out (from "working out" to reduce fat and cholesterol) effort made clear, first, that each division and its various parts had their own subculture and, second, that managers with 25–35 years of experience in GE were not going to change their fundamental way of thinking and managing just because of a few announcements, seminars, and hard conversations with the boss. After several years of effort and with some good progress in hand, GE management had to accept more modest results on the goal of revamping the culture of some 200,000 employees. In the twenty-first century, Jeff Immelt is trying to reengineer the GE culture more toward one of innovation and creativity. After a decade of trying, this effort has proved a difficult task.

In the end, culture is the *indirect* result of organizational design efforts. If the design is conceived and implemented carefully, the resulting culture may reflect more rather than less the leaders' original intentions. If the design is not carefully thought out, one may get a variety of unintentional outcomes that over time become cemented in the culture and make it even more sintractable in the future. In the end, the leadership, its organizational design, and the culture that emerges will all be evaluated by their results.

Another common model for thinking about organizational design is the once-famous 7-S model developed by Tony Athos of the Harvard Business School and colleagues at McKinsey and Company.[23] In the 7-S model, strategy, structure, and systems (the so-called "hard S's") interact and relate to the "soft S's" of staff, style, skills, and shared values as depicted in Figure 22-2. Careful attention to the nature of each *S* was thought to be critical to getting all of these elements aligned, that is, pointed in the same direction and not pulling against each other.

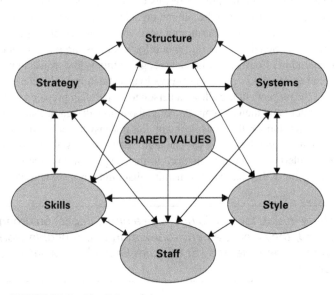

FIGURE 22-2   The 7-S model

---

[23] See Richard Pascale and Anthony Athos, *The Art of Japanese Management* (Clayton, Australia: Warner Books, 1982); and R. Waterman Jr., T. Peters, and J. R. Phillips, "Structure Is Not Organization," *Business Horizons*, 23, no. 3 (June 1980): 14–26.

Organizational Results

Organizational design decisions create a context in which people work and perform. In the midst of that context, leaders strive to encourage and guide. This effort eventually produces some results. One challenge is to figure out what kind of results you want and whether you are focusing on the results that will accurately and comprehensively reflect how the organization is doing in meeting its mission or purpose.

Historically, the most broadly accepted indicator of organizational results has been profitability. Despite many suggested variations on this theme (e.g., sales, return on equity, and growth in earnings per share), in the end the underlying focus is on profitability. Many, if not most, executives will say that the primary mission of their business is "to make money." Chapter 4, on strategic thinking, explored how this view of an organization might be helpful—and hurtful. If managerial conversations and reward systems focus exclusively on profitability, leaders can find themselves paradoxically working with an organization that is becoming less and less profitable as they and their employees make short-term decisions that undermine the company's competitive advantage. In some ways, this discussion is like the discussion on resonance in Chapter 13: a prescribed way of focusing on the task can weaken a person's ability to perform.

Ralph Waldo Emerson's often-quoted comment about happiness illustrates the point. He said that happiness is like a butterfly: the more you chase it around the meadow in the noonday sun, the more exhausted you become and the less able to catch the butterfly. The act of running and darting about swiping with your net makes the butterfly more skittish and less easy to catch. Paradoxically, after pursuing this approach unsuccessfully for a while, when you fall exhausted on the grass and lie still, the butterfly often alights on your shoulder. In Chapter 13 I described how a focus on internal experience can enhance performance. In Chapter 4 on strategic thinking, I pointed out how focus on customer service is a powerful precursor to profit—when profit focus might undermine customer service—and hence profits.

When leaders focus on profitability as the primary purpose of the organization, they are in danger of losing the inspiration and motivational power that resides in the expression and grasping of a high, organizational vision or purpose. Take, for example, the senior executives who declared to their subordinates that unless the stock price rose to a certain number by the end of the year, no one would get their annual bonuses. By demanding that subordinates get to work and get to work fast, they overemphasize results to the detriment of those results.

More recently, scholars and leaders point out the virtues and practical productivity of a more balanced approach to assessing organizational results.[24] The balanced scorecard approach introduced in Chapter 5 recognizes that unless leaders understand the relationships among the reasons why people go to work every day, meeting and exceeding customer expectations, and the importance of learning and improving ways of doing business, their financial results will not truly reflect what the organization is capable of.

The balanced scorecard approach does not ignore financial results. Instead, it simply links financial results the relationships between people and the development of organizational capabilities that deliver on the customer value proposition. Here's the linkage:

---

[24] See R. S. Kaplan and D. P. Norton, "Balanced Scorecard: Measures that Drive Performance," *Harvard Business Review*, January 1992, 92105.

Determine your Customer Value Proposition (Why would people come to us?) → Choice of Key Core Capabilities (What do we have to do really well to satisfy our customers?) → Invest in people and learning appropriately (What kind of people, culture, and organization do we need to build those capabilities?) → Use your people, culture, and organization to build the key capabilities → Use your key capabilities to delight your customers → Enjoy the additional revenues that happy customers bring you.

Every investment whether it's in hiring, training, IT infrastructure, reorganization, and so on should recognize those linkages. Investments should not be random; they should be strategic. The focus on short-term profitability at the expense of the other elements in the balanced scorecard linkages can be self destructive. Short-term profitability turned out to be a disastrous focus, for instance, for many overseas companies' efforts in Central and South America before the 1980s. When local governments grew tired of the exploitation of financial results and nationalized those investments, many companies lost millions of dollars in equity and in future income streams. A more balanced approach that included local learning and development, community involvement, and reinvestment might have produced a lower level of profitability in the short run, but a larger net present value when long-term future revenue streams were considered in the equation.

ORGANIZATIONAL GLUE

A former human resources executive for Circuit City stores, during their phenomenal growth, taught the importance of "organizational glue."[25] Consider for a moment the glue that holds the various organizational design components together. In other words, why do people stay with organizations? What forces keep them connected as opposed to luring them away to other pursuits or enterprises? Clearly, rewards are on this list; people stay, in part, because they're paid. Some people stay because of charismatic leadership; they identify with and want to be a part of the leader's team. Rules, regulations, procedures, and systems can also be powerful forces that shape employee's behavior and keep them "in line." Shared values and purpose are a fourth and powerful glue that can help keep an organization together. If we array these forces in a table and consider how much of each in any particular organization seems to be contributing to its cohesion, we can see the strength of that organization.

Attracting and retaining talented employees is an important strategic challenge to companies. The mix of "glue" that an organization offers can well determine the "stickiness" with which employees bond with the company. Some of the most powerful organizations in the world offer no rewards. They use leadership, rules, and common values to bind their members to them. Others may mostly use rewards to attract and retain people—and realize perhaps too late that lack of leadership, common values, or purpose leaves the employees feeling "flat" or "unmotivated." Table 22-1 shows various configurations of organizational glue, each with different strengths and weaknesses. What might those strengths and weaknesses be for each of the glue profiles? Take column 1 for example: What are the strengths and weaknesses of an organization held together primarily by financial rewards? Considering column 2, what are the strengths and weaknesses of an organization held together primarily by one strong charismatic leader?

---

[25] Thanks to Bill Zierden for this perspective.

TABLE 22-1 Organizational Glue				
	Company A	**Company B**	**Company C**	**Your Company**
Charismatic leadership	10	60	30	
Rewards	40	10	0	
Rules and regulations	20	10	20	
Common values and purpose	30	20	50	
Total glue	100%	100%	100%	100%

Consider organizations for which you've worked. As you think about why you worked there, how long you stayed, and why you left, how would you allocate the "glue" that bound you to the organization across these categories? Use the last column to estimate the glue that generally held your organization together. Perhaps you saw other kinds of glue. You could add one or more rows to complete a description of the cohesion you saw.

Conclusions

The shape and construction of the organizations that leaders intend to lead have an enormous impact on the outcomes of any leadership situation. Effective leaders understand the importance of the design demands of their jobs and work hard to create contexts in which their visions can be realized. Their Level Three philosophies about business and people inform those decisions and, in turn, influence the culture of the company. Effective leaders also understand that they do not have direct effects on their companies' results or even on the development of the dominant cultures that operate in those companies. Rather, they make design decisions that not only address the immediate problems at hand, but also leave a legacy that adds to, augments, or shifts the momentum of the organization's cultures and subcultures. When reviewing the results that emerge from any organizational or leadership situation, effective leaders realize that a balanced perspective may not optimize profitability in the short run but, in fact, produce a more stable and therefore larger net present value of that profitability over the long run. To realize that stream of profits, organizations need to survive and thrive. Leaders pay attention to the glue that holds their organizations together and manage it to strengthen the bonds between employees and organizations (the south–west axis of our general model).

Concepts Introduced in This Chapter

1. Leaders are architects of effective organizations.
2. Organizational design involves much more than structure.
3. There are hundreds of organizational systems in organizations that need careful attention and refinement in order to allow the capabilities of the organization to be unleashed.
4. Leaders have only an indirect effect through their design decisions on organizational outcomes.

5. Organizational culture is the result of the collision between management's organizational design decisions and the people who work in them.
6. The 7-S model is one way of thinking about how to align the various aspects of design.

7. Organizational glue consists of at least four elements: charismatic leadership, rewards, rules and regulations, and shared values or VABEs.

Questions for Personal Reflection

1. If you owned a company, what percentage of your organization's employees would you want to control? Zero percent? 100?
2. How well were the organizational design elements in your last organization aligned? Why or why not?
3. Can you identify an organizational design system, process, or procedure in your company that gets in the way of your doing the kind of work you know you could and should be doing? If so, what are you going to do about it?

CASELET FOR DISCUSSION

You've been assigned (tasked) to create the design for a new company that will manufacture toys in China and then distribute them to five different countries: Argentina, Egypt, Greece, Thailand, and Mexico. Create an organization for this venture, and describe the major systems you'd want to put in place.

WORKBOOK

Consider the simple form in the workbook (page 398) designed to help you identify organizational processes or designs that need fixing in your organization.

CONTRIBUTING YOUR OWN CASELETS

Have you seen or experienced a situation involving the concepts introduced in this chapter? If so and if you'd like to contribute your experience/situation to our case data bank, please visit http://faculty.darden.virginia.edu/clawsonj/ and click on the "Contribute new caselets" button.

23 | HUMAN RESOURCE MANAGEMENT SYSTEMS

All the physical assets—the things owned, the structures, and systems—pale beside the newly energized, motivated, determined workforce of the future, the men and women, the people of the organization.

—FRANCES HESSELBEIN[1]

Most organizations acknowledge verbally that people are their most important asset. At the same time many do not follow up their espoused theories with effective organizational designs that are consistent. So whereas we might acknowledge that without people, it's hard to have an organization of any kind, we can also note that it's hard to have an effective organization without carefully designed human resource management systems. As of this writing, the phraseology in vogue is "human capital management," but over the years, similar concerns have been

---

[1] Frances Hesselbein, "Leading Change: An Imperative of Leadership," in *The Future of Human Resource Management: 64 Thought Leaders Explore the Critical HR Issues of Today and Tomorrow*, edited by Mike Losey, Sue Meisinger, and Dave Ulrich (New York: John Wiley & Sons, 2005), 345.

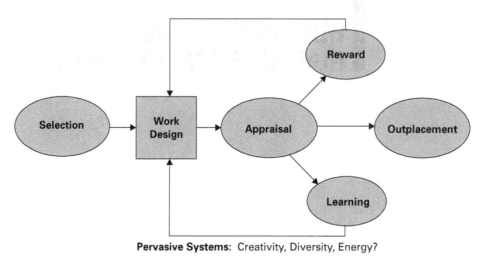

Pervasive Systems: Creativity, Diversity, Energy?

FIGURE 23-1   Human resources systems   Based on Tichy et al.

labeled "personnel," "human assets," and "human resources." Whatever you call it, without people, you have no real organization.

Every organization has human resource management systems. That is, *every* organization must decide how to bring people in, how to orient them to the company, what kind of work to give them, how to assess their work, how to reward them, how to teach them, and eventually how to let them go. These various functions may not be well thought out, may or may not be on paper, and may or may not be contributing to the organization's ability to build and maintain a competitive advantage. But they're there. Noel Tichy and others described a "human resources cycle" that captures these basic elements consisting of hiring, work design, appraisal, reward, and development elements. I've adapted his model as shown in Figure 23-1.[2]

SELECTION AND HIRING

Every hiring decision by a company represents a significant investment and, potentially, a constraint or an encouragement on the company's future. People with the right talent and personality to succeed at a company and help the company succeed are hard to find and difficult to identify. As I've worked with executive teams throughout the world, one of the most common challenges they mention is "attracting and retaining talent." We are, with the retiring Baby Boom generation and smaller cohorts of subsequent waves in the population, entering an era of a "war for talent." The ability to attract and retain talented people who fit a specific organization has become an increasingly important source of competitive advantage. Some companies go through elaborate processes to screen out inappropriate applicants; others seem to hire almost as an afterthought any warm body that comes along. Whether part-time, full-time, contracted, or

---

[2] Noel M. Tichy, Charles J. Fombrun, and Mary Anne Devanna, "Strategic Human Resource Management," *Sloan Management Review*, Winter 1982.

volunteer, each employee can become either a hindrance to the organization's strategic intent (assuming it has one) or a help that can push the company along in the direction it wants to go.

Sometimes companies use traditional methods for finding new employees without realizing the consequences of their actions. Effective leaders understand that every system in the company should support and accelerate the company's strategic intent and that if it doesn't, it should be a target for reengineering or surgical removal. Hiring is one such system.

Most companies that need a certain kind of skill will advertise for that skill. Usually, these needs are technical skills. If a company needs a welder, it advertises for welders and then screens applications for welding credentials. The same is true in accounting, marketing, and other technical areas. Usually the process involves interviews in which the interviewers try to determine the applicant's "fit" with the company. Human resource professionals, who may not know the working environment of the department in which a successful candidate would work, often conduct this interviewing. If line managers, who know the working environment, interview the applicants, they may not see the value of paying attention to the "softer" criteria—the human aspects of the candidates. One problem with this approach is that you may get the technical skills you desire, but the technician may not have the social and leadership skills you wanted.

The ability to attract and retain talented people who fit a specific organization has become an increasingly important source of competitive advantage.

If, for instance, you're trying to build a collaborative, team-based organization and you hire a skilled welder who turns out to be a loner and distrustful of others, this lack of social skills will be a hindrance to the organization's goals, even though the technical skills may contribute. You see the development of a collaborative team-based organization as a part of your strategic intent for building a sustainable competitive advantage, so the social skills of the new welder may actually inhibit your company's development more than the technical skills help. Belbin's work on effective teams showed clearly that teams comprised of the most "clever" individuals did not necessarily make the best team.[3] This so-called Apollo Syndrome points out to a team or organization the importance of hiring with a broad range of criteria in mind, including team and social skills as well as technical skills.

For this reason, many firms are paying much closer attention to the psychological, social, and organizational skills of new applicants than they did in the past. At FMC Aberdeen, for instance, new applicants underwent a four-hour psychosocial testing program administered by regular employees to see whether their personal philosophies and tendencies matched the organizational goals of the plant. In several cases, they hired people with minor technical skills and superior social skills, using the philosophy that it was easier to teach technical skills than psychosocial skills.

WORK DESIGN AND PERFORMANCE

Industrial Age organizations made great efforts to specify job demands and requirements. Modern infocratic organizations, on the other hand, are much more likely to offer more autonomy to employees to define and shape their jobs, especially at the managerial level. New managers who ask too many questions about what they can and cannot do are sending signals

---

[3] Meredith Belbin, *Management Teams: Why They Succeed or Fail* (Woburn, MA: Butterworth Heinemann, 1981, 1999).

that maybe they aren't managerial material after all. If you experience a gap in your understanding of what your job is, my advice would be to take the Leadership Point of View (LPV) described earlier, look around, see what needs to be done, analyze the relevant forces at play, and then initiate action. Don't wait to be told what to do. In some companies, even at the entry level, people who ask for definitions of their jobs are viewed as hiring mistakes and seldom last long. Jim Collins asserted this same principle in "First Who, Then What," in *Good to Great.*[4]

That said, if you are in a position to be designing jobs and shaping what people do, build on the research from the Industrial Age to ensure that jobs have measures of autonomy, holism, variety, immediacy of feedback, and direct contribution.[5] People want to have some say in what they do (autonomy), a sense of doing a complete job (holism) rather than a tiny part of it (putting nuts on bolts), some variation and creativity in what they do, clear indications of how well they're doing, and a feeling that they are doing something worthwhile and important.

The issue of autonomy brings us to the problem of "empowerment." Many employees chafe with their perceived lack of empowerment. Some of this disenchantment and confusion stems from a binary view of empowerment, both in the minds of management and in the minds of the employees. A more complex view of empowerment is that it is an analog concept rather than a binary one (either on or off, you are either empowered or not). A consideration of the much vaunted Japanese management system that seems to have high levels of empowerment will make the point.

Whereas Japanese managers are touted for being more empowering than American managers (given their use of nominal groups, consensual decision making, etc.), Japanese society is highly stratified and dependent on hierarchical controls. A closer look at the Japanese empowerment system shows that up to certain points, the traditional Japanese system is more inclusive, but beyond that, perhaps less so. The Japanese tend to include employees in problem identification and analysis much more than American managers, but perhaps less so than American managers in decision making, implementation, and assessment.

Consider whether one might be included in each of the following steps: problem identification, problem analysis, alternative identification, decision making, implementation, solution assessment. We can consider the degree of employee involvement (i.e., empowerment) for each individually. Table 23-1 displays this analog perspective of empowerment. The further

TABLE 23-1 An Analog Perspective on Empowerment

Problem solving step	Nature of empowerment (Who considers these questions? Management, employees, or both?)
Problem identification	What needs fixing around here? How do we know? Nominal work groups, suggestion boxes, town meetings, etc.
Problem analysis	What does the current system do and what are its consequences? Why do we need to fix this?
Alternative generation	What other approaches might we take?
Decision making	Who decides which alternative we will pick?
Implementation	Who will run the experiment?
Results assessment	Who decides whether the experiment worked or not? Who decides whether we continue with the new approach?

[4] Jim Collins, *Good to Great* (New York: HarperCollins, 2001).
[5] For a brief summary of the research on job design, see "An Introduction to Job Design" (UVA-OB-0091).

down the list employees are involved, the more we can say they are "empowered." If they are only involved in problem identification, they might be more empowered than in other traditional organizations where it's the job of management to find and solve problems, but they are certainly not deeply empowered.

This perspective on empowerment makes it easier for managers and employees alike to talk about the level of empowerment in the company and how it might be modified. This issue is linked to the centralization/decentralization and the degree-of-control issues discussed in Chapter 22.

However work is designed in the organization, eventually, it must be assessed in some fashion. How do we know if our employees are, or are not, doing well?

APPRAISAL

Few systems in organizations have been more maligned and misused than performance appraisal systems. The motivation for creating them is clear: if you have people working, how can you tell how they're doing? Superior–subordinate performance assessment systems attempt to identify the job requirements of each job (the result of the design work) and then to assess the employee on each of those requirements. It's not as easy as it may sound.

Many problems cropped up over the last 100 years in this process. Employees felt a lack of input into their job descriptions. Bosses felt uncomfortable giving straight feedback or negative feedback. They feared being seen as overly subjective in what is intended to be an "objective" process. Evaluations escalate, like the so-called grade inflation in schools: more and more people get the highest rating and the distributions rise. Rewards may not be tied to the evaluation—for any number of reasons—so employees see no connection between what they do and what they're paid. Employees may be discouraged rather than motivated by the process. Further, feedback from one's boss is clearly incomplete. What about what one's peers say? What about what customers say? What about what the employee's subordinates (if any) say?

Companies have tried many remedies to these problems: management by objectives; better training for bosses who give performance reviews; designing ever tighter evaluation systems in the attempt to reduce bosses' subjectivity; forced curves in the process ensuring only 10 percent, for example, will get "excellent" ratings; tightening up the links between appraisal and reward systems; separating the reward announcement from the developmental conversation; creating 360° feedback systems that include data from bosses, peers, subordinates, customers, and suppliers; and finally, even doing away with performance appraisal altogether![6]

Appraisal systems are powerful in that they reflect the philosophy of the leadership regarding how an organization tries to track its internal performance. Basic assumptions about workers and their attributes like trustworthiness are embodied and manifest in the appraisal systems and therefore send signals to employees about their relationship with management. Appraisal systems can also be a powerful negative influence, clogging communication and creating awkward, discouraging conversations that can harm rather than help the company. In some companies, they work well; in others, they don't. Whether they help or hinder will depend on their design, implementation, and alignment with other systems, especially the reward system.

---

[6] See, for example, the case of SAS Institute (Stanford case study, HR-6, January 1998), a highly successful software company that has done away with performance appraisals on the grounds of their inaccuracy and ineffectiveness.

REWARDS

Reward systems play a big part in directing the attention of an organization's employees. Strangely, many organizations design or keep existing reward systems that direct employee attention away from the goals of the organization or its strategic intent.[7] Unless the reward systems—including the decision making that goes into salary increases, bonus awards, promotions, public recognitions, and other forms of positive feedback to employees—are aligned with the strategic goals of the organization, people will feel confused and fragmented in their efforts and in their daily labors.

Despite the logic of this simple principle, many organizations, with good intentions, put in place and continue to use reward systems that seem perhaps unintentionally at odds with their goals. Consider, for example, the case of a company that had in place a $500 prize for new ideas that the company would use. At the same time, the company's forecasting and planning system used demographic behavior to predict possible sales for the following year and a "low base pay, high bonus for exceeding quota" system that actually, in effect, punished people for selling more or for submitting ideas that would increase quota allocations. The company's systems were working against the company.[8]

In another firm, in an attempt to improve customer service, senior management declared that 80 percent of all incoming phone calls were to be answered within 20 seconds. The management installed electronic systems to monitor calls and call length by operator. Paradoxically, in order to meet management's request, employees manning the phone lines began cutting their conversations short in order to answer the next incoming call. As a result, employees cut customers off before they got their problems solved and overall customer satisfaction actually declined. These examples of unintended consequences emerged from positively motivated design decisions meant to focus attention and reward people for behaving in one way, but which actually encouraged the exact opposite kind of behavior.

The challenge is to make sure that the reward systems in operation are reinforcing strategic intent instead of being a drag on it. Although senior management or specialists in human resources may think they have the answers, it is logical to include in the design process those people who will be working in the system, especially after they've been fully educated regarding the goals and strategic intent of the firm.[9] Employees are deeply affected by perceived fairness and justice in their reward systems.[10] Further, reward systems seem to be remarkably long-lived. The more a team can build flexibility into a reward system, allowing it to adjust rewards for changes in behavior needed, the more likely the organization will be able to direct employee attention to the current strategic challenges facing the organization.

LEARNING SYSTEMS

In a turbulent environment, the ability to learn is perhaps the only source of sustainable competitive advantage. This general principle is true at the individual, work-group, and organizational levels. Effective leaders understand that unless people are growing, learning, and expanding their skills and talents, the firm will gradually fall into obsolescence.

---

[7] See Steve Kerr, "On the Folly of Hoping for A While Rewarding B," *Academy of Management Journal*, August 15 (1988): 298.
[8] See the "Hausser Foods Company" case written by David Nadler of Columbia University, for more details on this non-aligned system. Available from Darden Educational Materials Services, University of Virginia.
[9] See C. Meyer, "How the Right Measures Help Teams Excel," *Harvard Business Review*, May 1994, 94305.
[10] See, for example, Joe Harder, "Organizational Reward Systems" (UVA-OB-0667).

An organization's learning systems, including its training programs, are critical, therefore, to the realization of strategic intent. The story of IBM, including its decline during the 1980s, surely is testament to the fact that just any kind of training is insufficient. For many years, IBM had a policy that all employees should receive a certain number of hours of training annually. Despite this seemingly laudable goal with the intent of ensuring an ongoing learning culture in the company, the company became increasingly out of touch with its markets.

IBM's experience points out the necessity of having training programs that are the result of and that match the firm's strategic intent. Again, at FMC Aberdeen, Bob Lancaster wanted to create an organization where people could work without fear of their own management. He knew employees would have to understand FMC's markets and the nature of its business. He could understand how they might fear competition and the fallout from not meeting or not exceeding customer desires, and he saw that they would have to be able to work together in significantly more efficient and productive ways.

Consequently, he designed with the aid of a professional consultant a training program that began with how to relate to people. Now, most adults going to work for a new company and being informed that they had to go through nine days of training on how to talk with each other might think it completely unnecessary. Lancaster, however, was convinced that unless all employees understood the basic principles of the organization he envisioned and could implement them in their daily work lives, they would not be able to build the kind of facility he envisioned.

These nine days of specialized training introduced the principles of respectful, fact-based communication, taught people how to avoid judging others, and taught how to engage them in mutually respectful, joint problem solving. The program dealt with responding nondefensively to feedback as "data" and managing change within one's self as opposed to trying to change others. Part of effective feedback included describing the potential consequences of unchanged continuation of dysfunctional patterns of behavior. The program was based on Level Three principles such as "All feedback is data, and no one has to respond unless they want to," "We're not trying to change anyone; we think people are fine the way they are," and "If we continue behaving this way, what will happen?" Through systematic exploration of these VABEs and how to communicate and behave, new employees were trained to view, to think of, and to behave in relationships in ways consistent with the organization's desired culture. Hiring the right people was an important first step in this process; adding targeted training was an important follow-up. Regardless of their training, though, unless employees have accurate and relevant information, they will be unlikely to capitalize on that training.

Learning about and the creation of learning organizations have become increasingly important in the rapidly changing Information Age. In fact, learning and the capacity for individuals, teams, and organizations to learn efficiently may well be the single most important source of sustainable competitive advantage. Arie deGeus, member of the famous Royal Dutch/Shell strategic planning group that developed scenario planning (described in Chapter 4 on strategic thinking), commented, "the only real source of competitive advantage may be the capacity to learn."[11] Peter Senge has written extensively about this subject,[12] and Marcia Conner described how to develop stronger learning cultures.[13] Effective leaders such as Garry Ridge at WD-40 pay attention to how well they are encouraging and supporting employees to learn and thereby stimulate the capacity to adapt and adjust within their organizational cultures.[14]

---

[11] Arie deGeus, *The Living Company* (Boston, MA: Harvard Business School Press, 2002).

[12] See Peter Senge, *The Fifth Discipline* (New York: Doubleday Currency, 1990).

[13] See Marcia Conner and James Clawson (eds.), *Creating a Learning Culture* (Cambridge: Cambridge University Press, 2004).

[14] See "WD-40" case series (UVA-OB-0764-0765), available from Darden Business Publishing.

Pervasive Systems

There is another category of human resource management systems that needs mention here. These are what we might call "pervasive systems" in that they are evident, or not, in each of the elements outlined earlier in this chapter. These pervasive systems can be designed or not, clear or fuzzy, helpful or hindering, just like all of the other elements in Tichy's model. These include systems related to diversity and creativity among others.

The role of diversity in an organization is a critical one. Whereas this discussion began some 70 years ago in the discussion of race in America, today when we talk about diversity in organizations we mean that and more. How management thinks about managing racial diversity, gender diversity, and ethnic diversity is a complex set of topics about which many other books have been written.

Part of the issue is whether one looks at one's human resources, or rather people, with an eye to "functionally relevant criteria" or "functionally irrelevant criteria." By "functionally relevant criteria" I mean whether or not the person can do the job in question regardless of their "functionally irrelevant criteria" (e.g., skin color). Some systems over the years have been intentionally and perhaps unintentionally but nevertheless inexorably oriented toward functionally irrelevant criteria. This orientation varies, of course, from country to country and company to company. My belief is that effective managers pay closer attention to functionally relevant criteria than they do to functionally irrelevant criteria. Of course, in life, these are often confused and comingled so that it may be difficult to parse out a person's or an organization's systematic reasoning. In general, organizations that rely on functionally relevant criteria (what does it take to get the job done) rather than functionally irrelevant criteria (appearance) have available to them a much broader spectrum of talent and resource and therefore a competitive advantage.

Diversity in functionally relevant criteria is a healthy feature. It allows for diversity of thinking, diversity of perspectives, and the opportunity to challenge assumptions and expectations and to serve broader audiences and customer bases. If management tends to hire only people who think like they do, the ability, the capability, of strategic thinking and of adapting to changes in the environment declines.

Diversity also enhances creativity. In the chapters on strategic thinking and innovation, I noted that creativity is essential in a rapidly changing world/environment. Excessive control that leads to groupthink can squelch creativity and innovation. Diversity of thought and approach tends to counterbalance that tendency.

Of course, too much diversity of thought can lead to chaos and paralysis. Every management team faces the trade-offs of strategic stagnation on the one hand and loss of control on the other. Historically, it seems that the tendency has been to err on the side of groupthink. There are psychological and sociological reasons for this. In today's world, though, the global manager must be aware of and comfortable with balancing these tensions.

Conclusions

Managing human resources or human capital is a critical set of issues for any leader. There are some universally common issues that every management team must face if it wants to be successful. Unfortunately, many of the decisions related to this area are made in an off-handed manner. Wise managers will recognize the import of designing their human resource systems carefully and with a broad view of the future. The organization that has a superior human capital management system in place has a competitive capability[15] that is rare.

---

[15] Dave Ulrich and Dale Lake, *Organizational Capabilities: Competing from the Inside Out* (New York: Wiley, 1990).

Concepts Introduced in This Chapter

1. Human resource management systems are a bundle of systems critical to an organization's success.
2. All organizations must deal with the issues of recruitment, orientation, work design, performance appraisal, rewards, learning, and outplacement.
3. In addition to the elements of the human resource management design model, there are pervasive systems that also need attention. These include diversity and creativity.
4. Empowerment is an analog, not binary, process that includes various levels of involvement for problem identification, problem analysis, alternative generation, decision making, implementation, and assessment.

Questions for Further Reflection

1. Most organizations worldwide are worried about their ability to attract and retain talented people. How well does your organization recruit and retain new people?
2. How would you rate your company's efforts at designing interesting and engaging work for people to do? What could be done better?
3. What are the employees in your company evaluated on? Individual work? Team work? How do these assessments affect the morale and energy in the organization?
4. What kinds of rewards does your organization offer? What is their impact on the organization?
5. Describe the learning systems in your organization. How robust are they? What do people learn? What support does the company have for learning? Is yours a learning organization? Why or why not?
6. How do you let people go? What has been your reaction to the process so far? What impact does it have on others?
7. Describe the diversity in your organization. What is going well and what needs to be done better? What would you recommend be done to improve the healthy diversity in your organization?
8. Describe your organization's creativity. How is it encouraged? How is it discouraged? What would you recommend be done to enhance creativity in your organization? What role could you play in that?

CASELET FOR DISCUSSION

You and a friend have decided to start your own business. Pick an industry for your business. Then design the major systems mentioned in this chapter. Be sure to include as many details as you can. Consider their implications on financial results as well as energy of the organization.

CONTRIBUTING YOUR OWN CASELETS

Have you seen or experienced a situation involving the concepts introduced in this chapter? If so and if you'd like to contribute your experience/situation to our case data bank, please visit http://faculty.darden.virginia.edu/clawsonj/ and click on the "Contribute new caselets" button.

24 LEADING CHANGE

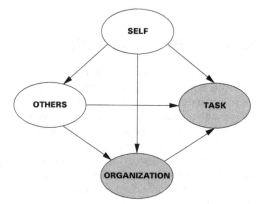

It's not the critic who counts. It's not the man who points out where the grown man stumbles, or how the doer of deeds could have done them better. The credit belongs to the man who actually is in the arena, who strives violently, who errs and comes up short again and again, who knows the great enthusiasms, the great devotions, and spends himself in a worthy cause, who if he wins knows the triumph of high achievement, but who if he fails, fails while daring greatly, so his place will never be with those cold and timid souls who know neither victory nor defeat.

THEODORE ROOSEVELT,
26th president of the United States

Leadership is nothing if not about change. No change, one could argue, means no leadership. We don't talk about "leadership for the status quo" or "maintenance leadership." Change and its related concepts and principles are inextricably intertwined with leadership and its concepts. In a world that continues to change rapidly, effective leaders are masters of the change process; they understand, embrace, and lead change. Ineffective leaders struggle with change and find that many of their efforts at managing change fail. It behooves every aspiring leader, therefore, to understand his or her own attitudes toward change and to become a master of the change process.

A GENERAL MODEL OF CHANGE

Over the course of our lives, we become comfortable with a certain set of behaviors, the habits we identified earlier. We used these habits before, and they seemed to work well enough, so they become a part of our common routines. The same pattern is true of organizations. Organizations develop ways of doing things that work well enough so those routines become institutionalized. These sets of comfortable routines become boxes that not only allow us to be productive and to move forward efficiently without testing everything we do, but also constrain us and inhibit our thinking about trying new things. We can call these sets of routines our comfort zone, our baseline behavior, or our organizational culture (Figure 24-1).

As long as we continue to get positive, confirming feedback from the outside world about our baseline behavior, we feel little motivation to change it—unless, of course, we are simply curious and want to learn and grow. In that context, we can speak of internally motivated change and externally motivated change. Internally motivated change generates from our innate curiosity and desire to improve things (see the chapter on innovation earlier). Externally motivated change is "forced" upon us by external forces (parents, teachers, bosses, investors, competitors, governments, etc.). The dangers of externally motivated change—responding rather than leading—are many: being too late in the market, taking an obedient instead of an excelling mind-set, missing a market altogether, half-hearted compliance, and haphazard implementation.

In business, many managers, especially Industrial Age managers, ascribe to the maxim "If it ain't broke, don't fix it" and see in stable, historically successful routines a way of generating steady cash flows, building leverage, managing margins, and realizing returns of past investments. The danger is that these comfort zones can reduce our flexibility—in which case it's just a matter of time until the market shifts and we're left behind. Unless these investments in our historical means to success build into our personal and organizational systems an enhanced ability to adapt to our environment, they become strategic blockades rather than sources of competitive advantage.

Again, we all want to think well of ourselves. Our minds develop remarkable techniques for maintaining a positive self-image. If what we did in the past worked and helped us succeed in some sense, then we naturally seek to maintain that positive self-image. This desire to think well of ourselves connects to our view of the outside world. If after long periods of receiving confirming data about our baseline behavior, we get some disconfirming data, we face a choice about what to do.

FIGURE 24-1   Comfort zone and baseline behavior

Disconfirming data are a challenge to our self-concept, because they say that what we just did doesn't work anymore. These data try to pull us away from our baseline behavior and signal to us that we should try something new. The data may be in the form of a monthly profit report, the establishment of a new competitor, feedback from a spouse or peer, angry facial expressions from a subordinate, a weak performance review, an appointment request turned down, or a myriad other sources. Whatever the source of the disconfirming data, these data challenge our view of ourselves and invite us to do something about it.

We decide in a variety of ways whether to accept or reject this "invitation." Accepting it can be painful because it means that we will have to rethink our self-image, perhaps change our behavior, move out of our comfort zone, and experiment with untried and unproven behaviors that may or may not work. It is risky business.

Accepting disconfirming data or, even before receiving them, breaking out of the comfort zone and trying to do difficult, somewhat painful, new things is the subject of Scott Peck's *The Road Less Traveled.*[1] Because most of us want to stay in our comfort zone, we persist in our baseline behavior. Breaking out of it is uncomfortable and threatening. Peck argues that the road less traveled is the path that leads to this discomfort, to breaking out of our baseline patterns and trying new things, and that it is the road to learning and growth. Without the courage to take the more difficult, uncomfortable path, he argues, we are destined to become little more than we presently are. Some welcome disconfirming data because they view these data as an opportunity to learn, to break out of their comfort boxes, and grow.

Many people, however, choose to stay in their comfort zone and respond to disconfirming data by systematically discounting them, distorting them, or ignoring them altogether. If the disconfirming data are discounted, distorted, or ignored, a person can continue behaving as always without interruption. Having encountered the disconfirming data, a person's behavior continues along the old baseline unchanged and undeviating. It's as if our behavior, like a rubber band stretched from the baseline, snaps back; we fall back into our old behavioral patterns. These concepts are shown visually in Figure 24-2.

Of course, the strength of the disconfirming data will have something to do with whether we can discount them, distort them, or ignore them. If the disconfirming data

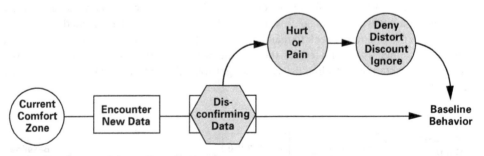

FIGURE 24-2   Reactions to disconfirming data

[1] M. Scott Peck, *The Road Less Traveled* (New York: Touchstone, 1978).

are very strong, we may not be able to ignore it. At the same time, we all know of people who received enormous disconfirming data, such as heart attacks or divorce or counseling interventions, and have been quite able to ignore it. Our attitudes about change and our comfort levels with change may shape our response to disconfirming data. At some level, though, we must choose whether to accept it. In Collins' terms as described earlier, we must "confront the brutal facts."

If we accept the disconfirming data, that is, if we recognize the need to change our behavior, then we have to do something about this need. Changing our behavior will involve, by definition, a search for alternative ways of behaving and then some experimentation on our parts. We will be electing to try out things we haven't done before. It means getting out of our comfort zone and trying something new, which can be threatening, scary, and undertaken with trepidation. We try the experiment, and it, in turn, generates more feedback data. If the data disconfirm the validity of the experiment, even if we didn't do the experiment "correctly," we are likely to abandon the new approach and our behavior will snap back to the former baseline. It's as if the baseline were a bow string—when you pull on it, it wants to snap back to its original position.

Think about your personal efforts to change, whether it be losing weight, stopping smoking, studying more frequently, exercising regularly, contacting family more often, or whatever it is. If the new behavior doesn't bring some positive results to you, you probably concluded that it didn't work and so slipped back into the former comfort zone.

If the new behavior produces positive results, though, a new pattern begins to be established. With reinforcement, one begins to see that the new approach works. As the positive feedback continues to come in, the new baseline is established and one continues on it until new disconfirming data come in. This evolution of our overall general model of change appears in Figure 24-3. In typical unsuccessful change efforts, attempts to do new

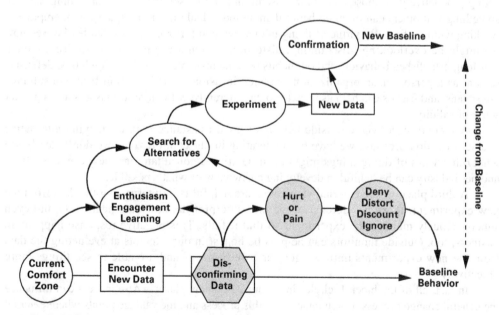

FIGURE 24-3   General change model

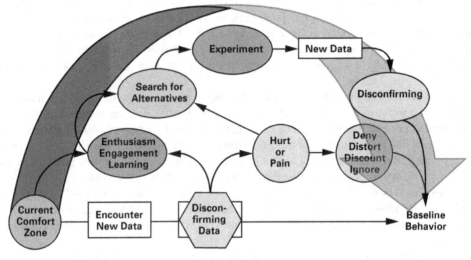

FIGURE 24-4 Unsuccessful change

things fail, and with those disconfirming data, people tend to snap back to their old ways as shown in Figure 24-4.

THE ROLE OF OUTSIDE HELP IN MANAGING CHANGE

Outside help can greatly assist a person or an organization in recognizing disconfirming data and acting productively on those data. First, assembling and presenting the disconfirming data are something that others can often do better than an individual or, for an organization, employees working within a firm. By virtue of living in our own comfort zones, it's often hard to see how we might be overlooking (discounting, distorting, or ignoring) bits of disconfirming data. Our long-established behaviors and our habits become invisible to us. If we tend to be defensive (again, as a person or an organization), outside infusions of information from consultants, physicians, and friends can help us view the data differently, with more seriousness and a greater sense of validity.

A second place where outside help is of great assistance is in identifying alternative courses of action. Because we have been operating in our comfort zone, we don't clearly see what other ways of doing things might exist. Getting a consultant or a new executive from another industry can be helpful in developing a new view of what's possible.

A third place where external viewpoints are helpful is in interpreting the data from the new experiment. If we are defensive, we may interpret the new data negatively and even subconsciously manage the experiment so that it fails. This negative response happens in business, too. Outside monitors can help us be honest in our attempts at evaluating the data from the new experiments until we get our own bearings and are able to see things more objectively.

In fact, all of the block L circles in Figure 24-5 show places where leaders can influence the general change process. If you understand this process and the vantage points where external influence can make a difference, you can have a big impact on change efforts.

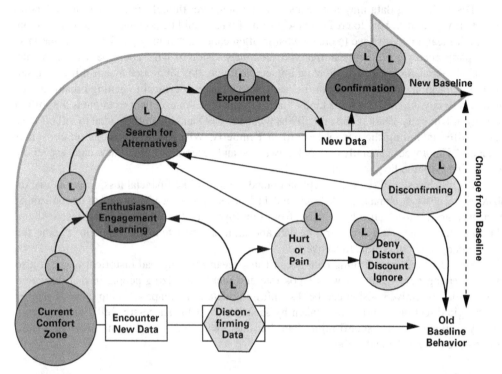

FIGURE 24-5 Leading change

LEADING THE CHANGE PROCESS

Given these points of influence in the change process, we can infer the following steps for managing change:

1. Clarifying disconfirming data
2. Building a change team
3. Designing and leading change experiments
4. Relentlessly reinforcing the results with the new vision

Clarifying Disconfirming Data

Effective leaders are able to clarify and publicize, even popularize, disconfirming data. Many organizations demonstrate massive capacity for discounting, distorting, and denying disconfirming data. Even natural scientists show remarkable resistance to new data that disconfirm their old views of the world.[2] Depending on the resistance to change in an individual or an organization, a would-be change leader may have to expend enormous energy to get people to see disconfirming data and their implications. Hal Leavitt at Stanford Graduate School of Business noted that in many cases, the role of modern leadership is less to find and solve problems and more increasingly to create problems for their employees—that is, help them see how they need to change before the market forces it.[3]

---

[2] See Thomas Kuhn, *The Structure of Scientific Revolutions*, 3rd ed. (Chicago: University of Chicago Press, 1996).
[3] Harold Leavitt, *Corporate Pathfinders: Building Vision and Values into Organizations* (Homewood, IL: Dow Jones-Irwin, 1986).

Disconfirming data may not necessarily be negative, though. Faced with a leadership opportunity, you may want to create a new vision of what could be possible for an organization. It doesn't mean that you have to create what is often called a "burning platform" or some false "third-party enemy"; it may mean that you see a new vision of what could be if the company were able to transform itself. Without an immediate threat, this kind of change is difficult to sell in an organization, so the strength of the leadership's vision is critical to getting organizational members to buy into or accept this kind of new information. An excellent example is the shift in strategy at Kimberly-Clark in the mid-1990s, when the CEO and his staff decided to sell off their paper mills, including the namesake mill in Kimberly, Wisconsin, and focus on consumer products.[4] Employees generally are not likely to see and accept this kind of new data, especially when things seem to be going well.

It's much easier to see and accept an immediate threat like financial loss, losses in market share, rising costs, or unmanageable levels of debt. The leader who bears this kind of disconfirming data may get a more willing response from employees or the unions that represent them. Unfortunately, when such disconfirming data appear, it may be late in the competitive game and the company may not be able to recover.

So asserting disconfirming data doesn't just mean bringing bad historical news; it also means creating new visions of what's possible and then galvanizing people in that direction. A new chief executive's vision can be disconfirming data to a company's employees. Changes in strategic direction such as those taken by Jack Welch or his successor, Jeff Immelt, would qualify as this kind of disconfirming data that those who had "bought" the previous vision would have to consider and embrace.

Building a Change Team

Carol Rubin was, for a time, the chief operating officer of the Chicago Park District during a period when it underwent dramatic changes from a patronage system that was highly dysfunctional to an organization that was dramatically improved on virtually every measure. The general superintendent of this change team was Forrest Claypool. During an interview about this change process, Rubin commented on Claypool's approach:

> The first thing that he did was that he spent a lot of time recruiting good people. As soon as he knew that he had this job, he spent months recruiting good people. And that is the only way that you could turn a bureaucracy around. I know people who have gone to other bureaucracies here and in other cities and it's always a telltale sign for me that whether they will succeed or fail, if they brought in a good team. I've had people say, you know, "I'm the only one that the new director brought over." Well, if I hear that I know they're really not going to get to do anything because, to turn a place around, you need a band of revolutionaries and you need a lot of people. One person can't do it alone, and there is so much to do that you really need to spend time bringing in a good team of people. Because if you have good people, you know, while strategic planning is great and it's very important, if you have good people, the job will get done. They have to share your vision; they have to share your values; they have to be your people. But they will come in and they will be the ones that will get the job done. They will also bring in good people.[5]

---

[4] Jim Collins, "Level Five Leadership," *Harvard Business Review*, December 2000.
[5] "Chicago Park District A" (UVA-OB-0618TN), teaching note.

Leading change is like dropping a pebble in a pond. After the initial splash, concentric waves emanate out from the center. The leader with the vision is that center, and the team he or she assembles becomes the waves that affect the rest of the pond. Leading change is like guerilla warfare: the leader assembles a small band of revolutionaries, imbues them with a common vision and purpose, organizes their efforts, and relies on them to "spread the word." You cannot lead change by yourself.

Designing and Leading Change Experiments

Change means doing something new. By definition, changes are experiments for the people who try. If the experiments aren't well designed and managed, participants can come out and conclude, "See, I told you! I knew it wouldn't work!" This experience happened to many companies that over the years tried the latest managerial process as a "program" or "Band-Aid" stuck on the surface of the underlying, persistent organizational culture. Management by objectives, nominal groups, self-managed teams, total quality management, and benchmarking, to name a few, worked in some companies, and not in others, in part because the experimental trials were not well designed or well led in the first place. In one situation, a general manager was asked by his boss to delegate more because the general manager was trying to do too much. A year later, after the manager had tried his definition of delegating, the company's financial indicators were down. His probably erroneous conclusion was that delegation didn't work. The experiment for him was unsuccessful. We might ask his boss how he designed the change attempt and how much coaching and guidance he gave during the experiment. Announcing a change and then disappearing does not constitute experimental design and leadership.

Well-designed experiments require clear goals and objectives, substantial training for how to achieve those goals, coaching and support when fledgling attempts don't go well, and lots of positive reinforcement when the behavior moves in the desired direction.

Relentlessly Reinforcing Results with the New Vision

People want and need positive reinforcement, especially when they are trying something new. It is clear that positive reinforcements have a powerful effect on behavior. Sometimes the innate, natural results of a situation (the final score in a game, the ability to ride a bike, the quarterly results) will be sufficient to "reward" people for their efforts. Few would disagree, however, that positive reinforcement, even in small doses,[6] can have a powerful influence on people. Hardcore Skinnerians would argue as well that positive reinforcement is the only kind of reinforcement that has lasting power; punishing may teach someone what not to do, but it does not teach them what to do—they face too many options besides the one that the leader may desire.

Given these fundamentals of a basic, general change process, we can explore the popular and documented change models used in business organizations today.

CLASSIC AND CURRENT CHANGE MODELS

Historically, probably the most popular change model has been to order people to do something different. If an army, a police force, a dungeon, or a guillotine stood behind the leader, many

---

[6] See, for example, Ken Blanchard, *The One Minute Manager* (New York: William Morrow and Company, 1982).

would comply. Telling or threatening as a means of initiating change remains a powerful, simple model today. Compliance, however, is not Level Three change and certainly not the route to world-class performance.

In the business world, a dominant change model was the simple three-step process articulated by Kurt Lewin. He noted that a change effort began with an unfreezing process, contained a transformation process in the middle, and ended with a refreezing stage. Nowadays, with the rapid rate of change taking place around us, most observers agree that the refreezing is dangerous and that we probably should think more in terms of allowing the new processes to gel, not freeze. The gel image is more flexible and responsive to future change while still giving some stability. Others argue we should simply give up on unfreeze–retrain–refreeze process and accept the reality of today as unfreeze–change–change. The implication of this notion in our general change model is that each new baseline will constantly be challenged by the events changing around it.

In today's changing world, unless an individual or organization has a deep-seated Level Three value for change, life will be a constant series of irritations and frustrations. People who have or develop a value for change, on the other hand, will begin to understand this process and manage it to their benefit.

A more recent, widely used change model comes from Michael Beer at the Harvard Business School. Beer asserts an equation that suggests that the amount of change in a system equals the amount of dissatisfaction with the status quo times the clarity of the model of where we want to go, times the strength of the change process when that product exceeds the cost of making the change.[7]

$$C_v = D_{sq} \times M_f \times P_c > C_c$$

where:

C_v = Volume of change

D_{sq} = Dissatisfaction with the status quo

M_f = Model of the future

P_c = Process of change

C_c = Cost of the change

This model is useful because it tells us that unless people are unhappy with the way things are, they aren't likely to change, and even if they are unhappy, unless they can see how they want to change things, they aren't likely to engage in the process. Change leaders can see specific things in this approach that they can do to raise the probability of success.

ROLES IN THE CHANGE PROCESS

Other roles besides problem creator are important in the change process: change leader, change agent, change manager, and change model.[8] Any one person can play all of these roles. A *change leader* is one who initiates a change process. This role may have come about by virtue of a significant event, a bolt of inspiration, or simply doing one's strategic homework. Senior

---

[7] See Michael Beer, "Leading Change," Harvard Case Services, 488-037.
[8] Alex Horniman introduced me to these ideas.

executives are often change leaders in corporations. Change leaders may, for instance, commission studies, request a new process for developing company strategy, or decide to acquire new kinds of businesses.

A *change agent* is one who causes the change to begin in a person or an organization. This person actually begins the change effort. It may or may not be the change leader. Consultants or senior staff members are often change agents—they both respond to a change leader's request or initiative.

A *change manager* is the person who has the day-to-day responsibilities of implementing and overseeing the change effort. This change manager could be a staff or a line person. The change leader will look to this person for reports and progress. This person has to influence others in the organization to make the changes take place.

A *change model* is a person who exemplifies the change effort. Change models are consistent in their repetition of the disconfirming data (the need for change), in their language in encouraging the change, and in their behavior in acting in a manner consistent with the change objectives and principles.

These various change roles interact. For instance, if the change leader is not a change model—if the senior executive recommending an organizational change does not behave the requested changes—the strength of the change effort is greatly undermined. Identifying each role in a change effort and assessing how the various role holders' behaviors and communications are consistent or inconsistent can help explain why many change efforts succeed or fail.

We should also recognize the *changees*, the individuals who are being asked to change what they do and how they do it. This role is as difficult and as important as any of the others, yet it is often overlooked by those in the first four roles. People being asked to make significant changes often go through some predictable phases.

RESPONSES TO CHANGE

Dying "Little Deaths"

When a person or an organization changes, they let go of some part of their historical comfort zone and begin to embrace a new pattern. This letting-go, in a significant way, is like letting a part of the self die. We can speak of experiencing change, then, as if it were like dying a little death.

Powerful parallels emerge between the research of Elisabeth Kübler-Ross on the stages of experience of terminally ill cancer patients and the experience of individuals and organizational members with the change process.[9] Although neither individuals nor groups of employees go through all these stages in exactly the same way or even in the same sequence, a general pattern is present. Knowledge of this pattern helps leaders manage change processes better.

People experiencing significant change typically go through periods of denial, anger, bargaining, despair, experimenting, resignation, and integration. Again, please note that not everyone experiences these stages in this order, and certainly not everyone goes through all of these stages. Some, for instance, get hung up in denial.

---

[9] See Elisabeth Kübler-Ross, *On Death and Dying* (New York: Collier Books, 1993).

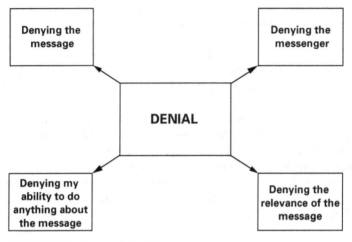

FIGURE 24-6   Forms of denial

The Many Faces of Denial

Some people react to disconfirming data by denying them. Many of the forms of denial are shown in Figure 24-6.[10] First, one can deny the credibility of the messenger, in effect discounting the validity of the source of the data. If one rejects the message before even considering the content, one is easily able to avoid thinking about the content of the message. If one is able or forced to admit that the messenger is credible, one can deny the content of the message, holding on to a belief that the data are false. Again, it's easy to avoid doing anything about data one doesn't believe. If one is forced to accept both the message and the messenger, one can deny the relevance of the message to one's own situation. "Yes," we may say, "it's true, and I acknowledge that you brought this to my attention, but it really doesn't concern me." Finally, however, if we are forced to acknowledge that the data source is credible, that the data are true, and that they relate to us, we may then deny our ability to do anything about it. These four successive hurdles to receiving and seriously considering disconfirming data are defense mechanisms that we often use to protect our self-image.

   People can stay locked in denial for long periods. Some refuse ever to come out. Addictions are, in part, a form of denial inasmuch as they are an attempt to seek alternative forms of peace or resonance from what the nonaddictive world presents. People who ignore health warnings from the Surgeon General's office are in a form of denial. Employees and/or managers who ignore competitive signals from their industries and persist in old routines are in a form of denial.

Anger and Bargaining

If the disconfirming data are strong enough to pierce a person's denial, the first typical emotional response is anger. Anger arises when the changee realizes that the disconfirming data cannot be denied and must be dealt with. This realization forces individuals to leave their

---

[10] Thanks again to Alex Horniman.

comfort zone and move into a new, unknown arena, and if navigated successfully, it will require giving up something of the old self and moving on. To change, an individual gives up an investment of time, energy, and emotion in a pattern that no longer works as well. This process can be infuriating. People don't want to give up their former investments, and they may vent this related anger at any number of targets that may not have anything to do with the real source of the problem. Employees may get angry with employers instead of with the competition. They may get angry with customers instead of trying to serve them. They may get angry with their colleagues, their families, their counterparts in other departments, and so on. As outlined in Chapter 12, people with higher EQs and CQs are more likely to be able to manage this anger and move ahead. Moving ahead usually means a failed attempt to move backward.

Anger in response to a recognized need for change often leads to bargaining. Having been forced to recognize that the old way doesn't work so well anymore, people will often try to bargain their way out of the change. "Maybe if we just cut back on expenses, we could continue as we are," is one common bargaining ploy. Another is, "Maybe we can work harder, and the data will get better." Others include, "This is a short-term phenomenon; we'll get back to the old way soon," "We've managed changes before, and we'll manage this one by doing what we've been doing," "The customer doesn't really know what he wants, we need to educate him," and so on.

Bargaining is an attempt to reverse the disconfirming data and retreat to the original baseline. In the resonance model presented earlier, bargaining is related to the ping-pong effect between Preparation and SOS barriers. Disconfirming data are manifestations of barriers. If short-term bargains are made and the data begin to show some responsiveness, bargaining can be dangerous to change efforts because people want to believe that things will get better without their changing. When bargaining fails, though, as it will in all fundamental change situations, they realize that they truly have to change, and this realization often leads to despair.

Transition Through Despair and Grieving

Despair for most is a watershed transitional stage between attempts to go back and willingness to go ahead. In this hopefully brief period, most people realize that there is no going back, that the former comfort is gone, and that however uncomfortable, they must go ahead.

Some argue that people need time to grieve at this point, to vent their despair, to cry, to reflect on the good old times, and to lend a sense of completion to the past before going on to the next stage. Although grieving is necessary, at some point a person must say, "Enough crying for the past. I must live in the present and prepare for tomorrow." The sooner a person finishes grieving for the past and begins to see possibilities for the future, the sooner progress will be made. Making changes in our lives and in our organizations is like dying small deaths, and like deaths, these changes require some grieving and attention if we are to move ahead with some psychological wholeness.

When the grieving is coming to an end, most people begin, however timidly, to see possibilities. Seeing possibilities in the future is the beginning of exploration and experimentation. As mentioned already, it is a place where outside, less involved, expert assistance can be of enormous help. As individuals begin to see new, manageable routes of progress, they take a few steps in that direction and begin to see the possible results. These alternative directions help generate some hope that the despair of the recent change will be replaced with a new sense of comfort and capability.

Hope and the Change Process

Hope is the anticipation that one's efforts can yield results. If people in the midst of a major change cannot see how the world will get better, it will be difficult for them to find something to work for in the new state of things and they will begin to look to the past for comfort and support. False hopes aren't any help. If management deviates from the moral rock described in Chapter 6 and allows or constructs false hopes, employees will soon become disenchanted and disengaged and slip back into despair. Realistic hope, achievable hope, and small but tangible hope are better than promises made lightly and without much expectation of fulfillment.

As they realize hope and positive data start coming in from the new experiments, people begin to integrate the new way of doing things into their network of assumptions and values. Ghosts of the old assumptions begin to fade, and the new principles take their place. Often this integration occurs so subtly that we don't even notice it. Although as powerful as anger and despair, integration is much less obvious. One day, you might notice that you have been using the new principles for a while and things have been going okay. The new order seems almost comfortable. Celebrating this ethereal transition is an important part of helping people understand what has happened, that they are veterans of managing change, and that together they have created a new reality.

The process just described can be diagramed as shown in Figure 24-7. It represents an oscillation between behavior and emotion, each in turn typically triggering the next. Overcoming denial leads to anger. Overcoming anger leads to bargaining. Overcoming bargaining leads to despair. Working through despair leads to new options. Working those options can generate new hope. Hope and work together produce the kind of behavior that leads to a new pattern of doing things. Effective leaders not only understand this process, but actively plan for and anticipate the reactions so their downside effects are minimized and their upside possibilities maximized.

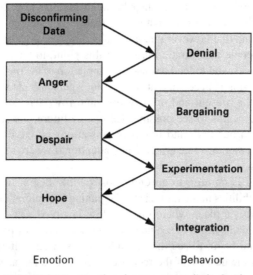

FIGURE 24-7 Emotional responses to little deaths

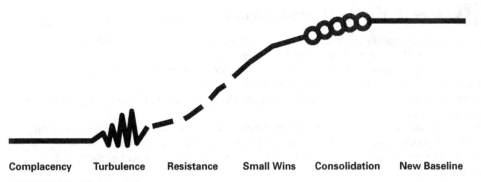

| Complacency | Turbulence | Resistance | Small Wins | Consolidation | New Baseline |

FIGURE 24-8 Phases of change

Another way to depict this process of change is as shown in Figure 24-8. Here, a smooth, flat line represents the early complacency of past successes. Disconfirming data become like rocks in a river causing chaotic rapids. Despite the evidence, people resist the need for and efforts to introduce change. If leadership is strong and good processes are put into place, short-term positive results begin to emerge. Then, lest the new efforts snap back to the old way, an iterative consolidation of the new way into a new habitual way of doing things establishes a new baseline. Unless the new baseline includes processes of continuous change, before long it can become its own complacency—and the process begins again.

LEVELS IN CHANGE

Similar to the way that we earlier talked about Level One, Level Two, and Level Three Leadership, we can talk about Level One, Level Two, and Level Three change. If the target of our change effort is behavior only, we are working on a Level One effort, but Level One change efforts can often have unintended Level Three consequences if the formal changes requested affect people at a deeper level. Effective leaders recognize that powerful change invites people to change not only their behavior but also their thoughts and beliefs and so target their attempts at Level Three. A Level Three change is any change that modifies the basic values and assumptions of an individual or organization.

John Kotter's Model of Change

John Kotter at the Harvard Business School would call this kind of change "anchoring the changes in the culture of the organization." Kotter's research outlined eight reasons that corporate change efforts fail—and eight corresponding ways of managing them.[11] Kotter's counsel was that change leaders should (1) establish a sense of urgency, (2) create a guiding, powerful coalition, (3) develop a clear and powerful vision and strategy, (4) communicate the change vision at every point possible, (5) redesign the organization to remove obstacles to change, (6) find short-term successes to celebrate, (7) consolidate short-term wins into new change initiatives, and (8) ensure that the changes are incorporated into the underlying

---

[11] John Kotter, *Leading Change* (Boston, MA: Harvard Business School Press, 1996).

TABLE 24-1 Kotter's Eight-Step Plan for Implementing Change

1. Establish a sense of urgency by creating a compelling reason for why change is needed.
2. Form a coalition with enough power to lead the change.
3. Create a new vision to direct the change and strategies for achieving the vision.
4. Communicate the vision throughout the organization.
5. Empower others to act on the vision by removing barriers to change and encouraging risk taking and creative problem solving.
6. Plan for, create, and reward short-term wins that move the organization toward the new vision.
7. Consolidate improvements, reassess changes, and make necessary adjustments in the new programs.
8. Reinforcement the changes by demonstrating the relationship between new behaviors and organizational success.

organizational culture. These eight steps, repeated in Table 24-1, correspond well to the principles introduced earlier in this book. Although Kotter provides a well-informed, empirically based view, the next model shows a similar supporting perspective from industry.

The Four P's

The president of the largest division of one of the most successful financial services firms in the United States summarizes the change process as the "Four P's" of change: purpose (derived presumably from some felt pain), picture, plan, and part. They represent, in essence, a manager's view of Beer's equation: if people don't see a purpose for the change, if they don't see where they're trying to go, if they don't see a plan for how to get there, and if they don't see a part that they can play in the plan, they're not likely to participate in the change effort—and it will flounder and/or founder.

The MIT Model

Just down the road from Kotter's Harvard office, researchers at MIT developed a powerful seven-step model of managing change.[12] They view change as a three-dimensional phenomenon involving a developmental process, seven tools for effecting change, and the importance of managing resistance to change.

According to the MIT team, major change efforts typically progress through four clear phases. The first phase is the traditional phase when employees and management are just learning that the old ways aren't working anymore. It means coming to grips with disconfirming data coming in from the environment. Once this realization sets in, management begins searching for new approaches in the second, exploratory phase. In the third, generative phase, key pieces of the change effort are generated out of new processes and approaches, so that the new processes become the source of energy for change. Finally, in an internalization phase, the new processes become so well ingrained that they become a natural part of the organization.

Nevis and his colleagues argue well that successful change efforts utilize not one or two, but seven sets of skills related to change, as shown in Table 24-2. Each of these skill sets has its strengths and weaknesses, and each might be more or less appropriate at each of the four phases. The challenge for effective change managers is to understand and be able to use each of these tools appropriately.

---

[12] Edwin C. Nevis, Joan Lancourt, and Helen G. Vassallo, *Intentional Revolutions* (San Francisco, CA: Jossey-Bass, 1996).

TABLE 24-2	The Nevis MIT Model of Process Change

1. Persuasive communication
2. Participation
3. Use of expectations
4. Modeling
5. Extrinsic rewards
6. Making structural and organizational changes
7. Coercing

Nevis and colleagues include coercion on the list of change management skills. On the other hand, coercion is a use of power that moves one out of the realm of leadership. You may or may not feel that coercion is necessary for a short period. Some managers say that sometimes you have to force people to do what they don't want to do when you know that the effort will eventually lead to their acceptance of the "right" way of doing things. The concern here is that if a manager gets comfortable using coercion as a crutch, as a last means of creating change, then it becomes easier and easier to use the next time, and, soon, a manager is leading almost exclusively at Level One. It's faster in some sense, but in the long term, it's less effective.

The MIT team notes that many change efforts fail because they ignore predictable resistance to change. Peter Senge and colleagues, in the learning organization research that's been done at MIT, suggest that a powerful way of recognizing this common feature is to encompass the principle of multiple realities. In other words, subgroups in an organization see the change efforts differently. Some are in favor of, and some opposed to, the changes—each for its own reasons. If change leaders can recognize that each of these groups has good reasons for its viewpoints, they are better armed to select and use change tools that fit that group's perspective. The keys to this approach are to legitimize diverse perceptions rather than to demand a singular view. If management takes this approach, it can find richer solutions through using these various viewpoints and can thus reduce resistance.

Prochaska's Model for Positive Change

Prochaska presents a modestly different approach in which the central idea is that people spiral toward change, often "recycling" the steps in his change process (see Table 24-3 and Figure 24-9). In fact, he argues that 85 percent of people will retreat to an earlier stage and begin anew. In his

TABLE 24-3	Prochaska's Spiral of Change

Stage	Key activity
Precontemplation	Unaware of the problem, much less the solution
Contemplation	I want to stop feeling/doing this
Preparation	I will do something very soon
Action	I am doing something about this
Maintenance	Careful attention to maintaining the change and not recycling
Termination	Temptation and threat have disappeared

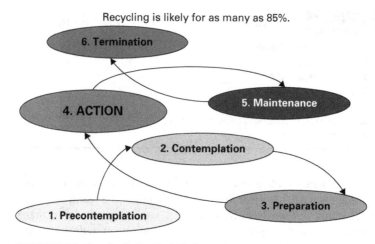

Recycling is likely for as many as 85%.

FIGURE 24-9   Prochaska's spiral of change

view, it's unlikely that people will make a sustained change with a single effort/jump cycle. Prochaska's steps are similar to others' and include precontemplation (no interest in changing), contemplation (I want to change something), preparation (here's what I plan to do to change), action (I am doing something about this), maintenance (how can I hold onto the changes I'm making), and termination (temptations disappear, and there is no recycling).[13]

Fighting Your Inherent Fears of Changing

Finally, we note the work of Robert Maurer, who argues that most change efforts fail because we try to do too much at once. Maurer argues that in managing individual change, we should begin with tiny, incremental changes that are not threatening or difficult in any way. When we choose bigger steps, he says, our natural, innate flight-or-fight response system kicks in and we are likely to relapse. On the other hand, when we begin with things that are utterly nonthreatening we can easily get some small wins, and these gradually build to the point where we can do more.[14]

Conclusions

As there were many models of strategic analysis, there are many models for managing change. The challenge here is not to memorize them all, rather to understand them all and then develop your own model borrowing here and there from those who've gone before you. To ignore this process—that is, to have no model of managing change at the individual, work-group, or organizational levels—is to overlook the importance of becoming a master of the change process in becoming an effective leader. Understanding and managing change is an integral part of effective leadership. Leadership seeks to change what people do, and if it is effective, it will change what people think and believe. People naturally tend to settle into a

[13] James O. Prochaska, John Norcross, and Carlo DiClemente, *Changing for Good: A Revolutionary Six Stage Process for Overcoming Bad Habits and Moving Your Life Positively Forward* (New York: Collins, 1994).
[14] Robert Maurer, *One Small Step Can Change Your Life The Kaizen Way* (New York: Workman, 2004).

comfort zone using personal, interpersonal, and organizational techniques that have served them in the past. Changing from this historical pattern usually begins with disconfirming data. Those who attend to these data and interpret them as meaningful begin a change process. In so doing, they leave behind a part of their former self, as if they were dying a little death. Making real change, especially Level Three change, triggers a common and emotional response pattern of denial, anger, bargaining, despair, experimentation, hope, and integration. Leaders who understand this process and can

develop skill at managing people through it can manage their mutual changes more effectively.

Go back to the opening sentence of the book: Leadership is about managing energy, first in yourself and then in those around you. The same can be said for managing change. If you want to change the world around you, recognize that the way you have dealt with the world in the past has produced the world you now experience. If you want to change it, you're going to have to change yourself first. If you are unwilling or unable to change the way you do things, the odds are that the world around you will continue the way it is.

Concepts Introduced in This Chapter

1. Leadership, by definition, is about managing change.
2. Effective leaders understand and master the skills of managing the change process.
3. Changing is like dying a little death—part of us must be let go and a new part created.
4. Change begins with disconfirming data. We then choose how we respond to those data, whether to ignore them or consider them.
5. Recognizing and managing various change-effort roles—including change leader, change agent, change manager, change model, and changee—are helpful in mounting a successful change effort.

6. Disconfirming data often lead to a series of predictable reactions to the change process: denial, anger, bargaining, despair, experimentation, hope, and integration into a new way of doing things. People can get stuck along the way, and outside help is often useful in moving through each phase.
7. People need strong and consistent reinforcement in the experimentation phase in order to settle on the new way of doing things.
8. Outside agents are often helpful in managing change because they can see things that have become invisible habits to those in the change arena.
9. Level Three, or value-level, change is the most enduring.

Questions for Personal Reflection

1. What kinds of disconfirming data have you encountered either personally or in your work group over the last six months? What was your response to it?
2. What change roles are you playing in your work group? What data do you see, that maybe others don't see, that invite you to become a change leader?
3. What has been helpful for you in the past when you have needed support getting through the reactions to change process? How could you provide those functions to others?
4. List the most significant changes you've made in your life. Think through the process that you used to navigate each change. How well did you manage those changes? What did you learn from them and what would you like to know how to do better?

CASELETS FOR DISCUSSION

Caselet 1

Marianne was excited about her new job as the manager for an urban-center store for a nationwide chain. As she arrived on location and began to get acquainted with her three employees, however, it was clear that there were some problems to be dealt with. First, Bob was very talented and technologically current, but he didn't like reporting to a woman. When Marianne asked him to do something, he often ignored her or waited until she'd asked him several times and then sighed or grunted his compliance. Suzanne, on the other hand, had a hygiene problem. Customers had complained to her two co-workers that she smelled and that they didn't want to be around her. And Rosy seldom smiled and was grouchy with customers. She seemed to have a dark cloud over her and seldom made a positive or cheerful comment. Marianne's sales had been flat to declining for the first three months of her administration and although each of these would be difficult conversations, she knew she had to do something.

Caselet 2

Consider that you have just been made the new police chief in your city. How would you find out what the problems are? What would be the areas in which you would want to explore to identify changes that needed to be made? How would you go about organizing your efforts? (Use your own amalgam of the change theories introduced here to guide your thinking.)

WORKBOOK

Consider page 362 in Workbook. What aspects of your personal style and leadership style would you like to work on moving forward? How will you attempt to do those things?

CONTRIBUTING YOUR OWN CASELETS

Have you seen or experienced a situation involving the concepts introduced in this chapter? If so and if you'd like to contribute your experience/situation to our case data bank, please visit http://faculty.darden.virginia. edu/clawsonj/ and click on the "Contribute new caselets" button.

Suggestions for Additional Reading

Hammer, Michael and James Champy. *Reengineering the Corporation*. New York: Harper Business, 1993.

Kotter, John. *Leading Change*. Boston, MA: Harvard Business School Press, 1996.

Maurer, Robert. *One Small Step Can Change Your Life the Kaizen Way*. New York: Workman, 2004.

Nevis, Edwin C., Joan Lancourt, and Helen G. Vassallo. *Intentional Revolutions*. San Francisco, CA: Jossey-Bass, 1996.

O'Toole, James. *Leading Change*. San Francisco, CA: Jossey-Bass, 1995.

Prochaska, James O., John Norcross, and Carlo DiClemente. *Changing for Good: A Revolutionary Six-Stage Process for Changing Your Bad Habits and Moving Your Life Positively Forward*. New York: Avon, 1995.

Quinn, Robert. *Deep Change*. San Francisco, CA: Jossey-Bass, 1997.

Schein, Edgar. *Process Consultation*. Reading, MA: Addison-Wesley, 1969.

Watzlawick, Paul, John H. Weakland, and Richard Fisch. *Change*. New York: W. W. Norton, 1974.

SECTION VI

CONCLUSION

CONCLUSION

The key to managing people in ways that lead to profits, productivity, innovation, and real organizational learning ultimately lies in how you think about your organization and its people. It lies in mind-set and perspective.

—JEFF PFEFFER[1]

Level Three Leadership is about managing energy, first in yourself and then in those around you. To manage energy, one must get below the surface to deal with the fundamental reasons why people do what they do. Without understanding where individual energy comes from, one will not be able to bring it out for collective focus and deployment. That means you must understand and be comfortable with influencing people's core values, assumptions, beliefs, and expectations (VABEs) about the way the world is or should be. Unless you do

---

[1] Jeffrey Pfeffer, *The Human Equation* (Boston, MA: Harvard Business School Press, 1998).

that, you are dealing at a relatively superficial level. And that may be good enough to pay the bills and get by, but it won't lead to world-class performance—and in today's flat, competitive world, excellence is what the market demands.

Level Three Leadership is about making a fundamental and lasting difference in yourself, in your work group, in your organization, and in society. This suggests that leadership begins with leading self; it's not just about changing the way others do things. Many people in positions of power over the last 200 years focused on leading at Level One, visible behavior. The unfortunate result of that approach is that millions of people dislike their work, hate going to work, and perform at a low-energy disengaged state of being. Whereas Level One Leadership focuses on and may get short-term behavioral results, Level Three Leadership targets what people think and believe and this, I say, has a more lasting effect.

Level One Leadership worked well enough for a long time—well enough to guide the Industrial Age and to form large corporations that supplied the world with a plethora of products and services. Level One Leadership gives a manager a sense of immediate accomplishment. A manager can see what people are doing and doesn't have to worry about what they're thinking and feeling. Level One Leadership is inherently visible; you can see what people do, and most people can see what the consequences are if they don't respond. In a relatively orderly world, if you have enough power, Level One Leadership works well enough.

In the turbulent, fast-changing world of today, however, where decisions need to be made throughout an organization and where the information needed to make those decisions can be rapidly distributed, the principles and consequences of Level One Leadership are breaking down. One person, one boss; vertical hierarchies; limited spans of control; clear functional and organizational boundaries; certainty about what to do; limited sharing of information; and clear repositories of expertise are fading. Multiple "bosses," including suppliers, customers, people from various functions, and even subordinates; much flatter organizations based on ever-forming and re-forming teams and the importance of current databases; broad spans of influence rather than control; fuzzy boundaries between functions and organizations; mounds of uncertainty about what to do; widespread information sharing and exchange; and constantly shifting pools of knowledge and insight are replacing them.

In this kind of environment, the Industrial Age leadership notions of command-and-control or planning-organizing-motivating-and-controlling are becoming absurdly out of date. Huge political entities in the former Soviet Union have broken down and been replaced with widely distributed, self-determined, more democratic countries. Large industrial corporations have been disassembled and reorganized into smaller, more independent firms. Although the political and industrial borders will continue to be mapped and melded in various ways, the people of the world will no longer accept circumstances in which they have less control over their lives and futures. Controlling is giving way to coordinating, and coordinating implies a respect for underlying beliefs and values in a way that controlling did not.

Level One Leaders will continue in the world (although in our lexicon, this phrase is a misnomer because a person who exercises power without regard for followers' voluntary responses is no longer a leader, but merely an "authoritor"). Part of the reason for the continued existence of Level One Leaders will be psychological. Many people grow up needing to control their environment and view people as a part of that environment. Further, Level One companies in the world will be run by Level One Leaders. These companies' cultures will continue to care little for the thoughts and feelings of the people who work within them, and they will continue to focus on short-term financial goals, which will hinge upon the shareholders' rewards to the subversion of other worthy objectives. Many of them may even survive for lengthy periods.

The organizations that will thrive and grow in the Information Age, however, will increasingly be based on Level Three Leadership. Their employees will not only do what they are asked, but also believe in what they do and believe in it deeply. Successful Information Age organizations will borrow from the nonprofit organizations of the Industrial Age to understand why people will work hard yielding their best efforts for little or no pay. These Level Three firms will understand the causal networks that encourage people to voluntarily work their hardest and will know that unless they can successfully elicit this kind of work, they will fall farther and farther behind their competitors who understand how to do it. Examples exist today at small, medium, and large scales. Pike's Place Fish Market in Seattle, Washington, is an excellent example of a high-energy, high-profitability small business. SAS in Cary, North Carolina, is an excellent medium-sized example. And Southwest Airlines is the often-studied example of a large, high-energy, profitable firm in a difficult industry. There are others, but they are in the minority.

It seems clear that no individual would use one and only one level in their attempts to influence others. We all have a profile of leadership-level focus. Each person may emphasize one level more than another. I've tried to make a case in this book that people who emphasize Level Three techniques more than Level One techniques are likely to succeed more in business and in more lasting ways.

People in Level Three organizations will be bonded to their companies by more than paychecks and fear of unemployment. They will believe in what the company is doing. They will have information available to them about how the company is doing, and this will strengthen the bond they have with their company. They will understand the importance of delighting the customer in a world where alternative sources are proliferating. And Level Three organizations will understand that unless the employees are delighted, the customers will not be. It will be the leadership of those organizations who will have defined and promulgated the purposes and missions, the visions and values, and the strategies and operating goals that employees respond to.

Those who desire to create Level Three organizations will face many challenges. First is the historical momentum of the Industrial Age and the principles that it taught. If Thomas Kuhn is right about the nature of scientific revolutions and the time it takes to realize one, it will take one or more generations in each organization before a new Level Three model of leadership will take hold.[2] This process will spread slowly through each industry. Richard Walton, a longtime researcher of high-performance workplaces, noted the slowness of this transition.[3] On the other hand, amid today's rapid communications and global outsourcing, we no longer have the luxury of waiting a generation for change. Each of us will be forced to consider how, if at all, we will change or else be relegated to the masses who are little more than conduits passing on genetic and memetic material to the next generation—and material that may be obsolete, outdated, and dysfunctional. And the challenge remains that each newborn is a blank slate upon which the family, neighborhood, and surrounding culture will begin to imprint their VABEs. The irony is that many will imprint the VABE "Don't pay attention to VABEs."

---

[2] In *Thomas Kuhn, The Structure of Scientific Revolutions*, 3rd ed. (Chicago: University of Chicago Press, 1996). Thomas Kuhn discovered that even after irrefutable scientific evidence backing up a new paradigm had been amassed, scientists who had been raised in the old paradigm literally had to die off before the new one was accepted and incorporated into general scientific thought. The same may be true of business organizations, especially given the larger and therefore stronger momentum of organizational culture that exists in many corporations. Although scientists often work in smaller organizations and even in relative isolation, corporations have a strong institutional learning process that propagates former thinking through myriads of processes and policies.

[3] See Richard Walton, "From Control to Commitment in the Workplace," *Harvard Business Review*, March 1985, 85219.

Second, the poverty endemic to many parts of the world will slow the spread of the Information Age. When people are unable to access and use computer-based information links, they are left to the information-sharing processes of the Industrial Age and remain subject to its, or its predecessor's, Level One characteristics. Yet education and the resultant power to access the Internet will accelerate this process. Television and nearly global satellite-based broadcasting have already changed the way people in previously isolated areas see the world and their personal possibilities. A major challenge of the Information Age will be to manage the increasingly obvious differences between the haves and the have-nots. When people in Eastern Europe or Southeastern Asia view *Lifestyles of the Rich and Famous* on television and see the opulent homes rich people live in, the lovely places they visit for vacations, and the total lack of care they have for financial details, it creates aspirations, desires, and even demands. Increasingly, people will insist on self-determination, politically and economically.

The Information Age will make this shift possible. Unlike the Industrial Age, in which people could be kept in the dark about options, the Information Age will inform poor people about how others live—and therefore about how they could live. So what we have is the collision between the Information Age and the Experience Economy. I recently asked a class of 30-year-old MBA candidates what it was that the United States produced or sold in an economy characterized by off shoring and outsourcing. Their answer was, "our lifestyle." Hmm. To them, we sell an experience, an experience made known by the Information Age technology. The challenge then will be to manage the perceived gaps in effort and reward, to create a world in which fairness based on contribution will guide reward systems. Since we know that human nature is not likely to change dramatically, this economic experiential system of fairness will require oversight. Left to their own devices, most leaders are self-serving. Level Three Leaders will understand this issue and, with help from the ethical foundation of leadership, will recognize and codevelop reward systems in which all can participate and thus provide for a sustainable competitive advantage.

A third challenge to face in the Information Age/Experience Economy will be the flexibility with which technology and information both invade and protect people's lives. With cell phones, PDAs, and Internet connections, people can work from anywhere. This capability can be a help or a hindrance. Some people will allow their work to control their lives no matter where they are. Others will face the dilemma of balancing their personal and professional lives. This is the most commonly mentioned issue in my seminars worldwide. It's not just a North American issue. With access to growing volumes of work-related data from any location, it becomes more difficult to manage the other aspects of life—health, family, rejuvenation, and relationships. The messages sent when one says, "Hang on for a moment, the other line is ringing" or "I'll be out in a minute dear, I just need to clear my [58] e-mail messages" are decidedly more invasive to personal and family life than working overtime during the Industrial Age. Worldwide, the challenge of balancing work and family life is the number one mentioned issue in my leadership seminars—regardless of race, gender, culture, or ethnicity.

Identity theft has already become an issue in industrialized societies, and hackers all around the world are attacking the structures of the Information Age economy. In the meantime, the principles of the Experience Economy are spreading across the globe. People want more than work—they want to live and enjoy life. And instantaneous communication allows them to see how the "other half" lives. With a new vision of what life could be like, people everywhere want it.

Fourth, Information Age leaders will need to find ways of developing Level Three influences in a population that might not be so willing to respond. University of Virginia's graduate school of business administration is a good example of this kind of development. During the construction of a new building during the early 1990s, the decision was made to put Internet and e-mail connections at each seat in the new classrooms. Later, in a case discussion–oriented environment, the entire tenor of the classroom was changed. Instructors entering the room found that they were not looking at the faces of 60 students. Rather, the faces had been replaced with 60 laptop lids. Some joked that the students should be required to paste their photographs on their laptops so the faculty could tell who they were. Furthermore, the faculty soon discovered that the students were e-mailing each other *during* class. While one student was speaking, several others were commenting and carrying on a simultaneous live virtual discussion with e-mails, text messages, and Tweets. Students were e-mailing their friends in other sections learning what was going on in other classes at the same time. The faculty began worrying about this loss of control, and a similar phenomenon has hit leaders of corporations.

Whether they want it to or not, the Information Age has changed the face of power in institutions by distributing power more widely and deeply than ever before. People at lower ranks of organizations are now able to communicate with each other and to get information about the business that makes it much harder for leaders to control them. Orwell's fear of Big Brother should have been, according to many a disgruntled modern manager raised in the Industrial Age, a fear of Little Sibling.[4] For many managers living during the present transition from the Industrial Age to the Information Age, coming to terms with this loss of control is a major career and professional issue.

Level Three Leadership also implies getting below the surface by not just accepting the first suitable solution that comes along. Although Herb Simon won a Nobel Prize for his clarification of the concept of satisficing, Level Three Leaders are not willing to settle for the first tolerable solution they hit upon. Forcing people to go to work, to break a strike, to stay late, and so on may be the easiest thing at the moment, but in the long term, this Level One approach creates much more difficulty. Level Three Leaders will think beyond the immediate and work hard, mentally and emotionally, to identify other avenues that ultimately affect their associates' hearts and heads as well as their bodies. If all human interaction is some form of exchange in which the currencies may be ill-defined, what kind of currency is necessary for a person to exchange part of his or her innermost motivations?

Herein lies a paradox. On one hand, we can argue that if all human interactions are exchanges, they are all intrinsically Level One phenomena. On the other hand, if we accept that each human can become the primary controller of his or her own motivations, values, and beliefs, then the question is, "What currency does that person need to voluntarily exchange with an institution or leader in order to be a member?" In other words, how much of one's core VABEs must one compromise in order to be included? Only when the institutional offerings are consistent with the individual's underlying motivations and values will that individual give his or her utmost for the institution. Consider all those who work for little pay in charity organizations, such as rescue squads, across the country. In Albemarle County, Virginia, most of the rescue squads are completely voluntary. People have full-time jobs and then offer to serve on the rescue squad vehicles, which often involves lengthy training and long night hours and weekends. Consider the PJs (pararescue jumpers), the rescue swimmers who work with the U.S. Coast Guard who are willing to risk their lives and families' livelihoods (modest as they are) for the lives of others at sea.[5] Consider the volunteer health-care providers throughout the world who give their own time, talent, and energy to help others, many of whom are admittedly dying.

---

[4] George Orwell, *1984* (New York: Harcourt, Brace and Jovanovich, 1949), published at the birth of the Information Age, told a story of how information was supposed to give control to a centralized authority, nicknamed "Big Brother" by the masses.
[5] See Sebastian Junger, *The Perfect Storm* (New York: W. W. Norton, 1997), for a description of the training and professional lifestyles of these extraordinary individuals.

Why do people do these things? Because they *believe*, at Level Three, in what they're doing. These activities match their highest values for human life and service. These extraordinary commitments yield world-class energy and service.

Perhaps you believe that this kind of commitment is not possible in business. You may be right in many corporations. How can one compare saving people's lives at sea in a storm to making ball bearings or fire extinguishers? On the other hand, what is the alternative? If a competitor in your industry can figure out a way to create a working environment in which people can bring their bodies, minds, and hearts to work and in which they can work wholeheartedly for a bigger purpose, what will your organization do? Over time, unless you find a similar way to engage people, your company will fall behind. The service, the quality, the customer focus, the enthusiasm—all of which characterize a Level Three organization—will not be there, and your customers will slowly, at first, and then more rapidly, migrate to the companies that can give superior value for the same cost.

This purpose is also the origin of this book: to outline a structured set of ways in which one can begin to think about and perhaps begin to practice leading below the surface. Level Three Leadership is not about trying out the latest fad and sticking it like a Band-Aid™ over a deep wound. Instead, it's about thinking beyond the superficial and developing a set of skills that will allow one to create a strong vision when none is apparent, to develop deeper relationships where none historically have been invited, and to organize in a way that will tend to perpetuate those deeper connections when one moves on.

To this end, the book describes the changing context in which we now find ourselves. This description outlines the ways in which deep underlying beliefs about business and enterprise are shifting. It includes a consideration of the ways in which rapidly changing information technology is shaping the new organizational forms. And it implies the need for a sturdy, general "four wheel drive" model of leadership that incorporates much of what we learned in the Industrial Age and yet leaves room for the new realities of the Information Age/Experience Economy.

This four-wheel-drive model of leadership includes four main elements: self, task, others, and organization. The book argues that who you are makes a big difference in whether you can lead. We've delved perhaps more than you thought you would into the inner workings of the human personality and psyche. This was the northern ball in our Diamond Model. We also argue that personal characteristics are, alone, not enough. A big part of an effective leadership outcome is the view that you, as the leader, take of the strategic tasks facing you, your work group, and your organization. This is the north–east axis in our basic model. Do you have, for instance, a habitual Leader's Point of View? The book offers a summary of historical ways of thinking about strategy and some newer principles of strategic thinking and invites you to practice them. The book maintains that unless you are able to develop these strategic thinking skills, you will be at a disadvantage compared with your peers.

The book then posited that the quality of your relationships with others has a major impact on whether they will accept your view of the strategic challenges facing them. If you are able to build your attempts to influence on a moral foundation and then communicate clearly and effectively with some stamina, you might be able to make something happen. More importantly, you might be able to release energy in an organizational setting.

The book argued that unless you are an organizational designer, your efforts at influencing and guiding others will be hampered by the constraints that every organization imposes on its employees. Unless you can design organizations that fit your view of the strategic challenges and also understand and master the change process that is continually necessary to move collections of people from one way of doing things to another, your efforts at leadership will fail.

Finally, leaders must be masters of the change process—able to understand the pieces of it and able to help others through it. They need to know how to initiate change, to lead change, and to manage change—not only in others, but also in themselves.

These four thrusts—strategic thinking, leading others, leading by design, and managing change—are presented as critical causes of the variations in energy level in organizational culture and the related business outcomes. Outcomes can be measured in terms of energy and its impact on customer satisfaction, internal operating efficiencies, organizational learning, and financial return, in the same order. Unless authoritors can see below the surface and develop deeper skills in these four areas, their efforts and results will tend to be superficial and fleeting.

My sincere hope is that the concepts, ideas, models, and principles presented in this book will help you become a more effective leader in your personal life, your professional life, and your community. It will happen if you think about and accept the principles of Level Three Leadership, that world-class leaders influence VABEs, that they think about and intend to influence the central VABEs of those they work with. They understand that unless they do these things, their efforts will be like small meteor showers, scarring the surface but leaving no deep and lasting change.

Summary of Concepts Introduced in This Book

1. Leadership is about managing energy, first in yourself and then in those around you.
2. People are creatures of habit, so the challenge in life is to rise above your unproductive habits.
3. You can choose whether you want to take a Leadership Point of View or some other habitual perspective.
4. Human behavior occurs at three levels: (1) visible behavior, (2) conscious thought, and (3) core values, assumptions, beliefs, and expectations (VABEs).
5. We are in the midst of a major managerial paradigm shift from an Industrial Age to an Informational Age that is transforming what it means to be an effective leader.
6. Leadership is a function of more than individual competence and charisma. Leadership is the result of many elements working together, including individual characteristics, forces in the environment, strategic opportunities envisioned by the leader, quality of relationships with followers, and appropriateness of the organization for the leader, task, and followers.
7. Leadership is the ability and the willingness to influence others to do what you want them to do voluntarily.
8. Leadership is about change, and change requires persistence in the development of new habits and routines. Effective leaders understand and use the mechanics and processes of managing change.

9. Leadership is also about ethics and moral behavior. You cannot be an effective leader without taking a moral stand. Effective leadership and extraordinary performance are based on a foundation of moral principles: truth-telling, promise-keeping, fairness, respect for the individual, and respect for demonstrated competency.
10. Your personal leadership emanates from your central beliefs, core values, and assumptions. In effect, who you are as a person defines who you are as a leader.
11. Individual leadership skills can be clustered into three groups: visioning, garnering commitment, and managing progress toward the vision.
12. People's behavior is a function of their genetics and memetics. Their underlying VABEs shape what they do. Level Three Leaders understand and use this perspective.
13. Motivating leadership is, in large part, a function of a clear and compelling vision of what could be. This need for a vision applies to yourself in terms of your life's dream and purpose as well as to your work group and your organization.
14. Leadership is an act of engagement. When you truly engage in something, you become a leader. Engagement is a function of personal commitments usually based on personal resonance.
15. Leadership involves mobilizing the talents of others, which means clarifying what others have to

offer and offering attractive invitations to them to engage in your cause.

16. People work at things they are rewarded for; they work hard for things they believe in.

17. Leadership is closely related to time. Although many speak of future-oriented leadership, much of leadership is about getting people to deal with the present.

18. Language is the primary tool of leadership. Effective leaders know, understand, have skill with, and can wisely use various forms of language.

19. Interpersonal leadership skills are based on respect for competency, trust in consistent caring, fair exchanges, and genuine willingness to be influenced.

20. Level Three Leaders are effective strategic thinkers. They are able to articulate the mission, vision, values, and strategy as well as the short-term operating goals of their organizations. They realize that these elements which together form a charter are essential to connecting with their followers.

21. Leadership is about designing organizations that support what others have to offer to the leader's enterprise. Most of these organizational forms are different from the forms developed in the previous era.

22. Leaders are, first, leaders of themselves. They work hard to see a higher vision and to make it happen.

23. These principles have certain implications for your individual behavior as a leader. They suggest that if you are to be an effective leader, you will engage in these activities:
    1. Clarifying your center
    2. Clarifying what is possible and desirable
    3. Clarifying what others can contribute
    4. Supporting others so they can contribute
    5. Being relentless
    6. Measuring and celebrating progress

24. The first three of these implications involve clarifying, which means bringing into sharper focus, developing, realizing, and using. Thus, the action implied is not a one-time thing, but an ongoing process of discovery and utilization. Effective leaders do not, for instance, simply clarify their center and then leave it for the rest of their career. Rather, they must be periodically reviewing, renewing, and recommitting to what lies at their core. We used the participial form of the verbs to imply this meaning.

25. Leadership is demanding and draining. It requires intense mental, physical, emotional, spiritual, and social effort. Many retreat from these demands, and our world, our businesses, and our communities are the worse for it. I hope that your exploration of leadership through this volume will have challenged you, changed you, and motivated you to reach for higher ideals and visions. I hope it will have tested and stretched your leadership skills, and because of this effort, you more clearly see yourself, your visions, the value others have to offer, and ways and means of combining those to make the world, your business, your community, and your life better places. Each of us can choose to make a difference, can be effective within our circles of influence, and can improve the situation around us. What will you do?

Questions for Further Reflection

1. Write your personal charter. Are you able to identify your purpose in life? How you want to feel? If you cannot put on paper how you want to manage your own life, how could presume to do so for others?

2. Write a charter for your department or work group. How could you do that? Whom would you involve? Why?

3. Can you write a charter for your organization (even if you're not the CEO)? If you can't, you'll be listening (following) while others make the key decisions. If you've thought through the issues and challenges that a charter structure brings up, you'll be able to participate in strategic discussions.

4. What's the central lesson you've taken away from your use of this book? Page 401 in the workbook is a place you can capture this central point.

WORKBOOK

Although the space is minimal, the structure for writing personal, work-group, and organizational charters is presented in the workbook on pages 349–351.

CONTRIBUTING YOUR OWN CASELETS

Have you seen or experienced a situation involving the concepts introduced in this chapter? If so, and you'd like to contribute your experience/situation to our case data bank, please visit http://faculty.darden. virginia.edu/clawsonj/ and click on the "Contribute new caselets" button.

SECTION VII

WORKBOOK AND EXERCISES

26 | LEVEL THREE LEADERSHIP WORKBOOK

THE DIAMOND MODEL OF LEADERSHIP

Here's the basic leadership model developed in the book for your review (Figure 26-1).

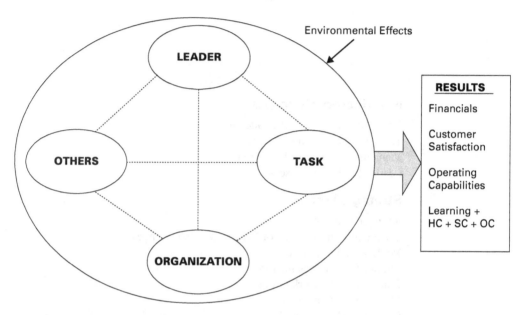

FIGURE 26-1   Diamond model of leadership

THE LEADERSHIP POINT OF VIEW

1. Do you *see* what needs to be done?
2. Do you *understand* all of the forces at play?
3. Do you *have the courage to act* to make things better?

OUTSIDE-IN VERSUS INSIDE-OUT: MANAGING THE FEAR OF REJECTION

Given the discussion in Chapter 1 on living outside-in versus inside-out, note here the things that you've done in the last week to avoid rejection. When have you changed what you would have said or done in order to be acceptable to others? How does this tendency impact your ability to lead?

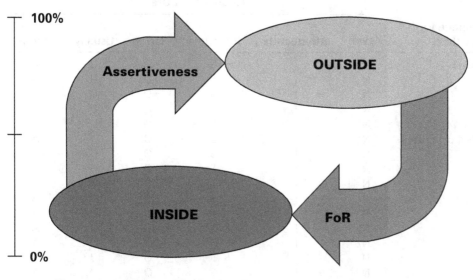

How much of your life do you live inside-out vs. outside-in?

FIGURE 1-1 Locus of control

LEADERSHIP LEVELS ASSESSMENT

Note how often you use the leadership tools and techniques listed below. If you have time and energy, ask five of your associates to rate, on the same scales, your attempts to influence others. Later, you can collect their answers anonymously and average them to compare with your self-perception.

Tool or Technique for Influencing Others	Frequency of Use					
	Never	**Infrequently**	**Sometimes**	**Often**	**Usually**	**Always**
Clear Commands	N	I	S	O	U	A
Telling stories	N	I	S	O	U	A
Data	N	I	S	O	U	A
Evidence	N	I	S	O	U	A
Careful listening	N	I	S	O	U	A
Threats (explicit or implied)	N	I	S	O	U	A
Arguing	N	I	S	O	U	A
Candor	N	I	S	O	U	A
Debate	N	I	S	O	U	A
Clarifying vision	N	I	S	O	U	A
Manipulating	N	I	S	O	U	A
Coercion	N	I	S	O	U	A
Yelling	N	I	S	O	U	A
Analysis	N	I	S	O	U	A
Self-disclosing	N	I	S	O	U	A

Theory

The theory behind this self-assessment tool was explained in different ways in Chapters 3, 16, 17, and 18. Each of the tools and techniques mentioned above tends to represent attempts to influence people's visible behavior, conscious thought, or underlying VABEs. Authoritors use a variety of tools and techniques. This instrument will give you a rough estimate of the proportion with which you use techniques of Levels One, Two, and Three. Because this is a self-report, it is susceptible to benign self-deception and lack of awareness of how others see you. If you collected data from associates, you'll be able to compare your answers with the average of your associates'.

Scoring Your Responses

Use the table below to score your responses above.

Q. no.	Tool or Technique for Influencing Others		Never	Infrequently	Sometimes	Often	Usually	Always
					Frequency of Use			
1	Clear Commands	L1	1	2	3	4	5	6
2	Telling stories	L3	1	2	3	4	5	6
3	Data	L2	1	2	3	4	5	6
4	Evidence	L2	1	2	3	4	5	6
5	Careful listening	L3	1	2	3	4	5	6
6	Threats (explicit or implied)	L1	1	2	3	4	5	6
7	Arguing	L2	1	2	3	4	5	6
8	Candor	L3	1	2	3	4	5	6
9	Debate	L2	1	2	3	4	5	6
10	Clarifying vision	L3	1	2	3	4	5	6
11	Manipulating	L1	1	2	3	4	5	6
12	Coercion	L1	1	2	3	4	5	6
13	Yelling	L1	1	2	3	4	5	6
14	Analysis	L2	1	2	3	4	5	6
15	Self-disclosing	L3	1	2	3	4	5	6

Totals			Percentage
Level One Scores			
Q1 + Q6 + Q11 + Q12 + Q13 =	___+___+___+___+___=		
Level Two Scores			
Q3 + Q4 + Q7 + Q9 + Q14 =	___+___+___+___+___=		
Level Three Scores			
Q2 + Q5 + Q8 + Q10 + Q15 =	___+___+___+___+___=		
		TOTAL =	100%

Calculate the percentage of each score by dividing each of them by the total and multiplying by 100. Please report your scores at http://faculty.darden.virginia.edu/clawsonj.

Interpreting Your Scores

Given your percentages above, what inferences can you draw about your typical attempts to influence others? Do you tend to use Level One, Two, or Three? What are the implications of this profile for your long-term leadership effectiveness?

STRATEGIC CHALLENGES

Everything we know about adult learning suggests that adults learn best when dealing with issues that are immediate and current for them. So what strategic challenges are you facing? "You" means your organization, your work group/function, and you personally. A strategic challenge is anything that affects your ability to develop and maintain a competitive advantage. A competitive advantage is defined by (1) superior value added, (2) difficulty in imitation, and (3) enhanced flexibility.

Organization	
Work Group	
Individual	

LEADERSHIP IMPLICATIONS OF MY STRATEGIC CHALLENGES

What *kind of leadership* traits and abilities will be necessary to meet the strategic challenges you identified above? In other words, what kind of leader do *you* need to become to meet and overcome the challenges you identified?

Organization Leadership	
Work-Group Leadership	
Self-Leadership	

MY LEADERSHIP FUTURE

Organizations I Expect to Lead	My Core Leadership Principles
In a reasonable scenario, what organizations will you be called on to lead over the course of the rest of your life? What's the next organization you expect to lead after the one you are in charge of now? The one after that? And so on.	What has your life taught you thus far about what it means to be an effective leader? What are your core leadership principles as of this moment?

CHARTER FOR MY ORGANIZATION

Mission (short)	
Vision (several pages: financial, customer, operations, people, etc.)	
Values (half page)	
Strategy (longest section: financial, marketing, operational, public image, rankings, tied to vision pieces)	
Short-Term Operating Goals (What metrics are key? Not too many)	
Leadership (Who's deciding all of these elements?)	

CHARTER FOR MY WORK GROUP

Mission	
Vision	
Values	
Strategy	
Short-Term Operating Goals	
Leadership	

MY PERSONAL CHARTER

Mission/Purpose & LD*int* (How I want to feel?)	
Vision	
Values	
Strategy	
Short-Term Operating Goals	
Leadership (Who's deciding all of these elements?)	

SURVEY OF MANAGERIAL STYLE[1]

Managers constantly identify desirable behavior both in themselves and in others with whom they work. Much of this behavior takes on a characteristic pattern. Knowing something about these different patterns may help us to become more-productive professionals. This instrument measures an aspect of managerial style. Please complete all items, and then score and interpret them according to the instructions that follow.

Note that people will often rate questions like those included in this packet in terms of how they think they **should** answer or in terms of the way that they would **like** to be. This approach is not the objective here. Please answer the items in terms of how much you agree with a statement as it applies to what you **actually do**. Give careful thought to your answers and remember that your results are only valuable to the extent that they reflect what you do, not what you think you should do. If you are a student now, consider the last job you held while you answer these questions. If you have not worked before, think about what you think your first job experience will be like.

As you complete the survey, please answer ALL items. You will probably note that some of the items on the survey are similar; this repetition is necessary to ensure that the survey information is statistically reliable. Please rate each item independently without regard to your responses to previous items. Finally, please note that there are no right or wrong answers on this survey.

SECTION I: GENERAL INFORMATION

1. How many major organizational levels are there in your organization, from the chief executive to the lowest rank?   _____

2. If the chief executive is at level one in your organization, at what numerical level are you?   _____

3. How many people report directly to you?   _____

4. Overall, how many people are in your reporting line or cone of authority? For example, in item 3, if you mentioned four direct reports and the first has 30 employees, the second has 49, then the overall number in your line of authority is 83.   _____

---

[1] This exercise was prepared by S. Gail Pearl under the supervision of James G. Clawson. I acknowledge the ideas and previous, related drafts contributed to this work by Paul D. McKinnon of Novations, Inc., and Dell Computer and Quentin Englerth of The World Group, Inc. Registered with Darden Publishing as "Survey of Managerial Style" (UVA-OB-0358). © 1988, 2001 by the University of Virginia Darden School Foundation, Charlottesville, VA. All rights reserved. To order copies, send e-mail to sales@dardenbusinesspublishing.com or visit www.dardenbusinesspublishing.com. No part of this publication may be reproduced, stored in a retrieval system, used in a spreadsheet, or transmitted in any form or by any means—electronic, mechanical, photocopying, recording, or otherwise—without the permission of the Darden School Foundation. Rev. 5/01.

SECTION II: MANAGEMENT-STYLE QUESTIONS (ITEMS)

Directions: For the following 30 items, read each item and rate it in terms of how much you agree that the item **describes you**.

On the scale, **SA** = Strongly Agree, **MA** = Moderately Agree, **LA** = Slightly Agree, **LD** = Slightly Disagree, **MD** = Moderately Disagree, and **SD** = Strongly Disagree.

Item	Agreement			Disagreement		
1. Managing company progress toward a vision represents a major portion of what I do in my job.	+SA	+MA	+LA	–LD	-MD	-SD
2. I am methodical in the way that I carry out my job responsibilities.	+SA	+MA	+LA	–LD	–MD	–SD
3. Most of my work-related activity is in thinking about the future of my organization.	+SA	+MA	+LA	–LD	–MD	–SD
4. I am a real "take charge" type of person.	+SA	+MA	+LA	–LD	–MD	–SD
5. Garnering commitment in people toward meeting some organizational goal represents a major portion of what I do in my job.	+SA	+MA	+LA	–LD	–MD	–SD
6. I am very decisive. When I must make a decision, I stick to it.	+SA	+MA	+LA	–LD	–MD	–SD
7. Whenever I must present information to a group, I typically speak without notes or outlines.	+SA	+MA	+LA	–LD	–MD	–SD
8. I focus my professional energies on envisioning the future of the organization.	+SA	+MA	+LA	–LD	–MD	–SD
9. Whenever I must present information to a group, I write out the speech, then read it to the group.	+SA	+MA	+LA	–LD	–MD	–SD
10. I am self-confident.	+SA	+MA	+LA	–LD	–MD	–SD
11. I focus my professional energies on getting people in my organization to build their commitments to our organization and its goals.	+SA	+MA	+LA	–LD	–MD	–SD
12. I learn best by diving in and seeing whether something works or doesn't work.	+SA	+MA	+LA	–LD	–MD	–SD
13. Most of my work-related activity is watching and managing indicators of organizational activity.	+SA	+MA	+LA	–LD	–MD	–SD

Item	Agreement			Disagreement		
14. I spend most of my professional time considering views of what my organization can become.	+SA	+MA	+LA	−LD	−MD	−SD
15. Most of my work-related activity is in pulling people together for the purpose of attaining an organizational goal.	+SA	+MA	+LA	−LD	−MD	−SD
16. I think that the most important aspect of my job is preparing for future needs of the organization.	+SA	+MA	+LA	−LD	−MD	−SD
17. I manage my professional time efficiently.	+SA	+MA	+LA	−LD	−MD	−SD
18. I think that the most important aspect of my job is persuading people to accept my vision for our organization.	+SA	+MA	+LA	−LD	−MD	−SD
19. I make an effort to participate in group activities.	+SA	+MA	+LA	−LD	−MD	−SD
20. I focus my professional energies on managing and monitoring my organization's progress toward a goal.	+SA	+MA	+LA	−LD	−MD	−SD
21. Thinking about what my organization might look like in the future represents a major portion of what I do in my job.	+SA	+MA	+LA	−LD	−MD	−SD
22. I am a predictable person. I think that people know what to expect of me.	+SA	+MA	+LA	−LD	−MD	−SD
23. At work I try to foster close personal relationships with my co-workers.	+SA	+MA	+LA	−LD	−MD	−SD
24. I spend most of my professional time in managing company progress toward a vision.	+SA	+MA	+LA	−LD	−MD	−SD
25. Solving problems in unstructured situations is an important part of what I do.	+SA	+MA	+LA	−LD	−MD	−SD
26. I would rather do something myself than delegate responsibility to someone else.	+SA	+MA	+LA	−LD	−MD	−SD
27. I learn on my own first, then apply what I have learned.	+SA	+MA	+LA	−LD	−MD	−SD
28. I spend most of my professional time convincing others in my organization to carry out a plan.	+SA	+MA	+LA	−LD	−MD	−SD
29. Whenever I must present information to a group, I speak while using an outline as a reference.	+SA	+MA	+LA	−LD	−MD	−SD
30. I think that the most important aspect of my job is looking at how my company is performing and determining what it needs to do to stick to the company plan.	+SA	+MA	+LA	−LD	−MD	−SD

NOTE: Do not read the rest of this note until you have completed the preceding questions!

SCORING AND INTERPRETING YOUR DATA

The Theory

This questionnaire was designed to measure aspects of your leadership style and preferences. Measuring leadership is not easy. Social scientists have been arguing for decades, even centuries, about the answer to the question, what makes a good leader? Out of this debate have emerged numerous theories about what makes a good leader. These theories, however, are often contradictory and confusing. We believe, in spite of the controversy about what the concept of leadership comprises, that a practical, immediate model of leadership would help focus the developmental efforts of managers on things they can begin doing now.

Given our reading of leadership studies and our observation of leaders in the world, we have concluded that leadership includes three fundamental clusters of skills and abilities: creating vision, garnering commitment to that vision, and monitoring and managing progress toward the realization of that vision.

Vision

Powerful leaders have a clear vision of where they want their organization to go. Vision is the view a person holds about what the organization will look like and do in the future. Obviously, some people have greater visions than others, and some have visions that extend further into the future than others. And some have visions that don't work or come to fruition. Each manager can, and we believe, ought to have a vision of his or her organization, what it can become, where it is going, how it should be operating, and what it should be like to work within it.

Vision is an essential part of leadership. Having a vision requires creativity; one must be able to think and see beyond the present timeframe and beyond the usual options. The ability to see ahead and the ability to see nontraditional alternatives are creative parts of leadership. So is the ability to frame the context of a business problem in broader terms that question current assumptions. The ability to incorporate these often unusual thoughts into a cohesive vision of the future of the company defines the first set of leadership skills.

Commitment

The ability to garner the commitment of others to one's vision is a key cluster of leadership skills. A leader may have a vision of what an organization can become, but unless others receive and become committed to that vision, it is unlikely to be realized. Leaders can create visions, but commitment, on the other hand, is offered by followers. This commitment allows leaders to build their visions into organizational realities. A key task of the leader, then, is to garner commitment from those people who are critical to his or her success.

Leaders may foster commitment in a variety of ways: public communications, one-on-one interactions, involving others in the decision-making process, and by modeling commitment to an idea, to name a few. However successful leaders go about it, they are able to develop and maintain strong commitments from others to their vision for the organization.

Monitoring and Managing Progress toward the Vision

The third cluster of skills in leadership that we see is the ability to monitor and manage progress of the organization toward the vision. For us, it is the bulk of "management" education today: ascertaining what the right measures are to monitor and the techniques and tools of getting those indicators to yield the right results. This aspect of leadership focuses on the details of the business. That we classify monitoring and management as a subset of leadership does not denigrate it. Instead, it points out that although managers can indeed be leaders, in our view, they need to augment their skills with the visionary and commitment-building skills as outlined. To us, management is a component of leadership. Ensuring that deadlines are met, objectives are achieved, and budgets are used appropriately are valuable and necessary (but not sufficient) leadership skills.

Leadership and the Survey of Managerial Style

Although some writers draw a provocative and dichotomous distinction between leadership and management, we believe they are closely related and that a consideration of the fluid relationship between them is more productive. Hence, we assert that leadership is not so much a question of whether someone is either a manager or a leader, but rather how much emphasis one places on the component skills of leadership including management. Knowing something about how a person tends to emphasize creating vision, garnering commitment, and monitoring and managing progress toward the vision can help that person in several ways. We will outline some of those elements, but first, let's score the data you generated.

Parts I and II of the Survey of Managerial Style (SMS) are designed to gather general information about you and to measure your self-perception of your work behavior regarding each of the three clusters mentioned. From these data, you can begin to construct a picture of your leadership profile, that is, how much you emphasize leadership overall and how much you emphasize the three different clusters of leadership as outlined previously. With these data, you can begin to consider how strong your desire to be a leader is and how your behavior is distributed across the three dimensions of leadership.

SCORING YOUR DATA

Step 1: On the Scoring Form that follows, you will see that values are associated with each point on the scale used in Section II of the survey:
For each section of the scoring form, indicate the score for each of the items listed. For example, if you checked "slightly agree" for item 3 and "agree" for item 8, your scores for these items would be 4 and 5, respectively. Please note that in Section II scoring, not all items are scored. The extra items in Section II of the survey are included to control measurement error and are not included in the individual scoring procedure.

Step 2: Sum the scores in each column to derive scores for vision, commitment, and management.

Step 3: Sum the scores for vision, commitment, and management to derive your total score.

Step 4: Compute proportional values for vision, commitment, and management by dividing the scale score by the total score.

Step 5: Next, complete the SMS Profile (Figure 26.2). The concentric circles represent varying strengths of leadership: the larger the circle, the greater the interest in leadership. The letters associated with each circle correspond to the total score obtained in Section II of the survey. Find the circle that corresponds to your total score in Section II and trace the circle with a heavy marking pen.

Step 6: In the scoring profile, there are 16 pie segments that you can use to create your profile. First, starting anywhere, draw a solid line from the center of the profile diagram out to the circle corresponding with your total score (A, B, C, D, or E). Note that each dotted pie segment represents about 22 degrees (22.5° exactly) out of the 360 degrees in a circle. If your V score was 40 percent of your total score, then $0.40 \times 360 = 144$ degrees. $144 \div 22$ degrees for each dotted segment = 6.5, so you would count 6.5 segments around the circle from your first line and draw a second one from the center to the circumference. This will be your "V" segment. Do the same for each of your other scores to produce a pie chart with three segments, one each for V, C, and M. Label each segment with their corresponding V, C, or M.

Note: When you finish scoring your data, you should have a pie chart with three divisions in it. The size of the pie reflects your overall interest in being a leader. The size of each of the three wedges (one each for creating vision, garnering commitment, and monitoring and managing progress toward the vision) indicates the relative strength of each leadership skill area. When you have completed the profile, proceed to the interpretation section.

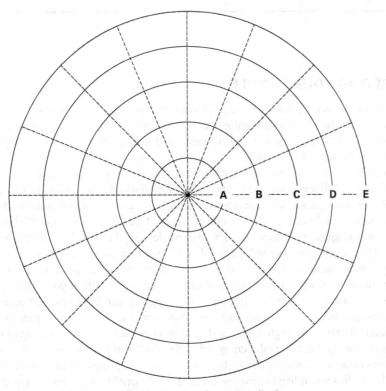

FIGURE 26-2 Survey of managerial style scoring display

SMS Scoring Worksheet

Item	Score	Item	Score	Item	Score
Item 3 _____ Item 8 _____ Item 14 _____ Item 16 _____ Item 21 _____		Item 5 _____ Item 11 _____ Item 15 _____ Item 18 _____ Item 28 _____		Item 1 _____ Item 13 _____ Item 20 _____ Item 24 _____ Item 30 _____	
Sum Vision _____ +		**Sum Commitment** _____ +		**Sum Management** _____ =	**Total Score**

Note: Maximum scale score = 30; minimum scale score = 5.

Score ÷ Total Score	% Score	× 360 = Degrees	÷ 22 = Number of Segments
Vision			
Commitment			
Management			

INTERPRETING YOUR PROFILE

The SMS Profile shows a graphical image of your current, self-assessed interest in leadership overall (the size of the circle you highlighted) and the relative strengths of your self-assessed skill clusters in visioning, garnering commitment, and managing progress toward your vision. Let's begin with the size of your circle.

The first thing to note is that it is not necessarily good or bad to desire to be or not to be a leader. People play different roles in life and in fact have influence in a wide variety of different situations. Leadership roles place demands on individuals just like all positions in life do; some people enjoy that set of demands, whereas others do not. Regardless of how superficially attractive the recognition and apparent influence of leadership roles may be (e.g., Wouldn't it be nice to be the divisional president?), unless one's personal skills and interests fit the demands of a particular leadership position, one is not likely to be happy or successful in that position. Thus, the size of your leadership pie is not a value judgment about you or your worth in your organization or in society. Rather, it is a description of your present preferences regarding leadership activities and as such can be used to make more-sound decisions about you and your work. If your pie is smaller than you "want" it to be, you might consider the various demands placed on leaders as reflected in the items in the survey. Do you really enjoy doing those activities? If not, perhaps you are not as enamored with being a leader as you may think at first blush. If you conclude you want your pie to be bigger; that is, that you'd like to have more interest in leadership activities, you might lay out a plan for involving yourself in more of those activities. Practice in leadership is like practice in other skill arenas—there's no substitute for it.

As for the relative strength of your V, C, and M segments, knowing something about your relative skills at visioning, garnering commitment, and managing progress can certainly help you to clarify where you're strong and where you might want to create a developmental plan. If your three V, C, and M segments are roughly the same size, you might conclude that your development as a leader so far has been relatively balanced. If one of the segments is, in your view, too large or too small, you might begin thinking about how you could develop that side of your leadership skill set. We offer some suggestions shortly.

Remember that these relative strengths are not fixed, nor are they necessarily equally desirable. Each profile, of course, will have different implications for your planning, development activities, and perhaps for the way you manage your work. Each profile will have certain strengths and weaknesses. The goal here is to be more aware of your leadership skill set and to be consciously managing your development in each arena.

Sometimes people will generate a small V score and comment, "Well, my current job doesn't require me to be visionary or to think strategically, so it's more a function of my job than of my personal characteristics." This hypothesis is interesting, because if it were true, we might expect to find a highly correlated relationship between "level in your organization" and "V score." The hypothesis seems to be that the higher our level, the more visioning our jobs will demand, and the more V we will manifest. In fact, after collecting data from around 600 business executives over several years and testing this hypothesis, it seems not to be true. A scatter diagram of the data points on "level in the organization" and "V score" shows points all over the quadrant, nothing approaching a diagonal trend line. This result suggests that people with strong visioning skills and habits can be found at virtually any level in most organizations. If this is the case, we might surmise that when it comes to being promoted, presumably to higher level jobs that require more visioning skills, all things being equal, the candidate with the stronger visioning skills is likely to be chosen. The implication here is clear: it's never too early to begin developing and strengthening your visioning skills.

Let's review some of the common VCM profile patterns. Look at the sample profiles shown here. What are the strengths and weaknesses of each of the profiles? Can you think of people, either at your work or in the public business eye, who seem to fit those profiles?

Now, compare your profile to the ones shown and your analysis of them. What strengths and weaknesses did you list for "your" profile? If you wanted to "strengthen" your profile, what could you do?

INTERPRETIVE ALTERNATIVES

For each of the following alternative profiles, write your interpretation of what it might mean to the individual or corporation that has it. See if you can identify individuals who fit each pattern.

SUGGESTIONS FOR STRENGTHENING YOUR SMS PROFILE

If one of your VCM segments is smaller than you'd like, you may be thinking about things you could do over time to "round out" that flat spot on your profile. Again, it is a choice you make, not something you "have" to do in any sense. If you set this goal, here are some ideas for helping you strengthen that area.

Skill Cluster	Suggestions for Strengthening
Visioning	• Read journals and magazines on future trends (e.g., **Futurist**). • Spend five minutes a day thinking about where your organization should be in 10 years. • Read books on strategic thinking (e.g., *Every Business Is a Growth Business, Leading the Revolution, The Art of the Long View, The Experience Economy*). • Engage in conversations with colleagues about where you and they think the business should go in 10 years. • Clarify where you'd like to be in 10 years. • Think about where your business was 10 years ago and the changes that have occurred, then try to project the same volume of the next 10 years. • Identify the strategic challenges facing your firm and then think through what you would do to manage each of them and why.
Garnering Commitment	• Reflect on your reputation among your peers. What is it? What would it take to clarify it? • What techniques do you usually use to influence your peers? How many different techniques do you use? What new ones could you add? • Practice listing and discussing the major pros and cons of key issues in the next several meetings you are in. See if you can demonstrate a balanced view to your peers on each topic/issue rather than just buttressing your opinion with a one-sided view. • Try listening for complete understanding of your peers' ideas before you present your own. • Pay attention to how often you interrupt people. Try to reduce that frequency.
Managing Progress toward the Vision	• List on paper at the end of each day what you did, however small, that moved your organization toward its goals. • List your goals (personal and professional) for the next three months. • Invite those who report to you to do the same and then discuss them. • Read your company's annual report in detail. Can you see progress? If not, what can you do to improve it? • What could you delegate to others so you could focus on getting the important things done? • How clear are you in performance reviews about exactly what you want the other person to do? How well do you listen to what they want to do and how you can help make that happen?

CONCLUSION

Leadership is comprised of many skills. This exercise was intended to help you identify your current self-assessment on three clusters of key leadership skills: visioning, garnering commitment toward your vision, and managing progress toward it. We hope that the scores on the V, C, and M scales and the graphical portrayal of their size and relative strengths will help you think about your own leadership profile and how you might go about strengthening it—if your goal is to do so. This instrument is only one among many. We encourage you to utilize all the data you can as you continue your quest to strengthen your leadership.

SMS/VCM DATA FORM

Group: _____   Date: _____/_____/_____

Directions: Please complete this data form, and mail it to Professor Jim Clawson, Box 6550, Charlottesville, VA 22906 OR you can enter your data at http://faculty.darden.virginia.edu/clawsonj/index.htm. Your data will be added to the SMS database for aggregate analysis and comparative database development.

1. Number of major levels in your organization: _____
2. Your organizational level (Please express level as a number):   _____
3. Number of direct reports: _____
4. Overall number in your reporting line of authority: _____
5. Your age: _____
6. Gender (Please encircle):   Male   Female

Source	Score	Source	Score	Source	Score
Item 3	_____	Item 5	_____	Item 1	_____
Item 8	_____	Item 11	_____	Item 13	_____
Item 14	_____	Item 15	_____	Item 20	_____
Item 16	_____	Item 18	_____	Item 24	_____
Item 21	_____	Item 28	_____	Item 30	_____
Total		**Total**		**Total**	
Vision	_____	**Commitment**	_____	**Management**	_____

Note: Maximum scale score = 30; minimum scale score = 5.

MY PERSONAL LEADERSHIP DEVELOPMENT GOALS
(KEEP, LOSE, ADD)

Following your class discussion of personal blind spots and the personal change process, consider your own leadership style as you now understand it and note the aspects of your leadership style that you'd like to keep, lose, or add. You can use this assessment as your personal leadership development plan.

Keep	Lose	Add

LEADERSHIP INTELLIGENCE SELF-ASSESSMENT

Following the discussion of leadership and intelligence and/or reading Chapter 12, assess your intelligence in each of the following categories by making check marks as appropriate. You may wish to check your self-assessment with others who know you well.

	Low	Medium	High
Intellectual Intelligence (IQ): Inherited abilities Curiosity Discipline Range of interests			
Emotional Intelligence (EQ): Recognizing emotions in yourself Managing your emotions Using productive self-talk Avoiding emotional hijackings			
Social Intelligence (SQ): Recognizing emotions in others Caring about the emotions of others Counseling others in managing their emotions			
Change Intelligence (CQ): Recognizing the need to change Understanding the change process Skill in managing the change process			

MANAGING YOUR ENERGY[2]

In the midst of their busy lives, most people focus their organizational efforts on time management. Books have been written about how to help people with this issue (e.g., *How to Get Control of Your Life and Your Time* and *The Time Trap*). Many consultants make a nice living advising people how to manage their time. Indeed, whole companies have sprung up and made a profitable existence trying to advise people about how to manage their time (e.g., Franklin-Covey, Inc.). Clearly, time is a critical resource and an important input into our productivity and enjoyment of life. But your productivity and enjoyment do not depend on your time management alone. Many factors affect our outputs and satisfactions in life. They include our talents, our choices, and surely, our personal energy level. In fact, the amount of energy we bring to our allotted time on the earth (beginning with the fixed 168 hours per week) may well determine much more about how much we give and get in life than our allocation and use of time.

The choices we make about how we eat, how we use our time, how we sleep, how we exercise, and how we manage our relationships all contribute to the amount of energy we have in life. We would probably be better off if we paid more attention to our energy management than to our time management. Consider, for example, the case of physicians. A typical emergency room–attending physician or a typical thoracic surgeon might work up to 110 hours a week. How do they have enough energy and stamina to live this kind of life, year after year? How would their energy level compare with that of an assembly line worker who spends 40 to 45 hours a week on the job? Is it just because physicians are dealing with life-and-death situations? Are they workaholics? Or are they managing their personal energy levels more effectively?

One of the best definitions of leadership is the ability to manage energy, first in yourself and then in those around you. If your interactions with people are building their energy, you are probably leading them. If your interactions are sucking energy out of people, you may be in charge, but you're probably not leading.

The goal of this exercise is to help you begin to clarify those things in your life that energize you and those that de-energize or debilitate you. Use the following table to help clarify how your choices affect your energy level. You may find the references at the end interesting in helping you to learn more about how you might manage your energy on a regular basis.

---

[2] This note was prepared by James G. Clawson, professor of Business Administration, Darden Graduate School of Business Administration, University of Virginia, and includes some ideas of Dr. Curt Tribble, M.D., formerly of the UVA Thoracic Surgery Department. It was written as a basis for class discussion rather than to illustrate effective or ineffective handling of an administrative situation. Registered with Darden Publishing as "Energy Management Exercise," (UVA-OB-0716). Copyright © 2000, 2003 by the University of Virginia Darden School Foundation, Charlottesville, VA. All rights reserved. *To order copies, send an e-mail to* or visit sales@dardenbusinesspublishing.com or visit www.dardenbusinesspublishing.com. *No part of this publication may be reproduced, stored in a retrieval system, used in a spreadsheet, or transmitted in any form or by any means—electronic, mechanical, photocopying, recording, or otherwise—without the permission of the Darden School Foundation.*

Category of Activities	Things That Energize Me	Things That Drain My Energy
Activities		
Foods		
Sleep		
Relationships		
Entertainment		
Exercise		
Other		

ENERGY ACTION ITEMS

Once you have listed as many items as you can under the categories in the table, reflect on the two columns. Identify one to five things you could do to increase your energy level. Try one or two of these things for the next week, and make daily, written observations about how your energy level is affected by them. These self-observations will be important in helping you see the connection between your choices and your energy level.

Energy management goals for the coming week:

1.

2.

3.

Reflections

Once you have tried one or two things for a week, make some written inferences about their impact on you and your energy level. Write down these insights so you can see them and refer to them.

Which ones do you want to continue?

What makes it difficult to continue doing them?

What can you do to ensure that these goals become positive, repeating habits?

ENERGY AND LEADERSHIP

If you agree with the notion that leadership is about managing energy, first in yourself and then in those around you, you might ask yourself, Do people see me as a net energy sucker or a net energy contributor? Why? This assessment may help you think about how you might raise your energy level when you're dealing with yourself and then others.

References

Covey, Stephen. *Seven Habits of Highly Effective People*. New York: Simon & Schuster, 1991.

Lakein, Alan. *How to Get Control of Your Time and Your Life*. New York: Dutton, 1974.

Maas, James B. *Power Sleep*. New York: Harper Collins, 1999.

MacKenzie, R. Alec. *The Time Trap*. New York: AMACOM, 1997.

Robbins, Anthony. *Unlimited Power*. New York: Simon & Schuster, 1997.

LIFE'S DREAM EXERCISE[3]

This exercise is designed to help you identify your life's dream(s). We will explore two definitions of "life's dream." First, we refer to an "external life's dream," or D*ext* based on achievements and accomplishments, which is the typical definition that most people understand. D*ext* relates to one's early dreams in life to become something or accomplish something. Sometimes people refer to their D*ext* as, "What I want to be when I grow up." The central question for D*ext* is, what do you dream of doing or becoming? Examples might be "CEO of a company," "a pilot," "wealthy," or "a good parent." Many people refer to their life's dream when they mean their "goal in life." Goals are not dreams, especially as we are using the term here.

Second, we will also refer to an "internal life's dream" or D*int*. An internal life's dream is defined by our emotional experiencing. In other words, the target for understanding D*int* is to focus on your feelings. For D*int*, the question is, how do you want to feel? Examples might be "fully engaged," "easy speed," "productive," or "peaceful."

A danger comes in focusing too much on either D*ext* or D*int*. If you focus on D*ext* to the exclusion of D*int*, you may find yourself one day wealthy and miserable. If you focus on D*int* to the exclusion of D*ext*, you may find yourself peaceful and poor. The challenge is to pay attention to both D*ext* and D*int*. In our experience, most people focus heavily on D*ext*, so the more common error is to live relatively unaware of one's experience.

The following questions are designed to help you identify your D*ext* and D*int* and to distinguish between them. In our experience, it is more difficult to define D*int* than D*ext*. So, if you cannot write satisfactory answers on your first try, don't despair. It may take considerable thinking and reflection before you settle on a D*int* with which you are comfortable. Some people seem to figure them out quickly; others may take a year or more to find the "right" wording and comprehensiveness.

---

[3] This exercise was prepared by James G. Clawson, adapted from ideas by Doug Newburg. Copyright © 2001, 2003 by the University of Virginia Darden School Foundation, Charlottesville, VA. All rights reserved. *To order copies, send an e-mail to* sales@dardenpublishing.com. *No part of this publication may be reproduced, stored in a retrieval system, used in a spreadsheet, or transmitted in any form or by any means—electronic, mechanical, photocopying, recording, or otherwise—without the permission of the Darden School Foundation.*

IDENTIFYING YOUR EXTERNAL LIFE'S DREAM

Use the following table to draft your external life's dream, or D*ext*.

1. What do you want to be doing at age _____? (Add 15 years to your current age.)	
2. What do you want to be at age _____? (Add 15 years to your current age.)	
3. What do you want people to remember you for?	
4. What do you want your epitaph to say?	
5. When you were little, what did you want to become? What happened to that dream?	
6. If you were independently wealthy now, what would you do?	
7. Meld all of the preceding answers into one description of your D*ext*.	

Note that all of these questions focus on things that you DO, or positions or titles that you HOLD. These can all be measured externally, that is, by observation by others.

IDENTIFYING YOUR INTERNAL LIFE'S DREAM

The next set of questions asks you to consider your emotional dream by focusing on feelings. Again, we presume that you have had a discussion in class exploring the concept of resonance. Try to be as descriptive as you can while still being concise. Finding the right words is key. Short answers such as "happy" may be true, but not especially helpful. How do you feel when you are happy? Long answers may be confusing and obfuscating. Try to distill your descriptions down to a phrase.

1. When in your life have you experienced "flow" or "resonance"? What were you doing?	
2. How did you feel when you were in flow? What aspects of it were satisfying to you?	
3. How are you feeling when you are performing at your peak and enjoying it?	
4. When were you most productive in your life? How did it feel?	
5. What kind of experience are you willing to work for?	
6. When you are "successful," how do you feel?	
7. Use your preceding answers to help you distill a single D*int* here: HOW DO YOU WANT TO FEEL ON A DAILY BASIS?	
8. What does it take to feel that way? (Preparation)	
9. What keeps you from feeling that way? (Obstacles)	
10. What does it take to get that feeling back? (Revisiting Your Dream)	
11. What are you willing to work for? (Energy Cycle)	

We expect that this will not be your final draft of either your D*ext* or your D*int*. We encourage you to keep these definitions handy and to reflect on them regularly. Revise and refine them as your "eyes-open" dreaming becomes clearer. The following table may help you track your life's dreams as they evolve over time.

Date	External Life's Dream (D*ext*)	Internal Life's Dream (D*int*)

IMPLEMENTING YOUR LIFE'S DREAM

The next challenge after identifying your D*int* will be to utilize it. In my experience, I have been so conditioned to focus on "to-do" lists and external achievements, it has become difficult to remember to focus on D*int* and then refer to it regularly. In other words, I, like millions of others, get caught in the "duty cycle," bouncing back and forth between work/preparation and obstacles and forget to "revisit my dream." Here are a couple of suggestions that will help you recognize how much you focus on D*ext* and how to focus more on D*int*.

1. Keep your D*int* definition posted somewhere in your morning routine, perhaps in your bathroom, to remind you of it.
2. Every time you find yourself making a "to-do" list for the day or week, be sure to add the full definition (not just "live my D*int*") to your list.
3. If you keep a daybook or a PDA schedule, mark each day that you live your D*int* with a symbol (perhaps a "D"). At the end of the month as you scan your daybook, you can see how many days out of the month you lived your experiential dream and whether you're getting better at it.

BALANCING YOUR LIFE[4]

Leaders in the modern era face the significant challenge of finding the right balance in their lives between work, family, self, and other interests. The constantly growing and competing demands of life on many fronts push us all to make daily behavioral decisions about how we spend our time and talents, often without taking the time to think clearly about the consequences of those decisions. Making those decisions without a clear picture of their consequences can be devastating for us all—leaders, managers, and employees.

Some people naturally seem to find a balance that fits them and their own definition of success over the years. Others have a more difficult time finding it. Far too many at middle or late-middle age find that they are deeply dissatisfied with the way their lives have turned out. Erik Eriksson in *Childhood and Society*, for example, outlined eight ages of humankind, each characterized by binary dilemmas. Even though it is admittedly and primarily a Western approach, his eighth stage in which older people wrestle with feelings of despair or integrity is instructive. His observation is that later in life we see that it's too late to change much in our lives. Either we realize that life has come together much in the way that we hoped and dreamed it would (integrity in the sense of integration into a complete whole) *or* we realize that life hasn't turned out as we thought it would, and because it's too late to change, we begin to despair. Eriksson's assertion is confirmed in the publication of books such as *The Failure of Success*; *Must Success Cost So Much?*; *Career Success/Personal Failure*; *Workaholics*; *Work, Family and the Career*; *Tradeoffs: Executive, Family and Organizational Life*; and the former Secretary of Labor's book, *The Future of Success*, quoted at the beginning. All of these books examine the ways in which our daily, weekly, and yearly choices repeated over and over structure our lives—sometimes in ways that we later deeply regret. The potential tragedy is to make those choices without thinking or anticipating their outcomes.

What we can learn from these commentaries is not to seek a common "right" balance. Instead, we should be aware of our current choices of time and energy allocation and make adjustments that point us toward our personal definitions of success in life, not just "career." The often-quoted line, "How many of us, on our deathbeds, with our last gasp will breathe, 'If only I had spent more time at the office!' " makes the point. No one wants to make daily decisions that add up over a lifetime to a balance that one realizes, in retrospect, was not what one would have consciously chosen.

This exercise is designed to help you see your current behavioral allocation of time and how it matches up with your personal definition of success. The exercise is built upon some fundamental assumptions:

1. We all have a limited, but equal, 168 hours per week of time.
2. We all have some freedom in choosing how we spend that time.
3. We all have some talent to apply to the time we have.
4. We all have various dimensions to our lives that we choose, consciously or unconsciously, to develop or ignore.

A list of these dimensions is given in Table 26-1. Some of the definitions may not be just what you immediately think, so please look at the parenthetical definitions so you'll know what we mean for each dimension. You may be able to think of other dimensions of life that should be

[4] This exercise was prepared by James G. Clawson. Copyright © 1986, 2007 by the University of Virginia Darden School Foundation, Charlottesville, VA. All rights reserved. *To order copies, send an e-mail to* sales@darden publishing.com. *No part of this publication may be reproduced, stored in a retrieval system, used in a spreadsheet, or transmitted in any form or by any means—electronic, mechanical, photocopying, recording, or otherwise—without the permission of the Darden School Foundation.*

TABLE 26-1 Aspects of Adult Life
Professional (working, earning in career and job)
Financial (managing money affairs)
Material (collecting things)
Recreational (playing)
Physical (exercising)
Sleep
Intellectual (learning, committing to memory, thinking)
Emotional (feeling, sensing, being aware of emotions)
Spiritual/Philosophical (praying, meditating, communing, reflecting)
Marital (with your spouse)
Parental (with your children)
Familial (with your parents)
Social (with your friends)
Societal (community work)
Sexual
Political (political work)
Ecclesiastical (church work)

added to the list. The point is that, because life consists of a number of facets, by choosing to spend time, energy, and talent in some areas, we necessarily neglect others. Alex Horniman often declares, "Excellence is a neurotic lifestyle," suggesting that to excel, most of us have to focus our time and attention in powerful ways. When we engage intensely and consciously, as in the case of an Olympic-hopeful athlete, we acknowledge the sacrifice that we are making in other aspects of life and become singular in our focus. Others prefer to have a more rounded lifestyle and, in so doing, may recognize the sacrifice of excellence in any one area. The challenge is to know what your choices are and what they mean for you. Perhaps this exercise can help.

Completing the exercise requires several steps:

1. Clarify your personal definition of success. Write it down in the following space. What does it mean to you now to be "successful?" Research shows that a person's definition of success may vary over that person's lifetime, but we need a place to start. You may not have thought about it before, so it may take some reflection to clarify what it means to you to be "successful." Approach this exercise broadly—consider what it means to be successful in life, not just your career. It's your life, only you can live it, and you are the primary shaper of it. What do you want it to be? Try to be specific as you can. "To be happy" may be true, but it's not especially helpful. What will make you happy? The clarity of the definition will make the exercise more powerful for you.

Success is:

Keep your definition where you can refer to it often; revise it as you feel it necessary. For the ship with no destination, any port will do, but the ship with a destination has a course and a purpose to its sailing. You may wish to consider the various aspects in Table 26-1 again as you write your personal definition. Reflect on the comment by the famous comedienne Lily Tomlin: "I always wanted to be somebody. Maybe I should have been more specific."

You may also wish to include some principles of measuring success along the way. That is, what if success were not a single place or condition? In that case, you may wish to define "success" in terms of the directions you're moving at any one point in time. This approach would not require you to define what you'd look like at age, say, 65, rather only what processes you'd like to have in place as you move toward that milestone. This is a process-oriented definition, not a "point" definition.

2. Assess your current level of development. On the wheel diagram in Figure 26-3 assess your current level of personal development on each dimension. Use a scale of 1–10, where 1 is completely undeveloped and 10 is perfectly developed, that is, at a world-class level. A "10" on the physical dimension, for example, would be an Olympic medalist; a "1" would be not being able to walk around the block comfortably. The zero point is at the center of the diagram. When you have marked your level of development on each dimension, shade in the area of your development across all dimensions. The result will show your perception of your life's developmental balance at this point. You may find the shape of your profile instructive as you think about how it compares with your definition of success. This diagram is the central piece of this exercise.

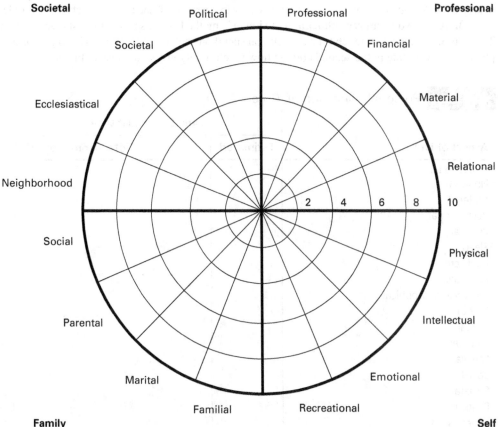

FIGURE 26-3 Personal developmental profile

TABLE 26-2 Stages of Growth

1. **Embryonic:** Unaware that the dimension exists and therefore pays no attention to it.
2. **Youth:** Aware that the dimension exists but does little intentionally to develop it.
3. **Adolescent:** Aware that the dimension exists but believes that it can be developed later; therefore, does a little about developing it now and then moves on.
4. **Young Adult:** Aware that the dimension exists and concerned about developing it. Has a superficial awareness that one must work at developing it all along and makes modest efforts to develop it.
5. **Mature Adult:** Aware that the dimension exists and concerned about developing it. Has a deep awareness of the need to develop the dimension constantly and is working hard to develop it.

Secondly, you can draw your goal or target profile on this same Balance Wheel using another color. This target profile will help you highlight the gaps in your present level of development.

One way of thinking about movement from the center of the diagram or embryonic level of development is in terms of "maturity." Using the following definitions, you can gauge your development on each dimension. These terms are intended to be descriptive, not evaluative.

The definitions in Table 26-2 suggest another way of delineating your development. You may wish to keep these definitions in mind as you determine how to assess and shade in your development profile.

3. Assess your current allocation of time. Using the list of aspects of life shown again in Table 26-3, estimate how much time a week you spend on each one. Without reviewing your day planner, just estimate in the second column how much time you spend on each dimension.

TABLE 26-3 Personal Allocation of Time

	Time Spent Last Week	
Aspect of Life	**Estimated**	**Total (from Table 26-4)**
Professional		
Financial		
Material		
Recreational		
Physical		
Sleep		
Intellectual		
Emotional		
Spiritual/Philosophical		
Marital		
Sexual		
Parental		
Familial		
Social		
Societal		
Political		
Ecclesiastical		
Total	(168?)	

TABLE 26-4 Allocating Time over the Aspects of Adult Life								
Time Spent during the Week of _____/_____/_____								
Aspect	**Mon**	**Tue**	**Wed**	**Thu**	**Fri**	**Sat**	**Sun**	**TOTAL**
Professional								
Financial								
Material								
Recreational								
Physical								
Sleep								
Intellectual								
Emotional								
Spiritual								
Marital								
Sexual								
Parental								
Familial								
Social								
Societal								
Political								
Ecclesiastical								
Other:								
Actual Total	24	24	24	24	24	24	24	168
Shadow Time								
Total Time								

Note daily your use of time in each of the following life dimensions: Working, Sleeping, Exercising, Managing Personal Hygiene (dressing, eating, bathing—you might include this in Physical if you don't want a separate look at your exercise), Reading and Learning (Intellectual), Managing Finances, Recreating (including most television), Attending to Material Things, Parenting, Being with Significant Other, Being with Parents, Being with Friends, Working in the Community, Working in Political Events, Being in Church, Meditating/Communing/Praying. Include your "shadow hours" in parentheses. Then summarize the results in Table 26-4.

If you have time, you may wish to actually keep track of your time for a week. Like our perceptions of our spending habits, our perceptions of how we spend our time do not often match up with the realities. You can use the form in Table 26-5 to keep a weekly time diary and then transform your results in Table 26-4 to show how much time you spent during the week on each dimension. Then enter the totals in the third column in Table 26-3.

As you work through this exercise, you will notice that some dimensions overlap, that is, you could be working on more than one dimension at the same time. If you work construction, you are probably getting lots of exercise while you are working. Likewise some aspects of work may involve new learning that stretches your mind intellectually, and spending time socially can be as emotionally powerful as when you are comforting grieving friends. You might deal

TABLE 26-5 Time Diary for One Week							
Time	Mon	Tue	Wed	Thu	Fri	Sat	Sun
12:00 midnight							
2:00 a.m.							
4:00 a.m.							
6:00 a.m.							
8:00 a.m.							
10:00 a.m.							
12:00 noon							
2:00 p.m.							
4:00 p.m.							
6:00 p.m.							
8:00 p.m.							
10:00 p.m.							

with this overlap by first allocating the 168 hours that you have each week to the dominant aspect and then returning to add "shadow hours" in parentheses to indicate that time spent elsewhere really had developmental impact in another area. For instance, if you find that your work requires you to be learning (not just repeating what you can already do), you might assess how much of your work time is like that and add that number to the Intellectual box in parentheses. In this way, your week of 168 hours is leveraged; you can assess how rewarding on how many dimensions your time choices are. If you play golf with your peers, for example, you can count that time as recreation, but probably not include any shadow hours in parental time. If you play golf as a family, you could have recreation time and shadow time with marital and parental aspects. You may find it interesting to see how much of your work time has shadow benefits to other aspects of life; that is, are you learning at work? Are you growing socially at work? You may find that you have no time, shadow or otherwise, for a particular dimension or that the only time you have for a dimension is shadow time. It may be that your shadow time is not as productive as "hard time" in which your attention and efforts are concentrated. You decide what to include and how effective both hard and shadow times are. When you're done, you can add up your total hard hours and your shadow hours in Table 26-5.

If you don't have time to complete an actual diary (which is also interesting—it's all data), think back on the previous week and try to allocate the time you spent on each dimension. Use Tables 26-4 and 26-5 to help you, and then enter your retrospective look in the third column in Table 26-3.

4. Create a profile of your current time allocation. You can create a profile in two ways. First, you could use the second wheel diagram in Figure 26-2 to mark and fill in your time allocations. The wheel is the same size and shape as the one in Figure 26-1, but the scale is now "Five times the hours of time" so that "10" means you spend 50 hours a week on this dimension. Include your shadow time in this calculation. I realize that some of you may be working 60, 70, 80, or even 90 hours a week. If so, extend your Professional pie segment beyond the outer circle in scale to your current level of work.

An alternative approach here would be to use a spreadsheet graphing program, if you have one, to create a pie chart of how much time you spent on each dimension last week using the data from step 3. The result won't match the format of your developmental profile, but you can use it to compare mentally. [You could also create a wheel by hand using a compass and protractor by drawing a circle and calculating the percentage of time for each dimension ((number of hours/168) * 100) and multiply by 360 to get the number of degrees around the circle for each dimension. For example, if you spent 55 hours working, then (55/168) * 100 = 33% * 360 degrees = 120 degrees of arc around the circle for that dimension.]

5. Compare and reflect. Now, consider the relationships between your definition of success, your goal or target profile, your current self-assessed level of development, and your current time allocations. The following questions may help guide your reflection:

1. What connections do you see? What disparities or gaps?
2. Do any "flat spots" on either wheel diagram concern you?
3. How do they relate to your definition of success and your allocation of time?
4. Do you want to do anything about them? How much time and talent will it take?
5. What will the impact of your current time allocation be on your development over the course of your life? That is, where logically does your present time allocation pattern take you 20 or 30 years into the future?

References

Derr, Brooklyn. *Work, Family and the Career.* New York: Praeger Special Studies, 1980.

Evans, Paul, and Fernando Bartolome. *Must Success Cost So Much?* New York: Basic Books, 1980.

Fassel, Diane. *Working Ourselves to Death.* New York: Harper Collins, 1990.

Greiff, Barrie S., and Preston K. Munter, *Tradeoffs: Executive, Family and Organizational Life.* New York: New American Library, 1980.

Korman, Abraham K. *Career Success/Personal Failure.* New York: Prentice Hall, 1980.

Lee, Mary Dean, and Rabindra N. Kanungo. *Management of Work and Personal Life.* New York: Praeger Special Studies, 1984.

Marrow, Alfred. *The Failure of Success.* New York: Amacom, 1972.

Machlowitz, Marilyn. *Workaholics.* Reading, MA: Addison-Wesley, 1977.

Reich, Robert. *The Future of Success.* New York: Alfred Knopf, 2001.

LEADERSHIP LANGUAGE EXERCISE

After a discussion of "The Language of Leadership" as outlined in Chapter 20, think about the basic concepts and consider how you'd like to strengthen your ability to communicate as a leader.

CLEAR: (How can I make my communications more clear?)	
RESPECTFUL: (How can I be more respectful to my audiences?)	
STIMULATING: (How can I be more memorable in my style?)	
CONGRUENT: (How authentic am I? Can I be more genuine?)	
LISTENING: (How could I learn to listen better?)	

LEADERSHIP STEPS ASSESSMENT (LSA)[5]

Leadership has many different components. This exercise offers the opportunity to assess your leadership activity on several of these dimensions. You will be asked in Part I to rate a series of descriptors (adjectives) for how well they currently describe you and then in Part II to rate a number of sentences as to how well they apply to you. You should answer regarding how you *currently* see yourself, not how you think that you should be or would like to be. There is no benefit to trying to "game" the assessment—just make the best assessment you can of how you *currently* are on items in the inventory.

Important: Please do not read ahead. After you have completed all of the items, you can go on to the theory, scoring, and interpretation sections. These sections will explain the nature of the instrument and what it is measuring. If you read ahead, you may bias your responses and reduce the value of the data to you.

The instrument will take between 30 and 60 minutes to complete. Please leave yourself enough time to complete the instrument and work through the scoring and interpretation. When you are ready, please turn the page and begin.

---

[5] This exercise, UVA-OB-0733, was prepared by James G. Clawson. Copyright © 2001 by the University of Virginia Darden School Foundation, Charlottesville, VA. All rights reserved. *To order copies, send an e-mail to* sales@darden publishing.com. *No part of this publication may be reproduced, stored in a retrieval system, used in a spreadsheet, or transmitted in any form or by any means—electronic, mechanical, photocopying, recording, or otherwise—without the permission of the Darden School Foundation.*

PART I: DESCRIPTORS/ADJECTIVES

For this part, please reflect on your activities at work and your relationships with your colleagues at work. This section consists of 18 items that are descriptors: adjectives that may or may not describe you. Rate yourself using the 7-point scales:

1 = Does not describe me at all

2 = Describes me rarely

3 = Describes me occasionally

4 = Describes me half of the time

5 = Describes me more than half the time

6 = Describes me usually

7 = Describes me all of the time

These Terms Describes Me:	Never			Half of the Time			Always
1 Anchored	1	2	3	4	5	6	7
2 Dreamer	1	2	3	4	5	6	7
3 Encouraging	1	2	3	4	5	6	7
4 Supportive	1	2	3	4	5	6	7
5 Relentless	1	2	3	4	5	6	7
6 Congratulatory	1	2	3	4	5	6	7
7 Centered	1	2	3	4	5	6	7
8 Visionary	1	2	3	4	5	6	7
9 Sees the good in others	1	2	3	4	5	6	7
10 Reorganizer	1	2	3	4	5	6	7
11 Determined	1	2	3	4	5	6	7
12 Praising	1	2	3	4	5	6	7
13 Self-aware	1	2	3	4	5	6	7
14 Trend Spotter	1	2	3	4	5	6	7
15 Good coach	1	2	3	4	5	6	7
16 Organizational architect	1	2	3	4	5	6	7
17 Persistent	1	2	3	4	5	6	7
18 Rewards Others	1	2	3	4	5	6	7

This completes Part I of the assessment. Please go on to complete Part II without skipping ahead.

PART II: DESCRIPTIVE PHRASES

The items in this section are statements which you may or may not agree describe you or your current beliefs. Remember that you are assessing your *current behavior and beliefs*, not how you think you should behave. As with Part I, you should rate each item on a scale from 1 to 7. Here, a score of 1 means, "I disagree completely with this statement" or, "I do not behave like this," whereas a score of 7, conversely, should be assigned to statements you fully agree with, or behaviors that match very much with how you behave.

It will take you about 15 minutes to complete the 18 statements in this section. Be honest with yourself. If in doubt, remember that first impressions are often the best guide. If you are not working now, answer with regard to your last job.

		Does NOT describe me or my beliefs				↔	Describes me or my beliefs VERY well	
19	I am clear on what I stand for.	1	2	3	4	5	6	7
20	I spend time envisioning what our company should become.	1	2	3	4	5	6	7
21	I look for the talents others have to offer.	1	2	3	4	5	6	7
22	I try to remove the barriers to getting good work done.	1	2	3	4	5	6	7
23	I am determined to achieve my goals.	1	2	3	4	5	6	7
24	I like to congratulate people on a job well done.	1	2	3	4	5	6	7
25	I could write down my core beliefs and values.	1	2	3	4	5	6	7
26	I enjoy imagining where we should be going.	1	2	3	4	5	6	7
27	I try to see what others have to contribute.	1	2	3	4	5	6	7
28	I often reorganize, trying to find a better way.	1	2	3	4	5	6	7
29	I am persistent in my pursuits.	1	2	3	4	5	6	7
30	Good leaders reward progress openly.	1	2	3	4	5	6	7
31	I am clear on what I will and will not do to succeed.	1	2	3	4	5	6	7
32	I have a clear picture of what the company should be.	1	2	3	4	5	6	7
33	I look for people's strengths rather than their weaknesses.	1	2	3	4	5	6	7
34	Good leaders work hard to support their people and their efforts.	1	2	3	4	5	6	7
35	I never give up.	1	2	3	4	5	6	7
36	One should always praise progress, however small.	1	2	3	4	5	6	7

This concludes Part II. Please read below to learn about the theory underlying the instrument and how to score your responses.

PART III: THE THEORY

There are many theories about the elements that make up leadership. The exercise you completed and the scoring you will do in a moment are based on a model of leadership designed not only to describe necessary components of leadership, but also to provide a framework for improving your own leadership ability. This framework identifies six key leadership principles:

1. Clarifying your center
2. Clarifying what's possible
3. Clarifying what others can contribute
4. Supporting others so they can contribute
5. Being relentless
6. Measuring and celebrating progress

Let's make sure the six concepts are clear; then we will lay out the scoring system. We use the term "clarifying" in the first three concepts because we believe that one may never really finalize one's core values, vision for the future, or the ways in which others can help achieve that vision. Each of these leadership principles will continue to emerge and evolve as we progress through life. The "clarifying" measures here refer to ongoing processes of leadership.

1. **Clarifying Your Center.** We use the term *center* in the sense in which it is often used in Asian philosophy to refer to one's center of gravity or one-point, either physically (as in martial-arts traditions) or spiritually (as in meditative practices). By "clarifying your center," we mean becoming clearer about what you stand for, what you value, and your personal ethical and moral rules. Clarity of core values is a key leadership characteristic, because if one is not internally clear about priorities, what is good to do, what is ethically acceptable, and so on, the influence of others may sway one's behavior away from achieving one's goals or from ethical means of achieving them. A clear set of personal values helps one have confidence in one's chosen course. The absence of a well-defined center is likely to encourage one to respond to others rather than to lead them.

2. **Clarifying What's Possible.** Leadership efforts will go nowhere if there is no target, no direction, or no vision of where one believes the organization (or one's part of an organization) should be headed. As with one's core values, seldom is a vision of the future fully formed at any one time. Rather, it emerges and evolves the more one thinks about how one wishes the future to be. Often, this visioning is intentional. Leaders work to clarify the futures they want to see created, first in their minds, and later in reality. This clarification is not so much trying to identify what will be as it is identifying what one wants to be.

3. **Clarifying What Others Can Contribute.** Leaders are not leaders without followers. People with a tendency to make immediate and negative judgments about others may miss what others have to contribute to their visions. The ability to see a wide range of possibilities in what others might add to your team is a key part of effective leadership. The challenge is to assess others in terms of their potential capabilities, rather than with a hypercritical eye. The question is, what can they do? rather than, what they cannot do? An initial critical and negative interpretation of others will tend to shut down possibilities and perhaps significant support for one's goals and visions.

4. **Supporting Others so They Can Contribute.** By support, we mean reorganizing the surrounding work context in a way that removes barriers and frees up employee creativity,

energy, and productivity. Effective leaders understand that even the best vision and the most motivated workforce will be hampered by poorly designed organizations. Consequently, they are working hard to make sure that organizational barriers to high performance are minimized or eliminated. Structure and the various organizational systems, including recruiting and selection, reward, appraisal, and education, need to be aligned and synchronized for the people in them to be working efficiently.

5. **Being Relentless.** Powerful leaders don't give up. Persistent striving for your goals in the face of adversity requires a high level of self-confidence and belief in the value of your goals. Without such strong commitment and an internal drive to achieve, one can become diverted from one's goals. Clarifying one's center is important here: if you know what you are aiming for and why, your commitment will likely be stronger and relentless pursuit of that ideal easier. A fine line divides relentlessness from stubbornness; they are not the same. Good leaders are flexible, especially on means, but rigidly determined when it comes to outcomes. Without a strong internal drive, however, would-be leaders falter before achieving their goals.

6. **Measuring and Celebrating Progress.** Most people need encouragement as they work. It's hard to keep plugging away at a distant goal without ever getting some sign that you're on the right track. Without some measure of progress, motivation dies. Strong leaders continuously identify and set appropriate intermediate goals on the path toward their vision or goal; they celebrate goals reached with the people who contributed to the achievement. The central feature of such celebration is the recognition of a job well done, as well as achievement and of the joy of doing, rather than receiving a tangible reward.

These six principles of effective leadership constitute values of leadership—principles that effective leaders hold to be true. The next section describes how to score your responses on items designed to measure these six principles.

PART IV: SCORING PROCEDURE

To calculate your scores, go back to Parts I and II and record the score for the items as numbered in each column here. When you have completed adding your scores, fill in the graph on the next page to create your profile.

	CYC	CWP	CWOCC	RTS	R	CP
Item Numbers	1 =	2 =	3 =	4 =	5 =	6 =
	7 =	8 =	9 =	10 =	11 =	12 =
	13 =	14 =	15 =	16 =	17 =	18 =
	19 =	20 =	21 =	22 =	23 =	24 =
	25 =	26 =	27 =	28 =	29 =	30 =
	31 =	32 =	33 =	34 =	35 =	36 =
Totals =						

Note that the maximum score possible in each column is 42 and the minimum possible score is 6. After you have calculated your total scores, turn the page and display them graphically.

PART V: DISPLAYING YOUR SCORES

Chart your scores on the following diagram to develop a profile of your LSA scores.

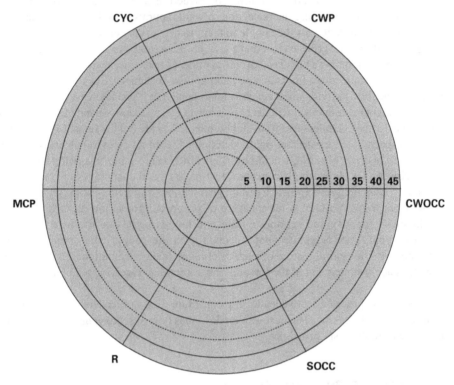

Leadership Steps Scoring Diagram

PART VI: INTERPRETING YOUR SCORES

The six concepts used as the basis for this self-assessment measure have been tested and discussed for many years in the classroom with practicing executives. We do not doubt their validity and usefulness as elements of leadership. This measure itself is a new tool, and we are in the process of establishing the norms for responses from people of different leadership abilities and strengths. Although we do not have enough data to provide normalized distributions of scores, we do have preliminary comparative data from 59 people from three executive education programs. These programs included middle-level and upper-middle-level managers. You can compare your scores with the maximums, minimums, averages, and standard deviations from these 59 executives from a variety of industries. See the data and chart in **Exhibit 1**. For each of the following concepts, consider your score, and if you feel you would like to work on that aspect of your leadership, read that section for some suggestions on how to do that.

Clarifying Your Center

People with strong core values have a calmness about them, tend to be less defensive, and are more likely to stand firm in a storm than those whose core values are more ambivalent or uncertain. People with clear values are more likely to adhere to those values in situations in which they are pressured to depart from the core values. In Stephen Covey's terms, people who have clarified their core values have won the private victory before the public battle.[6] If your score on clarifying your center was lower than you would have liked, you might consider some exercises that would help you clarify your core leadership values and principles.

1. Begin by sitting down and writing out a list of the core beliefs you have developed thus far in your life. Putting them on paper makes it easier to see and examine them, and subsequently to modify and polish them.
2. Complete the Life's Story Assignment exercise in which you are invited to write your life's story in 400 words or less, chart your ups and downs, and then draw some conclusions about the lessons you learned from those experiences. These major turning points in life tend to reveal our core values or to shape them.
3. Ask those who know you well, perhaps family members or work associates, to make a list of the things that they believe you stand for. Their take will be a behavioral one in that they will infer your values from what you do and how you behave around them. This list may vary from your "espoused values" in exercise 1. Reviewing the gaps, if any, can be enlightening as you consider what you think your core values are and what others observe them to be.
4. Take a week or a weekend and enroll in a seminar devoted to values clarification. These seminars are taught in many large cities periodically and can be helpful in guiding you to a deeper understanding of just what is important to you.
5. Pursue a specific values clarification exercise such as the Life and Career Values Card Sort, which is a chapter in the book, Self-Assessment, and Career Development.[7] It will ask you to lay out cards in a matrix and arrange them repeatedly until you get a "comfortable" picture of your values and their relative strength.

Clarifying What's Possible

This concept, ironically, is about "reflecting on the future." Higher scores indicate that you spend time thinking about what the future should hold for you and your company. Lower scores may indicate a lack of time or interest for such thinking or a tendency to restrict thoughts and plans

EXIHIBIT 26-1   Comparative Data on Six Steps to Leadership

The following data come from three executive education programs on leadership and include people with a variety of responsibilities. Respondents range in age from 54 to 29, averaging 42.4 years of age. There were 42 men and 17 women in this sample. The numbers of employees that report to them range from 405 to 0 with an average of 52. Additional comparative data are available on www.CareerNextStep.com.

	Center	Vision	Others	Support	Relentless	Celebration
Maximum =	40	40	41	42	41	42
Minimum =	21	12	20	25	14	13
Average =	31.86	27.20	32.34	31.42	33.12	32.46
Std Dev =	4.3	6.2	4.4	3.6	5.3	5.4
N =	59					

[6] See Stephen Covey, *The Seven Habits of Highly Effective People* (New York: Simon and Schuster, 1989), Chapter 2.
[7] James G. Clawson, John P. Kotter, Victor A. Faux, and Charles MacArthur, *Self-Assessment and Career Development*, 3rd ed. (Upper Saddle River, NJ: Prentice Hall, 1993).

to short-term goals or continuation of the present. People without a view of what they want to achieve will have a hard time convincing others of where to go. Clarifying for yourself and others where you want to go is in itself an act of leadership. Some call it dreaming. Robert Greenleaf (*Servant Leadership*) describes it this way:

> Not much happens without a dream. And for something great to happen, there must be a great dream. Behind every great achievement is a dreamer of great dreams. Much more than a dreamer is required to bring it to reality; but the dream must be there first.

Clarifying the future in part requires a willingness to break out of current thinking. As W. Edwards Deming once said, "Every system is perfectly designed to produce the results it is achieving." To get somewhere else, leaders must see a new and different future. If your scores here are lower than you would like, you might consider the following suggestions:

1. Set aside time weekly, perhaps an hour, to focus just on thinking about what your company, your part of the company, or you will look like in five years.
2. Read a futuristic novel like *The Gate to Women's Country*[8] or *A Canticle for Liebowitz*[9] or *Dune.*[10] Then reflect on what kinds of changes must have happened to have created those worlds and whether you see signs of them around you.
3. Learn about scenario planning and begin to practice its principles. It is much more than simply guessing about "best-case/worst-case" outcomes. *The Art of the Long View*[11] by Peter Schwartz is a good place to start.
4. Think of your parents or grandparents. What changes have they seen in their lives? What changes might you expect during your lifetime? What changes would you like to see?
5. Subscribe to a new magazine, for example, *The Futurist*, that you feel will stimulate your thinking about societal trends that may or may not affect your industry. Commit to reading one or two articles in each issue.
6. Go visit some places you've never been before: a soup kitchen, a rehab center for children, a ballet, a country with a different culture, or a business you've never been to. Ask yourself why things are working the way they do and what the underlying assumptions must be to make them so.
7. Seek out people unlike yourself at social functions, and ask them about their view of the world and what they see. This exercise is an easy thing to do—most people are quite happy to talk about their views. The challenge will be to listen to their new ideas without interrupting or tuning out.

Clarifying What Others Have to Contribute

This principle has to do with looking for what people can do rather than what they cannot do. Higher scores tend to indicate that you are willing to listen to a wide range of people, see their ideas for what they are worth, and look for abilities in people rather than their faults ("seeing the glass half-full rather than half-empty").

Many of us are professionally trained to find fault. Perhaps we learned it at an early age from our parents for whom our work was never quite good enough. Perhaps we learned it from our education where we learned systematic ways of striving for perfection or "six-sigma quality"

---

[8] Sherri Tepper, *The Gate to Women's Country*, reissue ed. (Dillon, CO: Spectra, 1993).
[9] Frank Herbert, *Dune* (ACE Charter, 25th Anniversary Edition: February 1, 1996).
[10] Walter M. Miller, Jr., *A Canticle for Leibowitz*, reprint ed. (Dillon, CO: Spectra, 1997).
[11] Peter Schwartz, *The Art of the Long View* (New York: Currency, 1996).

programs. Whatever the source, if we learned a habit of seeing what's not there as opposed to what is there, our attempts to lead may be thwarted. Followers who feel constantly "not good enough" find it difficult to be enthusiastic and motivated. If you would prefer higher scores on this dimension, you might consider the following:

1. For the next five conversations, consciously focus in your mind on the positive qualities of the person you're talking with. Find occasion in the conversation to compliment them even if the conversation doesn't seem to call for it. For example, if at the end of a conversation you haven't found an opportunity to compliment someone, try something like this: "You know, Elliott, I just wanted you to know that I really admire your ability to manage so many things. You do a great job at being organized."
2. You might also, at the end of a day, consider the subordinates who work for you and make a written list of their strong points. A simple list will do, but it's important to write it down. A translation occurs between thought and written expression that is important to cross.
3. In five conversations this week, discuss with your subordinates their potential skills. You might begin by asking what goals they have for developing skills in the coming year, and then you might suggest one or two that you think they could achieve—that would make them much more valuable to the organization. Identify ways in which you would like to see your subordinates grow, describing the specific skills that you'd like them to develop. Then, in a private conversation, mention to them your desires and beliefs that they could, in fact, develop those skills. Offer to help them if you can.
4. The next time you face a difficult task, identify those who could help you accomplish it and ask them if they feel up to it. Give them a significant responsibility and comment on how you are confident that they can accomplish the task. Most people will work hard to rise to this kind of occasion.
5. Think of the people at work of whom you may have a modest opinion. Stop for a moment and think of their strong points. Why did they get the job they have? What skills do they bring to their jobs? Can you identify what they *can* do as opposed to what they cannot do?

Our guess is that you may find some of these suggestions, at first blush, "silly" or "hard to do." That's the point. If they came naturally to you, you would have scored higher on "clarifying what others have to contribute." Try these simple suggestions for a week, and see if they don't make a difference in what you "see" in your colleagues.

True followership is a voluntary process; unless your followers are responding voluntarily, you are not really leading them. The challenge here is to see what others have to offer toward your goals. Some people in leadership roles are fundamentally negative, searching for things to criticize and ways to find fault with others. This tendency to overlook underlying strengths and skills can be demotivating for the people involved. Powerful leaders look and listen for possibilities in the people they work with, asking themselves what these people can do rather than what they cannot do.

Supporting Others so They Can Contribute

Sometimes organizational structures or systems can inhibit the efforts people make to accomplish the organization's goals. Jack Welch's well-known Work Out effort in the late 1980s and early 1990s was an attempt to remove the bureaucratic red tape that many said was slowing down decision-making and development cycles. Effective leaders look for ways to remove these organizational barriers by redesigning the systems that create them. Perhaps the reward system encourages behavior A while management hopes that behavior B will occur.[12] Or the information system produces a volume and range of reports that few can interpret and use. Or the decision-making structure stifles innovativeness and creativity. The list is potentially limitless. When leaders are oblivious to the ways in which their organizations constrain their workforce, they are thus tolerating the resulting cynicism and frustration in their workforce.

If you would like to improve your scores on this dimension, you might consider the following suggestions:

1. Survey your direct reports and have them survey theirs and find out what organizational systems they believe get in the way of getting key tasks done. Then, ask them to come up with better designs, sooner rather than later.
2. Walk around your organization and ask, What process, policy, or procedure recently has gotten in the way of you doing your best work? How might we change it?
3. In your performance reviews, include a series of questions that focus on the efficiency of your organizational processes, procedures, and systems. Expect that each subordinate will pay attention and be making suggestions—specific suggestions—for how to mend them. This activity is consistent with one of the four corners of the balanced scorecard.[13] If you pay attention to this aspect of your organization, so will your subordinates and you'll find yourself repeatedly acknowledging organizational adjustments here and there that you had no idea were getting in the way.

Being Relentless

Relentlessness is a hallmark of effective leadership. Powerful leaders don't easily give up. If you find that your score on this dimension was lower than you would have liked, you might try the following:

1. On your current to-do list, mark the items that are overdue. Ask yourself why, and write down the reasons. If you've overcommitted, consider the old saw, "Less is more." Even though it's true that people who do more often get more assignments, there is a point at which one's ability to produce declines. Pay attention to this point.
2. Review your New Year's resolutions and how often you've made them and not followed through. Spend some time thinking seriously about why that is. What do you need to do to follow through on a goal?
3. Identify a small thing you'd like to try doing differently (perhaps from the preceding lists of suggestions) and commit to yourself to try it for three days. If three days is too long, try one or two days. Then pick another—just to see if you can commit to something for more than a short period of time. Broken promises to ourselves on any dimension undermine our self-confidence and capacity for following through.
4. Identify the longest project or endeavor you have stayed with in your life. Reflect on why you stayed with it rather than others. What about it that captured your intensity and determination? How might you carry those characteristics to other endeavors?

---

[12] See Steve A. Kerr, "On the Folly of Hoping for A while Rewarding B," *Academy of Management Journal* (August 15, 1988): 298.

[13] See R. S. Kaplan and D. P. Norton, "Balanced Scorecard: Measures That Drive Performance," *Harvard Business Review*, January 1992, 92105.

Measuring and Celebrating Progress

Followers need to know that they are doing well. A few can make that assessment themselves, but most people thrive on positive feedback, whether it is from others or from the results of their work. Few of us have the stamina to persist in lengthy pursuits without some encouragement from positive feedback—whether it is social or natural. If you'd like to strengthen your skills in this area, consider the following:

1. List the celebrations you have at home or at work. What do you celebrate? How often do you celebrate? How long do you typically wait between celebrations?
2. How often do you praise the people around you? When was the last time you praised someone, a family member or a co-worker?
3. When someone you know achieves something, how long do you spend congratulating them? Do you tend to skim over their accomplishments and point to the next hurdle or assume that their progress was "normal" or "expected"?
4. How do you celebrate when you accomplish something you're working on? How long does your celebration last? How do you make the transition from accomplishment to commitment to the next objective?

CONCLUSION

We hope that this exercise has been of value to you by adding to your insights about leadership and your own leadership skills. Perhaps it has helped you identify an area or two in which you wish to work to improve your leadership abilities.

LSA DATA COLLECTION

Please take a moment to fill out the data page that follows and go to the Web site http://faculty.darden.edu/clawsonj and click on the LSA SURVEY button to input your data there. This will help us expand our database. Thank you!

Date and Group (course or program)	
Age	
Gender	Female/Male
College major	
Job title	
Job functional area (student, finance, marketing, operations, IT, etc.)	
Number of people who report to you in your responsibility cone (all the way down)	
Scores:	
Clarifying Your Center	
Clarifying What's Possible	
Clarifying What Others Can Contribute	
Supporting Others so They Can Contribute	
Being Relentless	
Measuring and Celebrating Progress	

LIFE'S STORY ASSIGNMENT[14]

People who are willing to share their life's story with others often find that this simple approach has powerful results. These short, biographical sketches help associates and subordinates understand the leader's background and "where they are coming from." These sketches also tend to be easy to remember and strong communicators of the storyteller's basic beliefs. In this sense, telling your life's story can be a powerful Level Three Leadership tool. This assignment is designed to help you clarify your Level Three Leadership story and has three parts.

1. Write your life's story in 400 words or less. This word limit will require you to condense, focusing on the highlights and major events. You can use the blank sheet provided if you wish.
2. In the table on page 395, list the key events you mentioned in the 400-word story in the left column, one event per row. Then note the extent to which each event was an emotional up or down or whether it was neutral. Then try to summarize the key learning from that event in the third column. How did this experience shape your life? What did it teach you? What did you learn from each experience about leadership? How did this event contribute to your current model of leadership?
3. Using the blank chart that follows, chart the key events in your life in terms of their emotional height, chronologically from left to right. Then, label the peaks and valleys with the events they represent.

    Your primary use for being clear about your life's major events and their impact on your leadership beliefs will be at various times and places in the future when, as a leader, you need to connect with your people and let them know why you believe what you do and where your motivations come from.

---

[14] This exercise, UVA-OB-0692, was prepared by James G. Clawson. Copyright © 1999 by the University of Virginia Darden School Foundation, Charlottesville, VA. All rights reserved. *To order copies, send an e-mail to* <u>sales@darden</u> <u>publishing.com</u>. *No part of this publication may be reproduced, stored in a retrieval system, used in a spreadsheet, or transmitted in any form or by any means—electronic, mechanical, photocopying, recording, or otherwise—without the permission of the Darden School Foundation.*

MY LIFE'S STORY IN 400 WORDS OR LESS

_____

_____

_____

_____

_____

_____

_____

_____

_____

_____

_____

_____

_____

_____

_____

_____

_____

_____

_____

_____

_____

_____

MY LIFE'S STORY KEY EVENTS TABLE

Key Event	Emotional Impact (+5 to 0 to –5)	Key Learning or Insight

LIFE'S STORY EMOTIONAL IMPACT CHART

Life's Story Emotional-Impact Chart

Source: Adapted from Noel Tichy, *The Leadership Engine* (New York: HarperCollins, 1997).

ASSESSING THE MORAL FOUNDATION OF YOUR LEADERSHIP[15]

After you have discussed the moral foundation of leadership, use this form to begin your leadership team assessment. First, make copies of the form and give one to each member of your team and have them assess your team. Second, answer each question according to your view of your current management team and its interactions. Third, collect each team member's answers (anonymously if you wish) and summarize the data. Fourth, hold a team meeting in which you discuss the results (average scores, variation, difference from expectations or hopes) and make joint plans for how to improve your scores. To answer, circle the number that represents the percentage of the time that each principle describes your leadership team.

Cornerstone Principle	Percentage of the Time That This Principle Describes Our Team									
1. Truth-Telling: We tell the truth to each other and don't hide things or talk behind others' backs. We know where each person stands.	10	20	30	40	50	60	70	80	90	100
2. Promise-Keeping: We keep our promises to each other no matter how large or small.	10	20	30	40	50	60	70	80	90	100
3. Fairness: We treat each other fairly and do not try to take advantage of each other.	10	20	30	40	50	60	70	80	90	100
4. Respect for the Individual: We show respect for each other and other members of our organization in our speech, action, and courtesy.	10	20	30	40	50	60	70	80	90	100

Team Scoring	Team Average	My Assessment	Difference
Truth-Telling Promise-Keeping Fairness Respect for the Individual			

Note again that each of these principles is really only a different window onto the same central concept. In other words, if you tell the truth, you have to keep your promises. If you are fair, you'll have respect for the individual.

[15]This instrument, UVA-OB-0734, note was prepared by James G. Clawson. Copyright © 2001 by the University of Virginia Darden School Foundation, Charlottesville, VA. All rights reserved. *To order copies, send an e-mail to* sales@dardenpublishing.com. *No part of this publication may be reproduced, stored in a retrieval system, used in a spreadsheet, or transmitted in any form or by any means—electronic, mechanical, photocopying, recording, or otherwise—without the permission of the Darden School Foundation. Revised 08-04.*

TEAM SELF-ASSESSMENT[16]

The following 17 items invite your assessment of your work team in terms of dimensions shown in the current literature to describe highly effective teams. Please rate your current team on each item as to how well the item describes what you do (where 1 = NOT TRUE about your team, 4 = TRUE HALF THE TIME, and 7 = ALWAYS TRUE about your team) and then follow your instructor's instructions for developing aggregate indicators.

ITEM	Not True			True Half the Time			Always True
1. We share leadership roles rather than relying on one strong, clearly focused leader.	1	2	3	4	5	6	7
2. We hold the team as well as individuals accountable rather than just looking at individuals for accountability.	1	2	3	4	5	6	7
3. We have developed a team purpose that we deliver rather than just assuming the team's purpose is the same as the organization's.	1	2	3	4	5	6	7
4. We have real collective products rather than a collection of individual products (strung together at the end).	1	2	3	4	5	6	7
5. We encourage open-ended discussion and active problem-solving in meetings rather than trying to run efficient meetings.	1	2	3	4	5	6	7
6. We measure our performance directly by assessing our collective work-products rather than measuring performance indirectly (e.g., financial performance of the business as a whole).	1	2	3	4	5	6	7
7. We discuss, decide, and DO real work together rather than discussing, deciding, and delegating real work to others to do.	1	2	3	4	5	6	7
8. We try to establish links with key resource organizations well BEFORE we need them rather than waiting for an emergency to make contact.	1	2	3	4	5	6	7
9. We only do real teamwork in teams rather than trying to get lots of people involved on basically individual tasks.	1	2	3	4	5	6	7
10. We don't refer to ourselves as a team when in fact we manage members as individuals (rewards, etc.).	1	2	3	4	5	6	7

---

[16] This exercise, UVA-OB-694, was prepared by James G. Clawson. Copyright © 2000, by the University of Virginia Darden School Foundation, Charlottesville, VA. All rights reserved. *To order copies, send an e-mail to* sales@dardenpublishing.com. *No part of this publication may be reproduced, stored in a retrieval system, used in a spreadsheet, or transmitted in any form or by any means—electronic, mechanical, photocopying, recording, or otherwise—without the permission of the Darden School Foundation.*

ITEM	Not True			True Half the Time			Always True
11. Our "leaders" only specify the desired end states and leave the means to the team members rather than trying to specify both means and ends.	1	2	3	4	5	6	7
12. We have a good mix of talent on our team. We have the right mix of people involved.	1	2	3	4	5	6	7
13. We ensure that our team has a discrete, identifiable job to do rather than dividing the work into such tiny pieces that members cannot see the "whole" that they are contributing to.	1	2	3	4	5	6	7
14. The things we "have to do" and "cannot do" are clear and unambiguous to all team members.	1	2	3	4	5	6	7
15. We ensure that the team has the appropriate organizational support it needs to get its job done rather than demanding big, hairy goals, but skimping on organizational support.	1	2	3	4	5	6	7
16. We assume that all team members need to be learning and growing rather than assuming that we have all the talent and learning we need.	1	2	3	4	5	6	7
17. We have devised internally real-time, analog measures of our performance which we monitor and watch continuously rather than relying on measures others have developed that only show historical performance after the fact.	1	2	3	4	5	6	7

References

Hackman, Richard J. 1998. "Why Teams Don't Work." *Leader to Leader* (Winter), 24 ff. Peter Drucker Institute, Claremont College, adapted from author's chapter in *Applications of Theory and Research on Groups to Social Issues*, edited by R.S. Tinadale, J. Edwards, and E.J. Posavac. New York: Plenum Publishers.

Katzenbach, Jon R., and Douglas K. Smith. 2005. "The Discipline of Teams." *Harvard Business Review* (July), R0507P.

Katzenbach, Jon R., and Douglas K. Smith. 2001. *The Discipline of Teams* (New York: John Wiley & Sons).

Kelley, Robert, and Janet Caplan. 1993. "How Bell Labs Creates Star Performers," *Harvard Business Review* (July–August), 93405.

Meyer, Christopher. 1994. "How the Right Measures Help Teams Excel," *Harvard Business Review* (May), 94305.

SYSTEMS AND PROCESSES IN MY ORGANIZATION THAT NEED REDESIGNING

After reading the chapter on leading organizations, think about the systems and processes in your organization that aren't working well. List them and begin thinking about how you'd redesign them if given the chance. The well-known GE Workout process included five steps: (1) describe the current system, (2) describe the results (—) produced by the current system, (3) describe the "new" system, (4) describe the intended benefits, and (5) describe what it would take to make the changes.

Dysfunctional Systems	A Better Design Would Be ...

MY PERSONAL MODEL OF CHANGE

In the space below, draw your personal model of how change occurs. You may or may not wish to draw from the models presented in Chapter 24.

WHAT DO I WANT TO DO NEXT?

Given your work with this book in a course or an executive education program, what few things do you wish to do next with regard to developing your Level Three leadership skills?

1.
2.
3.
4.
5.
6.
7.
8.

YOUR CENTRAL POINT

What's the most important thing you learned from the book about becoming a more influential leader to yourself, to your work group, and to your organization? If you focus on too many goals, you may not reach any of them. If you pick one and stick to it, you may make some real progress. What would that thing be?

APPENDIX

Leadership Theories

Leadership has been widely studied over a long period of time, yet it remains an elusive phenomenon to understand and develop. This note is intended to offer a relatively quick overview of some of the major leadership theories. The theories are grouped according to the research approaches behind them (as in *Leadership in Organizations*, 4th ed., by Gary Yukl, Prentice Hall, New Jersey, 1998). The six categories are the trait, behavior, power and influence, situational, charismatic, and transformational approaches. Simple direct statements of the main assumptions or conceptual points related to each theory comprise the bulk of the note. This note does not intend to portray these theories in their entirety nor to reflect their complexity, only to give you an introduction to the key points.

TRAIT APPROACH

The trait approach—one of the earliest used to study leadership—emphasizes the personal traits of leaders. The underlying assumption is that certain people possess innate characteristics that make them better leaders than others.

The "Great Man" Theory Of Leadership

Leaders are born, not made. Leadership ability arises from innate, internal traits. Some have them, and some don't. It is our job to figure out what these characteristics are so we can use them to identify potential leaders. No amount of training or coaching will make a leader out of someone who does not possess these traits.

Stogdill's Leadership Traits

From R. M. Stogdill, *Stogdill's Handbook of Leadership*, revised and expanded by Bernard M. Bass (New York: The Free Press, 1981).

This text summarizes more than 3,000 books and articles on leadership spanning the period from 1947 to 1980. Most attempts to pursue the "Great Man" avenue of research found difficulty in identifying specific traits; however, Stogdill was able to summarize some generally common traits among effective leaders.

> The leader is characterized by a strong drive for responsibility and task completion, vigor and persistence in pursuit of goals, venturesomeness and originality in problem solving, drive to exercise initiative in social situations, self-confidence and sense of personal identity, willingness to accept consequences of decision and action, readiness to absorb interpersonal stress, willingness to tolerate frustration and delay, ability to influence other persons' behavior, and capacity to structure social interaction systems to the purpose at hand. (1974 ed., p. 81)

TRAITS

Adaptable to situations	1 2 3 4 5 6 7 8 9 10
Alert to social environment	1 2 3 4 5 6 7 8 9 10
Ambitious and achievement oriented	1 2 3 4 5 6 7 8 9 10
Assertive	1 2 3 4 5 6 7 8 9 10
Cooperative	1 2 3 4 5 6 7 8 9 10
Decisive	1 2 3 4 5 6 7 8 9 10
Dependable	1 2 3 4 5 6 7 8 9 10
Energetic (high activity level)	1 2 3 4 5 6 7 8 9 10
Dominant (desire to influence others)	1 2 3 4 5 6 7 8 9 10
Persistent	1 2 3 4 5 6 7 8 9 10
Self-confident	1 2 3 4 5 6 7 8 9 10
Tolerant of stress	1 2 3 4 5 6 7 8 9 10
Willing to assume responsibility	1 2 3 4 5 6 7 8 9 10

SKILLS

Clever (intelligent)	1 2 3 4 5 6 7 8 9 10
Conceptually skilled	1 2 3 4 5 6 7 8 9 10
Creative	1 2 3 4 5 6 7 8 9 10
Diplomatic and tactful	1 2 3 4 5 6 7 8 9 10
Fluent in speaking	1 2 3 4 5 6 7 8 9 10
Knowledgeable about group task	1 2 3 4 5 6 7 8 9 10
Organized (administrative ability)	1 2 3 4 5 6 7 8 9 10
Persuasive	1 2 3 4 5 6 7 8 9 10
Socially skilled	1 2 3 4 5 6 7 8 9 10

"Great Man" Theory Traits

We offer a simple 10-point scale here in case you wish to assess yourself on some of these dimensions.

Maccoby's Leader

From Michael Maccoby, *The Leader* (New York: Ballantine, 1981).

I need hardly say much to you about the importance of authority. Only very few civilized persons are capable of existing without reliance on others or are even capable of coming to an independent opinion. You cannot exaggerate the intensity of man's inner irresolution and craving for authority.

—Sigmund Freud

The best of all leaders is the one who helps people so that, eventually, they don't need him. Then comes the one they love and admire. Then comes the one they fear. The worst is the one who lets people push him around. Where there is no trust, people will act in bad faith. The best leader doesn't say much, but what he says carries weight. When he is finished with his work, the people say, "It happened naturally."

—Lao Tzu

The four main ideal types of character orientation to work each carry positive and negative potentials:

Type	Positive Potential	Negative Potential
Craft	Independent and hardworking	Inflexible and suspicious
Enterprise	Entrepreneurial and daring	Instrumental and uncaring
Career	Professional and meritocratic	Bureaucratic and fearful
Self	Experimental and self-developing	Escapist and rebellious

Craft is the traditional orientation to independent, inner-directed, skilled work.... **Enterprise** is at best an entrepreneurial, risk-taking orientation.... **Career** is the orientation of the technical expert, at best with professional standards and a meritocratic belief that measurable performance should be rewarded by promotion.... **Self** is the orientation of the new man in an age where abundance is taken as a right and technology provides limitless possibilities. The self-oriented person sees himself in a world of constant change and few roots, where he must create his identity and relationships and use himself as an instrument at work. At best he is experimental, tolerant, willing to be involved in an equitable enterprise that promises enriching experience and continued personal growth. At worst, the self-oriented are indeed rebellious, disloyal, centerless, and escapist into an unproductive inner world of fantasy. (Preface)

Maccoby names four main types of leaders:

Administrators: Traditional expert engineer, accountant, lawyer/craftsman
Strongmen: Distrust can be overcome by bearing down: "jungle fighter"
Gamesmen: Risk-taking, innovative, adaptable, inspiring in competition
Developers: New products, develop people, participative

The new social character is evolving most rapidly in the affluent, technically educated, large urban populations here and in the other industrial democracies as well. Like all social characters, it contains both negative and positive tendencies. It is a social character more oriented to self than to craft, enterprise or career. (p. 42)

CHARACTERISTICS OF THE NEW LEADER   Intelligent, ambitious, willful, optimistic, persuasive, influenced by religious and political thought, an able competitor, critical of traditional authority, willing to take risks, but—most importantly—possessed of the following:

1. Caring, respectful, and responsible attitude
2. Flexibility about people and organizational structure
3. Participative approach to management: willingness to share power

John Gardner

From John Gardner, *On Leadership* (New York: Free Press, 1990).

John Gardner is a widely known and well-respected essayist and author on the topic of leadership. In this volume, he explores the leadership challenges in large organizations, in political arenas, in government, and in integrating them all. He posits a series of leadership attributes drawn from other researchers as essential to good leadership:

1. Physical vitality and stamina
2. Intelligence and judgment-in-action
3. Willingness (eagerness) to accept responsibilities
4. Task competence
5. Understanding of followers/constituents and their needs
6. Skill in dealing with people
7. Need to achieve
8. Capacity to motivate
9. Courage, resolution, steadiness
10. Capacity to win and hold trust
11. Capacity to manage, decide, set priorities
12. Confidence
13. Ascendance, dominance, assertiveness
14. Adaptability, flexibility of approach

Jim Collins

From Jim Collins, "Level Five Leadership," *Harvard Business Review*, December 2000.

Co-author of the best selling book *Built to Last,* Collins describes here his new findings about the kind of leadership that has taken mediocre companies to greatness. *Good to Great* describes a five-year study of 1,500 companies on the NYSE in which Collins found that only 11 companies in 30 years made this jump from average to extraordinary, and that all their leaders had two traits in common: a self-effacing humility and a dogged persistence, what he called "humility + will." He argues that Level One is the highly capable individual, Level Two is contributing team members, Level Three is competent manager, Level Four is effective leader, and Level Five is the executive who builds enduring greatness through a paradoxical combination of personal humility and professional will.

BEHAVIOR APPROACH

The behavior approach first rose to prominence in the 1950s as researchers grew frustrated with the trait approach. They switched their emphasis to observations of what effective and ineffective leaders actually *do* on the job.

Mintzberg's 10 Managerial Roles

From Henry Mintzberg, *The Nature of Managerial Work* (New York: HarperCollins, 1973).

The Nature of Managerial Work contains interviews and observations of five chief executives and talks about the roles that leaders must fulfill.

1. Figurehead Role
2. Leader Role: Integrating the organization, motivating
3. Liaison Role
4. Monitor Role

5. Disseminator Role
6. Spokesman Role
7. Entrepreneur Role
8. Disturbance Handler Role
9. Resource Allocator Role
10. Negotiator Role

Kotter's Leadership Factor

John Kotter, *The Leadership Factor* (New York: The Free Press, 1988) contains data from 900 senior executives in 100 American corporations. Kotter's leadership factor is also described in "What Leaders Really Do," *Harvard Business Review*, May–June 1990, p. 3. See also *The General Managers* and *Power and Influence* by the same author.

> . . . leadership is defined as the **process** of moving a group (or groups) in some direction through mostly noncoercive means. Effective leadership is defined as leadership that produces movement in the long-term best interest of the group(s). (*The Leadership Factor*, p. 5)

Using Lee Iacocca as an example, Kotter outlines this pattern:

1. Development of a bold, new vision
2. An intelligent—that is, workable—strategy for implementing the vision
3. Eliciting the cooperation and teamwork from a large network of essential people
4. Relentless work to keep key people in the network motivated toward the vision

> Great vision emerges when a powerful mind, working long and hard on massive amounts of information, is able to see (or recognize in suggestions from others) interesting patterns and new possibilities. (*The Leadership Factor*, p. 29)

CHARACTERISTICS OF EFFECTIVE SENIOR MANAGEMENT

Industry and organizational knowledge
Relationships in the firm and the industry
Reputation and track record
Abilities and skills (keen mind, interpersonal skills)
Personal values (integrity)
Motivation (high energy level, strong drive to lead)

> A surprisingly large number of the items [on the characteristics list] are developed on the job as a part of one's posteducational career. Almost all the knowledge, relationship, and background requirements fit this generalization. . . . (*The Leadership Factor*, p. 34)

Management is different from leadership. Management is about coping with complexity, and leadership is about coping with change. Both are invaluable to the well-being of an organization. Management and leadership are both focused on providing three crucial functions, but they accomplish these tasks in different ways, as outlined here:

Companies with weak leadership show these characteristics:

1. Managers who leave felt frustrated with neglect and/or abuse.
2. Middle management jobs are mostly fire-fighting.

Function	Management	Leadership
Deciding what needs to be done	Planning and budgeting (short-term focus)	Setting a direction (long-term focus; communicating a vision)
Creating networks of people and relationships to accomplish the agenda	Organizing and staffing	Aligning people (by communicating with them)
Ensuring that the job gets done	Control mechanisms (compare results to plan and make corrections)	Motivating people (appeal to human needs such as self-esteem and recognition)

Source: John Kotter, "What Leaders Really Do," *Harvard Business Review*, May–June 1990, 3.

3. Managers who wanted to be leaders were stymied by bureaucracy.
4. Without depth of management, people were promoted into positions they weren't prepared for.
5. Managers could not be moved across organizational boundaries.
6. Managers were rarely coached or mentored.
7. Managers had one chance only at promotion, regardless of whether that made sense.

In short, such companies manage by responding to short-term financial imperatives, and their efforts are often hampered by parochial internal politics.

Companies with strong leadership tend to emphasize the following:

1. Sophisticated recruiting efforts
2. Attractive work environment
3. Challenging opportunities
4. Early identification
5. Planned development

We need to

1. Abandon the notion of professional leadership.
2. Think of leadership with a small "l," something we all must do better.
3. Think more carefully about managerial careers.
4. Realize that human resource professionals are not professionals but rather advisors to the line management.
5. Think about how to manage global businesses and develop that talent.
6. Realize that the sources of competitive advantage have changed from the past.

STEWART'S THREE-PART THEORY OF MANAGEMENT
R. Stewart's theory is described in the following sources: *Managers and Their Jobs* (London: MacMillan, 1967); *Contrasts in Management* (Maidenhead, England: McGraw-Hill UK, 1976); and *Choices for the Manager: A Guide to Understanding Managerial Work* (Englewood Cliffs, NJ: Prentice Hall, 1982). Stewart outlines three forces that affect individual managerial roles to varying degrees, helping to shape the nature of those jobs:

Demands: These duties and responsibilities (e.g., standards, deadlines, bureaucratic procedures) are imposed by others in positions of power, which the manager must uphold.

Constraints: These elements in the organizational and external environment (e.g., policies, regulations, and labor laws, as well as the limited funds, supplies, and personnel available for a task) limit the manager's options.

Choices: These activities/ideas (e.g., objectives for the business unit being managed, prioritizing of tasks, and strategy) are the things a manager *may* do, at his or her own discretion.

The relative influences of these three forces affect managerial behavior and can make one management position distinctly different from another.

Kouzes and Posner's Leadership Challenge

From J. M. Kouzes and B. Z. Posner, *The Leadership Challenge* (San Francisco, CA: Jossey-Bass, 1987).

In a three-year study of about 1,500 managers, Kouzes and Posner inferred 5 practices and 10 behavioral commitments that characterize effective leaders. They developed a self-assessment and leadership assessment tool, the *Leadership Practices Inventory* (LPI), to measure these 10 dimensions. The LPI has become widely used in many schools and businesses.

The 5 practices and their 10 related behavioral commitments are the following:

Challenging the Process
  1. Search for opportunities
  2. Experiment and take risks
     Inspiring a Shared Vision
  3. Envision the future
  4. Enlist others
     Enabling Others to Act
  5. Foster collaboration
  6. Strengthen others
     Modeling the Way
  7. Set the example
  8. Plan small wins
     Encouraging the Heart
  9. Recognize individual contribution
  10. Celebrate accomplishments

Results-Focused Leadership

From Dave Ulrich, Jack Zenger, and Norm Smallwood, *Results-Based Leadership* (Boston, MA: Harvard Business School Press, 1999).

Ulrich and his co-authors assert here that whatever a person's characteristics might be, in the end, one must focus on results, on outcomes of an organization. They point out that at least four entities perceive results from an organization: employees, organizational capabilities, customers, and investors. A results-oriented leader will pay attention to all four of these stakeholders. Then they offer 14 suggestions to help one become a more results-oriented leader:

  1. Begin with an absolute focus on results.
  2. Take complete and personal responsibility for your groups' results.
  3. Clearly and specifically communicate expectations and targets to the people in your group.

4. Determine what you need to do personally to improve your results.
5. Use results as the litmus test for continuing or implementing leadership practice.
6. Engage in developmental activities and opportunities that will help you produce better results.
7. Know and use every group member's capabilities to the fullest and provide everyone with appropriate developmental opportunities.
8. Experiment and innovate in every realm under your influence, looking constantly for new ways to improve performance.
9. Measure the right standards and increase the rigor with which you measure them.
10. Constantly take action; results won't improve without it.
11. Increase the pace or tempo of your group.
12. Seek feedback from others in the organization about ways you and your group can improve your outcomes.
13. Ensure that your subordinates and colleagues perceive that your motivation for being a leader is the achievement of positive results, not personal or political gain.
14. Model the methods and strive for the results you want your group to use and attain.

POWER AND INFLUENCE APPROACH

This school of research studies the influence processes at work between leaders and other individuals. In general, the aim is to gain insight into leadership effectiveness by studying the power possessed by a leader, as well as the way that power is wielded.

Two Faces of Power

From David McClelland, "The Two Faces of Power," *Journal of International Affairs* 24, no. 1 (1970): 29–47.

> **Dominating Power:** Seeks to subjugate others by keeping them weak and dependent on the leader.
> **Empowering Power:** Seeks to enable the weak. Power is exercised cautiously; the aim is to build commitment to the organization and its ideals rather than to oneself.

Winter's Theory of Leadership

In an unpublished doctoral dissertation (Harvard Business School, circa 1978), Winter describes leadership as a function of the ability of the leader to empower the followers: to make them feel that they are more capable, more powerful, more able than they were.

> If you think about it, people love others not for who they are, but for how they make us feel. We willingly follow others for much the same reason. It makes us feel good to do so. Now, we also follow platoon sergeants, self-centered geniuses, demanding spouses, bosses of various persuasions and others, for a variety of reasons as well. But none of those reasons involves that person's leadership qualities. In order to willingly accept the direction of another individual, it must feel good to do so. This business of making another person feel good in the unspectacular course of his daily comings and goings is, in my view, the very essence of leadership. (Irwin Federman, quoted in Bennis and Nanus, *Leaders*, pp. 62–63)

The West Point Way of Leadership

From Larry Donnithorne, *The West Point Way of Leadership* (New York: Currency/Doubleday, 1993).

Colonel Donnithorne describes the leadership principles that West Point cadets are taught in each year of their education at the Academy. These lessons, taken sequentially and carefully, comprise, he said, the West Point Way of Leadership. Donnithorne's lessons include the following:

First Year

Followership is Job One
Finding courage in fear
Honor is the language we speak
Being a team member

Second Year

Positioning the leader inside the group/team
Just and unjust leadership
Face-to-face leadership

Third Year

Acquiring self-reliance to lead leaders
Pushing character to the extreme
Leading leaders

Fourth Year

Executive leadership
Serving as the organization's eyes and ears

Social Exchange Theory

From E. P. Hollander, "Conformity, Status, and Idiosyncrasy Credit," *Psychological Review* 65 (1958): 117–27; E. P. Hollander, "Leadership and Social Exchange Processes," in K. Gergen, M. S. Greenberg, and R. H. Willis (eds.), *Social Exchange: Advances in Theory and Research* (New York: Winston-John Wiley, 1979); and T. O. Jacobs, *Leadership and Exchange in Formal Organizations* (Alexandria, VA: Human Resources Research Organization, 1970).

Social exchange exists between a leader and the other members of the group: the leader champions a course of action, and the group affords the leader a greater (or lesser) degree of status and influence based on the perceived success (or failure) of the plan.

When an innovative plan succeeds, the leader wins not only greater power and influence but also **idiosyncrasy credits**—the allowance of greater latitude to deviate from normal procedures in the future. In other words, the group becomes more receptive to radical-sounding proposals, thanks to the trust that former success has engendered.

When the leader's plan fails, social exchange theory predicts that the leader will experience a loss of status and influence. The loss will be greater if the failure appears to be due to poor judgment, rather than factors beyond the leader's control; if the leader is thought to have pursued selfish motives; if the plan was especially divergent from group norms; or if the leader had a particularly high degree of status beforehand.

Strategic Contingencies Theory

From D. J. Hickson, C. R. Hinings, C. A. Lee, R. S. Schneck, and J. M. Pennings, "A strategic contingencies theory of intra-organizational power," *Administrative Science Quarterly* 16 (1971): 216–229.

Strategic contingencies theory looks at organizational subunits and their relative abilities to influence strategic decisions for the organization as a whole. In other words, what makes some subunits more powerful than others? The theory names three factors:

1. *Expertise in dealing with important problems.* This expertise is especially valuable when solving the problem is critical (essential for the survival and well-being of the organization) and when the subunits are highly interdependent.
2. *The subunit's centrality in the work flow of the organization.* This factor is particularly important if the subunits are not highly interdependent.
3. *The extent to which the expertise of the subunit is unique and not easily substitutable.*

SITUATIONAL APPROACH

The situational approach pays special attention to contextual factors: the nature of the work performed by the leader's unit, the individual characteristics of the followers, or the nature of the external environment. How, it asks, does the larger situation affect the leadership task?

Hersey and Blanchard's Situational Theory of Leadership

From P. Hersey and K. H Blanchard, *Management of Organizational Behavior* (Englewood Cliffs, NJ: Prentice Hall, 1977).

This theory is an extension of the leadership theories presented by Blake and Mouton (in the Managerial Grid approach) and Reddin's 3-D Management Style Theory. Hersey and Blanchard, like Blake and Mouton, use a two-dimensional grid with Task Orientation and People Orientation axes. They also argue that the maturity of the subordinate determines what mix of people versus task orientation is appropriate for that subordinate. Immature subordinates require a more directive, task-oriented leader, while mature subordinates who are willing to take responsibility will respond better to a more relationship- and people-oriented leader. The four Blanchard leadership styles are directive, managing, coaching, and delegating (from leading less mature to more mature subordinates).

House's Path–Goal Theory of Leadership

From R. J. House, "A Path-Goal Theory of Leader Effectiveness," *Administrative Science Quarterly* 16 (1971): 321–339.

> . . . the motivational function of the leader consists of increasing personal payoffs to subordinates for work-goal attainment, and making the path to these payoffs easier to travel by clarifying it, reducing roadblocks and pitfalls, and increasing the opportunities for personal satisfaction en route. (p. 324)

Path–goal theory is related to expectancy theory—the belief that people are motivated by their level of expectations that they can do the work, be rewarded, and value the reward offered—in that the leader must understand the subordinates' expectancies and clarify and magnify them toward the desired result. The latest version of the path–goal approach includes four basic types of leader behavior: supportive, directive, participative, and achievement-oriented.

Fiedler's Contingency Model of Leadership

From F. E. Fiedler, *A Theory of Leadership Effectiveness* (New York: McGraw-Hill, 1967).

Fiedler's work revolves around the collection of data on a "Least Preferred Coworker (LPC)" scale. Individuals are asked to name the person with whom they have worked least well in the past, and then to rate the personality of that person; those who do so critically receive low LPC scores, while those who are more positive in their evaluations receive high scores. The interpretation of the scores has changed over the years. Fiedler's belief is that one particular score is not necessarily a better indicator of leadership effectiveness; rather, that effectiveness is a function of the individual's score and several other factors in the situation. Hence, some leaders will be more effective in certain situations, while others will do better in other situations. Fiedler argues that leader–member relationships, positional power, and the structure of the task all contribute to the degree of fit between an individual and a situation.

Leadership Substitutes Theory

From S. Kerr and J. M. Jermier, "Substitutes for Leadership: Their Meaning and Measurement," *Organizational Behavior and Human Performance* 22 (1978): 375–403.

This theory explores aspects of a work situation that can reduce the importance of leadership by "formal leaders" such as managers. It involves two situational variables:

> **Neutralizers:** Factors in the work situation that hamper the effectiveness of a leader's actions.
> **Substitutes:** Factors that make the very role of a formal leader unnecessary.

Neutralizers and substitutes may be found in three different dimensions of the work situation. The following list provides a few examples of each:

1. **Subordinate characteristics.** Subordinates who arrive with extensive training (e.g., doctors) or who have high internal motivation may serve as substitutes for leadership: They may not require, or even want, supervision. Subordinates' values may serve as neutralizers for leadership: if they value time spent with their families highly, they may not respond to "time-and-a-half" payment incentives for working overtime.
2. **Task characteristics.** Certain tasks, by their nature, do not call for much leadership. Simple, repetitive tasks that can be mastered easily make leadership unnecessary. Extremely rewarding tasks, too, can serve as substitutes for certain types of leadership, by ensuring job satisfaction and enthusiasm without the presence of a formal leader.
3. **Group and organization characteristics.** Highly formalized organizations, with extensive regulations and policies, can serve as substitutes for leadership: once subordinates learn the rules, little need remains for the direction of a leader. Such formalized settings can also become neutralizers for leadership, if the inflexibility of the rules impedes the leader's efforts to make strategic changes.

MEINDL'S ROMANCE MODEL

From James R. Meindl, "The Romance of Leadership as a Follower-Centric Theory: A Social Constructionist Approach," *The Leadership Quarterly*, 6, no. 3 (Autumn 1995): 329–341.

James Meindl notes that leadership studies acknowledge the importance of the leader, the follower, and the context, but that most studies focus on the leader. His approach focuses more on the follower and how followers' thoughts create a "leader" in their minds. His theory emphasizes exploration of how followers develop commitments to a leader and how they define followership which leads to follower-like behavior. In this approach, he recognizes the inter-relationship between cognitive and affective processes, what we have called here Level Two and Level Three behavior.

The Multiple-Linkage Model

From G. Yukl, "Toward a Behavioral Theory of Leadership," *Organizational Behavior and Human Performance* 6 (1971): 414–440.

This model builds on several earlier theories, particularly the previously mentioned leadership substitutes theory. A leader attempts to influence the performance of a group, but with a class of **intervening variables** ultimately determining the performance outcomes. The six intervening variables are as follows:

1. Subordinate effort
2. Subordinate ability and role clarity
3. Organization of the work
4. Cooperation and teamwork
5. Resources and support
6. External coordination

Like the leadership substitutes theory, this model includes two additional **situational variables**: neutralizers and substitutes. Here, they exert influence at three points: they affect the behavior and effectiveness of the leader; they impinge directly on the intervening variables; and they determine the relative importance of the intervening variables. As an example of the last, a situation that requires subordinates to work in close quarters for long periods of time will make intervening variable 4 (in the preceding list), cooperation and teamwork, especially crucial.

Leaders can take actions to influence the variables and thereby bring about better outcomes. In the short term, they can correct deficiencies in the intervening variables. For example, they can affect intervening variable 2 by setting specific goals and giving feedback on performance. In the long term, they can modify the situational variables. For example, they can institute new recruitment systems to attract highly skilled people to the organization.

Cognitive Resources Theory

From F. E. Fiedler, "The Contribution of Cognitive Resources to Leadership Performance," *Journal of Applied Social Psychology* 16 (1986): 532–548; and F. E. Fiedler and J. E. Garcia, *New Approaches to Leadership: Cognitive Resources and Organizational Performance* (New York: John Wiley, 1987).

This theory explores the conditions in which two cognitive resources of a leader—**intelligence** and **experience**—have a bearing on group performance. The theory has three propositions:

1. Leader ability contributes to group performance only when (a) the leader has a directive style, and (b) subordinates require guidance in order to perform. When a task is complex, an intelligent leader will be able to devise a better strategy for performance than an unintelligent leader and should use a directive style to convey it. When the task is more routine, subordinates will not need much leadership, and leader intelligence will not have any bearing.
2. **Stress** affects the relationship between **intelligence** and group performance. In a low-stress situation, a high-intelligence leader will generate better strategies and decisions than a less intelligent leader. When stress is high, a negative relationship occurs between leader intelligence and the quality of decisions.
3. **Stress** affects the relationship between leader **experience** and group performance. In high-stress situations, leaders look to their own past decisions for guidance. Experience is positively related to decision quality in these situations, but is unrelated to decision quality when stress is low.

CHARISMATIC APPROACH

Charisma was rarely studied in a managerial context before the 1980s, but since then it has attracted a good deal of attention. In Greek, *charisma* means "divinely inspired gift," but theorists use a less colorful definition: the result of follower perceptions that are influenced by actual leader traits and behavior, situational context, and the needs of the followers.

House's Theory of Charismatic Leadership

From R. J. House, "A 1976 Theory of Charismatic Leadership," in J. G. Hunt and L. L. Larson (eds.), *Leadership: The Cutting Edge* (Carbondale, IL: Southern Illinois University Press, 1977).

Charismatic leadership is measured by the following:

1. Followers' trust in the correctness of the leader's beliefs
2. Similarity of followers' beliefs to the leader's beliefs
3. Unquestioning acceptance of the leader by followers
4. Followers' affection for the leader
5. Followers' willing obedience to the leader
6. Emotional involvement of followers in the mission of the organization
7. Heightened performance goals of followers
8. Belief of followers that they are able to contribute to the success of the group's mission

   Given these factors, charismatic leaders

- Have high self-confidence and strong conviction in their own beliefs.
- Create the impression that they are competent.
- Articulate ideological goals for subordinates.
- Appeal to the hopes and ideals of the followers.
- Use role modeling where they can "Be like me."
- Communicate high expectations.
- Arouse motives related to the group's mission.

Attribution Theory of Charisma

From J. A. Conger and R. Kanungo, "Toward a Behavioral Theory of Charismatic Leadership in Organizational Settings," *Academy of Management Review* 12 (1987): 637–647; and J. A. Conger, *The Charismatic Leader: Behind the Mystique of Exceptional Leadership* (San Francisco, CA: Jossey-Bass, 1989).

This theory describes five leader traits and behaviors that help make the leader seem charismatic in the eyes of followers:

1. Championing a vision that is **radically different** from the status quo, although not so different that followers will find it unacceptable.
2. Employing **unconventional** methods and strategies to realize the vision.
3. Taking personal **risk** and making **sacrifices**: followers trust a leader who may incur personal loss if the undertaking fails.
4. Projecting **confidence**.
5. Using **persuasive** appeals toward followers, rather than an authoritative or consensus approach.

The theory outlines two processes by which charismatic leaders actually influence followers:

1. **Personal identification.** Followers admire the leader, and as a result want to become more like him or her.
2. **Internalization of values and beliefs.** This process runs deeper than personal identification, which is often limited to the imitation of superficial leader traits. Followers who internalize the values and beliefs of the leader become motivated on their own to perform.

Finally, the theory names **dissatisfaction** as an important situational contributor to charismatic leadership. A charismatic leader is more likely to emerge when a crisis calls for drastic measures.

Self-Concept Theory of Charismatic Leadership

From B. Shamir, R. J. House, and M. B. Arthur, "The Motivational Effects of Charismatic Leadership: A Self-Concept Based Theory," *Organization Science* 4 (1993): 1–17.

This theory, which builds on some earlier, related works, attempts to explain how charismatic leaders are able to compel followers to put aside their own self-interest for the sake of the organization's betterment. It identifies four processes:

1. **Personal identification.** As in the attribution theory, the self-concept theory further says that those with low self-esteem are most likely to identify in this way with a leader.
2. **Social identification.** More important than personal identification, this process involves defining oneself in terms of one's membership in the group. High social identification leads followers to put the group's needs ahead of their own. Charismatic leaders inspire social identification through appeals to group values, and through the use of flags, uniforms, and other symbolic devices.
3. **Internalization.** In this theory, follower adaptation (internalization) of the *leader's* values is uncommon. More often, the leader plays up existing *follower* values by linking them to task objectives.
4. **Self-efficacy.** This process involves the belief in one's own competence and ability. By holding high expectations and projecting confidence that followers can live up to them, a charismatic leader inspires this trait in individuals and also in the group as a whole (*collective* self-efficacy).

FACILITATING CONDITIONS   Charismatic leaders are more likely to motivate when

1. Leader's vision harmonizes with existing follower values.
2. Organizational mission can be linked to follower values (e.g., defense-contractor employees believing they are helping to defend the country).
3. Work is unstructured and hazy.
4. Organization is facing difficulties.

TRANSFORMATIONAL APPROACH

Transformational leadership is seen as a process in which leaders and followers inspire one another to elevated moral conduct. It can be used to influence both superiors and subordinates. Those under its influence feel they are bettering themselves.

Warren Bennis's Theory of Leadership

From Warren Bennis and Burt Nanus, *Leaders: The Strategies for Taking Charge* (New York: Harper and Row, 1985). Ninety interviews with 60 successful CEOs and 30 outstanding public-sector leaders.

In *Leaders*, Bennis and Nanus describe leadership as occurring in a context defined by three elements: (1) commitment of the culture to excellence and improvement, (2) complexity of the culture/society (swirling maelstroms of technological, social, and business changes), and (3) credibility: the willingness of people to place trust and respect in public figures. With regard to the second element, the authors maintain that we are at a pivotal point in the world's industrial history: a transition from the Industrial Society to the Information Society.

> . . . power is the basic energy needed to initiate and sustain action or, to put it another way, the capacity to translate intention into reality and sustain it. (p. 17)
>
> Present problems will not be solved without successful organizations, and organizations cannot be successful without effective leadership. (p. 20)
>
> Managers are people who do things right and leaders are people who do the right thing. (p. 21)

Four leadership strategies were found to be used by all 90 interviewees:

1. **Attention through vision.** "Vision animates, inspirits, transforms purpose into action" (p. 30).
2. **Meaning through communication.** Regardless of how articulate they are in a conventional sense, leaders find a way to convey their visions and meanings in unmistakable terms to their constituents. "The main clue is that leadership creates a new audience for its ideas because it alters the shape of understanding by transmitting information in such a way that it 'fixes' and secures tradition" (p. 42).
3. **Trust through positioning.** Trust is a function of constancy. "Trust is the lubrication that makes it possible for organizations to work" (p. 43). "Every organization incorporates four concepts of organization . . . the manifest organization (on the charts) . . . the assumed organization (what we think we have) . . . the extant organization (what we really have), . . . the requisite organization (what we should have)" (pp. 50–51).
4. **Deployment of self through positive self-regard.** "To have self-respect is everything. Without it, we are nothing but unwilling slaves, at everybody's mercy, especially those we fear or hold in contempt" (p. 58). "Recognizing strengths and compensating for weaknesses represent the first step in achieving positive self-regard" (p. 58). "The second element of positive self-regard is the nurturing of skills with discipline—that is, to keep working on and developing one's talents" (p. 59). "[T]he third aspect of positive self-regard, the capacity to discern the fit between one's perceived skills and what the job requires" (p. 60).

FIVE CHARACTERISTICS OF EMOTIONAL WISDOM

1. The ability to accept people as they are.
2. The capacity to approach relationships and problems in the present rather than in the past.
3. The ability to treat those who are close with the same respect and courtesy reserved for those who are strangers.
4. The ability to trust others even if the risk is great.
5. The ability to do without constant approval and recognition from others.

James MacGregor Burns's Theory of Leadership

From James MacGregor Burns, *Leadership* (New York: Perennial, December 9, 1982).

No matter how strong this longing for unanimity, however, almost all leaders, at least at the national level, must settle for far less than universal affection. They must be willing to make enemies—to deny themselves the affection of their adversaries. They must accept conflict. They must be willing and able to be unloved. It is hard to pick one's friends, harder to pick one's enemies. (p. 34)

   . . . transforming leadership ultimately becomes moral in that it raises the level of human conduct and ethical aspiration of both leader and led, and thus it has a transforming effect on both. (p. 20)

   I define leadership as leaders inducing followers to act for certain goals that represent the values and the motivations—the wants and needs, the aspirations and expectations—of both leaders and followers. And the genius of leadership lies in the manner in which leaders see and act on their own and their followers' values and motivations. (p. 19)

   Leadership over human beings is exercised when persons with certain motives and purposes mobilize, in competition or conflict with others, institutional, political, psychological, and other resources so as to arouse, engage, and satisfy the motives of followers. (p. 18)

   We must see power—and leadership—as not things but as relationships. We must analyze power in a context of human motives and physical constraints. (p. 11)

   [Moral leadership] is the kind of leadership that operates at need and value levels higher than those of the potential follower (but not so much higher as to lose contact). (p. 42)

   Second, it is the kind of leadership that can exploit conflict and tension within persons' value structures. (p. 42)

   But the ultimate test of moral leadership is its capacity to transcend the claims of the multiplicity of everyday wants and needs and expectations, to respond to the higher levels of moral development, and to relate leadership behavior—its roles, choices, style, commitments—to a set of reasoned, relatively explicit, conscious values. (p. 46)

Transforming leadership must be distinguished from **transactional** leadership. Both appeal to values, but the latter only to values related to exchange (fairness, reciprocity). Some types of transforming leadership and their corresponding transactional types are listed here:

Bass's Theory of Transformational Leadership

From B. M. Bass, *Leadership and Performance Beyond Expectations* (New York: Free Press, 1985).

This theory, which builds on Burns's theory, distinguishes transactional leadership from transformational leadership. **Transactional leadership** is based on an exchange: the leader offers rewards for performance of a desired behavior. **Transformational leadership** (which differs from Burns's transforming leadership in that it does not necessarily have to appeal to *positive* moral values) lies in the leader's ability to inspire trust, loyalty, and admiration in followers, who then subordinate their individual interests to the interests of the group.

Transforming Leadership	Transactional Leadership
Intellectual leadership	Legislative leadership
Heroic leadership	Group leadership
Executive leadership	Bureaucratic leadership
Ideological leadership	Reforming leadership
Revolutionary leadership	

TRANSACTIONAL BEHAVIORS

1. **Contingent reward:** The use of incentives and rewards to induce task performance
2. **Passive management by exception:** The use of punishments and other measures to correct deviations from expected performance
3. **Active management by exception:** Monitoring subordinates to ensure that deviations from expected performance do not occur
4. **Laissez-faire leadership:** Not managing much at all; ignoring problems

TRANSFORMATIONAL BEHAVIORS

1. **Idealized influence:** Charisma
2. **Individualized consideration:** Support, guidance, encouragement
3. **Intellectual stimulation:** Increasing follower awareness and understanding of problems
4. **Inspirational motivation:** Conveying a compelling vision; using symbols and slogans to unite followers and intensify their efforts

DIFFERENCES BETWEEN CHARISMATIC AND TRANSFORMATIONAL LEADERSHIP

1. Bass sees charismatic leadership as the ability to inspire *superficial* identification only. Charisma is an ingredient of transformational leadership (see the preceding list of transformational behaviors); transformational leadership encloses it and goes beyond it. Transformational leadership arouses stronger emotions and appeals to values.
2. Charismatic leaders often try to keep followers dependent and weak. Transformational leaders offer empowerment.
3. Charismatic leaders are rare. Transformational leaders can be found at any level of an organization.
4. Charismatic leaders inspire extreme love and extreme hate. Transformational leaders inspire a less polarized response.

Tichy and Devanna's Transformational Leadership Process

From N. M. Tichy and M. A. Devanna, *The Transformational Leader* (New York: John Wiley & Sons, 1986).

Transforming and revitalizing an existing organization involve the following sequence:

1. **Recognizing the need for change.** Transformational leaders must identify significant changes in the environment and then be able to convince others that major organizational changes, rather than small adjustments, are needed. Four ways to increase the sensitivity of the organization to environmental change include the following:
   a. Encourage dissenting opinions.
   b. Listen to outsiders who can objectively critique the organization.
   c. Visit with and learn from other organizations.
   d. Measure performance against the competition, and not simply against the previous fiscal year.
2. **Managing the transition.** Determine what changes are necessary, and help followers deal with the emotional upheaval that accompanies them.
3. **Creating a new vision.** Communicate (through a mission statement as well as other means) a vision for the future that can inspire and unite followers. Express it not just as numbers but as ideology. Make it conducive to greater follower self-esteem.

4. **Institutionalizing the changes.** Ensure that the new vision has the support of top management and other key players in the organization. Develop a coalition of people who are committed to the vision, replacing people where necessary. Revise the structure of the organization itself if the current structure is an impediment to realization of the vision.

Seven attributes of transformational leaders:

1. They see themselves as agents of change.
2. They are not afraid to take risks, but are not reckless.
3. They believe in people and are attentive to their needs.
4. They are able to identify and articulate their own set of core values.
5. They are flexible and open to new ideas.
6. They are careful, disciplined thinkers.
7. They trust their own intuitions.

Schein's Model of Organizational Culture and Leadership

From Edgar Schein, *Organizational Culture and Leadership* (San Francisco, CA: Jossey-Bass, 1985).

Culture is invisible. Only its manifestations are visible. Culture stems from the enduring solutions to problems that have arisen historically. It also contains and reduces anxiety. "Leaders create cultures, but cultures, in turn, create their next generation of leaders" (p. 313). "[T]he unique and essential function of leadership is the manipulation of culture" (p. 317).

In early stages of culture formation, leaders need vision, the ability to articulate it, and the ability to enforce it. They need persistence and patience. They need the ability to absorb anxiety when things do not go as well as originally planned or hoped. They must also be able to provide temporary stability and emotional reassurance.

In mature organizations, leadership is defined by culture. The leaders of such organizations must understand their cultures insightfully. They must be able to skillfully motivate their followers. They must also have emotional strength to get the organization through periods of change. In order to do so, they must be able to change the culture's assumptions, which requires the paradoxical abilities to listen and to create involvement. They must be able to see the deepest parts of the assumptive framework of the organization.

The leader is a culture manager. He/she must understand culture formation and maturation. Cultures form around assumptions relating to humanity's relationship to nature, the nature of reality and truth, human nature, the nature of human activity, and the nature of human relationships. (p. 86)

BIBLIOGRAPHY

A Reading List on Leadership, Managing Human Resources, and Organizational Behavior

Selected by Jim Clawson, Darden GSB, UVA for more information see my Web site: http://faculty.darden.edu/clawsonj/

GENERAL PERSPECTIVES

Powered by Feel: How Individuals, Teams, and Companies Excel, James Clawson and Doug Newburg, World Scientific, Singapore, 2009.

On Leadership, John Gardner, Free Press, New York, 1990.

The Leadership Challenge, James Kouzes and Barry Posner, Jossey-Bass, San Francisco, CA, 1987.

Driven, Paul Lawrence, Paul and Nitin Nohria, Jossey-Bass, San Francisco, CA, 2001.

Executive Instinct. Nigel Nicholson, Crown Publishing, New York, 2000.

***Organizational Culture and Leadership*, Edgar Schein, Jossey-Bass, San Francisco, CA, 1985.

Outliers: The Story of Success, Malcolm Gladwell, Little Brown, New York, 2008.

PERSONAL PERSPECTIVES

Balancing Your Life: Executive Lessons for Work, Family and Self, James Clawson, World Scientific, Singapore, 2009.

The Virus of the Mind: The New Science of the Meme, Richard Brodie, Integral Press, Seattle, WA, 1996.

Flow: The Psychology of Optimal Experience, Mihalyi Csikszentmihalyi, Harper & Row, New York, 1990.

***The Evolving Self: A Psychology for the Third Millennium*, Mihalyi Csikszentmihalyi, Harper & Collins, New York, 1993.

The 7 Habits of Highly Effective People, Stephen Covey, Simon & Schuster, New York, 1989.

A Guide to Rational Living, Albert Ellis and Robert Harper, Wilshire Book Company, North Hollywood, CA, 1975.

Working Ourselves to Death, and the Rewards of Recovery, Diane Fassel, Harper, New York, 1990.

Choice Theory, William Glasser, Harper Perennial, New York, 1999.

Emotional Intelligence, Daniel Goleman, Bantam, New York, 1995.

Please Understand Me, David Keirsey and Bates, Marilyn, Prometheus Books, Del Mar, CA, 1984. Explains the Myers Briggs Type Indicator.

The Road Less Traveled, Scott Peck, Touchstone, New York, 1978.

Shadow Syndromes, The Mild Forms of Major Mental Disorders that Sabotage Us, John Ratey, and Johnson, Catherine, Bantam, New York, 1997.

On Becoming a Person, Carl Rogers, Mariner/Houghton Mifflin, New York, 1995.

The Drama of the Gifted Child, Alice Miller, Basic Books, New York, 1990.

You Just Don't Understand, Deborah Tannen, Ballentine, New York, 1990.

Necessary Losses, Judith Viorst, Fawcett, New York, 1986.

STRATEGIC THINKING

Every Business Is a Growth Business, Ram Charan and Noel Tichy, Rivers Press, New York, 1998, ISBN: 0812928792

The Innovators Solution, Clayton Christensen and Michael Raynor, HBS Press, Boston, MA, 2003.

Future Perfect, Stan Davis, Addison-Wesley, Reading, MA, 1987.

Competing for the Future, Gary Hamel and C.K. Prahalad, HBS Press, Boston, MA, 1994.

The Future of Management, Gary Hamel Harvard Business School Press, Boston, MA, 2007.

The Ultimate Advantage, Edward Lawler, III, Jossey-Bass, San Francisco, CA, 1992.

The Future of Human Resource Management, Mike Losey, Sue Meisinger, and Dave Ulrich, John Wiley, Hoboken, NJ, 2005.

The Human Equation, Jeffrey Pfeffer, Harvard Business School Press, Boston, MA, 1998.

The Experience Economy, Joe Pine, and Jim Gilmore, Harvard Business School Press, Boston, MA, 1999.

Competitive Strategy, Michael Porter, Free Press, New York, 1980.

The Art of the Long View, Peter Schwartz, Double-day Currency, New York, 1991.

CREATIVITY AND INNOVATION

Creativity at Work: Developing the Right Practices to Make Innovation Happen, deGraff, Jeff and Katherine A. Lawrence, Jossey Bass, San Francisco, CA, 2002.

Innovate Like Edison, Gelb, Michael J. Gelb and Sarah Miller Caldicott, Dutton, New York, 2007.

Learning to Think like Leonardo daVinci, Michael Gelb, Delacorte Press, New York, 1998.

Discover Your Genius: How to Think like History's Ten Most Revolutionary Minds, Michael Gelb, HarperCollins, New York, 2002.

What a Great Idea!, Charles Thompson, Harper Perennial, New York, 1992.

A Whack on the Side of the Head, Roger Von Oech, Creative Think, Menlo Park, CA, 1983.

INTERPERSONAL AND TEAM PERSPECTIVES

Organizing Genius, Warren Bennis, Addison-Wesley, Reading, MA, 1997.

Influence: The Psychology of Persuasion, Robert Cialdini, Quill, New York, 1993.

Influence without Authority, Allan Cohen and David Bradford, John Wiley & Sons, Hoboken, NJ, 1991.

Team Building: Proven Strategies for Improving Team Performance, Bill Dyer, Gibb Dyer, and Jeffrey Dyer, Jossey Bass, San Francisco, CA, 2007.

ORGANIZATIONAL PERSPECTIVES

The Living Company, Arie DeGeus, HBS Press, Boston, MA, 1997.

Managing Human Assets, Michael Beer, Bert Spector, Paul R. Lawrence, D. Quinn Mills, and Richard E. Walton, The Free Press, New York, 1984.

Punished by Rewards: The Trouble with Gold Stars, Incentive Plans, A's, Praise, and Other Bribes, Alfie Kohn, Mariner, New York, 1999.

"Strategic Human Resource Management," Noel Tichy, et.al., *Sloan Management Review*, 23, no. 2 (Winter 1982): 47–62.

**The Fifth Discipline: The Art and Practice of the Learning Organization*, Peter Senge, Doubleday, New York, 1990.

The Necessary Revolution, Peter Senge, US Green Building Council, New York (Senge), 2008.

Career Dynamics, Edgar Schein, Addison-Wesley, Reading, MA, 1978.

Control Your Destiny or Someone Else Will, Noel Tichy and Stratford Sherman, HarperCollins, New York, 1994.

MANAGING CHANGE

Leading Change, John Kotter, HBS Press, Boston, MA, 1996.

Good to Great, James Collins, Harper Collins, New York, 2001.

Reengineering the Corporation, Michael Hammer, & James Champy, Harper Business, New York, 1993.

Intentional Revolutions, Edwin Nevis, Jon Lancourt, and Helen C. Vassallo, Jossey-Bass, San Francisco, CA, 1996.

Leading Change, James O'Toole, Jossey-Bass, San Francisco, CA, 1995.

Changing for Good, James Prochaska, John C. Norcross, and Carlo C. DiClemente, HarperCollins, New York, 1994.

Deep Change, Robert Quinn, Jossey-Bass, San Francisco, CA, 1997.

Process Consultation, Edgar Schein, Addison-Wesley, Reading, MA, 1969.

Change, Paul Watzlawick, John H. Weakland, and Richard Fisch, Norton, New York, 1974.

** = books on my Top Five nonfiction list

INDEX

Note: The letters 'f' and 't' followed by the locators refers to figures and tables cited in the text.